D0757429

Transcultural Bodies

Transcultural Bodies

FEMALE GENITAL CUTTING IN GLOBAL CONTEXT

Edited by
YLVA HERNLUND
BETTINA SHELL-DUNCAN

RUTGERS UNIVERSITY PRESS
New Brunswick, New Jersey, and London

Library of Congress Cataloging-in-Publication Data

Transcultural bodies : female genital cutting in global context / edited by Ylva Hernlund and Bettina Shell-Duncan.

    p. cm.

Includes bibliographical references and index.

ISBN-13: 978-0-8135-4025-2 (hardcover : alk. paper)

ISBN-13: 978-0-8135-4026-9 (pbk. : alk. paper)

  1. Female circumcision.   2. Infibulation.   I. Hernlund, Ylva, 1962–   II. Shell-Duncan, Bettina, 1963–

GN484.T734 2007

392.1–dc22   2006025455

A British Cataloging-in-Publication record for this book is available
from the British Library

This collection copyright © 2007 by Rutgers, The State University

Individual chapters copyright © 2007 in the names of their authors

All rights reserved

No part of this book may be reproduced or utilized in any form or by any means, electronic or mechanical, or by any information storage and retrieval system, without written permission from the publisher. Please contact Rutgers University Press, 100 Joyce Kilmer Avenue, Piscataway, NJ 08854–8099. The only exception to this prohibition is "fair use" as defined by U.S. copyright law.

Visit our Web site: http://rutgerspress.rutgers.edu

Manufactured in the United States of America

CONTENTS

TABLES

PREFACE

THIS VOLUME HAS BEEN some time in the making, and we are deeply appreciative of the patience and perseverance of each one of our contributors. The idea for the project first arose as we were engaged in editing a previous volume, *Female "Circumcision" in Africa: Culture, Controversy, and Change*, and realized that its scope would not allow us to include chapters related to the practice of female genital cutting (FGC) "on the move."

We wish to thank Charles Piot for strongly encouraging us to take on this project, providing the initial push we needed in order to commit to another complex edited volume, and Janelle Taylor for her steadfast support at a critical juncture. Fuambai Ahmadu started out as coeditor of this volume, but unfortunately other commitments forced her to withdraw. Nonetheless, her influence on the work is unmistakable. Any errors, however, are naturally the sole responsibility of the editors.

In working on this project we have benefited from being able to observe discussions about FGC in a wide variety of sites. In particular, we gained a great deal of insight from several meetings and conferences. Ylva Hernlund in 2003 delivered a keynote address and made invaluable connections with European activists and academics at the FOKO (Network for Research on Female Circumcision, based at the University of Oslo, Norway) conference held in Sweden. Bettina Shell-Duncan participated in 2002 in a Rockefeller Foundation–sponsored meeting in Bellagio, Italy, on research directions for FGM, which brought together program managers, technical officers from international organizations, and academic researchers. Additionally, attending the 2004 USAID-sponsored Washington, D.C., conference commemorating the first anniversary of "Zero Tolerance Day," as well as the adjacent congressional hearing, provided valuable information about efforts to guide the global movement on FGC in particular directions. We have also benefited tremendously from our communications with Molly Melching and Gannon Gillespie of Tostan, a Senegal-based nongovernmental organization.

We wish to thank all those colleagues, too numerous to name here, who have over the years shared with us information, ideas, and insights on this topic. Most importantly, however, we must express our sincere gratitude to all those women and men who shared with the contributors to this volume their knowledge, concerns, and convictions regarding an issue that affects them most directly.

At various stages this manuscript or portions thereof have greatly benefited from the careful reading and insightful feedback of Fuambai Ahmadu, Nancy Hunt, Sara Johnsdotter, Caren Kaplan, Leslye Obiora, Arzoo Osanloo, Rick Shweder, Janelle Taylor, Lynn Thomas, Stan Yoder, and two anonymous reviewers. We are deeply grateful to Rutgers University Press, and, in particular, editors Kristi Long and Adi Hovav, for their expert guidance, consistent reasonableness, and unflagging support.

Last but not least we wish to thank our families, Ylva's Ron and Maya, and Bettina's Tim, Jack, and Luke, who—while incredulous that we would do this again—patiently put up with sharing us with another demanding and time-consuming project.

Transcultural Bodies

CHAPTER 1

Transcultural Positions

NEGOTIATING RIGHTS AND CULTURE

Ylva Hernlund and Bettina Shell-Duncan

IN AN EARLIER volume, *Female "Circumcision" in Africa: Culture, Controversy, and Change* (Shell-Duncan and Hernlund 2000), we sought to examine multidisciplinary perspectives on practices of female genital cutting (FGC) in Africa and how this topic has become a nexus for debates about gender, power, and cultural autonomy.[1] In the present work we are broadening this scope with the aim of adding to a growing literature that examines these practices in a global context (see also, for example, Boyle 2002; James and Robertson 2002; Shweder et al. 2002). The empathetic and ethnographically grounded contributions in this volume illustrate an expansion of focus to consider what FGC practices can tell us about the movements of bodies, ideas, resources, regimes, and desires.

The global movement to "eradicate FGM" has currently reached a point of increased critical reflection, involving the reassessment of intervention approaches, the reappraisal of priorities, and the resetting of goals. Particularly significant has been a gradual shift of justifying anti-FGC efforts based on human rights, rather than on medical, grounds. FGC scholars, in turn,[2] are wrestling with a number of issues which include the alleged and real health effects of FGC, its intended and actual effects on female sexual response, and the political and legal issues that arise with migration—when African asylum seekers in the West claim to fear coerced circumcision for themselves and/or their children if deported back to their home countries; when African women who have undergone various forms of genital cutting deliver their babies in Western health care facilities; and when "parental rights" bump up against the "rights of children" in novel ways within varied diasporic frameworks for child welfare.

DRAWING LINES OR STILLING THE PENDULUM?

It has been pointed out by a number of observers that few topics have the ability that FGC does to provoke calls for "drawing the line" of tolerance (see, for example, Gordon 1991 and responses). The rhetorical question "But what about FGM?" (see Shweder 2002) is presented as an "obvious counterargument to cultural pluralism and a clear limit to any feelings of tolerance for alternative ways of life" (ibid., 218); any further attempts at gaining understanding of difference can thus be effectively shut down. When substantive discourse *is* allowed to develop, it tends to get mired in dead-end arguments regarding universal values versus cultural relativism.

A number of scholars have made valiant attempts at moving beyond this impasse (see, for example, Gosselin 2000b; Gunning 1991; Renteln 1988), and the field of anthropology has struggled with the ethics of "prorights anthropology" since its early days (Gosselin 2000b). As we discuss in greater depth later in this chapter, we find particularly useful for the task at hand the ideas of anthropologist Marie-Bénédicte Dembour, whose work appears in a groundbreaking collection of essays on culture and rights (Cowan et al. 2001a). In an analysis of the often contradictory legal responses to cases of excision in France, Dembour argues that debates have exaggerated the irreconcilability of universalism and relativism; she argues that "neither is tenable without the other" (Dembour 2001, 75). She employs the image of the pendulum: as one is drawn to relativism, "there is a moment when getting too close to it, one is compelled to revert towards universalism—and vice versa" (ibid., 56).[3] This discomfort, she argues, stems from the limitations of each polar extreme.

In our own work reviewing scholarship on FGC, we have noticed, as well, a tendency for assertions—regarding the effects these practices have on health, sexuality, child welfare, and the empowerment of women—to at times swing rather dramatically from one pole to another and that, as Martha Minow so trenchantly remarks, "dueling accusations of false consciousness can escalate with no end" (Minow 2002, 256). While we agree with Dembour's analysis of the tendency for human minds to operate on the pendulum model rather than committing permanently to false dichotomies—such as the one between rights and culture—it is also our ambition that this volume add to the growing number of voices in the field of FGC studies and activism that call for a move "to the middle."

TRANSCULTURAL BODIES

It has been suggested that female and male initiations including genital cutting that have long been performed in parts of Africa in complex ritual contexts could well constitute a set of practices distinct from infibulating procedures in other parts of the continent, which seem to arise from different concerns (Hernlund 2003). Yet, typically, all of these practices are casually lumped together under the label of FGM/FGC/FC (see also Walley 2002).[4] This blurring of distinctions between diverse practices with varied consequences has had a confusing impact on evaluations of the effects that FGC can indeed have on health and well-being—physical in the short and long term, obstetrical, psychological, social, and sexual—as well as on how the individuals undergoing these procedures, and those close to them, subjectively experience pain and meaning and to what extent they perceive the experience as an assault on bodily integrity and human rights. These gradations take on new significance and urgency in the context of the increasing mobility of transcultural bodies.

The titles of both this chapter and the volume as a whole make reference to trans*cultural*—rather than transnational—bodies, although this was not an obvious choice. Recent scholarship on FGC, including our own, has tended to stress that the best predictor of FGC prevalence, type, and context is not nationality, but ethnicity or membership "in a culture."[5] We find, however, that this is increasingly too simplistic a picture as, in a number of contexts discussed in greater detail later in this chapter, national frontiers have indeed come to play an important role in whether and how FGC is practiced and with what consequences. In a range of continually evolving situations, it does indeed make more and more of a difference what side of a particular border you are on.

The emergent mosaic of nation-states' positionings on FGC does not, however, preclude the continued importance of affiliation with "culture." It is increasingly crucial *where* you are—at home or in exile, in the United States or in Norway, Ghana or Mali, The Gambia or Senegal. But it often remains equally significant how you are positioned *within* the nation-state—in urban or rural areas, in a marriage with someone from the same or a different ethnic group as yours, surrounded by neighbors who do or do not practice FGC, in communities that have experienced varying degrees of exposure to anti-FGM campaigns, out- (and perhaps return-) migration, biomedical health care services, and contact with agents of the nation-state. As bodies move through these different domains, they become subject to regimes that intersect in varied and sometimes contradictory ways.

Bodies on the Move

It is estimated that the current worldwide immigrant population is more than one hundred million (Suárez-Orozco 2002, 19), and these individuals are moving across boundaries in an increasingly fluid fashion. As Marcelo Suárez-Orozco points out, "that immigration takes place between remote, neatly bounded geopolitical spaces, where a clean break is inevitable, whether desired or not, may no longer be useful to assume." Instead, he cautions, we are currently seeing now more than ever a massive back-and-forth movement of people, goods, information, and symbols (ibid).

As the essays of this collection demonstrate, the various actors, arenas, and agendas involved in the global debates surrounding FGC interact in complex ways.[6] The many individuals on the move around the world whose origins are in circumcising societies are no different than other migrants in that they often "remain powerful protagonists in the economic, political, and cultural spheres back home" (Suárez-Orozco 2002, 27). Contributions to this volume illustrate the busy traffic in ideas and influence between home and exile communities in relation to what people perceive should be done about FGC. Michelle Johnson, for example, asks us to consider efforts to change or retain traditions as they are "'uprooted' and 'transplanted' in the process of transnational migration," and cautions us against falling into the trap of simply equating values "at home" with "tradition" and views in exile with "change."

Suárez-Orozco points to the importance of "social remittances" whereby "culturally, immigrants not only significantly reshape the ethos of their new communities but also are responsible for significant social transformations back home" (2002, 39 n. 8). It has been suggested by some that the eventual return of many emigrants to their home countries will gradually have a major effect on FGC practices on the ground. These are two-way flows, however, as, additionally, members of "home" communities often continue to exercise considerable influence over exile members, a context that has given rise to alarm in Western countries regarding the potential "mutilation" of Western-born girls of African backgrounds, what Unni Wikan has in a different context referred to as "the perils of dual citizenship" (2002, 140).[7]

Negotiations in Exile

Although, historically, men have often tended to be the first to move into new arenas, perhaps later sending for wives and female relatives from home, increasingly it is women, including those from circumcising societies, who are themselves on the move. This new mobility is affecting changes in gender, age, class, and family dynamics. Especially noteworthy for the discussion at hand are the shifts taking place in power differentials between immigrant adults and their children (see in particular the contributions to Shweder et al. 2002) and between women and men. A number of observers (for example, Fábos 2001; Dopico, Johansen, Johnsdotter, and Talle, chapters 10, 11, 5, and 4 respectively of this volume) point to the rapid and substantial changes in gender relations in many African diaspora communities. Women, they argue, often gain access more easily to work and other opportunities while, increasingly, some men "stay home" (Fábos 2001, 96). In addition, as we discuss in greater detail in the context of asylum law, gender-specific legal recourses have opened up, as women increasingly are able to gain political asylum based on the fear of undergoing FGM if they are returned home—a glaring anomaly in an otherwise hardening global climate for migration (see Kratz, Piot, Obiora, chapters 8, 7, and 3 respectively of this volume).

Some of the contributors to this volume engage with the thorny question of assessing and addressing the prevalence of FGC in the diaspora, although definitive answers are hard to come by. Numerous sources, from government to mass media reports, speculate on the numbers of African immigrant girls "at risk" in their new countries. Sara Johnsdotter in her chapter engages in a critique of assumptions regarding the extent to which immigrants continue to circumcise their daughters. Her assertion (see also Johnsdotter 2002) that Somalis in Sweden have for the most part stopped practicing FGC has been vigorously debated there (see, for example, Ahlberg et al. 2004 and 2005; Almroth et al. 2005; Johnsdotter and Essén 2005).

Alison Dundes Renteln, arguing in favor of the admissibility of a cultural defense in criminal cases involving immigrants, notes that different people become acculturated at varying paces (Renteln 2002). But in the same volume in which the Renteln piece appears (Shweder et al. 2002), Lawrence G. Sager also cautions against an overly simplistic view of cultural affiliation in immigrant communities. Immigrants, he argues, are likely to meld and move between cultures in a complex fashion, and their allegiance to any one group may vacillate according to time and circumstance. Consequently, the invocation of a cultural defense can be fraught with complexity (Sager 2002).

Several of the chapters in this collection engage with the complexity of the negotiations that members of exile communities are forced to engage in when they become caught between the values of home and host communities. As Anita Häusermann Fábos points out in an essay about Sudanese immigrants to Egypt: "there is clearly a relationship between geographic or cultural distance from a social environment that shapes and perpetuates people's attitudes" (2001, 106). She stresses the importance, when rethinking the need to infibulate, of the absence of immediate influences in uprooted communities from neighborhood and family members, especially being away from "the pressure of grandmothers" (ibid., 105).[8]

Shweder and colleagues argue that some migrants "leave because they wish to become cosmopolitan; others seek a safer place to preserve their traditions." Moreover they pose the profound question: "What does tolerance mean in liberal democracies?" (Shweder et al 2002, 1–4). They point to two often contradictory impulses in liberal democracies: the desire to protect personal freedom and multiculturalism versus the desire to protect individuals from exploitation and to promote social justice.

The chapters in this volume provide a wide spectrum of examples of just how these dilemmas are being played out in Europe, North America, and Australia. As Elise Johansen points out in her chapter, "research in an exile community can help throw new light on cultural processes that were less accessible in the home context, as in exile they are voiced and debated to a higher extent." It goes without stating that these issues have taken on a sharper focus and more urgent tone in the last few years, in light of recent global events and trends. Juliet Rogers, for example, stresses in her chapter that we must consider the current broader context of a peak in Western "fear of the 'Muslim scourge.'" In a similar vein, the author of a recent article in *The Nation* about the controversies in the Netherlands surrounding Somali-born parliamentarian Ayaan Hirsi Ali[9] suggests that in "what appears to be a Europe-wide pattern, some feminists are aligning themselves with the anti-immigrant right against their former multiculturalist allies on the left" (Scroggins 2005, 22) when approaching issues such as FGC, veiling, and so-called honor killings.

Examples abound in this volume of the power of the popular media in shaping public imaginings about FGC. In Portugal and Norway, France and Australia, African immigrants find it hard to escape distorted media images of "barbaric customs," and some report being treated differently by host country citizens after particular media events, such as TV documentaries (Ahmadu, Johansen, Johnson, Johnsdotter, Rogers, Talle, chapters 12, 11, 9, 5, 6, and 4 respectively of this volume; see also Grise 2001).

Equally significant, several of these chapters reveal the deep anxieties with which many members of African (and other) immigrant communities view some of the values of their host cultures, especially regarding sexual liberalism and the autonomy of young women. Interestingly, Suárez-Orozco shows that research with immigrant youth indicates that, indeed, "the more Americanized they became, the more likely they were to engage in risky behaviors such as substance abuse, unprotected sex, and delinquency" (2002, 31). Thus, as a Somali woman interviewed by Johansen so poignantly explains, a generation of families on the move find themselves involved in a "social experiment," especially regarding raising their daughters, as difficult adjustments are made between new and emerging freedoms and constraints.

Layers of Affiliation

Each of these families has passed through a series of concentric and cumulative circles of identity and their accompanying disciplinary regimes. Most have at some point used ethnicity and/or clan membership as a form of primary self-identification, although it is crucial to bear in mind the cautionary words of Jane Maslow Cohen and Caroline Bledsoe that "ethnicity is not a set of survivals from earlier cultural traditions, but rather a situational and perpetually emergent phenomenon" (2002, 117; see also Johnson's discussion of Mandingahood in chapter 9 of this volume).

Many of them identify religion—in the context of this volume, Islam is particularly central—as an overriding source of identity and solidarity, but there are no obvious or straightforward answers about how religious faith intersects with "culture" and "tradition." For example, the Mandinga women and men who spoke with Michelle Johnson about their journey from Guinea-Bissau to Portugal expressed a wide range of views on the relationship between being a proper Mandinga person and a proper Muslim. These positions are further complicated by gendered differences in access to Islamic scripture, pilgrimage, and contact with a broader Islamic community in which FGC is not universally, or even predominantly, practiced.

In addition, Johnsdotter and Essén stress that negotiations regarding the relationship between Islam and FGC are increasingly taking place among laypersons, and that it cannot, for example, be assumed that because a particular diaspora imam has expressed support for FGC that it is widely practiced among his followers (2005, 581). They refer to a study by Rema McGown that found that Somali women in London increasingly have "redefined their Islam. They read the Qu'ran themselves. They began to interpret it for themselves. . . . They did not need any man—neither their husbands nor other authoritative figures—to tell them how to think, what to do or how to do it" (McGown 2003, 169, cited in Johnsdotter and Essén 2005, 582). The Somali migrants in Australia, Norway, Sweden, and the United Kingdom who shared their thoughts with Dopico, Johansen, Johnsdotter, and Talle, as well, made often sharp distinctions between what is required by their faith and what is "just a tradition" (see also Ahlberg et al. 2005, Yount 2004).

In their far-flung diasporas, these individuals, families, and communities—often rapidly reduced to and lumped together as generic "immigrants" or "foreigners" by their hosts—then become subjects of country-specific legal and moral regimes that can vary greatly in their responses to the perceived threat of genital cutting practices taking place outside of Africa.

Above all these arenas, finally, hovers the moral discourse of a global civil society that has as its moral goal to "reconstruct, re-imagine, and re-map world politics" (Perry 2004, 48). As Donna Perry points out in an article on children's rights in Senegal, the alliance of activists focused on women's and children's rights increasingly engages in a strategic project of reframing their causes "for international legibility" (Perry 2004, 68). She urges us to bear in mind that these movements present "not a 'Western' narrative but a global one, formed through dialogue, debate, and concession across borders" (ibid., 66) Thus, as Henrietta Moore points out in her discussion (chapter 13 of this volume), "female genital operations raise with particular force the question of the nature of politics in a globalized world."

A number of the contributions to this volume indicate that those who come from circumcising societies and move into new arenas are often unfairly prejudged by a strict culturalist assumption (see Johnsdotter, chapter 5 of this volume; Renteln 2002) that their "culture makes them" do things such as infibulate their Western-born daughters, when the host culture constructs a "generic 'they' who conduct such practices and a generic 'we' who do not" (Walley 2002, 45). The chapters by Johnsdotter and Boddy offer further reflections on how we might unsettle the prevalent notion that "culture" is something in which African women, but not "we," are mired.

Reexamining Universalist/Relativist Debates: Moving Beyond the Impasse

In the enduring debate between universalism and cultural relativism, FGC repeatedly emerges as a "test case" for the limits of the latter. Elvin Hatch, for example, groups FGC with political executions, genocide, and honor killings as "situations in which ethical relativism in untenable" (Hatch 1997, 372, cited in Dembour 2001). While some scholars argue that the debate has been exhaustive and has reached an impasse (see, for example, Cowan et al. 2001; and Gosselin 2000b), recent work in legal anthropology has offered novel and intriguing perspectives.

The Right to Culture and the Culture of Rights

As Sally Engle Merry (2001) notes, the debate between universalism and relativism in the field of human rights has long been premised on a fixed conception of both culture and rights. Now familiar to many are anthropological critiques of essentialized and static constructions of the concept of "cultures" as discrete, bounded, or homogenous groups that uniformly share norms, ideals, and practices. This formulation is replaced by one that views "culture as historically produced, globally inter-connected, internally contested, and marked with ambiguous boundaries of identity and practice" (ibid., 41). Less familiar perhaps is the notion that in many instances the framework of human rights has, as well, been cast as essentialized and static. Merry points out that the concept of human rights can be traced historically to the Enlightenment idea of the Rights of Man, which emerged in late eighteenth century Europe and has never been static, but rather a "cultural phenomenon, developing and changing over time in response to a variety of social, economic, political and cultural influences" (ibid., 38). She adds that the concept of human rights has continued to change, and in the past fifty years it has grown to include an expanded notion of collective and cultural rights.

Transnational organizations such as the United Nations, as well as numerous nongovernmental organizations (NGOs), are viewed as constituting an international civil society and have contributed to the development and expansion of human rights (Merry 2001; Perry 2004). From this perspective, human rights are historical, fluid, contested, and continually negotiated in response to changing global circumstances (Cowan et al. 2001b; Merry 2001). Thus Merry argues that "considering cultures as changing and interconnected, and rights as historically erected and transnationally defined by national and local actors, better describes the contemporary situation" (43). It also reveals the artificiality of posing culture and rights as polar opposite positions."

Several commentators (for example, Merry 2001 and Shweder 2002) have conceptualized "human rights" as a Western construct employed in the international movement to end FGC, to be contrasted with African ideals such as personhood and self-determination. Yet, as Dembour notes, "the stark divide posited between the West and the rest of the world just does not exist. . . . The spread of the modern state makes human rights relevant throughout the world" (2001, 59). Cowan and colleagues concur: "As the human rights regime becomes increasingly entrenched at the global level in international declarations, conventions and agreements which are negotiated, implemented and monitored by national, international and transnational institutions, this understanding of rights as structuring discourse seems increasingly pervasive" (Cowan et al. 2001b, 12). Several scholars point out that a "human rights culture" has already become a central aspect of global, transnational culture.

Dembour outlines two main problems with the universalist stance on human rights. First, the existence of universal human rights "is constant with the faith in natural laws. . . . Natural law is a problematic idea, however, in that it assumes that everyone will arrive at the same conclusion as to what is natural/ natural law" (2001, 57). The difficulty in identifying natural law is, however, well understood in the field of the philosophy of human rights. Second, Dembour argues that positing the existence of universal human rights "ultimately leads to arrogance because it excludes the experience of the 'other'" (ibid., 58).

Cultural relativism, Dembour argues, when taken too far, is equally flawed, as it "tends to assume that people are more determined by their culture than they in fact are," by overlooking variation, choices, and change within cultures (2001, 59). She goes on to assert that a cultural relativist position risks making people immune to considerations of morality, allowing culture to become "an excuse for abuse" (ibid., 59; see also Honig 1999). Dembour therefore concludes that problems with either extreme position present a conundrum, and that "the way out of the conundrum is to err uncomfortably between the two poles represented by universalism and relativism" (2001, 58).

Dembour illustrates the vacillation of "the pendulum" in the "uncomfortable between" space through the recent history of legal decisions regarding FGC in French criminal courts, by examining the outcomes of several cases of prosecution of parents for having excision performed on a daughter. Although French law has been interpreted to ban excision under the framework of child abuse (rather than under a separate anti-FGM law), suspended sentences and some notable cases of acquittal indicate that the role of "culture" and actors' motives weaken a purely universalist stance. The pattern of a trend from milder to more severe sentencing across the late 1980s and 1990s and then a sudden acquittal illustrates that applying the image of the pendulum, "one can speculate that, having gone too far in one direction, it was driven to revert back towards leniency" (Dembour 2001, 68).

From "Excuse for Abuse" to "Margin of Appreciation": Situating a Right to Culture

Dembour argues that the "need for relativism is *so* fundamental" (emphasis in original) that it appears even in fora framed by universalist assumptions, such as the European Court of Human Rights: "Anyone familiar with the case law of the Court will have heard about the doctrine of 'the margin of appreciation.' Through this doctrine the Court recognizes that national governments can be better placed than itself to appreciate local circumstances and local needs, and thus human rights claims" (2001, 74). It is through such doctrines that it is possible to take into account local circumstances, or what some call "culturalist" claims—"claims which invoke notions of culture, tradition, language, religion, locality, tribe or race" (Cowan et al. 2001b, 9). Culturalist claims, and particularly minority group rights, have become part of familiar rhetoric in human rights discourse, and have reached an unprecedented scale in the past two decades (Cowan et al. 2001b; see also Okin 1999a; Shweder et al. 2002). Demands for group rights have been growing, particularly from indigenous populations, minority ethnic or religious groups, and formerly colonized populations (Okin 1999a).

The debate regarding group rights versus universalist formulations of individual rights (what Martha Minow refers to as "cultural defender" versus "liberal" arguments, 2002, 255) attained renewed vigor in the wake of Susan Okin's essay, "Is Multiculturalism Bad for Women?"[10] Okin's definition of multiculturalism holds that "minority cultures or ways of life are not sufficiently protected by the practices of ensuring the individual rights of their members, and as a consequence these should be protected through special *group* rights or privileges" (1999a, 10–11). She paraphrases the position of the foremost scholar on group rights, Will Kymlicka, who holds that "because societal cultures play so pervasive and fundamental a role in the lives of their members, and because such cultures are threatened with extinction, minority cultures should be protected by special [group] rights" (ibid., 11). Moreover, minority cultures should be tolerated and protected because a stable culture is essential for "the development of self-respect and for giving persons a context in which they can develop the capacity to make choices about how to lead their lives" (ibid., 20). Group rights have been invoked to claim exemption from laws binding other citizens, such as the exemption of Sikh men, who wear turbans, from the requirement by British law to use helmets when riding a motorcycle (Cowan et al. 2001b). More controversial examples cited by Okin, however, spotlight FGC, alongside polygamy and forced or early marriage.

Okin, along with other commentators, points to a paradox. Efforts to assure respect and tolerance for cultural diversity do so through legal measures that have strict definitions of group membership and tradition, "paying more attention to differences among groups than within them" (1999a, 12). This point has been elaborated by Tamir (1999), who notes that the notion of group rights as it is often used in the current debate and legal cases assumes that groups are homogenous static entities and that members' adherence to unifying tradition, beliefs, and practices becomes a precondition for exercising these rights (see also Cowan et al. 2001b and Piot, chapter 7 of this volume).

Okin's main critique of multiculturalism is based on the assertion that it reinforces gender inequality, thereby undermining advances made by feminists in recent decades. This argument rests on a series of premises. First, she asserts that "most cultures have as one of their principle aims the control of women by men" and institute discriminatory practices in order to ensure that control (Okin 1999a, 13). Second, sometimes "'culture' or 'tradition' are so closely linked with control over women that they are virtually equated" and form the basis of cultural claims (ibid., 16). Finally, she argues that the majority of cultural claims that are invoked in U.S. criminal cases are connected to gender and therefore aim to uphold discriminatory practices and in doing so violate women's right to equality. She concludes that many women born into patriarchal societies, "*might be much better off if the culture into which they were born either became extinct (so that its members would become integrated into the less sexist surrounding culture) or, preferably, to be encouraged to alter itself so as to reinforce the equality of women—at least to the degree to which this value is upheld in the majority culture*" (ibid., 22–23, emphasis in original).

While most commentators agree with Okin that respect for minority cultures cannot be entirely unconditional, several lines of criticism have emerged, some particularly relevant to the posing of FGC as an example of the "limits of multiculturalism." Bonnie Honig argues that "culture is something rather more complicated than patriarchal permission for powerful men to subordinate vulnerable women" (1999, 36), and critiques Okin for divorcing practices such as FGC from their context, meaning, and significance. Questioning Okin's assumption that Western liberal regimes are less patriarchal than those of minorities, she urges Western feminists to "hold their own practices up to the same scrutiny they apply to Others," and to "resist the all-too-familiar and dangerous temptation to mark foreignness as fundamentally threatening to women" (ibid., 38–40). Bhikhu Parekh (1999) additionally raises the point that those who do not share Western feminist views are often accused of culturally generated false consciousness, a critique that has been leveled at proponents of FGC (see, for example, Nussbaum 1999). She asserts that "what is clumsily called multiculturalism is a revolt against liberal hegemony and self-righteousness" (Parekh 1999, 73).[11]

Kymlicka (1999) agrees with Okin that it is important to look carefully at gender inequality, as well as other forms of inequality, when examining the legitimacy of minority group rights. He suggests, however, that it is possible to distinguish between two kinds of group rights: those that restrict individual choice and those that protect a minority group from economic or political oppression by the larger society. Robert Post (1999, 67) notes that it is unclear how one distinguishes enabling and oppressive cultural norms, and, importantly, asks: "When, exactly, do pervasive influences of a culture become 'impositions'?"

Is FGC Best Approached as a Human Rights Violation?

The classification of FGC specifically as an international human rights violation under the rubric of international law has been a subject of ongoing debate. This topic is, for example, the central focus of a book that makes the authoritative claim to being "a guide to laws and policies worldwide," by Anika Rahman, director of the International Program of the Center for Reproductive Law and Policy, and well-known anticircumcision activist Nahid Toubia. They investigate whether FGC violates human rights as protected by international instruments, and they claim to consider counterarguments of those who find that

FGC does not fall under the purview of international law (Rahman and Toubia 2000, 15). Unfortunately, they fail to cite the work of leading legal scholars who have often found the applications on U.N. conventions to the case of FGC to be problematic.

Kay Boulware-Miller (1985), for instance, analyzes arguments regarding the framing of FGC as a human rights violation, based on three claims: the rights of the child, the right to sexual and corporal integrity, and the right to health. For each claim, Boulware-Miller outlined a number of problems that can prevent each approach from being effective with respect to FGC. Gunning (1991) and Breitung (1996) have also reviewed international human rights doctrines that could potentially form the basis for opposing FGC; to the claims addressed by Bouleware-Miller they add prohibitions against torture and freedom from discrimination against women. Although Rahman and Toubia (2000, 30) conclude that "there is ample support under human rights law for holding governments accountable for the practice of FC/FGM in their countries," Boulware-Miller and Gunning found flaws in their application to FGC (see Gosselin 2000b for a discussion of the complications associated with each claim; see also Shell-Duncan and Hernlund 2000). Moreover, a UN Special Working Group assigned to study legal claims as applied to FGC concluded in its report that no international treaty could directly address this practice, finding that the issue raises a number of "challenging questions" (United Nations 1986). We revisit each of the varied approaches later in this chapter, although we discuss some aspects in greater detail than others to allow for a close engagement with the focus of the chapters.

HUMAN RIGHTS AND THE RIGHT TO HEALTH: AN UNSETTLED ALLIANCE

A number of observers have argued that the least controversial approach to the elimination of FGC is through a right-to-health argument (for example, Boulware-Miller 1985, United Nations 1986; see also discussion in Shell-Duncan and Hernlund 2000). There exists, however, an uncomfortable and uneasy alliance between health and human rights in debates surrounding the topic of FGC. Although many activists and international organizations have tried to distance their arguments from a health or medical basis, this has largely been unsuccessful. Debates surrounding the interpretation of health evidence and the medicalization of the practice, as well as discourses on female circumcision and human rights, are overshadowed by disquieting subjective interpretations and contradictions.

A Brief History of Health-Based Campaigns

Opposition to FGC can be traced back several centuries to early colonial campaigns (see, for example, Mackie 1996 and L. Thomas 2003). The current wave of opposition was launched by a series of conferences honoring the

United Nations Decade for Women from 1975 to 1985 (see Gosselin 2000b). It is widely recognized that there has, in general, been "greater success in raising awareness about the issue than in changing behavior" (Population Reference Bureau 2001), a surprising and perplexing—if not alarming—finding, given the volume of resources and now decades of effort aimed at eliminating female genital cutting practices.

The first international conference on female circumcision, organized by the World Health Organization (WHO) and held in 1979 in Khartoum, Sudan, launched what Shweder calls "the global campaign"—an international movement "with the aim of creating and enforcing universal norms according to which any socially endorsed surgical alteration of the genitals of a female child or adolescent is defined as either a) an intolerably harmful cultural practice, or b) an obvious and impermissible violation of human rights, or both" (forthcoming, 2). The initial phase of the global campaign framed opposition to FGC as a health problem—an "impediment to development that can be prevented and eradicated much like any disease" (Hosken 1978, 85)

Following a 1984 seminar in Dakar, Senegal, the Inter-African Committee (IAC) was formed to coordinate national and international efforts to eliminate what was referred to as "FGM." Recognizing that a specific focus on FGM would not work without simultaneously attacking other pressing health concerns, FGM became labeled one of four "harmful traditional practices," along with childhood marriage and early pregnancy, nutritional taboos, and certain child spacing and delivery practices. Using grassroots educational programs about negative health effects, the IAC education is credited with consciousness raising that resulted in an essential shift: a topic once considered a private matter beyond the realm of government policy became the subject of public debate and scrutiny (Boyle 2002; Merry 2001; Welch 1995). The IAC's health education approach focused largely on delivering a message centered on the adverse health effects, assuming that as people are made aware of the risks, they will acknowledge a need to abandon the practice.

Elisabeth Boyle (2002) argues that a health approach was, at the outset, essential for legitimizing intervention. She points to an important contradiction: "the institutionalized notion of individualism emphasizes human rights and calls for international organizations to intervene into national politics" (16). This stands in contrast to the institution of sovereign autonomy, "i.e., local rule without outside interference," a construct highly valued in the context of post-colonial Africa. Given the conflict between these two institutions, a "health discourse provided a compromise that promoted international intervention without undermining sovereignty" (43).

Rethinking Health Approaches

As an intervention approach, education on the adverse health effects of FGC has gradually fallen from favor for several reasons. In circumcising communities, people are often already aware of many, if not most, of the potential adverse health outcomes but feel that the risk is worth taking in light of the social and cultural importance of the practice (Obiora 1997, 359; Sargent 1989, 1991; Shell-Duncan and Hernlund, 2000; N. Toubia 1988). Additionally, health risk information delivered in anticircumcision campaigns is often drawn from extraordinary case studies of infibulation with extreme complications, resulting in perceived, and often real, exaggerations of health risks, the effect of which in some instances has been to undermine the credibility of such campaigns (for example, Ahmadu 2000; Boddy, chapter 2 of this volume; Gosselin 2000; Hernlund 2003; Johnson 2000a).[12]

CREDIBILITY GAPS. Boyle (2002, 55) reports that a 1995 Joint Statement on FGM first drafted by WHO, UNICEF, the UN Family Planning Association (UNFPA), and the United Nations Development Program "labeled the medical basis for anti-FGC policies a 'mistake'" and suggested that medical discourses had been exaggerated and counterproductive. A number of researchers of FGC have long witnessed on the ground the credibility gap that often appears between well-meaning propaganda and the real-life experiences of affected women. In many cases, local health care professionals also express skepticism regarding dramatic claims of harm, especially when procedures are noninfibulating. One physician interviewed by Hernlund, for example, questioned the utility of "borrowing arguments from Sudan that have nothing to do with what is practiced here" (Hernlund 2003).

Closer scrutiny of data on health problems associated with FGC shows that it is indeed difficult to establish the medical "facts" (see Shell-Duncan and Hernlund 2000). Information is available from several published sources, including case reports, clinic and hospital records, hospital-based case control comparisons, and self-reported retrospective survey data; each source of data bears serious limitations (see Shell-Duncan 2001 for an extensive discussion). Impassioned debates have arisen from scholarly claims and counterclaims regarding the effects of various types of genital cutting of both males and females. This is one area where the pendulum seems to be swinging with particular ferocity between poles that lie very far apart.

Carla Makhlouf Obermeyer completed the first systematic review of the biomedical literature[13] and found that, despite the "vast literature on harmful effects of genital surgeries . . . evidence on complications is very scarce" (1999, 92).[14] Only eight studies met her criteria for inclusion in her summary of major findings, and she concluded that "severe complications are relatively infrequent" (97) and that medical complications are "the exception rather than the rule" (92). Her interpretation of the available evidence launched a renewed debate over the interpretation of the "medical facts."

Shweder used this review to suggest that lack of evidence of harm is equivalent to evidence of lack of harm (see also Hernlund 2003) and claimed that

Obermeyer's review shows that "African genital modifications are not all that dangerous, and can in any case be done safely" (forthcoming, 8). Mackie, who deems the health risks to be "nontrivial," vehemently objected to Obermeyer's dismissal of complications as "infrequent": "Death from malaria is the exception rather than the rule, but no physician would put it that way to a patient about to travel to a malarial zone" (2003, 144). Arguments on each extreme range from, on the one hand, the examples given by Boddy in this volume that matter-of-factly state that operations are "frequently fatal" (Pugh 1983, 9) and use phrases such as "if she survives" (Lightfoot-Klein 1989b, 378), to Shweder's assertions that "African children do not die because they have been circumcised (rather, they die from malnutrition, war, and disease)" (2002, 228) and that "women are not typically injured . . . by the surgery" (ibid., 237).

Perhaps anticipating such divergent perspectives, Obermeyer states that "from a biomedical point of view, which powerfully shapes the evaluation we make of interventions on the body, no matter what the exact numbers are, any pain and suffering that accompany or follow the operations that are not medically prescribed, and even the lowest rates of complications are unacceptable" (1999, 92). She goes on to note, however, that "this assessment is not universally shared" (93) and points out that FGC may be valued by practitioners for reasons that have nothing to do with health (94). The central question, then, is: what is acceptable risk? And perhaps more importantly: who has the authority to decide what is acceptable risk?

ASSESSING HARM. Noting, again, that extreme cases of infibulation are often used to generalize about health risks associated with all forms of FGC, in 2001 Shell-Duncan published a comprehensive review of the literature reporting the frequency of complications differentiated by type of female circumcision (Shell-Duncan 2001). After considering the limitations of clinical and cross-sectional survey data, Shell-Duncan concluded that the then-available information on long-term and obstetrical consequences was quite sparse for all types of FGC.

She also noted that many of the reported conditions, such as chronic pelvic and urinary tract infections, may arise from factors other than genital cutting, and it was not possible to discern the causal role of FGC with the available evidence. This review showed that all forms of FGC are associated with short-term complications such as infection, hemorrhage, and severe pain. The main finding, however, was an extraordinarily wide range of reported incidences of complications associated with any one form of cutting: "For example, the percentage of women reporting hemorrhage following clitoridectomy ranged from 6–55 percent, and from 5 to 66 percent following infibulation" (Shell-Duncan 2001, 1018). Shell-Duncan further demonstrated that the literature to date failed to control for factors that may influence this wider range, such as training of the circumciser, location of the operation, and availability of medical support. These factors, along with the limitations of using self-reported, retrospective data, led to her conclusion that the information at the time provided only limited insight regarding the potential health risks, and that better data were needed.

A more recent, large-scaled community-based study conducted in The Gambia by Morison et al. (2001), which included physical examination of most of the respondents, confirmed the hunches of many researchers and their informants: there does indeed not seem to be a measurable connection between noninfibulating genital cutting and obstructed labor and other often repeated long-term medical consequences (but see also Yount n.d.). Intriguingly, some later research findings also seem to indicate that, even in the case of infibulation, health consequences are perhaps not as straightforward as has previously been assumed. Birgitta Essén, a gynecologist with extensive experience working with infibulated women in Sweden, claims that "the scar tissue after an infibulation, provided that the scar has healed well, is more elastic and thinner than scar tissue after episiotomies (where the cut is made in the vaginal birth canal through muscular tissue), regularly performed at Swedish hospitals in non-circumcised primigravidae women" (see Essén 2001).[15] She cautions, however, that claims of exaggerated medical complications of infibulation are not uncontroversial, given the moral discourse on female circumcision.

This more recent research on the health effects of FGC has also failed to find an association between these practices, especially clitoridectomy and excision, and several other purported long-term health outcomes, including fistulaes, tumors, infertility, painful intercourse, prolapse of the uterus, and reproductive tract infections (Morison et al. 2001). Morison and others see no reason, however, why this conclusion should interfere with efforts to address the practice and its elimination on the grounds that it is most commonly performed without real consent and causes irreversible bodily changes (see also Mackie 2003). Morison and colleagues conclude that "efforts to eradicate the practice should incorporate a human rights approach rather than rely solely on the damaging health consequences of FGC" (ibid., 652). Yet, as we argue, disentangling health from human rights is particularly challenging.[16]

Complications

Even seemingly straightforward appeals to the universal human desire for health and wellness tend, in the context of female genital cutting, to become entangled in a number of related complications: the slippery nature of the concept of "sunna"; the similarities and differences—legal and medical, actual and perceived—between female and male genital modifications; the contradictions inherent in judgments of FGC on the one hand and female genital cosmetic surgeries (FGCS) on the other; the impact that the "moral panic" (see Johnsdotter, chapter 5 of this volume) surrounding FGC has had on the quality of medical care—especially gynecological and obstetrical—received by already circumcised women in the diaspora; and, finally, debates over the morality of using medicalization of FGC as an intermediate harm-reduction strategy.

"IT IS ONLY *Sunna.*" One dilemma that is frequently raised at conferences where FGC scholars and affected health care professionals gather is how to approach the claim that a genital cutting procedure is "only sunna." Although the term is rooted in Islamic scripture that urges those who practice female circumcision to do so in moderation, attempts have been made to delineate precisely what the practice entails. While standard taxonomies define sunna as a nonwounding pricking of the clitoris, anecdotal evidence suggests that the term is used much more widely by practitioners. It has for example been claimed that in Somalia and Sudan, any procedure short of infibulation gets labeled as mere sunna. Reports of true symbolic circumcisions being performed in Africa have not presented published supporting evidence.[17] In the new diasporas, however, the concept has become highly politicized.

The federal anti-FGM law of the United States (further elaborated on later in this chapter in the section on legislative approaches), for example, is not worded clearly enough to definitively provide a platform to prosecute someone for performing a symbolic circumcision (see, for example, Fernandez-Romano 1999). However, this inclusion is likely its intent and, as we discuss in the context of medicalization, a Seattle hospital's proposal to perform symbolic circumcisions in a clinical setting became a political impossibility.

Johnsdotter (chapter 5 of this volume) points to a similar situation in Sweden, where the letter of the law also appears to not criminalize nonmutilating circumcision ("mutilating" here being defined as removing tissue). Rather than focusing on the actual medical consequences of a symbolic pricking and comparing this harm to what arises from fashionable genital piercings, routine infant male circumcisions, and female genital cosmetic surgeries, however, the decision to condemn any and all symbolic female circumcision is clearly an ideological one, argues Johnsdotter. Rather than being an issue of preventing actual harm, it becomes, she suggests, an issue of the authorities not being perceived as "sending the wrong message" to immigrants.

Hernlund witnessed a similar struggle over "sending the right message" at a Seattle seminar organized a few years ago for health care providers and for refugee women. Some of the Somali women claimed in a group discussion that sunna today entails a "nicking," others that there is only a "pinch" of the prepuce skin and a verbal declaration of altered status. While they all expressed strong opposition to infibulation and considered that practice un-Islamic, they failed to see the harm done by a purely symbolic act leaving no scars. The workshop organizers, however, were visibly uncomfortable and advised the women not to say any more about a potentially illegal practice.

In a private conversation later with two of the Somali women, who labeled themselves not only as refugees but also as social service providers in another city, they talked at length about this politically charged situation. It had not occurred to these extremely bright, articulate, and politically astute women professionals that a simple pinprick of the clitoris could be illegal under U.S.

law, while their own sons legally underwent much more invasive procedures. They concluded that it would be better to return to secrecy rather than share with North Americans the remarkable behavior changes initiated within the community itself. Particularly in the tense climate following September 11, in which Somalis have already been singled out as potential terrorists, they decided that this was yet another way that Somalis could risk deportation or the loss of their children.

MALE GENITAL MUTILATION. Eric Silverman has complained that anthropologists have neglected to study the impassioned debate over male circumcision, "a debate that resonates with the same issues as disputes over female circumcision" (2004, 426). A more recent article by Kirsten Bell expresses concern "with the *asymmetry* in discussions of [male and female] genital cutting and the problematic assumptions they perpetuate" (2005, 140). Shweder, as well, has engaged in a comparative analysis of the two practices, utilizing for both the criteria of consensual versus nonconsensual, major versus minor, and reversible versus nonreversible (2002, 239). Shweder and his colleagues ask whether the "unequal treatment of male and female circumcision demonstrate[s] hypocrisy, ethnocentrism, or unjustifiable limits to the tolerance granted ethnic minority groups in the United States and European nations?" (Shweder et al. 2002, 1; see also G. P. Miller 2002).

Of interest to discussions surrounding FGM is the growing trend of activism against what some refer to as MGM (male genital mutilation). Referring to themselves as "pro-intact" or as advocating for "genital integrity," a myriad of organizations have been formed to fight male circumcision (Silverman 2004, 435).[18] Silverman points out that many legal challenges to male circumcision in U.S. courts appeal on the basis of FGM law to the equal protection clause of the Fourteenth Amendment (ibid., 436).

While former Senator Carol Moseley-Braun has justified legislation against female-but-not-male circumcision by describing the latter as "quick, relatively painless, and without long-term consequences for men" (in Fernandez-Romano 1999, 153), others disagree. In the 1996 case of *Fishbeck vs. the State of North Dakota* (United States District Court for the District of North Dakota, Southeastern Division), for example, a mother whose son was circumcised against her will with only his father's consent seeks to show the unconstitutionality of an anti–genital mutilation law that offers protection only for infant females. In the court proceedings, she argues, "No one doubts that children should be protected from the needless and unconsented to mutilation of their genitals. The question presented here is whether males should be denied such protection solely because of their sex." Her medical expert witness, Dr. Van Howe, M.D., adds, "[T]he complications from surgical alterations of the genitalia are similar for both male and females. The only differences are related to the gender specific functions of menstruation, child birth, impotence, and premature ejaculation."

Dr. Van Howe adds in a concluding sentence that seems particularly relevant to the present discussion that "the reasons cited by families for altering the genitalia of their children is nearly identical whether it is a girl in Africa or a boy in the United Sates," that is "cleanliness, preventing illness, religion, looking like other children or like their parents, fear of promiscuity, and acceptance of the altered genitalia as more attractive by the opposite sex."

DESIGNER VAGINAS. If contradictory responses to nonconsensual genital surgeries on female and male minors respectively reveal inconsistencies, the same can be said when comparing FGC and an increasingly common type of plastic surgery, popularly referred to as female genital cosmetic surgeries or "designer vaginas." Such procedures include labia minora reduction, labia majora remodeling, pubic liposuction and lifts, and clitoral reduction (see www.altermd.com), some of which resemble quite closely—in results, if not in the context of the surgeries—genital cutting procedures done "traditionally" in African societies.[19]

Journalists commenting on this growing fad in places including the United States, Canada, and Sweden point out that such surgery is done—according to the surgery-seeking women themselves—for "aesthetic" or "practical" reasons, including "difficulty practicing certain sports, such as horseback riding or bicycling" (Kjöller 2005, translation by Hernlund; see also Klein 2005, Navarro 2004, Nilsson 2005, Summerfield 2004, and the contributions to *Jenda,* volume 1, 2001: Derrick 2001, Falcon 2000, Gorov 1999, Jen-Loy no date, Ollivier 2000).

Essén and Johnsdotter add that these novel beauty ideals seem influenced by pornography (2004, 612), which is confirmed in accounts from promotional materials for U.S. plastic surgeons offering such procedures: a Dr. Stern "runs ads in strip club magazines" (Navarro 2004), and a Dr. Matlock "uses billboard ads depicting women throwing their bodies back in sexual pleasure" (Summerfield 2004). The personal testimonies of women who have elected to undergo such surgeries for reasons other than to correct a pathology echo, in surreal ways, reports from infibulating societies: "'I'll just get graphic because that's what it's about,' [one patient] said. 'It's cleaner, it's more hygienic. . . . It's sculpted. It looks nice. It's perfect. Honestly, I feel sexier'" (Gorov 1999).

A number of observers point to the ironies of such widely varying valuations of related procedures. Women from the Horn of Africa living in Australia perceived labioplasty as a "double standard" in light of aggressive campaigns against any genital modifications, however minor, among women of African origin (Allotey et al. 2001, 197). Ahmadu, as well, in chapter 12 of this book wonders why the credibility of Western women is not questioned when they claim benefits from genital surgeries.

In Sweden, Essén and Johnsdotter question how the Swedish anti-FGM law, which bans any type of genital cutting on women regardless of age or level of consent, can allow genital surgeries to be performed on Swedish women (2004; see also Kjöller 2005, Nilsson 2005).[20] "Is it acceptable if her motive is about aesthetics and perceived difficulties bicycling," Johnsdotter asks, "but unacceptable if she refers to tradition or religion?" (quoted in Kjöller 2005). In this scenario, adult African women are seen as in need of protection, while adult Swedish women are considered capable of making their own decisions (ibid.).

A Swedish surgeon (quoted in Nilsson 2005) asserts, "Personally, I don't see any similarities between genital mutilation and FGCS. Genital mutilation aims to remove the clitoris. But the labia are simply a fold of skin. Genital mutilation, performed coercively for cultural reasons, is horrific, I think. But it is a completely different thing when *well balanced* people come here and want to have surgery on a voluntary basis" (emphasis added). Johnsdotter asks us to consider, however, the extent to which Swedish women's decisions to undergo such operations are as cultural in nature as are motivations behind other genital cutting procedures. "How should a plastic surgeon respond to an adult woman, seeking genital surgical modifications," Essén and Johnsdotter ask rhetorically, if she "has one Swedish and one African parent?"

These provocative questions have indeed had an effect in Sweden, where the "National Board of Health said it is considering declaring some of the vaginal cosmetic procedures illegal and a form of genital mutilation. It has yet to figure out where these procedures fit into law" (Summerfield 2004). In the United States (see also the section on legislation later in this chapter) the situation is a bit clearer, as any woman over the age of eighteen who has given consent can legally undergo genital surgery, regardless of her stated reasons. The American College of Obstetricians and Gynecologists, however, issued a letter in June 2004 expressing concern over the surgeries and, in particular, "the way in which these procedures are being marketed and promoted. The use of a business model that aims to control the dissemination of scientific knowledge is troubling. For physicians who perform these procedures, obtaining a patient's informed consent will be challenging, given the absence of medical literature about these procedures" (Klein 2005).

(E)QUALITY OF CARE. If some African women who have migrated to the West thus perceive a discrepancy in the level of medical decision-making power they are allowed vis-à-vis their hosts, of perhaps even greater concern are the disparities in the quality of care that seem to arise as a result of the "moral panic" surrounding genital cutting practices (see Johnsdotter, chapter 5 of this volume). A number of observers point out that circumcised women in the diaspora face unique challenges, particularly in relationship to gynecological and obstetrical care, when encountering host-country health workers who typically lack training in how to give proper care to circumcised women and who may let personal feelings of confusion and anxiety about these practices overshadow their professional demeanors.

Birgitta Essén and Charlotte Wilken-Jensen caution that there is "a risk that strong emotional feelings against the practice of FGC may obscure the rational way of evaluating obstetric and gynecological risks, and preempt the investigation of other factors that may play a causative role in morbidity among these immigrant women" (2003, 684). Likewise, Mmaskepe Sejoe, coordinator at the Department of Human Services in Melbourne, Australia, told Christine Mason that "'health professionals often assume that circumcised women must be a mindless vessel to be used and abused.' It is for this reason that many circumcised women can find the racism they experience in relation to their condition worse than the problem itself. Some therefore avoid doctors and health practitioners for fear of ridicule and embarrassment" (Mason 2001; see also Gunning 2002).

This assertion is backed up by empirical work. For instance, Beverly Chalmers and Kowser Omer Hashi write that among Somali immigrant women in Canada, 74.7 percent reported being afraid of seeking prenatal care during their most recent pregnancy. In general, these women wanted less intervention than they got—1 percent wanted a C-section, but 50 percent actually had one. A staggering 87.5 percent reported hurtful comments about their genital status by caregivers (2000, 232). Aud Talle, in chapter 4 of this volume, reports similarly troubling findings among Somali women in London.

At the Seattle workshop discussed earlier, as well, several Somali women expressed anger that 80 percent of the seminar time was taken up with information about the harmfulness of infibulation, while they wanted to know more about diabetes and asthma and how to apply for food stamps and subsidized housing. Although they were sympathetic to the project of training U.S. doctors to provide more skilled and sensitive care to those women who already have undergone infibulation (one of the goals of the event), they insisted that they no longer need to be reminded and reprimanded about how harmful something is that they have already undergone and cannot undo, but which they have no intention of doing to their daughters.

Widmark and colleagues (2002) point to communication problems between midwives and the women and their families and the fact that they found few or no official guidelines in place about how to provide appropriate care. Despite the high level of awareness of FGC-related issues in Sweden, the authors describe obstetrical care for circumcised (especially infibulated) women as a "marginalized issue." The only written information the midwives they interviewed claimed to have received consisted of "an elaboration of the law focusing mainly on what should *not* be done," that is re-suturing after being defibulated in order to give birth (Widmark et al., 2002, 119).[21]

It is very encouraging that many highly skilled and deeply compassionate caregivers in each of these diaspora settings are busy providing excellent care for their immigrant patients and that many are engaged, as well, in developing educational protocols for their colleagues and providing training and emotional support (see, for example, Horowitz and Jackson 1997; Lightfoot-Klein and Shaw 1990; and the clinical work of Dr. Nawal Nour). Nonetheless, this remains an area of great concern, as women who have already undergone genital cutting are in dire need of empathy and professionalism rather than lectures and condemnation.

MEDICALIZATION AS HARM REDUCTION. A final problematic aspect of the health approach as a rationale for abandoning FGC is that the emphasis on health risks is believed by anticircumcision advocates to have inadvertently promoted the conceptualization of FGC as a health issue amenable to treatment through medical care.[22] Opposition to all forms of medicalization has been and remains at the core of anticircumcision activities. A 1982 statement by the World Health Organization declared it unethical for FGC to be performed by "any health officials in any setting—including hospitals or other health establishments" (WHO 1982). In 1994 the International Federation of Gynecology and Obstetrics passed a resolution that calls on all doctors to refuse to perform "female genital mutilation," and was joined by many other major organizations such as the American College of Obstetrics and Gynecology, UNICEF, and the American Medical Association (ACOG Committee Opinion 1995).

Opposition to medicalization by anticircumcision activists and international organizations is based on numerous claims, including that it violates professional ethics of the medical profession (Toubia and Izette 1998); that promotion of less severe forms of cutting does not necessarily promote "eradication" (Dorkenoo 1994); that medicalization would overburden healthcare systems that are already taxed (Mandara 2000); that it legitimizes and perhaps encourages the practice; and that it hinders or undermines interventions designed to eliminate the practice (Gordon 1991; see Shell-Duncan 2001 for a discussion of these arguments against medicalization).

Perhaps the most major concern raised against any form of harm-reducing medicalization (as well as against "allowing" any form of sunna or symbolic cutting in general) is that cutting will become entrenched, which will prevent its eventual eradication. For example, in the context of a U.S. congressional hearing held in Washington, D.C., in 2004, a pamphlet states unequivocally, despite the unresolved questions regarding the effects of medicalization on anticircumcision campaigns: "Medicalization of FGC is ineffective and perpetuates the practice."[23]

A rare dissenting voice emerges in a commentary by physician Julia Valderrama (2002) in response to the controversy surrounding a 1999 newspaper report that Médecins Sans Frontières (MSF) had provided medical equipment for female genital cutting (529). Dr. Valderrama worked in Somalia in 1994, where she found traditional birth attendants (TBAs) surprisingly willing to "cut less," but not to not cut at all. While she asserts that the "medicalisation of female genital mutilation should not be officially incorporated into any organisation's policy," she goes on to argue that the "provision of medical supplies for surgical procedures may save lives and suffering." MSF stated that this action was the "decision of individuals" and that it did not reflect its policy; and Valderrama declares, "I think such individual decision is a wise intermediate position towards the eradication of female genital mutilation" (529). Providing such support, she argues, is a "harm-reduction strategy" and "international health workers should not turn a blind eye to the pain inflicted while awaiting other effective strategies" (530).

In an extensive review, Shell-Duncan found little empirical support for claims regarding the adverse effects of medicalization and argued that "we do not, at this juncture, have the grounds to advocate staunch opposition to medicalization of FGC" (2001, 1026). This review investigated whether the medicalization of FGC could be informed by the public health strategy of harm reduction, a paradigm that "aims to minimize health hazards associated with risky behaviors . . . by encouraging safer alternatives, including, but not limited to abstinence" (ibid., 1013). However, transitional measures that may make the practice of FGC safer have been rejected in the international community, based on the belief that they undermine "the urgency that originally motivated the eradication of the practice" (Boyle 2002, 55).

Shweder concurs, and argues that

> perhaps one good reason for separating the harmful practice claim from the violation of basic human rights is that those who want to eradicate the practice want to eradicate it even if genital surgeries already are, or could be made to be, medically safe. They think it is wrong for Africans to modify female genitals (although not male genitals), and it is wrong, many advocates will argue, even if the body modification can be done hygienically, with anesthesia and with no effect on sexual functioning. In other words, the human rights advocacy groups are not really interested in making the world safe for these types of medical procedures. Their goal is to eradicate the practice, whether it is medically harmful or not (forthcoming, 5).[24]

Boyle notes that "alternatives to complete eradication . . . have not been addressed by international actors, but may be important nationally and locally" (2002, 18). Proposals that were not explicitly labeled "harm reduction" but were offered in order to reduce more extensive forms of FGC and minimize health risks for African immigrants have been developed in the West. The first such proposal was made in the Netherlands, when a Welfare, Health, and Culture Ministry report recommended that doctors be allowed to perform symbolic circumcision, involving an anaesthetized pricking of the clitoris, as an alternative to infibulation for Somali immigrants (Hinge 1995; Obiora 1997, 285; see also discussion of sunna earlier in this chapter). A similar proposal was forwarded in 1996 at Harborview Hospital in Seattle, Washington. Both proposals drew a storm of protest and were subsequently rejected. There was little public reflection, however, on the fact that the very same hospital routinely performs infant male circumcisions involving far more removal of healthy tissue and no consent. Nor did the general public seem concerned with how the Somalis caught up in the controversy managed to find a solution.

Similarly, a Somali gynecologist practicing in Italy recently developed a proposal to offer symbolic circumcision for Somali women and obtained support from leaders of ten local communities of immigrants from Africa (Turone 2004). Nonetheless, this proposal ignited a political and media storm. While on December 5, 2003, the Bioethics Board of Florence had expressed support, the proposal was ultimately blocked by the Regional Council of Toscana, which on February 3, 2004, unanimously disapproved of Dr. Abdulcadir's proposal (Pia Grassivaro Gallo, personal communication to editors).

In many regions of Africa, however, medicalization is increasing, even in the face of opposition or formal bans (see, for example, Collinet et al. 2002 on Djibouti and Gosselin 2000b on Mali), a situation in which "those who are or would be entrusted with the task of educating the public on the health hazards of female circumcision (nurses, midwives, and doctors) are sometimes the very people who operate on girls" (Gosselin 2000b). In certain instances, the unfolding changes are consistent with harm-reduction principles, although the term "harm reduction" is not generally used (but see Valderrama 2002).

A qualitative UNICEF study on FGC in Somalia reports that religious leaders are preaching against infibulation and are urging sunna circumcision. The religious leaders argue that "sunni is good because it does not have health problems and is allowed by religion" (Kaphle 2000, 95). The study also reports that "health professionals are not in consensus for total eradication, and are denying to perform traditional circumcision, but not sunni" (ibid.). A small but growing number of Somali gynecologists are advocating symbolic circumcision as a transitional measure toward total abandonment of the practice (Roda Qumane, personal communication to authors). Similarly, an NGO in Tanzania has reportedly introduced a milder form of clitoridectomy "as a compromise to those who do not wish to end FGM" (*Awaken*, December 2002, 6). The emergence of such compromise proposals and practices has not, however, resulted in any change in the position toward medicalization by activists and international donor agencies, as staunch opposition to all forms of medicalization remains unwavering.

ZERO TOLERANCE VERSUS FREEDOM OF CHOICE. Such resolute opposition to any and all intermediate harm-reduction compromises is evidenced, for example, in the Inter-African Committee's 2003 pronouncement of February 6 as annual Zero Tolerance on FGM Day. This pronouncement was coupled with a conference in Addis Ababa at which the IAC made an express appeal to African heads of state and their wives to commit themselves to "eradicate all forms of HTPs (harmful traditional practices) and adopt **'Zero Tolerance to FGM'**" (pamphlet made available at the event; bolded in the original).

Major international donors, as well, have adopted unambiguous stances opposing FGC, as well as medicalization of the practice. This stance was publicized in particular by the United States Aid and International Development Agency (USAID), which sponsored a 2004 congressional hearing and conference to commemorate the first anniversary of Zero Tolerance on FGM Day on February 6. Representatives of USAID as well as of the Population Reference Bureau, interviewed by Shell-Duncan, stated that the express purpose of the congressional briefing was to maintain FGC on the United States's national agenda and to reenergize the seemingly dwindling commitment of the U.S. government to support further measures to eliminate the practice. In 1996 Congress passed several legislative measures, including making FGC a minor federal crime. According to the statement issued at the briefing, however, there has been insufficient follow-up on these activities since the late 1990s.

At the congressional briefing, Nawal Nour, a Sudanese-born physician, called for further protection of uncircumcised African girls in the United States by expanding the current federal anticircumcision law, which bans FGC on women under the age of eighteen. She argued that this law needs to go further, by preventing U.S. nationals from taking children to Africa or elsewhere to undergo FGC (see further discussion of extraterritoriality below).

It is interesting to note that among many anticircumcision activists the human rights framework for opposing FGC has been adopted wholesale, despite the potential problems surrounding this approach. Beyond questions of whether or how FGC should be conceptualized as a human rights issue in light of international laws and conventions, critics have called into question whether this approach protects or restricts women's autonomy in making personal choices. Shweder, for instance, argues that through the human rights framework, "activist organizations and governments in the rich nations of the world have tried to universalize their own cultural preferences and tastes with . . . forceful expansion and imposition of American and European cultural perspectives" (forthcoming, 5).

Law and ethics scholar Martha Nussbaum addresses attacks on universalism in general and specifically the claim that it advocates neglect or abrogation of women's autonomy. She argues that an "important way to answer this worry is to insist on the universal importance of protecting spheres of choice and freedom, within which people with diverse views of what matters in life can pursue flourishing according to their own lights" (1999, 9). However, she argues that "this does not mean maximizing the sheer number of choices people get to make for themselves. . . . The choices that liberal politics should protect are those that are deemed of central importance in the development and expression of personhood" (ibid., 11).

According to this perspective, protection from FGC secures autonomy over central human functional capacities such as life, bodily health and integrity, and control over one's environment (both political and material). Zero tolerance is indeed apparent in Nussbaum's forceful concluding statement: "We should keep FGM on the list of unacceptable practices that violate women's human rights, and we should be ashamed of ourselves if we do not use whatever privilege and power that has come our way to make it disappear forever" (ibid., 129). The obvious question is: who exactly is "we"? One might question whether this is another instance of what Gayatri Spivak (1988), in another context, labeled "white men saving brown women from brown men" and what other critics have referred to as "the white woman's burden."[25] Clearly, the denunciation of foreign traditions as morally retrograde and the importation of changes that are "for your own good" under the name of international human rights can be interpreted as disquieting echoes of the legacy of colonial imperialism.

Shweder puts forth the notion that the global eradication campaign itself appears to violate several human rights, including "the right of people and nations to autonomy and self-determination, rights of parents to raise children as they see fit, the right of members of a family to be free of government intrusion into decisions that are private, the right of members of a group to favor their own traditions in the education and socialization of their children, their right to freedom of religion" (forthcoming, 10). At the same time, it is important neither to draw up overly simplistic dichotomies between "Western activists" on the one hand and "African women" on the other—as such identities often coincide—nor to trivialize the powerful and committed engagement of those "insiders" with a true stake in the practices who are working for their elimination.

RECONCEPTUALIZING RIGHTS

Since the early 1990's, the global anti-FGM campaign has actively attempted to divorce itself from the health approach, largely adopting instead an alternative human rights framework for opposition to FGC. As discussed above, these rights have been further defined by legal scholars as anchored in the following areas: the rights of children, the rights of women, the right to sexual and bodily integrity, and the right to be free from torture.

The Rights of Children

A standard approach to opposing FGC practices performed on minors is rooted in claims of child abuse and violations against the UN Declaration on the Rights of the Child (UNDRC). This approach is not entirely unproblematic, however (see, for example, Boulware-Miller 1985; Breitung 1996; Gosselin 2000b; Shell-Duncan and Hernlund 2000). Such claims risk alienating and putting on the defensive parents and other relatives who—while believing that they are acting in the best interest of the child—become accused of being incompetent and/or abusive (Breitung 1996, 9). Simply referring to the assertion in the UNDRC that every child has the right to "develop . . . in a normal manner" becomes challenging in cultural contexts in which being circumcised *is* to develop in a "normal" manner. In addition, the issue of informed consent is complicated by diverse cultural ideas regarding age of maturity and the decision-making powers of children versus parents.

Alison Dundes Renteln has pointed to the irony inherent in the fact that "according to international law (the Convention on the Rights of the Child), children have both a right to practice their culture under Article 30 as well as a right against traditions prejudicial to their health under Article 24(3)"; she concludes that "the obvious difficulty is to decide when the parent's right to their exercise of culture outweighs the child's right to protection from the culture" (2002, 05). Sharon Stephens, as well, draws attention to the interesting paradox that children are increasingly seen as having cultural rights, along with more basic rights to, for example, food and shelter. She argues that, on the one hand, children may have "the right to culture," but it can also be argued that children have "rights not to be constrained within exclusionary cultural identities and not have their bodies and minds appropriated as the unprotected territory upon which cultural battles are fought" (Stephens 1995, 3–4; see also Hernlund 2003).

In exile, of course, the issue becomes more sharply focused, and we are perhaps forced to ask, as do Shweder et al.: "Does the state's assessment of a child's best interests include the child's membership in a given culture or does it abstract the child from that membership, as if the child had no such connection and was really a 'citizen of the world'?" (2002, 13). In the case of the United States, Shweder and colleagues point out that regarding cases involving the family and the raising of children, the "U.S. Supreme Court has at times favored toleration for diverse practices by parents, and at other times ordered restraints on parental control over children's access to liberal democratic values" (ibid., 10).

A number of observers point out that were girls to be made to undergo genital cutting procedures in exile settings without the strength of previous community support, the procedures are likely to be perceived as far more traumatic than would have been the case "at home." Renteln opines that "when a tradition requires an irreparable harm or change and the child has moved from one society to another, my view is that the child should not be subject to the tradition until reaching the age of majority. At that point the child can opt to have the ritual scarification, genital cutting, or other permanent bodily change" (2002, 206); although as we discuss, this is not a legal option under some current European laws. For Boddy (chapter 2 of this volume), part of the problem lies in the fact that what one child may experience as a fulfilling "traditional" coming-of-age ceremony associated with her "home" country, another child, born or raised in a "host" country, may experience as traumatic violence and alienation. Therefore, even those critical of a blanket condemnation of all FGC procedures agree that allowing any such operations would have to be tied to an age of consent (Shweder et al. 2002; see also discussions earlier in this chapter regarding sunna, male circumcision, and FGCS).

As in any assessment of prevalence, host countries are faced with the difficult challenge of protecting their new citizens in a nondiscriminatory manner. Several of the chapters in this volume engage with the on-the-ground situations that arise as African families in the diaspora are suspected of, at the very least, the intention to circumcise their daughters, including Rogers's discussion in chapter 6 of a 1993 case in Australia, in which the issue of the infibulation of two Eritrean girls was brought to the attention of the courts and the Australian media. Johnsdotter (chapter 5 of this volume) recounts a case from Sweden that illustrates how FGC has become treated as a form of child abuse, justifying state intervention. Janice Boddy, in chapter 2, reports, as well, on a situation in which she as a researcher became affected by child-abuse-prevention measures when proposing to conduct research among Sudanese immigrants to Canada.

The Rights of Women

If FGC in relation to the rights of minor children presents complex legal and moral conundrums, things become even more problematic when those being protected are adult women. Several contributions to this volume discuss "the central role of women in the process" and the fact that "just as they are the primary enthusiasts that give force to the practice either as circumcisers or circumcised, they have become the key engines for its renunciation" (Obiora, chapter 3 of this volume).

While "FGM" has become a cause célèbre of many Western feminists, their interventions are often shockingly unself-conscious, and frequently arrogant. A number of African scholars have in recent years offered scathing critiques of the "maternalistic" approach of Western women out to "save" their African "sisters" (see for example R. M. Abusharaf 2000; Ahmadu 2000; Amadiume 1987; and the contributions to Oyěwùmi 2003). In chapter 12 of this volume, Fuambai Ahmadu likewise indicts the tendency of some Western feminists to accuse the Other of false consciousness. There is no indication, however, that certain Western feminist critiques are not going to continue to address FGM as an extreme example of global misogyny. These critiques and activist agendas tend to be concentrated primarily in two areas: the right of women to be free from violence and the right of women to sexual and bodily integrity.

VIOLENCE AGAINST WOMEN. At the 1993 Vienna World Conference on Human Rights, two important historic events occurred. First, "female genital mutilation" became classified as a form of violence against women; second, the issue of violence against women was for the first time acknowledged to fall under the purview of international human rights law. Prior to the 1990s, violence against women (VAW) was nearly invisible in international law and traditional understandings of human rights because both originally operated on the assumption that public and private domains are sharply divided (Human Rights Dialogue 2003; Kapur 2002; Perry 2004). The beating, rape, or "mutilation of women in their home at the hand of relatives" was viewed as a private matter, and beyond the scope of international human rights law (Human Rights Dialogue 2003; see also Kapur 2002).

The 1993 Vienna World conference was a landmark event in which a co-alition of groups with diverse interests in domains of VAW joined efforts to seek judicial protection. Four previously separate gender-based issues became united under the label VAW: victims of armed conflict, including rape and sexual abuse in war; global trafficking of women; domestic violence and rape; and violence due to customary practices and religious law (Coomaraswamy 2004). According to Radhika Coomaraswamy, the former UN Special Rapporteur on Violence against Women, violence due to customary practices has been the hardest to address because culture comes under attack (ibid.). Yet inclusion of FGC in this category firmly aligns the international campaign to eliminate FGC with the global movement to fight VAW. Activists have successfully challenged the traditional concept of human rights issues as state perpetrated only and expanded the legitimacy of the human rights movement (Human Rights Dialogue 2003).

GENDER AND AGENCY. In the decade since FGC became reconceptualized as a human rights issue, critiques have been leveled at developments regarding FGC specifically, as well as more broadly at the anti-violence against women movement. What these critics are concerned with is what Moore refers to in chapter 13 of this volume as the "larger difficulty of the relationship between gender and agency." While acknowledging significant gains in protection of women's rights, several scholars (Coomaraswamy 2004; Kapur 2002) argue that the anti-VAW movement has transformed the image of Third World women into one of powerless victims incapable of self-determination, self-expression, or reasoned decision making. Ratna Kapur points out that "the image that is produced is that of a truncated Third World woman who is sexually constrained, tradition-bound, incarcerated in the home, illiterate and poor. It is an image that is strikingly reminiscent to the colonial construction of the Eastern woman. . . . In striking contrast to this emaciated image stands the image of the emancipated Western woman; she has 'control over her income, her body, her sexuality'" (Barry 1979, cited in Kapur 2002, 18–19).

Critics charge that the anti-VAW movement has increasingly acquired an arrogant tone that can create more obstacles than it eliminates (Coomaraswamy 2004; Kapur 2002). Such arrogance is believed to lead to policy that ignores to the plight and reality of women and to methods of intervention that are insensitive to the struggles of women in their own societies. Coomaraswamy argues that such arrogance also brings back fears of the legacy of imperialism, where the freedom, autonomy, and right to self-determination of non-Western people are crushed by the belief in the superiority and power of one culture over another.

Critiques have also emerged along this line specific to FGC. Kratz has in-
dicted many writings on FGC for their failure to recognize differences in African women based on nationality, class, ethnicity, education, and age. Instead
what emerges is an image of a homogenized, essentialized African woman who
is "powerless, constrained by tradition, defined by men, unable to think clearly,
and having only problems and needs, not choices" (Kratz 1999a, 108). She further argues that conceptually, women become classified and defined by shared
victimization by FGC (ibid., 109; see also Obiora 1997, 303, 327–328).

Kratz concludes, "The underlying premise is that only women who have no
choice or agency . . . would submit to such practices. Because they are unable to
act for themselves, others must deliver them through *international action*. This is
a rhetorical argument that . . . justifies *interventions* of a range of people and dis-
misses the beliefs and wishes of those involved as 'false consciousness'" (1999a,
109; emphasis in original). Nowhere, perhaps, is this argument regarding agency
and false consciousness more prominent than in the area of women's sexuality,
to which we turn next.

The Right to Sexual Integrity: The Contested Clitoris

One of the most ardently articulated aspects of feminist opposition to FGC
is that the practice erases a woman's sexual enjoyment. Gosselin (2000a) and
others have pointed out that for many Western feminists the clitoris as a site
for orgasm has become a powerful icon of female agency and power. Important
critiques, however, have interrogated the notion that priorities are necessarily
the same for women everywhere (see for example R. M. Abusharaf 2000 and
the contributions to Oyěwùmi 2003). As with discussions about the long-term
health consequences of FGC, sexuality is an area in which it seems tempting for
various stakeholders to resort to deceptively simple arguments about the "natural" body with its "intact" genitals.

As for the actual effects that genital-cutting procedures have on sexuality,
however, the data have—not surprisingly—tended to be incomplete, contradictory, and difficult to interpret. We have previously pointed out (Shell-Duncan
and Hernlund 2000) that diverse stakeholders in the practice variously claim
that genital cutting has no effect on sexual drive or pleasure, that it tempers
a woman's sexuality or even suppresses it, that it ends up leading instead to
more promiscuity because of women's lack of satisfaction, or even that there is
no explicit link between sexuality and FGC (see, for example, Hernlund 2003,
Johnson 2000, Skramstad 1990).

In addition, a number of researchers have been told by respondents that,
whatever the intended effect on women's sexuality might be, in reality there
is not much difference, on average, in the way circumcised and uncircumcised
women conduct themselves sexually (see, for example, Gosselin 2000b, Hernlund 2003; for a critique of assertions of lack of harm to sexual health, see,
for example, Morison and Scherf 2003). Dopico, Johansen, and Johnsdotter in

their chapters (10, 11, and 5 respectively) in this volume draw our attention to the ambivalence between sexual ideals and realities, as well as to the gaps in discourse between what women believe that men want versus what men themselves state (although it is wise to note Ahmadu's cautioning words in chapter 12 about taking too seriously the comments men make about women's sexuality).

Toubia and Izette document a broad range of findings: in some cases, up to 90 percent of infibulated women reported pleasurable sex with frequent orgasm (Lightfoot-Klein 1989b); in others 50 percent claimed diminished sexual pleasure (El Dareer 1982b). Mansura Dopico, in chapter 10 of this volume, discusses the "orgasm puzzle" and presents an extremely comprehensive survey of literature on the clitoris and female sexual response, which reveals a wide range in sexual responsiveness among both circumcised and uncircumcised women, echoed in chapter 12 by Fuambai Ahmadu.

We find it useful to distinguish between female sexual desire, action, and pleasure—that is, between what women want, actually do, and feel. We also agree with Ahmadu's assertion in chapter 12 that it is impossible for any woman (or man for that matter) to truly know what any other woman—circumcised or not—feels during sex. Nonetheless, three in-depth studies presented in this volume, based on lengthy interviews with circumcised women about their experiences of sex, go a long way in providing some insight into the relationship between sexual pleasure, the clitoris, the rest of the body, the mind, and the surrounding culture. These are Ahmadu's latest study, based on her own experiences, those of her Sierra Leonean relatives in Washington, D.C., and of the women she and her team interviewed in The Gambia; Mansura Dopico's work with Eritrean women in Eritrea and Australia; and Elise Johansen's with Somali refugee women in Norway.

A report from The Gambia asserts unequivocally that one intention of FGM is to curb the woman's sexual feelings, giving "the impression that women are owned chattel who should only be used for male satisfaction and whose own personal pleasure does not matter" (Daffeh et al. 1999, 25). The authors concede, however, that the "sexual experiences of mutilated women are very difficult to assess or research in our communities. Talking about sex remains a traditional taboo." Nonetheless, Ahmadu's respondents in a study carried out recently in The Gambia on sexual exploitation speak with remarkable candor about the most intimate matters, as Hernlund also found, on a smaller scale, to be true in her own discussions with some Gambian women.

Thus, Ahmadu's "insider" view of healthy post-FGC sexuality is a previously muted one. With an admirable mixture of wit and indignation, she describes in chapter 12 encounters with skeptical colleagues and friends who simply cannot or will not believe her assertions that her own sexual enjoyment has not been reduced or compromised by undergoing excision. Assertions from women such as Ahmadu (although few have had her courage in speaking so directly about these issues) are indeed met with skepticism, if not patronizing pity. In fact, what Ahmadu asserts has been reported in more than the rare context but has usually been dismissed as "false consciousness." It will be most interesting to see to what extent her well-articulated personal experience is as easily brushed aside.

Instead of unquestioningly succumbing to new narratives of sexual normalcy, many of the immigrants who spoke with these researchers appear to continue to experience deep anxiety about the sexual liberalism of their host societies. Stereotypes and misunderstandings may well be flourishing in both communities. Ahlberg et al. write that sex education is "compulsory in Swedish schools and is one forum where FC is often introduced, using visual aids to show the mutilated female genitals" (2004, 54). They relate how some of their respondents expressed shock at their own perception that Swedish girls casually begin having sex at the age of thirteen although, interestingly, a survey shows that the actual average age of sexual debut for Swedish women is sixteen and that the age is going up (Levin 1996). Michelle Johnson (chapter 9 of this volume) also discusses some of the changing conceptions regarding uncircumcised women's sexuality expressed by circumcised Mandinga people living in Portugal, where, just as "at home" in Guinea-Bissau, uninitiated people are seen as lacking self-control. Although not presenting any definitive solution to "the orgasm puzzle," these contributions begin to offer an alternate reading to a simplistic assumption that all circumcised women, or uncircumcised ones for that matter, experience sexual desire and pleasure in the same way.

Freedom from Torture and the Right to Asylum

A final human rights approach increasingly used to address FGC is the right to be free from torture. Although international statutes created after World War II were primarily designed to offer members of vulnerable groups protection from state persecution, they are now commonly used, as well, by individuals seeking protection from violent customary practices. Asylum seekers and refugees, referred to as ASRs (see, for example, Powell et al. 2004), struggle to gain sanctuary under widely varying legal frameworks around the "Western world." Once again, in very pragmatic ways, it matters on which side of international boundaries you find yourself.

Richard Powell and his colleagues point to the need for an integrated European Union agenda. The European Parliament has called on fear of FGC as constituting a right to political asylum; on September 20, 2001, it adopted a resolution on FGM that is not legally binding but can "prepare the ground for a EU-wide FGM policy" (Powell et al. 2004, 154). In actuality, however, they stress that there is "no internal consistency from a EU perspective; one can be a bona fide EU citizen in one member state for fearing FGC, and not in another, despite the fact that free movement of all EU citizens enables that same person to relocate within the EU" (ibid.).[26]

GENDERED SANCTUARY. In the United States a few highly publicized cases, notably those of Kassindja and of Abankwah, have served to crystallize the conditions under which a woman can be granted political asylum if she claims to fear FGM for herself or her children if returned "home." These cases are discussed in depth by Charles Piot and Corinne Kratz in chapters 7 and 8 of this volume (see also Obiora, chapter 3). Edwidge Danticat, in an article in the *Nation,* explains: "The United States still has no uniform, binding regulations or statutes on gender-based asylum, only advisory guidelines that do not need to be considered by higher-level decision-makers such as immigration judges, the Board of Immigration Appeals or even the Attorney General, whose authority over the detention process has expanded thanks to the aggressive efforts of John Ashcroft in the wake of the September 11 attacks" (2005, 15).

Danticat relates a quote from Karen Musalo, director of the Center for Gender and Refugee Studies at the University of California Hastings College of the Law and former attorney in the Kassindja case: "The way we think about refugees is a male paradigm. If a man is tortured with electric shock during war, most people would say of course he deserves asylum. If a woman is raped during war, or is a victim of domestic violence, we don't consider it a form of persecution" (quoted in Danticat 2005, 15). Interestingly, however, in the case of FGM, the legal situation has gradually become gendered in a different way, offering a female-only basis for asylum. Claire Robertson points out that this has become "the *sine qua non* without which African women whose immigration status is questionable will be deported, in part because feminists are less likely to get involved in helping them fight deportation if FGC is not an issue," a sentiment echoed in Obiora's chapter (James and Robertson 2002, 74).

Kratz alerts us in chapter 8 to the way in which judicial standards come to be applied in the context of political lobbying and media pressures. Charles Piot interrogates, as well, the potentially problematic role that anthropologists come to play when recruited as expert witnesses in asylum cases. Although he praises an emergent literature in FGC scholarship that presents a more nuanced view, Piot expresses concern that anthropologists may become complicitous with an agenda that leads to fewer women gaining asylum.

While Piot raises important concerns regarding the ethical position of "the expert" in mediating representations of "African culture," it does appear that recent trends in asylum rulings are actually moving in a reverse direction to what he predicted. A Ninth Circuit Court of Appeals ruling in the case of *Mohamed v. Gonsalez* dramatically widens the grounds for FGM-related asylum (National Immigration Law Center 2005, henceforth NILC). In this "reopening of removal proceedings in the case of a Somali woman based on her claim that her attorney's failure, when she was applying for asylum, to raise the issue of her genital mutilation as a child constituted ineffective assistance of counsel" (NILC 2005, 1), the U.S. Court of Appeals for the Ninth Circuit determined that already having suffered genital mutilation constitutes ongoing persecution;

in a previous, similar ruling, the court ruled that having been made to undergo forced sterilization constitutes ongoing persecution, as well, thus making many more women potentially eligible.

A number of observers have refuted the idea of the "opening of the flood-gates," pointing out that it is going to be the exceptional African woman who has the opportunity to travel to the West to seek asylum based on FGM. None-theless, Kratz asks in chapter 8 whether the issue of FGM-based asylum has become so politicized that, quite literally, different standards of evidence are applied than in other types of cases. Offering a detailed analysis of the similari-ties and differences between the cases of Kasindja and Abankwah, she asks us to contemplate whether different standards of evidence come to apply when the case involves Africa and FGM.

ACTION AND ADVOCACY

In the wake of more than two decades of international campaigns and nu-merous national and local intervention efforts, Toubia and Sharief (2003) have posed a question that is also asked by donors, technical agencies, program man-agers, activists, and scholars: "Have we made progress yes?" Although we attempt in this volume to point to other considerations for the well-being of affected women and girls, in the zero-tolerance climate of anti-FGM activism "progress" is generally defined as movement toward the complete eradication of all female genital–cutting procedures.[27] Empirically, the Demographic and Health Survey data show that overall declines in FGC are, in most instances, small and slow, and that the practice is still favored by large segments of practicing populations (Carr 1997; Yoder 2004).

Recently, there have been some reported cases of community abandonment in, for example, Egypt (Abdel-Hadi, 1998). Perhaps better known are the devel-opments in Senegal, where the NGO Tostan has been implementing a nonfor-mal education program that integrates an anticircumcision component within a broader context of training on health, literacy, problem solving, and community development (see Obiora, chapter 3 of this volume). In Senegal, as of 2005, 1,571 villages had at least declared their commitment to abandon FGC, and the Tostan program has been extended to other African countries, including Guinea and Mali (www.tostan.org).

A key question that has been raised, however, is how to define "progress" or "success." In the climate of zero-tolerance anti-FGM activism, Toubia and Sharief (2003, 256–257) propose a rigid definition: "The only acceptable suc-cess or 'outcome' indicator is irrefutable proof of irreversible abandonment of the practice in a family or a community." This arguably impossibly high stan-dard of success is, however, problematic on several levels, including the fact that an endpoint for measuring success is ill defined. For the purpose of evalu-ation, an Egyptian project suggested that marriage without circumcision was a valid endpoint for defining permanent abandonment (Toubia and Sharief

2003). Assessments of behavior at predefined endpoints, however, overlook the fact that arenas of decision making can shift over a woman's life. Our current research in Senegambia, for example, has shown that a family's decision to not circumcise a daughter can be revisited at numerous times, including after marriage, when a new constellation of decision makers (often including the woman herself, as well as members of her husband's family) negotiate the proper course of action. Our data reveal a surprising number of cases in which women undergo FGC after marriage, and in some instances, even after bearing several children (see also Thomas 2003 about similar cases among Kenyan Meru).

Toubia and Sharief "recommend that monitoring of successful behavior change should start at the point at which successful action is taken. . . . A public declaration by an individual, a family or a whole community should be considered as the action, that is, the declaration not to circumcise" (2003, 257). Mackie (1996 and 2000), too, emphasizes the importance of a public declaration to abandon FGC as signaling a convention shift, whereby FGC is no longer locked in place as a prerequisite to marriage. Obiora, however, offers in chapter 3 a poignant critique of any simple reading of such declarations, and stresses the importance of material incentives, drawing our attention to what she refers to as the "full-belly quotient."

A recent evaluation of Tostan argues that "the prevalence of FGC among daughters of women who participated in the program decreased, and the proportion of uncut girls ages 0–10 increased significantly" (Diop et al. 2003, 43) However, the timing of the Senegalese law against FGM, which was implemented after the Tostan campaign had already gained momentum, makes it challenging to ascertain the extent to which people have stopped practicing due to a fear of the law, a commitment to the Tostan declarations, a true internalization of the messages of the campaign, or a combination of all of these.

Legislative Approaches

Since the early 1990s African countries have faced growing interest in their human rights records, including pressure to demonstrate actions taken to eliminate "FGM." Human rights NGOs such as Amnesty International, Article 19, and Africa Watch regularly publish reports of governments' human rights performance. The U.S. Department of State, as well, requires for its human rights report that individual countries produce evidence of legislation or bans against FGC. Therefore, national-level policies regarding FGC are no longer isolated from scrutiny by the international community or NGOs (Welch 1995).

A decade ago Welch predicted that "there will come a time when IAC strategy must seek allies for legislation—that is, when popular attitudes have shifted. That day is coming. Education about human rights can lead toward their implementation through legislation and legal enforcement" (1995, 101). This shift is now indeed occurring: an increasing number of countries are passing anti-FGM laws, and there are indications that popular attitudes have begun shifting in significant ways. The IAC mission has now been broadened from education to also include advocating for enforcement (1995). The effects of varied approaches to such legislation are not fully understood, however.

REACTANCE. Reviews of strategies for eliminating FGC (for example, Mackie 2000; Shell-Duncan and Hernlund 2000; Toubia and Sharief 2003) have often concluded that legislation is a poor tool for evoking behavior change. Several well-known examples of responses to laws enacted under colonial rule provide evidence that legislation can be ineffective or counterproductive, failing to act as a deterrent, and instead sparking negative reactance. For example, Lynn Thomas's compelling account of responses to the 1956 ban on excision in Meru, Kenya, reveals that girls defied the ban by circumcising one another (Thomas 1996, 2000). Other reports document public protests and backlash reactions so strong that they actually resulted in an increase in the practice, at least temporarily. Janice Boddy's account of Sudan on the eve of legislation being enacted banning infibulation reveals that scores of parents rushed to have their daughters infibulated (Boddy 1991, 16). Gunning suggests that the failure of early legislative efforts "lies partly in their colonial origins. Such a history has led African people to view outside interests in the surgeries as just another form of imperialism" (1991, 228). She further predicts that the problem is likely to plague even current attempts to enact legislation, despite the growing involvement of African feminists and indigenous activists.

Yet the past decade has witnessed a proliferation of legislation specifically banning FGC in both African and Western nations. Boulware-Miller in 1985 predicted that the enactment of legislation in the West would not be met with the sort of reactance seen in colonial Africa: "European governments may find it easier to prohibit a practice which is 'new'[28] to their culture rather than, as African countries must, condemn a tradition that has existed for centuries" (160). She also suggests that the lower prevalence of FGC in non-African countries may facilitate regulation and enforcement.

Boulware-Miller (1985) argues that legal measures should not be disregarded as a possible means of ending FGC but should be employed in conjunction with health and education programs. Rahman and Toubia concur, adding that "law can be a useful tool for change, giving NGOs and individuals greater leverage in persuading communities to abandon the practice" (2000, 13). The intended effect of legislation as a tool for eliminating FGC appears to be twofold: first, to provide a deterrent effect for supporters of FGC and, second, to "provide [for those already opposed to the practice] that extra needed support against social pressures to circumcise their daughters" (Gunning 1991, 228–229).

The success of laws in Africa and the West in terms of eliminating the practice of FGC is unclear, however. This is partly because the climate of intolerance and threat of legal sanctions serve, in certain instances, to drive the practice underground. Although a WHO survey of eighty-eight agencies with anti-FGC programs found that two-thirds of respondents felt that national anticircumcision legislation would have a positive impact on their programs, most respondents also expressed concern that a law would drive the practice underground (WHO 1999).

ENFORCEMENT. Mackie argues that "criminal laws work because thieves and murderers are a minority of the population" (2000, 278). By contrast, he views laws against FGC, which is often nearly universal within circumcising groups, as unenforceable: "It is not possible to criminalize the entirety of a population or the entirety of a discrete and insular minority of the population without methods of mass terror" (ibid.). Our current research in Senegal reveals, however, that large-scale enforcement is not necessarily needed in order to generate widespread fear of prosecution. Instead, we find that awareness of a few highly publicized cases of prosecution and even, in some cases, simply rumors or imaginings of enforceability engender fear of prosecution.

Even in the presence of specific laws against FGC, enforcement is variable. The 2004 Human Rights Report noted enforcement of the law in only five African countries in the year preceding the report: Senegal, Burkina Faso, Cote d'Ivoire, Ghana, and Tanzania (U.S. Department of State, 2004). The targets of enforcement are varied as well. In Burkina Faso, for example, prosecution has largely been directed at circumcisers. Moreover, a convicted circumciser was given a twelve-month suspended sentence, reflecting the fact that culture and local context are being weighed against the law (see also Dembour 2001 on variable sentencing in France). In Senegal and Tanzania, the law has recently been targeted at parents of the circumcised girl, rather than at circumcisers.

The 2004 Tanzania Human Rights Report elaborates on the complex and varied problems that surround enforcement of the law: in some cases police officers were unaware of the law; "victims" were often reluctant to testify against their own family members; bribes, in some instances, were purportedly given to leaders to assure freedom from prosecution; court cases often failed to offer an adequate standard of evidence despite having testimony from victims and confessions from parents and circumcisers (U. S. Department of State 2004).

In European settings, controversy has arisen around enforcement mechanisms, in particular proposals to conduct physical exams on immigrant girls to detect any genital cutting. Mason reports that some states in Australia "allow the court to make an order preventing a person from removing a child from the State; seizing the child's passport and subjecting her to 'periodic examination' to ensure surgery has not taken place" (2001, 62). Essén and Johnsdotter report that genital screening of all children starting school is taking place in some cities in Denmark (2004), and Elise Johansen relates that such screenings are being performed in France and are contemplated in Norway (personal communication to editors).

In the United States there have, to our knowledge, been only two cases to date of individuals being charged with female genital mutilation. The first, in 1995, did not involve African immigrants, but rather a Southern California couple who, according to the man's Web site "enjoy the psychosexual aspect of piercing and body modification" (Costello 2004). According to a posting on www.womensenews.org (September 26, 2005), the two were arraigned in a Los Angeles federal court on charges of conspiring to circumcise two female minors after "undercover FBI agents posing as the girls' parents offered the couple $8,000 to perform the procedure" on two fictitious girls. Costello reports that, "although heartened by the government's enforcement of the law, FGM activists say the alleged crime is not a typical case of genital mutilation."

The second case involved charges of cruelty to children against an Ethiopian immigrant man in Atlanta who is accused of having performed a clitoridectomy on his two-year-old daughter. As this volume goes to press, we are not clear on the final outcome of this case, but interesting developments have followed from the publicity surrounding it. The defendant did not plead a cultural defense but denied that he committed the genital cutting (Hansen 2005). His former wife, a South African, has become engaged in anti-FGM intervention efforts (see www.amirahsvoice.org). Although the case was argued under existing child abuse statutes, heavy criticism was leveled at the state legislature of Georgia for not having passed specific anti-FGM legislation (Hansen 2005). As a result, in February 2004, Georgia's state senate passed the Amirah Joyce Adem Act, named for the girl. Interestingly, a last-minute add-on to the bill also outlaws voluntary genital piercings on adult women, but not on men (www.amirahsvoice.org, March 26, 2004).

Some have argued that even if a law is not broadly perceived as enforceable, it bears a positive effect by way of creating a climate of intolerance. Gusfield (1986, cited in Boyle 2002, 80) states in warlike terms, "Even if the law is not enforced or enforceable, the symbolic import of its passage is important to the reformer. It settles the controversies between those who represent clashing cultures. The public support of one conception of morality at the expense of another enhances the prestige and self-esteem of the victors and degrades the culture of the losers."

Isabelle Gunning (1991) worries, as well, about the broader negative ramifications of enforcement: What is the psychological effect on a young, newly circumcised girl witnessing the arrest of her parents? What is the financial impact of imposing fines on people who are already poor? Given that women are the prime initiators and practitioners of FGC, would enforcement lead to the systematic imprisonment of women? Consequently, beyond the question of whether international or national laws *can* be interpreted as grounds for condemning FGC lies the question of whether they *should* be used to eliminate the practice.

Gunning notes that the imposition of law, with its attribution of right and wrong, exoneration and punishment, "can easily be construed as barely disguised ethnocentrism or cultural imperialism" (1991, 189). She goes on to argue that "domestic legislation attempting to abolish surgeries is still perceived as the imposition of alien values, and not the result of change in values" (ibid., 231). She raises a critical question: "Even if one can inject a multicultural perspective and set of values into the law, how can mutual respect be maintained if the 'losing' cultural value can be punished or even forced to change?" (ibid., 193). The solution proposed by Gunning is to forego the use of punishment in favor of dialogue and education. Rahman and Toubia suggest that the debate over whether law should be used as a tool to combat FGC is not moot, arguing that "the fact that many Africans and Western cultures have recently enacted laws prohibiting the practice creates a *de facto* role for legislation, the effects of which should be closely observed and documented in the coming years" (2000, xiv).

PROLIFERATION OF LAWS. Despite the unproven effectiveness of legislation in bringing about change in the practice of FGC, an increasing number of nation-states around the world have adopted legislation specifically banning FGC in the wake of mounting international pressure to protect girls and women from human rights violations. A 1999 WHO review of programs to eliminate FGC stated unequivocally that "protecting the rights of each and every citizen is the responsibility of national governments" and specifically recommended that "governments must enact and/or use anti-FGM laws to protect girls" (WHO 1999, 14–15).

Boyle (2002) points to the different factors motivating the proliferation of anticircumcision laws in Africa and the West. Although it is often assumed that laws in the West were motivated by an influx of immigration from practicing societies, figures on migration rates do not actually support this. In the United States, for example, in the decade preceding the passing of the 1996 federal law against FGC, immigration from countries in which FGC is commonly practiced was extremely low (see also Obiora, chapter 3 of this volume). Instead, Boyle argues that legislation was motivated by international influence evoked by high-profile asylum cases, most notably that of Fauziya Kassindja (see Kratz, Obiora, Piot, chapters 8, 3, and 7 respectively of this volume). The proposal to medicalize symbolic circumcision at Harborview Hospital also drew a storm of protest and heightened international attention to the practice of FGC within the United States.

Another compellingly motivating factor for African governments to pass anti-FGM legislation lies with policies linking foreign aid to FGC policies (Boyle 2002; Obiora chapter 3 of this volume; Shell-Duncan and Hernlund 2000). As Boyle puts it, "hegemonic definitions of proper national action may spread through coercive action" (2002, 92). Thus, African governments are increasingly pressured by, for example the United States, as certain forms of aid and loans are tied conditionally to presenting evidence of combating FGM. House Bill H.R.3540 (the Foreign Operations, Export Financing, and Related Programs Appropriations Act of 1997) states that the "Secretary of the Treasury

shall instruct the United States Executive Director of each international financial institution to use the voice and vote of the United States to oppose any loan
or other utilization of the funds of their respective institution, other than to
address basic human needs, for the government of any country which the Secretary of the Treasury determines" not to be in compliance with such demands
(see also Obiora's chapter).

Boyle (2002), Leye and Deblonde (2004), and Rahman and Toubia (2000)
have summarized national anticircumcision laws and policies for numerous nations worldwide. For African countries it is possible to assess updated legal status
from the annual U.S. Department of State Human Rights Reports; although
the State Department has required all countries to report the status of "FGM"
activities each year since 1994, it is no longer consistently reported for non-
African countries. Of particular interest are the varied ways in which laws are
being constructed. In Mauritania and Egypt, for example, the practice of FGC
has been restricted to bans on the practice in government health facilities and
by medical practitioners.[29] In Kenya and Tanzania (as in some Western countries, including the United States) FGC is illegal for women under the age of
majority. Laws banning FGC at any age have now also been passed in thirteen
African countries (Benin, Burkina Faso, the Central African Republic, Chad,
Cote d'Ivoire, Djibouti, Ghana, Guinea, Niger, some states in Nigeria, Senegal,
Somalia, and Togo).

In Ghana, the first African nation to pass legislation specifically against
FGC, there have been calls to tighten the 1994 ban. After a Khartoum symposium sponsored by UNICEF and Japan's government, Sudan, too, has recently
vowed to tighten laws already passed in 1946 and 1974 and to introduce "stiff
penalties" (Moszynski 2003, 580). Meanwhile, in Mali, Claudie Gosselin reports
that "the official position of the government so far has been against legislation,
and we can assume that politicians would not legislate against excision unless
they felt that a majority supported ending the practice—which is clearly not
the case at the present time" (2000b, 55). Likewise, there is no indication that
the Gambian government is contemplating passing anti-FGM legislation (see
Hernlund 2000 and 2003).

In Europe, FGC is either punishable under general criminal law (in Finland,
France, Greece, Ireland, Italy, Luxemburg, the Netherlands, Portugal, and Germany) or with specialty legislation (Austria, Belgium, Denmark, Spain, Sweden,
and the United Kingdom), although there is discussion in Ireland and Portugal
about creating special laws (from Leye and Deblonde 2004, 8–9). To date, prosecution has taken place only in France (ibid.), where thirty-one cases have gone
to court since 1988 (see Dembour 2001), and Italy (Leye and Deblonde 2004).

In the United States, most FGM statutes were enacted between 1996 and
1999. In addition to the conditional aid discussed above, federal law makes any
practice of FGM on a minor a felony and requires the government to compile
data and engage in education and outreach, as well as to provide information

to immigrants which relays "the serious harm to physical and psychological health." According to the 2004 Human Rights Report, members of the legal community have asked not only that loopholes in the existing law be closed, but also that culpability be extended to "citizens who commit the crime outside the country's border" (U.S. Department of State 2004). Powell and colleagues argue that the lack of such a clause makes it difficult to prosecute cases of circumcision when it can not be proven where the procedure took place (Powell et al. 2004). In Europe, all the countries' laws now include a clause on extraterritoriality except those of Finland, Greece, Ireland, Luxemburg, and Portugal; in the Netherlands and Germany this takes effect only if the practice is also against the law in the country where it is done and the perpetrator has German or Dutch citizenship (Leye and Deblonde 2004).

"CONSULTATIONS." As anti-FGM legislation has been drafted in various Western contexts, attempts have been made to show that consultation has taken place with affected communities. Several scholars, however, have pointed out that such consultations have typically been deeply flawed, as is powerfully demonstrated in Juliet Rogers's chapter in this volume about Australia. She argues that "*a dialogue amongst equal representatives was never possible*" (emphasis in original; see also Kratz' chapter in this volume), as no attempt was made to incorporate the poignant suggestions of immigrant activist women already deeply committed to anti-FGM work. It is useful, Rogers points out, to ask why, in that context, a law was seen as necessary. Likewise, Chalmers and Hashi report from Canada that even among Somali women, many of whom oppose the practice, only 34 percent agreed with the Canadian anti-FGM law (2000, 231).

In the United States, as well, the federal anti-FGM legislation was created in a highly politicized and media-driven climate. Fernandez-Romano cautions that "senators who advocated the need for this piece of legislation were not fully informed as to the different types of female genital surgeries, the reasons for which they are performed and the methods through which they may be performed" (1999). Gunning, as well, has published a fascinating account based on her own experiences of trying to affect the California state law against FGM, the creation of which she feels "reveals disdain and disrespect for African women and their cultures" (2002, 114). Like Rogers, she refers to the "invisibility" of the eradication efforts of African immigrant and points to the glaring absence of input from the very African women for whom legislation was being drafted. Instead, a participatory symposium was not held until the bill had already been signed into law.

Gunning points out by way of comparison that when in the mid-1970s "the American Academy of Pediatrics (AAP) determined that male circumcision had no health benefits whatsoever, one could have asked, Then why not pass a law outlawing the practice of male circumcision under threat of fines and imprisonment?" Instead, it was determined that "in light of deep-seated religious, aesthetic, and cultural norms" the approach should instead be educational (I. R. Gunning 2002, 117). This leads Gunning to conclude that through a selective and ethnocentric process, some cultures and groups are respected enough to be allowed self-determination, whereas others are treated as "childlike," requiring others to make decisions about what is in their own best interest.

After describing the frustrating process of participating in attempting to amend the law, Gunning concludes that its ultimate value is "cynical and symbolic" (2002, 121). "The ease with which the bills passed," she argues, "meant that conservatives—otherwise busy trashing welfare, health care, and other issues of vital importance to women, immigrants, minorities, and working and poor people—had suddenly found concern for colored women." Finally, she points out, such a vote was an empty gesture of concern as no financial backing from either the state of California or the federal government was placed behind such programs.

CONCLUSIONS

We have in this chapter attempted to untangle some of the complex ways in which the migration of people from circumcising societies is giving rise to challenging transcultural encounters in areas that include health care and child rearing, asylum law, sexuality, and human rights. We have wielded two overlapping metaphors. On the one hand we invoke Dembour's image of a pendulum swinging between exaggerated claims on both "sides" of a contentious issue, and advocate for a clearheaded approach more firmly grounded "in the middle." Likewise, we seek to problematize the dominant tendency to "draw the line" when it comes to FGC, as politicized ultimatums often inform absolutist judgments that resonate poorly with interrelated issues.

We firmly believe that scholars who have devoted their energies to this challenging topic have a profound responsibility to use their knowledge to demonstrate, as do the contributors to this volume, that research rigor and compassionate engagement are in no way mutually exclusive. As Kratz so trenchantly remarks in chapter 8, the long-standing debates about FGC are "difficult to resolve and do not stand still." Although these practices are commonly referred to as "ancient" and "entrenched," it is clear that in actuality they are in flux and constantly being renegotiated. In the current world climate of paranoid discourses about the "clash of civilizations," it is more important than ever to avoid sensationalism and exaggerated judgments. Instead we must remind ourselves that "culture" is something that all of us do, and that most of us are confronted with multiple cultural narratives from which we must determine the "right" thing to do.

NOTES

1. We would like to extend our gratitude to those who have offered suggestions, ideas, practical assistance, and/or encouragement as we thought about and wrote this introduction, in particular Fuambai Ahmadu, Nancy Hunt, Sara Johnsdotter, Caren Kaplan,

Crystal Nam, Arzoo Osanloo, Rick Shweder, Janelle Taylor, Anthony Tessandori, Lynn Thomas, Kathy Wander, Stan Yoder, and two anonymous reviewers. Although we were not able to incorporate all their suggestions, we are deeply appreciative of their insights and, naturally, we take full responsibility for any shortcomings in this work.

We tend to use the term "female circumcision" when referring to emic accounts about these practices, "female genital mutilation" or FGM when discussing activism for their abolishment, and "female genital cutting" or FGC in an attempt to be purely descriptive (but see Kratz 1999a and chapter 8 of this volume for a poignant critique of this term). For a more detailed discussion of the pitfalls of various politicized terminologies, see for example Shell-Duncan and Hernlund 2000.

2. We are not suggesting, however, that the positions of "activists" and "scholars" are necessarily mutually exclusive; we recognize that many individuals, including some of the contributors to this volume, struggle with negotiating their own positions within and between these categories (see also James and Robertson 2002).

3. Similarly, Victoria C. Plaut points out that "in America, group life is seen largely as a matter of choice, and therefore belonging to a group is not seen as natural; what is basic and natural is the individual" (2002, 374), but she goes on to argue that "the question of individual versus group is not really a question of either-or but rather how . . . [and the solution is one of] tacking back and forth between individual and group-based perspectives" (ibid., 388).

4. These types have been extensively discussed in a number of works (see, for example, Shell-Duncan and Hernlund 2000; Toubia and Izette 1998; WHO 1979, 1986; also Boddy, chapter 2 of this volume). We find it more productive, however, to think of the variations of genital cutting as falling on a continuum, rather than into discrete types.

5. There are, of course, also limits to "ethnicity" or "culture" as a predictor of the practice. For example, central Kenyan Kikuyus and Merus illustrate that ethnic groups may be divided on the practice (we thank Lynn Thomas for reminding us of this point).

6. See Kratz, 1999a and chapter 8 of this volume, for a useful model to think with about actors, arenas, and agendas with a stake in FGC.

7. It is important to bear in mind, as well, that these migration patterns do not only move north and west, but often within the global South itself. See for example Anita Häusermann Fábos's insightful 2001 study on constructions of Sudanese identities and FGC in Cairo, Egypt.

8. Powell et al. (2004, 157) point out that "some researchers have found that acculturation and abandonment of the practice appears to be associated with age on arrival" (referring to Morison et al. 2004) but also caution that "there has been a substantial increase in the number of Somalis in exile in the UK, which has increased the size of the Somali community. This increase could potentially have altered the dynamics within which cultural change is expected to occur, possibly increasing the pressure and reducing the opportunities for cultural abandonment by reawakening the fear of social criticism and ostracism" (ibid., 154).

9. Ali has been at the center of controversy after making a series of highly critical remarks about Islam, as well as collaborating on the film *Submission* with slain filmmaker Theo van Gogh.

10. This essay was first published in the *Boston Review* in 1999 and subsequently, along with a series of response essays, in a 1999 volume edited by Cohen et al. .

11. We deeply regret that space constraints prohibit us from engaging in a discussion of the important emergent scholarship of African women interrogating local constructions of sex, gender, and power, and challenging the supposed universality of gender relations and patriarchy. We urge the reader to refer to the important work of, for example, Ahmadu (2000, 2005), Amadiume (1987), and Oyěwùmi et al. (2003).

12. In a particularly extreme example of an alarmist but "data-free" (Shweder 2002, 227) approach, a 1979 report published by the Swedish aid agency SIDA includes the remarkable assertion, entirely unsupported by evidence, that "according to some

medical research approximately 25 percent of women in Africa become infertile after these operations" (Halldén 1979, 30, translation by Hernlund).

13. These included hospital studies, as well as epidemiological studies and population surveys that met the following criteria: adequate description of sampling and methods, large sample size, clear description of genital cutting and complications, and clearly presented results.

14. More recently, Kathryn Yount (in an article under review with *Studies in Family Planning*) has undertaken to assess the quality of studies spanning from 1999 to 2003. She examined fifty-seven articles with empirical evidence, 43 percent of which dealt with immigrants, and concluded that her review "has uncovered a reasonable body of evidence suggesting that more severe forms of genital cutting increase the risk of selected obstetric complications" (n.d., 23).

15. This statement refers to first-time pregnancy.

16. As this manuscript was going to press, the World Health Organization study group on female genital mutilation and obstetric outcome released a six-country study that did find that women with FGM, compared to uncut women, experienced an elevated risk of certain complications such as postpartum hemorrhage, stillbirth, or early neonatal death (WHO 2006).

17. While this information has not yet been published in English, we have learned in a personal communication with Pia Grassivaro Gallo (referring to a talk by Mana Abdurhaman in Padua, Italy, on May 4, 2005) that in Merka, Somalia, the "new rite" of *sunna gudnin*, involving a simple needle-prick of the clitoris, has become accepted and established.

18. Silverman (2004, 434) refers to the "acronymic flamboyance" of groups with names such as: INTACT (Infants Need to Avoid Circumcision Trauma); UNCIRC (Uncircumcising Information and Resources Center), MUSIC (Musicians United to Stop Involuntary Circumcision), Boys Too (as in "Boys Too Deserve the Same Protection as Girls"), OUCH (Outlaw Unnecessary Circumcision in Hospitals), to which Bell adds BUFF (Brothers United for Future Foreskin), RECAP (Recovery of a Penis), and DOC (Doctors Opposing Circumcision). Many of these organizations have created Websites, she points out, and there is also a journal, *Foreskin Quarterly,* devoted to similar activist activities.

19. Just how different the settings, if not the outcomes, of such surgeries are is illustrated by this description from Dr. Alter's Web site: "Outpatients spend the night after surgery in a plastic surgery recovery center, a hotel room with a friend, or at the home of a trained surgical attendant. Multiple hotels with a wide range of prices are within a short distance of each office. Superb shopping and sight-seeing is available in both Beverly Hills and New York, so friends and family can be entertained during your recovery."

20. Three U.S. states—Minnesota, Rhode Island, and Tennessee—also prohibit FGM on adult women. We have not been able to ascertain whether FGCS is legal under these statutes.

21. The midwives interviewed stressed generally, however, that requests for reinfibulation are getting less common as awareness of its illegality grows.

22. It is important to note that the term "medicalization" here actually refers to a spectrum of interventions that can range from simply providing circumcisers with clean razorblades to full-fledged clinicalization (see Obiora 1997) in which health care personnel perform the procedures in hospitals.

23. Interestingly, however, we have been informed by our Italian colleague Pia Grassivaro Gallo that in the context of sunna gudnin in Merka, Somalia (see note 17), the newborn daughters of mothers who have accepted the alternative rite are left without any kind of circumcision. This demonstrates, according to Dr. Gallo, the possibility of eradicating infibulation via the compromise of symbolic circumcision (Gallo, personal communication, citing Mana Abdurhaman).

24. In a 2002 conference on research directions on FGC in Bellagio, Italy, Nahid Toubia voiced a similar stance. Arguing that FGM should not be framed as a health issue, she forcefully (and rhetorically) questioned, "Is there anyone here who would still not oppose FGM even if the health risks could be averted?"

25. Although in the case of anti-FGM activism things become far more complex as, additionally, it is in large part African women and men who are trying to save other African women from the practice.

26. In some countries, such as Sweden, actual asylum is not given because of a fear of FGM, but residency permits are granted based on "humanitarian" grounds.

27. For a survey of campaign strategies to date, see, for example, Shell-Duncan and Hernlund 2000.

28. Boulware-Miller denotes the practice as "new" in terms of being introduced by immigrants from Africa. Others, however, note that FGC has a long history in many Western nations. Gunning (1991), for example cites the work of Barker-Benfield, who describes the social context in which clitoridectomy and other procedures on female genital organs arose as cures to "afflictions" such as masturbation in nineteenth-century America and Europe.

29. See Yount 2004 (1068–1069) for an excellent overview of the complicated recent history of the legality of FGC in Egypt.

CHAPTER 2

Gender Crusades

THE FEMALE CIRCUMCISION CONTROVERSY IN CULTURAL PERSPECTIVE

Janice Boddy

IN THE MID-1990S, an Internet message entitled "An Open Letter to a Middle-Class White Woman" circulated widely among feminist interest groups. Its author, identified only as "Waiyego," confronted a gulf of privilege and authority that presumably divides Western from African women over the issue of female circumcision. Waiyego's words were caustic, but salutary: "I am writing this letter to you to thank you very much for the compassion you have been showing lately for the hardships I have to go through as an African black woman.... If it was not for you, I would still be thinking that genital mutilation was circumcision and that it was an integral part of my culture. I'm glad you opened my eyes to the fact that circumcision was in fact a male conspiracy to reduce my sexual drive, kill me at childbirth, and a means of passing on AIDS to me. For coming to my rescue I'm eternally grateful."

This chapter explores the failure Waiyego identified: the apparent lack of understanding that Western feminists, medical practitioners, and media, on the one hand, have of African women on the other. I recognize there are dangers in granting Waiyego's presumed antitheses: clearly not all Westerners, middle class and white or not, lack appreciation of African women's perspectives and are unsympathetic to their claims. Nor are African women necessarily unaware of the harm genital cutting can do. Neither group is internally monolithic in background or belief. My intent in regarding them as opposed is heuristic: to draw out some of the subtleties of misapprehension that continue to plague the female circumcision debate.

My argument focuses on one form of the practice in its specific sociocultural and political context, that of rural northern Sudan, where I have lived and worked. I will also describe some problems I encountered with a university ethics committee when I sought to continue my research among Sudanese women living in Canada. Along the way I reflect on why Western commentators—especially the popular feminist press—are so often disdainful toward the societies where female genital cutting is done. Let me be clear: I do not endorse these practices; in fact, like the analysts I critique I am eager to see them stopped. This is something that African women—such as Nahid Toubia and her colleagues, and the faculty and students of Afhad University for Women in Sudan—are at work on at home and abroad; they know better than I how best to proceed. I, however, like Waiyego, am suspicious of some Western critics' motives and means. As an example of the rhetoric to which Waiyego refers, consider the following passages from Fran Hosken's perennially cited *Hosken Report:*

> It is evident that female genital mutilation can be abolished and wiped out in our lifetime. We are able to teach those who cling to distorted beliefs and damaging practices some better ways to cope with themselves, their lives, reproduction and sexuality. We know that everyone on earth has the capacity to learn. . . .
>
> "Why am I pursuing this?" . . . I feel that my own personal sense of dignity and worth as a woman and human being is under attack by these mutilations, inflicted on helpless children for no other reason than that they are female. I cannot tolerate this. I find it impossible, indeed absurd, to work for feminist goals, for human rights, for justice and equality, while ignoring senseless attacks on the essence of the female personality, which these operations represent. . . .
>
> These operations have continued for 2,000 years to the present time only because they are demanded by men. (Hosken 1982, 2, 14, 15)

To whom is this message directed, to what intent? On what assumptions—about personhood, gender, humanity, knowledge, power, truth—is it based? If the practices have not ceased in the wake of vigorous international condemnation, official censure, national health and education programs and the like, then why do they persist, albeit with diminishing severity in some locales? Posing such questions requires us to expand horizons of inquiry to the agency and consciousness of those who participate in the admonishing discourse as well as of those they reprove. It means stepping back from the fray to interrogate why and how female circumcision in Africa is constructed as an issue for the West.

Before jumping in, a caveat: throughout this chapter I prefer the terms "female circumcision" and "female genital cutting" to "female genital mutilation," because the lattermost contains an analysis I want to unsettle, challenge, and explore. True, "female circumcision" carries a bias too, but, although it comes closer the perspective of Sudanese women with whom I worked, it does not conform to their description of the operation, which they in Arabic call *tahara* or *tahur:* "purification." All terminologies are political, and my terminology steers uneasily between competing ideologies while trying to remain sensitive to practitioners' views.

PARAMETERS AND PROPOSITIONS

It bears repeating that while female genital cutting (FGC) is widely practiced in Africa, the custom is not confined to that continent. It is also performed by groups in Oman, Yemen, the United Arab Emirates, Malaysia,
Indonesia, India, and Pakistan (Dorkenoo and Elworthy 1992; Ghadially 1991;
Toubia 1995). Increasingly, it is encountered by health professionals in Europe
and North America, where people from these regions have moved. Although it
is often observed to have religious significance, its practitioners adhere to a variety of faiths, among them Islam, Christianity, Judaism, and indigenous African
religions. African Muslims account for a sizable number of these, however, and
the custom is popularly linked to premarital chastity, which is strongly valued
in Islam. Still, although prevalent among Northeast African Muslims, neither
infibulation—the severest forms of genital cutting—nor clitoridectomy is sanctioned by the tenets of Islam.

Most procedures are held to purify the body, prepare it for reproductive
maturity, and mark the person as belonging to a social group. They are generally
performed on children: on infants or, more commonly, when girls are between
four and ten years of age. In parts of West Africa, however, excision of the clitoris takes place shortly before marriage or just before the birth of the first child
(Dorkenoo and Elworthy 1992, 7; Myers et al. 1985). Several researchers have
observed that the operations are being conducted on girls ever younger in age,
and with less ritual fanfare than before, owing possibly to parents' increased fears
of outside intervention. Yet the traditional age typically coincides with that preferred for the circumcision of boys, with which female genital cutting is, to my
knowledge, invariably associated. Although this pairing is discounted by critics
who observe that female circumcision is not the anatomical equivalent of male,
it nonetheless provides an important window onto some cultural significances
of the practices, as we shall see.

Despite recent amendments in classification (World Health Organization 1996, hereafter WHO), varieties of female genital cutting are commonly
grouped into three broad types (Cook 1979; Shandall 1967; Verzin 1975; WHO
1979, 1986), with "sunna circumcision" the least harmful or extreme, and infibulation, or "pharaonic circumcision," the most. Some popular accounts elide
these differences, letting infibulation stand for female genital cutting, *tout court*.
This conveys a misleading impression that all genitally cut women are prone to
effects of the severest form, when only an estimated 15 percent of procedures
conform to this type.

Infibulation is prevalent in Somalia and Sudan and is practiced by the
women with whom I conducted research. It enjoins removal of the clitoris
(sometimes not in its entirety), plus all of the labia minora. The labia majora are
then pared or incised and stitched together, leaving a sheath of skin covering
the urethra and obstructing the vaginal orifice to a greater or lesser extent (see

Toubia 1994). In some locales, all external parts may be scraped away and remaining skin is stretched and fastened over the wound (Boddy 1989, 51; Lightfoot-Klein 1989a, 87). A reed or other narrow implement is usually inserted to
allow for the passage of urine and menstrual blood. As the wound heals it forms
a fibrous layer of tissue, and a midwife may be needed to enlarge the woman's
vaginal opening when she weds. Moreover, during labor a birth attendant must
be present to cut through the scar and release the child.

Grave consequences to health can attend infibulation, and contrary to
popular belief, those who have undergone it yet advocate its continuance may
be well aware of these. Immediate complications can include hemorrhage and
severe pain, which may lead to shock and death. Blood loss can result in anemia
and adversely affect the growth of an already undernourished child (Toubia
1994, 713). Septicemia and tetanus have been reported, for even when performed by trained midwives, unhygienic conditions may prevail (Aziz 1980;
Boddy 1982; El Dareer 1982b; Gruenbaum 1982 and 2000; Toubia 1994).
Physicians sometimes do the surgeries in hospital, knowing that with skilled
techniques and sanitary conditions children suffer less than in the hands of
untrained practitioners (Hall and Ismail 1981, 99). Ironically, however, once
medicalized the procedures may gain new dimensions of legitimacy, and WHO
therefore strongly discourages health professionals from doing all but remedial
operations (1986, 35).

This is a grim picture, indeed. Yet it would be irresponsible to leave the
matter there. For although infibulation, like other forms of genital cutting, is
traumatic and intensely painful, it seldom results in immediate death, despite
what might be inferred from popular accounts. Empirical studies are surprisingly scarce but suggest that even long-term complications may be less prevalent
than previously thought (Obermeyer 1999). The dearth of scientific evidence
can be linked to investigators' assumptions; as Obermeyer and her associates
note, "the harmful effects of female genital surgeries are so often assumed to
be indisputably true that they are rarely posed as questions to be investigated"
(ibid., 24). Indeed, it is precisely because they are rarely lethal that the practices
can persist. WHO (1986, 31) has in fact identified several customs it deems more
pernicious, among them early and frequent childbearing, to which many circumcised women are also disposed.

Yet infibulated women are clearly at risk over time, for complications resulting from improper drainage of urine and menstrual blood may well contribute to maternal and infant death. Childbirth is difficult, as the inelastic scar
may prolong the second stage of labor when the baby is leaving the womb; even
when a midwife is present, the outcome can be brain damage to the child. A
lengthy delivery may cause fistulae (passages) to develop between the mother's
vagina and bladder or rectum, leading to incontinence for which she might face
ostracism and divorce (El Dareer 1982b, 38; Toubia 1994, 713). In order to ease
the approaching birth, some women in the third trimester cut back on their

food, resulting in low birth weights and a doubtful start for the child, plus a slow recovery for the mother (Mohamud 1991, 208; van der Kwaak 1992, 780).

Despite such hazards, apparent fertility levels in northern Sudan are high: on average a woman experiences seven live births, and the region enjoys an annual rate of increase on the order of 3 percent (see also Balk 2000; Gruenbaum 2000; Spencer 1994, 123; Sudan Government 1982, 60–67). So, while individual women face obstacles bearing children, it is not at all clear that infibulation compromises reproductive success. This observation helps sustain local understandings that the practice socializes procreativity and conveys a moral boon, while affirming a girl's emergent sense of herself as implicitly fertile. Indeed, those who perform the operations and most resolutely defend them are women, although the number of indigenous women who oppose them and press for change is certainly on the rise (see Abusharaf 1998). Whereas no rural woman I spoke to in the 1970s or 1980s was willing to abandon infibulation, when I visited Sudan in 1994 some mooted that sunna circumcision would one day come to prevail.

Still, I found few women and men who were apprised of what sunna, or "circumcision proper," entails: cutting only the prepuce or hood of the clitoris. Toubia (1994, 712) is similarly skeptical, noting that in her medical practice in Sudan she never encountered a case of sunna that involved no damage to the clitoris itself. Since the term "sunna" refers to the "way" or "path" that Muslims follow in their daily lives, it is often attached to customary practice in a given Islamic society. Thus it may be conflated with excision or, as in the case of my informants, a modified pharaonic operation (El Dareer 1982b; Gruenbaum 1982, 2000).

This is not to say that change has not occurred. In Sudan during the 1920s and 1930s, British midwives urging eventual cessation devised an attenuated form of infibulation as a cautiously remedial first step. Called ṭahūr al-wasiṭ or ṭahūr al-mitwassiṭ—"intermediate purification"—it has largely replaced the more radical form throughout the riverine north (Boddy 1998a). In view of my informants' contrasts between their own and their daughters' operations, it requires less cutting of the labia than before (Boddy 1982, 1989); moreover, only anterior parts of the outer lips are joined, resulting in a larger genital opening (see Toubia 1994, 712). In the late 1970s I was told of a city practice wherein the labia majora were reversibly joined so that otherwise intact daughters of Western-educated parents could save face before their infibulated playmates at school (Boddy 1982). A related compromise arose in 1980s, also in urban Sudan. Following clitoridectomy the labia minora were roughened and lightly stitched to provoke adhesion; the result was called a "sandwich" (Lightfoot-Klein 1989a, 35). In 1991, Gruenbaum (1991, 642) reported a variant in which the clitoris remains intact, sewn beneath a small flap of tissue, for, according to one Sudanese midwife she interviewed, the rising demand for true sunna circumcisions that followed the 1989 Islamist coup was nonetheless accompanied by a request for some covering of the urethra "in order to avoid the sound of urination, which is considered unfeminine" (1991, 642). Modifications to infibulation have been possible not only because the practice is officially un-Islamic, but also because many men are unfamiliar with the unaltered adult female body and what the procedures entail. This lack has given women space in which to maneuver and still behave in a virtuous way. Nonetheless, many Sudanese (and Somali) women request reinfibulation after each birth because they "feel naked," impure, or ashamed when their bodies are no longer "closed."

In places such as rural Sudan, where virtually every female over the age of ten is infibulated, those undergoing the operation receive considerable support. Indeed, the experience is indispensable to becoming marriageable, a full adult, *normal*. A Sudanese girl becomes "clean" and "pure," and withstanding the trauma shows her to have attained responsibility and social agency (Barnes and Boddy 1994; Boddy 1989; see Snively 1994; Talle 1993). While children unquestionably fear the operation (R. M. Abusharaf 1998), the prospect of not being circumcised can be more disturbing still, and girls have been known to beg reluctant parents to allow them to be circumcised or even attempt to circumcise themselves (Barnes and Boddy 1994; Hall and Ismail 1981; van der Kwaak 1992).

Yet when infibulation is performed on an immigrant child living in the West, the psychological impact can be dire. If she does not belong to a close community of compatriots, she will surely lack a sympathetic environment, and the idea that her genitals have been socialized, clarified, and refined may not be sustained. She will surely be seen as abnormal, different from uncircumcised peers (see also Johnsdotter, chapter 5 of this volume). Even where the procedure is customary, rapid social change may be weakening community support, and controversy over the proper form of cutting may be deeply troubling to those already circumcised in a more radical manner.

Two oft-described effects of infibulation are pain during intercourse and lack of satisfaction from the act. According to Toubia (1994, 714), many infibulated women in Sudan are chronically anxious and depressed "from worry over the state of their genitals, intractable dysmenorrhea, and the fear of infertility" (see also Baasher 1979; Sanderson 1981). In the 1980s doctors in Khartoum reported seeing more and more women who were apprehensive lest their lack of sexual sensation and response prevent them from becoming pregnant (Light-foot-Klein1989b, 384). These observations imply two things: that female sexuality is now a medical as well as a moral issue in Sudan, and, more significantly, that concern over fertility rather than sexual pleasure *per se* is fueling women's doubts about circumcision. I return to the last point later in this chapter.

The pain of initial deinfibulation can be excruciating, particularly should the husband resort to brutal means (see Abdalla 1982; Barnes and Boddy 1994; El Dareer 1982b; Dopico, Johansen, Talle, chapters 10, 11, and 4 of this volume). Where marriages are arranged between families with permanent interests in the match, this likelihood may be reduced; it may be further diminished where, as is often the case in Sudan, spouses are close kin who have known each other from birth. Still, infibulation constitutes an implicit test of manhood in societies where it is performed. Failure to meet virility norms is deeply shameful for a man, who, like his wife, may dread the prospect of "disvirgining" her. Some men who repeatedly fail to penetrate their brides resort to suicide rather than suffer the scorn of family and peers (Lightfoot-Klein 1989a, 95–96). Moreover, for a man to oppose his wife's reinfibulation after childbirth, a long-standing practice in Sudan, signals weakness on his part, whatever his personal desires. In a study of three hundred Sudanese men, each of whom had one wife who was infibu-lated and one who was not, subjects voiced an overwhelming sexual preference for the uninfibulated partner (Shandall 1967). Thus the widely cited rationale that pharaonic circumcision is performed to enhance the husband's sexual plea-sure may be more rhetorical than real. Something else must be at stake in con-tinuing the practice, however reasonable the implication of male sexuality might appear to outside observers.

CONTESTED PERSPECTIVES

Female circumcision came to common attention in the West not in the wake of contemporary feminism's second surge, as some believe, but of its first. As early as the 1920s, metropolitan women were speaking out on behalf of their colonized sisters whom they deemed voiceless, oppressed, and unhelped by co-lonial policies designed to placate and rule through native men. Missionaries in Kenya, parliamentarians in England, British nurses, midwives, and teachers in Sudan—all publicly condemned the "barbaric," "backward" practices of female circumcision and worked within their own conceptual horizons to hasten those customs' demise (Boddy 1998a and 2007; Pedersen 1991; C. M. Shaw 1995; Snively 1994). But their efforts largely failed to produce the desired result. The practices continued. In the 1970s they were rediscovered by the West and again became an international issue, giving rise to a spate of popular commentaries, advocacy initiatives, human rights resolutions, and uncharitable denigrations of Africa and Islam.

The global feminist movement is presently divided on the practices' import. Many non-Western women wax indignant when "female genital mutilation" (FGM) commands center stage at international meetings, while the pernicious effects of Western neocolonial policies are left waiting in the wings. Too often the social and historical contexts of African women's lives go unexamined, and their enduring political and economic hardships remain unaddressed. This has engendered resentment toward those who identify female genital cutting as the ultimate form of woman abuse under patriarchy and presume to define the cir-cumcised as hapless victims of male control (Gilliam 1991; Mohanty 1991).

Much popular writing on female circumcision is polemical, preachy, advo-cacy driven, and endlessly self-referential. "Facts" culled from earlier publications are regularly summarized without exploration or critique. However inaccurate and judgmental, they acquire from repetition the patina of truth (Shell-Duncan and Hernlund 2000; Obermeyer 1999; van der Kwaak 1992). One recognizes such activity as diagnostic of a discourse in Foucault's (1979, 1980, and 1990) sense of the term: a system of interwoven ideas and practices that is productive of further knowledge; a segment of a conceptual apparatus that powerfully shapes the thoughts and behavior of participants by defining the world of permissible assertions (the regime of truth) within which they live and meaningfully interact (cf. DuBois 1991; Ferguson 1990; Rogers, chapter 6 of this volume; Said 1978). Through this discourse, the discourse of FGM, power relations are seemingly subverted even as they are maintained. Sisterhood is invoked, a caring, humanitarian "we" that masks continuing relations of dominance; African societies are normalized as "barbaric" and needing Western guidance. Foucault suggests that for the modern state to exercise control as it does, "there must be, between male and female or adult and child, quite specific relations of domination which have their own configuration and relative autonomy" (1980, 188). Power circulates through such relations not so much in representational or homological form, as where a father is to his children as the state to its subjects, but as complex and unstable refractions, partly independent of wider relations and simultaneously informative of them. If we accept a decentralized concept of power but broaden the observation, we might propose that for the conjunctions of global capitalism or secular modernity to work the way that they do, there must be, between the West and the rest, as between state and subject, etc., "quite specific relations of domination which have their own configuration and relative autonomy" (ibid.). FGM discourse contributes to such a project despite the intentions of its practitioners. Decades after being repudiated by scholars, ideas about social evolution that shaped European responses to African societies and justified their colonization in the nineteenth and early twentieth centuries are here promiscuously reinvoked. And, of course, the dichotomy between civilized and barbaric, or developed and underdeveloped in its recent more genteel guise, has long created openings for Western intervention and control (DuBois 1991). It is the appeal to social evolutionary thought in all its arrogant certainty that is the most troubling feature of FGM texts.

What is it then, specifically, that these texts say and do? First, indigenous explanations for genital cutting are presented out of context, simplified, and hyperbolized, then dismissed as irrational or based on superstition. The voices of affected women and children are either absent or carefully chosen for horrific impact; rarely do we hear from those who wish to maintain the practice, and when we do their concerns are trivialized. Even African women who oppose circumcision for health reasons or endorse a sunna procedure on religious grounds may be chastised as missing the point, or accused of false consciousness as in the earlier quote from Hosken. Authors regularly declare that the operations are "frequently fatal" (Pugh 1983, 9) or use phrases like "if she survives"

(Lightfoot-Klein 1989b, 378) without providing a basis for their claims, thus disclosing their own investment more than reliable "fact" and losing credibility with the millions of circumcised women whose counterindicative numbers feature saliently and ironically in their prose. FGM discourse also typically describes circumcised women as having been robbed of all sexual pleasure; yet scientific studies are equivocal as to the effects of the operations on sexual response even among the infibulated. Some clearly experience pleasure to the point of orgasm or "finishing" (Ahmadu, Dopico, Johansen, chapters 12, 10, and 11 of this volume; Gosselin 1999; Gruenbaum 1996, 462, and Gruenbaum 2000; Lightfoot-Klein 1989b), while others do not. Several disciples of FGM discourse are, however, undaunted by the cautions of such research (for example, Accad 1989; Hosken 1982; Walker 1992; Walker and Parmar 1993). Although African women's voices and experiences may be muted in FGM texts, their bodies and body parts are omnipresent. Even otherwise culturally perceptive publications include prurient photographs of disembodied female genitals; alternatively, terror-struck little girls are shown undergoing circumcision or in anguish from resulting pain. Seldom are we shown the smiling faces of their mothers and sisters, even the girls themselves, rejoicing at their accomplishment. Scarcely less problematic are the ubiquitous sketches of "normal versus circumcised" genitalia. While these may serve a legitimate purpose in medical texts, they nonetheless produce the unintended effect of reducing African women's bodies to savage curiosities for the scrutiny of powerful foreign elites. By the same token, uncircumcised Western women—readers and authors alike—implicitly have their bodies, and their sexuality reconfirmed as normal and ideal (see also Rogers, chapter 6 of this volume)

The resilience of images of African barbarity perpetuated in FGM discourse and the service they provide in affirming Western canons of normalcy were brought home to me when I was awarded a grant to conduct research among Sudanese women living in Toronto and my project underwent the standard university ethics review. Part of the project was concerned with whether the issue of female circumcision had overdetermined the relationship of Sudanese women to Canadian society as a whole. Moreover, prior contact with the community had shown that its women, almost all of them political refugees, were engaged in rethinking traditional parameters of gender, religion, and ethnicity, while publicly re-visioning a future non-Islamist but by no means anti-Muslim nation of Sudan (Boddy 1995). The women had met several times to discuss human rights abuses in their homeland, among which they included female circumcision. Their use of the language of universal human rights, coupled with their support for certain parochial customs, such as *zar* spirit possession rites banned as "superstition" by the Islamist government in Sudan and from which, as elites, the women had distanced themselves in the past, suggested that a syncretistic cultural shift was underway, of which the women were primary agents. I felt that research among them might shed light on how gender ideology was being transformed in the process of refashioning national or ethnic identity vis-à-vis the state the women had fled and the one to which they had come. But the research did not get far.

The ethics board informed me that because in Canada female circumcision was legally considered child abuse, if, during the project I came to suspect a child was at risk of undergoing the procedure, I was obliged to report her family to child welfare authorities, who would then take steps to intervene, possibly by removing the child from her family. Risk could minimally be defined as having an older sister who was circumcised and a mother or father who favored the practice. I was therefore required to notify those I interviewed of the custom's illegality and of my responsibility to report them if I acquired the knowledge described here. In other words, I was asked to become an agent of the state, when it was the relation of these women to the state that I sought to understand. The demand put me in the awkward position of being part of the very problem I was hoping to investigate. Moreover, the experience actually confirmed my working hypothesis that the issue of female circumcision had overdetermined the position of Sudanese in Canada. One member of the ethics tribunal wondered if I might not find that Sudanese adults practice "other forms of child abuse as well," implying that they are a deviant population with an aberrant culture, who wish to do their children harm. (Most came to Canada at great personal expense to ensure their children a safer life.) When, following the committee's request, I contacted two regional children's aid societies to see how they would handle the situation should it arise, one social worker suggested I let Sudanese couples know that she and her colleagues could teach them how to parent properly. However well-intended such statements, they are clearly patronizing and ill informed. They reflect how insidiously the ladder of social evolution shapes interactions between dominant and non-elite groups of different backgrounds, how this apparently anachronistic "master-narrative" exerts continuing if unconscious effect.

It is the hubris of the position just described, its inattention to cultural nuance and social context, its zealous polarization of African women and men, parents and children, "us" and "them," but even more, its proponents' claim to hold monopolies on truth and righteous conduct, that are so vexing to African feminists and feminist anthropologists alike. What, then, is at stake for Western popular writers who engage the debate on such terms? To tackle this requires us to consider some epistemological grounds of their position—its historically specific cultural context—in relation to the premises of those whom they confront.

Gender Images

In his provocative book, *Making Sex: Body and Gender from the Greeks to Freud* (1990), Thomas Laqueur explores a shift in Euro-American thought toward the end of the eighteenth century, when what he (with poetic license) calls a "one-sex" model was gradually replaced by our current notion that there exist two explicit and distinct sexes. Importantly, Laqueur links this change not to an unalloyed growth of scientific knowledge but to transformations in the cultural and political processes that both constitute subjects and social relations and generate the problems that scientists seek to solve. For thousands of years Europeans imagined that women and men were equipped with similar reproductive equipment, but spatially reversed—placed inside or outside the body in complementary ways. But as the old social and cosmic order faltered under the pressures of industrialization and the sexual division of labor was remade, the obvious differences between women and men assumed new meanings.

Where before the sexes' social and natural differences were seen as relative, hence commensurable if hierarchically arrayed, now they became discrete and incomparable, antitheses rather than asymmetric complementaries. Further, suggests Laqueur, scholars were spurred to seek evidence to establish such claims, in keeping with a growing belief in "positive knowledge" by which the material world—biology, sex, the body—furnishes decisive ground for contingent, variable traits such as culture, gender, or "the mind." Laqueur writes, "The dominant, though by no means universal, view since the eighteenth century has been that there are two stable, incommensurable, opposite sexes and that the political, economic, and cultural lives of women and men, their gender roles, are somehow based on these "facts." Biology—the stable, ahistorical, sexed body—is understood to be the epistemic foundation for prescriptive claims about the social order" (1990, 6).

In the earlier "one-sex" model there was gender hierarchy, to be sure, but its grounds were subtly skewed. Women had been seen as imperfect men, and gender was not epiphenomenal or derivative of biological sex; rather, the physical and the social were complexly interwoven, "explicitly bound up in a circle of meanings from which escape to a supposed biological substrate—the strategy of the Enlightenment—was impossible" (ibid., 8).

The conviction that the sexes constitute ontological categories from which a host of social corollaries arise grounds Western commonsense understandings of women and men today: we may dispute what comprises their essences— whether the sexes are inherently different or alike, the scope of men's nurturance or women's aggression—but that they have certain innate predilections seems intuitively obvious and banal. Moreover, in Western societies the organs of reproduction are metonyms of this sexual essence, constituting it and representing it at the same time. In the late nineteenth and early twentieth centuries, woman's essence was associated with childbearing and the womb; from the mid-twentieth century on, when medicalized contraception unlinked sexual intimacy and childbearing, it has come to focus on the clitoris as a site of sexual pleasure, signifying the unencumbered individual relative to the world. Likewise, whereas in 1920s and 1930s Western campaigns against female genital cutting focused on infibulation and its consequences for childbirth (Boddy

2007; Pedersen 1991), by the 1970s emphasis had shifted to clitoridectomy and its consequences for sexual fulfillment.

Habitually, we consider an organic two-sex pattern natural, the way things really are. But as Laqueur and others have shown, it is a cultural construct that, like the one-sex model earlier described, arose under specific historical and political conditions. As such, assertions of its accuracy miss the mark. "Facts" are always filtered through language and cultural premise, knowledge is never perfect, claims to "truth" are inherently provisional. In our everyday lives the extent to which received ideas about sex are constituted by social processes is obscure. We tend to assume that sex is prior, fixed, and given, based in a "positive" biology; in the Western world, sex is what you start with, gender what you, and society, make of it. Yet much of the time the dynamic works in reverse: we project gender (social roles, cultural images) onto sex, reading sex through the lens of gender (J. Butler 1990). Think, for instance, of some cinema depictions of conception: anthropomorphized sperm in Woody Allen's *Everything You Wanted to Know About Sex (But Were Afraid to Ask)* are played by male actors; in the two *Look Who's Talking* films, the personified ovum acts coyly, "femininely," and has a female voice; sperm "swimming" or "racing" up the birth canal have male voices and act "masculinely," urging each other on as in a football match. Yet high school biology reminds us that sperm are not strictly male: each carries an X or Y sex-determining chromosome. Moreover, since genes sort randomly, any ovum or sperm is a composite, a mix of characteristics inherited from male and female forebearers. From comedy to science: Emily Martin (1991) convincingly shows how the commonsense notion that sperm are male and ova female plagues "objective" research, burdening laboratory investigations of human conception with romantic images of "typical" masculine and feminine traits. All this is part of a process by which we affix culturally specific gender roles to nature, anchoring them in material reality to the point where they seem inevitable, universal. We remain largely unaware of how dependent our notions of sexual difference are on such taken-for-granted ideas (Butler 1990; Grosz 1987; Martin 1987), or, as Laqueur puts it, of how "everything one wants to say about sex—however sex is understood—already has in it a claim about gender" (1990, 11). And here is my point: we may be quite ready to grant that this applies to other societies, but we are less prepared to concede it applies to our own. African women are mired in culture; "we" hold the light of truth.

Some conventional ideas common to societies in the contemporary West: that we possess our bodies; that each body is the site of a person, an individual bounded self who is the bearer of rights and responsibilities; that important aspects of the self's essential identity—key to what rights and responsibilities it can and cannot claim—are vested in its sex from birth. A baby's genitals are evidence of the incipient person beneath the skin; society's role is to nurture the child's inherent potential according to its sex, or to surmount sex typing

and ensure the same opportunities for girls and boys. Such are a few of the assumptions that female circumcision exposes and defies.

Earlier I noted that some infibulated and clitoridectomized women report
experiencing orgasm or at least enjoyment of sexual relations. While such findings challenge Western expectations, explanations exist that do not. Midwives
seeking to prevent excessive blood loss may leave the clitoris relatively intact
beneath the infibulation seam (Gruenbaum 2000). And the closeness of the
marital bond may assuage reduction of the organ responsible for orgasm while
heightening the cerebral components of sex (see Dopico and Ahmadu, chapters
10 and 12 of this volume; Bonaparte 1953; Hite 1976; Lightfoot-Klein 1989a
and 1989b). But if we take seriously the suggestion that bodily experience is
interactively produced *through* culture and is not simply culture's natural base,
we must also allow that desires and pleasures can be culturally and historically
specific. The questions raised by findings of sexual enjoyment in circumcised
women are unsettling precisely because "they imply that what is presented as
an indisputable physiological reality may itself be socially constructed" (Obermeyer 1999, 24).

We could also turn the point around and wonder why *these* findings seem
so instantly counterintuitive. Moreover, what do we invest in the clitoris that
contemplating its loss augurs such serious personal diminishment? Part of the
answer has been suggested earlier in this chapter, with the historical shift from
womb to clitoris as organs metonymic of female personhood, yet I think there
is more. In the 1950s North American surgeons routinely removed children's
tonsils because they held them to be vestigial and to cause ill health, and although the operation was risky and traumatic, and the removal of functioning
organs can hardly be justified as promoting health, I do not recall it being suggested that the loss of one's tonsils would irreparably damage one's personality.
But tonsils are not genitals. Still, we customarily amputate babies' foreskins, now
with some controversy but little alarm. And people in a number of societies
routinely alter the penises of boys more radically than we: there is subincision,
where the organ is slit along the underside to the point where the urethra is
permanently exposed; and in some societies the penis is partially flayed.

Yet global censure of these practices is scarcely comparable to that leveled at
female circumcision. Nor do they receive FGM's level of media attention. Why
not? Why is there no outrage remotely parallel to that which leads some writers
to insist that circumcised women are entirely alienated from the essence of the
female personality (Hosken 1982; see Hashi and Silver 1994, Walker 1992)? Is it
because these excisions are performed on boys, and only girls and women figure
as victims in our cultural lexicon?

Gender in the contemporary West tends to be imagined in terms of di-
ametric contrasts and closely tied to anatomy. In biology and psychology—
sciences laden with cultural import—such distinctions have tended to focus on
the sexual organs of the male, on having or not having a penis. "Male" is defined

by presence and "female" by absence, by being "not-male" (see Ardener 1986). So significant is this presence and so strict its parameters that a child born with an undersized penis (but a penis all the same) is likely to become a candidate for sex reassignment surgery (Fausto-Sterling 1997). The anomalous organ/sign is reduced in order to ensure that the child's body better fits existing categorical criteria; female is, by this cultural logic, the "default" sex.

Anthropologists and others have argued that Western societies evince a deep division between "culture" and "nature" to which gender and other axiomatic principles are linked. Hence, "culture" is typically associated with mind, reason, agency, self, social creativity, and maleness; and "nature" (the given, precultural or primitive) with body, procreation, instinctual emotion, passivity, receptivity, "the other," and femaleness (Bordo 1993; Grosz 1987; Mascia-Lees and Sharpe 1992b; Ortner 1974 and 1996). Males are by definition actors and females the "acted upon." When such definitions are referred to anatomical difference (if sometimes surgically enhanced), the models naturalize asymmetric social constructs and uneven distributions of power: intuitively, men and boys are not "natural" victims.

Although considerable research in anthropology and feminist philosophy has exposed these ideas' ideological roots, it has barely reduced their relevance. They are mobilized even in certain feminist camps, albeit in backhanded ways: for some, the very existence of the clitoris serves to disrupt established gender hierarchies, intimating a world in which neither sex prevails (Mascia-Lees and Sharpe 1992b, 149, 162) and where both are creative, rational agents. This observation derives from the "rediscovery" of the clitoris as a site of sexual pleasure by the women's movement in the 1970s and its consequent transformation into a robust symbol of female emancipation; it is hardly surprising that female circumcision in Africa was "rediscovered" and recondemned at about the same time (see Scheper-Hughes 1991).

In effect, accounts that ground personal autonomy in the clitoris invoke a one-sex model, based on alleged similarity of function: the clitoris is the female analogue of the penis, hence both sexes are endowed with qualities the penis represents. Yet far from unseating the binary archetype, they seem to sustain it by implicitly valorizing the male, subsuming the female, and advancing a model of gender that stakes presocial anatomy as its (cultural) ground. Still, it is understandable that for those committed to this view, removal of the clitoris entails an irreparable diminution of feminine value—the ultimate violation of natural female "essence" (for example, Hosken 1982; compare R. M. Abusharaf 1995, 1996; Ahmadu, chapter 12 of this volume; D. Fraser 1995; Rogers, chapter 6 of this volume).

Patently, we are discussing a socially meaningful clitoris, not (were it possible) an unmediated, precultural one. Yet many writers abjure. Rather than situate their epistemology, they mobilize it to envelop the clitoris in a mantle of biomedical—seemingly culture-free—fact, deploying science to refute others' "cultural mistakes," which can only be remedied by "education" (for example, Armstrong 1991; Anonymous 1992; Hosken 1982; Koso-Thomas 1987; Kouba and Muasher 1985; Slack 1984). I do not for a moment deny that circumcision harms women's health; the entailments of infibulation, with labial excision and attenuation of the vagina, are, as we have seen, particularly severe. But the suggestion that "science" is untainted by cultural content and, with Western culture generally, intrinsically superior and beneficial, is both disparaging and fallacious: the canons of normality that nourish a quest for physical perfection leading girls to risk their health through dieting, women to painful cosmetic surgery, and doctors to unnecessary caesarean deliveries are by no means culture free. Moreover, as Gruenbaum pithily remarks, "social customs ... are not 'pathologies,' and such a view is a poor starting point for change, since it is not one necessarily shared by the people whose customs are under attack" (1982, 6).

What, then, are some indigenous views? First, recall that where female circumcision is performed, so is the circumcision of males. To my knowledge there is no African society where the former takes place but the latter does not, and this perhaps furnishes a clue to their meaning. Many such groups adhere to models of gender complementarity not unlike that which Laqueur (1990) describes for pre-eighteenth-century Europe. Indeed, Egypt and Arabic-speaking Sudan share with Europe the Galenic medical tradition that depicts the sexes as homologous, and humoral medicine remains a popular alternative to biomedicine in North African societies today. Beyond this, several peoples hold that humans are born unfinished. Dogon in Mali (Griaule 1965), for instance, and Sudanese and upper Egyptian villagers (Ammar 1954; Boddy 1989; Kennedy 1978) perform circumcisions to complete the social or spiritual definition of a child's sex by removing anatomical traces of ambiguity, thus differentiating socially what is deemed "naturally" similar (see also Ahmadu 2000). Thus Sudanese remove the "masculine" clitoris and labia in the case of girls and the "feminine" foreskin in the case of boys. In the village of Hofriyat where I lived, male and female children undergo their respective operations upon gaining a minimum of reason ('aql) or "social sense." They are expected to realize that their bodies are being "purified," made discrete by the social group. Here, excision of the clitoris is followed by infibulation designed to "cover" and protect the female reproductive tract, where the male's organ is opened or "unveiled." Hofriyati consider the operations complementary (Boddy 1989).

This is the sort of indigenous account that Western analysts typically dismiss: removing the clitoris, they rebuke, is not physically equal to removing the foreskin but to amputating the penis (see, for example, Bardach 1993; Hosken 1982; Kellner 1993; Slack 1984; Winkel 1995; compare Winter 1994). Unwilling to think beyond a biomedical view that privileges anatomical function per se, such critics miss the cultural point. Moreover, if disposed to what Sacks (1976) calls "state-bias"—the proclivity in industrial polities where commodity logic prevails, to conflate equivalence with sameness—they may distort gender complementarity too. Hence they perform a double reduction to absolute physical terms: if Hofriyati claim that the clitoris and foreskin are comparable, surely they must think them physiologically alike. Yet Hofriyati are not poor observers. I doubt they regard the parts they remove from one sex as physically equivalent to those they accent in the other; this is remote from their concerns. Rather, they deem them morally and cosmologically analogous. Circumcision creates a certain kind of difference, or lack, in order to affect a specific sort of relationship, or fit. Instead of presuming to derive gender from "presocial" sex, Hofriyati shape anatomical sex to the exigencies of gender, thereby endowing bodies with the potential for appropriate sociality. In short, where the "naturally" sexed body is primary in Western thought and gender is derived, gender is primary and the conventionally sexed body its derivative in northern Sudanese (Boddy 1989, 1998b; Holy 1991, compare Laqueur 1990, 8). Villagers' perpetuation of female circumcision is not a simple consequence of inadequate scientific knowledge: culturally specific premises of both science and circumcision counsel the poverty of that view.

Still, insofar as a global economy dedicated to satisfying people's physical needs and desires requires that bodies be universally intelligible, the biomedical discourse enlisted by Western critics seeks not only to "other" circumcising peoples but to normalize them (compare Foucault 1979, 136). By drawing attention to their aberrance and discounting alternate modes of thought it seeks to implant in them the desire to become what they "should" be. In the same breath with which it castigates Africans for failing to modernize, it seeks to colonize their bodies and, wittingly or not, perpetuate their exploitation (Kirby 1987).

Hofriyat

I want now to describe one indigenous context more fully, to the extent that I was able to comprehend it. Hofriyati women who endorse female circumcision do so for reasons at once both material and ideological. In Hofriyat, as in most African societies, the state has not displaced kinship as the principal means of social organization and support. Moreover, the corporate family is upheld by Islamic law. Thus the defense of one's rights and obligations, property allotments, economic prospects, health care, and social security all flow largely from relations among close or extended kin. The lineage—a patriline, whose male and female members trace or assert descent from a common ancestor long deceased—is a basic source of personal identity and economic well-being. Marriages establish alliances between different descent groups or, more often in Hofriyat, between close kin wishing to build upon existing moral, political, and economic commitments. In kinship-based societies, virtually all important political and economic relations are produced and reproduced through conjugal ties. Thus, genealogies chart corporate connections, and great care may be taken to avoid indeterminate parentage. Sexuality poses a dilemma: insofar as it generates people, hence labor, numerical strength, new marriages, and potential wealth, it is a tremendously valuable resource; yet insofar as it is the domain of the individual its realization can threaten collective interests (Abdalla 1982; Abu Lughod 1986; Boddy 1989 and 1994; Gruenbaum 1982; Hayes 1975). Hence marriage is largely by parental arrangement, subordinating the sexuality of younger women and men to the interests of the social group as defined by its elders.

In Hofriyat, sexual restraint is a matter of family honor. Where the superintending polity is weak, a family's relative honor is a measure of its ability to command essential resources (Bourdieu 1977). A family that loses honor risks being deemed unmarriageable, which endangers its economic status, political leverage, and very continuity. Not surprisingly, honor is vested mainly in the conduct of women: daughters and sisters, less so women who marry into the group. Women's lives are more circumscribed than men's and more vigilantly patrolled. Yet women are by no means powerless: compulsion too is shameful; subordinates must *want* to act appropriately. A woman's misbehavior condemns her guardians as not having earned her respect; reciprocally, her obedience constrains their responsible conduct (Abu-Lughod 1986).

Women may, however, have few options outside of marriage and the reproductive role that this entails. For her to be marriageable, a woman's morals, hence the social value of her fertility, must be above reproach. In Somalia, for instance, a husband's family has the right to inspect the bride's body prior to marriage; mothers regularly check their unwed daughters to ensure that they are "closed"; a girl accused of indiscretion may publicly expose her genitals so as to prove herself chaste (Barnes and Boddy 1994; Talle 1993). Thus, by continuing circumcision women shield themselves from the effects of potential or implied deviance (Toubia 1985, 151). Where circumcision is the norm, uncircumcised women are prostitutes and pariahs, and mothers circumcise their daughters out of a desire to do the best for them, not because they wish to do them harm.

A number of Western writers vilify the precedence of collective over individual ends that this ethnographic context reveals (for example, Hosken 1982, Slack 1984). Here the Western idea of the person as a bounded entity possessed of rights and a social identity that increasingly resides in the appetites and pleasures of the singular body clashes with notions in which the person is unthinkable except in relational terms. Those who condemn circumcision as violating the person's right to sexual and corporal integrity risk presuming their own construction of self to be the ideal or "natural" human state (Boulware-Miller 1985). And, unless they equally censure all deleterious body modifications, including those at home, they risk accusations of duplicity.

At this point it may be objected that collective ends are men's, and invariably override women's interests. Yet a strict gender division is illusory, born of assuming the universality of our own contested ideology dividing "domestic" [female] from "public" [male] spheres, itself the counterpart of a now outmoded anatomical dualism. In Hofriyat a woman gains public status as her sons and daughters mature, marry, and reproduce. Grandmothers (*ḥabōbat*) achieve respect and considerable authority over family and village affairs, the principal realms in which villagers can exercise control. Still, respected elderhood can only be attained through the bodies of kin. Insofar as genital surgery is a condition of marriage and reproduction for both women and men, the precedence of the older generation is supported by the operations they perform on the young. Importantly, women's power and social agency—as well as their economic well-being—have hitherto rested with continuing the practice.

The impression of duress I may have conjured needs to be contextualized, if not dispelled. Pressures at work in Hofriyat resemble disciplinary power in which subjects are schooled to self-surveillance more than coerced from without. Hofriyati, like the rest of us, internalize constraints on their behavior in learning to inhabit an already meaningful world. Yet societies create meaningful worlds in various ways. As noted above, the proclivity in Western representational practice is to reduce cultural meanings to underlying "truths." Hofriyati logic, however, tends to work not reductively but recursively: images resolve to other images and yet other images, reprising Laqueur's aforementioned "circle of meanings from which escape to a supposed biological substrate . . . [is] impossible" (Laqueur 1990, 8). Villagers' cultural logic is raveled in the skein of daily life, informing its most banal and intimate details. It is embedded in habits of body and mind, more felt, intuited, than willed. It constitutes, as I claim elsewhere (Boddy 1998b), an embodied cultural aesthetic, shaping visceral sensibilities and imbuing them with political effect. For aesthetics are never neutral; they are judgments of value and conduct that suggest suitable—"normal"—inclinations toward others and the world.

What follows draws briefly from my earlier work (Boddy 1989 and 1998b) to show how Hofriyati consensual notions of propriety—purity, integrity, closure—govern not only human behavior but also ideals of physical form, food, architecture, odors, the familiar objects of everyday life. The tracings of such values in seemingly disparate domains converge to create a horizon of intelligibility that confronts participants as self-evident, real. Thus is the social order internalized "by the hidden persuasion of an implicit pedagogy" (Bourdieu 1990, 69), and power embodied, made self.

Genital cutting aligns girls and boys to their incompletely shared social world, establishing differences in their sensibilities and adult perspectives. A girl's body is feminized, enclosed both by infibulation and the courtyard walls behind which she should now remain; a boy's body is masculinized, opened to confront the world. Hereafter, the space they inhabit is explicitly gendered: girls are oriented to interiors, boys to fields, streets, and public areas in the family home. Prior to circumcision a child must have attained a modicum of *'aql,* reason or social sense, hence begun to discern its future roles. To be *'aqil(a)* is to be socially aware: able to anticipate others' needs and respond in appropriate ways, to internalize and demonstrate the reciprocity of perspectives that is the basis of human sociality. Once circumcised, boys and girls lead more segregated lives, and their complementary dispositions mature. Their continuous engagement with humanly ordered spaces, meaningful objects, and socialized elders ensures their progressive implication in this world. The girl's body, however, is the more symbolically marked: it has become a metonym and icon of village society, guarded against external threat by its own scar tissue, compound walls, and the defensive efforts of kin.

Homes and infibulated bodies are isomorphic, heeding a common aesthetic form. This is expressed both in practice—as in the custom of burying miscarriages within the compound's walls—and in words, for the men's door to the courtyard is called "the mouth of the house" (al-khashm al-bayt), a term that also denotes descendants therein sired and raised, while a woman's vaginal meatus is "the mouth of the house of childbirth" (al-khashm al-bayt al-wilāda). The front part of the courtyard is the men's place, where strangers are received; as the vagina is to the female body, it is the part of the house that is penetrable, under controlled conditions, from without. The house's protected inner part—its "belly" (buṭon), by implication its "womb"—is women's domain, an informal, private space where kin and close friends mix. The honor and integrity of a family are best preserved when women remain within courtyard walls and external forces are kept at bay. Then too is the village—an extended family, expanded house—protected and safe. Importantly, women are housed within their own bodies when they are bodily present in the house (Boddy 1998b).

Houses, families, and bodies require openings lest the process of life should cease; yet openings—doors, marriages, bodily orifices—make people vulnerable: to other villagers, foreign colonizers, and powerful spirits that cannot be kept out by walls, human skin or closed doors. Illnesses result when physical and architectural defenses are breached and spirits, especially, intrude. Certain physical disorders are attributed to bodies "opening" inadvertently: headache, for example, is an "opened head" and mended by binding (a remedy now eclipsed by aspirin). Bodily "closure" is considered health promoting, curative: during one of my stays in the village an ailing toddler was precociously infibulated in order to make her well. And parturition hemorrhage can be staunched if the patient sees a group of objects having gender-complementary significances—like water and grain, the respective products of women and men—proclaiming completeness, closure, balance.

Infibulation, by enclosing the womb, contains and safeguards uterine blood, the source of a woman's fertility and her village's well-being. According to local concepts of procreation, a child's bones and sinew (hard parts) are formed from the semen or "seed" of its father, while its flesh and blood (soft parts) are formed from its mother's blood (compare Holy 1991). Such contributions are complementary, if differently weighted: flesh and blood are evanescent, bones relatively enduring. Like the skeleton that structures the body, patrilineal descent structures village relationships in lasting ways. Although marriages with patrilineal cousins are preferred, in practice those traced through close female kin are highly desirable, even should prospective spouses belong to different lineages. Indeed, relationships traced through flesh and blood—through women—bind the village's skeletal descent groups, providing the tissue that succumbs over time to decay unless renewed by successive intermarriages. The social body—the endogamous village—is a physical body writ large; both are moral entities. But equally, the physical body is the endogamous village writ small. Each person's body is a composite of maternal and paternal substance: bone, flesh, blood, received from preceding generations of male and female kin. Persons are thus aggregate and socially androgynous, conditions that circumcision refines in creating the potential for marriage and social continuity.

Ideas about the village and the body round back again to the house, which is physically linked to childbirth and the womb through practices that resolve failed pregnancies. A stillbirth is buried outside the "mouth of the house" against the courtyard wall, and a miscarriage is placed in an impervious rounded pottery jar that is then buried inside the courtyard near the kitchen, intimating the life that has stopped in the womb. Importantly, this type of jar is also used by women for mixing flour (seed produced by men) with water (fluid—like blood—associated with women) to produce the dough that, when poured onto a hot metal plate and baked, becomes the bread that nourishes human life with the fertility of the land.

Such practices and objects of everyday life are implicit media of socialization. Engaging them helps shape and sustain a woman's profound identification with her fertility and persuade her of the need to protect it so that it can be transformed into life under appropriate social conditions. Ideal bodies are at once "closed" and integral, and interdependent, intimately and complexly relational. The village is an organism through which gendered physical substances circulate and are shared by kin of varying degrees. Closely related women may experience their shared material selves acutely: a woman whose daughter has died in childbed may fall ill herself from a malady called *du'f,* "weak" or "diminished blood." Further, ideas about circulating body substances intersect with notions of harmony, balance, and purity: health, hence propriety and closure, requires an internal balance of complementary forces—cold and hot, light and heavy, wet and dry—achieved by ingesting appropriate foods or smelling suitable odors. Foul odors or impure foods—those that are neither white nor enclosed by skins, jars, or tins—can lead to illness and render the body assailable by spirits. Smells of human sweat or blood indicate physical openness and are hazardous to health. In short, closure is an axiomatic value in Hofriyat, underwriting a range of practices and ideas, salient among them infibulation.

CONCLUSION

Hofriyati cultural models refer to human physiology, like our own, yet their trajectory tends to be elliptical, rather than reductive as is typical in the

West. In Hofriyat, biological traits belong to a wider set of motifs that weave through disparate realms of meaning without resolving to essences or absolutes. Enough has been said by now to convey a sense of how villagers' conventional ideas shape their sensibilities, which in turn render their conventions natural, inevitable, real. That the conventions of Western observers are similarly informed—albeit by other priorities and assumptions—should also be clear, granting Western critics no Archimedean leverage on the customs they decry. Moreover, the fact that a society practices female genital cutting cannot be left to "stand for" that society in its entirely—to act as its reductive truth. Clearly, Hofriyati culture is a complex process, often coherent if not always consistent, and as deeply premised as any other. Only when scientists, scholars, and advocates fully embrace these understandings might Western engagement with the practices do less harm than good.

As a hint of what may follow should we refuse, I end with a report circulated to a Sudan-focused Internet discussion group, dated June 25, 1998. It is attributed to Nhial Bol, International Press Service, Khartoum, and begins thus: "Sudan's Islamic clerics have urged the people to resist a new campaign by a group of non-governmental organizations in the country to challenge the age-old practice of Female Genital Mutilation (FGM)."

The report notes that Sheikh Mohamed Abbas, a respected cleric, has "urged Sudan's 60 percent Moslem community to resist Western culture and to uphold their traditional practices, like FGM"; moreover, it claims that his plea (however conventionally un-Islamic) is backed by some influential Muslims in the Islamic state. Tellingly, the censured NGO campaign is local, not foreign-led. When the abolition of female circumcision became a grail in the new crusades, its political reclamation might well have been foretold.

NOTE

I am grateful to Rogia Abusharaf, Claudie Gosselin, Carla Obermeyer, Jackie Solway, and Judy Whitehead, who helped in different ways; the faults in this chapter are mine, not theirs. The Social Sciences and Humanities Research Council of Canada, the Connaught Fellowship Fund of the University of Toronto, and the H. F. Guggenheim Foundation have funded my research; I gratefully acknowledge their support. I am most indebted, however, to the women of Hofriyat, Sudan.

CHAPTER 3

A Refuge from Tradition
and the Refuge of Tradition

ON ANTICIRCUMCISION PARADIGMS

L. Amede Obiora

Complex notions like culture . . . inhibit an analysis of the relationships among the variables they pack together. . . . [I]f the
elements of culture are disaggregated, it is usually not difficult
to show that the parts are separately tied to specific administrative arrangements, economic pressures, biological constraints, and so forth. . . . In short, it is a poor strategy to separate out a cultural sphere, and to treat it in its own terms.

—Kuper 1999

Does the overwhelming disgust at clitoridectomy signal an
emerging social commitment to structural change—to ensuring equal social, economic, and political status of women? I
am afraid not. Of course the absence of such commitment is
no justification for clitoridectomy.

—Tamir 1996

The attention given FGM seems to me somewhat disproportionate, among the many gross abuses the world practices
against women. . . . Surely Tamir is right that we should not
focus on this one abuse while relaxing our determination to
make structural changes that would bring women closer to
full equality worldwide.

—Nussbaum 1996

SOME YEARS AGO, I presented some arguments that were featured as the centerpiece of a symposium about the limitations of the campaign against female circumcision (Obiora 1997). In a companion piece, I
chronicled the chain of events that coerced my involvement in the debate

and triggered my critique of abstract anticircumcision rhetoric (Obiora 1996).
These endeavors reinforced my appreciation of the paramount need to implement concrete measures to substantiate the gender equity agenda in respective
African contexts. Having shared the views I deemed expedient to articulate
on female circumcision, I resolved to disengage from extensive scholarly ru-
minations about the matter and to devote my immediate energy to outlining a
viable framework that would contribute to the improvement of the objective
conditions that underpin practices like female circumcision. Subsequently, I
accepted an offer to manage the Gender and Law Program at the World Bank.
The core of this assignment was to explore and define ways to best mobilize law to promote gender equity. In the course of my tenure at the Bank, I
gained a heightened awareness of the contingency of law and of its operation
as a dependent variable.[1] The experience sealed my conviction about the imperative for nuance vis-à-vis efforts to substantiate gender equity in general
and about the place of practices such as female circumcision as prisms through
which to comprehend the complexity of gender as an analytic category in
particular. By the same token, I became all the more persuaded of the futility
of discussions that prioritize gender as an overarching cleavage instead of examining its interface with other variables that acquire differing salience from
time to time.[2]

     The preceding epigraphs capture the thrust of my present contribution,
which can be restated as an invitation to critically address an enduring dilemma
of anticircumcision campaigns. The insights delineated in these epigraphs echo
sentiments that have been repeatedly expressed by Africans. For example, in a
piece that was published several years ago, Achola Pala [Okeyo] recounted and
lamented scenarios depicting considerable dissonance between the approaches
of anticircumcision campaigners and the putative beneficiaries of their endeavors (or the primary stakeholders so to say). Pala's intervention went to length to
highlight the relevance of historically sensitive and materially grounded critiques
of the practice (Okeyo 1981). Interestingly, reactions exemplified by Nussbaum's
concession aptly demonstrate that moral outrage regarding the question of female circumcision is dynamic.

     A decade or so ago, it was commonplace for the public to be assaulted by
graphic depictions of female circumcision.[3] Juxtaposed against a series of provocative strategies, these images came to define the heart of certain campaigns
presumably aimed at sensitizing the world about the tragic consequences of
the practice. The perceived extremities of these campaigns in turn triggered
a set of controversies that threatened to jeopardize the vision of reform that
informed the campaigns. At the height of these controversies, it was rather easy
to yield to pessimism and assume that the prospect for meaningful change was
dim. This was in spite of the fact that the practice in question had not been
frozen in time or space but had been marked by considerable fluidity. Even
at times when the controversies were most charged and riveting, the practice

maintained its dynamism, and significant transformations about various elements of the practice were gaining grounds in diverse arenas.

Currently, it appears that much of the passionate disputation that engulfed research and policy discussions pertaining to circumcision is subsiding as relevant constituencies learn to better engage each other.[4] At the same time, as emerging evidence casts new light on terms of reference that were once taken for granted,[5] there are grounds to expect further refinement and retreat from trends that once overshadowed the bottom line of issues. It is becoming increasingly obvious that female circumcision is a practice marked by the negotiation of competing interests in the interstices of power, authority, and resistance. Women give into it presumably to gain something else for their lives, and there are substantial trade-offs. Evolving knowledge about winning formulas for change suggest some leads about what works and demonstrate the artificiality of acontextual, ahistorical, and abstract approaches.

Snapshots of organic transformations relating to female circumcision capture instructive facets of societies in transition, offer glimpses into some of the factors that contribute to the politicization of the practice, and illuminate its material concomitants in ways that counter highly problematic representations. Understandings of the why, when, and how of successful social reform are enriched by innovative strategies that have considerably mediated and galvanized a reorientation of core commitments in specific terrains. Sample highlights of these innovations include emergent replacements such as "ritual without cutting" in The Gambia, "circumcision with words" in Kenya, and similar symbolic substitutions in Uganda and Somalia. These trends suggest the gradual demise of the practice as a functional rite of passage and signal transformative points of entry.[6]

Euphoria about encouraging trends is equally tempered by the sobering failure of celebrated schemes and by the risk of backlash that attends reform interventions.[7] In the same vein, evidence of modification or abandonment of the practice in some quarters is matched by the paradox of its recent adoption in communities where it was previously unknown.[8] Mere cursory reviews of these contradictory outcomes, especially of initiatives that are fueling the discontinuation of the practice, verify the central role of women in the process. Just as they give force to the practice through their roles as circumcisers or circumcised, they have become the key engines for its renunciation. Even in the face of fierce opposition, women armed with the courage of their convictions have fought against gender-biased vulnerabilities encoded in a variety of traditional practices. The more valiant of these women have in fact invoked the resources of culture to ameliorate the constraints of its dictates.

Beginning with Ousmane Sembene's cinematographic interrogation of the nuances of cultural formations and conscientious objections, this chapter addresses the manipulation of culture within certain epistemological sites. Problematizing the persistence of orthodox racist ideology in asylum jurisprudence, the second part offers a critique of the apparent refuge from tradition that has resulted from virulent condemnations of female circumcision. The third section discusses the activities of Tostan, a popular grassroots strategy, which, like Sembene's film, is set in Senegal. Tostan draws from the resources of cultures in localities that practice female circumcision to advance gender empowerment in ways that complicate other-defined agenda to negotiate a refuge for girls and women. The third part of this chapter also examines the shortfalls of a theorem that, approaching circumcision as critical capital in the marriage market, locates the impetus for the renunciation of the practice in select communities in public declarations. The fourth section of this chapter explores the extent to which culture counts and analyzes the material underpinnings that inform apparent allegiance to female circumcision for insights into the logic for its dislocation.

Circumcision in the Creative Industry

A little over a decade ago when Alice Walker and other commentators were receiving critical acclaim for their forceful denunciation of the practice (Walker 1992; Walker and Parmar 1993),[9] it was easy to assume that they invented such opposition. Recuperating African agency, Ousmane Sembene's very well received film, *Moolaade,* celebrates an age-old mechanism that possibly predates the advent of genital modification surgeries to which women can recourse as a bulwark against the coercive reaches of culture. The heroic maneuver that lies at the heart of the film culminates in the invocation of this sacred stricture by cordoning off the threshold with a strand of yarn. This simple act offers a refuge, sanctuary, haven, or safe harbor for four girls resolute to opt out of the rite of female circumcision.

In *Moolaade,* Sembene comes into his own as an octogenarian par excellence in a gerontocracy for the facility with which he attempts to referee the struggles surrounding female circumcision. Drawing on a wealth of knowledge becoming a seasoned elder statesman, he presents a refreshing alternative to narratives that typically construe the practice as overdetermined by the vested interests of the elite and portray African women as monolithically condemned to slavish conformity. The film vividly showcases how the collision of values and attendant anxieties in a Senegalese village positions women to act as change agents precisely by virtue of their location at the site of contradictions. In this context, the film best animates the possibilities for change that inhere in a culture and illustrates the reality of indigenous transformative paradigms that often lie latent, even as arguably less efficient and effective reform aspirations are pursued. At once depicting culture as a surrogate for oppression and culture as a spontaneous zone of empowerment and resistance, the film extols knowledge as power, tracing how the culturally competent deploy the rich repertoire of cultural knowledge to fund radical challenge.

Relevant for our immediate purposes is the film's critical engagement of the thick of daily life to illuminate the rituals of exit and voice in a face-to-face society. As one perceptive commentator observes, the "village in 'Moolaade' has an interesting division of power. All authority allegedly resides with the council of men, but all decisions seem to be made by the women, who in their own way make up their minds and achieve what they desire" (Ebert 2004). The extent to which the protagonist, Colle, is socially constituted and deeply embedded in multiplex roles and relationships underscores the intricate intertwining of social structures and the structure of motivation they shape. Watching the film, one is curious about what fortifies the courage of Colle's conviction. In interrogating what her indomitable spirit reveals about the context for its formation and expression, one comes to terms with the salient aspects of the community that conceded the protagonist the space to "be," even in the face of the tyranny of the majority, and mediated the volatility of the fierce self-assertion that marked her messianic intervention.

The possibility of a Colle, let alone the notion of an indigenous refuge such as the one signified by *Moolaade,* is inconceivable in the realities that account for the resilience of images of African barbarity in the discourses of female circumcision.[10] These images abound in literature on immigration policies in the United States. So pervasive are tropes of inherent misogyny that they subsume formidable acts of resistance by African women whose travails catalyzed some of the modest gains against exclusionary immigration policies and practices in the United States. The bid to secure refuge for these women from the scourge of their natal ancestral tradition have on occasion yielded modest concessions that promise to simultaneously dislodge restrictions replete with bias. In some respects, these restrictions share close affinity with established traditions of discrimination that arbitrarily burden immutable traits. Accordingly, putative efforts to save African women from the scourge of their native traditions inadvertently save the West from some scourge of perennial prejudice.

There is instructive irony in the fact that it takes the repudiation of the gender bias of African custom to attenuate the potency of the staple of racism routinely enforced under the veil of law in the U.S. immigration arena, for example. More precisely, the past decade has seen innovative assaults on biased exclusionary policy that have resulted in the recognition of circumcision as persecution in asylum jurisprudence. In the celebration of such a landmark decision, the tendency is to lose sight of the extent to which asymmetric immigration standards are on a continuum, with circumcision as points of contestations. It is noteworthy that an important lesson of *Moolaade* is that to respect the autonomy of individuals and the significance of their membership in local cultural worlds is to empower them to engage in critical deliberations of their positioning and commitments. This lesson is, arguably, subverted by the tenuous but relative expansion of the menu of options achieved for African immigrants by promoting female circumcision as evidence of persecution in the U.S. immigration process.

CIRCUMCISION AND IMMIGRATION POLITICS

The recent past in the United States has witnessed the introduction of a broad spectrum of reforms to curb the influx of immigrants. In some respects, the anti-immigration backlash represents the invocation of errant assumptions, jaundiced perceptions, and bogus inferences to construct code-bonded hierarchies and galaxies of existence that are manipulated to provide a smoke screen for prejudice, paranoia, and exoticism. Asylum, refugee status, and withholding deportation are different legal categories that allow an alien to enter and remain in the United States. In this framework, an alien petitioner must prove that he or she cannot return to the country of origin because of a well-founded fear of persecution on the basis of race, religion, nationality, membership in a particular group, or political opinion (8 U.S.C. §1101a.42.A). To be cognizable, the persecution must be at the hands of an incumbent government, unless the government is unable to restrain the violence or is unwilling to protect the alien.

The criteria and procedures for U.S. asylum and refugee laws developed with a gender bias in favor of circumstances that are more typical of male experiences of persecution. Given the prevalence of sexist and patently extreme alien exclusionary measures, many applauded the recognition of female circumcision in the matter of *Kasinga* (21 *Immigration and Naturalization Decisions* 357, 1996) as valid evidence of well-founded fear of persecution. More recently in 2005, the Ninth Circuit affirmed the precedent in *Mohammed v. Gonzales* (400 F. 3d 785, 801), noting that female genital surgery is a permanent and continuing act that establishes an unrebuttable presumption of well-founded fear. Canada was the first country to adopt a set of guidelines that favorably accommodated petitions by women who fear persecution as the consequence of failing to conform to, or for transgressing, certain gender-discriminating religious or customary laws and practices in their country of origin (Macklin 1994; Immigration and Refugee Board 1996).

Considering the perennial role of U.S. immigration and refugee policy in determining the content, meaning, and importance of racial categories and the disproportionality of African admissions, the recognition of circumcision as persecution has prompted some to ponder why the case against female circumcision found such resonance. It is somewhat telling, therefore, that in the emerging accommodation of gender exceptions, a handful of African women seem only able to beat discriminatory immigration regimes by croaking the age-old but still appealing tune of "save me from the ravages of my savage culture." Analogues of this tune historically offered the classic ideology for patterns of chauvinism that justified crusades championed by the West in the name of saving African women from culture-bound and doomed existence (Obiora 2004).

In his contribution to this volume, Charles Piot tracks mutually reinforcing discourses and networks to show how female circumcision and asylum jurisprudence align with a technology of power that conflates complex local realities to fictionalize and fetishize Africa as the antithesis of the West. Piot's pertinent analysis revolves around the notorious judicial precedent relating to the granting of asylum to Fazuiya Kassindja on June 13, 1996. Reviewing this matter, Piot contends that meanings were created in the courtroom for a larger public and that the self-iterating demonizing narratives evoked to support the opinion became so normalizing that counterdiscourses about the meaning of genital cutting is today for most Westerners utterly unthinkable. According to Piot (chapter 7 of this volume), the fact that no standard scholarly research or testimony was adduced to help decide key issues gives some indications about the house of cards on which the Kassindja case was built. Particularly profound is this so-called expert's disclaimer that "[m]uch to my astonishment—for I had said nothing of substance about Kassinga [sic] herself, and used literature that was a half a century old—my letter was used right through the trial process, and was cited in the [Bureau of Immigration Affairs'] final opinion as expert testimony that reinforced the case Kassindja's lawyers were trying to make."

Piot further expressed concern that the emergence of nuanced literature that complicates simpleminded reading of the practice may be co-opted by the Bureau of Immigration Affairs (BIA) to validate its exclusionary tendencies (chapter 7 of this volume). Insofar as the goals of circumcision-as-persecution proponents are in conflict with the BIA's restrictive agenda, activists' ratifications of Orientalist discourses ultimately subvert a paradigm of inclusion sensitive to multiculturalism and reinforce reactionary gatekeeping. Indeed, echoing somewhat similar sentiments, Audrey Macklin predicts a backlash from seemingly protective anticircumcision enterprises in the form of hostility that overtly limits visas to certain prospective immigrants (Macklin 2006).

Corrine Kratz offers an array of questions that are apt to raise consciousness and build competence for reviewing circumcision-as-persecution cases adjudicated on playing fields skewed by differences of knowledge, influences, resources, and cultural outlooks. These questions include the following: How are different actors portrayed and represented? Who speaks for whom, who gains a hearing and how, which perspectives are not recognized, and how are different actors involved? How do the complex social and political processes and interconnections of the debates enter court cases and how much of the flux in practice registers there? How do cases draw on and become part of broader debates about female circumcision, and how are they seen from various perspectives and settings? How do they figure in the production and circulation of knowledge and values? Do different standards of evidence and expertise apply to Africans?

Against this backdrop, Kratz critiques another case that illustrates the complicity of law in perpetrating and perpetuating highly problematic representations of Africans (chapter 8 of this volume). In that case, *Abankwah,* the agency then known as the INS granted asylum on grounds that genital operations were used to punish "women of Nkumasa tribes who did not remain virgins." Within months of the decision, the Board of Immigration Appeals (BIA) assembled

overwhelming evidence of fraud. The woman claiming to be Adelaide Abankwah was really Regina Norman Danson, a former hotel worker from a town
where female circumcision is not performed. The real Adelaide Abankwah is
a former college student whose passport was stolen. Danson feigned a fear of
persecution to avoid deportation, and her scheme merely found fertile ground
in the ethic steeped in racist stereotypes and in the carefully orchestrated gullibility of relevant actors who, persuaded by a collection of fragments and factoids, reneged on their sworn obligation for due diligence. The after-the-fact
verifications of perjurious "truths" betrayed the absurdity of insistently filtering
a diverse continent of complex dimensions through the looking glass darkly.
Marveling at the sworn affirmation of knowledgeable people for Abankwah's
contrived testimony, Kratz took solace in an Akan proverb that enjoins active
support for one "fighting to bring home property."

This perspective is a poignant commentary against the limitations of current
immigration reform models that isolate and attribute the flow of migration to
individual push factors. By ignoring the systemic relationships at the root of migration patterns, the models exonerate the receiving country from responsibility
for the dysfunctional integration of sending countries in the global political
economy. Accordingly, the decision to admit immigrants is construed as some
favor or privilege bestowed upon aliens in search of greener pastures. Structural
interpretations of emigration approach it as a localized epiphenomenon em-
blematic of structural violence that derives from a complex web of historical
specificities and interdependencies. This approach implicates the United States
as a locus of global hegemony and underscores the value of radical policies that
address the causes of extreme growth inequity as a more compelling alternative to symptomatic Band-Aids. Inquiry into historical particulars that config-
ure cultural elements demonstrates the centrality of removing constraints and
improving access to resources to harness decision-making power and change
gender ideologies. The effectiveness of this paradigm is exemplified by initiatives
that seek to correct for vulnerabilities indexed by female circumcision.

EMPIRICAL SHIFTS IN AFRICA

As far back as 1992, village leaders, religious clerics, circumcisers, and wom-
en's groups in an Egyptian community signed and publicly declared a resolution
to refrain from female circumcision. Abdel Hadi identifies the paramount factor
for the growing discontinuation of the practice in the Egyptian village as a fundamental value shift and power dislocation that reconfigured gender relations
in the community (2006). Apparently, the village had been a long-standing site
for integrated development interventions by the Coptic Evangelical Organization for Social Services (CEOSS) that promoted women's participation. A large-
scale study undertaken by the Cairo Center for Human Rights found a positive
correlation between involvement in comprehensive development activities and
abstention from circumcision.

In 1997, women, men, and traditional and religious leaders in thirteen Senegalese villages enacted public declarations to end female circumcision; eight years later, the number grew to 1,527, representing 30 percent of Senegalese communities that adhere to the practice (Crawley 2005). The radical change is credited to a grassroots development and education initiative facilitated by Tostan, a nongovernmental organization domiciled in Senegal (Melching 2001). Tostan's holistic human rights program provides participants with the resources to improve their standard of living and helps them to acquire and effectively employ a framework to scrutinize their individual experiences and arrive at their own conclusions about the merits (or lack thereof) of practices such as female circumcision.

Tostan's accomplishments aptly illustrate the essence and process of self-determination. These accomplishments earn Tostan close examination as a best-practice example, especially insofar as they offer instructive insights into the political economy of circumcision and change strategies. At its Web site, www.tostan.org, Tostan explains that its name means "breakthrough" in Wolof. Its mission statement articulates its aspiration to provide learners with the knowledge and skills to become confident, resourceful actors in the social transformation and economic development of their communities. The statement identifies a guiding principle of Tostan's pedagogy as "based on the African tradition of participation and respectful consultation of all those concerned and affected by the implementation of any eventual decisions or policies. Villagers themselves determine their future goals and obstacles to overcome in order to achieve their goals." Drawing upon learner-generated materials and pedagogical values inspired by local cultural traditions, the program presumably facilitates systematic scrutiny of the preexisting intuitions and knowledge of its trainees. By the same token, the program promotes integrated nonformal education, which helps equip its participants to tackle everyday realities, of which genital cuttings are just a sample (World Bank 1998).

Without any particular reference to female genital cuttings, Tostan enacted specific learning modules that illuminated the need for change and enabled the participants to exert and assert themselves as agents of requisite social transformations. Tostan's nonformal education program, which was originally developed in 1982, primarily consisted of six learning modules implemented over a period of eighteen months. The first module concentrates on problem-solving skills. The second module addresses health and hygiene. The third deals with preventing child mortality caused by diarrhea or lack of vaccination. The fourth entails financial and material management for various types of village projects. The fifth targets leadership and group dynamics. The sixth focuses on how to conduct a feasibility analysis to predict whether proposed group projects would result in net gains (Mackie 2000, 259).

Several years after its inception, Tostan initiated a seventh module presumably in response to the solicitations of village authorities in Malicounda

Bambara who had seen the impact of its training programs on women in neighboring communities. In 1995, Tostan inaugurated the nonformal education program in Malicounda Bambara in collaboration with UNICEF and the Senegalese government. Tostan developed the women's health and human rights module in 1996. Following the implementation of this module, Tostan participants advocated the inclusion of a session addressing female genital cutting. The session that was introduced involved the adaptation of a theatrical play about a girl who died as a result of circumcision. Mdey Diop, the program facilitator, recalls that the women hesitantly broached the issue, acknowledging that circumcision was an ancient tradition that they were able to evaluate through the lenses of their growing appreciation of their right to health.

Shortly after completing their training, the women of Malicounda developed an arsenal of arguments that eventually convinced the village council to promulgate an official policy abolishing female circumcision, and no circumcision was performed in that community during the annual season. When Tostan got wind of this, it "visited the village with trepidation to confirm the impact of its program" (Tostan 2005) Even then, its "representatives were hesitant to broach the subject because of the cultural sensitivity of [female genital cuttings]" (ibid.) Subsequently, the program disseminated a report announcing that the "women of Malicounda have made up their minds. They will no longer practice female genital cutting on the young girls of the village." Reflecting on the "reasons making the historic change significant," Tostan states on its Web site that the

> women had made this decision of their own free will and not because Tostan had tried to impose it. . . . A *public declaration* was made and signed in a ceremony attended by villagers. The decision came after the women had already spent two years in the basic education program. They were accustomed to working together, trusted the program and one another and would be able to defend their decision with information gathered from their modules on hygiene, health, problem-solving, leadership and human rights. (ibid.)

Tostan goes on to note that the "story did not end here. UNICEF and Tostan invited twenty journalists to visit Malicounda Bambara and the women spoke publicly . . . [standing] firm in their decision to cease practicing FGC" (Tostan 2005). Apparently, what became known as the "Oath of Malicounda" opposing female circumcision was formalized at this press briefing. The formalization of the maiden corporate commitment was precipitated by the participation of the members of these communities in the Tostan program. According to Molly Melching, the executive director of Tostan, by the end of the program the villages "had made important changes to improve the health and well-being of all members of the community" (Melching 2001, 167). Some of the collateral changes that accrued from the program included acquiring financial and material management skills, implementing income-generating projects, "ending violence against women, vaccinating children and pregnant women, using local health facilities more frequently, and practicing family planning (ibid.). The significance of these changes in the logic of transformation is conveyed by the participants' appeal for material input as "measures necessary to ensure a total and sustainable respect" for the decision to abstain from circumcision (ibid., 169). The participants became vectors of sorts for the propagation of the groundswell of opposition to neighboring villages that were not yet substantively exposed to Tostan's program.

The Pledge Factor

Diop and Askew submit that effective strategies designed to change practices like female circumcision that are based on and enforced by social conventions, rather than merely predicated on individual preferences, require attentiveness to social dimensions and the provision of support for those who opt for change (Diop and Askew 2006). Conceding the role of education in stemming circumcision, the authors suggest that converting knowledge generated in the educational process into behavioral abandonment of circumcision necessitates an additional sequence of components to foster and sustain the buy-in of a critical mass of families. They go on to discuss social mobilization activities that build community-wide consensus against circumcision through the incorporation of several initiatives that enhance life chances. Apparently, the social mobilization model that informs their analysis culminates in public denunciations that replicate the dynamics of social conventions that derive force from trust and openness.

Curiously however, the authors endorse a claim by Gerry Mackie that public declarations are the most important factor facilitating the abandonment of the practice. A comparable attribution found on Tostan's Web site identifies Mackie as an "influential figure in this movement" (Tostan 2005). This acknowledgment paid tribute to the role of an article that Mackie published in 1996 in which he analogized circumcision to Chinese foot binding, the eradication of which he links to the commitment of collectives to support the eligibility of women who had not conformed to foot binding to marry within their ethnic group. What is unclear is the nature and scope of Mackie's influence, particularly in light of the time line that Tostan furnishes. This dates the establishment of the Malicounda initiative to 1995 and gives July 1996 as the time when the women of their own volition agitated for the introduction of Module 7. By September 1996, it appears that the women of Malicounda had already taken a categorical stance against circumcision. It was not until May 1997, almost a year after the women had "made up their own mind," that Tostan coordinated an evaluation to confirm that no circumcision was performed. It took another couple of month for Tostan executives who could have served as purveyors of Mackie's theorem to venture timidly to rally the change agents for media ceremonials.

Mackie understands female circumcision as a strategy that mothers adopt to optimize the prospects for their daughters. In this scheme, mothers refrain from circumcision when competing alternatives hold better promise for life enhancement. Nonetheless, he valorizes pledges above their determinants. The gist of Mackie's argument is that female circumcision is a convention maintained by interdependent expectations in the marriage market and deeply entrenched because of its role in determining access to reproduction. Pursuant to this hypothesis, he insists that in the absence of a collective shift, female genital cuttings would persist indefinitely even if every individual wanted to abandon the practice, since those who fail to comply also risk failing to reproduce. In his opinion, the eradication of the convention primarily depends on forming associations of parents who pledge not to engage in the practice or to allow their sons to marry uncircumcised women (Mackie 2000, 36–38).

Identifying public oaths and pledges as the pivot for reform, Gerry Mackie finds a tight correspondence between a convention theory he posits and the trend unfolding in Senegal. He contends that, without the right reform program, female genital cuttings might take many generations to end, regardless of the degree of economic development or cultural internationalization. "Fortunately," he continues, "after a period of credible non-directive education about its health consequences, *the way to end FGC is as simple as the formation of associations whose members pledge to abandon the practice*" (Mackie 2000, 254, emphasis added). Notwithstanding this confident assertion, much about the Senegalese experience as it manifested among the Malicounda demonstrates that it is more complicated than some readings of Mackie's claim suggest. My own work on the subject extols the profound value-added element of comprehensive education, while recognizing that the relationship between education and circumcision is not invariably linear (Obiora 1997). My point of departure with Mackie revolves around the seminal and dispositive value he ascribes to the public pledges in the shift in convention that trigger the displacement of female circumcision.

This weighting of the formal oaths is all the more questionable in light of Mackie's assertion that the convention theory suggests a tripartite strategy of abandonment which incorporates basic education, public discussion, and public declaration (Mackie 2000, 279). In fact, he affirms the basic education program designed by Tostan as the most important factor in its multidimensional approach. Details of this program show how it builds up, boils down to, and revolves around imparting useful skills and information that empower the trainees to confront the material conditions of their daily lives. Nevertheless, identifying public declaration within the local pools of marriage eligibles as the distinctive value added by his approach, Mackie takes pains to credit it as the paramount signifier and determinant of collective shift.[11] In material respects, therefore, it would appear that this analysis mistakes the consequence of the process for the cause of its outcome. For one, if women are willing to defy legal convention at the risk of death,[12] it is not certain how formally undertaking an oath to desist from the practice offers a more compelling deterrent.[13] This is not to insist that the coercive authority of the state that underpins law as an institution is necessarily superior to social sanction as a control mechanism (Obiora 1997).

It is telling that the Diabougou Declaration that ensued on the heels of the official inauguration of the regime of public pledge as part of the rituals for renegotiating the rite of passage was mainly ushered into existence at the instigation of Demba Diawara. Diawara is a religious leader and graduate of the Tostan program. Reflecting on the situation in his own village of Ker Simbara, Diarwara explained that they could not effectively bring the practice to an end without consulting kin in a network of neighboring villages. Following a laborious mission to enlist converts across the spectrum, Diawara became instrumental in the formulation of the declaration. The enforcement measures elucidated in this and subsequent declarations lend little support to the hypothesis privileging pledge determinism or fundamentalism.

This is coupled with the fact that the social mobilization and empowerment at the heart of the Tostan activities worked before the integration of the conventions. Obviously, Tostan's basic education program thrived and achieved renown independent of, and much before, the incorporation of the declaration, which may actually appeal to some as more of an adjunct to the pioneering interventions. Objective proof that the emergent ethic of abstinence from circumcision predated the advent of ceremonial pledge has already been marshaled. Molly Melching's retrospection on the circumstances that inspired the commemoration of the oath dimension is further revealing (Melching 2001,163–166). The pledge conventions have reinforced the efforts of Tostan, but there is not ample empirical basis to verify their autonomous and unambiguous impact as harbingers of enduring change. Even in villages where training was not an antecedent of oath, the reality remains that the declarations and pledges renouncing genital cuttings in Senegal were neither stand-alone prescriptives nor manufactured in isolation out of thin air. To the contrary, they were part of a self-consciously attained "broader movement for social justice" (ibid., 161). Indeed, it is reasonable to conclude that the contagious pledge associations were essentially contingent fragments of a comprehensive process.

Mackie's location of the nucleus of change in the pledge association is a meaningful point of entry into the examination of the significance of women's agency in the pertinent processes and outcomes. Informed by a host of reasons, including its perception as a prerequisite for marriage,[14] female circumcision is indeed perpetuated by the power of social conformity. It is the same pull of social convention that is galvanizing the movement instigated by Tostan that builds on the momentum of prior public declarations to mobilize for and enlist fresh denunciations of female circumcision. Mackie's pledge or oath theorem captures the importance of attenuating the opportunity costs of self-expression in close-knit communities overwhelmingly regulated by conventions. This is even more the case concerning largely symbolic goods that certify and embed lives in a quantum of honor (Bourdieu 1986). However, the theory is encumbered by presuppositions that fall short of adequately interrogating the nature, impact, and implications of the social processes that determine the social practice impinging on the well-being of women. The same variables that catalyze and crystallize the pledge associations hint at conditions for effective action for reform and transformation.

Like the cosmetic concession in the immigration sphere that neglects the factors that constitute the so-called center and its gravitational pull, the consideration of circumcision as capital in the marriage market eclipses critical elements entering into individual women's cost-advantage calculus. My point is not to dismiss the value of gender-sensitive immigration guidelines or the role of pledges but to illuminate the vital importance of contexts—often subsumed under the rubric of culture—for the emergence of these processes and to direct attention to the fundamentals that render these contexts conducive for change-inducing autonomy.

The Full-Belly Quotient

The events that culminated in the oath of Malicounda Bambara suggest some linkage between cultural reorientation and material benefits. In more ways than one, Tostan signals that it would have had difficulty sustaining its initiatives had it not spoken realities that the participants deemed relevant. Cessation programs devoid of a structure of incentive floundered across Africa just as much as the promise of incentive in and of itself has not heralded a miracle cure.[15] The effectiveness of Tostan is directly related to the extent to which its message resonates with and could be verified as credible by the participants. Wrestling with impoverished options and formidable barriers to the development of their capabilities, the women's attraction to the opportunities offered by participation in the activities sponsored by Tostan makes sense.[16] The legitimacy or "trustworthiness" (Mackie 2000, 259) of its message is strong enough to motivate prospective enrollees to eke out moderate fees from their modest existence in advance for the program. In so doing, the enrollees nurse unequivocal expectations that as a consideration for their bargain, the program will help them cultivate the capabilities to overcome the constraints of their time and space as well as to solve the practical and strategic problems precipitated by the circumstances of their being.

The pull of this perceived return somewhat parallels the magnitude of appeal that makes circumcision trump competing considerations in the eyes of its adherents. For example, some have observed that the determination to adhere to the dictates of culture is sufficiently intense to render initiates deaf to their own intuitions and recognition of the possible health hazards of the procedure (Sargent 1991 and 1989). It seems that, all things considered, the "loss of [their] genitalia is not too high a price to pay" (Toubia and Izette 1998, 102). Whatever compels the subordination of a vital asset like health must be something that is not merely perceived as superior but something that is so integral to the enjoyment of health that its absence functionally diminishes the expedience for health and its availability presupposes or defines a good [read healthy] life.

The anticircumcision impact of the activities championed by Tostan demonstrates the enormous dividends of enhanced socioeconomic assets and corroborates the importance of what I identify as the full-belly quotient. Earlier proposals to couple the promotion of socioeconomic health with the specific agenda to eradicate female circumcision may have struck some as misguided and diversionary. Nonetheless, affirmative reports about Tostan and similar programs vindicate this position. Insofar as the educational process Tostan implemented was truly nondirective and the decision of the communities to abandon female genital cutting was internally generated as opposed to being coerced by some outside authority, the voluntary abandonment constitutes an eloquent case for empowerment. Empowerment refers broadly to the expansion of freedom of choice and action or the expansion of assets and capabilities of poor people to participate in, negotiate with, influence, control, and hold accountable institutions that affect their lives (World Bank 2002). Tostan's record stands for the proposition that individuals without any formal education, from villages with minimal resources, can improve their lives and environment through a solid program that deepens autonomy and self-sufficiency.

The decline in the incidence of female circumcision influenced by Tostan's program reinforces the emerging consensus among scholars and development practitioners that effective intervention strategies are not discrete and mutually exclusive, but rather multidimensional and integrated (Sen 1999, Obiora 2004). In this light, the fight against female circumcision is best pursued within the context of larger transformative projects that holistically attack persistent gender disparities. Evidently, when Tostan set out to provide skills and information that help people better define and pursue their own goals, eradicating genital surgeries was not a paramount goal or preliminary concern that the initial recruits brought to the program (Mackie 2000, 261). They arrived with their own agenda not unrelated to the urgent challenge of leveraging resources that would better enable them to guarantee a full belly, presumably conceptualized to encompass an expansive view of socioeconomic health for themselves and their dependents. Tostan met them where they were, and the abandonment of female circumcision evolved out of this "dialogic democracy" (Giddens 1994; cf. Melching's accent on the uses of love and respect).

The Irreducibility of Voice

It is difficult to discount the role of the activities spearheaded by Tostan in the decision of its trainees to abandon female circumcision. However, the cause-and-effect relationship between Tostan's intervention and the ratification of parallel decisions in villages that did not receive the benefits of the training is not very clear (Diop and Askew 2006). The opportunities to enhance economic viability are not a sufficient explanation for denunciations in terrains where Tostan's programs had not been administered. Indeed, extant literature demonstrates that the influence of socioeconomic status on adherence to female circumcision (or the lack thereof) is ambiguous. Similarly, studies of domestic violence and the analyses of other forms of gender inequity suggest a consensus among feminists that socioeconomic mobility does not necessarily ensure increased autonomy for women. However, it is plausible to reason that the autonomy, dialogic, and consensus-building skills that women hone or cultivate by virtue of interacting in empowerment initiatives exemplified by Tostan have implications that extend beyond narrowly construed socioeconomic parameters. It is these skills, tools, and/or resources that they deploy "as license to recirculate" their insights in ways that help refurbish tradition. The same skills facilitate and institutionalize self-determination by opening up space that is hospitable to envisaging a different conception of the ethics and aesthetics of womanhood (Meyers 2000, 480).

Relying on trends that suggest a correlation between the expansion of women's autonomy and the erosion of female circumcision, Diana Tietjens Meyers proffers a view of autonomy that respects people as self-determining agents (Meyers 2000, 487). Meyers identifies the distinct advantage of educational programs developed by cultural initiates who rely on traditional modes of expression and appeal to traditional values. Illuminating how these programs honor women's understanding of what matters to them and how best to proceed in light of their values and commitments, Meyers reasons that the programs foster the examination of subjective experiences with supportive associates and the engagement in a safe environment of unorthodox ideas that deepen self-knowledge, self-confidence, and empathy. While contending that the programs are designed to promote autonomy within culture, Meyers equally calls attention to the extent to which the programs enrich the repertoire of concepts and interpretive schemas beyond the culturally furnished stock (ibid., 483). Within this framework, the context that emerges for interaction, communication, and deliberation advances collective and individual self-definition in ways that allow for the recognition, articulation, and furtherance of pertinent interests.

Many social theorists agree that increasing the democratization of decision-making processes increases substantive freedoms. Democratization elicits marginalized voices and entrenches channels through which the underrepresented can more effectively influence social choices and shape social institutions (Hill 2003, 123).[17] Public discourse equips individuals and groups with frames of reference to conceptualize, interrogate, and invigorate their interests (Hamilton 1999). Building on the notion that social relationships as structured institutions largely determine our ability to lead the kinds of lives we value, Hill argues that agency engenders changes through the promotion of shared understanding (Hill 2003; Collins 2000; Hartsock 1998). As she put it, democratization changes embedded institutions and the bases of society, nurturing fresh understandings

of social reality and altering self-definitions.[18] Just as individuals reproduce social institutions by conforming to conventional practices, change ensues when
individuals who share a perception that change is necessary or desirable initiate
new practices, and the process is completed when the practice attains normativ-
ity (Peterson 2002).

Since female circumcision is something one does, but seldom discusses,[19]
even in places where strong resistance to ending the practice has engendered a
backlash to the opposition, reform outreaches have in turn precipitated debates
that signal a major shift from the reticence that once characterized the practice. The civic opportunities to brainstorm, dialogue and dissent in the public
sphere about a practice that had been historically mystified and clandestine is
profoundly constructive and emancipatory. Nancy Frazer concedes that emancipatory outcomes in social processes such as the restructuring of decision-
making hierarchies and changes in ideology depends on the development of
new contexts of interaction, achieved through communication (Fraser 1989).
To this end, she submits that equity in the exercise of institutionalized power
involves more than increasing the input of individuals into social decision-
making; it involves the empowerment of individuals through their self-orga-
nization and through increasing their self-determination in all areas of activity
(Fraser 1989). As she notes, if power is instantiated in mundane social practices
and relations, then efforts to dismantle or transform the regime must address
those practices and relations.[20]

THE FULL-BELLY QUOTIENT REVISITED

I will postulate the usefulness of what I have designated the "full-belly quotient" as an enduring antidote for gender inequity and for essentializing anticircumcision discourses that are not sufficiently attentive to context. Privileging the full-belly quotient is a functional response to the political economy of
gender oppression. A full belly amplifies the possibilities and strategies for exit
from the material conditions that constrain the lives and choices of women in
communities that practice female circumcision. By the same token, it minimizes
the opportunities for the discursive gymnastics that have come to define success in the U.S. immigration processes. As already demonstrated, an unfortunate
ramification of the rhetorical tactic is the attraction it holds for advocates who
would ordinarily spurn brute accommodations that ultimately deepen marginalization and asymmetric power relations. Attending to the objective conditions
that drive the influx of immigrants to the United States enriches the capabilities
of women to be and do what they want within the frameworks of their cultures
and counters trends that trade one form of bias for another.

The incidence of female circumcision among the privileged and elite establishes the need for caution in find a causal connection between improved socioeconomic status and changes in the practice of female genital cutting (van der
Kwaak 1992; Balk 1996). Insofar as correlation is not cause, changing material

conditions are not enough to dislodge deeply embedded beliefs and values about circumcision, and enhanced socioeconomic status does not invariably guarantee conversions to anticircumcision camps. The success of Tostan's arguably veiled attack illustrates the radical potentials and consequences of empowering women to leverage resources that facilitate their informed participation as autonomous agents within their spheres of influence. The promise of empowerment as a mode of containing, if not eradicating, health-impairing forms of circumcision far exceeds competing alternatives.[21] Given the empirical knowledge accruing from projects such as Tostan, one would be hard pressed to sustain an argument that empowering rural development preempts or poses an impediment either for the specific goal of ending circumcision or for the gender-equity agenda in general. Shifting the focus of attention to address some of the material conditions that enable and entrench the practice reduces responses to it as some illogical and curious pathology that calls for draconian measures (Gruenbaum 1988).[22]

While contemporary exigencies are redefining the meanings and nature of female circumcision, it remains a rite of passage that helps secure access to productive and reproductive resources in some communities.[23] The instrumental role of female genital cutting, as illuminated by its rationalization as a prerequisite for marriage and motherhood, foregrounds empowerment as an important step in this displacement.[24] The emphasis on empowerment enables the generation of more coherent strategies and efficient iterations of programs that exemplify the best evidence of commitment to gender equity in situated domains. By the same token, it is arguable that empowerment is as much a right as it is a rite of passage and personhood for that matter—for women in communities that practice circumcision. To the extent that empowerment is invoked as a catalyst for comprehensive well-being, it offers an alternative to shallow symptomatic treatments. Approached from a holistic perspective, empowerment can be seen as having varied but decidedly interdependent components; all the parts are equal, and it takes the integral functioning of the whole to guarantee the efficiency of any part. This paradigm of empowerment recasts debates over the prioritization of genital modification surgeries as a paramount concern of the international community. As such, it signifies a common denominator that reconciles the bottom line of the proponents and opponents of female circumcision and celebrates their mutual interests in the well-being of women in communities that adhere to the practice. The convergence of views about the pivotal place of empowerment for the feminist agenda in general corroborates the finding of a similar nexus in the matter of circumcision.

From the standpoint of empowerment, I posit exit options as a corollary of the full-belly quotient thesis. A wealth of research on human agency affirms a preexisting potential for the exercise of such options. The "full belly" stimulates women's ability to rearticulate the rite of circumcision or renegotiate their right of passage from its strictures, and thereby consolidates the exit options of women from compromising situations. Interrogating the correlation between exit options and the quotient in the present context entails the recuperation of culture. As I have argued elsewhere (Obiora 1998 and 2004), the commonplace reification of culture as the prime site and source of gender oppression exhausts its usefulness at some point, and the denigration of culture implicit in such representations becomes all the more wrongheaded insofar as it obscures the attributes of culture that can catalyze desirable change. Tostan's reliance on indigenous knowledge and its community-based focus vividly bear out the beauty of culture as an organic and dynamic entity that is at once amenable to influence and can calibrate and accelerate a meaningful reform agenda. Insofar as evaluations of the elements that explain the progress of Tostan give precedence to its deep valuing of African culture as the foundation of its program (World Bank 1998), it is instructive as a model that embraces culture as a space for empowerment and transcends its facile vilification as a surrogate for oppression.

Maximizing the efficiency of deploying culture as a reform strategy mandates the effective mobilization of the community as a whole, including local religious authorities, village elders, and youth. This may take the form of creatively courting the support and intermediation of the larger community and actively reorienting formal indigenous institutions and apparatus of governance. Leveraging preexisting resources is especially expedient in light of the emphasis on capacity building and the resources invested in the formation of new institutions to enforce anticircumcision directives. Incidentally, the vital lessons of anticircumcision campaigns underscore the costs of noninclusion.[25] If the practice is indeed as embedded in cultural traditions as critics have observed, it stands to reason that achieving its denunciation as an unequivocal outcome requires some level of engagement with the authority of tradition. Historically, tradition and its custodian have functioned as purveyors of patriarchal privilege and as potent forces of resistance to gender-balancing initiatives. However, there is nothing inherently oppositional about them.

CONCLUSION

Female genital surgeries can pose significant health hazards. Yet women engage in them. Interrogating some of the variables that account for gravitation to the practice offers insights into the nature of corrective measures that can viably counter its appeal and force. It is in interrogating the dynamics of the range of factors that underpin the incidence of genital surgeries in contemporary Africa and how these material conditions can be effectively dislodged in keeping with the emerging global consensus that the notion of culture is less ambiguated and the objective of gender reform substantiated beyond rhetoric. In an instructive analogy between gender oppression and the structure of a birdcage, Marilyn Frye contends that a bird is not necessarily entrapped by the individual wires of a cage, but that it takes a network of wires to constitute an effective barrier. There are discernable parallels between Frye's analogy and the lived experiences of women implicated by the controversy around female circumcision.

It is not uncommon for international campaigns against the surgical modifications of the female genitalia to highlight the predicaments and portray women in contexts where it occurs as "prisoners of culture." Yet the resilience of this practice demonstrates that its eradication calls for strategies far more substantive than fancy iterations of "Just Say No" campaigns. What then is the key to "freedom" for the so-called prisoners of culture? While the self is socially constituted, human beings have demonstrated enormous capacity to overcome the constraints of time and space. What factors facilitate this ability? How can the prospects for such conditions and the dividends thereof be maximized? How can the international community facilitate the creation of a civic space within which women who oppose collective practices feel empowered to exercise meaningful exit options, and those who desire to affirm or adhere to the practices have the leeway to dialogue and critically interrogate their commitment?

A wealth of experiences demonstrates that the modest, albeit historic, gains applauded in the realm of immigration fall short and best operate as stopgap measures. Chronicles such as Fauziya Kassindja's speak volumes of the indelible "warrior marks" of her emigration to the United States. Indeed, the fact that the question "Do They Hear You When You Cry," the title of the book that she co-authored, stands on its own as a sad commentary on the treacherousness of her occidental passage suffices to induce nostalgia for the era when African women more readily availed themselves of sanctuary within the comfort of their own homes and within the integrity of their cultures of origin. This was the manner of refuge portrayed in Sembene's film. The fact that the invocation of *Moolaade* involved neither dislocation nor needlessly dehumanizing routines reinforces the fundamentals for viable empowerment. It remains to be seen whether African women will go to great lengths to subject themselves to the functional equivalent of attempting to "pass through the eye of a needle" if they otherwise find relative voice and succor.

A key lesson of an intervention such as Tostan's is that the symbiotic relationships between the variables that mediate gender experiences cannot be ignored in the articulation of gender reform initiatives. Instead of addressing the deeply embedded cultural practice in isolation, Tostan fashioned a program that seemed to have targeted its political economy and approached the phenomenon as integrally intertwined with the manifest problems of development. The outcome that opened up the space for the participants to challenge the enterprise reflects more than just morally informed personal decision making or political commitment; it foregrounds women as strategic actors prone to benchmark and operationalize aspirations for autonomy. Tostan's covert eradication strategy promoted the outcome it championed through a series of reinforcements, earning it a place of honor among the broader interventions to redress structural violence in the setting where it operates. Its robust sensitivity to the complexity of the practice formed the nucleus of the transformative process that helped transfigure the participants from captives of the thick circumstances of their daily lives into active arbiters of their own destinies equipped with the knowledge and skill sets necessary to formulate their own conception of good and make choices accordingly. Its program of empowerment, which could be likened to a refuge, tempered the potentially coercive reaches of culture and social control while creating the space for individual self-assertion and determination.

Cognizant that women's capacity to exercise their agency is not in question, the program steered clear of prescriptivism, marshaling instead strategies to stimulate self-realization and facilitate the elimination of the formidable handicaps in the way of translating this capacity into potent political capital for women to leverage life options vis-à-vis participation and productivity. More concretely, the program increased women's awareness, helped them set their own goals, gain the skills to solve their problems as autonomous agents of change, and become more self-reliant. These shifts in turn boosted their self-confidence, built capacity to foster solidarity and mutual support, and contributed to the emergence of a public sphere that enabled women to organize effectively for greater involvement and influence. It may well be that one cannot change society by a sequence of individual self-transformations. However, the bulwark that precipitated the counter-hegemonic maneuvers of the women who participated in Tostan and accounted for their ability to assert the courage of their convictions is telling about the dynamics of power and resistance and about the rituals of exit and voice.

Failure to address the complex ways conditions of poverty constrain the action potentials and choices of women in settings that form the backdrop for interventions such as Tostan's mystifies and romanticizes resistance. A political-economy approach illuminates the structural conditions that underpin the practice and the promise of indivisible human rights norms, illustrating the need for the articulation of correctives within a comprehensive framework. Conversely, insofar as human rights are contested, the challenge of achieving the aspirations of pertinent pronouncements is directly related to the extent to which they can be grounded in concrete domains. Some critics equate the paucity of enforcement mechanisms for human rights with the failure of the regime. The finding of a seminal study that so-called tribal wars or ethnic conflicts are overwhelmingly triggered by resource constraints could be essentially construed as corroborating perennial grassroots sentiments about the centrality of socioeconomic considerations for human rights protection (World Bank 2000, 2). At core, the case for a full-belly quotient is a restatement of the interdependence and indivisibility of human rights.

NOTES

This piece is dedicated to the memory of Susan Moller Okin—notwithstanding the differences in our perspectives, we shared a fierce commitment for the well-being of women and sought to collaborate on this common ground.

1. See L. Amede Obiora, "Firing on All Cylinders" (work in progress presented at several forums)—this piece draws on primary research data to demonstrate the importance of the indivisibility and interdependence of international human rights norms. See

also L. Amede Obiora, "When Rights Become Sexy" (unpublished manuscript on file with the author)—this work explores the opportunities and constraints that mark the mobility of gender equity norms across cultures, structures, and histories.

2. Obiora, "Africa and the 21st Century: The Imperative of Gender" (work in progress on file with the author). Informed by a ministerial conference that I convened at the World Bank, this manuscript analyzes the configuration of variables that impinge on the autonomy of women and the invaluable returns of the agency of women for Africa's renewal.

3. The major forms of the practice range from sunna, which is the least severe, to infibulation and pharaonic circumcision. For detailed descriptions of these types of the procedure, see Obiora 1997 and Shell-Duncan and Hernlund 2000.

4. Perhaps the salience of pertinent discourses helped illuminate a core convergence of interests that may well have tempered the stridency.

5. Several commentators have addressed the informational discrepancies of anticircumcision critiques. Obermeyer 1999 is an epidemiological study that challenges dominant understanding about the nature and distribution of hazards.

6. My entry in the *International Encyclopedia of Social and Behavioral Sciences* maps the landscape of evolving changes vis-à-vis female circumcision (Obiora 2001).

7. The popular promise of efforts to retrain traditional practitioners who perform the procedure has given way to serious questions about the effectiveness of the interventions (Diop and Askew 2006).

8. In one report, pharaonic circumcision is rapidly becoming the norm in Mayerno, which is a Fulani and Hausa settlement in central Sudan. An ethnographic study found that no woman older than 35 years of age was circumcised. One-sixth of women between ages 35 and 25, one-fourth of those between 24 and 18, and three-quarters of those aged 16 and 17 were circumcised. More significantly, however, all girls between the ages of 7 and 15 were circumcised (El Bashir 2006).

9. These books epitomized ill-conceived anticircumcision campaigns and merited numerous incisive reviews (Obiora 1996; Oyěwùmi 2003).

10. For additional insights into the service they provide in affirming Western canons of normalcy, see Boddy 1999.

11. Standing alone, the pledges could only make a dent as a cessation strategy and that is especially if Mackie's subsequently discussed assumptions about marriageability are valid. In keeping with this, the force of his analysis derives from the strength of the marriageability premise and depends on the scope of its applicability. For a critique of the marriageability premise, see Obiora 1997, 318. The mutual reinforcement or symbiotic relationship between marriage and motherhood as both causes and consequences of circumcision also makes for some tautology.

12. In Guinea, for example, adherents have not been deterred by the death sentence that is decreed as the penalty for the practice (Masland et al., 1999; Greer 1999).

13. Understandably, the proclamation of oath is a ritual that externalizes the commitment of its undertakers. However, the implications are different for peers who do not share this commitment, but are targeted for influence. In this vein, the diffusion effect of the learning experience can be said to vary where it influences the behavior of members from when it determines the responses of nonmembers living in program villages or satellites.

14. Later I will discuss the implications of Mackie's accentuation of marriage, irrespective of the contentiousness of the justifications for the practice, which casts some light on why he sees ties that may well be more reflective of trust as engendered by the dynamics of intermarriage. The assumption of the preeminence of marriage does not explain exogamous marriages that are entirely outside the culture.

15. See Diop and Askew (2006) for a critique of supply-end interventions. A comparable initiative spearheaded by a local NGO and three arms of the World Bank group seeks to provide so-called village cutters in Kouroussa, Guinea, with the opportunity to find

alternative means to generate income, maintain their social standing, and take leadership in improving life in the community. The main goal of the initiative is to prepare circumcisers to become entrepreneurs through grassroots management training and by developing the resources of the village (World Bank 2000).

16. Even sovereign entities that command far more resources than ordinary individuals respond to material incentives. The adoption of punitive legislation as a barometer for allocating development aid saw the machination of African governments to position themselves as sensitive to Western sensibilities and deserving of corresponding benevolence. In Senegal, for example, drafts of Article 299A of the Penal Code were carefully vetted by local offices of western aid organizations to reflect and accommodate the perspectives of their home governments. Unfortunately, the preemption of criminalization as an ally prerogative undermined delicate local efforts to discourage the practice and engendered enough resistance to prompt Tostan to suspend its work. Remarkably, in defiance of the law just before it was passed, one southern village reportedly circumcised 120 girls en masse.

17. According to Marianne Hill, democratization involves the creation of new knowledge and values, in effect a paradigm shift, that brings about the meaningful empowerment of groups who ordinarily lack voice.

18. Democratization can be analyzed as a process of change in institutionalized practices, following a path of innovation and diffusion (Hill 2003, 124).

19. As Aud Talle put it, "it is just one of those practices that are not the object of conscious dialogue." See chapter 4 of this volume.

20. Fraser's point reinforces the proposition that the restructuring or complication of decision-making hierarchies reflected in the pledge associations derives from the processes for self-definition and self-determination influenced by Tostan. The study by Diop and Askew (2006) elaborates on materials that give some sense of the reciprocity between procedural ethics and substantive outcomes.

21. An emphasis on health impairment precludes a tension between my apparent endorsement of cessation in this chapter and the painstakingly nuanced reform recommendations of my earlier work. My argument in this arena is consistent and on a continuum with my previous position that reform must be conditioned and informed by empirically grounded studies of the demographic distribution of harm and the correlation between the incidence of harm and different kinds of circumcision.

22. The allusion of a participant in Tostan to the connection between the deficiencies of the political economy and the scapegoating of culture is on point in this regard. As she clarified, "'the tradition' doesn't lead to infection; it's the transmission of germs from non-sterile razor blade from one girl to another that can lead to infection" (Melching 2000, 158).

23. Maurice Godelier refers to initiation rituals to illustrate the extent to which social relations exist as a means to attain certain ends (Godelier 1986). Given that "tradition was once a bright new idea," it is useful to understand what imbues a practice with the kind of significance that galvanizes deference to it as custom and sustains its momentum as such. Historical studies demonstrate how quickly the imputation of cultural significance can accrue (Hobsbawm and Ranger 1983). In an investigation of whether female circumcision overdetermines the position of Sudanese women in Canada, Janice Boddy historicizes the abstraction of the clitoris as a site of sexual pleasure, spotlights the ideological subtext for castigating Africans for clitoral modifications, and situates genital cuttings within a complex cultural aesthetic that shapes pertinent sensibilities (chapter 2 of this volume).

24. While controvertible, assertions that circumcision "is a matter of proper marriage" or enhanced eligibility for motherhood and the elements that go into the individual's cost-advantage calculus betray material motivations for the practice. Several analyses of the rationales for female circumcision point up linkages with marriage. In contexts where material benefits are attached to marriage and motherhood, the

economic utility of membership status in these institutions contributes to their glorification. For instance, if marriage has practical implications for subsistence and children ultimately provide some form of social insurance and augment the prospects for subsistence, such externalities intensify aspirations for marriage and motherhood. The interplay between these externalities and their reciprocal explanation for circumcision locates some pressure for the practice in the necessities conferred by the social roles of marriage and motherhood. This reading adds significance to the description of the practice as a rite of passage that helps secure access to productive and reproductive resources.

25. The generational struggle epitomized by the *Ngaitana* movement is revealing of this component (Thomas 2000).

CHAPTER 4

Female Circumcision in Africa and Beyond

THE ANTHROPOLOGY OF A DIFFICULT ISSUE

Aud Talle

FEMALE CIRCUMCISION IS a cultural practice that has not concerned anthropologists a great deal in the past. Even anthropologists who did
research in areas where circumcision was widespread chose to ignore the issue.
One relevant example of this is I. M. Lewis's studies from Somalia in the 1950s.
In his celebrated monograph on nomadic politics, *A Pastoral Democracy,* female
circumcision is not mentioned at all, and in the slightly later publication *Marriage and Family in Northern Somaliland* circumcision is referred to only once in a
footnote (Lewis 1961 and 1962). Lewis's work is, however, not an isolated case.
When I wrote my master's thesis on the pastoral, Nilotic-speaking Barabaig in
Tanzania, I sensed that female circumcision was not an issue to be noted in spite
of the fact that household organization and male-female relations were a major
theme of the thesis (Talle 1974).

This conspicuous silence surrounding female circumcision is not a coin-
cidence. In Somalia, as in other places where circumcision is practiced, female
circumcision is something one does, but seldom discusses (Talle 1993). It is not
a matter of excluding outsiders from esoteric knowledge—circumcision is just
one of those commonplace social practices that are not an object of conscious
dialogue, neither among people themselves nor, until recently, among researchers in the region.[1] On the surface of it, female circumcision belongs to what
Pierre Bourdieu calls the *habitus* of social life—actions inscribed in body practice and moral form, and which are reproduced without much further reflections (Bourdieu 1977).

Female circumcision is a difficult anthropological issue chiefly because it
both calls for and challenges a conventional cultural relativistic perspective as
we know it from Franz Boas and onward, one that still, although much debated, informs anthropological practice and analyses. It must be understood that

knowledge and understanding of female circumcision are grounded in people's own concepts and forms of knowledge, their cultural preferences and values, as it were. Nonetheless, female circumcision is a bodily intervention involving considerable pain, suffering, and health consequences—experiences and feelings that move on the margins of a cultural explanation.

Inspired by, among others Mary Douglas's analysis of the body as a metaphor for "society" (Douglas 1966 and 1973), I have written about female circumcision in Somalia, particularly about the relationship between the individual female body and the patrilineal group as a social body (Talle 1993). When Somali girls are circumcised, the "male"–and thus "unclean"—parts are removed from the female body, while simultaneously a male image is bodily inscribed through the infibulation scar in the form of a fake penis. I argue that the male insignia enclose the girls in their lineages, not as politically active members, but as "pure" agnates and worthy representatives of the collectivity (ibid.).

The human body, however, is not only a source of representation, but also one of subjective and intersubjective experience, and of action and intentionality. It is through the body we "are" in the world and that we fix our look beyond ourselves and engage in others (cf., for example, Csordas 1994). The intense bodily experience of female circumcision draws participant and observer into a common experiential space where boundaries between subject and object become blurred. This intersubjective room has the potential to overarch—and mark—cultural differences, as well as to establish solidarity (Hastrup and Hervik 1994; Shweder 1991).

In this chapter I give some brief glimpses into my field research in Africa and in Europe. These intersubjective ventures embedded in anthropological fieldwork have become moments of clearing in how I understand female circumcision as a cultural and embodied practice. The glimpses are ordered chronologically, from fieldwork in Tanzania at a young age, via Kenya and Somalia, to being an experienced anthropologist in London. My mode of description is "phenomenological and ethnographic" (Lindsay 1996, 192). It aims to combine experience with representation. The text is an explorative journey of sorts into a highly complex ethnographic landscape where the journey itself, and not its end, is the primary aim of traveling. To me, a "truthful" analysis of female circumcision seems to lie where the ways part next. In London, my latest stop on the journey, female circumcision has come threateningly close to my European life, adding yet another dimension to its complexity.

UNEXPECTED EVENTS

Female circumcision was for a long time considered too intimate, culturally marginal, and eccentric an object for serious anthropological analysis. It was, rather, something that the anthropologist would stumble over while doing field research, one of those events that are detected because one simply is there. However, in most cases, the idea that with closer inspection such events may turn out to be the key to valuable knowledge for cultural and social analysis was ignored (cf. Falk Moore 1994). Female circumcision is the sort of cultural stuff that informants seldom think of telling visitors unless they explicitly ask for it.

I can still remember my feeling of surprise and vague disappointment when my Barabaig host in Tanzania in 1972 told me that his two youngest daughters, Gulu and Shangu, who were then about three and four years old, had been circumcised the same morning while I stayed in my tent a stone's throw from the homestead. I was taken aback by this news. How was that possible? So near, but still so distant. For a moment my position as a fieldworker felt shaky. I never asked my host why I had not been told beforehand (so that I might have participated), simply because I was uncertain about how much interest I should show such an issue. At the same time I felt that even the family preferred the incident to pass without further comments or questioning. Perhaps I should have been relieved to not have to watch the bloody intervention. I, like my host, let the event remain in silence. It was easiest thus.

After Shangu and Gulu's circumcision, I never encountered female circumcision again while I lived among the Barabaig. I was, however, invited to participate in a large male circumcision ceremony where more than one hundred boys were circumcised. One by one the young boys, most in their early puberty but also some very young ones, were brought forward to the two circumcisers who worked in parallel. Afterward the newly circumcised were celebrated by several hundred guests in a ceremony that lasted the whole day and far into the next. The difference in ceremonial and social worth between the circumcision of girls and boys was striking, but for the Barabaigs themselves the operations are complementary. Both are necessary to create productive persons able to procreate children and tend to animals.

A PAINFUL MOMENT

After two periods of field research among the Barabaig and one among the pastoral Maasai in Kenya, circumcision was an issue I had encountered several times. Female and male circumcision—although different in form and cultural content—were part of the order of the day and a cultural phenomenon that no longer raised feelings of anxiety or indignation. In Geertzian terms I could remain "experience-distant" to that sort of bodily intrusion (Geertz 1983). Particularly when confronted with this piece of ethnography, it felt safe to repose in the cognition of cultural differences.

The first female circumcision I witnessed was in 1978 in Kenya, and it was a shocking and deep-felt experience, chiefly because it did not proceed "normally," as the Maasai would have it. This account, I think, brings out issues of hegemonic power and subjugation of women, which, although they are profoundly significant aspects of female circumcision, are seldom overtly contested in places where the practice is socially accepted.

The girl to be circumcised was a young and athletic woman of fourteen to fifteen years of age. I noted that she was tall with a particularly well shaped body and beautiful face. She was operated upon in the house of her mother, which is common both among the Barabaig and the Maasai (as well as among the Somali described later). As soon as the circumciser began cutting her flesh the girl started to fight back. That is the point in time when "normality" took its own course. The women who participated in the operation did not manage to hold her down in spite of the fact that they were several who thronged around her.

Finally, the elder brother and guardian of the girl (her father had passed away) approached the house with long and resolute paces—in a typical masculine Maasai way—and shouted at his sister to stop crying for "nothing." Pain is something the Maasai must learn to tolerate and be proud to endure from an early age. From a male perspective, circumcision constitutes the ultimate sign of courage and bodily control. The brother told the women that if they could not hold the girl by their own strength, they would have to use ropes to bind her. The operation had to be executed immediately because the cattle were restlessly waiting to get out to the pastures, and all the guests who had gathered were eager to begin the feasting.

Another brother, slightly older than the girl, had been circumcised in the cattle corral the same morning—outside, under the bare sky, and in front of everybody. He had endured the operation without the slightest sign of protest or pain—all in accordance with the expectations of the onlookers. The Maasai boy who dares flicker as much as "an eyelid" during this ordeal of manhood becomes an object of public ridicule, and the shame may be transmitted to his family for generations to come.

One of the women assisting with the operation on the girl ran over to another house and came back with a bundle under the beaded skin gown she was wearing in honor of the day. She was an elderly woman, and I still remember her forward bending way of running, particularly typical for women in East Africa with back trouble from heavy loads. Only the powerful orders of the guardian brother and the old woman's running broke the tense silence of the homestead. In the bundle the woman grasped onto while running were the leather ropes the brother had asked for—the same ropes women used for fetching firewood and water.

The women made a loop on each rope end and tried to lock these around the ankles of the girl, who at the same time tried desperately to kick them off. The struggle continued for a while before the girl tired and the rope loops were securely fastened around her ankles. It was, however, difficult to hold her legs stretched out inside the narrow house. One of the men watching the scene from a distance and waiting for the women to get finished with the work approached the house to offer his assistance. (It is likely that her prospective husband was also among the men, and he, as is common among the Maasai, probably had paid for part of the expenses for the celebration of her circumcision.) The man who joined the women forced his stick through the mud wall of the house, made a hole, and pulled out one of the rope ends. The other rope was fastened to a roof beam at the entrance of the house. At last, the circumciser could proceed with her work. With tiny movements she carved away the clitoris and the labia minora, while the women in loud voices instructed her how to cut. The blood rushed forward, and for us outside the actual scene, it was as if the excited voices of the women and the heavy breathing of the girl would never come to an end.

I had been invited inside, but to come so close to the operation had seemed threatening. The Maasai house is small and the entrance low, and I knew that if I stayed inside, I risked being squeezed between bodies without being able to move in or out. Besides, I had experienced the invitation partly to be a polite gesture toward a foreigner (*ekashumpai*) who had come to participate in the celebration. Intuitively, I felt a great resistance to fulfill the role of observer.

The limit of my participant observation was thus a cracked wall of mud and branches. When I gathered courage, I peeped through the opening in the roof that the women had made beforehand to lighten up the room. There were others, in particular children and boys of the same age as the girl, who tried to get a peek at the scene through the roof. The man, all the time holding tightly on to the rope, gazed into the narrow room to check that the women did a proper job. The spectators outside said nothing; glances were exchanged and some broke into uncertain smiles. The nervousness of the women who executed the operation had spread to the observers, and it was as if we sought support in each other's glances and presence. The smell of blood and sweat forced itself through the wall and incorporated us into what was happening inside. My own pulse beat more quickly than normal. Instantly, I understood what a personal challenge anthropological fieldwork could be. I was witnessing "torture," and the fact that I remained standing with the others outside somehow sanctioned what happened inside the house.

When the operation finally came to an end, the girl was helped to get up and a black piece of cloth was placed around her naked shoulders. Among the Maasai, black is a blessed color, and in this ritual it symbolizes growth and fertility. The cloth indicates that the newly circumcised girl now is an adult person, ready to be married and give birth to children. (Maasai girls are usually married away—that is, they leave their home and are given away in marriage—three or four months after their genital operation.) While standing up, the girl bowed her head and looked down on her body with an apprehensive, almost curious look and was obviously relieved that the intervention was over. The blood, which continued to run down her legs, had collected in a small pool on the earthen floor underneath her together with the cut genitals, which were later gathered and buried under the bed in the house. The women, whose voices had waned, were busy tidying up and bringing the house back to its normal state of peace and well-being.

The Maasai house is practically and symbolically a female domain. The women build it themselves, manage its allocated property (livestock), and it is inside the house that women conceive, deliver, and foster their children. In fact, woman and house are so intimately associated in Maasai cultural thought that they both semantically and metaphorically substitute for each other. The flesh that was severed from the body of the young Maasai woman continues to belong to her by becoming part of the house but is now placed in another moral context. The severed body parts are buried in the house, which initially gave her life, and now, by being removed from her physical self, constitute her as a gendered and active person able to procreate (Strathern 1993). Among the Maasai, the reproductive capacity of a woman is activated by the cutting of her clitoris.

The family of the girl lived in an area I did not visit regularly during my field research, and thus I never saw her again. Hence, I did not manage to find out what she thought or felt during the ordeal she had been through. It is not unlikely that her answer would have been similar to others I heard afterward in the homestead: "We the Maasai have always circumcised our children." This is how it has been since time immemorial and this is how it must be continued; any alternative is incomprehensible and not to be contemplated (cf. Horton 1967).

It was the excruciating pain that made the girl protest against the circumcision—an impulsive reaction of the body and in no way a conscious resistance against a cultural practice. The people present in the homestead that day also interpreted the girl's fight during the operation as a sign of fear and a low threshold for pain. Her protests were nonetheless an effect of bodily agency and intentionality. By opposing the pain of circumcision or "the pain of the knife"—a metaphor of adult status in many places in East Africa (cf., for example, Heald 1999)—the young Maasai woman demanded attention in an indirect protest against cultural hegemony.

The brother's determined but merciless intervention in a critical moment, which at first glance may appear brutal, was agency of another order. His action was both an effect of and a source of power—as the judicial guardian of the girl he could act and drive the event forward. His word gave the women strength and the moral responsibility to act (Ortner 1999). When the world had turned chaotic, he brought meaning into the situation by normalizing and interpreting what had become unclear (cf. Douglas 1966; Horton 1967).

SOCIAL SUFFERING

In the early 1980s I began studying female circumcision more systematically. I participated in a Somali-Swedish collaborative research project on female circumcision in which we interviewed one hundred women, men, circumcision practitioners, and religious leaders. I also did a study among camel nomads about five hundred kilometers from the Somalian capital, Mogadishu, close to the Ethiopian border.

The Somalis practice the infibulation form of circumcision, which in surgical terms is considered the most severe intervention. It is a risky undertaking and often implies considerable medical and health consequences for those who undergo the operation. The Somali are meticulously preoccupied with the form of the infibulation scar: it should be without unnecessary scar tissue—forming a straight line—and the opening should be as small as possible. An attractive female body should bear smooth and nicely sewn genitals. One may be tempted to speculate that an ugly scar evokes a memory of an "ugly" event, and thus instills uneasiness and doubt in the beholder.

Those parts of the female body that are cut away are culturally labeled childish and unclean and are sometimes compared to the hump of the camel or the cock's comb (because they "stand up"). They have to be removed in order to humanize and feminize the woman, to secure her moral uprightness and bodily beauty. The girls are operated upon when they are still young, between six and eight years old, and they remain sewn until they get married ten to fifteen years later. A tight opening is a sign of distinction for a Somali woman. It elevates her body to an aesthetic ideal and only as a "sewn" woman may she represent her family later in life at marriage (cf. Talle 1993).

Infibulation is a cultural practice deeply imprinted in the life of the Somali population. In every family context the operation on a daughter or sister is an "extreme situation" embodying anxiety, violence, and pain—in all senses a "normal" situation, but still an event surrounded by risk and ambiguity. There are women who do not want to see any operations executed in their homes because of "all the blood." The operation forces women to transcend appropriate female behavior as they exercise violence, handle weapons (a male attribute), and draw blood. That the intervention is judged risky and painful is confirmed by the popularity of modern circumcisers in towns where such services are available. These practitioners, in contrast to local ones, use modern surgical equipment and anesthetics and apply tetanus injections.

At each operation, which lasts some twenty minutes, every possible precaution is taken in order to minimize the adverse effects of a hazardous intervention. However, bad luck is unavoidable. In the course of our interviews in Somalia we came to a house where a newly operated girl was resting. She and her sister had been infibulated the day before, but the young girl revealed that her sister "died yesterday." The sister was a little bit older than she and had not uttered a sound of pain during the whole operation because she dearly wanted to have the gold necklace her aunt had promised the one of them who did not shout when being operated upon. During the ordeal the sister said several times "Look, I do not cry," as if to tell herself and those present that she was working wonders. Other than knowing that "her time [to die] had come," we never learned the reason why she passed away.

Later in life, difficult deliveries and chronic abdominal pain torment many Somali women. It may appear as if the pain of the first intervention forever guides the body in a certain direction—cultural models are embodied. Every Somali woman carries in her a circumcision tale of her own. "How can I forget the day which had so much pain?" said one woman we interviewed. Women can verbalize their tales, but these are more clearly retold in female bodily praxis of indeterminate illness conditions (cf. Scheper-Hughes 1992). Pain and infibulation are one and the same thing for women in Somalia; in fact the link is so obvious that it does not have to be spoken out loud (cf. H. Summerfield 1993, also Dopico and Johansen, chapters 10 and 11 of this volume). To retell the pain is somehow to evoke it anew.

MEANING AND EXPERIENCE

The anthropological explanation is to find meaning in events and practices that appear meaningless to cultural outsiders. In all human interaction it is meaning that defines life and gives it its purpose (Ortner 1999). For me it has always been right to see female circumcision in a contextual and relativistic perspective. It has been important to come as close as possible to the "reality" of the informants. How otherwise could we understand that mothers and grandmothers, generation after generation, subject their daughters and granddaughters to the violent treatment of circumcision and additionally risk that they will bleed to death or become disfigured by infections? Indeed, it is the women themselves who often insist that the operation should be performed.

For the Barabaig, the Maasai, and the Somali the circumcision of girls as well as of boys—male and female circumcision are often constituted as analogous practices—are an overall positive act. Circumcision produces moral individuals who may be included in an adult community. The establishment of a single-sex community and community across the sexes is a fundamental precondition for action and creation, for material and social reproduction (cf. Strathern 1988). In a large part of Africa, circumcision has a given place in such cultural models of reproduction.

The "cultural" explanation, however, tends to disregard the concrete and the individual. Within social theory it is more important how people think and categorize, that is, order and represent their world, than how they experience and live it. The ubiquitous tension between the individual and the social, between experience and theory, subjectivism and objectivism, becomes particularly challenging in the study of female circumcision. Because circumcision is to such a great extent a bodily and individual experience, any anthropological analysis built "only" on representation would become less than "truthful." An analysis of female circumcision without social meaning and cultural conceptualization quickly becomes meaningless, however. The two approaches must go together in order to forward our understanding of this practice.

OTHER PLACES, OTHER MEANINGS

When the civil war in Somalia broke out on a large scale in 1990, it became impossible to work anthropologically in the country, and two of my closest collaborators fled to England.[2] I had some unused funds from my research project on nomadic women and decided to use them to study "female circumcision in exile." My experience and knowledge of this cultural practice in the Somali context spurred me to hypothesize that a study of circumcision in exile would produce meaningful knowledge on this anthropologically difficult and rather enigmatic social reality. Without being certain of what to find beyond the Somali scene, my decision was an "imaginative investment" (Hastrup 1995, 67) in an unknown landscape via the detour of the known. The anthropological experience of Somalis in Somalia helped me imagine Somalis in exile and to make room for "novel connections" (ibid., 63). I was launching a comparative exercise of probing one Somali cultural instance by way of the other. The fact that my Somali collaborators—one of them being Sarah—were forced into exile became an opportunity for continued and new research on a familiar theme. The recent immigration of Africans to Europe also added urgency to the production of knowledge on female circumcision.

In 1999, I met Sarah in London and we continued our dialogue on female circumcision. Sarah is a gynecologist and works at different refugee centers in the suburbs of Camden and Leyton in north and northeast London respectively. At the time Sarah was living in the area on the thirteenth floor of a high-rise building together with her elderly mother, unemployed husband (a former civil servant at the foreign ministry in Somalia), and two college-age sons. In London I visited Sarah's different working places, called on her friends (other Somali refugees), and drank tea at a volunteer center for Somali women.[3] We had lunch at a restaurant colloquially known as Khadiya's place, an apartment decorated in Somali style where Somali food is served to Somali customers. My field research in London depended upon Sarah and her network of friends and acquaintances. Being a sensitive subject in the exile context, research on female circumcision must be grounded in trust and personal relationships. The material I present below derives mainly from adult and educated women who have experienced a downward social mobility after migrating to London.

The first time I met Sarah in London, we visited the premises of the London Black Women's Health Action Project, which provides many different activities for women and young people within the health and education sector. The project has, among other things, issued the publication *FGM [female genital mutilation] Is a World Wide Issue.* I hesitated when I read "world wide issue." Female circumcision has generally been associated with the African continent, but in recent years "primitive practices," as it were, are no longer confined to distant and exotic places. Such practices have "come home" to Europeans, posing some specific methodological and epistemological problems for anthropology (H. Moore 1999).

I noticed that the publication uses "FGM" in the title, and commented to Sarah that I preferred the more relativistic "circumcision" for the practice. Sarah turned against me and said, "But *it is* mutilation!" Her sharp answer surprised me. I could do nothing but agree. Sarah's comment brought to mind the introduction to the anthology *Anthropological Theory Today,* which problematizes the entire foundation of anthropology as a discipline, namely the idea that cultures can be compared because they exist independently of each other (H. Moore 1999, 8). Which culture does Sarah in London belong to then, in contrast to the anthropologist? The question has little relevance. In London Sarah is neither a "carrier" of Somali culture nor a "hybrid" or outcome of British and Somali amalgamation (that is, of two original cultural instances), but rather an experiencing subject who engages in and interprets the world from different positions and locations (cf. Hastrup 1995). In the office of the Black Women's Health Project it is Sarah—not a newcomer to the place, as the anthropologist is—who has the power of definition, and it is in such concrete situations of "subject positions" that social meaning and identity are generated (cf. H. L. Moore 1994). Sarah was always against female circumcision, even when she lived in Somalia, but in London she appeared more determined, and particularly so in the premises of the Black Women's Health Project. It was as if the place itself, packed with anticircumcision pamphlets and posters and memories of previous discussions and seminars in which she often had been a participant, spurred Sarah to enforce her point one bit further. The Black Women's Health Project was not a place in which to compromise her arguments.

In the discussions I had with Somali refugee women in London, I noted that a great majority of them took a firm stance against female circumcision. This was not only the case in public places such as the refugee centers; even in their homes they would air strong anticircumcision views. The fact that I, a European, and Sarah, known for her opposition to circumcision, were present during the discussions may of course have influenced how women at those particular instances reported on the issue. Considering the cultural deep-rootedness of female circumcision, one may be tempted to interpret such views as lip service to overdetermined listeners. I do not think, however, that this was the case, and my rather impressionistic data from London do correlate with observations and interviews done in other places outside Somalia. In an interview study conducted among Somali refugees in the southern Swedish town of Malmö there was clear resistance against female circumcision among both women and men (Johnsdotter et al. 2000). Furthermore, it is common in the Somali diaspora for outreach services conducted among refugee women by other Somali women (routinely elite women) to make anticircumcision campaigns an important part of their activities (cf., e. g. El-Sohl 1993; Griffiths 1997; Summerfield 1993). There are also indications of changes in actual practice.

A survey study done in 1998 of ninety-four women by the London Black Women's Health Action Project and the London School of Hygiene and Tropical Medicine found that 70 percent reported being circumcised. Of females born in the United Kingdom or who had arrived before the age of eight, less than half had been circumcised, whereas among those arriving after the age of nine, 84 percent had been circumcised. Girls are still circumcised after they arrive, although less frequently than girls who grow up in Somalia.

Not surprisingly, the resistance to circumcision is more pronounced in the exile community than in Somalia. Some (such as Sarah and her educational equals) were already opposed to the practice while they lived in Somalia; others just "found themselves against it when they arrived in London." One woman, now against the practice, told us that to convey her steadfast wish to be operated on, when she was a girl of seven, she had run to the shop and bought the razor blade herself in order to speed up the operation. She said that she even endured the operation without anybody holding her and she demonstrated how she had sat with legs widely spread when she was operated on. "I did not cry either," she boasted. For her, the pain came afterward, when she married and had children. "This was an experience of agony," she added. In Somalia this woman had lived a sheltered family life without material worries (her husband was an army officer, now unemployed in London), and female circumcision was just something that "existed everywhere," even among educated people in the capital where she resided at the time. The pain she had suffered in Somalia, however, became meaningless when she moved to England. She claimed, without bitterness, that she had suffered "in vain," while she pointed to her four-year-old daughter, noting that she "at least" should be spared from being "sewn." This woman had an unusual clarity when she spoke; it was as if she had been exposed to a sudden revelation—as if her present resistance had just waited to be awakened.

In Europe, female circumcision is an awkward practice, raising questions and causing embarrassment and often anger. In the hegemonic FGM discourse, the practice draws a sharp line between "us" and "them." We are all acquainted with the "Western" cum global discourse on female circumcision through the tabloid media—in the press, the radio, and television—where the Somalis and others who perform such operations count as less than human. The fervent media coverage that followed a Norwegian TV documentary in October 2000 is a case in point (*Rikets tilstand* 2000). The documentary was made by a young female Somali, resident of Norway, who clandestinely interviewed Muslim religious leaders on their opinions of female circumcision (see also Johansen, chapter 11 of this volume). She approached them, pretending to be seeking advice on whether to be circumcised. Her family wanted her to be cut, but she herself was doubtful. Of course, the imams advised her not to go against the authority of her parents. The ensuing agitated media discussion praising the "courageous" (*modige*) girl and castigating the "false" (*falske*) imams led to government involvement and establishment of institutions to forcefully fight the "cruel" (*brutale*) practice. The debate in the media lingered for weeks, and its tenacity, in addition to its fanatical zeal, leads one to speculate that the major concern was not the health and well-being of the Somali and other African women, but rather the moral standing of the Muslim community (which has recently grown at a rapid rate in Norway).

A tenacious aspect of the media debate in Norway and elsewhere in Europe is that it notoriously focuses on Somalis who presumably continue to circumcise their daughters even in exile and less on those who have stopped doing it (see also Johnsdotter, chapter 5 of this volume). A focus on the latter group would have put Somalis and other Muslims in a much more favorable light, and probably been far more instrumental to the abolition of the practice.

There are, of course, Somali families who continue to circumcise their daughters after they arrive in England or Norway. However, since female circumcision is criminalized and there are examples in France of African parents who have been jailed (see, for example, Lionnet 1992), the operations are done secretly in private clinics or, more commonly, girls are sent abroad to be operated upon. Some also see to it that girls are circumcised before they arrive in Europe, with the risk that the circumcision age is lowered. A case I heard about was a four-year-old girl who was already circumcised when she came to London. "She was only a baby when they did it to her," the women deplored, implying that she was far too young for such an ordeal. Their agitated discussion seemed to disregard the fact that Sarah herself was only four when she was operated upon in Somalia, now almost forty-five years ago. Her case was comparable in its practical considerations; being a town girl, she was infibulated together with another girl of the family while she stayed with her grandmother in the rural area.

The fact that an elite Somali woman in exile opposes female circumcision and has stopped circumcising her own daughters and relatives, I take as an important sign of a gradual eradication of the practice. There are simply no "good reasons" for continuing to circumcise females in the context of contemporary, modern Europe, where such practices strongly associate to primitivism and non-humanistic values. There are, though, the few who find it important to be "true to their culture" and stand up against the encompassing mainstream society which they often feel discriminates against the Somalis as an immigrant group (El-Sohl 1993). Or there are those who envision a return to Somalia "with all their cultural baggage intact" (Rousseau et al. 1998, 403). It is impossible to predict exactly which girls will be circumcised and which will not, as there are a number of circumstantial factors leading to the decision in each individual case. This gray zone of decision making reflects "encounters and experiences across boundaries [that] engender new interpretations of fundamental cultural principles" (Griffiths 1997, 20), as well as practical contingencies.

THE VEIL AND THE PAIN

The infibulated women in London are an object of great worry and negative attention, which is a situation that the women I met detested and that rendered them very uncomfortable. Somali women in general encounter perpetual gynecological problems (real and imagined), and their relationship to health authorities in Britain, as it was in Somalia, is frequent and intense. "We do not like all the fuss about circumcision," despaired many, and recounted experiences of humiliating and embarrassing episodes in hospitals and with general practitioners (GPs). For one reason or another they particularly disliked the Asian doctors, who were found in abundance in the area where they lived.

There are practicing doctors in London who are still unaware of the practice of female circumcision. One medical practitioner in a hospital ran to seek advice from his colleagues when he got a circumcised woman as a patient. After much excitement he found a Nigerian doctor who could explain the situation. There are also the stories of Somali women who bring relatives to hospitals to deliver and who have to tolerate words of abuse and reprimand from shocked hospital personnel. "We came to give birth, not to discuss female circumcision," said one. This, as far as she was concerned, was not the right moment to reflect on a century-long tradition, to which they had acceded in "ignorance." My impression was that the women, although not all of them could recount offending situations or rude doctors, just felt uncomfortable and uneasy in their relationship to the health authorities. A few had not even been to a doctor but could still imaginatively sense the abashment of presenting their bodies to uninformed health personnel. An African Women's Health Clinic at a refugee center in Leyton where Sarah worked was established for the simple reason that "the health personnel has not known how to treat a woman with female circumcision" (Bourne and Edmans 2000).

The situated lives of Somali women in London make them acutely aware of their bodily difference from mainstream society, which may reinforce a general skepticism toward the host community. The scar of circumcision, a sign of excellence inscribed in their bodies when they were still very young, has become a mark of deficiency and difference—of less worth on a global scene. By being infibulated, Somali women are marked and marginalized as incomplete and inferior women. In the streets of London they are not "in the world" with a perfect body as they were on the savannah in Somalia. Now they wander forward as "lacks"—mutilated souls in mutilated bodies. They are signs of a story they have not written themselves; in fact, their bodies have become sites of a worldwide discourse on morality.

Exile and the displacement of populations are embodied processes: people move and cross boundaries with their bodies, and in this particular case of Somali refugees we are witnessing a transnational flow of circumcised female bodies. In other words, the traumatic uprootedness of the Somali population is about the displacement of persons and about a dislocation of bodies. I am not referring to a "natural setting" problematic, but to the fact that when Somali women arrive in London the body is the first and foremost instrument through which they perceive and experience themselves as positioned subjects—and as members of a global world.

One telling episode is a haphazard encounter on the street in Leyton between Sarah and a man she knew from Mogadishu. He told her that he wanted to marry a second wife (the first was still in Somalia, while he resided in London). "But," he said "I do not want a 'Somali' woman—they are no good, because they have no clitoris." By using "Somali" in this context he meant an infibulated or "sewn" woman. "He said it abruptly, and I was shocked," said

Sarah when she quoted the dialogue between them. His straightforward remark
had pained her. In defense of Somali women, she, as a doctor, tried to explain to
him that sexuality and desire are located in wider areas of the human body than
the genitals. But she spoke in vain; she knew that her arguments would poorly
counter the sort he had thrown at her. This brief rendezvous between Sarah and
her male acquaintance highlights the experience of Somali culture in exile as a
series of "sites of contested representation and resistance within fields of power"
(H. Moore 1999, 11). For Somalis living in London, female circumcision is
negotiable, where female morality and beauty are constituted through another
kind of bodily accomplishment than cutting away of genitals.

   During my first visit to London I could not fail to notice the clothing style
of Somali women. Many of them dress in an orthodox Muslim fashion: long
one-colored dresses covering arms and legs, and a matching scarf tightly folded
around head and face in veil-like fashion (*jellaba*). Their covered bodies give the
women an unfamiliar look, different not only from how they used to dress in
Somalia but also from the surrounding British society (see also Johansen, chapter 11 of this volume). To my questioning about this striking change in clothing,
many claimed that they wear the veil because they have become more truly
religious after they fled. One young woman, herself heavily veiled in dark gray
clothes, explained while laying her hand on her heart that they had become religious in a "deeper sense." This "deeper sense" referred not only to an emotional
state but also to the fact that they had begun to read the Qu'ran more actively
than they used to in Somalia. And more of them had become devoted practitioners of the religious faith.

   This dress style has not hampered Somali women, however, in driving cars,
seeking employment, meeting friends, or attending language classes. In a study
comparing Somali and Bangladeshi women, another large Muslim immigrant
group in the United Kingdom, it was found that Somali women are in general
far less dependent than are Bangladeshi women on husbands and relatives (Summerfield 1993). Somalis are on the whole more outgoing, forming women's associations for combating circumcision or teaching English for easier integration
with the mainstream society; above all, their community is much more permissive toward divorce (ibid.). These factors, particularly the ease with which Somali
women can get a divorce, contribute to greater independence and well-being
among Somali than Bangladeshi women in exile (see also Johansen, chapter
11 of this volume, for similarities in Norway). The Somalis in Northeast London, who mainly come from the southern parts of Somalia, continue to marry
relatives, a tendency reinforced in exile, I was told. This tendency was related to
a perceived vulnerability as residents in foreign lands. The closeness in kin relations between husband and wife, however, does not prevent a high divorce rate
among Somalis, even in exile.

   "You just feel you have to, or the other Somalis will look at you as if you
were indecently dressed [naked]," said one woman about the recent change in

style of dress. She was hinting at the pressure of a common morality, and also at the vulnerability of the exile situation. The women's insecurity and continuous exposure to foreign people, coupled with the turbulence and grief of migration, require protection. One refugee woman who personified the image of this collective vulnerability was Halima. She was in her mid-thirties and had fled with her husband and two children in a car from Mogadishu southward toward the Kenyan border. About a hundred kilometers along the road from Mogadishu, their car was shot at, and Halima's husband and two children were killed. She had to continue the journey toward Kenya on her own; through benevolent assistance in Nairobi she managed to get on a plane to England. She did not know any English and no relatives or friends waiting for her. Sitting in front of me at a Somali women's support center, tightly shrouded in her clothes—her face barely visible—Halima iconized the burden of an exiled and deprived woman. She had had to bear all this suffering on her own—no wonder she sought comfort in warm wrappings. Her withdrawn bodily appearance, suggested by her clothing as well as by her remarkably dispassionate face, bore witness to great distress.

CONCLUSION

I argue that the displacement of circumcised bodies in London is the displacement of bodies in pain. Traces of pain that occurred in women's bodies a long time ago at the operation of circumcision, and later at marriage and childbirth, surface through the gazes of others—on the streets, at the health centers, and in the media. The public noise of the global debate around circumcision is painful, intimidating exiled women and drawing boundaries between "healthy and unhealthy bodies" (see also Rogers, chapter 6 of this volume). For individual Somali women in London the experience of difference and of being in an outsider position is terribly concrete and tormenting. A predominant theme in their discourse of female circumcision is pain—the pain they experienced at the operation and immediately afterward, the pain of fleeing a beloved homeland, and the pain of meeting with the British health authorities.

The flight to London and the subsequent repositioning of Somali bodies rekindle thoughts and sentiments deeply sunk in consciousness. The surfacing of curbed experiences may lead to "natural phenomena" being debated, and often to action (cf. Comaroff 1985; Hastrup 1995). The increasing use of the veil (and islamization in general) among Somali women in the diaspora (and recently even in Somalia) can be considered as a protection against views from outside and against looking toward distant horizons. It is also worth noting that orthodox Islam does not prescribe female circumcision. On the contrary, many Muslim groups in Europe denigrate African Muslims for such nonreligious practices (see also Johnson, chapter 9 of this volume). The reworking of a Somali female identity in the diaspora suggests a new area of meaning and representation where female circumcision is a contested element (Griffiths 1997, 19). In London the words I heard from a Somali male colleague many years ago in Mogadishu gained new relevance: "We the Somali do not have to confine our women [as the Arabs do], we circumcise them instead." Circumcision or veil? The question may lead us into a blind alley, but in the present narrow back streets of London the veil certainly constitutes a better protection for Somali women than does the scar of circumcision.

MY TEXT HAS traveled far in time and space, giving accounts of different meanings and representations of female circumcision in and out of Africa. These are disconnected instances—abbreviated stories from individual lives—that come together as a result of my life in a coherent story in the present text. The movement in space as well as time is important for drawing a better understanding of an extraordinary predicament. In her book *A Passage to Anthropology,* Kirsten Hastrup argues that we should be careful not to conflate our texts with the objects we describe: the distance between theory and lived life is abysmal (1995, 83). The abyss may appear particularly deep in the encounter with the ethnography of female circumcision. The intensity of female circumcision as a bodily experience encourages a narrative ethnographic form that manages to capture "the dialectic between the particular and the universal as it makes its appearance in the interpersonal life of peoples" (Jackson 1998, 4). Writing about female circumcision cannot be anything other than a blend of rigid scholarship and "sympathy" writing. The founding stone in ethnographic method, participant observation, requires that the anthropologist and the informant enter an intersubjective room and become imaginable to each other (Shweder 1991). By describing and interpreting events in this intersubjective space, the anthropological account of female circumcision has the potential to become a meaningful story.

NOTES

A shorter version of this chapter has been published in Norwegian (Talle 2001).

1. From the 1970s onward, feminist anthropology gained momentum and demanded a gender-balanced description of societies and cultures: female life should be described and analyzed on par with male life. Over the last twenty-five years or so, female circumcision has become an object of anthropological analysis (cf., for example, Boddy 1982; Hayes 1975; and Talle 1993, as well as contributors to this volume). Presently there are at least six or seven graduate students in Norway and Sweden writing theses on various aspects of female circumcision, and drawing on material from Africa as well as Europe. The waxing academic interest for the issue must be seen partly in connection with increasing immigration to Europe and elsewhere from African countries where female circumcision is practiced.

2. It is estimated that perhaps as many as three million Somalis were displaced during the civil war of the 1980 and 1990s—one million to Europe and North America, one million to neighboring East African countries, and one million internally within Somalia. These figures may be overstated, but nevertheless they indicate the magnitude of the problem. In Britain alone there are about eighty thousand Somalis, of whom perhaps 80 to 90 percent live in London.

3. Somalis have a long history of immigration to Britain (London included), but my research mainly concerns Somali refugees who arrived more recently as a consequence of the collapse of the Barre regime in 1991 (cf. El-Sohl 1993).

CHAPTER 5

Persistence of Tradition or Reassessment of Cultural Practices in Exile?

DISCOURSES ON FEMALE CIRCUMCISION AMONG AND ABOUT SWEDISH SOMALIS

Sara Johnsdotter

THERE ARE SEVERAL possible scenarios if one wants to specu-late about what is going on with the practice of female circumcision among immigrant groups in Sweden. One extreme view is that no female circumcision takes place among African immigrants in exile. The other extreme is one that sees female circumcision as widely practiced among immigrants in their new environment, leading to the alarming conclusion that thousands of girls risk having to go through the procedure.

In Sweden, not a single illegal case has, as yet, been authenticated and brought to court. Yet the general understanding among the actors in the field—activists, officials, politicians, and journalists—is that the practice is maintained on a large scale among Somalis in exile. The aim of this article is to describe the discourse on female circumcision among Somalis in Sweden and contrast it to public views. A few aspects of these public views will be suggested and discussed. I shall also argue that discrepancies between internal Somali debates and public understanding of the issue form an obstacle in the process toward a complete abandonment of female circumcision among Somali immigrants in Sweden.

EXILE DISCOURSES ON FEMALE CIRCUMCISION

The description of internal Somali discourses on female circumcision is based on data from interviews with Somalis in Malmö, Sweden's third largest city, during the last years of the 1990s.[1] I conducted fieldwork, living with my family for three years in an area called Rosengård, well known for being popu-lated almost exclusively by immigrants. During the summer of 2000, a research group including four interviewers was formed to study internal debate on fe-male circumcision among Somalis in the area: the groups included two women

(Asha Omar and Sara Johnsdotter) and two men (Ali Elmi and Aje Carlbom), two of Somali background and two of Swedish origin. This qualitative study included taped in-depth interviews with thirty Somalis, half of them women and half men. Working in pairs and alone (women interviewing women and men interviewing men), we focused on issues concerning attitudes to pharaonic and sunnah circumcision and the situation in exile.[2] Some themes from the group of women were presented in later interviews to the men, and vice versa. In this way we confronted men with many of women's ideas about male preferences concerning female circumcision, and women—a great share of them convinced that Somali men in general are in favor of pharaonic circumcision—with our male interviewees' solid opposition to this procedure. This step generated further understanding of the complex nature of this sphere of people's lives, not least of the discrepancy between notions emanating from, on one hand, Somali public discourse on gender relations and sexuality and, on the other hand, specific individuals' personal relations and experiences in life. It was also obvious that the extensive segregation between men and women in Somali society supports systematically false beliefs about the views of the opposite sex. The separation of sexual spheres prevents the emergence of a public life where these incorrect stereotypes about the other sex's views can be ironed out.[3]

The general discussion in this chapter is further based upon interviews, some taped and others informal, conducted by me, primarily with Somali women in Malmö, but also with men, and with Somalis in other parts of Sweden. These interviews took place in a variety of situations, including during a period when I was course administrator of a training course for Somali women in Malmö and while I was a secretary for a local Somali women's organization in Rosengård.

According to a strict culturalist view, people think and behave in certain ways because "it is their culture." In exile, it is believed, most people tend to cling to their cultural habits and values even more firmly, in order to save their original identity in a strange environment, as will be discussed later in this chapter. In an empirically oriented study the question must remain open: what values seem to be cherished in exile, and what values are exposed to revaluation? Even if it is impossible to make categorical statements about an entire ethnic group, it may be possible to discern tendencies within the group.

SOME VALUES PRESERVED IN EXILE

It is evident that some traditional values, associated with the field of female circumcision, are upheld in Sweden, even when these are not in harmony with the mainstream mentality of Swedish society. One example of this is the appreciation of female virginity before marriage and the fact that an unmarried pregnant girl almost without exception becomes "socially dead" in the Somali community: that is, she is left without any social support at all from her family or clan. Some of the more integrated women talk about this fact with sorrow and helplessness, but most female informants express the feeling that a strict attitude in this matter is the only possible standpoint according to Islamic principles, with their ban on extramarital sexual relations. But the patrilineal principle of Somali society is also crucial here. Affinity runs through the paternal side of the family, so every child inherits his or her father's clan affiliation. A child born outside marriage—marriage being the only culturally and religiously legitimate context for sex to take place within the Somali community—is born with no blood ties. The birth of a *wacal,* a child without a father, is seen as one of the most disastrous things that can happen to a Somali family, also in exile:

[I ASK:] "What happens if a Somali girl here in Sweden has a child while she is unmarried?"
[SOMALI WOMAN:] "A child? While she is unmarried? She may as well die."
[ANOTHER SOMALI WOMAN, shocked by the other woman's statement:] "Oooh."
[FIRST SOMALI WOMAN:] "Should the girl have a child without a father? It's so horrible, it cannot exist. She has to go, move away, she can't stay with her family. Without a father . . . it's impossible. [. . .] I know many in Somalia who got into this . . . these women never returned to their families, ever. They disappeared."

The consequences of having an illegitimate child, when they result in a girl being declared "socially dead," are grave but seem to be perceived by many Somalis as in proportion to what the girl has done. A young unmarried woman, raised in Sweden, describes this kind of behavior in a way that resembles discourses on criminality:

Girls who behave like this, they must be . . . kind of outcast right from the beginning, I'd say. . . . What has influenced her to behave like this, to be what she has become? That she has gotten pregnant . . . what's the reason behind that she suddenly spent time with boys and had sex without marriage? There must be something behind it. . . . If everything is right, if you raise your children well and teach them right from wrong, this shouldn't happen.

Some informants argued that the dreadful instance of a premarital pregnancy is easier to deal with in Sweden than in Somalia. If the man who impregnated the girl can not be persuaded to give *maher,* a husband's gift to his wife-to-be and equal to a marriage contract according to Islamic law, a safe and secret abortion can be a possible solution for a family stricken by this disaster in Sweden. When this is not an option (perhaps because of ethical misgivings), the girl is left to manage without the social and financial support from her community.

REASSESSING FEMALE CIRCUMCISION

In contrast to a general maintenance of values regarding virginity and the repudiation of pregnant unmarried girls in the Somali community, notions about female circumcision seem to have undergone some drastic changes among Somalis in Sweden.

Our enthusiastic pursuit of informants who favored the practice of pharaonic circumcision failed. Information received about people who allegedly
could be in favor of female circumcision was seldom reliable—or they were opposed to pharaonic circumcision but found a symbolic sunnah circumcision to
be acceptable. However, the few informants who could be found to be in favor
of more extensive forms of female circumcision than a symbolic pricking did
not hesitate in any way to speak out. In a surprisingly open way, they, too, were
willing to explain the motives for their opinions.

Nor were any of the informants who are positive toward a symbolic sunnah
circumcision (here defined as pricking of the clitoris to cause a minor bleeding)
afraid to talk about it, even though this procedure is considered illegal in Sweden.[4] Most informants emphasize that this procedure is unnecessary and state
that they will not let their own daughters undergo any form of circumcision.
This type, however, is generally considered consistent with Islam—as long as no
genital parts at all are removed—and an acceptable form of female circumcision
for those who do not want to give up the traditional practice entirely.

Pharaonic circumcision, on the other hand, is considered to be in opposition to Islamic values. Even the only person who could be found in favor of
pharaonic circumcision, a woman not yet a mother of daughters, claimed that
Islam forbids infibulation: "I'm afraid of God's punishment. Yet I would choose
tradition." This distinction between (Somali) culture and (Islamic) religion was
emphasized by almost all the informants as an explanation of how it is possible
to just abandon an ancient tradition. Religion takes precedence over culture according to the interviewees (except for the woman just cited). Often this state
of affairs was expressed in terms of female circumcision being "only" a cultural
tradition and therefore susceptible to change, while religiously commanded traditions carry implications of being eternal and unchangeable. In Somalia, most
people comprehended the two spheres as merged with respect to female circumcision (female circumcision was understood as a Somali tradition *and* a religious duty), but in Sweden this idea has been challenged. When there is a
clash between the two spheres, almost everyone seems to place "religion" above
"culture." If pharaonic circumcision is classified as *haram* (forbidden) according
to Islam, then it must by necessity be abandoned, no matter how ancient it is. It
is generally argued that any idea about a religious obligation to infibulate girls is
a historical misinterpretation of Islam.

In a traditional Somali context, pharaonic circumcision is said to enhance
the possibility that the girls will behave like "good girls," and so to make sure
that no children without fathers are born within one's family. The key issue here,
then, is: why have attitudes to female circumcision changed among so many Somalis in exile in Sweden? Why has a practice that was for ages considered to be
a religious duty suddenly become questioned and abandoned in exile?

Some informants, both women and men, state that they had already reas-
sessed the practice in Somalia. Many claim that they were informed about the

Islamic ban on pharaonic circumcision through the governmental campaign in Somalia in the 1980s.[5] A substantial share of the women convey how the exile situation itself made them reassess the practice. Quite a few of them have given vivid and often distressing descriptions of their encounters with the health care system in Sweden:

> I started thinking about it some ten years ago when I got married. Well . . . then I went to see a doctor [for defibulation]. He thought it was . . . that it was horrible. It made me ask myself, "What is it about this that is so horrible?" Well, I did know that this practice doesn't exist in Sweden or Europe . . . but still . . . where I come from it's just considered to be something natural. And then I got an admission note for a visit at a gynecological clinic, and there everybody was really curious. . . . And I kept asking myself what this curiosity was all about. Until then I had thought about it as something completely normal. I mean . . . you were born into a society where . . . this is the way it should be, and if you are not shaped in this way, then you are an outsider . . ." Oh, she hasn't had it done, how disgusting!" If you haven't had it done, there is no way you can tell your friends; you just try to hide it. So . . . I didn't really think about it until I came here and was to be opened.

A common trait in these descriptions is that most women did not understand at first what the fuss was about.[6] In ignorance of what was going on, speculation set them in a mental state of fear and shock: "I thought something was wrong with me and my pregnancy. I felt like I had a stone on my heart. Before the doctor had explained to me why she was upset, she summoned several others. I couldn't breathe, I couldn't talk."

Others claimed that they had started pondering the matter when they, in exile, were faced with Muslim Arabs, who have a special status in Muslim circles (because the Prophet was Arab and the Koran is written in Arabic). Generally, unmarried daughters of Arab Muslims in Sweden do not get pregnant, even if they are uncircumcised. This has been one aspect of the wide internal debate on an Islamic view, ending up in a general understanding that any extensive forms of female circumcision are practices forbidden by God (*haram*). A frequent argument used is the Koranic ban on destruction of God's creation, an argument that many see as counter to any accusations of a failure of one's cultural heritage:

[I ask:] "What about your daughters in the future?"
[Somali woman:] "They should stay the way they were created by God."
[I ask:] "Won't they get into problems?"
[Somali woman:] "No, I don't think so. It depends on how I raise them, if I can manage to make them understand. I'll explain to them what circumcision is about and the difficulties and that being circumcised won't give them anything important. I want them to understand what it is all about. That my parents had it done to me because they thought it was Islamic, but my

children will know that this has nothing to do with religion. [. . .] There are many religious men who talk about this, that it's not Islam and you know . . . so I don't think anyone would say that I've become more Swedish than Somali, because I don't circumcise my girls."

Another aspect of the matter is the marital patterns of today. Arranged marriages may occur in rural villages in Somalia, but the usual way to form a marriage nowadays is that young people meet, get to know each other, and choose each other as future spouses, whereupon they ask their parents to arrange their marriage. In such marriages there is a mutual sense of trust, where it is unnecessary for the woman to prove her good nature by showing an infibulation. Moreover, many women claim that their unmarried daughters in Sweden have another way of showing courting men that they are trustworthy and have a good personality: simply by refusing to get involved in sexual activities before they are married (see also Johansen, chapter 11 of this volume). A still-unmarried woman, who was already circumcised when she arrived in Sweden as a young teenage girl, expresses it in this way:

Women who live in Sweden should think about raising their girls well, so the girls respect themselves. No circumcision and stuff like that. But make the girls understand the importance of virginity. She can tell the man "I won't sleep with you until we are married," and then he'll know she is a good girl. If she is a good girl she should not [have sex] . . . the most important thing is that she is a virgin. That's what matters. You should wait until you are married, our religion and culture demand that. "I'm not circumcised, but I am virgin and I won't sleep with you until I'm married." I don't think there is any man who would reply "No, I don't want you" . . . no.

Even if a great share of the Somalis in Sweden tend to be oriented toward their own community, they are certainly not isolated from Swedish society; nor are their children. Some women stated that they could never make the decision to have their daughters circumcised while living in Sweden, as this would be a stigma for their daughters in their new society. An important reason for circumcision in Somalia—fear of social criticism—is turned inside out in Sweden. A woman in her thirties, mother of two daughters, explained it in this way: "In Sweden it's easier for uncircumcised girls; no one will tease them and point at them for being different. Here the circumcised girls are the ones to be different and feel ashamed. That's one of the reasons behind my decision to never circumcise my daughters. In this society they would be the ones deviating if I did."

The same woman expressed her feelings of embarrassment when there are articles in Swedish newspapers or reports on television about female circumcision. She says she can imagine how Swedes perceive the tradition: "'How can they do these terrible things to their own daughters?' . . . They don't understand . . . and I can see why." This feeling of being abashed at the existence of the tradition, looking at it with the eyes of the Swedes, appears to be one of the reasons behind some Somalis' strong reactions when their countrymen have appeared in the mass media talking about circumcision: 'Do they have to insist on paying attention to this practice?' Continuous attention will create a bad image of the Somalis in Sweden: portraying them as monstrous people torturing their own flesh and blood (see also Johansen and Johnson, chapters 11 and 9, respectively this volume).

Yet another crucial aspect when it comes to decision making in this field is the widespread and deep fear of the Swedish social authorities, especially among the women, who give the impression of being convinced that their children can be taken away from them by the state for almost any reason. If there are Swedish Somali girls who are at risk of having to go through infibulation, some argue, this procedure would take place in Somalia and these girls would never return to Sweden; their mothers would simply be too afraid of disclosure and of losing custody of all their children. Consequently, it is argued, these hypothetical persons probably refrain from the operation (or postpone it).

Practically all Somalis I have talked to about female circumcision claim that it is important to strengthen discussions leading toward a total abolition of the practice, at least all types more extensive than a symbolic sunnah circumcision. An important aspect of this study is the fact that even if every informant knows a lot about this issue, nobody has all-embracing knowledge of the opinions of Swedish Somalis in general. Somalis talk about female circumcision, but only with their closest friends and kin. There are occasions of larger meetings where this issue has been discussed, but these are extremely few and generally do not include both sexes.

Hence, what I refer to as an internal debate in the Somali community should not be confused with the kind of debate conducted in a Swedish or European "public sphere" of media, experts, politicians, and the public. It is not a debate mainly characterized by open meetings or public writing; rather, the Somali debate is the sum of all the private discussions at the micro-level, involving an individual and her or his closest circle of kin and friends. This lack of a genuine Somali public sphere can explain the curious misperception among some Somalis regarding circumcision, whereby they insist that while they themselves, their spouse, and their close friends are opposed to female circumcision, there may be many other Swedish Somalis who are in favor. It remains an open question how many of these Somalis are in fact supporters of pharaonic circumcision, and how they can be found.

My data indicate that an overwhelming majority of the Somalis in Sweden are truly opposed to pharaonic circumcision, but that many of them themselves are unaware of this fact. They have taken a stand against the practice as individuals, and they have seen their kin and friends take a similar stand, but many of them believe that there are others who still cling to old traditions. These assertions of Somalis about their own community have been based on speculation. This was especially obvious in relation to Somali women's ideas about men's opinions and preferences, and many of the men's assertions that the whole issue is dependent on women's opinions. If Swedes have limited knowledge about Swedish Somalis' opinions regarding female circumcision, so too have the Somalis.

Practically all Somalis I have talked to claim that female circumcision is a redundant practice in Sweden. As long as Somali families do not know whether they will go back to Somalia in the future or keep living in Sweden for a very long time, there is no reason to circumcise the girls. The Swedish Somali girls grow up in a society where they do not run the risk of becoming social outcasts for being uncircumcised, and in the future they will probably marry someone who is familiar with the new view of the practice. Many interviewees even stressed expected future changes in Somalia: they believe that the practice of infibulation already is in decline, or will decline, especially considering that a great number of Somalis live in exile all over the world. In the future, when many of them return, they will bring the new views of the practice into the already changing Somali society, speeding up the process.

MACKIE'S MODEL: FEMALE CIRCUMCISION AS STRATEGY

A key to a more profound understanding of the practice of female circumcision—and also of its abandonment—has been offered by political scientist Gerry Mackie (1996 and 2000). His starting point is that parents all over the world love their children and want to do what is best for them. Female circumcision is to be understood as a strategy, and mothers choosing female circumcision for their daughters in a specific situation are doing so to optimize their daughters' future prospects. This means that mothers choosing female circumcision do so when this option has a better outcome for their daughters than if they (the mothers) decide not to have their daughters circumcised. This also means that mothers will refrain from having their daughters circumcised when giving it up will lead to a better life, all aspects regarded, for their daughters. Mackie's model is instructive in trying to understand both the persistence of circumcision in Somalia and its abandonment among Somalis in Sweden.

Another aspect inherent in Mackie's model is *ambivalence;* it includes both negative and positive feelings toward a phenomenon. Thus, this model can account for the ambivalence surrounding female circumcision in both Somalia and Sweden. A critical question I often encounter at presentations of my empirical data is: "Why would Somalis in Sweden so suddenly have changed their minds and become antagonists of a practice they not long ago advocated?" This view implies that practicing female circumcision in Somalia means favoring all aspects of it, and that refraining from practicing female circumcision in Swedish exile means disliking all aspects of it. In reality, people's views are much more complex and ambivalent, as emphasized in Mackie's model. A more balanced understanding can account for the feelings of relief experienced by Somalis at the possibility of not having to expose one's daughter to female circumcision, and also for feelings of fear about the negative aspects of raising an uncircumcised daughter, especially in a Western society characterized by sexual liberty.

The specific exile situation makes most Somali mothers in Sweden choose strategies other than female circumcision to optimize their daughters' future prospects, as their life circumstances—for instance the role of the clan system and the relation between the sexes—have changed so drastically in exile.

To conclude this section about how Somalis in Sweden reassess the practice of female circumcision, an attempt to summarize the complex processes is presented in Table 5.1. Western ideas about general maintenance of the practice of female circumcision in exile are often put forward with the main argument used that "they do it because it is their culture." I would like to emphasize that the aspects of the "culture" upholding the practice of female circumcision among Somalis in Somalia are context specific—and that each and every one of these aspects is challenged in exile.

In the table, the left-hand column could be seen as the traditional "culture" of Somalis, as described in academic writing on female circumcision in Somalia (for example, Dirie and Lindmark 1991; Gallo and Abdisamed 1985; Ntiri 1991 and 1993; Omar 1991; and Talle 1991and 1993). The right-hand column represents my own conclusions about what Somalis are faced with in their exile life in Sweden. The purpose of the table is to emphasize how altered circumstances and experiences in exile lead to altered values, strategies, and opinions.[7] The statements in the two columns are made at a general level. The motives for circumcision of girls listed in the left-hand column are not universal among Somalis in Somalia; nor do the statements to the right about experiences of exile Somalis in Sweden pretend to include all Somalis on Swedish soil. It is, however, an attempt to illustrate general trends.

THE POLITICS OF FEMALE CIRCUMCISION

Once one has realized that circumcision is a strategy (and not an end in itself, something people do only because it is their "culture" to do so), and that strategies may change when life conditions change, the idea that this practice may be abandoned in exile is not so hard to grasp.

However, since the procedure is constantly presented to the public as a meaningless and cruel archaic cultural trait, there are firm expectations, put forward by authorities, activists, and journalists, that this practice is upheld on a large scale among Somalis in Sweden. In September 2001, a documentary was broadcast nationwide as part of the highly prestigious series *Dokument inifrån* (*Report from Within*): *The Forgotten Girls*. In it, it was alleged that probably thousands of Swedish African girls are circumcised, even if born or raised in Sweden, and that "mutilators" are imported from African countries and go on circumcision tours in Sweden. The program gave rise to a storm in the Swedish mass media and forced politicians and officials to declare with one voice that all steps possible were to be taken to stop this "barbaric" tradition on Swedish soil.[8]

TABLE 5.1

Motives and Circumstances in Somalia and Sweden

Motives for circumcision of girls in Somalia	Circumstances behind changed attitudes in Sweden
• An experience of being circumcised as the "normal" and "natural" state	• The "normality"/"naturalness" of the state becomes questioned when living in exile
• A conviction that Islam demands circumcision	• Encounters with other Muslims (especially Muslim Arabs) not circumcising their daughters → reflection upon Islam and circumcision
• A fear that the daughter will be rejected at marriage	• Changed marital patterns: nowadays young people know each other before marriage. Future husbands can be found among Somali men who have grown up in Western exile
• The fact that practically all other girls are circumcised, which leaves an uncircumcised girl exposed to stigmatization	• In Sweden girls are generally not circumcised → if circumcised, the girl would be the one deviating from most of her peers
• A social context in which female circumcision is widely accepted and not counterchecked by authorities	• A deep fear of Swedish social authorities and the risk of losing custody of the children

Sweden passed the first law on female circumcision in 1982 and became the first Western country to legislate against the practice. In 1998 the law was revised with a change in terminology, from "female circumcision" to "female genital mutilation," and more severe penalties were imposed. The law was further reformulated in 1999 to allow prosecution in a Swedish court against someone carrying out female genital mutilation even if the act was performed in a country where it is not declared criminal. For many years, it has been a general duty for employees in the public sector to report any suspicion of child abuse to the social authorities, a legal obligation overriding the usual professional confidentiality in, for example, the health care system. There is also the more general act stating every citizen's duty to safeguard children. Again, not a single case of female circumcision has been authenticated and brought to court. The Somalis in Sweden number about 20,000, and many of them have lived in Sweden for ten years or more. If female circumcision were as widely practiced as alleged, it would probably have been possible to take at least a few cases to court.[9] The question here, then, is why the belief that thousands of Swedish African girls are being circumcised, or are on the verge of being so, is so firmly rooted. It is a view so strongly accepted that criticism of it is stigmatized as either naïve, immoral, or a bizarre product of cultural relativism.

I argue later in this chapter that possible explanations of this firm belief have their base in a culturalist perspective. This culturalism is combined with a moral discourse, which carries a voyeuristic bent. There is also a structure of actors who benefit, financially, morally, or otherwise, from propagating the view that female circumcision is a practice widely upheld among immigrants in exile.

I would like to point out that the discussion that follows is not intended to argue that *no* Swedish Somali girls are subjected to female circumcision. It is an attempt to analyze some aspects of the public discourse on female circumcision in Sweden. Whether the practice is abandoned or maintained by exiled Africans in Sweden, it is a fact that, up to the present, we lack any documentation of illegal circumcision. Hence, we must try to grasp the basis of this public discourse. If it is not based upon documented cases, what are the motivational powers behind it?

THE ACTORS IN THE FIELD

The moral mission to expose the evil of female circumcision and save the thousands of girls who risk being subjected to circumcision is carried out by a host of actors. Many of these actors articulate positions that tend toward preserving the idea that the practice of female circumcision is widely upheld among exile Africans in Sweden. Each one of these positions is tied up with moral elements, but I have deliberately downgraded these moral characteristics, such as sincere interest or true devotion to the cause, in order to make the structural conditions of each position more evident.

Processes of change often require human commitment—people who want to change a perceived social evil and act accordingly. In Sweden, collective action is organized around voluntary associations, which may receive public funds for all or some of its activities, if the state shares the opinion that their objectives fall under the rubric of dealing with a social problem or cultural issue. This is certainly the case for organizations that work for the elimination of female circumcision, as they touch on the key vulnerable groups and issues of immigrants, children, young girls, and what is regarded as sexual violence.

When it comes to the issue of female circumcision in Sweden, there exist both large and small organizations working for change. Some organizations deal with the issue as one among others, often within a scheme of women's rights. RISK (Riksförbundet Stoppa kvinnlig könsstympning [National Association Stop Female Genital Mutilation]) has initiated projects with informants: Swedish African women who are experts in matters associated with female circumcision and who work as molders of opinion in their own native exile groups. Without intending to denigrate their work in any way, I argue that it is in their interest to claim that many girls in Sweden are at risk of circumcision. If a problem is not serious, then they might risk a decrease in their financial support. When an activist from such an organization tells a journalist that every other girl in Sweden whose parents come from the Horn of Africa is mutilated, she is at the same time optimizing the possibilities for future financing for her organization.[10] Her only risk is a loss of credibility in case someone disproves her statement as an exaggeration. Yet in the morally charged atmosphere of female circumcision there are few people who feel the need to investigate such claims, as this would hardly entail a positive picture in the mass media or parts of the academic world. No journalist or historian achieves prestige by trying to downgrade the scope of a disaster or human tragedy.

Journalists are another group of actors in this field. While I am not trying to generalize about a whole occupational group, there is nevertheless a broad recognition within the mass media that sensational news items generate more publicity than does more balanced coverage. Today's competitive news reporting often demands sharp and simplistic angles and easily comprehensible messages. The titillating story of how the horrible practice of female circumcision is going on right among us is, to many journalists, an irresistible topic, approaching the voyeuristic.

The official posture is that female circumcision is a practice widely maintained in exile; at least this is the conclusion to be drawn as the Swedish National Board of Health and Welfare officially declares that at least 5,000 girls risk being subjected to circumcision.[11] The authority ultimately responsible for the female circumcision issue in Sweden is a department at the national Board of Health and Welfare, the Unit for Individual and Family (Individ- och Familjeenheten). This unit provides one among many voices molding public opinion, but the official statements coming from this department have, naturally, a certain authority. The department allocates funds for a variety of activities concerning women's rights and, like all state departments, grants funds under constant pressure from various lobbying groups. Regional and local authorities may be engaged in this issue as well, organizing seminars or diffusing information to employees in the public sector. All authorities involved must be able to point out an urgent problem, if they are to spend tax revenues, and they must be able to defend the expenditure to higher quarters. Again, it must be reiterated that not a single case of illegal female circumcision has so far been authenticated and brought to court in Sweden, which means that the authorities have to use speculative arguments to justify financing of projects and activities. Stating that thousands of girls *risk* being subjected to circumcision is a quite safe stand, as there is no need to support the statement with identifiable examples. The category of girls who are "at risk" is thus very extensible.

Politicians make up another group of creators of public opinion. The logic inherent in this issue more or less forces a politician to take a moral stand based on the idea that this practice is maintained in Sweden. Relatively few voters seem to care as much about African girls in Africa as about African girls in Sweden; if there are any political points to be made, the issue must be presented as relevant to Swedish society and its citizens. For a politician, the reward is not to be measured in votes as such, but in a gain of moral capital (taking a clear stand on a matter of basic human injustice, which generally leads to a rise in prestige).

There are also some people, project staff and researchers (myself included), who may obtain grants or lecture fees for diffusing information about female circumcision in various settings. Obviously, issues that generate social indignation demand experts who can interpret them, and these experts have an interest in keeping the issue alive.

Clinging to the belief that there is a huge number of girls who risk being subjected to circumcision is beneficial for all those who work in one way or another with the issue. Many people put a lot of effort into this work, most of them idealistically with no economic gain, and I am quite sure that a vast majority is convinced that there really are thousands of girls at risk. But no matter how people think about this at heart, declaring that many girls in Sweden risk being subjected to female circumcision is also a statement that produces short- and long-term benefits for those who propagate such views. Conversely, if authorities were to be convinced (by, say, a group of anthropologists) that this practice more or less vanishes in exile, the resources given today for activities aimed at the elimination of the tradition in exile would probably disappear.

Subsidies from the state and other public institutions contribute in many ways to sustaining female circumcision as a field of political and economic interests as well as scientific inquiry. When one applies for funds, however, some statements are more lucrative than others. Claiming that "resources are needed to help Swedish Somali women who live with medical complications due to infibulation" is not as alarming as "resources are needed to rescue small Swedish Somali girls from genital mutilation." The belief that there are thousands of Swedish girls of African origin who are being subjected to circumcision will probably prosper as long as it is the most profitable statement to make on applications for public funds.

A basic legal principle holds that an individual is presumed innocent until found guilty. For the Somalis in Sweden, however, the entire exile group is tacitly accused of being potential torturers of their own children, with weak or nonexistent support for this allegation. In the culturalist perspective prevalent in Sweden, the behavior of ethnic Swedes is judged on the basis of their individual characteristics and personal social situation, while behavior of people of Somali origin is judged *and predefined* on the basis of the culture they "have."

After the broadcast of *The Forgotten Girls* documentary, the assumption that Swedish Somali girls are being circumcised on a large scale, some of them even in Sweden, will probably be regarded as an established fact.[12] The Somalis have no forum for rejecting this depiction and no way to clear themselves of suspicion. Furthermore, the group, seen as a collective, has come to Sweden relatively recently and has very few representatives within the Swedish political system. Nor does the group have advocates with access to the editorial debates in the newspapers. Thus, Somalis in Sweden have a weak position, struggling to represent views that may countervail the hegemonic discourse about them as a group. There is no way that Somalis in Sweden can defend themselves from such labeling. How can they refute these statements? Certainly not by refraining from circumcising their daughters. Whether they "cling to tradition" or not, in the public eye, they are found guilty.

A CULTURALIST PERSPECTIVE

Culturalism can be understood as a perspective characterized by an understanding of the relations between ethnic groups (majority and minorities) in Western societies in terms of their "culture" (Duffield 1984, cited in Schierup 1993, 165). "All of a sudden, everyone got 'culture,'" as Marshall Sahlins (1999, 401) has framed the general tendency of cultural politics in different settings all over the world.

A kindred aspect of this discussion is when the notion of culture is ascribed properties of agency. "Culture" is seen as an independent intrinsic force in people, a specific set of values that they will not reassess and that guides them toward a specific behavior almost impossible to change. Furthermore, culture is seen as more important in the specific social situation known as "exile," or "migration," because it is something the immigrants "hold onto" in the face of their difficult social situation. Presumptions that immigrants maintain the practice of female circumcision are, in the culturalist view, explained as a way in which people tend to strengthen their traditions living in a foreign country: *they do it because it is their culture, and culture gets more important in exile.* Such reasoning seems to underlie some Swedish scholars' explanations of the persistence of female circumcision. The theologian Hedin is an example: "While there is [cultural] development in the native country, it ceases among the emigrants. They often lack power and education for changing themselves when confronting the new [circumstances]. Instead they stand up for the old [habits/values]. To eliminate all kinds of change, the national traditions are raised to religiously commanded rules. Female circumcision is an example of this" (Hedin 1994, 143, my translation from Swedish).

In *The Forgotten Girls,* the culturalist view was the perspective underpinning the whole narrative. A clip from the trials in France, where West African immigrants were sentenced for practicing female circumcision, was used to illustrate the logic of maintenance of the practice in exile:

[A BLACK MAN shouting in French into the camera:] "What has been sentenced here in France is the African culture. Eight years—for what? This is not a crime. They haven't killed anybody. She [the circumciser] has not killed anybody. Are you supposed to get eight years for circumcision? This is the culture we have!"

This selection of images strengthened the impression of evil Africans, obsessed with cultural ideas, hiding their faces. The Swedish broadcast made no mention of the fact that the trials in France were held against West African immigrants, while the African groups in Sweden come largely from the Horn of

Africa; or that exile groups in France are generally not political refugees but labor immigrants from ex-colonies and, thus, have another history in another host country; or that there are large numbers of French West Africans who bitterly and openly oppose female circumcision.[13] The program gave the impression that if one is African, coming from a country where female circumcision is practiced, one is forced to stick to this cultural practice.

Culture, it seems, inhabits people and forces them to live in accordance with old traditions, especially when groups live in segregation abroad. The statement "There are indications that the strong force of tradition leads parents, coming from countries where genital mutilation is practiced and who have children in Sweden, to persist in maintaining the custom" is found in a government bill presented to the Swedish Parliament (Prop. 1998/99:70, 9, my translation from Swedish). This view gives "culture" a property of agency; "culture" in itself is regarded as sufficient to explain why people do certain things. The anthropologist Jonathan Friedman has argued, "Cultural specificity can never be accounted for in terms of itself. It can never be understood as an autonomous domain that can account for the organization of behavior" (1995, 81). To further emphasize that the understanding of culture must be based upon what people do and not upon a notion of culture as an object, Friedman suggests a reformulation of the concept of culture in terms of a "return to the verb" (ibid., 80).

Friedman's view stands in contrasts to the essentialist view, which sees culture as having a "deeply rooted" static existence inside people. The contrast between the essentialist and the dynamic understandings of culture is also addressed by Gerd Baumann (1999). According to Baumann, there are two basic theories of culture: the *essentialist* one, which is popular in the media and in much political rhetoric, but also among minorities; and the much less popular *processual* theory. Basically, it is a question of whether we see culture as something people "have" or culture as a process shaped by people.

Ellen Gruenbaum, who has conducted research about female circumcision for decades, focusing on Sudan, has come to the conclusion that the culturalist perspective—"'tradition' as the sole explanation" (1996, 456)—is problematic when it comes to efforts to change circumcision practices: "When reformers assume that people follow 'tradition' for no conscious reason, they overlook the complexity of decision-making processes within a culture and the competing demands on individuals (ibid.). Culture is always dynamic, and that is even more the case when the issue at hand is the subject of international controversy, health education, and political discord (Gruenbaum 2000, 51).

In a discussion about female circumcision and about claims that "culture" demands that girls be circumcised, the Norwegian anthropologist Unni Wikan (1995 and 1999) points out that "it," culture, always consists of people's opinions, people's choices, and people's decisions. Wikan is critical of the fact that the culturalist perspective has been utilized in the courts in attempts to justify or "explain" criminal acts, as defenders have pleaded for lenient sentences or verdicts of not guilty as the acts are said to be part of the defendants' "culture."[14] According to Wikan, in a Western society where there are laws against female circumcision, there is no reason to accept justifications of incidents of female circumcision when formulated in terms of "culture" (1996, 58).[15]

Turning Wikan's argument upside down, it is possible to argue that there is no reason to make assumptions about what entire (exile) groups are up to based on what is supposed to be their "culture." Female circumcision, traditionally a taboo topic in Somalia, has been defined as a problem in Western Europe in connection with African immigration, and, thus, becomes a practice reflected upon and debated among exile Somalis.

A related phenomenon is the traditional versus exile contexts of giving birth. According to tradition in Somalia, giving birth is an activity exclusively restricted to the women's sphere. During a study on experiences of pregnancy and delivery (Essén et al. 2000), however, practically all the Somali women who had given birth in Sweden stated that their husbands were present at delivery. Most of them claimed that this was a positive experience; some conveyed that sharing this moment was a good thing, and a few stated that it was good for the husband to really know what women go through during childbirth, a fact that they claimed had made the husband more sensitive to his wife's needs after delivery. According to one of the midwives involved in the state Göteborg Project for preventive work against female circumcision, about 99 percent of the husbands in these groups (groups coming from countries where female circumcision is practiced) are present when their wives give birth.[16] Wiklund et al. (2000) discuss the abandonment of traditional practices in this field, reporting both positive and negative reactions to the husbands' presence in the delivery room among the female and male interviewees in a study about Somalis giving birth in Sweden: "Both women and men explained that childbirth in Somalia is strictly female business in which no men were allowed to participate. Because of the special cultural and social circumstances in Sweden, the Somalian men often behaved as the women's primary support in contact with Swedish maternity and delivery care. In other words, both the woman and the man broke the strong Somali tradition of clear division between female and male spheres" (ibid., 109). In contrast, "childbirth in Somalia is a strictly female matter, carefully hidden by a strong female culture" (ibid., 111).

Here we see again that cultural patterns—even time-honored customs— do not need to be preserved at any cost in new social contexts, even though they have seemed well founded and rational in another context not long ago (and still are considered so by many). Customs do not even have to change slowly—a change may occur quite drastically. Rationales change with changing context, even those grounded in seemingly "fixed" traditional systems, such as "Islam." A qualitative study among Somalis in Canada and London showed how growing opposition to female circumcision revolved to a large extent around new interpretations of an Islamic point of view (McGown 1999 and

2003). Similar processes of change after migration to other Muslim countries have been reported by Fábos (2001) regarding Sudanese people migrating to Cairo and mentioned by Kassamali (1998) regarding Sudanese and Egyptians abandoning the practice at migration to the Gulf States. Morison et al. (2004) on Somalis in London render a more complex picture but largely confirm that migration gives rise to changed attitudes.

In Israel, a study was undertaken in which qualitative interviews were combined with genital examinations. The group studied, Ethiopian Jews (Falashas), claimed they had abandoned the practice at once after migration to Israel, and the researchers could not see any signs of "distress or nostalgia" (Grisaru et al. 1997, 214). The genital examinations, including 113 fertile women, confirmed the abandonment of female circumcision.[17]

It is an essentialist view of culture that lurks behind the culturalist conviction that the practice of female circumcision necessarily is maintained in exile; the only argument used is that "they do it, because it is their culture."

A Moral Discourse

There is an implicit and sometimes explicit moral discourse attached to the issue of female circumcision. Almost any critique can be made if its purpose is to act against a tradition that is deemed harmful or evil. It is not surprising if analyses concerning social and cultural conditions have a moral undertone; such reasoning is always highly dependent on subjective experience and interpretation. But in the field of female circumcision, "hard facts," such as statements about medical consequences of the practice, are also often presented within a moral context.

In the greater part of the literature on female circumcision—in activist as well as many scientific texts—there is a laundry list of medical complications, where some assertions are made without scientific support.[18] Carla Makhlouf Obermeyer has made a thorough scrutiny of medical articles in this field (1999). She concludes that many sources, which have acquired "an aura of dependability through repeated and uncritical citations," in reality suffer from serious shortcomings when it comes to, for example, the methods used in the studies. She had expected to find a wealth of studies documenting mortality and morbidity resulting from female circumcision, but she has to conclude: "This review could find no incontrovertible evidence on mortality, and the rate of medical complications suggests that they are the exception rather than the rule. This should be cause to ponder, because it suggests a discrepancy between the forceful rhetoric, which depicts female genital surgeries as causing death and disease, and the large numbers of women who, voluntarily or under pressure, undergo these procedures" (ibid., 92).

Obermeyer asks herself why the harmful effects of female genital surgeries are so often assumed to be indisputably true, while their occurrence is so poorly investigated. She suggests that "the reasons have to do with political, economic, and ethical factors at both the local and international levels" (1999, 97).[19]

British anthropologist Melissa Parker (1995) presents a similar critique—posing the question of why researchers in this field accept other scholars' deficient studies—and goes on to speculate about what the acceptance of this misuse of scientific tools is really about. She blames the "emotionality of Euro-American-Canadian culture" (1995, 506) and argues that it is necessary to pay attention to the strong emotions attached to the issue of female circumcision, as these emotions influence fieldwork and data analysis. Her own view is that European and North American concepts of sexuality include "a tendency to define the self in sexual terms" (ibid., 518). She points at the symbolic importance of the clitoris among Westerners, a point also made by Obermeyer (1999, 96), Shell-Duncan and Hernlund (2000, 21–22), and Fuambai Ahmadu (2000, 304) among others. Parker concludes that these "intense emotions aroused by the subject among Western researchers are, to a large extent, influenced by Euro-American discourses and debates which have little or nothing to do with the study populations" (ibid., 520). Her point is that scholars conducting research on the biomedical and social aspects of this tradition have to accept these intense emotions and deal with them.

The often cited statement that infibulation leads to prolonged labor, which in turn leads to an increased risk of brain-damaged or malformed infants, is a hypothesis whose casual connection remains to be demonstrated.[20] An attempt to scrutinize some of the facts often cited—perinatal mortality and prolonged labor induced by the scar tissue of infibulation—has been made in a study by Dr. Birgitta Essén, specialist in obstetrics and gynecology at MAS University Hospital in southern Sweden. She found no support for these assertions; at least they are not valid in a country with a high level of medical emergency resources, such as Sweden. Essén compared the actual time of the second stage of labor and found it was actually shorter among infibulated women in comparison with a control group of noncircumcised women (Essén 2001, 157–161; Essén et al. 2005).[21] Being an experienced obstetrician, these findings were not very surprising to her. The scar tissue after an infibulation, provided that the scar has healed well, is more elastic and thinner than scar tissue after episiotomies (where the cut is made in the vaginal birth canal through muscular tissue), which are regularly performed at Swedish hospitals in noncircumcised primigravidae women. Nobody expects *them* to have a prolonged second stage of labor due to scar tissue in the actual birth canal.[22] This is consistent with what WHO states: that there should be no reason for obstructed labor as a result of female circumcision (1998, 42). Cases of perinatally dead infants of infibulated women are more often associated with incidents of mothers refusing cesarean sections or with insufficient obstetric care, such as misinterpretation of intrapartal cardiotocography, or CTG (Essén 2001, 145–153; Essén et al. 2002).[23]

Pointing out that often-cited medical complications of infibulation may be undocumented or exaggerated is not uncontroversial, given the moral discourse on female circumcision. Essén's remarks were presented at an oral defense of a doctor's thesis in September 2001 (Essén 2001), about two weeks after the television broadcast of *The Forgotten Girls*. The whole issue of female circumcision had been highlighted and charged with indignation due to the TV program, and some colleagues at the hospital advised Dr. Essén to tone down her remarks, as the subject was "somewhat delicate." Her colleagues implied that in the eyes of the public she might be categorized as a supporter of a harmful practice. Questioning well-established but poorly supported statements might lead to one being seen as an advocate of this harmful tradition. Medical research highlighting the bad outcomes of this harmful practice is welcomed and seldom questioned, while studies with results contradicting our intuitive ideas may be associated with feelings of uneasiness and suspiciousness about the researcher's moral standard. In this way, moral and medical statements become intertwined.

Certain things should *not* be said, it seems, as the speaker runs the risk of being suspected of inability to grasp the horrible reality of the traditions involving female circumcision. At a conference on FGM in Stockholm (12 October, 2000), a midwife showed pictures of a vagina before and after a defibulation to demonstrate that it is a minor operation at a gynecological clinic. A woman in the audience, who had met many infibulated women in her work in public health, stated—completely unconscious of the prevalent moral discourse surrounding the issue: "Circumcisers seem to know what they're doing, they don't damage the birth canal and so on, this area often looks fine." I interpreted her utterance as stating an experience from her field, while at the same time trying to console infibulated women in the audience. Immediately another woman stood up to reprimand her, talking about half-blind circumcisers cutting through urethra, vagina and rectum. Turning to the audience she rebuked the woman as if she were an errant child: "Your description sounded so good. But it *must not* be described in that way."

It is hazardous to refute generalized, "self-evident," statements in public. They counter most people's intuitive, and often morally charged, views about the consequences of such brutal practices: "Of course going through something like that gives a girl psychological problems!" (regarding critiques of statements about psychological disorders as an almost automatic result of female circumcision). And "Isn't it bad enough if only one girl dies?" (on highlighting the fact that there is no reason to list "death" as a common consequence of female circumcision, as long as there only exists anecdotal evidence and no established relation between the practices and mortality; see, for example, WHO 1998, 41). The result of such generalized statements is that practically all circumcised women are tacitly categorized as suffering from psychological disorders, and African parents who have their daughters circumcised are depicted as people who do not care whether their children live or die. Nevertheless, a critic appears as a person completely indifferent to the suffering resulting from female circumcision. Almost anything about the horrifying consequences of these practices can be alleged in the public discourse without evidence to support it; those who question the statements and refute them with actual findings will automatically appear to be devoid of empathy.

An example of the moral-ideological-political tension in the discourse on female circumcision is the discussion about "symbolic sunnah," pricking, in Sweden. The official posture in Swedish society is that the law against female genital mutilation in Sweden includes a ban on pricking. According to the law, all procedures leading to permanent changes of the female genitals, performed for other than medical reasons, are illegal, regardless of the age of the female.[24] There is no way to know exactly what this law permits and forbids, as it has never been applied. Pricking the clitoris to induce minor bleeding does not, generally speaking, lead to permanent changes. Besides that, such a procedure is far less invasive than what is done to male infants at Swedish hospitals during male circumcision and what is permitted on young women who have their genitals pierced, as well as on women who go through genital plastic surgery.[25] In a strictly medical sense, then, there is no reasonable motive to forbid pricking of girls' genitalia while permitting male circumcision, genital plastic surgery, and genital piercing for aesthetic or erotic reasons. Yet the public posture in Sweden is that pricking is forbidden according to Swedish law.[26]

The motive behind choosing to label pricking as a form of mutilation seems to be ideological, originating from feminist politics. The Swedish law is formulated in accordance with the WHO classification (which includes "pricking" in category IV), a classification that is a result of radical feminist lobbying. There are some practical reasons for taking a stand against symbolic sunnah circumcision; for example, if the legislation allows a symbolic pricking, there is a risk that more extensive operations will be performed under the pretense of being just "symbolic." There would probably not be much risk if these procedures were performed at a Western hospital. The reason for allowing and performing male circumcision at hospitals while forbidding female symbolic sunnah circumcision is, then, purely ideological. It reflects a prohibition against any contact with girls' genitals, a prohibition by which any such contact is an abuse.

Another aspect of the public attitude has to do with a desire among some of the activists and officials to educate African immigrants morally in Sweden; this is often expressed in terms of what kind of "signals" Swedish society ought to give the exile communities. Activists and officials dealing with the issue of female circumcision sometimes articulate the idea that "we" have to teach "them" basic facts about bodily integrity. This whole discussion about symbolic sunnah circumcision and the comparatively prosaic way in which male circumcision, genital piercing, and plastic surgery are dealt with complicates the enterprise of teaching this basic morality. In discussions about my Somali informants' views with Swedish activists—particularly the Somalis' opposition to genital mutilation but more accepting views of symbolic sunnah circumcision—I sometimes encounter reactions stating that if I talk about a widespread opposition to female genital mutilation, while not including pricking, I may be sending "hazardous signals" to the Somalis. Revealing the nuances of the circumcision debate may be interpreted as condoning an immoral practice.

We thus see the potential explosiveness of the circumcision issue in Western societies. Some things need to be said; other things must not be said for fear of giving the wrong signals. Symbolic sunnah circumcision is not illegal in Sweden, if one reads what is really stated in the act on FGM. Yet no Swedish official or activist could ever publicly say, "If you want to have your girls go through a symbolic sunnah circumcision, go ahead." The public posture then, is to pretend that the legislation includes a prohibition of pricking.

Along the same line, there is an overwhelming force attached to the belief that thousands of girls risk being subjected to female circumcision. A person who criticizes a harmful practice will automatically be categorized by most people as a good human being with a high level of morality. This logic holds, regardless of whether there are any victims at hand. Claiming that five thousand girls in Sweden risk being subjected to female circumcision is an act of moral goodness. There is no need to scrutinize the figures, it seems, as the estimates are made for a "good cause."

A VOYEURISTIC BENT

Among writers with a background in medicine, there is a tradition of giving vivid descriptions of incidents of female circumcision. Early medical accounts have provided a voyeurist Western gaze . . . "sanitised through a medical discourse" (Kirby 1987, 37, quoted in Shell-Duncan and Hernlund 2000, 18). The most famous example is perhaps the article published by Worseley, a male gynecologist who worked in Sudan in the 1930s, in the *British Journal of Obstetrics and Gynaecology:* "The naked girl is laid across a bed, being securely held by the arms and ankles, while the midwife, with a deft sweep of the razor, removes the anterior two-thirds of one of the labia, together with the clitoris. The unfortunate girl's shrieks are drowned by loud shouts of 'That's nothing to make a fuss about!'—and the midwife proceeds the other labium in the same way. There is always a sadistic smile of delight upon the face of the operator, and the whole business is thoroughly enjoyed by the privileged spectators" (Worseley 1938, 687).

This description displays several themes central to a discussion about voyeurism. Traditionally the term "voyeurism" is applied to describe a sexual perversion: some people get sexually excited by watching other people's sexual activities. The term as used here will have a wider meaning. Here the subject does not aim at sexual excitement; it is a more general state that includes sensations of curiosity, amazement, and thrill. The object is not purely sexual by nature, but involves traits of exoticism and evil as well.

The Swedish state aid agency SIDA (Swedish International Development Cooperation Agency) published an information booklet about female circumcision in 1979. It is one of the few texts written about female circumcision in Swedish and is therefore, despite its age, widely used by the innumerable students all over the country who write their papers in anthropology, public health, cultural studies, and so forth about female circumcision. The descriptions of circumcisions carry morally charged formulations such as: "Analgesia and hygiene are not priorities" (Halldén 1979, 22, my translation from Swedish). This specific article continues by quoting another article by Jacques Lantier, commenting that most descriptions of operations in the literature "are as good as identical" (Halldén 1979): "The little girl screams from extreme pain, but nobody cares. . . . If the girl faints, the women blow *pilipili* (spice powder) into her nose to wake her up. But this is not the end of the torture. The most important part of the operation starts now. After a short break the operator takes up the knife again and cuts away the labia minora, without taking the slightest consideration to the tremendous pain she inflicts on the girl" (Lantier, quoted in Halldén 1979, 22–23, my translation from Swedish).

One may claim that these stories are "true," as they portray real events and mirror the horrifying reality of many girls' experiences. Yet there are as many stories about female circumcision as there are girls being circumcised. Postmodernist critiques of generalizations in social science have led to an upswing of narratives in ethnographic writing. Commenting on the apparent particularity of such narratives, D'Andrade (referring to Burke 1945) argues that "the world is 'summarized by' and 'reduces to' the story one tells about it" (1995, 405); that is, we are dealing here with "reductive anecdotes." A story in this genre—about a specific girl at a specific point of time—makes generalizing statements about what takes place at circumcisions: a single anecdote represents the entire spectrum. In the field of female circumcision, such stories fit well with a more comprehensive scheme of "the enlightened world and the dark continent" (Shweder 2002, 229), where Africans choosing circumcision for their daughters are depicted as uneducated, ignorant, and in acute need of Western enlightenment (ibid., 229–231).

In its typical form, the anecdote of female circumcision only captures the worst-case scenarios (Obiora 1996, 53). It is little wonder that descriptions involving sadistic circumcisers are popular. They have elements of mythological tales of innocent victims and evildoers. These "horror stories," while illustrating a practice and entertaining or thrilling the reader, also serve to localize and personalize the source of the evil: a practice involving so much suffering and pain must have an evil agent. Fran Hosken (for example, 1993 and 1994) and other radical feminist writers, who entered the stage with a strong ideological framework before other researchers challenged their perspective, announced the global male collective as the source of the evil, and this explanatory model still has a stronghold in the public understanding of these practices. In a simplified version of the radical feminist model, the mothers involved are not the real co-conspirators: they are victims with false consciousness. In much of the Western discourse, however, it is not only a matter of indicating Somali exiled women as "mutilated"; there is also the image of them as "mutilators." These are allegations about "disgusting practices" taking place "in our very midst," among "our own" citizens and residents.

The closer the perpetrators, or practitioners of evil, come, the trickier it gets to label them as evil. This is what happens when African groups, such as Somalis, come to live in a Western society such as Sweden. What makes some public descriptions "politically correct," in spite of their obvious attacks on already marginalized groups in the Swedish society, is their localization of evil: they generally do not in any explicit way ascribe evil intentions to the Swedish African parents. Instead, "religious leaders" and evasive "mutilators" are the ones to blame for these evil deeds—helping to picture ordinary Swedish Africans as victims of religious submission and sociocultural pressure.

In Somalis' own accounts of circumcision, as is evident in the empirical data from this study, there is no intent to localize the evil. Their accounts may describe pain, suffering, and agony—but a mother is often pictured as "good," a father as "good" or absent, and the circumcisers as people doing their job. My Somali informants' accounts reveal a more nuanced experience of circumcision practices in all their complex dynamics. What makes Swedish and Somali discourses about circumcision so different is their attribution of agency and power. Swedish, and Western in general, public discourses on this practice desperately seek the source of evil, while narratives of Somali origin generally display a more varied and complex depiction of what happens when girls undergo this procedure.

Western interest in these practices has often been expressed in an objectifying way, rendering an image of a circumcised woman as someone essentially different from "us" as she is "genitally mutilated" and often even alleged to be "deprived of her sexuality" (see Ahmadu and Dopico, chapters 12 and 10 respectively of this volume). It is a process of objectification that in a way reduces the woman to the mutilated organs (see, for example, Shell-Duncan and Hernlund 2000; also Rogers, chapter 6 of this volume). The Norwegian anthropologist Aud Talle (2001) also highlights this, when she describes the experiences of Somali women in London. Being circumcised was once a sign of social solidarity and has now become a sign of difference: "In their circumcised state they are pointed out and marginalized as incomplete and inferior women. In the streets of London, the Somali women 'are' no longer 'in the world' (Merleau-Ponty, quoted in Csordas 1994) with a body perfect in form, as they used to be in the savannah in Somalia. Now they walk around as 'defects,' a mutilated soul in a mutilated body" (Talle 2001, 31, my translation from Norwegian; see also Talle, chapter 4 of this volume).

For individual women, this experience of being outsiders is most tangible and painful (Talle 2001, 31). With the migration from African countries to Western countries, this process of objectification, from a Western perspective directed toward African women, takes place in the same geographical area; it is no longer a matter of "us" here describing "them" over there. In a column with the head-line "Glittering Journalism or Gleaming Victim Porno?" a debater and stand-up comedian, Shabana Rehman, comments on a Norwegian televised documen-tary about female circumcision among Norwegian Africans: "They used to be-lieve that we were beaten black and blue every day. Now they believe none of us have a clitoris" (2000, my translation from Norwegian). Some scholars have reacted to this situation: "Can it possibly be a good thing for thousands of Afri-can immigrants who must soak in images of their nether regions literally spread open in 'education' pamphlets, women's magazines and so-called documentaries for the modern world to ponder?" (Ahmadu 1995, quoted in Shell-Duncan and Hernlund 2000, 19). This everyday voyeurism is excused by a perceived need to inform people about this practice: only if we know about it we can fight it—we must not hush this issue up, that would be to let potential victims down.[27]

I argue that this kind of interest in the topic is voyeuristic, because it in-volves certain ingredients specific to the realm of peeping on the sly: the issue involves genitals, it is exotic and spectacular. It helps keep the conviction alive that there are thousands of girls who are at risk of being subjected to circumci-sion. Highlighting this kind of topic may be considered unethical, if it were not for the perceived urgent need to deal with this issue. Our locally based fascina-tion with the subject is justified by the allegation that this is a practice main-tained in exile. The same moral warrant was at work when Swedish national television exploited the subject with a poorly researched program: it broadcast this program for the sake of the "forgotten" girls.

Even when no evidence that the practice is maintained in exile can be presented, material from other parts of the world is used instead, for instance in televised documentaries. There is an abundance of films, pictures, and narratives of female circumcision at an international level that can be used to thrill West-ern citizens with the claims that this is going on right here in our own society. Our interest in the issue of female circumcision, an interest of an unmistakable voyeuristic bent, can only be explained if we can claim that it has its basis in a true concern about Swedish African girls. Being a voyeur is an unpleasant trait, while being committed to saving girls who risk being subjected to mutilation is a respectable mission. If it could be proven that the practice of female circum-cision tends to vanish in Swedish exile, the public interest in the topic would seem somewhat misplaced.

This is not to argue that seminars on female circumcision should be abol-ished, or that no programs or popular articles on the topic ought to be published. Nor is it an attempt to claim that no Swedish Somali girls are circumcised. But there is reason to be aware of the connection between everyday voyeurism and our moralistic attempts to excuse this interest by invoking some higher purpose. The practices of female circumcision are associated with titillating ingredients in-volving ideas of evil, the exotic Other, sex, and genitals. The locally based interest in these components becomes socially acceptable only when we can legitimize it by talking about thousands of girls who risk being subjected to circumcision. Thus, we take on a mission before we have analyzed the scope of the problem.

CONCLUSION

Anticircumcision campaigns in Sweden may have had considerable effects in Somali groups, for example, when it comes to informing immigrants about medical consequences of the practice and spreading awareness about the Swedish law against female circumcision. However, there have been no follow-up studies to measure the results—that is, to determine whether attitudes in the target groups have changed. Consequently, the figures for girls who risk being subjected to circumcision in Sweden have been adjusted upward rather than downward during these years; adjusting for the influx of African immigrants but not taking into consideration the effect of campaigns and, even less, what have been the results of the internal debate within the Somali community.

Such an attitude from official quarters may be counterproductive in the preventive work against female circumcision in Sweden. One aspect of Mackie's (1996 and 2000) model on conventions and convention shifts, an aspect that deserves some reflection, is that the tipping point—the moment when the great mass becomes aware of the overwhelming advantages of giving up a practice—is advanced to an earlier point in time through educational campaigns. But the motivational power of the process itself, resulting in a convention shift, depends on estimations about what decisions "all the others" take at the same time. In Sweden, this process may be complicated by the fact that there are activists, officials, and journalists who constantly assert that female circumcision is a practice upheld among Swedish immigrants and even takes place in Sweden. A better way to deal with the situation would be to establish—through research—that an overwhelming majority of the people involved have reached the conclusion that female circumcision ought to be abandoned. Such a public message (what kind of "signals" to give to the exile groups) would probably encourage the minority of Somalis still in favor of the practice to dissociate themselves from the practice.

Today's policies and measures all over Europe are concerned with anxious estimations of numbers of girls who risk being subjected to circumcision. Before more campaigns are launched, there is an obvious need for more insights into what happens to female circumcision in different exile contexts—and there is a need to sort out the discourses about the issue. Renouncing culturalist, morally charged, voyeuristically tinted, stigmatizing standpoints will certainly facilitate a complete abandonment of female circumcision among Somalis in Western exile.

NOTES

1. For further presentation of the study, see Johnsdotter (2002) in English, Omar et al. (2001) in Somali, and Johnsdotter et al. (2000) in Swedish.

2. Among Somalis, there are basically two distinct concepts of female circumcision. Pharaonic circumcision is equivalent to infibulation. Sunnah circumcision covers all other types, ranging from a symbolic pricking of the clitoris or its foreskin to procedures that resemble infibulation.

3. Among the Somalis in Malmö, however, it seems as if some of these beliefs are discussed more openly today, even if it still is a delicate topic.

4. According to the letter of the law, this procedure is not criminalized. In official interpretations of the law, however, the procedure is classified as illegal (further discussed later in this chapter).

5. For a brief account of the governmental campaign in Somalia in the 1980s, see, for example, Dorkenoo (1994, 118f).

6. Also, many health care professionals seem to have been perplexed trying to understand what they were confronted with. Several women have told me about how they were questioned by the doctor trying to understand what had happened to them, for example, asking if the genitals had been accidentally burned.

7. In a study about medical complications arising from female circumcision, twenty-nine Swedish Somali girls aged thirteen to twenty were interviewed (Ismail 1999). Twenty-two had been circumcised (fourteen of these infibulated). "The remaining four [of the uncircumcised girls] had been born in Somalia but had left the country at an early age before they would normally be circumcised (two to five years old). The twenty-two girls who had been circumcised had migrated when they were older (seven to sixteen years old)" (ibid., 16). Even if it is impossible to draw any conclusions from such a limited number of informants, the obvious tendency in the material is that growing up in Sweden from an early age enhances the girls' opportunity to escape the procedure of circumcision.

8. In reality, evidence presented in the documentary was indeed fragmentary and brittle. For a critical analysis of the allegations in the documentary, see Johnsdotter (2002).

9. In 2003 a study was undertaken in five EU member states to investigate how legislation regarding unlawful female circumcision is implemented (Leye and Deblonde 2004). The Swedish part of the study included all police reports dealing with suspected cases of female circumcision through the years, including "hearsay cases" reported by interviewed health care providers, social workers, municipal legal experts, hospital legal experts, police officers, and other key actors working in the field in Sweden (Johnsdotter 2004). In most cases, it could be established that no circumcision had been performed. In other cases, it seemed unlikely, and in a few cases there was a possibility that illegal female circumcision had been performed but no way to prove it. The large share of unfounded suspected cases shows that the level of alertness is high in Sweden. It is unlikely that there is a substantial, but hidden, incidence of female circumcision, since most cases handled by the authorities turn out to be groundless.

10. "She [an activist] estimates that as many as every other girl with parents from Eritrea, Somalia and Ethiopia is genitally mutilated—even if they were born in Sweden" (Vallgren 2001).

11. One of the later estimations suggests that 7,500 to 8,000 girls in Sweden are at risk. The basis for the figures is the number of girls aged from infancy to twenty in Sweden who come from countries where more than 60 percent of the women are circumcised (Olsson 2000, 4694).

12. Without any further commentary, a journalist gives the following depiction of Swedish Africans (Somalis) in an editorial column in Sweden's most important daily paper: "It is not Anders and Greta Svensson [names representing 'typical Swedes'] who have their five-year-old daughter circumcised on the kitchen table, by a Somali circumciser on tour in Sweden" (Kjöller 2002, my translation from Swedish). This allegation about African circumcisers touring Sweden is highly improbable simply on the grounds that Swedish regulations regarding tourists from Africa are extraordinarily strict. It is

practically impossible for an African person, resident in Africa, to obtain even a short tourist visa to Sweden.

13. For accounts of the cases of female circumcision in France, see Bloul (1996); Gallard (1995); and Winter (1994). France is, to the best of my knowledge, the only Western country where cases of female circumcision among immigrants have been documented and taken to court.

14. The American political scientist Susan Moller Okin has also warned against too loose and instrumental a use of the concept of "culture," arguing for instance that "the self-proclaimed leaders of a cultural group are in no way representative of all or even most of its members" (Okin 1999a, 121).

15. For a review of the culturalist arguments used in the French trials on circumcision, see Winter (1994).

16. In 1993, the Swedish Board of Health and Welfare initiated a three-year-project called "Health Promoting Measures for Women and Children: Prevention of Female Genital Mutilation." The project was in response to increasing needs from officials and school staff, health care staff, and other professionals who come in contact with a growing number of immigrants from countries where female circumcision is practiced (above all, Somalis). The project, run by the Immigrant Service Administration of Göteborg, had the aim of creating methods for prevention of FGM and working for adequate care of circumcised women in Sweden.

17. Approximately 85,000 Ethiopian Jews live in Israel today. A majority were transferred from Ethiopia by the Israeli state during Operation Moses in 1984–85, Operation Salomo in 1991, and Operation Quara in 1999 (Wymark 2003).

18. The expression "laundry list" is from Shell-Duncan and Hernlund (2000, 15), discussing the "recitation of short-term, long-term, and obstetrical complications" (ibid., 14) in the activist literature.

19. See also Obiora (1997 and 1996) for critical discussion.

20. This alleged causal connection has been widely spread by Fran Hosken among others (for example, Koso-Thomas 1987, 27). In *The Universal Childbirth Picture Book,* translated into French, Arabic, and Somali, there are pictures in the study material, including a drawing of a hand holding a vigorous newborn, below which there is a drawing showing a hand holding a lifeless baby: "In the top row is a happy, lively, newborn baby delivered by a mother with natural genital organs. The pictures below show a baby delivered by an excised mother. She had to be cut open to let the baby out. The baby is limp and its head is flattened. Will it be able to live?" (F. P. Hosken 1995).

21. An average of thirty-four minutes was found in the group of circumcised women having their first baby (n83), fifty-three minutes in the group of uncircumcised women having their first baby (n2779, Essén 2001, Essén et al. 2005). In our study (Essén et al. 2000) the women did not associate their circumcision with experiences during delivery. This overall depiction is supported by a study by Wiklund et al. (2000): "All the women in the study were circumcised and the majority did not relate complications during delivery to this fact" (ibid., 108).

22. Personal communication from Dr. Essén to author (December, 15 2001).

23. Cardiotocography is a technique for monitoring the rate of the baby's heart in relation to the contractions of the delivering mother's uterus during labor (personal communication from Dr. Birgitta Essén to author, September 18, 2001).

24. Law (1982:316 is a prohibition of genital mutilation of women. Revision of the law took place on July 1, 1998 (SFS 1998, 407): "1§. A procedure involving the external genitals aiming at mutilating these or at bringing about other permanent changes of them (genital mutilation) must not be performed, whether or not there is consent to the procedure" (my translation from Swedish).

25. See Atoki (1995, 233) and Ivan (1997, 71) for a similar argument. Regarding piercing, the Swedish National Board of Health and Welfare recommends a minimum age of eighteen years to piercing establishments. The general acceptance of male

circumcision at the same time that symbolic pricking is labeled "mutilation" is discussed by the Danish historian of religion Helle Hinge (1995) as a result of the fact that the Western world accepts the religious foundation of the practice of male circumcision, for example, in Judaism—while female circumcision is established outside the Judeo-Christian cultural sphere (ibid., 30).

26. "According to the law all types of female genital mutilation are illegal, ranging from the most extensive, where large parts of the genitals are cut away and the vaginal opening is stitched together (infibulation), to pricking of the clitoris with a sharp or pointed object" (information sheet from the Gothenburg Project, my translation from Swedish). See also the government bill, Prop. 1998/99:70, 8.

27. In the Swedish context, one of the loudest-voiced activists is an EU commissioner and former member of the Swedish parliament. In one of her debate articles she discourses on about clitoris and labia being "carved out" in this "torture," and implicitly she describes African mothers as evil, while emphasizing that shutting one's eyes to this torture would be to abandon all the Swedish African girls who are being subjected to mutilation (Theorin 2001).

CHAPTER 6

Managing Cultural Diversity in Australia

LEGISLATING FEMALE CIRCUMCISION, LEGISLATING COMMUNITIES

Juliet Rogers

For the purposes of the *National Agenda,* multiculturalism is defined as a policy for "managing the consequences of cultural diversity in the interests of the individual and society as a whole."

—Family Law Council's statements in reference to federal government's *National Agenda for a Multicultural Australia* (Family Law Council 1994b, 30)

IN 1993, THE practices of female circumcision appeared in Australian newspapers as an issue to be attended to on Australian shores. In 1996, "female genital mutilation"[1] was legislated as a criminal act in Australia under the Crimes (Female Genital Mutilation) Act 1996. In this chapter I will argue that the move to legislate, and the process that resulted in the implementation of the legislation—known to some as "consultation"—enabled the representation of particular cultural groups in Victoria as people who were socially and politically mutilated in terms of their capacity to speak for or about issues related to female circumcision, or indeed to represent themselves. Further, I will argue, it enabled the construction of "others"[2] in Australia as "violent" and in need of "management," thereby justifying legislative processes both past and pending. It also contributed to the representation of the 1996 law as an entity essential to the protection of women and, perhaps indirectly, the Australian population "as a whole" (Family Law Council 1994b, 4). However, as I will argue in this chapter, the movements toward and subsequent implementation of the legislation on female circumcision were not strategies for "managing the consequences of cultural diversity"; rather, they were strategies to represent "cultural diversity"—broadly understood as a divergence from

135

the dominant culture—as forms of dangerous and barbaric acts, and therefore something to be managed.

In this chapter I will initially describe the strategic development and implementation of the Crimes (Female Genital Mutilation) Act 1996 and later explain this strategy within the context of the historical and contemporary management strategies applied to both Aboriginal people and immigrant communities in Australia. In doing so, I want to emphasize the distinction between the types of engagement that might be considered a relationship of respect and management strategies that are spectacularly not about a relationship of respect, but are instead about the management of people who are other than the dominantly Anglo, Christian-identified (if not defined) population in Australia, in order to regulate, and indeed assimilate, their differences in ways that have been described by Sanjay Seth, in relation to (multi)culturalism, as "domestication" (Seth 2001, 74). In this chapter I employ the term "management" to best describe a dynamic between the dominant culture in Australia, which, through the implementation of the legislation on "female genital mutilation," exemplifies and reifies the right of white Australians and Australian systems to manage Australia's social and political space, simultaneously defining "others" as people requiring management. I will argue that the processes of "consultation" and the implementation of the Crimes (Female Genital Mutilation) Act 1996 exemplify the assertion of this right in legal, social, and political domains.

To best illustrate and unpack some of the methods of management applied to people considered "other," I will focus on the work of the African Women's Working Group (AWWG), the Eritrean Women's Group (EWG), and the Family Law Council.[3] I will discuss some of the processes of consultation, research, and advocacy employed by these groups with an aim to exhibiting the silencing of the EWG and AWWG, and the power to produce others as silent, enacted by the Family Law Council. I will also examine aspects of the Victorian political and social climate of the 1980s and 1990s that enabled the conception and implementation of the legislation in relation to "FGM" or "female genital mutilation." This focus will enable an exposition of the role of the Family Law Council in providing the framework for the development of the legislation. It will be argued that the work of the Family Law Council existed within a system that reifies the silencing of the voices of community organizations such as the AWWG and EWG in Victoria. This silencing enabled the management of complicated, and arguably dangerous, cultural divergences to be delivered to the Australian public. I will also explain the significance. within this system and in the current political contexts, of the representation of these divergences as Muslim.[4]

The processes of the Family Law Council, the EWG, and the AWWG could in one sense be seen as exclusive mechanisms operating with their own agendas and frameworks. This view, however, does not consider the necessary interrelatedness of language and power, as discussed by Michel Foucault (1990, 93–102), which (re)produces discourse in an *always already* existing system of meaning production. It is my argument, therefore, that the social, political, and economic factors that both enabled and resisted the work of these organizations are intertwined and informed by each other through sites of discursive encounter. I do not suggest that these sites represent "pluralism." As I will explain later, a dialogue amongst equal representatives was never possible. Rather, I argue that the existence and performance of the various groups informed each other, along with the many other entities speaking about the practices of female circumcision in the Western world.[5]

In this chapter I will use the work of Ghassan Hage to explain some of the languages and legal gestures that surround female circumcision as ways of representing "others" within social, political, and legal discourses as objects—or perhaps even noncitizens—requiring management (Hage 1998, 42–44). I will argue that this management was—and arguably still is—achieved through processes that can be called domestication. That is, similar to the "assimilation" strategies of earlier Australian governments, women who are described as "mutilated women" by the Family Law Council in Australia, are represented as objects to be managed. It is the processes of representation, the ways and means that the languages around female circumcision in Australia are enacted, that can be called "domestication." The very term "mutilated women" already assumes that there is a "whole" woman somewhere, a woman against whom the other can be measured. This "whole" woman becomes the center, the yardstick of what is a "woman." As Chandra Talpade Mohanty has discussed, the "third-world woman" inhabits the margins of the discourses of the West, in order that a Western self/identity can be produced (1994, 215–216). And for Gayatri Spivak, this "third world woman" is measured against the Western woman as a whole "individual" (1985, 246). This process enables Western legal representatives to be produced in a particular role, with a particular identity. They are managers, that is, as nonmutilated; and "mutilated women" become objects to be managed.

The task of this chapter is both to examine the production of "others" as nonspeaking objects, as "mutilated women," and to displace the notion of the "mutilated woman," fixed and silent, by speaking of the work and resistance of the EWG and the AWWG. When "the other" speaks, she/he displaces and disturbs both her or his representation in the West and representations of the Western self. In utilizing the published and unpublished writings and discussions of the AWWG and EWG, I will explore the varied meanings of responses to the representation of "female genital mutilation" in Victoria, examine the implicit and explicit practices of silencing and producing the voices of group members (both individually and collectively) as objects, and emphasize the diversity of opinions and responses to the practices of "female circumcision."[6] Further, I aim to document the work of these groups in order to highlight the dynamism of cultural practices and dialogues that exist within African communities in Victoria, thereby undermining the notion that those who embody "diversity" are a monolithic entity whose dimensions are only a reflection of a Western gaze, and—in the discourses of "female genital mutilation"—mutilated objects to be managed.

COURTING EXPERTISE: THE MAKING OF MANAGEMENT

By the late 1980s, the migration of people from the Horn of Africa to Australia was well established. Communities of people from Eritrea, Sudan, Somalia, and Ethiopia—including Hararian and Oromian—were becoming both socially and politically visible as groups with needs and voting power, particularly in local electorates. By the early 1990s, the various communities had their own consultative mechanisms to discuss contentious issues. One of these issues was female circumcision.

Debates around female circumcision had gone largely unnoticed by the Australian media and were not present in Australian legal discourse until the 1990s. Yet for many generations in Africa, the practices have been evolving and dissolving into various forms, through dynamic discussion and complex cultural developments that are both internally and externally influenced. "Activism" by people working for the discontinuation of the practices in their own culture was well established in many cultures both before and after migration to Australia. The debates had long been present in the relevant communities before their migration to Australia in the 1980s and 1990s, and certainly long before the Family Law Council recommended legislation as a necessary "first step in the educative process" (1994, 50). Such a recommendation immediately represented African communities as either unaware of or intransigent on the issues, and the Family Law Council as a necessary entity to lead the way.

Giving lie to this representation, the Eritrean Women's Group was formed in the late 1980s in response to the needs of a large number of Eritrean women migrating to Australia. The group's aim was to respond to the social and psychosocial needs of Eritrean women. It was also a forum for women to continue to discuss both opposition to and desire for the continued practice of female circumcision. In 1988, representatives of the EWG began approaching Victorian organizations to sponsor projects around issues related to female circumcision for Horn of African women in Victoria. While the EWG group was arguably already engaged in an educative framework in the form of dialogue and debate, it was neither an incorporated nor authorized organization in Victoria, and was not itself able to secure funding for its work until several years later.

Before funding was secured, however, the EWG had already developed many formal and informal mechanisms to engage Horn of African communities in Melbourne in questioning the continuation of the practices. These mechanisms were well established and were readily formulated into an official proposal. In 1992, the EWG documented and implemented the Eritrean Women's Project. This was a three-pronged project, with a primary focus on community education about issues related to female circumcision. The aim was to enhance the dialogue between women from Eritrea about the importance of ceasing the practice of female circumcision. In 1996, when the project was evaluated, the authors stated that the aim of strategies developed by the group were "to ensure that the practice [referred to as 'female circumcision'] did not continue" (Adams et al.1996, 2). The second element of the project was dialogue with Western medical personnel who were seeing women from the Horn of Africa for pre- and postnatal care. The third element—education of the broader Australian community—would become a major focus for the group in 1993, when the broader Australian community responded, at times with vitriol, to the issue's very presence in Victoria.

In 1993, the issue of the infibulation of two Eritrean girls was brought to the attention of the courts and the Australian media. In an investigation by Community Service Victoria (CSV)—later the Department of Human Services (DHS)—in relation to suspected child abuse, it was discovered, through medical examinations, that the girls had been infibulated. The children's father was charged with child abuse, and the case went to court. The Australian media, and particularly the Melbourne media, were not interested, however, in the various "standard" forms of child abuse that had allegedly been perpetrated on the children—only in their infibulation. Indeed, the case was described in the media as the "child abuse/infibulation case," thereby conflating the two terms, or certainly investing them with the same significance.

The media's reporting of this case was instrumental in constructing many of the meanings of infibulation as associated with violence and "barbarism."[7] The children's infibulation was always—in the media's representation—a mutilation. This representation both reflected and reproduced the subsequent privileging of the knowledge of Western legal and medical experts to speak about the meanings—both contemporary and historical—of female circumcision/"female genital mutilation." It followed that if one was to understand the practices of circumcision as a "mutilation," then one would already be knowledgeable. If we analyze this representation within a Foucauldian frame, we can employ what Foucault described as the "power, right, truth triangle" (Foucault 1980, 93), in which the power to know the "truth" on a particular issue and to inform meaning production is attributed to entities—in this case the Family Law Council—whose arguments already articulate with the dominant position on "female genital mutilation." The dominant position is, of course, authorized by those who believe themselves to know the truth, which is attributed to those who hold a powerful social/political position. In white Australia, this is undeniably held by representatives of the British legal system.

The prejudice exercised in the privileging of Western legal knowledge because of the already assumed knowledge of Western legal experts and anti-FGM activists became clear at this time in relation to the positioning of a group calling itself Women Lawyers against Female Genital Mutilation (WLAFGM). WLAFGM and its assumed expertise were sanctioned by the magistrate in this case, enabling legal representatives to cross-examine witnesses from this group and to offer their knowledge to the court in relation to "female genital mutilation." The members of the group described themselves as a "friend of the court" (Pegler 1993, 1). Their expertise was not derived from any experience of the practices or from formal study. No member of the group was from a community, or even a country, that practiced female circumcision. As is apparent in the statement of the expertise and objectives present in the group's title, they were women, they were lawyers, and they were against "female genital mutilation"; this apparently qualified them as "experts" on the matter before the court. What was absent from their title, and indeed from any debate about their expertise, was their whiteness; so flush was their position with existing systems of British legal thought that their obvious experiential ignorance in the matter was rendered unmentionable. Their "sameness" to the whiteness of the court offered them a credibility and status that contributed to their positioning as experts. In explaining his position in relation to the acceptance of the presence of the WLAFGM in the proceedings, the magistrate stated that it was important to enable "as much evidence to be tendered to the court as possible" (ibid.). If we consider, however, the position of the WLAFGM in the court from a Derridean perspective, and examine what is presented through its absence (Derrida 1981, 19), we can also see how the presentation of the WLAFGM as experts presupposes the positioning of the EWG at this time as "nonexperts," thereby effectively denying the possibility of many types of evidence being tendered to the court.

The EWG was never asked to present evidence or to cross-examine witnesses. They were not-lawyers, not-white, and their representation as "women" was arguable—as I shall explain later—because of their own "mutilated" subject position. Despite advocating for the abolition of female circumcision, they did not describe the practices as a "mutilation," thereby assuming the language of expertise. They were not represented as "experts" within legal discourse at this time, which enabled a particular type of expertise to be rendered legitimate on this issue. I am not suggesting that this action of the court was the origin of the "mutilation" of the expert status of the EWG or the AWWG. They were always already not experts within a Western legal system, which validates its own expertise within its own systems of representation (Derrida 1990). Rather, this was a moment in which the WLAFGM became recognized by the Western media as experts on the issue of "female genital mutilation"; the knowledge emanating from WLAFGM became all there was to know about the practices of female circumcision; and the Australian population "as a whole" articulated their decisions and opinions accordingly.

The Age newspaper[8] published twenty-six articles in relation to the issue in 1993 and 1994. In only one of those articles did the voice of a representative from the African communities appear. However, many "nonexpert" opinions of both journalists and the broader Australian public appeared unreferenced in articles and letters to the editor, along with many comments solicited from the WLAFGM. Comments ranged from claims of scientific knowledge in the form of statements about the practices' impact on women's sexuality, about the practice originating with the pharoahs in Egypt, through to descriptions of the practices as "barbaric." In the *Sydney Morning Herald* the practices were likened to slavery, the cutting off of hands, the stoning of adulteresses, and the death penalty (February26, 1994).[9] I would argue that perhaps the most contentious commentary on the matter—which reproduced the idea that members of "migrant" communities are ignorant, intransigent, and in many ways uneducated about the "seriousness" of the practices—came from Karen Kissane, a senior writer for *The Age*. On December 3, 1993, Kissane wrote, "Genital mutilation should be criminalized if migrants are to get a clear message about how serious a practice it is."[10]

Kissane's comment enables the Western imagination of a particular type of migrant. This migrant, who is neither a social nor a political agent with whom to engage in dialogue, is represented here as a stagnant object who must be told—and clearly—how to think about the practice of "genital mutilation." This migrant is unspeaking on the issues of female circumcision—in that s/he must be educated—and one who is unspeakable, in necessitating legal intervention—in that s/he cannot be engaged with as a thinking, speaking being. Ghassan Hage's discussion of spatial management (Hage 1998, 37–47) can be employed here to consider the position of the manager as one who represents "the other" as an object to be managed, and him- or herself as both capable of and entitled to manage. In Kissane's statement there is the articulation of both the objects who must be told, and perhaps criminalized if they don't understand, and the manager who knows the truth and assumes the position of manager through the need to manage this unknowing object before it hurts itself, or others. Kissane also makes no distinction between migrants on either the basis of ethnicity, gender, political, or religious affiliation, cultural location through age, sexuality, or life experience, as if they were indeed all the same. In her statements, all migrants need to "get a clear message" (3). Since we can assume she does not believe that all migrants practice circumcision, perhaps the message they are to get might relate more to the importance of the implementation of legislation, and the necessity of the 1996 law, and its affiliates, to act as manager.

THE FAMILY LAW COUNCIL'S CONSULTATION:
THE MAKING OF SENSE

In 1993, the Family Law Council was summoned by the attorney-general to research the issue of "female genital mutilation" and to make recommendations accordingly. In 1994, the Family Law Council produced *Female Genital Mutilation: A Discussion Paper,* which was published in January of that year and requested responses by March. *It was printed only in English.* In response to criticisms about this, the Council stated:

1.14 A complaint was also made to the Council that its discussion paper
was available only in English and that this prevented many members of the
vulnerable communities (especially recently arrived refugees) from making
their *view* known. Council does not have the funds to produce its discussion papers and reports in multi languages. Council considers, however, that
in this instance funds should be provided to enable Council's *final report* to
be produced in several languages. This would enable the report to be used
more effectively in the education process within the relevant communities.
(Family Law Council 1994b, 3, emphasis added)

It would not, however, enable the discussion paper or the intermediate report
to be used more effectively in the consultation process. Notably, the emphasis
is on education, not discussion, and the reference to "recently arrived refugees"
as having a singular "view" on the issues conspicuously implies an assumption
that all the communities think the same, or indeed are the same—an assumption
similar to that in Kissane's representation of "migrants."

In June 1994, the Family Law Council published *Female Genital Mutilation:
A Report to the Attorney-General,* outlining recommendations to legislate "FGM"
within the Victorian Crimes Act 1958. The report stated that it had received
sixty-four responses from "government departments" and "concerned doctors,"
and twelve responses from "communities concerned" (1994b, 62–63). Only one
of the comments from the "communities concerned" was documented in the
report. This came from the Eritrean Community in Australia (ECA), which
stated that the two months allocated to respond to the discussion paper "essentially prevented adequate community consultation from taking place" (ibid.,
2). Despite this comment from the ECA, the Family Law Council stated in its
report that it is "in no doubt that the Australian community's view *as a whole* on
the issue of female genital mutilation is clear" (ibid., 3, emphasis in original).

These criticisms and responses articulate an already existing attitude toward
"consultation" from the Family Law Council, which denotes an obvious resistance to the notion of dialogue with the relevant communities, who were themselves already discussing the practices. This attitude is justified and represented
within the pages of the report itself. Far from it being a discussion, or even a
reflection of a discussion (in the form of the report), the Family Law Council's
document—some of which I examine in this chapter—exposes the attitude of
the Council to the communities, by positioning them as unspeaking, by ignoring community concerns already articulated, and by representing communities
and their representatives as unspeakable, as always already mutilated in terms of
their capacity for understanding, analysis, and dialogue.

The Family Law Council acknowledges early in its report that there are
many different types of "the practice." However, the Council chose to adopt
the term "female genital mutilation" to "embrace all types of the practice" in
its Report (1994b, 5). There is no reference to any consultation with Victorian

communities on this naming issue, despite the ongoing work by the EWG objecting to the use of this term. Nor does the Family Law Council's "embrace" allow any room for the recognition of the EWG's work to reduce the severity of the practices by practicing forms such as sunna. In the Family Law Council's representation, sunna, too, is a mutilation. The Council's representation of the practices as singular also exhibits a particular attitude common to discourses on "female genital mutilation," in which all practices are reduced to a singular term or acronym as if—despite the disclaimers—they can be considered "the same," and as if, by extension, the communities that practice "FGM" can be considered "the same." This enables the construction of many diverse communities as a singular object, one that articulates a singular view, according to the Family Law Council. The Council also employs a single system to measure the values of all cultures—one that is readily understood within Western systems of meaning.

In the Family Law Council's report this reduction is followed by a half-page diagram of a "normal adolescent vulva" (1994b, 6). The report contains no discussion of to whom this vulva is normal, the implication being that only uncircumcised vulvas are normal. This universalization of Western sensibilities of "normalcy" is extended in the report to statements about the purpose of the clitoris and experiences of "pleasure." These statements are exhibited as if they are self-evident, without acknowledgment of their culturally and individually contextual meanings (ibid., 22).[11] The argument is extended further into the meanings of the practices when the Council verges on engagement in a struggle with its relationship to "neo-colonialist attempts to impose Western human rights standards on Third World countries." This struggle is, however, efficiently short-circuited by a reinforcement of the Council's measurement of female circumcision as "cultural practices which are no different from practices in the West through which women are valued less than men" (ibid., 32). This measurement system enables the construction of cultural practices as viewable not as "different," with their own meanings and status, but as commensurably "the same" as some unspecified and unreferenced practices in the West. The "incommensurability of difference" that I will discuss later, enables what Vicky Kirby has eloquently described as a strategy to "dissolve the difference between women and between cultures into a nonsense, which the West alone can rein-scribe with sense" (Kirby 1987, 44). It is precisely this representation of a type of sense and sense-making that is apparently known to Western legal, medical, and political representatives—although it is never declared—and that enables the delegitimation of the work of the EWG and AWWG, as if their opinions and work are a non-sense, and should therefore be disregarded.

THE EWG AND THE AWWG: STRUGGLING WITH SENSELESSNESS

In contradiction to Kissane's assertion that "migrants" need legislation to understand the "seriousness" of female circumcision, the EWG, prior to the

Family Law Council's "consultation process," was implementing the Eritrean Women's Project and discussing the issues with health professionals, politicians, community workers, and members of the broader African communities. One result of these discussions was the decision to develop the group into the larger umbrella group, called the African Women's Working Group. This group was established in February 1995 in order "to be a voice for African women on female circumcision" (African Women's Working Group 1997). The group incorporated representatives from the Eritrean, Somali, Hararian, Oromo, and Sudanese communities who were already active in groups such as the Somali Women's Association and the Oromo Women's Association. Also included in the group were members described as "independent African women and two non-African resource women."

The aims of the group were defined as being:

- To increase awareness about the issue amongst the general community.
- To promote affected women in the planning and implementation of programs that address the issue as they are in the best position to know which strategies will be most effective in stopping the practice from occurring in Australia.
- To develop and implement effective education models which will successfully increase the awareness of affected communities about female circumcision and enable the women to choose not to continue the practice (African Women's Working Group 1997).

The only funding that the group received was from the Victorian Women's Trust, for a project officer working just four hours per week. Yet the AWWG managed, in its three-year lifespan, to present at several conferences; to produce, implement, document, and evaluate a "Community Legal Education Project"; to liaise with the Inter-African Committee in Geneva; and to consult with the State Department of the Attorney-General, the prime minister's advisory body the Office of Women's Affairs (OWA), and the Royal Australian College of Obstetricians and Gynaecologists (RACOG). This work, while certainly contradicting the assumptions held by Kissane, nevertheless did not disturb the representation of the groups and their members as nonexperts within Western legal (and arguably social) discourses of "female genital mutilation." While the work and the existence of the groups were recognized by some government representatives as significant enough to invite consultation, the opinions and arguments of AWWG members were rarely acknowledged as relevant expertise or professional opinion. Their suggestions were systematically discounted and misrepresented, and their status as a representative body for Horn of African communities was constantly discredited, despite being funded to research and represent the perspectives of those communities.

In its discussions with the OWA, RACOG, and the State Department of the Attorney-General, the AWWG brought up some key reoccurring topics. These can briefly be described as: the lack of need for, and the possibly detrimental effects of, legislation; the need for the communities to themselves define and manage strategies for the elimination of the practices; the problematic defining of the practices as psychologically damaging; the description of women who had experienced the practices as "mutilated" through the use of terms such as "female genital mutilation" or "FGM"; and the lack of consultation with the communities about proposed legislation or the implementation of a DHS program to work with communities on the issues. Responses to these concerns could be generously described as varied. In one meeting with RACOG representatives, AWWG representatives were invited to consult on a training manual intended to help health professionals understand and work with the communities on issues relating to the practices. The AWWG recommended that the practices should be referred to as "female circumcision" rather than "FGM" or "female genital mutilation." This recommendation was noted, but not taken up (personal communication to author).[12] Recommendations at meetings, and in writing, for communities to be consulted in relation to the recommendations for legislation and the development and implementation of the DHS program were similarly noted and ignored (Idris 1996; Mohamed 1996, 2). Criticism came from the DHS and OWA in the form of statements about the capacity of the AWWG to represent the communities on the issues. This criticism was often interjected in forums in which the AWWG had been invited to provide comments on the work or perspectives of the DHS and OWA. Such statements about the group's capacity to represent were often articulated in response to criticisms by the AWWG about the practices of these bodies. Perhaps one of the most pernicious aspects of the "consultation process," however, was the reference to women who had experienced circumcision as "mutilated." This type of construction, together with discussion of the "psychological damage" of the "mutilation," was accompanied by the expectation that women could or would comment within an already existing system that referenced them as psychologically less. While this can be viewed as an insidious (and offensive) strategy to manage the AWWG's appearance as an informed and informing expert on the issues, there were other strategies that can be understood as more disturbingly pragmatic in their implementation. One of these is exhibited in the interactions of the AWWG with the OWA.

The AWWG—under the auspices of the Ecumenical Migration Centre (EMC)—was funded by the OWA to produce a report on the impacts of the legislation on Horn of African communities. After completing the report, the OWA released a summary (Office of Women's Affairs 1996a) of its findings. The AWWG described the summary as inaccurate and inadequate because it did "not have adequate and sufficient information about the Legal Education Project, as presented by the initial Project Report. . . . [It] also makes some inaccurate statements about the project" (African Women's Working Group 1996b). The criticisms of the summary were presented to OWA representatives at a meeting in October 1996. The OWA did not alter its summary and responded strongly to the request to release the original report:

> The recommendation to supply a copy of the report could not be supported because of contractual arrangements between the Department of Justice and the Ecumenical Migration Centre. There was also concern that some individuals who made personal comments at sessions with few participants from each community, may be identified by the detailed report and it would be inappropriate for this information to be published (Office of Women's Affairs 1996b).

The "concern" for the individuals who made "personal comments," while apparently well meaning, articulates a representation of the groups as a collection of individuals rather than a professional body made up of women representing their communities. The statement that the comments were "personal" also suggests members' inability to articulate their positions without it being "personal." This implies that only people who are not directly affected by the practices can rationally speak on the issue. Notably, these concerns for the "individuals" were not discussed with those who made the comments. Also, the AWWG accepted the "contractual arrangement" before beginning the project in "good faith," not with the assumption that the report would be inaccurate or misleading (personal communication from members of AWWG in January 2002). Despite the AWWG's criticisms, the OWA did not alter its summary, did not release the original report written by the AWWG to the communities, and did not authorize the use of the report by the AWWG itself. In an effort to redress this issue, the AWWG wrote a second document from the information it had acquired during the project, entitled "Report on Community Legal Information Project on Female Circumcision" (1996b) and produced and distributed its own document from the research on the original project, entitled "The Implications of the Legislation on FGM for the Affected Communities" (Mohamed 1996). Neither report was ever published or referred to in any media reports or publicized legal debates on "female genital mutilation." This is not to say that they were not valuable documents for health and community workers who were able to find out about their existence. Rather, I would argue that the suppression of the original document and its inaccurate representation by the OWA was instrumental in positioning the AWWG as powerless to inform decisions about the implementation of programs and legislation in relation to the practices of female circumcision in Victoria.

After the recommendations of the Family Law Council were presented, the matter of legislation was not debated. Victoria Attorney-General Jan Wade appeared before the communities in a "consultative forum" about the legislation in Melbourne in 1995; although her manner was described as receptive, the forum was a presentation of the legislation, not a discussion. There was no debate. Indeed, the forum might best be described as a strategy to manage any objections to the legislation that might exist. The Crimes (Female Genital Mutilation) Act 1996 was passed in 1996. In July 1997 the AWWG publicized the group's predicament in an "Important Notice" circulated among community members, requesting that members attend a meeting to discuss the group's fate. The notice stated that the group believed that they were being undermined and that "Few women (members) are committed to (or feel powerless to) promote the aims and philosophies of the group" (African Women's Working Group 1997). Although the group was renewed in terms of energy and commitment after the meeting, the AWWG disbanded in 1998.

The AWWG's predicament can be understood as common to many community groups at this time; it seems certain that economic and social pressures of the Liberal (conservative) Victorian government were influential in disabling the group, as with many community groups during its term in office. The statement by the AWWG in this notice reflects the positioning of women who had experienced "circumcision" in many ways during the Victorian debates as "mutilated" in terms of their political position on this issue. The decision to disband the group was also informed by the impossibility of its political position: by this stage, the legislation was a foregone conclusion, as was the implementation of the DHS program, the Family and Reproductive Rights Education Program (FARREP), which both undermined the AWWG and created a social and economic dilemma for some of the groups members. As Mohamed describes:

> Many of documents produced by AWWG were provided to DHS as a way of show-casing AWWG capabilities to develop & implement efficient & effective community education programs for affected communities with the aim of eradicating the practice. DHS used many of AWWG reports as a base to develop their own "FARREP" projects without any acknowledgement of AWWG work; both verbal and written work. Yet, many of DHS employed strategies in developing FARREP project has lead to many AWWG members feeling marginalised, undermined and discriminated against (Personal e-mail communication from Mohamed to author, 2001).

The FARREP program was an important employment opportunity for women from Horn of African communities, who might otherwise have had difficulties because of language, structural racisms, and the existing political climate. This meant that criticism of the FARREP program or attempts to alter it would impact heavily on many friends and relatives of AWWG members, who were seeking and securing necessary employment in the program. The AWWG, in this sense, was in an impossible position.

"STRATEGIC MANAGEMENT": A BRIEF INTRODUCTION

There are many ways to read the issues and incidents of the period in Victoria preceding the passing of the legislation. In this chapter I have endeavored to represent some of the discursive and procedural issues that served to enable the legislating of female circumcision in 1996. I want to now shift to a spatial and temporal analysis of the factors that have both represented and perpetuated the management of the many forms of cultural diversity in Australia. I will do so through a description of some of the practices of management designed and implemented for assimilation and domestication of "others" since the invasion of Australia by the British in 1788. Within this context we can begin to analyze some of the actions of the Family Law Council and the OWA as not simply a desire to avoid work that might result in the extension of the time frame of the report and the legislation. This expediency can easily be understood in light of government pressure to be seen to have done something about this "barbaric practice" before the following election. However, by considering the multilay-ered histories of Australia and the location of many types of "others" as socially and politically mutilated, it becomes apparent that many factors were involved. The actions of the Family Law Council, OWA, and the judiciary were not re-moved from the already existing attitudes toward "others" exhibited contempo-rarily and historically.

In particular, it is essential to consider the management of these "others" within the context of the post–Gulf War period in Australia, when Australia's fear of the "Muslim scourge" was at a peak.[13] During this period, Arabic and Muslim communities were commonly the targets of many direct forms of rac-isms. The Australian public as a whole reacted to the presence of these com-munities and individuals as if they presented a constant threat, if not militarily, then certainly culturally. This was reflected in assaults, such as the tearing off of women's hijab in public spaces, spitting on women wearing the hijab in the street, and several motor vehicle attacks in which people were either driven into or dragged out of cars and beaten when wearing the hijab (National Inquiry into Racist Violence in Australia [NIRVA] 1991).[14] In the interests of appeasing the Australian public, the desire to be seen to condemn anything that might be viewed as an Arabic/Muslim threat to the "Australian way of life" was high on the political agenda of the Australian and Victorian governments.

The need for Australian—and, historically, British governments—to con-demn threats to the image of an "Australian way of life" should be considered against the historical backdrop of the mutilation and wholesale slaughter of divergences from the fantasy of a White Australia through the implementation of various legislative policies over time. In the early 1900s, the emergence of the fantastical idea of a White Australia—which had in fact never existed—re-sulted in the implementation of what became known as the White Australia Policy. This term embraced a series of policies that encouraged the emigra-tion of predominantly British citizens to Australia and discouraged (and often rejected) the applications of would-be migrants from other countries apart from Northern Europe and the United States. The White Australia Policy was ended in its official form by the federal government in 1973. While this policy can be seen as an overt attempt to ensure domination, at least in quantity, of whiteness in the Australian population "as a whole," it can also be viewed as a discursive site in which the right to manage was asserted and exercised through the representation of Australian governments as necessary managers of cultural diversity. The latter interpretation presupposes that divergence from whiteness necessitates management.

The construction of a divergence from whiteness requiring management can be seen in many of the policies, both contemporary and historical, of Australian governments. One recent high-profile example in contemporary Australia is the construction of asylum seekers from Arabic and/or Muslim backgrounds—including children—as possible terrorists, therefore requiring refusal of entry, or interrogation and detention. The mandatory detention of all asylum seekers without a valid visa, sometimes for up to three years, is akin to imprisonment. Most recently, the Australian federal government used the concern about potential terrorists to justify a breach of the United Nations Convention on the Protection of Refugees 1951: armed Australian troops were deployed to turn away 438 Afghani and Iraqi asylum seekers rescued from international waters by the *Tampa,* a Norwegian cargo ship, off the northwest coast of Australia. This was followed by the high-speed production of legislation that enabled the removal of ships containing asylum seekers from Australian waters.[15]

Legislative interventions that manage divergences from whiteness can also be viewed in the historical and contemporary treatment of indigenous Australians. The long-standing legal description of Australia as *terra nullius* (empty land) is perhaps the most obvious example. It has the literal meaning and practical implication that the more than 250 separate indigenous nations already inhabiting the continent did not exist in law and certainly had no claim on the land and its resources, or any rights to participate in the political decisions of Australia. This representation framed the justification for the slaughter of hundreds of thousands of indigenous people, from the first encounters in the 1700s until recent history.[16] The representation of Australia as "empty" also enabled the British legal system and Australian governments to assert domination over forms of cultural dissent that might imply that the land was not empty. These broad and complex policies were implemented through a series of violent encounters and discursive representations, beginning with *terra nullius.* They can briefly be listed as: the massacre of many thousands of indigenous people in many separate (and recorded) incidents until the early 1900s; the forcible removal of indigenous children from their families to situations often akin to slave labor from the early 1900s until the 1960s;[17] the collusion with and alleged frequent facilitation of indigenous "suicides" and assaults in custody;[18] the existence of many forms of social and economic apartheid that have been compared with those of South Africa in the late 1900s; the dispossession of indigenous people from their land, heritage, and language through the quashing of Native Title legislation under the current federal coalition government under the leadership of John Howard; and the ongoing enforcement of laws that are clearly discriminatory and assist in the disproportionate criminalizing of Indigenous people.[19] In the arguments for the implementation of these legislative actions there existed, and still exists, the implication, and sometimes explicit requirement, that indigenous Australians must be managed. The assumptions are that they are a potential danger to themselves and to the Australian population because they cannot manage themselves, and that it would be impossible for indigenous Australians to exercise political and social agency according to Western understandings.

The construction of "others" as incompetent to manage themselves, and of their actions as potentially dangerous to the Australian population as a whole, cultivates a landscape in which the authority of Australian governments is an essential component in ensuring the Australian way of life. The authority of the state is assured through the construction of its necessity, and "others" are represented *always already* within this system as dangerous or in need of management, because they cannot manage themselves. This argument also extends to the authority of the Law particularly in relation to the Crimes (FGM) Act 1996 and can be considered in light of the intense criticism of the courts that was present in the early 1990s.

MEASURING MANNERS AND THE ESSENTIAL CLITORIS

In considering the expedient move to legislate "female genital mutilation" without consideration of relevant community voices, it is essential to acknowledge that the court processes and the perceived impartiality of the legal system had come under heavy attack from feminists in the early 1990s, as a result of comments made by magistrates in recent rape cases.[20] These comments were criticized for implying that certain women have lesser experiences of harm from sexual assault because of their profession or their sexual history (Troup 1993). It can be argued that much of the impetus to expediently pass legislation to prohibit "female genital mutilation" arose from the view that this was likely to appease Western (liberal) feminists and promote belief in the necessity of the legal system as a vehicle to protect women.[21] It might seem that the lack of consultation with women from communities that practice circumcision should itself have been a feminist issue, deserving of debate from both "community development"[22] and "human rights"[23] perspectives. In analyzing what happened in the 1990s in Victoria through the representation of "female genital mutilation," it is important to look at the absence of such debates. Why did Western feminists not see the active silencing of the perspectives of women in decision making about their own communities' fate as a feminist issue? Why did human rights activists actively participate in the debates around "saving the children" from this "barbaric practice," without themselves seeking the perspectives of the women who would possibly be imprisoned for perpetuating their cultural practices? (Amnesty International 1994 and 1997a). It is also, perhaps, useful to ask "why a law?" when women from the communities in question were already actively encouraging the discontinuation of the practices. To discuss these questions I want to consider the frameworks used by Sanjay Seth in relation to liberalism and (multi)culturalism (Seth 2001) and propose that the difficulties with the employment of ambivalent frameworks for the issues around female circumcision are problems of economics in relation to migration, of politics in relation to migration and the defense of nationalism, and of the inescapability of profound "difference" that female circumcision embodies in Australian social and legal politics.

First, we must consider the debates around female circumcision in a broader context; I acknowledge the work of Janice Boddy in critically highlighting the representation of the "clitoris" as the site of feminine agency in the West. As Boddy discusses, "the clitoris is the female analogue of the penis, both sexes are marked by 'presence,' creativity, agency . . . which make this body part a powerful symbol of women's emancipation" (1998b, 89). The clitoris has been viewed in the West—since feminists and sexual liberationists (re)discovered their own— as the integral part of a woman's capacity to assert herself as a woman. Indeed the anti-"female genital mutilation" activist Fran Hosken—described by Kirby as "the source most relied upon by other writers" (Kirby 1987)—describes the clitoris as the "essence of the female personality" (Hosken 1982, 14). The point here, however, is not to debate what the clitoris actually means. In fact, it is the representation of the clitoris as a singular universally understood and experienced entity that is precisely the problem. As Grosz states, "culturally specific grids of power, regulation and force condition and provide techniques for the formation of particular bodies" (1990, 72); the particular body being marked will therefore adopt a specific position in relation to the cultural significance of those markings. This applies to both the absence and the presence of the clitoris, and the practicing or not practicing of female circumcision. In Victoria in the 1990s, however, the debates were reduced to the explanation of the clitoris and the practicing of female circumcision as culturally explainable within Western systems of reference; these issues were made sense of through Western legal and social discourses of the time. When the Family Law Council located the clitoris within particular discourses of "womanhood" and later defended its own position as "neocolonialist" with the reference to "female genital mutilation" in relation to "cultural practices which are no different from practices in the West through which women are valued less than men" (Family Law Council 1994b, 32), it was reducing female circumcision to supposedly comparable practices, and thereby representing women's experiences as universally explainable within Western systems of reference.

While these arguments are useful for understanding the many racisms inherent in the debates regarding female circumcision in Victoria at this time—indeed they may also be useful when considering the processes of legislating the practices in other states and nations—they are also important components in understanding the construction of the voices/work of the AWWG and EWG as "mutilated." Here I want to use the work of Sanjay Seth in depicting the construction of the historical Western subject under a liberalist scheme, and the relationship of this construction to (mutli)culturalism and the legislating of female circumcision. In Seth's discussion, the subject under liberalism has been understood within discourses that represent particular types of subjectivities as recognizable in civil and political society in the West. Both his description of a Kantian perspective of liberalism in which the subject is defined as socially meaningful through its capacity for Reason (Seth 2001, 66) and the earlier depictions of a liberal subjects defined by their "level of social-cultural development" (67) are important to the positioning of the "mutilated woman." In both frames, there is an inherent assumption of the capacity for reason and reasonableness. If we understand the presence of the clitoris through the Western feminist representation, which links its existence with agency and the capacity for women to perform as social/political subjects, then it becomes associated with a type of Western feminist reason.[24] Through the act of circumcision, reason is therefore unequivocally "mutilated" from a Western feminist perspective. The endeavor to speak from the position of the "mutilated" is, it follows, categorically unreasonable. Indeed, the "reasonableness" of women who are "mutilated" can only be displayed in feminist discourse by their lack of capacity to speak, or at least their consciousness of this position. This position is also mirrored in the violence of law, through the operations of legislating against the practices of female circumcision.

The subjugation of the work of the two African women's groups was enabled through the delegitimation of their expertise. Where knowledge is subjugated, however, there is also the ascendance of another type of knowledge. As Foucault describes, this knowledge exists always already through its representation as truth. The disavowal of the work of the AWWG and EWG operated through the representation of the groups' work as lacking in knowledge, or as the opinions only of individuals. It reified the necessity of law, and denied the capacity of black/Muslim/others to intelligently articulate their beliefs and their social and political perspectives within complicatedly intersecting racial and legal discourses. The Family Law Council, OWA, and the Victoria judiciary did not simply perpetrate a silencing of the already existing voices speaking on female circumcision; they were also enabled by it. Their positioning as experts was/is authorized not only by their capacity to silence but by the imperative to silence, or in this case to protect, the Australian population as a whole. "Female genital mutilation," therefore, needed to be represented as a "mutilation" and a violent act to be managed through the essential presence of law. Horn of Africa women therefore had to be understood as "mutilated"—unspeaking and unspeakable—in order to enable the display of the capacity of "female genital mutilation" to damage their "womanhood."[25] Indeed, what would it have meant for Horn of African women to both be articulate, whole women *and* be "mutilated"? Their presence as such would have grossly undermined the necessity of having a law, for what then was/is it that the Australian population was/is being protected from? It also would have demanded a questioning of what "difference" meant. How could these women be seen as so utterly different if they were speaking, writing, and discussing issues with policy makers, legal representatives, and the media without the "essence of the female personality"?[26]

"Strategic Management": A Brief Conclusion

In analyzing the management of "cultural diversity" in Victoria at this time, I have highlighted some of the issues and incidents that enabled and resisted the representation of women who have experienced female circumcision as physically, psychologically, and intellectually "mutilated." The legislating of "female genital mutilation" in Victoria was a process of community consultation, manipulation, and subjugation that represented the authority of law as essential to protect Australia from "barbarous practices" and simultaneously constructed "others" as barbaric and as "mutilated" social agents who were not entitled to the rights of citizenship—that is, to participate in political and legal debates that affected their lives. These processes enabled the construction of a type of "other" whose practices and presence demanded management, potentially in the form of imprisonment; this construction allowed for a retrospective perception of the violence of Australia's colonization of Australia and subsequent human rights abuses as legitimate. What is perhaps most alarming about this type of representation, however, is its capacity to facilitate the construction of "others" to the Australian "self" as always already produced within representations of violence that are both culturally stagnant and unable to be dialogued with. Diversity, as a divergence from the Australian population as a whole, is not an experience to be encountered and respected.

In Seth's discussion of the domestication of difference (2001, 76), we can understand the fantasy of plurality articulated through a type of liberalist position on the legal subject, which enables the perception that difference is accommodated in contemporary Australia. The consideration of legislation was, of course, considered a "consultative process" by the Family Law Council, yet it was by no means a dialogue. The AWWG and the EWG were silenced in Victoria on the issues of female circumcision precisely because their embodied difference was seen as necessarily manageable by law. In order for this to occur, however, their position had to be established through their representation as "reasonable," indeed "civilized," subjects before the law; in order to do this they had to be seen as "mutilated" rather than differently embodied, and be seen to accept their position as "mutilated." As "mutilated," their subjectivity is both recognizable and representable within the discourses of "female genital mutilation." Their mutilation, as measured against the nonmutilation of white women, makes their difference (re)cognizable. To displace their own social and psychological "mutilation" would have not only disturbed the authority of law (or at least its progressive necessity) but would also have demanded an engagement with a "difference" that cannot be readily assimilated to, or domesticated within, Western value systems and as such must be managed.

ACRONYMS

AWWG—African Women's Working Group

CSV—Community Services Victoria

DHS—Department of Human Services

ECA—Eritrean Community of Australia

EMC—Ecumenical Migration Centre

EWG—Eritrean Women's Group

FARREP—Family and Reproductive Rights Education Program

MP—Member of Parliament

NIRVA—National Inquiry into Racist Violence in Australia

OWA—Office of Women's Affairs

RACOG—Royal Australian College of Obstetricians and Gynaecologists

UN—United Nations

WLAFGM—Women Lawyers against Female Genital Mutilation

NOTES

A version of this chapter was presented at the Encounters with Law Conference, La Trobe University, Melbourne, Australia, 2000, and developed with consideration of the feedback received there. Thanks to those who offered comments at this presentation. Thanks also to Amuna Abdella, Jacques Boulet, Cara Brough, and Sarah Lowe for their comments and support, and I am always indebted to the brave and rigorous work of the African Women's Working Group. Their generosity, collegiality, and friendship have been essential, important and inspirational in the writing of this work.

   This chapter was written in consultation with Munira Mohamed and Nikki Marshall, with the assistance of members of the Melbourne-based Eritrean Women's Group and African Women's Working Group.

1. Throughout this paper I will use the terms "circumcision" or "female circumcision" where I am referring to the actual practices that have come to be translated into these English terms. While this does not comprehensively list the practices, it is the term used by the African Women's Working Group (AWWG) and the Eritrean Women's Group (EWG) to describe the many practices that do not have equivalent English terms. For a more comprehensive discussion of some of the different types of practices, see, for example, Shell-Duncan and Hernlund (2000, 3–7). I use the terms "female genital mutilation" or "FGM" when I am referring to these concepts as discursive productions or where they are used within other texts.

2. For the purposes of this chapter, "others" is used to refer to people represented through discourse as not white, not Christian, not of European descent, and embodying particular qualities or capacities that I shall outline in the chapter.

3. The Family Law Council is a federal body in Australia that researches issues and recommends legislative changes or alterations to government policy to the attorney general on the basis of its research. It is able to initiate its own research topics or can be invited by the attorney-general to explore areas related to "family law." It is not,

however, outside the constitutive frameworks that we might understand as discourse. It is not a mind to the body, as it were, but a site that both produces and is produced by legislative, medical, and political discourse.

4. While it is well documented that the practices of female circumcision are not exclusively or even predominantly associated with Islam, it is the perception of the Australian population as a whole that mattered in Australia in the 1990s. Testimony to the practices' association with Islam has been not so much the direct statements of this in media reports, but the constant disclaimers that it is "not a Muslim practice," and the somewhat inaccurate statement in the Family Law Council's report that "*female genital mutilation is not a religious practice*" (1994, 8, emphasis in original).

5. For the purposes of this chapter the use of the terms "Western" or "West" is intended to refer to locations and mentalities that are commonly defined through white, European, largely Christian-identified, and/or colonial histories. However, it is worth using Bourdieu's articulation of "fields of power" in *Language and Symbolic Power* to best engage with the varied and competing mechanisms ascribed to representations of power in relation to "the ruling class," or in this case to dominant whiteness or Western-ness. Also see Ghassan Hage's use of "fields of power" in relation to whiteness (2000, 55–67).

6. I want to emphasize here the distinction between the representations of "female genital mutilation" and "female circumcision." The latter is the term preferred and articulated by the AWWG and the EWG to include all the practices articulated within their communities. "Female genital mutilation" or "FGM" has its own particular meanings, produced through the ways in which it is represented in discourse, as I discuss in this chapter.

7. See "A Barbarous Practice" in *The Age,* Opinion—Analysis, March 23, 1994.

8. *The Age* is a leading Melbourne newspaper, which has the second largest readership in Melbourne.

9. Notably, this "letter to the editor" by Louise M. Steer was cited uncritically in the Family Law Council's report (1994b, 36).

10. Kissane (1993). It is worth noting here the similarity between Kissane's type of comment and the much-criticized practice in Australia of speaking loudly, slowly, and firmly to people from non-English speaking backgrounds, which is often explained as an attempt to bridge language difficulties, but is well established as a practice that constructs "others" as intellectually inferior to people of Anglo descent, rather than perhaps struggling with the fluency of a second language.

11. See Boddy (1998a and 1998b) for further discussions of the universalizing of the meanings of women's bodies in relation to female circumcision, and Grosz (1994) for a further critical discussion of the positioning of bodies as having objective and understandable meanings.

12. From Dr. Chris Boyly of the Royal Women's Hospital in Melbourne during discussions about the events of 1996. These discussions took place in February and March of 2002.

13. See Hage (1998) *White Nation* for further discussions of the reactions and responses to the perceived threats following the Gulf War.

14. *"Hijab"* is used here to indicate the hair-covering veil worn by some Muslim women in Australia.

15. For a discussion of this incident see Marr and Wilkinson (2003).

16. This question of when the last recorded massacres took place is highly contentious in Australian historical communities, although many indigenous people claim that the last massacres occurred in the early twentieth century and that the "deaths in custody" of indigenous people are an ongoing participation in the slaughter of indigenous people by and through Western systems of governance including police practice. See Whimp (1997) and Amnesty International (1997b).

17. See Commonwealth of Australia (1997).

18. See Whimp (1997), and Amnesty International (1997b).
19. These issues are only a limited citing of many of the discussions and complaints that have been brought to entities such as the United Nations and have been described as "genocide" by many indigenous and nonindigenous writers, academics, politicians, health workers, and activists. It is impossible within the limits of this chapter to articulate all the known and unknown incidents of violence toward the indigenous people in Australia. For further discussion and historical documentation, see Dick (2001), Johnson (2000), Langton (2001b), and D. Johnson and Zdenowski (2000).
20. See *R. v. Hakopian,* August 8, 1991, County Court of Victoria, and *R. v. Harris,* August 11, 1981, Court of Criminal Appeal, Victorian Supreme Court.
21. It is not within the parameters of this chapter to discuss the inherent violence of the law in its capacity to represent juridical issues within an *always already* existing system that demands the authority of law. For further discussion of the "authorization" of law see Derrida (1990).
22. The principles of community development in Victoria involve the perception that communities have the best knowledge about their own needs and the processes that govern their lives from both individual and group perspectives. These philosophies are, at least theoretically, fundamental to the development of best-practice models and policy decisions produced within the community and welfare sectors in Victoria.
23. According to the United Nations Convention on the Elimination All Forms of Discrimination against Women, specifically Article 7,
    States Parties shall take all appropriate measures to eliminate discrimination against women in the political and public life of the country and, in particular, shall ensure to women on equal terms with men, the right:
    (b) To participate in the formulation of government policy and the implementation thereof and to hold public office and perform all public functions at all levels of government.
24. Reason, articulated by Kant (as discussed by Seth), is not directly represented in feminist values of reason; however, while a comprehensive articulation of Western feminist reason is beyond the scope of this chapter, it is perhaps best represented—in relation to the matter of this chapter—as the existence of the clitoris as the location of personality and agency, and as associated with a consciousness that involves the desire for "liberation." These arguments are well integrated into the work of Fran Hosken, but they are also reminiscent of the work of Mary Wollstonecroft and the types of feminism articulated in the 1960s and 1970s in North America. See also Boddy (1998b).
25. Notably, the Family Law Council directly related "female genital mutilation" to "womanhood" (1994b, 23) in a severely edited quotation from a woman's comments on an Special Broadcasting Service (SBS) program, *The Cutting Edge* June 29, 1993.
26. I do not mean to suggest here that all the women represented in the groups had specifically experienced the practice of clitoridectomy, but that they were represented as such.

CHAPTER 7

Representing Africa in the Kasinga Asylum Case

Charles Piot

THIS ESSAY FOCUSES on the landmark 1996 case in which Fauziya Kasinga (Kassindja[1]), a Togolese woman, sought and won political asylum in the United States in order to escape genital cutting and forced marriage in Africa. The arguments advanced by the lawyers involved in the Kasinga case and the images in the media reporting on it circulated widely and came to define much more than Kasinga's travails or the practice of female genital cutting itself. Like Robert Kaplan's demonizing piece in the *Atlantic Monthly* in 1994, "The Coming Anarchy," they evoked and inserted themselves into a genealogy of racist stereotypes about Africa that have long mediated the West's relationship to the continent. In so doing, they glossed over complex local realities and once again fictionalized and fetishized Africa as the West's Other.

In what follows, I examine two principal sites: first, the court transcripts of the arguments presented by Kasinga's lawyer and by the lead attorney for the Immigration and Naturalization Service (INS) before the Board of Immigration Appeals (BIA) on May 2, 1996; and, second, the articles about the case that appeared on the front page of the *New York Times* throughout the spring, summer, and fall of 1996. These two sites were intimately tied together, indeed fed off one another, and provided mutually reinforcing "truths" about Kasinga and female genital mutilation (FGM) for the wider public. I then contrast the portrayal of Kasinga and her ordeal in these two venues with those details of her story I came to know through discussions with one of her lawyers and with an official at the American Embassy in Togo, whom I met in July of 1996 just after the case had been decided, at a time when the State Department was trying to decide whether it should take a stand on genital cutting, and at a time when reporters from both the *New York Times* and the *Washington Post* were in Togo to do after-the-fact background stories on Kasinga's family. This embassy official had been charged with investigating the case so that the embassy could not only respond to adverse publicity surrounding it but also generate new policy that would bring pressure to bear on the Togolese government to pass a law against the practice. His involvement indicates the global reach of this debate; a hearing before the INS was connected not only to a Western public through the media and the Internet but also to an embassy in a backwater region in West Africa and, thence, to the intimacies of life in rural Togolese villages.

I should mention at the outset that I myself played a minor role in the Kasinga case. Since I had conducted ethnographic fieldwork in northern Togo, near the homeland of Kasinga's ethnic group, the Tchamba, I was contacted early on by one of her lawyers to see whether I might be willing to serve as an expert witness during her initial hearing at the Immigration and Naturaliza-tion Service. After listening to the facts of the case, however, I was reluctant to become involved. While I was sympathetic to Kasinga's plight, I had never been to the area Kasinga was from, and the people I have worked with do not practice female genital cutting (Piot 1999a). Moreover, I sensed that, if I testi-fied at her hearing, I would be forced to seriously compromise my own views and, in the process, reify those images about Africa that many of us work hard to undo in our classrooms and in our writing, or else I would do damage to her case. Nevertheless, I agreed to file a letter with the court based on a reading of the ethnographic literature, which affirmed that the Tchamba of northern Togo practiced clitoridectomy and that it was likely that a Tchamba woman would be expected to undergo the procedure before she married. Much to my astonish-ment—for I had said nothing of substance about Kasinga herself, and I had used anthropological scholarship that was a half-century old—my letter was used right through the trial process and cited in the BIA's final opinion on the case as expert testimony that reinforced the case Kasinga's lawyers were trying to make (see U.S. Dept. of Justice 1996). This gives some indication of the house of cards on which this legal case was built.

KASINGA'S STORY

I begin by describing some of the facts of Fauziya Kasinga's life and trans-national ordeal. She grew up in a Muslim family in the town of Kpalimé in southern Togo. Her mother was a petty trader and her father a successful busi-nessman. Her father's income from the transportation business enabled him to build a spacious eight-bedroom house, which Kasinga described as "one of the finest" in Kpalimé (Kassindja and Bashir 1998, 12), and to send his daughter to boarding school in neighboring Ghana during her high school years. However, when she was sixteen, her father died. Kasinga returned to Togo to find that her mother had been banished to her natal home in Benin and that she was now under the guardianship of her father's sister. Unable, or unwilling, to pay the school fees, Kasinga's aunt kept her home and arranged for her to marry a local man with three wives.[2] She was also expected to undergo clitoridectomy at the time of marriage. Opposed to both marriage and to being cut, Kasinga fled with the help of an older sister. They borrowed money from their mother and crossed the border to Ghana. Kasinga purchased a plane ticket and flew to Germany. She spent two months in Germany, and then, with the aid of a Nigerian man she met on the street, obtained a British passport and flew to Newark, New Jersey.[3]

Upon arrival in the United States, she told immigration officials that she was fleeing forced FGM in her home country and wished to seek political asylum. As is routine for someone entering without a visa, she was detained. She spent the next sixteen months in detention facilities in New Jersey and Pennsylvania, where she not only shared cells with hardened criminals and murderers but also was repeatedly strip-searched, shackled, denied sanitary napkins, put in isolation for washing herself at dawn before her morning prayers, and beaten and tear-gassed during a prison riot. A cousin of Kasinga's found an attorney who was willing to take her case and pressed for an asylum hearing. At this hearing in August 1995, for which I submitted my letter, her claim was denied by an immigration judge who found her story "inconsistent" and "irrational." At that point, Layli Miller Bashir, then a law student at American University in Washington, D.C., took up Kasinga's cause and contacted Karen Musalo, a lawyer at American University's International Human Rights Clinic. Musalo agreed to take the case and appealed the earlier decision. On May 2, 1996, she and the INS presented arguments before seven members of the Board of Immigration Appeals. The appeals board, unlike the earlier judge, found Kasinga's story credible and the arguments of the lawyer who presented her case compelling, and granted her political asylum on June 13, 1996.[4] During the spring and into the summer and fall of 1996, Kasinga's case was publicized throughout the media and by human rights and feminist organizations on the Internet. This attention focused not only on Kasinga's flight from forced FGM but also on the horrific treatment she had been subjected to while detained in this country. Though this publicity was never mentioned by the lawyers during their arguments, or by the judges in their ruling, it clearly played a major role in the case's outcome.

THE CASE BEFORE THE BOARD OF IMMIGRATION APPEALS

The case heard by the BIA in May 1996 turned on five sets of arguments. First, whether or not Kasinga was a credible witness—that is, whether the inconsistencies in earlier accounts she had given to INS officials and at her earlier hearing[5] were serious enough to impugn her testimony about what had happened. Second, whether the Board itself should rule on the case or whether, in light of new evidence, it should remand it to the lower court judge who had heard the case previously. Third, whether or not Kasinga's situation (and FGM more generally) fit within the framework of political asylum law. Asylum law requires that an individual establish a well-founded fear of harm or persecution involving "a threat to life or freedom" because of his or her race, religion, nationality, politics, or membership in a social group. Fourth, whether, if returned to Togo, Kasinga would be forcibly subjected to FGM, or whether she could find safe haven elsewhere in the country. And fifth, whether in deciding this specific case, the board should restrict its ruling to the narrow facts of the case at hand or attempt to establish a broad framework for future cases as well.

Much of the discussion by both of the lawyers and between lawyers and judges revolved around the third of these issues: whether Kasinga had been subjected to harm based on her membership in a "social group."[6] For me as an anthropologist, this was the most interesting part of the debate. The pressing issue here was that gender—unlike race, religion, nationality, and politics—is not a recognized group category under asylum law. Thus, the board had to decide whether a gender-based claim was covered by the vague fifth "social group" category.[7] In arcane discussions that called to mind a certain Fortesian anthropology but were notable for their inattention to any of the anthropological literature, both lawyers and judges were drawn into debate about what social group category into which to place Kasinga. Kasinga's lawyer, Karen Musalo, suggested that the group in question was defined by "gender and tribe": the social group of women of the Tchamba people of northern Togo. INS attorney David Martin wanted to narrow the definition of the group in question to include only Tchamba women who were uncircumcised: "young women of the Tchamba Kusuntu tribe who have not been circumcised in accordance with tribal custom." His concern was that legal precedent would be established by a favorable ruling and that such precedent might enable thousands of women to make asylum claims in the future. Furthermore, he wanted to narrow the group to those uncircumcised Tchamba women who had resisted cutting and who had a "country-wide fear of persecution" for their resistance. This last point was key, for mere social ostracism or economic hardship that might result from noncompliance could not, he argued, constitute grounds for asylum. Karen Musalo protested the INS's attempt to narrow the definition of the social group in question, although not too vigorously, for she was caught between her desire to establish a general framework for FGM jurisprudence that could be applied to future cases and her more immediate desire to win this case for her client.

But is this a "true social group?" one of the judges asked Martin. Is it a "cognizable group" that has any reality outside of this context? asked another. "For what other societal purpose does the particular social group exist?" asked a third. These questions were motivated by the fact that individuals cannot bring asylum claims unless they can show that they are members of social groups. It is ironic that human rights law, from which asylum law derives, is based on the rights of the individual. In this case the INS could not accede to a definition of group—women of the Tchamba tribe—that is arguably the only definition that might correspond to some locally "cognizable" social grouping, precisely because it was so broad as to invite thousands of asylum petitions. By narrowing the definition to uncircumcised Tchamba women who resist cutting and justly fear they will be persecuted countrywide, the INS was proposing an invented social category—indeed, a group that might only consist of a single person, Kasinga herself. The contradictions at play here were never resolved, for both lawyers were under time constraints (each had only a half hour for argument) and wanted to return to other arguments they needed to make. Finally, what was remarkable to me as anthropologist, who worries about such esoteric questions as the nature of group identity in a place like West Africa, was that there was no expert testimony adduced to help decide the issue. None of the standard scholarly questions about group identity were raised: how homogeneous it might be? is there universal compliance with ritual practice? with genital cutting? and so on.

In addition to the central matter of defining group identity, other interesting issues were raised during the hearing which I only allude to here. The question of the motive of the so-called persecutors came under discussion, for in classic asylum cases involving persecution for religious or political beliefs the claimant must show malicious and punitive intent on the part of his or her persecutors. Thus, the issue raised in this context was whether the "harm of mutilation" was carried out with malignant intent. INS attorney Martin suggested that not only was it difficult to divine the nature of a person's subjective beliefs but also it was probable that those responsible for the practice of genital cutting had "benign" motives—that is, that they were likely merely carrying out the dictates of their culture. In order to get around this stumbling block, he proposed what one of the judges referred to as the "novel" idea that there might be certain cultural practices that, whatever the motives of those involved, were so appalling as to "shock the conscience of a great part of the world community," and that should therefore be considered a form of persecution. Notice, however, as with the discussion of group identity, the notion of intent that is key for asylum law is here dismantled: persecution might be unintentional and "benign." But the implications of this deconstructive move, again for lack of time, were left unresolved.

The judges briefly raised the question as to why genital cutting is practiced in the first place. INS attorney Martin responded, "I don't know . . . we are at a loss to come up with a reason that would explain it . . . it's part of a cultural practice." Karen Musalo objected to this vacuous response by stating, "FGM is performed purely for the purpose of gender subjugation . . . to control women's sexuality and reproduction." Martin then conceded that "some sociologists" describe it that way. Here, too, none of the anthropological literature on genital cutting was invoked.

The issue as to whether Kasinga would be subjected to a countrywide threat of persecution was key, because a claimant who could meet all of the other criteria for asylum would still be deported back to her home country if she could find a safe haven anywhere in that country. On this matter, the lawyers argued that in a country with a 50 percent rate of female circumcision, finding a safe haven would be well-nigh impossible. How they arrived at this figure, I do not know. State Department statistics for Togo in 1996 reported a 12 percent rate countrywide (U.S. Department of State 1996), though even this is likely inflated; I have heard from more reliable Togolese sources that the figure is closer to 5 percent.

Given the momentous nature of this hearing, the silences in this text are mind boggling and the list of anthropological howlers long. There is no discussion whatsoever of Tchamba and what they are like (the nature of groups, of ritual, of how they might respond to those who resist ritual practice), no testimony by anyone familiar with present-day Togo,[8] no inkling that discussion by Africanist scholars over two decades has established as orthodoxy that homogeneous social groups do not exist and that group identity is often fluid and shifting, and no reference to any anthropological literature on female genital cutting.

Moreover, these silences are filled by the crudest, most essentializing images and stereotypes. Kasinga was assumed by all in attendance to be a member of a "patriarchal tribe" with "immutable cultural norms" that practices "forced polygamy" and "mutilates" its women. Women of the tribe, it was suggested, "are brainwashed into believing that mutilation is good for them." These terms and images cycled through the entire discussion like shadows in the background, remaining utterly uncontested and uninterrogated, and providing a bedrock of understanding and a set of normalizing assumptions that filled the void of incomprehensibility, the utter inability of anyone in the room to conceive of anyone anywhere engaging in a practice like genital cutting. The only uncertainty during this courtroom hearing was whether the particulars of Kasinga's case would enable her to fit into the rigid, albeit ill-defined, categories of asylum law.

THE MEDIA

My larger concern as a scholar of West Africa is with the fact that this reification of false image and stereotype about Togo, and metonymically about all of Africa, is not confined to a hearing in a federal courtroom with a handful of attorneys and judges in Falls Church, Virginia. Meanings were created in this courtroom for a larger public, and this opinion was (and is) widely cited in the press and beyond. Its demonizing images have become hegemonic, and so normalized in the print media, on the radio, and on the Internet that counter-discourse about the meaning of female genital cutting is today for most Westerners utterly unthinkable.[9]

Moreover, the fact that the same self-iterating narrative emerges across all these sites is no accident. In the spring of 1996, Kasinga's lawyers sought help from a media-savvy New York–based feminist human rights group, Equality Now, which put them in touch with *New York Times* metro-area correspondent Celia Dugger. Immediately the lawyers realized they had a sympathetic ear and arranged for Dugger to interview Kasinga in her Pennsylvania detention facility. The article that emerged from this interview was published on the front page of the *Times* on April 15. It not only brought the case to the attention of a wider public (which the intense petitioning and Internet activity of human rights organizations throughout the spring had been unable to achieve) but also significantly influenced the INS and the BIA.[10] Within ten days Kasinga was released from detention (an event that produced another Dugger article on the front page of the *Times* on April 25, 1996), and within two months she was granted asylum. I do not have the space here to fully analyze Dugger's four *Times* articles on Kasinga and her case published on April 15, April 25, June 14, and September 11, 1996, but they are fascinating, powerful narratives and mimetic (albeit more fully fleshed out) iterations of the same story told in the courtroom. They move from Kasinga's treatment under detention to her flight from arranged marriage and forced FGM in Togo, and, in the article that appeared after the BIA ruling and following a trip Dugger made to Togo (Dugger 1996c), all the way back to the courtyard of the family "patriarch" chastising Kasinga's mother for facilitating her daughter's escape. This piece was emblazoned with pictures of dirt roads and submissive women, with heads bowed before male patriarchs; it was punctuated by subheadings such as "The Tradition," "The Escape," "The Patriarch," "The Apology," "The Village." Its evocation of images of the immutable nature of patriarchal tradition in a timeless Africa was extraordinary.[11] Dugger had never been to Africa before her July trip, spoke neither French nor Tchamba, and spent only a few days in the country. Yet she wrote an article read by millions that spoke the "truth" not only about Kasinga's personal odyssey and Tchamba culture but also about an entire continent. It also seemed to validate the BIA ruling retroactively.

RETELLING KASINGA'S STORY

But how otherwise to portray Kasinga's travail? Based on what I heard about the case from one of her lawyers and from the U.S. Embassy official I met in Togo in the summer of 1996, I am fully prepared to believe that Kasinga was being coerced into a marriage and into a ritual practice that she did not want to undergo. However, I read this coercion in a different register, for it took place within a long family history of jealousy and exclusion, of strained relations between her well-to-do father and his brothers and sisters with whom he refused to share his wealth. This family conflict was characterized by the sort of snobbery and greed that typifies many struggles on the edges of the bourgeoisie in African cities today, in which self-interest is disguised behind a proclaimed rejection of tradition. "I don't do those rituals any longer because I am modern and no longer believe in Tchamba tradition" is the refrain, when the underlying reality is often "I have money and don't want to share it with you." The coercion to which Kasinga was subjected after her father died and her mother was banished was the family's indirect revenge on Kasinga's father.[12] Her refusal to submit to their wishes to marry further incited their anger. This is not in any way to justify what they did; indeed, I am deeply compelled by Kasinga's situation. Rather, it is an attempt to renarrativize Kasinga's story as one that is not about a timeless tradition of mutilating rituals and unyielding patriarchy in remote rural villages but rather about a nasty family dispute and about issues of class and modernity in Togo today.

But here's the rub. In the United States, an applicant cannot get asylum based on his or her status and claims as an individual. Kasinga's lawyers could not have argued that their petitioner was caught in an ugly family dispute and was being coerced into an arranged marriage and into engaging in a ritual act against her wishes. The law requires that asylum claims be based on membership in a cognizable social group that comes under persecution. This contradiction is the proximate cause of the demonizing imagery that Kasinga's lawyers were forced to draw on. To win their case, they *had* to portray her as coming from an unchanging patriarchal society of mutilators. And because the lawyers got Celia Dugger to write the story they had scripted and the human rights organizations to reiterate this narrative endlessly on the Internet, it is this contradiction that I see as responsible for producing this global discourse. (Needless to say, this cultural script transcends the courtroom and borrows racist, imperialist, and missionary images of Africa that are centuries old. Nevertheless, it was here produced in a new register, and with a focus and visibility that is unprecedented.) This traveling narrative and truth telling is hegemonic and thoroughly fetishized, in both Marxian and Freudian senses of that term, a story that utterly erases its origins in a past and different family history.

WHOSE POLITICS?

I end by raising a question about the role of the anthropologist in writing about this overdetermined issue. It is clear, at least to me, that before long anthropologists will be more fully brought into the FGM asylum process, if not by the lawyers of those seeking asylum, then certainly by an INS (now renamed United States Citizenship and Immigration Services [USCIS], a bureau of Homeland Security) that worries about being deluged with asylum claims. A more robust and nuanced literature is beginning to emerge (Boddy 1998a and 1998b; Gruenbaum 2001; Kratz 1994 and 1999b; Shell-Duncan and Hernlund 2000; C. J. Walley 1997) that, while not supporting genital cutting, complicates any simpleminded reading of the practice. This literature will surely be cited and invoked by the INS/USCIS. Thus, we will risk finding ourselves in the uncomfortable position of being used by, even of being complicitous with, what many of us regard as a deeply conservative arm of the U.S. government. Indeed, I imagine that when this emerging literature begins to circulate and comes to the attention of the INS/USCIS, few women will be able to get asylum under current definitions of the law. How, then, as anthropologists *and* feminists, are we to think about our role in this debate? Is there, as Marilyn Strathern (1986 and 1988) suggested over a decade ago, an irreconcilable difference between feminist and anthropological agendas, between a global, universalistic feminism and an anthropology committed to communicating the nuance and meaning of local cultural worlds? And at what cost?

NOTES

This is a reprint of an article published in *Female Circumcision: Multicultural Perspectives,* edited by Rogaia Mustafa Abusharaf (2006). Reprinted with permission of University of Pennsylvania Press.

1. In her 1998 autobiography (written with Layli Miller Bashir), *Do They Hear You When You Cry,* she spelled her surname "Kassindja." In the press at the time, and often still today, she was referred to as "Kasinga," a misspelling (and mispronunciation) that apparently resulted from an Immigration and Naturalization Service official's error. Since this essay deals with documents that use the erroneous spelling, I retain it here.

2. Accounts of the identity of Kasinga's "husband" are confused and contradictory. Kasinga claimed during trial that he was forty-five years old, although he told two U.S. journalists that he was twenty-eight (Dugger 1996c; C. Coleman 1997). Kasinga claimed that he was a well-to-do builder and politician with connections to local police, while he claimed to be a petty trader who didn't even "know what a district assemblyman is" (C. Coleman 1997).

3. To add one more twist to a complicated personal story, the embassy official I spoke with (see also C. Coleman 1997) told me that during his investigative work, he had sought out a woman in the Togolese government who had always been a reliable source of information. Upon hearing his description of the facts of Kasinga's case (about which she was previously unaware), she said it was likely (since she knew others similarly situated) that Kasinga was part of an international prostitution ring that worked the Togo-Germany-U.S. triangle. "They are told that if they are caught without papers, they should say they are fleeing FGM," he repeated her having said.

4. The case before the board was made easier for Kasinga and her lawyers by the fact that INS general counsel David Martin was himself willing to grant asylum to Kasinga if it was based on sufficiently narrow grounds so as to ensure that the INS would not be flooded with FGM asylum requests.

5. There was some ambiguity in Kasinga's earlier statements concerning her marital status (whether or not she was *already* married to the man in question), whether or not her father was still alive, who performed genital cutting among Tchamba (an old man or an old woman), and exactly what had happened when she was in Germany. There was also concern about the fact that portions of the taped transcript from the earlier hearing were inaudible, and that the record included an untranslated document (in French) from the Togolese police.

6. All of the other issues, except for whether the Board of Immigration Appeals should establish a broad framework for future policy, were dealt with briefly, both during the hearing and in the court's final opinion.

7. As INS general counsel Martin put it, classic asylum cases focus on someone "who is the political opponent of a dictator and has fled for fear of his/her life" or "a minority group subjected to a life-threatening campaign of ethnic/racial hatred."

8. Kasinga's lawyers submitted an affidavit by Merrick Posnansky, an archeologist, which asserted that FGM was common in Tchamba, that Tchamba women who chose not to undergo the procedure would be forced to do so, that because "Togo is a very patriarchal society" young women Kasinga's age would have no say in their marital fates, and that if returned to Togo she would be subjected to countrywide persecution. Although he conducted archeological work in Togo, Posnansky has never to my knowledge conducted ethnographic work there, speaks none of the local languages, and has never lived among Tchamba.

9. See Grewal and Kaplan (1996) for a postcolonial feminist critique of the Orientalist assumptions that similarly inform Pratibha Parmar and Alice Walker's 1993 film *Warrior Marks.*

10. Other articles published during spring 1996 include those of Judy Mann and Linda Burstyn in the *Washington Post* (January 19, March 17), Ellen Goodman in the *Boston*

Globe (April 10), and A. M. Rosenthal on the Op-Ed page of the *New York Times* (April 12).

11. The article is peppered with phrases such as *"for millennia,* girls across Africa" and "it has been the custom *since antiquity,"* all suggesting timelessness and stasis (Dugger 1996c, emphasis added).

12. Even Dugger's account (1999c) suggests such a retelling: "Mr. Kasinga's decisions [to not have his daughters cut, and to educate Fauziya] brought stinging disapproval from his own extended family. They accused him of trying to act like a white man. His girls would never be considered full Tchamba women until their genitals had been excised, the elders said, and he was wasting money by sending them to high school. But Mr. Kassindja kept a distance from his relatives, including his cousin, who lived a few blocks away. 'He was a rich man, so the family couldn't tell him anything,' said the cousin, Mouhamadou Kassindja, now the family patriarch."

CHAPTER 8

Seeking Asylum, Debating Values, and Setting Precedents in the 1990s

THE CASES OF KASSINDJA AND ABANKWAH IN THE UNITED STATES

Corinne A. Kratz

INTERNATIONAL DEBATES HAVE swirled around practices of female genital modification for decades, since early last century, variously calling the practices female circumcision, female genital cutting (FGC), or FGM—female genital modification to those seeking a neutral descriptive term, female genital mutilation to activists opposing the practices.[1] The contests burgeoned particularly in contexts that entail intercultural encounters and cultural pluralism. In such situations, fundamental values and interests often conflict, raising questions and debates about the judgments inevitably made about the practices, people, and communities that clothe abstract values in daily experience. When these disputes land in the courts, decisions must define new issues in terms of existing legal principles and precedents. At the same time, however, they might also set other precedents that begin to reshape the circumstances of intercultural exchange, throwing into relief the differences of power, status, and resources that define such encounters, and setting limits to pluralism. Case studies provide critical ways to understand conflicting values and norms from the diverse perspectives of those involved, as well as to trace social processes over time to determine how and when such contradictions arise.

In the past twenty-five years, international campaigns against female genital modification reached new prominence, and debates about the practices became far more widespread. These developments were bolstered by extensive media attention in the United States and Europe in the 1990s, the formation of new advocacy groups, and changing patterns of international migration and interaction. With political action groups and media coverage importantly fueling and shaping the dynamics of the debates, ideas and issues related to female genital modification were increasingly incorporated into public culture in the United

States. Yet given the fraught character of the debates and the fundamentally different understandings at stake, it makes sense to ask which perspectives, understandings, values, and interests have been most saliently voiced and embedded in public culture. Media stories and advocacy groups often simplify complex and contradictory issues. In dealing with cultural practices and ideas that run counter to their own deeply held notions, those involved may be unable or unwilling to see beyond their own values or to consider information that contradicts their assumptions. This can result in misinterpretation, misrepresentation, or reducing a range of cultural perspectives and practices to try to make them fit more comfortably, too often falling back on stereotypes. What, then, are the implications of the striking involvement of advocacy groups and media in these debates in recent decades? How do their representations of circumcising practices influence particular cases and situations, help replicate or heighten controversies and disagreements, or advocate for more equal dialogue and understanding?

The late 1980s and 1990s also saw prominent legal cases about female genital operations in Europe and North America, as growing immigrant communities brought traditional customs to new locales. Defendants were charged with assault in France,[2] but most legal cases in the United States have been framed in terms of immigration, refugee, and asylum law. Fauziya Kassindja and Adelaide Abankwah were the protagonists in two asylum cases heard in the United States during this time. The Kassindja case was conducted from 1994 to 1996, soon followed by the Abankwah case from 1997 to 1999. The cases, the first of their kind to be heard, set legal precedents that were cited and incorporated in subsequent cases. Contrasts and continuities between these two cases provide a way to consider the roles that media coverage, advocacy groups, and the ongoing debates can play in such critical situations.

For participants, such legal cases can be extremely unsettling: understandings are turned topsy-turvy, familiar assumptions and ways of reasoning are fundamentally contested. It might seem they have passed through the looking glass into another world, mirroring experiences described in Lewis Carroll's classic books. Yet what hangs in the balance is highly consequential for some participants. International debates about circumcising practices contain similar disjunctions. In the courts, however, the collisions between different values, social organizations, and religious and aesthetic convictions undergo further translations into specialized legal language and procedures. In considering such disputed practices and contentious circumstances it is vital to separate their different dimensions and divergent perspectives and to identify the basic grounds of dispute and moral/ethical principles at issue (Kratz 1999a). This underlines "just how complicated inter-cultural dialogue on rights questions actually becomes *when all cultures enter the dialogue on grounds of moral and intellectual equality*" (Ignatieff 1999, 34, emphasis added). Such equality has rarely been part of the international debates, however, and this worrisome inequality in representation and power has been exacerbated by lobbying efforts and media blitzes aimed at the courts. The two legal cases considered in this chapter illustrate the shape, scope, and effects of these efforts.

In this chapter I consider both international debates and legal cases because they represent different aspects of the long, far-reaching social processes through which issues related to female genital modification have been defined. The debates are typically formulated through a broad division between "Western" and "traditional" cultures; anticircumcision campaigns usually ignore both differences among circumcising practices and differences among and within the many societies that practice them.[3] Court cases often rely on these same simplified, polarizing characterizations, though the very situations presented demonstrate their fallacies. Societies that practice female genital modification are not uniform, homogeneous, or unchanging, and these debates occur in multiple settings—local, regional, national, international, and global, with alliances and interconnections across settings. Indeed, divisions, alliances, and changes in societies and settings where genital modifications are practiced and debated have already shaped the representation of a case when it reaches court.

These diverse perspectives and situations are illustrated in the following ten quotations that show how a range of people describe genital modifications, including African men and women in the United States and in Africa, journalists, activists and lawyers:

"I was circumcised at eleven with my cousin. We were lucky to get anesthetics. . . . Everybody in the family was very happy—my mom, my dad. (What about you?) I was happy. Everyone would call you names, saying that you are not a grown woman. The ones who were circumcised had more honor. So you feel alone and ashamed if you're not circumcised. (Young Somali woman, quoted in Mire 1994)

All my friends were getting circumcised. I felt that if I was left out I would become the laughing stock. So I ran away from home and went to stay with grand mum who gave me the green light to become a woman. (Mary Nyamboki, Kenyan woman who ran away at fifteen because her mother refused to allow her to be circumcised, quoted in Wachira 1995)

In the U.S., when you tell your new friends that you have been circumcised, they seem to avoid you and they feel uneasy with you, thinking that something's wrong with you. It's difficult to make them understand. (Young Somali woman, quoted in Mire 1994)

It is important . . . that we not be looked at as . . . victims. . . . There's a wide spectrum of opinion among women—Somali men and Somali women—on this, but I think I can safely say, as for who perpetuates the actual tradition, that's firmly in the hands of women. . . . . And so what you, I guess, need to take yourselves to is this leap of faith that there's an incredible amount of love that's involved in this experience. (Young Somali woman, quoted in Mire 1994)

The most widespread existing violation of human rights in the world. (*New York Times* editorial columnist A. M. Rosenthal 1993)

Female circumcision is the popular but medically incorrect term most frequently used in Africa and the Middle East for a variety of genital mutilations of female children and young girls. . . . The real purpose is to reduce or extinguish sexual pleasure and keep women under male sexual control. (Anticircumcision activist Fran Hosken n.d.)

Ahmadu argues that many women (herself included) who had sexual experiences prior to excision perceive either no difference or increased sexual satisfaction. She also points out that many Western women who have clitorises are unable to achieve orgasm. (Kirsten Bell 2005, 132)

No evil intent should be read into excision. They do it because they love their children. Parents think they're doing the right thing. (Hélène Liehnard, technical adviser to the Department of Population and Migration, Interior Ministry, France during 1991 trial of Sory and Sémité Coulibaly and Aramata Keita from Mali, quoted in Peyrot 1991)

Frankly, I don't give a damn if opposing this is a violation of someone's culture. To me, female genital mutilation is a violation of the physical and spiritual integrity of a person. (Mr. Hasche, lawyer for Nigerian Lydia Oluloro's immigration case in Oregon, quoted in Egan 1994)

A judge's role is to maintain public order, but by combating excision, he would disturb public order. (Mr. Fofana, Justice Ministry, Côte d'Ivoire, quoted in Dugger 1996c, A5)

This range of outlooks raises critical questions for legal cases. How are different actors portrayed and represented in court? Which gain a hearing, and how? How should parents' rights, children's rights, and community rights be weighed against one another? How do universal rights apply to the judicial process itself? How do such cases modify definitions of these rights? How should the multiple locales and understandings shaping participants' situations be taken into account?

The various local, national, and international spheres of practice and debate have long been joined in larger, shared fields of social action (cf. Gluckman 1958). Their connections are complex, for the larger social fields are composed of semi-autonomous arenas (Moore 1978), interacting yet structured and defined differently.[4] This means, for example, that actions by U.S. organizations might influence the way African national policies or local disputes play out. But despite Ignatieff's ideal (noted above), neither debates nor cases involve even and equal playing fields. Participants are characterized by differences of knowledge, influence, and resources as well as different cultural outlooks and values. It is critical, then, to consider from a variety of social positions both the moral, ethical, and aesthetic values in conflict *and* the social processes that constitute debates and cases about circumcising practices.

When I consider the Kassindja and Abankwah asylum cases in the next section, I distinguish these social positions with the framework I developed to define the crosscutting contexts and multiple perspectives involved in circumcision debates. It distinguishes three broad interacting arenas: home countries, Euro-American countries (including Australia), and international campaigns (Kratz 1999a):[5]

1. *Home countries* are countries in Africa, the Middle East, and Southeast Asia where circumcising practices have traditional standing. There may be various traditions and practices within home countries and different positions within communities. Actors might include national government and politicians, local nongovernmental organizations (NGOs) and action groups, international action groups, churches, and members of ethnic and religious communities with their own differences of age, gender, education, religion, wealth, and so forth. Debates about genital modification also have long histories in some countries, for example, Kenya and Sudan (Abusharaf 1999; Murray 1974 and 1976; Thomas 1996; Thomas 1997).

2. *Euro-American countries,* the second arena, also have a history of genital operations for both girls and boys, histories related to changing understandings of health, class, ethnicity, gender, and sexuality. Clitoridectomy was a recognized medical treatment in these countries through the 1950s, and even into the 1960s, used to treat insomnia, sterility, and masturbation (Bell 2005, 129; Morgan and Steinem 1979, 293–296; Pederson 1991, 672). Contemporary concern about female genital operations within these countries is related particularly to immigrants from the home countries just discussed. The operations are subject to specific laws in an increasing number of countries, with legislation passed now in Sweden (1982), Switzerland (1982), the United Kingdom (1985), Australia (1996), Norway (1996), the United States (1996), Belgium (2001), Austria (2002), and Italy (2004). The European Parliament also adopted a resolution in 2001 seeking to harmonize legislation throughout European Union countries (Powell et al. 2004, 154). In this arena, actors include national and state governments and courts, agencies dealing with immigrants (for example, INS, Health and Human Services), immigrants from "home countries" with different histories and circumcising practices, various host communities in Europe, Australia, or the United States, immigrant community organizations,

national action groups, and organizations concerned with women and children, and international action groups. Differences of gender, generation, and wealth within immigrant families and communities may be exacerbated through differential engagement with educational systems, job opportunities, and other features of host countries.

3. The third arena, *international campaigns,* is related to the others yet constituted by its international reach and involvement in several domains of debate at once. Key actors include international action groups based in different countries, international agencies such as the UN and WHO, as well as some religious officials, journalists, and others.

Even this skeletal description of the three arenas and their participants makes clear how complicated, contentious, and inherently multisided disputes and decisions about genital modification must be. It also points to serious questions about who speaks for whom in the debates and cases, which perspectives and interests are not recognized, and how different actors are involved. Numerous shifts in circumcising practices and debates in home countries show increasing interconnection both among home-country settings and among home countries and the other two arenas.[6] Ritual practice has always been historically and socially adaptable—even if practitioners claim unchanging "tradition." Yet this wide wave of change is notable, if variable in direction and type. Further, there is a common shift discernable in the terms of discussion about genital modification in many home countries: local practitioners and communities increasingly discuss practices in ways that separate ritual into different segments to consider separately—thinking about and debating whether genital modification or the other ritual events in which it is embedded are the more important. Such discussion underlines the fact that many individuals and families everywhere are making difficult decisions about and conscious adaptations in their circumcising practices.

The courts are also making difficult decisions, but how do the complex social and political processes and interconnections of the debates enter court cases and how much of this flux in practice registers there? While international debates about female genital modification encompass and cross the three arenas, particular areas of national law define horizons for most court cases. This affects and limits legal strategies. Although influential, the broader contexts and debates might be unknown to lawyers or judges or not seem germane or admissible in a narrower legal sense. To explore the implications of these issues and consider how particular cases look from other perspectives in and across other arenas, I turn now to the 1990s asylum cases of Fauziya Kassindja and Adelaide Abankwah in the United States. These landmark cases received considerable media attention and attracted involvements that embroiled them in the politics of the international debates as well. Comparing the cases also illustrates just how elusive are the "grounds of moral and intellectual equality."

Two Cases for Asylum: Fauziya Kassindja and Adelaide Abankwah

Kassindja and Abankwah are not the only immigration cases concerning female genital modification heard in the United States,[7] but they have certainly been the most widely discussed, and both set legal precedents. Kassindja's was the first case in which the Board of Immigration Appeals, the highest tribunal of the INS, recognized fear of genital operations as a valid basis for an asylum claim, changing guidelines for all immigration judges. Abankwah's case was the first time a federal court supported an asylum petition based on this fear. For the two young women, the cases were part of life-changing experiences that included stressful departures from their homelands, years of detention in the United States, and, eventually, lives in a new country.[8] In considering them here, however, I am concerned less with individuals than with how these cases draw upon and become part of broader debates about female genital modification and how they are seen from various perspectives and settings. My concern is with how they figure in the production and circulation of knowledge and social values.[9] This section outlines the chronology of events in both cases. In the following section, I consider how different actors, arenas, and criteria of evidence were invoked in the two, as well as moments where conflicts of value and cultural outlook crystallized. Since I seek to show the complex social and political processes at work in both cases and debates, I maintain a descriptive and analytical tone. The imbalances and biases evident from comparing the cases are nonetheless of grave concern.

Before the cases began, public attention to and familiarity with debates about female genital modification increased dramatically in the United States in the 1990s. In 1992 and 1993, the practices were hotly debated in editorial pages of the *New York Times; Warrior Marks,* the book and film by Alice Walker and Pratibha Parmar, appeared;[10] and *Time* magazine ran a story on the heightened American debates (Kaplan et al. 1993). In 1994, the case of Lydia Omowunmi Oluloro made national news, again including *Time,* the *New York Times,* and television profiles.[11]

A Yoruba woman from southern Nigeria, Oluloro moved to Portland, Oregon, in 1986 to join her husband, who had permanent resident status. They divorced in 1993, with two daughters born in the United States, and deportation proceedings were begun against Oluloro because her own residency papers had not been filed. She requested suspension of deportation on the grounds that her daughters, American citizens, would be forcibly circumcised if returned to Nigeria with her. She was circumcised herself as a girl[12] and supported the practice but said materials from anticircumcision campaigns had changed her mind. Her husband claimed "her change of heart had coincided with the Government's move to deport her," but she "won support from feminists and human rights advocates across the United States" (Egan 1994). Her deportation was suspended in March 1994, a decision "controversial among many Africans, who said that Oluloro was from the Ijebu branch of the Yoruba in southern Nigeria, where FGM is not practiced" (Fokkena 1994). Such distinctions, relevant to African realities, did not enter American legal arenas, though they might have been pertinent.

The *Time* article about Oluloro quotes Colorado Congresswoman Pat Schroeder, who in 1993 introduced federal legislation prohibiting and criminalizing female genital modification. Similar bills were soon introduced in the Senate (1995) and several state legislatures. The congressional bill passed in late September 1996 and took effect six months later. Schroeder and others also involved themselves in the fall 1996 controversy over proposals by Harborview Medical Center in Seattle. Harborview sought to work with the local Somali immigrant community to devise a simple, largely symbolic procedure that addressed their need and wish to "circumcise" their daughters without harming them (D. L. Coleman 1998). When their efforts were publicized, the ensuing furor foreclosed the solution.[13]

When seventeen-year-old Fauziya Kassindja arrived in Newark, New Jersey, in mid-December 1994, this was the context for her case. Journalist Celia Dugger wrote of the 1996 legislation, "Support for these measures—included in an end-of-session spending bill—mounted this year as the case of Fauziya Kassindja, a young woman who fled Togo to avoid having her genitals cut off and sought asylum here, gained attention in the American news media, Government officials said" (1996c).[14] Kassindja's case continued until June 1996, when she was granted asylum. Adelaide Abankwah's immigration case began soon after, when she arrived in March 1997, and continued until she received asylum in August 1999. Kassindja herself became a figure in Abankwah's case, visiting her with Gloria Steinem while Abankwah was in detention.

The Kassindja and Abankwah cases are complex tales involving many people, places, and organizations. The following sketches reconstruct events, although the interconnections and timing of events are not always clear from material available. Tables 8.1–8.3 show time lines for the cases and for 1990s media and legal developments in the United States.

The Kassindja Case

Fauziya Kassindja was the youngest daughter of a well-to-do family of the Tchamba-Koussountou people living in Kpalimé, a town in northern Togo.[15] Her father had long-standing disputes with his brother and sister over his marriage to her mother, education of his daughters, and circumcision of the family's daughters. Kassindja was caught in those disputes after her father died in January 1993. Her father's siblings gradually took over his affairs, sent her mother away after the prescribed mourning period, removed Kassindja from her secondary school in Ghana, and arranged for her to marry and be circumcised in October 1994. With the help of her older sister and money from her mother, Kassindja fled as her marriage and preparations for her circumcision were being finalized.

TABLE 8.1

Time Line of 1990s Media/Legal Developments in the United States

1992–1993	Debates in U.S. news (Rosenthal, Walker, Mekuria, Dawit, and others)
1993	*Warrior Marks* book and film (after *Possessing the Secret of Joy* in 1992)
1993	Congresswoman Shroeder and Senator Reid propose federal legislation prohibiting and criminalizing FGM
March 1994	Oluloro case
December 1994	Kassindja arrives in U.S. and is detained
1995–1996	Kassindja campaign
June 1996	Kassindja granted asylum
September 1996	Congress passes law (takes effect six months later)
Fall 1996	Harborview controversy
March 1997	Abankwah arrives in U.S. and is detained
Spring 1998–1999	Abankwah campaign
August 1999	Abankwah granted asylum

Her sister arranged for her to be taken illegally into Germany; two months later she bought a fake passport and continued to the United States, hoping to be given political asylum and to contact an uncle in New Jersey.

On her arrival in December, she asked for political asylum and was sent to a detention center. Her first hearing, in Philadelphia in late August 1995, was argued by Layli Miller Bashir, then a law student at American University who had worked on the case for some months as clerk for the lawyer Kassindja's cousin had retained. Asylum was denied; Kassindja's account was found inconsistent and not credible. Miller Bashir sought help with the appeal from Surita Sandosham of Equality Now, an organization dedicated to action for women, human rights, and refugees, and from Karen Musalo, acting head of the International Human Rights Clinic at American University. Sandosham "agreed to work her media and political contacts to bring attention to the case" (Dugger 1996b), and Musalo agreed to handle the appeal pro bono.

A request for parole in mid-October was denied a month later; an appeal brief and accompanying affidavits were submitted in early December. The case was mentioned briefly in a *New York Times* article around the same time. Equality Now had Kassindja write notes to key reporters, and coverage began to increase in 1996. It also organized letters from Congress to the attorney general and a public letter-writing campaign. The first full news article about the case appeared in the *Washington Post* in mid-March 1997, just after Kassindja's lawyers filed a writ of habeas corpus trying to get her released. In April the Justice Department defended continued detention. That same month, the U.S. Embassy in Togo sent staff to interview Kassindja's family in Kpalimé; contacted Suzanne

TABLE 8.2

Time Line of Fauziya Kassindja Case

January 1993	Kassindja's father dies
October 1994	Kassindja flees home during wedding period; leaves Togo for Germany
December 17, 1994	Arrives in the U.S.; on illegal entry, sent to New Jersey detention center
August 1995	First hearing in Philadelphia, represented by Miller Bashir; asylum denied
Fall 1995	Miller Bashir seeks help from Sandosham of Equality Now and Musalo of American University's International Human Rights Clinic. Musalo takes on appeal; Equality Now agrees to help
October 1995	Request for release on parole
November 1995	Request for release on parole denied
Fall 1995–	Equality Now mounts letter-writing campaign to U.S. Justice Department
Spring 1996	Equality Now contacts members of Congress and media (including Mann of *Washington Post* and Dugger of *New York Times*)
December 1995	Appeal brief and affidavits filed; first brief mention of case in *New York Times*; Equality Now has Kassindja write notes to reporters
March 1996	Writ of habeas corpus filed; *Washington Post* article, then other coverage
April 1996	*In the United States:*
	April 5 — Justice Dept brief filed defending continued detention ("risk for flight")
	mid-April — *New York Times* stories by Rosenthal and Dugger add to attention and pressure to release
	April 24 — Kassindja released from detention pending resolution of appeal
	next — Kassindja appears on Nightline, CNN, CBS; Gloria Steinem and others meet and champion Kassindja
April 1996	*Meanwhile in Togo:*
	U.S. Embassy in Lomé (a) sends staff to interview Kassindja family; (b) sends Justice Department a study on incidence in Togo; (c) contacts Suzanne Aho, director of Togo's Office for Protection and Promotion of the Family, who talks to Kassindja's father's brother
May 2, 1996	Appeal heard
June 13, 1996	Political asylum granted

Aho, director of Togo's Office for Protection and Promotion of the Family,[16] who also spoke with Kassindja's uncle; and sent the Justice Department a new report on the incidence of "female genital cutting" in Togo (Dugger 1996b).

Further media attention had come in the wake of the *Post* article, including a column by A.M. Rosenthal in the April 12 *New York Times. Times* reporter

Table 8.3
Time Line of Adelaide Abankwah Case

July 1996	Abankwah's mother dies
Later in 1996	Abankwah moves to Accra
Starting five weeks later	Dispute over money with employers, who contact people in Abankwah's village; fearing people from village will come, she leaves
March 29, 97	Arrives in the U.S.; on illegal entry, sent to New York detention center
June 1997	Narymsky, attorney for Hebrew Immigrant Aid Society, takes case
September/October 97	Immigration hearings, Otumfuor testimony/affidavits submitted, pleas for asylum and withholding of deportation denied
Spring 1998	Women's Commission for Refugee Women and Children, celebrities, and media draw attention to the case and begin campaign (*Marie Claire* article in May)
July 1998	Board of Immigration Appeals denies appeal
August 1998	Appeal filed with Second Circuit Court of Appeals
Spring 1999	Campaign by Equality Now; Jonathan Rauchway, new lawyer for appeal, recruited by Women's Commission for Refugee Women and Children; internet and letter campaigns; protests by immigrant rights groups and New York legislators; media coverage; joint visit to detention center by Kassindja and Steinem; press conferences held by NOW-NYC; New York legislators write to attorney general and hold press conference
May 3, 1999	Second Circuit Court case argued
July 9, 1999	Second Circuit Court decision reverses appeal (sending it back to BIA)
August 1999	Asylum granted by BIA
December 2000	Further INS investigation finds "Abankwah" to be false identity and her claims to be fraudulent
September 9, 2002	Regina Norman Danson (aka Adelaide Abankwah) is indicted on nine counts of perjury, false statements, and passport fraud
January 15, 2003	Danson is found guilty of all nine counts
August 12, 2003	Criminal sentencing in Danson fraud case
Several months later	INS files to reopen Danson's asylum case, rescind asylum, and enter a removal order. The case was still pending in January 2005.

Dugger visited Kassindja in mid-April and published the first of several front-page stories on April 15, catapulting the case into full media scrutiny. Kassindja was released from detention nine days later, "because she has developed in recent months strong ties to religious and human rights groups who have promised to support her and insure she shows up for legal hearings" and/or because "an

April 15 article in the *New York Times* detailing the case and the conditions of her detention led to a public outcry, a barrage of news accounts, and the promise of continuing protests by an array of advocacy groups" (Dugger 1996a). Coverage continued, with television appearances for Kassindja on *Nightline,* CNN, and CBS, and support from such public figures as Gloria Steinem.[17]

Kassindja's appeal was heard in early May; the decision granting her asylum was issued in mid-June. Celia Dugger did an extensive follow-up in the *New York Times* in September after visiting Togo and interviewing Kassindja's relatives and government officials there (1996b). Among the developments and repercussions in Togo that she describes are these: Kassindja's mother asks forgiveness from her husband's brother; he holds a contentious meeting of the extended family about abandoning female genital modification since the attention is "spoiling the family reputation"; Fauziya herself receives a substantial book contract. Dugger also learned that in recent years, girls in Koussountou were being circumcised between the ages of four and seven instead of in their teens because of opposition to the practice. A family elder explained, "We don't want to let them . . . run away." Dugger continued to write about "female genital cutting" until the end of 1996, focusing on Côte d'Ivoire, the new congressional law, and finally on African immigrants in the United States.

The Abankwah Case

Adelaide Abankwah arrived in the United States in late March 1997; she was twenty-seven years old. After she passed through immigration, an inspector called her back to check her documents again (Sikes 1998, 56). Arrested for traveling on a false passport, she asked for asylum and explained why she had left Ghana. Newspaper reports repeatedly describe her as sobbing and speaking in "broken English" during her account (English is a national language in Ghana, but Abankwah only finished primary school, Waldman 1999).

She said she belonged to a small (six-hundred-member) tribe in central Ghana called Nkumssa; her mother had been the queen mother. When her mother died in 1996, Abankwah's grandmother told her she would take the office, although no elders approached her about it. Becoming queen mother was said to involve a virginity test and later marriage to a man the elders would select. Abankwah had had sexual relations with her boyfriend and so would fail the test; she reported that circumcision would be her punishment.[18] To avoid this, she went to Accra, the capital, stayed with a friend's family, and found employment. After five weeks her employers accused her of stealing money, reported her to the Nkumssa, and members of the tribe came to find her in Accra. At this point, about eight months after her mother's death, she purchased a fake passport, visa, and a plane ticket and fled to the United States. No available court decisions or newspaper stories provide names for anyone mentioned in the account or for Abankwah's home in central Ghana. The INS hearing transcript, however, notes that her village is called Briwa (Matter of Abankwah transcript, 55).

Abankwah had eight short immigration hearings between April and July and was given a list of legal aid groups; the case was postponed each time because she had not yet found representation. After two short court appearances in July with both a lawyer and an interpreter, her hearing was postponed at the request of Olga Narymsky, an attorney with the Hebrew Immigrant Aid Society (HIAS) who had just taken the case and needed time to prepare. The case was heard in September, with a Fanti interpreter. Two Ghanaians gave supporting evidence in October: Victoria Otumfuor, a Pentecostal minister living in the Bronx, and her son, Kwabena Danso Otumfuor, who had met Abankwah in Accra shortly before she left Ghana.[19] The request for asylum and withholding of deportation was denied, as was Abankwah's initial appeal heard nine months later, in July 1998, by the Board of Immigration Appeals. An appeal was filed with the Second Circuit Court of Appeals a month later.

In spring 1998, *Marie Claire* magazine featured Abankwah's case in a story on women refugees, noting that the Women's Commission for Refugee Women and Children was trying to bring attention to it and that celebrities (for example, Vanessa Redgrave) were becoming involved. *Marie Claire* photography editor Nancy Weisman, "who visited Abankwah when the magazine ran [the] story . . . inadvertently became an activist on Abankwah's behalf. 'I sent out press packets, color photocopies of stories, facts on the case, legal documents, pleas to people'" (McCarthy 1999, 22). Jonathan Rauchway, recruited by the Commission from "a prestigious law firm" in New York, also agreed to argue Abankwah's appeal in federal court (McCarthy 1999; Thompson 1999a).

By spring 1999 Equality Now had joined the campaign and a range of supporters "made her case a cause célèbre" (Waldman 1999). NOW-NYC held press conferences, as did Senator Charles Schumer and Representative Carolyn Maloney, surrounded by a dozen people wearing "Free Adelaide Now" T-shirts, to announce their letter to the attorney general about Abankwah's release (Thompson 1999b). Fauziya Kassindja and Gloria Steinem visited Abankwah together; Rosalyn Carter and Julia Roberts also lent their names to the effort. The president of Equality Now also reported that Hilary Rodham Clinton "was very helpful in ensuring that INS was aware of the case at the highest level" though Clinton's spokeswoman said she did not "believe it was appropriate to inject herself into the immigration service's ongoing process" (Branigin and Farah 2000a, 2000b). Between April and August, the *New York Times* ran seven articles about the case by several reporters but placed them in the Metro section, not on the front page as it had earlier stories about Kassindja. Media coverage was extensive, but Abankwah did not find a Celia Dugger who followed her case closely, writing prominently and sympathetically about characters and places involved.

Abankwah's appeal was argued before the Second Circuit Court in May and granted in July. The judge agreed that Abankwah's fear was subjectively grounded but overturned the earlier ruling of insufficient objective grounds.

The earlier ruling found no credible evidence that genital operations were used, as claimed, to punish lack of virginity or that they were common practice in Abankwah's home area, noted that the practice was outlawed in Ghana in 1994, and found that Abankwah had not established membership in a particular, cognizable social group subject to persecution, as required for asylum. (The group membership claimed was "women of the Nkumssa tribe who did not remain virgins until marriage.") The circuit court judge determined that Abankwah's own testimony could be the basis not only for the subjective component of "well-founded fear" but could also establish the necessary objective basis of the fear as well, supported by Otumfuor's testimony. Otumfuor gave general evidence about "FGM," but admitted she had no specific knowledge of Abankwah's ethnic group or area.

The circuit court decision sent Abankwah's case back to the Board of Immigration Appeals for consideration. She remained in detention for ten days while supporters demanded her release; Senator Schumer's staff was "relentlessly pressing the agency [INS] to grant Ms. Abankwah's release" (Jacobs 1999). Released on parole, she was granted asylum the next month. Soon after, she appeared with supporters at a news conference at *Marie Claire* magazine (Hu 1999) and went to stay with Otumfuor.

INTERSECTING ARENAS, ETHNOGRAPHICA, AND THROUGH-THE-LOOKING-GLASS MOMENTS

As seen from the United States and portrayed in American media, the Kassindja and Abankwah cases were dramatic, clear-cut examples of how young women could be threatened and oppressed by "tribal customs." Extended detention in the United States—Kassindja's under harsh conditions—heightened their plights. The two cases also created narratives and trajectories of involvement stretching from West Africa to the United States. Their similarities and differences can help in considering relations among international debates and court cases about genital modification and different perspectives on the cases. In analyzing the cases, I first map actors and arenas involved, then consider what I call the ethnographica—fragments of cultural and historical information—about Togo and Ghana invoked in producing knowledge, narratives, and social values through the cases. This also involves "through-the-looking-glass moments" where common understandings and assumptions seem upside down, incompatible, or irrelevant. In comparing actors, arenas, representations, and values in these cases, I also consider patterns and trends in the social and political processes linking debates and cases. This includes the ways that advocacy groups and media have been involved.

Tables 8.4 and 8.5 summarize the actors involved in the Kassindja and Abankwah cases. In both, actors come from all three arenas discussed, though international campaigns seem primarily involved as sources of literature submitted in court.[20]

TABLE 8.4

Actors and Arenas in the Kassindja Case

Home countries—In Togo:

Locations:

Kpalimé (and Koussountou in later developments)—towns in northern Togo Lomé—capital of Togo

Family/communities:

Tchamba-Koussountou people

Kassindja family (her father, mother, father's brother, father's sister, sister were all named and/or interviewed)

Husband-to-be (named)

National government, NGOs, and organizations:

No law in Togo against female genital operations at the time

Officials report no request for aid in such a case yet, though constitutional provision ensuring physical integrity could be applied (Dugger 1996b)

Media:

Little coverage in Togo (Dugger 1996b)

Euro-American countries—In Germany:

Kassindja spent several months in Germany, befriended by German woman and bought passport there

Euro-American countries—In the United States:

National government, NGOs, and organizations:

Immigration and Naturalization Service (including Board of Immigration Appeals)

Initial law firm where Miller Bashir got involved in the case

Equality Now (letter campaign; contacts with politicians and media)

International Human Rights Clinic (of American University)

Congressional representatives (Congresswoman Pat Schroeder and others)

Attorney general (letters addressed to)

Media:

Newspapers: *Washington Post, New York Times, Los Angeles Times,* and others

Television: *Nightline,* CNN International

Public figures/celebrities:

Gloria Steinem

Congressional representatives and other politicians (see above)

Crossing locations—Togo/US:

Family:

Cousin in United States hires first lawyer

National governments and NGOs:

U.S. Embassy in Togo—interviews family and groom; sends recent study showing highest incidence of genital cutting in Kassindja's ethnic group

Office for Protection and Promotion of the Family (in Ministry for the Promotion of Women and for Social Services) —talked with father's brother at embassy's request

(continued)

Table 8.4. Actors and Arenas in the Kassindja Case *(continued)*

Media:
  New York Times reporter Dugger travels to Togo for follow-up story
International campaigns:
  Exhibits include material produced by international campaigns

Although situations begin in Kassindja's and Abankwah's home countries, American organizations and actors have the major involvement in their court cases; U.S. law defines the horizon of relevance once they arrive there. Only in Kassindja's case is assistance and information sought in her home country during the case, crossing arenas through the U.S. Embassy in Lomé. Information on Kassindja's situation in Togo is specific and detailed in media reports and court materials (for example, relatives and locations are named and described). Information on Abankwah is vague and general; it is not even clear at times that Adelaide Abankwah is the real name of the woman in court.

Some U.S. organizations and public figures were involved in both cases. For instance, Equality Now heightened attention to both but joined Abankwah's case when other organizations were already seeking public notice and high-caliber legal assistance. Kassindja herself joins celebrities visiting Abankwah. Similarly, Karen Musalo is an expert commentator in media coverage of Abankwah. Now directing the Center for Gender and Refugee Studies, her legal representation of Kassindja is not noted when she is quoted in the later case (McCarthy 1999; Sachs 1999; Thompson 1999a).[21]

Comparing the two cases, however, suggests both repetition and escalation. The precedent the Kassindja case created was not only legal; it also demonstrated how a media/political action campaign could gain attention and apply pressure in other cases of genital modification (Abankwah most immediately) and elsewhere (C. Kaplan 1999). The Abankwah campaign followed a similar pattern but involved more organizations and celebrities, even as the Justice Department seemed to put less effort into examining her specific home country situation.[22] Taken together with the 1994 Oluloro case, the three suggest a trend of increasing media coverage and involvement by rights organizations. This parallels the trend within home countries toward increasing contact and interaction across settings and arenas over the same period.

Media coverage of Oluloro, Kassindja, and Abankwah also shows decreasing representation of the cases and circumcising practices as contested and debated. Stories about Oluloro in the *New York Times* and *Time* mention both larger debates about genital operations and disagreements specific to the case. Coverage of Kassindja's case makes clear that there were family disagreements; Dugger's follow-up story quotes several people who believe the practice is right and important (1996b). In Abankwah's coverage, however, the contested nature is

TABLE 8.5

Actors and arenas in the Abankwah case

Home countries—In Ghana:

Locations:

Village in central Ghana (usually unspecified; named as Briwa in INS transcript)

Accra—capital of Ghana

Family/communities:

Nkumssa people

Abankwah's family (mother, grandmother, unspecified elders—no names or backgrounds provided)

Family of a friend in Accra (unspecified name and circumstances)

Employer in Accra (unspecified name)

National government, NGOs, and organizations:

Law passed in Ghana in 1994 against female genital cutting

Media:

Newspapers: *The Ghanaian Chronicle* (other articles reported)

Euro-American countries—In the United States:

National government, NGOs, and organizations:

Immigration and Naturalization Service (including Board of Immigration Appeals)

Second Circuit Court of Appeals

Hebrew Immigrant Aid Society (lawyer for first hearings)

Women's Commission for Refugee Women and Children (recruited lawyer for federal appeal and sought initial media attention)

Orrick, Herrington, and Sutcliffe   "prestigious law firm" in N.Y. (lawyer for federal appeal)

Equality Now

NOW-NYC

Congressional representatives (Senator Charles Schumer, Representative Carolyn Maloney and others)

Attorney general (letters addressed to)

Media:

Newspapers & magazines: *Marie Claire, New York Times, Washington Post*, Newsday, *Village Voice, Ms.*

Television: WWOR-TV

Public figures/celebrities:

Gloria Steinem, Vanessa Redgrave, Julia Roberts, Rosalyn Carter

Congressional representatives and other politicians (see above)

Crossing locations—Ghana and U.S.:

Ghanaians living in U.S.:

Victoria Otumfuor and Kwabena Danso Otumfuor befriend and testify for Abankwah as "expert witnesses"

Exhibits include material produced by international campaigns and country-specific reports from State Department

---

largely absent or muted. This might be related to Abankwah's description of genital cutting as punishment. It might also indicate a shift in U.S. public understandings that have come with increasing coverage and familiarity with the debates, especially the well-advertised standpoint of campaigns against genital modification. The starting point for Abankwah coverage, then, seemed not to be the debates and disagreements—still ongoing in home countries and in immigrant communities overseas—but a certain position in those debates.[23]

This shift in the extent to which genital modification is portrayed as contested had parallels in court hearings as well. The Kassindja case included an exchange on reasons for female circumcision that mirrors one impasse between conflicting cultural values and outlooks that is prominent in the larger debates. In this case, however, INS general counsel was put in the position of explaining cultural and moral beliefs he did not hold when asked, "Does the Government have a view as to why FGM is imposed?"[24]

INS: Well, no. I mean, it is part of a cultural practice there. It's not necessarily for us to try to justify. We are trying to submit–

BIA: Well, I'm not asking you to justify it. I'm asking you does the Government have a position as to why this cultural practice is imposed?

INS: No, we—we do not. But we—we are at a loss to come up with a reason that would be regarded as legitimate and—and that's another reason why this particular circumstance—the practice should be regarded as meeting the threshold of—of shocking the conscience.

BIA: Well, some of the background evidence in front of the Immigration Judge, for example, characterizes FGM as a form of sexual oppression based on manipulation of women's sexuality in order to assure male dominance and exploitation. Does the Government disagree with that?

INS: Well, we indicated in our brief that—that there are important sociological insights and descriptions of that kind. We do not think that it's necessary for us to take a position on that one way or another. We suggest in particular that we are not—that the Board is not required to analyze the practice in those particular terms. Certainly, there's an element of that—of exactly what that description is—and again, it's our position that there is no particular reason that our society is prepared to regard as legitimate—that entails it even as a practice. (In Re: Kasinga transcript, 17–18).

In rebuttal, Kassindja's lawyer stated her position quite emphatically: "[T]here is much evidence in the record to explain the reason why FGM is inflicted . . . the practice of FGM is purely for the purpose of gender subjugation and the perpetuation of social injustice" (ibid., 23).

The contested nature of genital modification was indicated. The pertinent question in court, however, was not whether it was deplorable or whether the anticircumcision background literature submitted was accurate, but whether this case fit the framework of asylum law: could Kassindja be defined as a member of a social group suffering persecution? [25] In relation to the notion of persecution, INS counsel proposed a new "shocks the conscience" test to grapple with questions of intentionality—a point of cultural contention and misunderstanding in broader debates and central to objections to the term "female genital mutilation." "The advantages seen by the Service [INS] of this test evidently include: 1) the ability to define FGM as 'persecution' notwithstanding any lack of intent to 'punish' FGM victims on the part of the victims' parents or tribe members who may well 'believe that they are simply performing an important cultural rite that bonds the individual to the society'" (In Re: Kasinga, 21). The Abankwah case did not deal even tangentially with the contested nature of reasons and intentions related to the practices. When Abankwah described the Nkumssa practice as punishment, it came closer to standard understandings of persecution. As argued in Kassindja's case, "Persecution usually means deliberate infliction of suffering or harm. It's often equated with punishment" (In Re: Kasinga transcript, 17). Instead, Abankwah's case focused on the objective basis of her claims, whether or not genital modification was practiced in her home area and in the ways recounted. [26]

Contested cases transform in meaning and implication as they move through different arenas; presentation and evidence come to fit the arena at hand. As narratives are told and retold in communicative interaction during the asylum process, the salience of particular actors, situations, and notions of responsibility might shift, foregrounding aspects most relevant to the asylum claim (Kratz 1991, 2001; D. A. Martin 2005, 248). Both Kassindja's and Abankwah's accounts were questioned, particularly in their early forms. The first immigration judge found Kassindja's account inconsistent because he did not understand premises relevant to her situation in Togo. [27] Abankwah's "broken English" and tears made her initial account difficult to understand. Further, when her first asylum claim as a member of the social group "candidates for the queen mother position who are unable or unwilling to accept that position" was found too narrow and cast her situation as "'an individual predicament' or 'personal problem,'" the social group was redefined on appeal as "women of the Nkumssa tribe who did not remain virgins until marriage" (In Re: Abankwah 1998, 2–3). As Piot (1999b, 8; see also chapter 7 of this volume) notes, a situation that might best be seen as a family dispute in the original context must be recast into defined social groups for a viable asylum claim. In a judicial setting and particular national arena, certain aspects are defined as important and legitimate while others are devalued and rendered irrelevant. These criteria and judgments feed back into other arenas and discussions.

Mapping actors and arenas in these two cases reveals a complicated web of social and political relations and transformations. Involvements and influences interconnect both within and across arenas: the Kassindja family meets in Togo to reconsider genital modification because U.S. publicity is spoiling its name; basic information submitted into evidence comes from international organizations campaigning against genital modification; to influence and draw attention to court cases, advocacy organizations "work media and political contacts" and politicians "relentlessly" press government agencies; judicial decisions and legislative decisions reverberate with one another. Tracing the web of social connections and relations in these cases shows that the different arenas cannot be seen as separate and that differential access to key social connections in each arena can significantly influence attention to and treatment of a case.

Such interconnections are part of the workings of society and the very processes through which cultural understandings and expectations are redefined. But how and by whom particular social webs are woven can have real implications for a broad range of people. Other immigrant residents' preferences, practices, and possibilities are caught in that same web, for instance, although their influence in shaping these social circumstances is far less. The question of how judicial standards are applied in the context of increased lobbying and media pressure is particularly important. It should lead us to consider carefully the role of the judicial system in the production of knowledge and values and how that system is caught up with larger debates concerning genital modification as well as other issues.[28]

The full web of connections results from many actions and decisions over time, not fully coordinated or planned. Well-meaning efforts toward worthy goals can have unintended consequences, however. In turning now to consider how particular narratives, forms of knowledge, and values were produced in the Kassindja and Abankwah cases, I focus on one of these: how existing stereotypes of Africa and Africans fed into the cases, not only being re-created and reinforced but perhaps influencing standards of evidence and critical evaluation as well. It would take another paper to fully discuss representations of African societies and cultures in the two cases, but Piot notes of the Kassindja case

> There is no discussion whatsoever of Tchamba and what they are like, no testimony by anyone familiar with present day Togo, no inkling that two decades of discussion by Africanist scholars has established as orthodoxy that homogeneous "social groups" don't exist and that group identity is often fluid and shifting, and no reference to any anthropological literature on genital cutting. Moreover, these silences were filled by the crudest, most essentializing images and stereotypes. Thus, Kasinga was assumed by all in attendance to be a member of a "patriarchal tribe" with "immutable cultural norms" that practices "forced polygamy" and "mutilates" its women. (1999b, 6; see also chapter 7 of this volume).[29]

In the context of a more general debate about multiculturalism, Katha Pollitt notes that such assumptions are typically applied only to "cultures that most Americans know comparatively little about: cultures that in our ignorance we can imagine as stable, timeless, ancient, lacking in internal conflict, premodern. But where on the globe today is such a society?" (1999, 28).

One way to recognize how such stereotypes figured in the production of knowledge and values in the two cases is to compare the ethnographica and expert witnesses used in them, keeping in sight the effects over time of this increasingly interconnected web. I also consider several through-the-looking-glass moments that bring material in Abankwah's case into conversation with opinions and perspectives from other arenas, foregrounding questions of evidence and critical judgment. I call the cultural and historical information invoked in the cases "ethnographica" because it often seems, to an anthropologist, to be a collection of fragments and factoids, not pieced together in ways that provide coherent or comprehensive understanding of circumstances under question.[30] Indeed, the absence of basic information is astonishing at times, but those joined in legal contest are not ethnographers or historians, their time for argument and investigation is limited, and their goal is not to demonstrate the changing complexities and nuances of cultural practice.[31] But that is also why they have recourse to expert witnesses.

In cases like these, expert witnesses often include people who themselves cross arenas, with experience and knowledge of both home country and the United States. Kassindja's counsel submitted affidavits from two experts, Charles Piot and Merrick Posnansky. Piot, an anthropologist who started doing research in northern Togo in the 1980s, prepared a brief review of literature on the Tchamba people (Piot 1999b, 1; In Re: Abankwah 1998, 6). His affidavit became part of the record early in the case; Posnansky's was submitted with the appeal brief to help counter the initial ruling about Kassindja's credibility. Posnansky is an archaeologist who worked at universities in Uganda and Ghana for years, with extensive research and administrative experience in Togo (but see also Piot, chapter 7 of this volume).[32] Kassindja's counsel calls him an expert on Togo (In Re: Kasinga transcript, 4) who "analyzed her case on the basis of her affidavit . . . [and] was meticulous in explaining the facts and reasoning underlying each of his conclusions" (In Re: Kasinga Reply Brief, 7).

As noted earlier in this chapter, Abankwah's expert witnesses were Victoria Otumfuor, a Ghanaian immigrant to the United States who had recently become a Pentecostal minister, and Kwabena Danso Otumfuor, who sent an affidavit from Ghana. National origin seems to have been the main basis of their expertise, although Ghana is home to dozens of cultural groups and languages. Kwabena Danso Otumfuor's expertise was dismissed in the BIA decision as "based only on what the applicant told him" with "no indication that he is . . . an expert in the traditions of the applicant's tribe" (In Re: Abankwah 1998, 3–4). The later decision did not challenge this assessment.

Victoria Otumfuor's affidavit and testimony were discounted in the BIA decision as not material to Abankwah's situation. She "specifically stated that she did 'not know a great deal about [the applicant's] tribe.' Moreover, when asked if she knew that the applicant's tribe practiced FGM as punishment, she replied, 'No, really, I can't say I know it specifically'" and indicated that punishment for premarital sex in her own village would be banishment, not FGM (In Re: Abankwah 1998, 4). In fact, the hearing transcript shows that the word "expert" was expunged from her affidavit (Matter of Abankwah transcript, 61). However, the Second Circuit decision found that specific knowledge was not necessary and accepted Otumfuor's expertise because she visited her own home in Ghana biannually during the twenty years she lived in the United States. Although no background information submitted indicated that genital modification was used as punishment anywhere in the world, the court took as sufficient corroboration her explanation "that 'Ghana is a country of many ethnic groups. We speak ten languages and forty dialects, and every village has a little practice. . . . [I]t's not all the practices that are being put to the government. . . . It would take time. There are some up in the limelight, and some are still in the distant'" (*Abankwah v. INS 1999,* 7).

Many scholars of Ghanaian culture and history would have disagreed, but they were not expert witnesses. Historian Jean Allman sent *The Ghanaian Chronicle* a copy of her letter to *Marie Claire* magazine shortly after Abankwah was granted asylum.[33] Former head of the Ghana Studies Council, Allman has been doing research in Ghana for several decades and was there when Abankwah's case was most highly publicized in the United States. She began, "Surely a magazine of your stature employs investigative reporters capable of fleshing out the facts of a story," and continued,

> I am disgusted that your magazine has made Adelaide into a cause celebre when there is every indication that her story is contrived. Female genital mutilation is not only NOT practised in the area of Ghana from which Adelaide claims to come, but NEVER has been. . . . Nowhere in Ghana and, in fact, nowhere on the African continent, is FMG [sic] used as a punishment against those who have lost their virginity. Her claims are preposterous and any glance at any relevant literature or a conversation with any one of the Ghanaian immigrants in NYC, or the Ghanaian Consulate, would have made this clear, [it] is a felony offence in Ghana (Anonymous 1999, emphasis in original)

Yet Otumfuor *was* one of those Ghanaian immigrants in the New York City area. What kinds of facts and fact checking were part of these cases, then?

Kassindja's circumstances were described with considerable detail; people and places were named and characterized. The various ethnographica relating to the Tchamba people and area from which she came—customs regarding widows (hence Kassindja's mother), excision in the mid-teens, details of marriage ceremonies—were well documented. The account was specific enough for representatives of both the U.S. and Togolese governments to corroborate it and speak with some of the principals in Togo. In comparison, Abankwah's account (as told in court decisions and media) was vague; no particular places or people were identified or described in detail. Despite the ambiguity, it seems no inquiries were made by American or Ghanaian officials in Ghana, or by Ghanaian officials in the United States. As the Ghanaian press noted, "Adelaide also failed to tell the U.S. authorities and the rest of the world exactly which village in the Central Region she ran away from, a very important detail that would have required just a phone call from the Ghana Embassy in Washington to cross check" (Anokye 1999).[34] The ethnographica of Abankwah's case were also quite peculiar compared to other available information and research on Ghanaian society, culture, and history.

When I first heard of the case, I was struck by three aspects of the Nkumssa tradition of genital modification as described. These features were unusual, perhaps unique, and as far as I could tell unattested in the ethnographic record: limiting the practice to a small group of women within an ethnic group, using genital modification as punishment, and circumcising an adult woman of Abankwah's age (twenty-seven years old).[35] They also made me doubt the reported story. Intrigued, I began to consider the entire account more carefully. Initial searches for information on Nkumssa (with various spellings) turned up nothing in major library collections on African studies, anthropology journal indexes, general reference books on Africa, or the *Ethnologue* index of world languages. I turned next to literature on Ghana and to colleagues (Ghanaian and American) who study Ghanaian culture and history. On closer look, much of Abankwah's other ethnographica also seemed rather strange.[36]

- The office of "queen mother" is part of the institution of chieftancy among Akan-speaking peoples in southern Ghana. When a new chief or queen mother is installed, there are usually several candidates. If one was unwilling, s/he would not be forced to serve. Another candidate would take the position.
- A virginity test for queen mother is documented nowhere else in Ghana, although a candidate might be expected to have demonstrated her fertility by having children.
- There are many queen mothers and chiefs, each associated with a particular community and organized into larger hierarchical systems or networks within Akan groups. It would, thus, be unusual if Nkumssa and their queen mother, said to be Abankwah's mother, were not known more widely, even if Nkumssa are a small group.
- The *bragoro* puberty rite for girls is rare now, but still practiced in certain Akan-speaking areas. Girls were presented to the queen mother, but it did not involve circumcision. Young women were prohibited from becoming pregnant before *bragoro,* but not from losing virginity. Punishment for early pregnancy was banishment, as Otumfuor noted (Matter of Abankwah transcript, 111).
- My first inquiry to colleagues was about the name "Nkumssa" because my searches had been fruitless. Was there such an ethnic group or was it

the name of Abankwah's village or clan? No one knew of an Nkumssa ethnic group, community, or clan in Ghana. Further, Abankwah's name and claimed home area identified her clearly to them as Akan. A Ghanaian linguist offered further analysis, breaking the word down to translate: "The word Nkumsaa subjected to Akan morphological analysis will be N (negative particle) + kum (kill) +me (me) + saa (that way), meaning 'Don't kill me this/that way.' Nkumsaa is thus a well-made Akan word to fit the story" (personal communication, Obeng to author, September 3, 1999). Fauziya Kassindja did not correct misspelling of her name ("Kasinga") by the first immigration officers she encountered, a mistake carried through her case. I wondered if the "tribal" name Nkumssa reflected misunderstanding of Abankwah's tearful account in "broken English," similarly perpetuated. This seemed unlikely, however, once I read the hearing transcript because Abankwah states and spells the name through the Fanti interpreter.

- The hearing transcript raised still other questions about Abankwah and her identity. She said she usually used the name Kukwa Norman; Abankwah came from her father's father, Adelaide was used occasionally at school. The birth date given in testimony differs from the one on the fake passport, made through photo-substitution. Questions to Abankwah and Otumfuor in the hearing sought to determine whether the name Adelaide Abankwah had simply been adopted since it was on the passport she received (Matter of Abankwah transcript, 54, 63–64, 86–89, 100).

With all these peculiarities, Abankwah's account presented another world as far as other Ghanaians and scholars of Ghana were concerned, with elements of familiar practices and customs twisted and combined in bizarre ways.[37] Ghanaians did not find it amusing, however, but "a national embarrassment" where "the country's name and integrity are compromised" (Anokye 1999). A colleague who was in Ghana at the time said "people were quite upset at the slander of their cultural reputation" (personal communication, Clark to author, September 4, 1999).[38] For Americans to recognize these peculiarities, however, they needed more than ethnographic fragments and had to look beyond popular American images of Africa.[39]

Popular stereotypes were evident both in American newspaper reports and in details of other accounts of the case. For instance, when Abankwah was accused of stealing money from her employers in Accra, it was said they "reported it to her tribe"[40] so they could come after her. My guess at the situation behind this description was that Abankwah found employment through kinship and friendship networks of people she knew at home and/or at school. When she got in trouble, they tried to resolve it through the same networks rather than go to the police—which would either create more serious trouble or simply be ineffective. The notion of "reporting someone to their tribe" makes little sense without explanation of the social and political relations involved.[41]

Abankwah's appeal lawyer, Jonathan Rauchway, also made very clear the framework of stereotypes through which Abankwah's case was interpreted in his comment to the *New York Times:* "In places like Ghana, Mr. Rauchway said, people do not have basic identification papers like birth certificates or driver's licenses. Ms. Abankwah's identification is a tattoo on her forearm that reads 'Marmenorman Briwa.' The first word, she said, translates loosely as 'older sister.' The second is the name of her village. 'If I am dead somewhere,' she said, showing the tattoo, 'they can look at this and they will know where I come from'" (Thompson 1999a, 41). Ghanaians would not recognize their country in these remarks. They present another through-the-looking-glass moment for citizens of the first African country to declare independence from colonialism (in 1957), home of Kwame Nkrumah, Kofi Annan, and four universities, where adult citizens in even the most rural parts of the country hold identity cards and vote in national elections. Anokye's comment (1999) in *The Ghanaian Chronicle* is an apt rejoinder:

> With Adelaide's case all doubts I had before about the ignorance of many Americans about Ghanaian and other African societies have evaporated. It requires a lot of education to correct the jaundiced view of many on the other side of the ocean. I hope it will not be too much to ask of the people who can believe Adelaide's story right away, without checking her story, that they should know that people this side of heaven also live in skyscrapers, drive cars, wear Calvin Klein and Gucci and watch television. Indeed, I wish to have all know that it is possible to e-mail the White House from Adelaide's village or, for that matter, from a mine deep in the forest of the great Asante Kingdom of the Ashanti Region of Ghana.

Yet Victoria Otumfuor gave sworn testimony supporting Abankwah. Could these other knowledgeable people be mistaken? Abankwah's account was so vague that all were extrapolating to some extent—how else to explain Otumfuor's deposition? While Abankwah's lawyers argued her membership in a social group that would support her asylum claim, other social group memberships might have encouraged or shaped supporting testimony. Ghanaian colleagues raised this possibility with me, introducing yet another through-the-looking-glass moment—one that turns certain American assumptions about the legal process upside down.

Legal systems differ in many ways, and understandings of what it means to be a witness and give testimony are not universal. The American legal system defines allegiance to "fair and impartial justice" as an overriding concern for witnesses, with serious sanctions for perjury. Exceptions are made for close relationships that might create conflicts of allegiance (for example, spouses need not testify against one another). But those experienced in the legal system find that ideals of impartiality and fairness must be vigilantly pursued, and organizations working for international social justice and democracy regularly protest corrupt or biased legal systems in other countries. Similarly, other forms of allegiance might influence witnesses and their testimonies.

In Abankwah's case, a colleague advised, "Learn from these two Akan proverbs: (a) If you can tell lies which resemble the truth, you always have an escape route; (b) She who is fighting to bring home property should not be prohibited but should be helped. . . . Remember what constitutes a crime in one society may not be a crime or an insult in another." The second proverb suggests that Ghanaians, especially Akan (assuming Abankwah to be from an Akan group), who testified publicly against Abankwah might be seen as hindering a fellow Ghanaian, not helping her prosper. Historically, colonial courts in Ghana and elsewhere also provide cases where people agreed to a story that helped someone needing aid. Kwabena Danso Otumfuor's testimony was deemed to repeat what Abankwah had told him, with no other expertise or independent knowledge. Victoria Otumfuor's expertise was eventually accepted, but what understandings of court, testimony, allegiances, and social groups informed her testimony? Were American and Ghanaian understandings somehow combined?

As the different assessments of the Otumfuors' testimonies suggest, notions and standards of evidence are also debated in American courts, and decisions about evidentiary standards were important in the Kassindja and Abankwah cases. Kassindja's appeal lawyers remarked on her extensive objective evidence, "more corroboration than most asylum applicants" can provide (In Re: Kasinga Transcript, 3).[42] As noted, the appeal decision overturned an earlier judgment that applied assumptions based on American life to find Kassindja's account unbelievable. If interpretation of evidence became more reasonable and responsive to case circumstances in successive Kassindja rulings, however, Abankwah case rulings seemed to take a reverse trajectory. Her BIA appeal judge seemed to have read case material closely, pointed out disjunctions with Abankwah's claims, and raised questions about the expert witnesses. The decision made several of the points raised by Ghanaians and scholars of Ghanaian culture and history. However, the Second Circuit Court felt "the BIA was too exacting both in the quantity and quality of evidence that it required" (*Abankwah v. INS* 1999, 6), for "it must be acknowledged that a genuine refugee does not flee her native country with affidavits, expert witnesses, and extensive documentation" (ibid., 7). Applying a much more forgiving evidentiary standard, that decision found Abankwah's own testimony to be sufficient objective evidence for her account, backed by Otumfuor, as well as subjective evidence of her fear. From the perspective of some Ghanaians and scholars, that standard suspended critical evaluation and judgment and took little account of contemporary Ghanaian realities.

Those who found Abankwah's account puzzling or implausible, including myself, often supported broadly tolerant decisions about immigration and asylum. The point is that each case has to be made, taken seriously, and stand up to fair, knowledgeable, but critical evaluation. Abankwah's vagueness turned her case into both a Rashomon tale and a Rorschach test for American ideas about Africa and about genital modification. Why was there no apparent effort to clarify or verify such an account? The high level of media and advocacy attention seemed to bring greater clarity and detail to Kassindja's case but not to Abankwah's. Although it is hard to predict how intensified media scrutiny and lobbying might influence rulings, they can certainly make a difference.

When the clamor subsided after Abankwah's release, the district INS officer began looking into her background. Within months, agency investigators had interviewed people in Ghana, located relevant records, and assembled "what one called 'overwhelming evidence' of fraud" (Branigin and Farah 2000a; National Public Radio 2000). When this news came out, the *Washington Post* sent a reporter to Ghana. The woman claiming to be Adelaide Abankwah was really Regina Norman Danson, a former hotel worker from the town of Biriwa (eighty miles from the capital, Accra). She was never a candidate for queen mother (not being from a royal family), her mother was still living, and she had married in 1996. The local chief, Nana Kwa Bonko V, confirmed that "female circumcision plays no role in his tribe's tradition and that there is no punishment for rejecting nomination as a queen mother" (Branigin and Farah 2000a). As Danson's former employer in Biriwa summarized, "Her whole story is a complete lie . . . she left because she wanted to go to the United States."

Investigators recommended in late 1999 that Danson be prosecuted for fraud, but the "Justice Department has been reluctant to proceed for fear of embarrassing politicians and top administration officials who weighed in on Danson's behalf" (Branigin and Farah 2000a; Murphy 2000). In December 2000, Danson was selling French beauty products in New York, studying for her high school equivalency certificate, and sticking to her story.[43] Twenty months later, on the day before the statute of limitations expired in September 2002, Danson was finally charged with nine counts of perjury, making false statements, and passport fraud—crimes for which she could spend ten years in prison and be deported. Witnesses from Ghana were brought to testify during the trial, with media coverage both in Ghana and in the United States.[44] Found guilty of all charges in January 2003, Danson was sentenced in August to two years of supervised release, a small fine, and the time she had already served in INS detention (D. A. Martin 2005, 265).[45]

Nonetheless, Danson remained in New York. The fraud conviction did not void her grant of asylum. INS has filed to reopen Danson's case in order to rescind asylum and enter a removal order, but a hearing had yet to be scheduled as of January 2005 (D. A. Martin 2005, 265). Although the ultimate outcome of the Abankwah-Danson saga is not yet clear, the belated INS inquiry did resolve the questions her story raised. Yet it also raises other, more troubling questions. As a Ghanaian colleague asked: "If they could investigate afterward, why not before?"

Did political lobbying and media outrage short-circuit judicious reasoning? Do different standards of evidence and expertise apply for Africa?

For her part, Fauziya Kassindja has spent the years since her landmark case attending college and speaking on issues that were central to her case—the mistreatment of asylum seekers and female genital modification. With a B.S. in accounting and business law, she is now married, mother of male triplets, and goes by the name Kassindja Tijani (Danticat 2005, 15–16). She maintains a continuing connection with Equality Now and currently serves on the board of the Center for Gender and Refugee Studies, which Karen Musalo (her former lawyer) directs.[46]

The Kassindja and Abankwah cases set legal precedents that will continue to be used in other asylum decisions, but they created other precedents as well. If Kassindja showed how political advocacy groups can combine with relatively responsible journalism to make a sometimes flawed legal system more accountable, Abankwah showed how misplaced support by the same alliance might help subvert careful examination and due process. Legal scholar David Martin observes, "The story of Adelaide Abankwah reveals both the real strengths and the disquieting weaknesses in the institution of political asylum and in the American system for receiving and resolving asylum claims" (2005, 245). How will the Abankwah legal precedent be applied now that the objective basis of her case has been undermined?

One troubling indication comes in Judge Reinhardt's March 2005 opinion in Khadija Mohammed's petition for review of a BIA order, which cites both the Kassindja and Abankwah cases frequently. Abankwah provides the foundation in his opinion for understanding female genital modification as punishment—despite this being disproved by testimony at her fraud trial. The judge then extends the sense of "persecution" to characterize any genital modification as a "permanent and continuing" act of persecution by likening it to forced sterilization. This would give a woman who has already undergone genital modification, like Mohammed, the same potential grounds for asylum as someone like Kassindja who sought to avoid the procedure. Yet his reasoning is based on perjury and the fallacy of genital modification as punishment. How can the damage of Abankwah's misrepresentations and stereotypes be expunged from other cases when it increasingly becomes embedded as precedent?

However, one aspect now common to both the Kassindja and Abankwah cases should become a standard for future practice. When the Abankwah-Danson story was finally investigated, what made the difference was trying to ascertain and understand the Ghanaian circumstances from which she had come. Kassindja's story was confirmed through similar efforts, with support from undisputed experts. Asylum cases inevitably cross international arenas, but home country contexts cannot be ignored when they involve unfamiliar customs and circumstances. To act responsibly, legal investigations, journalists, and advocacy groups alike must take account of the multiple groundings and social relations involved, not rely on fragmented ethnographica or projected American stereotypes.

DEFINING CIRCUMSTANCES AND DISPLACED DEBATES

These two cases have shown how debates and cases about genital modification intersect and interact within and across arenas, linked moments in the sociopolitical processes through which these practices are defined and redefined in various settings. Although focused in the United States, such cases and actions in the Euroamerican arena reverberate both within that arena and elsewhere. This analysis has implications beyond circumcising practices as well, for it suggests how possibilities for understanding a range of cultural practices and immigrant communities are shaped, narrowed, or broadened. Taken separately, these cases offered instructive comparisons and contrasts. But it has been equally important to see them as different points in a larger social process.

Taken together, the Kassindja and Abankwah cases suggest shifts over time in U.S. public understandings of female genital modification. The shifts seem to favor perspectives promulgated by advocacy groups and international campaigns, along with their highly problematic representations of Africans and of circumcising practices. They might be paralleled by changing standards for evidence and critical evaluation in court cases involving genital modification. In looking at the Oluloro, Kassindja, and Abankwah cases, I noted that debates about the practices recede in Abankwah.[47] Only outside or after the court case, when other perspectives and arenas were brought in, did debates and contradictions again became prominent. But those debates were about Abankwah-Danson's account and American gullibility, not about genital modification per se.

The long-standing debates about genital modification are difficult to resolve and do not stand still. As stances, stakes, and participants change, defined in particular situations, issues and debates might also be displaced. For instance, understanding why people practice genital modification presents a fundamental intercultural impasse in international debates. When raised at Kassindja's appeal hearing, interlocutors did not understand or believe the stance of practitioners in home countries. The original stakes and stances were much attenuated in this new setting; the perplexed INS counsel was at a loss to explain practitioners' social and moral convictions and values. Through-the-looking-glass moments also transform in different settings. In Abankwah, they encompassed a wide range of cultural practice for Ghanaians and scholars, but had little to do with issues fundamental to ongoing debates about genital modification.

Comparing the Kassindja and Abankwah cases suggested what a difference thorough, grounded knowledge can make when it goes beyond fragmented ethnographica whose vague contours are easily filled in with stereotypes. Yet debates about genital modification are full of obfuscating representations and assertions that are unsubstantiated, though repeated incessantly.[48] If the images and rhetoric of anticircumcision campaigns have now circulated so relentlessly that "counterdiscourse about the meaning of genital cutting is today for most Westerners utterly unthinkable" (Piot 1999b, 6, and chapter 7 of this volume), what does that mean for "facing up to a demanding inter-cultural dialogue in which all parties come to the table under common expectations of being treated as moral equals" (Ignatieff 1999, 40)? Female genital modification is often taken as an extreme case that tests the limits of pluralism and tolerance for Euroamericans (Shweder 2002), but shouldn't that mean extra care is taken with arguments, evidence, and enabling dialogue?

Exploring questions at the limits can throw into relief problems, processes, and assumptions that may be harder to recognize in other circumstances. This discussion of debates and cases about female genital modification has shown how tangled the webs of interconnection can become and how important it is to consider these complex social dimensions when looking at contested cultural practices and at the very debates and cases themselves. The changing nature of social relations, cultural understandings, and circumstances involved mean that questions about cultural pluralism and intercultural encounters may be impossible to answer in the abstract. However, situationally defined guidelines should recognize that the playing field is never even and take careful account of its contours and shifts. Given the role that advocacy groups and media involvement can have in shaping public culture, it is particularly important that a full range of perspectives and balanced arguments be part of these fractious debates and critical cases.

NOTES

Discussions with Ivan Karp helped me formulate and clarify arguments presented in this chapter; I thank him for our ongoing conversation and for reading drafts. Peter Brown, Arthur Eisenberg, Anni Peller, Charles Piot, Rick Shweder, and Beverly Stoeltje commented on an earlier version. Jean Allman, Anthony Appiah, Gracia Clark, Christine and Ross Kreamer, Samuel Obeng, and Beverly Stoeltje offered guidance on Ghanaian customs, history, and politics. I also appreciate Ylva Hernlund and Bettina Shell-Duncan's enthusiasm and kind patience as this volume took final shape. An earlier version of this chapter appeared as "Circumcision Debates and Asylum Cases: Intersecting Arenas, Contested Values, and Tangled Webs" in *Engaging Cultural Differences: The Multicultural Challenge in Liberal Democracies,* edited by Richard A. Shweder, Hazel R. Markus, and Martha Minow (New York: Russell Sage Foundation).

1. Never neutral, the choice of terms always implies a stance toward the debates. See Kratz (1994, 1999a, 2003) on their history and rhetorical and political implications. I use the term "female circumcision" to refer to specific community traditions where practitioners view male and female circumcision as parallel practices (and often translate their own term into English as circumcision). Otherwise, I use "genital modification," "genital operations," and "circumcising practices" for the broader array of practices grouped together in international debates. Occasionally I use "genital cutting" or "FGC," but this is not as neutral as it is intended to be. Journalist Celia Dugger helped popularize that term, yet combined it with lurid descriptions of women having "their genitals cut off." I use quotation marks when following terminology used in sources mentioned.

2. See Winter (1994) for an overview of French cases, which began in 1983, and Simons (1993) for an American news account.

3. I analyze the rhetorics and representations of the international debates closely in earlier papers, as well as ways to approach such fraught controversies in the classroom (Kratz 1994, 1999a, 1999b). This paper moves beyond these concerns to consider their further implications and other domains affected by (and intertwined with) the debates.

4. Anthropologists have long used notions such as semiautonomous fields (S. F. Moore 1978) to understand the structure and processes involved in complex, large-scale social and political interactions. These concepts could be combined in profitable and illuminating ways with more recent, structurally amorphous formulations of global phenomena in terms of "flows" and "scapes" (Appadurai 1990).

5. Rogers (chapter 6 of this volume) provides a case study of the workings of these intersecting arenas in the Australian context and shows how differences and distinctions within home countries and within immigrant communities can be overlooked by actors in other arenas. Johnsdotter (chapter 5 of this volume) also notes the range of agencies and actors at work within Sweden, particularly in relation to Somali immigrant communities

6. Looking across different home countries, shifts in practice go in all directions imaginable: adoption of genital modification by noncircumcising communities (Leonard 1999); modification of long-standing rituals toward what I call "circumcision by pronouncement" or "performative circumcision," that is, substituting a verbal formula for actual cutting (Abusharaf 1999, 7; Hernlund 1999); modification through medicalization (Obiora 1997; Shell-Duncan 2001); and recontextualizing ceremonies with genital modification within refugee camp settings. Many other social, political, and economic transformations in home countries have coincided with increasing pressure from anticircumcision campaigns. These have often been more significant than campaign pressure in producing shifts.

7. In 2001, twenty were noted on the Web site of the Center for Gender and Refugee Studies; the site listed seventy-eight in August 2005 (www.uchastings.edu/cgrs/summaries/persecute.html, site accessed August 6, 2005).

8. For Kassindja, this included sudden financial success. She received more than half the proceeds of a $600,000 contract for a book coauthored with the law student who first presented her case (Dugger 1996b; Kassindja and Bashir 1998).

9. I base this discussion on material readily available about the cases, mainly U.S. media coverage and copies of court decisions. I could not visit libraries with Ghanaian or Togolese newspapers before writing this chapter; on-line archives are very limited. I am not a legal scholar and do not dwell on judicial issues, but discussion of the Abankwah case with Arthur Eisenberg, Larry Sager, and others in the SSRC-Russell Sage working group on Ethnic Customs, Assimilation, and American Law from 1998 to 2001 was a great help. Thanks to Charles Piot and Beverly Stoeltje for sending helpful sources and to the Center for Gender and Refugee Studies for sending the Abankwah hearing transcript and other material. While I made final revisions on the original version of the paper that became this chapter, news broke that further INS investigation showed Abankwah's claims to be fraudulent (Branigin and Farah 2000a; Murphy 2000). David A. Martin kindly confirmed some of the final developments in efforts to reopen the Abankwah grant of asylum after she was convicted of fraud.

10. Efua Dorkenoo, who works with the Minority Rights Group in London, was consultant for the film. In 1983, she coauthored the group's report, *Female Circumcision, Excision, and Infibulation: The Facts and Proposal for Change,* revised and reissued in 1992 as *Female Genital Mutilation: Proposals for Change.* The title change indicates shifts that occurred as debates heightened during the intervening decade.

11. Media coverage and incorporation of the debates into popular culture continued after the two court cases discussed here as well, including a piece in *Readers Digest* and a 1997 episode of the television series *Law and Order* (K. Bell 2005, 128; Shell-Duncan and Hernlund 2000, 32–34).

12. Yoruba boys and girls are circumcised when small. Circumcision and excision are not connected with initiation for the Yoruba people but are related to moral concepts associated with shame and fertility.

13. More recently, a proposal for the same such symbolic substitute was made by a Somali doctor in Italy, to be performed at a public hospital in Florence (Powell et al. 2004, 153). See also Grande (2004, 3 n. 11).

14. Dugger probably refers to excision, but such descriptions make it hard to tell.

15. Tchamba-Koussountou combines the two areas where the extended Kassindja family live. In her book, Kassindja also mentions relief at speaking Éwé with another woman from Togo who arrives at the detention center. None of the media or case material identifies the language(s) she speaks, but a search of *Ethnologue*, an extensive data base on world languages, shows (a) that Tchamba is the name for a language also known as Akaselem, with Tchamba as its main center; (b) Koussountou is the name for a language also known as Bago, with main centers in areas bearing those names; (c) Éwé is spoken in both Ghana and Togo (by 20 percent of Togo's population), is widely known as a second language, and has a main center at Kpalimé, where Kassindja's family lives.

16. This seems to be part of the Ministry for the Promotion of Women and for Social Services.

17. At the same time that media attention was growing, developments within INS led to a fuller review of legal issues related to female genital modification (Martin 2005, 256). David Martin was general counsel of INS at the time and argued the Kassindja case at BIA (ibid., 273 n. 49).

18. It is hard to know what kind of operation this was supposed to be. Abankwah spoke Fanti, an Akan language, in court proceedings, and said people from her village traded in Kumasi, a major Asante/Akan town. Knudsen notes that very few Akan groups, who make up the population of southern and central Ghana, practice female genital modification. Those that do either practice sunna circumcision (taking "off the hood of the clitoris—or the prepuce—with precision") or else make four scarification marks "on the clitoris without cutting the hood or the prepuce off" (1994, 54–56). These are the mildest forms of female genital modification.

19. Only the hearing transcript specifies the relation between these two; they figure little in news coverage. The final *New York Times* story (Hu 1999) refers to Victoria as Otumfuor-Neequaye and notes that she left Ghana twenty-two years ago. Victoria testified that her son introduced her to Abankwah at a funeral in Accra in early 1997 and then called her when he knew Abankwah was in detention (Matter of Abankwah transcript, 115–117). This portion of the testimony also sought to determine whether she was using the name "Adelaide Abankwah" in Accra.

20. Given the problematic representations of circumcising practices in some campaign literature, this has important implications for how the debates and practices were understood. Note that "mutilation" was the term used throughout Abankwah's hearings.

21. More recently, Musalo has coauthored *Refugee Law and Policy* (Musalo et al. 2001), a casebook. She has also received several awards in recognition of her legal work in support of human rights and civil rights. See cgrs.uchastings.edu/about/staff.php (site accessed July 28, 2005).

22. These are not necessarily linked, except coincidentally. I do not know if the Justice Department and the U.S. Embassy in Accra communicated during the case, as with the embassy in Lomé. Nonetheless, the belated investigation that disproved "Abankwah's" story shows that this could have made a difference (Branigin and Farah 2000a). The number of organizations devoted to women's rights and refugees has also increased over the past decade as problems have both increased and received greater attention. The Women's Commission was founded in 1989, and Equality Now in 1992.

23. When Abankwah was later charged with fraud in connection with her asylum claim, her case became part of other debates and disagreements. Her fraudulence provided

an opportunity for antifeminist commentators and anti–Hillary Clinton conservatives to gloat (see, for example, Malkin 2002). Abankwah's name even entered several online encyclopedias under the category of "Impostors" (Anonymous 2005). In the Ghanaian press, the fraud case was regarded as a triumph in ongoing battles over misrepresentation and stereotyping of Africa and Africans by the U.S. media ("We Are Not Savages" 2003).

24. Note the language of this exchange, with all here describing the practice as "imposed" or "inflicted" and taking FGM as standard, uncontested terminology. Kassindja's lawyer's use of "inflict" escalates the sense of intentionally causing suffering. The court opinion in a more recent (2005) case creates another escalation that follows the reasoning and language of anticircumcision campaigns. The opinion not only takes FGM as the standard term but refuses to use the acronym with the comment, "We see no need for using initials rather than the full three word phrase. We are short neither of paper nor of ink. The use of initials, if it has any effect, serves only to dull the senses and minimize the barbaric nature of the practice" (*Mohamed v. Gonzales* (9th Cir. 2005), 3068).

25. Similar grounds for asylum claims are in effect in other countries as well. A 2002 Austrian case, for instance, defined the social group of a woman seeking asylum as "women from Cameroon who feared being subjected to FGM" (Powell et al. 2004, 155). A recent U.S. opinion in the Ninth Circuit Court of Appeals seems to lay the basis for taking a broader view that would recognize "females" as a social group relevant for asylum claims, though two narrower social groups were emphasized as well ("young girls in the Benadiri clan" and " Somalian females" (*Mohammed v. Gonzales* 2005, 3081–3083). This opinion also takes it for granted that female genital modification is persecution, simply asserting it, in contrast to arguments presented in Kassindja's case that contended with the issue of how to make it fit such a definition.

26. As noted elsewhere, there were many objective questions about her claims.

27. For instance, he found it incredible that Kassindja did not know where her mother was, not understanding that her father's family could properly send the widow away after a reasonable mourning period and that this happened while Kassindja was away at school. Her lawyer argued, "Togo is not the United States and the Judge's reliance upon U.S. cultural norms to judge Ms. Kasinga's credibility regarding the whereabouts of her mother was totally improper" (In Re: Kasinga transcript, 4).

28. It is clear from the Gore/Bush presidential election in 2000 and from contests over judicial appointments that even the highest U.S. court can be embroiled in partisan advocacy. Mikva (2000) discusses other threats to judicial integrity.

29. Abankwah may be from a matrilineal society, like most Akan in southern and central Ghana; discussions of the queen mother position during her case showed no recognition of this.

30. In fact, there is little sense that history is relevant to "traditional" customs. "Traditional" is often assumed to mean unchanging, rather than seen as ascribing value to certain domains of practice (Hobsbawm and Ranger 1983; Kratz 1993).

31. D. A. Martin notes that trial attorneys with heavy caseloads may only have a few hours to prepare for an initial asylum hearing (2005, 6).

32. Posnansky is professor emeritus of history and anthropology at UCLA. His affidavit notes that he visited Togo sixteen times in the past sixteen years, sometimes for over a month, and had visited Kpalimé on several occasions (1998, 419).

33. *Marie Claire* did not publish or respond to the letter (personal communication, Allman to author, July 13, 2000).

34. The hearing transcript has more information, including the village name (Briwa) and nearby place where Abankwah attended school (District Konso), but hearing participants did not have the background or experience to relate these details or Abankwah's account to regional, social, cultural, and historical patterns in Ghana.

35. Societies that practice female genital modification typically prescribe it for all women, although some women do not participate because of church membership, opposition,

or other factors. As Allman's letter underlines, more than a century of research has failed to identify any society in Africa that defines genital operations as punishment. Circumcising practices are usually understood in terms of initiation into adulthood, fertility, and sexuality. Usual age varies across different societies, but puberty and late teens are the top of the range. In isolated cases, older adult women decide to be circumcised when they marry into a circumcising society (Gosselin 1999, 7). These are individual exceptions and actions taken by the women concerned, however, not accepted customs prescribing genital modification for older women. Knudsen notes examples of this in Ghana, with observations of particular relevance to Abankwah's claims. "In such marriages the Akan woman has other problems. *In some cases, the Akan woman's children may become chiefs or queen mothers one day among her own people. Therefore, they must not have any scarification on their faces, bodies or on the outer genitalia*" (1994, 50, emphasis added).

36. See Stoeltje (1997) on the Asante queen mother institution, Yankah (1995) on Akan chiefs and royal language, Dakubu (1988) on Ghanaian languages, Nukunya (1992) as an overview, and Ardayfio-Schandorf and Kwafo-Akoto (1990) for an extensive bibliography on women in Ghana. The following comments are based on these sources and e-mail discussion with scholars of Ghanaian culture and history.

37. When the story was later shown to be fraudulent, these peculiar elements were disproved (see below).

38. There was lively on-line discussion of the case in a chat group that *The Ghanaian Chronicle* sponsors (personal communication, Allman to author, July 17, 2000).

39. See Kratz (2002, 104–111) on these images and how stereotypes are recreated and circulated.

40. The BIA decision describes this differently, more neutrally: "The applicant also apparently fled because of a problem she had in Accra regarding lost money. She claimed that she was assisting the individuals with whom she was staying in Accra, and when some money was lost, she was accused of losing or taking it. She then fled from Accra. These individuals then went to her village to look for her and it was in this way that the villagers learned she was in Accra (Tr. at 72–73). The applicant acknowledged that no one from her village came to look for her until after they had been visited by the individuals who claimed she took or lost their money (Tr. at 82–83)" (In Re: Abankwah 1998, 2). This episode, which relates Abankwah's flight to other circumstances, is not mentioned in most news accounts or in the Second Circuit Court decision.

41. Appiah talks about how people adjusted to the decline of the Ghanaian state in the 1970s, providing relevant social and historical context for interpreting the notion of "being reported to the tribe":

> Life went on. Not only did people not "get away with murder" even though the police would usually not have been in a position to do anything about it, but people made deals, bought and sold goods, owned houses, married, raised families. If anything could be said about the role of state officials (including the army and the police), it was that by and large their intervention was as likely to get in the way of these arrangements as to aid them, as likely to be feared and resented as welcomed. . . . Disputes in urban as well as in rural areas were likely to end up in arbitration, between heads of families, or in the courts of "traditional" chiefs and queen mothers, in procedures that people felt they could understand and, at least to some extent, manage: once the lawyers and magistrates and the judges of the colonial (and, now, with little change, the postcolonial) legal system came into play, most people knew that what happened was likely to pass beyond their comprehension and control (1992, 168–169).

> Much has changed and improved since the 1970s. Ghana is now seen as having one of the most efficient and reputable electoral systems in Africa and having made "considerable progress . . . [from] a near 'failed state' in the late 1970s toward becoming a stable, integrated, constitutional, and democratic polity" (Joseph 2002).

42. It included letters, an unsigned marriage certificate, and photographs as well as background material on female genital modification in Togo.

43. The real Adelaide Abankwah is a former college student whose passport was stolen in Accra in 1996 (Branigan and Farah 2000a).

44. See Glaberson (2002); Hays (2002); Sheridan (2003); Ghanian [sic] Found Guilty (2003); "We Are Not Savages" (2003). The indictment *United States of America v. Danson* is available on line at news.findlaw.com/hdocs/docs/ins/usdanson90902ind.pdf (site accessed August 8, 2005).

45. In March 2003, "INS was abolished and its functions were taken over by the Department of Homeland Security" (D. A. Martin 2005, 270 n. 8). Since most of the Abankwah case was handled by INS, I continue to refer to that agency in narrating these final developments even though Homeland Security has handled them since that time.

46. See Equality Now's 2003 Annual Report (www.equalitynow.org/reports/annualreport_2003.pdf) and cgrs.uchastings.edu/about/staff.php (sites accessed July 28, 2005). The Equality Now report also includes a photograph of Kassindja Tijani's triplets.

47. The recent opinion in the Muhammed case seems to continue this trend.

48. Some of the main issues involved in these assertions and representations have to do with the range of explanations offered for genital modification, effects on sexuality, and documentation of the health consequences of various kinds of operations (Bell 2005; Grande 2004; Kratz 1994, 1999a; Morison et. al. 2001; Mugo 1997; Obermeyer 1999 and 2003; Obiora 1997; Parker 1995). A number of parallels might also be found in the politics of representation and rhetorics associated with debates about human rights and the traffic in women that burgeoned in the 1990s and early 2000s. It is worth noting that as the literature on the social construction of sexuality grew, the findings and assumptions of that work were not applied to women's experiences with female genital modification in a range of cultural settings. See A. M. Miller (2000 and 2004) and Miller and Vance (2004) on the ways debates about the traffic in women have been shaped in recent decades.

CHAPTER 9

Making Mandinga or Making Muslims?

DEBATING FEMALE CIRCUMCISION, ETHNICITY, AND ISLAM IN GUINEA-BISSAU AND PORTUGAL

Michelle C. Johnson

BAFATA-OIO, GUINEA-BISSAU (1997). We finish the last round of tea, and everyone leaves but Binta. She and I sit together on a woven mat in the shade of a mango tree. Binta tells me that her eight-year-old daughter has been asking her when she will be circumcised, lamenting that all of her friends have already been through the ritual. Binta smiles and says, "I just tell her to be patient, that you can't rush this thing. When your daughter is circumcised, you have to work hard so you can buy her cowry shells, nice cloth, and food—the girls must have meat in their sauce every day. It's difficult, but you just leave it all up to God." I ask Binta to recall the day she was initiated. "I wasn't afraid, and it didn't hurt. When it was all over, I asked the ŋamaanoo [traditional circumciser] to cut off the tip of my pointer finger because I didn't feel a thing. To this day, the old woman smiles when she greets me. People say that circumcision is a bad thing for women, but we know the truth. If a woman isn't circumcised, she is unclean and her prayers are worthless. When you are circumcised, you become a true Muslim."

Queluz-Belas, Portugal (1999). I join Alaaji in the suburb of Queluz-Belas, located twenty minutes by train from central Lisbon. As he brews the afternoon tea, his seven-year-old daughter, Maraŋ, shows me pictures of her family back home in Guinea-Bissau. Maraŋ recently joined her father and his second wife in Portugal in July of 1998, shortly after the start of the armed conflict in Guinea-Bissau. "This is my little sister, Sali," she says, pointing to the photograph. Pouring the tea, Alaaji tells me that his mother just had two-year-old Sali circumcised against his will. "Had I been there, she would not have had the courage to do it," he explains. I ask Alaaji if he is angry at his mother for what she did. "How can I be angry at her? She is my mother. Circumcision is our women's custom. They say that a woman must be clean in order to pray, in order to be a Muslim. But we Islamic healers have all been to Mecca, we have studied, and we know the truth. Circumcision is not mandatory; it is optional. If God doesn't distinguish a circumcised woman from an uncircumcised one, then why should we? Our mothers don't know what we know about the Qur'an."

INTRODUCTION

Anthropologists have recently shifted their focus from studies of peoples and cultures in bounded, local contexts to the movement of people between locales and to the contested relationship between place and identity in transnational or diaspora settings (for example, Appadurai 1996; Gupta and Ferguson 1992; Lavie and Swedenburg 1996; MacGaffey and Bazenguissa-Ganga 2000; Olwig and Hastrup 1997; Piot 1999a; Rasmussen 2003; Stoller 2002). This shift has brought with it new questions and challenges for anthropologists interested in religion and ritual. What are the continuities and ruptures in both the structure and meaning of ritual and religious practices as they are "uprooted" from one locale and "transplanted" into another by their practitioners (for example, Ahmadu 2000; Bruner 1999; Delaney 1990)? What roles are ritual and religious practices currently playing in the reconfiguring of identities in transnational spaces (D'Alisera 2004; Johnson 2006; van Dijk 1997; Werbner 1990; Yalçun-Heckmann 1993) and in local understandings of modernity (Comaroff and Comaroff 1993; Geschiere 1997)?

In this chapter, I explore these questions by focusing on the multiple and conflicting discourses centered on one ritual practice—female circumcision[1]—among Mandinga in Guinea-Bissau and among Mandinga immigrants living in and around Lisbon, Portugal. Specifically, I explore how changing notions of the meaning and practice of female circumcision and recent global efforts to end it are currently understood and discussed by Mandinga as they move between the increasingly interconnected spaces of Africa and Europe. I apply here what Edward Bruner terms a "culturally and symbolically sensitive [approach to] transnationalism, one that takes account of the [local] people's own understanding of . . . global forces" (1999, 462).

I consider changing perceptions of female circumcision as a backdrop for examining wider discourses and ensuing debates centered on ethnicity, Islam, and Mandinga life-course rituals. In examining the flow of local meanings and global images between Africa and Europe, I show how the transnational debate surrounding female circumcision is creating divisions between men and women, elders and youth, and between those who aspire to "modern" Islam (as defined and practiced by Muslims outside of Africa) and those who resist this model, preferring to remain rooted in Mandinga "custom." These debates are both currently shaping and being shaped by recent changes in how Mandinga imagine themselves as members of a distinct ethnic group and how they practice the world religion of Islam, whether in the village or the metropole. These current debates underscore the fluidity of ritual practice and religious doctrine

in an increasingly globalized world. Furthermore, they reveal the inherent contradiction and ambiguity involved in the making of modern identity.[2]

MANDINGA "AT HOME" AND "ABROAD"

Before discussing female circumcision as it is understood, practiced, and
discussed by Mandinga in Guinea-Bissau and Portugal, it is first necessary to introduce briefly the research and the people in both places. This chapter is based
on nearly two years of ethnographic research—eleven months in Guinea-Bissau
in 1996–1997 in the capital city of Bissau and in the village of Bafata-Oio and
surrounding areas, and ten months in 1999 with Mandinga immigrants and refugees living in Lisbon, Portugal. This was followed by shorter stays in Portugal
in 2001 and 2003 and in Guinea-Bissau in 2003. In both field sites, my research
combined long-term participant observation, interviews, and in-depth examination of life-course events. While in Lisbon, I recorded women's experiences of
initiation and female circumcision and their stories of how migration or flight
has influenced their plans to initiate (or not initiate) their own daughters.[3]

The Mandinga are the fourth largest ethnic group in Guinea-Bissau, making
up 13 percent of the country's population of approximately 1.4 million (Central Intelligence Agency 2005). They make their living primarily as subsistence
farmers, merchants, and as Qur'anic teachers and healers. Although the northern
Oio region is home to the largest concentration of Mandinga in Guinea-Bissau,
Mandinga live in all regions of the country, including the capital city of Bissau. Mandinga occupy a unique position in their "home" country of Guinea-
Bissau when compared with indigenous coastal peoples.[4] During my research,
members of this latter group often informed me that the Mandinga, like other
Muslim groups, such as the Fula and Beafada, "came from abroad" (in the local
language of Kriolu, *e bin di fora*). Mandinga themselves are well aware of their
"outsider" status in Guinea-Bissau. They speak a southern Mande language and
trace their origin to the Mande heartland (in present-day Mali). As such, they
stress their "oneness" with other Mande peoples in neighboring Senegal, The
Gambia, and Guinea-Conakry (as well as with other Muslim groups in Guinea-
Bissau) and their difference from non-Muslim groups in Guinea-Bissau, such as
the Manjaco, Pepel, or Balanta.[5] Matt Schaffer and Christine Cooper note that
the Mandinka, despite their tendency to live in permanent villages, are "great
travelers" who have "a history of migration for purposes of conquest, trade, and
religious proselytizing" (1987, 5).[6]

Their diasporic identity in West Africa is strengthened further when Mandinga migrate to Portugal. In Lisbon, they make up part of the large population of
African immigrants from all of Portugal's former colonies—Angola, Cape Verde,
Guinea-Bissau, Mozambique, and São Tomé—which in 1981 was estimated at
45,222 (cited in de Sainte-Maurice 1997, 55). Antonio Machado (1994) distinguishes three waves of African immigration to Portugal. The first wave began
before April 25, 1974, the date marking the end of Portugal's fascist regime, and

included a privileged group of students and skilled laborers. The second wave corresponded with the independence of the former colonies (1974–975) and included primarily political refugees and *antigos combatentes,* Africans who aligned themselves with the Portuguese during Guinea-Bissau's war of liberation. The third and largest phase took place after 1980 and consisted mainly of unskilled laborers who found employment in construction and public works. According to Machado, it was not until the 1980s that Portugal became "a country of immigrants" (ibid., 112). Since this time, African immigration to Portugal has steadily increased. In 1996, Machado estimated the number of Guinean immigrants and "Luso-Guinenses" (children born in Portugal of Guinean immigrant parents) alone to be between 22,000 and 23,000 (1998, 17).[7]

Muslims—Mandinga, Fula, and Beafada peoples—make up approximately 22 percent of the total number of Guineans in Portugal (Machado 1998, 47). There are two distinctive features about this group when compared to other Guineans in Portugal. First, they are the most recent immigrants to Portugal, most arriving after 1990. Second, whereas most Guineans (approximately 80 percent) currently residing in Portugal lived in the capital city of Bissau prior to migrating, Muslims have tended to immigrate directly from the rural areas, passing through Bissau only briefly (ibid., 49). It is important to keep these factors in mind when examining Mandinga ritual practices in Portugal, as constructions of homeland and identity are inherently tied to Mandinga "custom" and village life.

Population estimates by ethnic group are not currently available and are difficult to obtain, especially considering the flow of people between Portugal and Africa. Based on Machado's figures, however, I would estimate that Mandinga make up at least 10 percent of the total population of Guinean Muslims in Portugal, which would place their numbers at anywhere between 2,000 and 2,500. Mandinga are ambivalent about the issue of officially counting themselves. On the one hand, they link the systematic counting of bodies to forced labor and other atrocities suffered during five hundred years of Portuguese colonialism. Furthermore, they fear that participating in official censuses may lead to the discovery of inadequacies in (or the absence of) documents required for legal residence in Portugal or for freedom of movement within Europe. On the other hand, Mandinga take pride in knowing that they constitute a sizable population in Portugal. Indeed, when I asked several informants to estimate how many Mandinga currently live in Lisbon, they replied, "So many that you could never count us all."

The Mandinga community in Lisbon is dispersed, with some people living in rented apartments or rooms in central Lisbon and others in neighborhoods in Lisbon's surrounding suburbs. Known locally as *barracas,* these neighborhoods are settled almost exclusively by immigrants from Portugal's former African colonies. Each neighborhood typically has its own restaurants, markets, and shops that provide immigrants a steady supply of goods from back home.

For Mandinga in Portugal, as in Guinea-Bissau, Islam is a principal organizing force in the shaping of identity and in the experience of daily life. For
example, Mandinga immigrants have transformed many parts of Lisbon—a
city dominated by increasingly secular Roman Catholics—into "Muslim
spaces" (Metcalf 1996). At Rossio Square in central Lisbon, for example, Fula
and Mandinga merchants sell kola nuts, palm oil, and other goods from Guinea-
Bissau. On Fridays, African Muslim merchants transform the sidewalk across
from the mosque into a bustling market where they sell religious paraphernalia,
such as rosary beads, prayer carpets, and wall hangings. Furthermore, Muslim
immigrants from Guinea-Bissau have formed their own associations in Lisbon.
While conducting my research, I worked closely with members of one of these
associations, the Badim Culubo.[8]

The Mandinga men I know in Lisbon earn their living primarily as construction workers, musicians, shopkeepers, and Muslim healers (mooroolu). Many
of these latter men, who often call themselves by the Portuguese term astrólogos
("astrologers"), operate their own businesses out of their homes. Using the di-
vining tools of cowry shells, rosary beads, and dreams, they diagnose and offer
remedies for all types of misfortune, ranging from drug addiction to a cheating
spouse. Many of the Mandinga women I know in Lisbon work as cleaning ladies in businesses or private homes. Others are successful merchants who make
regular trips to Dakar or Mecca to purchase the latest clothing styles and other
goods, which they sell in Portugal. Many women own restaurants in Lisbon
and surrounding areas, where clients savor traditional dishes from home. Others
work as full-time wives and mothers or assist their "astrologer" husbands by an-
swering cell phone calls, booking appointments, or translating for Portuguese-
speaking clients.

CONTEXTUALIZING FEMALE CIRCUMCISION: INITIATION, ETHNICITY, AND ISLAM

I have argued elsewhere (Johnson 2000 and 2002) that female circumcision
as practiced by Mandinga must be seen in relation to girls' initiation rituals. In
Guinea-Bissau, the physical act of circumcision (kuiandiŋo in Mandinga; fana-
dusiñu in Kriolu, both meaning "little initiation") most often consists of partial
clitoridectomy (see Carreira 1947, 82; Urdang 1979, 185–6). The practice was
historically linked to marriage and took place within the context of initiation
rituals (kuiaŋbaa in Mandinga; fanadu garandi in Kriolu, both meaning "big initiation"). As one step in the gradual transformation from childhood to adulthood,
Mandinga girls' initiation involved an educational period in the bush lasting
from three to four months, followed by public "coming out" dances. At the level
of discourse, virtually all of my informants in Guinea-Bissau and Portugal emphasize the connectedness of circumcision and initiation rituals for both boys
and girls. In practice, however, very few people experience these events simultaneously. Most women I spoke with told me they were circumcised between

the ages of three and seven and attended a shortened initiation ritual when they were older. Others never experienced this second part at all (for similar situations among other Mande-speaking peoples in West Africa, see Hernlund 2000; Ahmadu 2000; and Gosselin 2000a).[9]

Comments about the recent separation of female circumcision and girls' initiation rituals converge on two factors, the first being recent campaigns to end female circumcision in Africa. Although the government of Guinea-Bissau does not officially outlaw the practice, it does support and encourage development organizations working to end it. Many women told me that girls' initiation rituals in the past were nearly as frequent and public as the boy's rituals, which remain quite elaborate today. Women claim, however, that holding girls' initiation rituals nowadays is "big trouble," especially in the capital city. Out of fear, many women in Bissau opt for a more private, even clandestine, form of circumcision for their daughters.[10] Others link the separation between circumcision and initiation rituals to socioeconomic changes brought about by urbanization and modernization. There are fewer traditional circumcisers (*ŋamaanoolu*) around today, people claim, especially in Bissau because women no longer "have the head" for such work. That is, few women today know how to conduct initiation rituals in the proper manner. Loss of traditional knowledge aside, this is often a matter of personal choice. Mandinga women maintain that a circumciser's job is a difficult one. She must posses an extraordinary connection to the supernatural world, which allows her to battle witches and evil spirits who might attack the initiates at their most vulnerable time. Considering the difficulty associated with traditional initiation, most women would rather earn a living by selling goods at the market.

Despite the fact that few Mandinga are circumcised in the context of initiation, most people still agree that initiation rituals are crucial for the shaping of ethnic identity. Although initiation does not mark adulthood, it is linked to the fostering of knowledge and behaviors that adult Mandinga are thought ideally to possess (see Jackson 1977; Beidelman 1997; Ottenberg 1989; and Kratz 1994, for explorations of the relationship between initiation, personhood, and adulthood in other African societies). For example, initiation is an important process whereby a person comes to "know the eye" (*ñaa loŋ* in Mandinga, *kunsi udju* in Kriolu). This term refers to the moral and educational component of initiation, through which children are taught their position in society and the proper ways of behaving in a variety of social situations relative to gender, age, and clan or "caste" membership. To "know the eye" also involves being socially graceful, sensitive, and perceptive. As one woman in her thirties from Bissau told me, "You know the eye when you can see inside someone. You know what they are feeling, even before they say anything."

Although Mandinga consider "knowing the eye" to be a gradual process beginning in early childhood and ending in late adolescence, it is cultivated most actively during initiation rituals, to the extent that the phrase is often used as a euphemism for initiation itself. Initiated people are contrasted with uniniti-ated people (called *solimaa* in Mandinga, *bulufu* in Kriolu) who are thought to be unrefined, disrespectful, and simpleminded. They have no sense of shame or awareness of the powers and dangers of sex, evident in the way they frolic about naked in the compound with playmates of the opposite sex.

The hardships of traditional initiation, including circumcision for both boys and girls, are also said to teach children to "suffer," which Mandinga link to strength, perseverance, and the enhancement of self. Each person is said to learn and to grow stronger with each episode that he or she is made to suffer. Before they can become teachers or healers, students must complete the ardu-ous task of memorizing the Qur'an. Before they can savor millet porridge for breakfast, farmers must endure the heat and backbreaking labor of the plant-ing season. Before a woman becomes a mother—her true initiation into social adulthood—she must bear the pain of childbirth, ideally without any outward sign of distress.

Among the Mandinga, emotional and physical fatigue caused by hardship of various kinds is invariably met with the encouraging statement *i sabari,* or "suffer it." This phrase acknowledges the difficulty of the situation and reminds people to rely on God and other people to get through it. As Paul Riesman (1998, 148) argued for the Fulani of Burkina Faso, speaking openly about pain and the inherent difficulty of life eases the suffering, since once pain is made public it can be shared with others.

Despite the importance of traditional initiation rituals to ethnic identity, however, most Mandinga women in Guinea-Bissau and Portugal consider ini-tiation to be less important than the physical act of female circumcision itself, which they link explicitly to religious identity (Johnson 2000; see Dellenborg 2004 for a parallel case in Senegal). Although many women claim that ini-tiation rituals may soon no longer be practiced in Guinea-Bissau, they confi-dently state that female circumcision, like male circumcision, will never end (cf. Hernlund 2000). I suggest that the tendency to emphasize female circumcision over initiation rituals can best be explained by the explicit link made by many Mandinga between female circumcision and Islam. I will soon show, however, that Mandinga immigrants' changing assessments of this link are beginning to unsettle in complicated ways the certainty of this link, which may effect the future continuation of the practice.

Is Female Circumcision an "African" or a "Muslim" Practice?

Members of three ethnic groups in Guinea-Bissau—the Mandinga, the Fula, and the Beafada—practice some form of female circumcision. Since members of these ethnic groups define themselves as Muslims and are defined by others as Muslims, Guineans consider female circumcision to be a Muslim practice. Stephanie Urdang estimates that 30 percent of the population in Guinea-Bissau has undergone some form of female circumcision (1979, 185). Citing figures reported by Fran Hosken (1982), Leonard Kouba and Judith Muasher estimate the percentage to be about 50 (1985, 99). The status of female circumcision as a "Muslim practice" contrasts sharply with male circumcision in Guinea-Bissau, which is practiced by everyone, despite religious affiliation. Female circumcision is thus a principal means through which Muslims distinguish themselves from *kristons*—the Kriolu term for non-Muslims, whether "Christian," "animist," or both—in the village and in the metropole.[11]

When asked why they practice initiation rituals, Mandinga claim that it is by way of this "custom" (*aadoo*) that children come to "know the eye" and learn to "suffer," thus becoming full Mandinga persons. When asked why circumcision forms a part of these rituals, however, Mandinga more commonly evoke Islam. If a boy is not circumcised, Mandinga maintain, he is "not clean" (*a man seneyaa*) and is thus unfit to pray, slaughter animals in the proper manner, and keep the Ramadan fast. Mandinga explain that the Prophet Mohammed was circumcised as a rite of purification. It is their duty as practicing Muslims to follow his example.

As I have explained elsewhere (Johnson 2000 and 2002), Mandinga women describe female circumcision as a cleansing rite that enables women to pray in the proper fashion, making them "true Muslims." My female informants claim that an uncircumcised woman's genitals produce an odor that renders them ritually unclean and "spoils" her prayers. Similar beliefs have been reported elsewhere in West Africa. Claudie Gosselin (2000a, 54) writes that circumcision for both sexes in Mali is commonly termed *seliji* ("prayer water"), which refers to the necessary ritual ablutions performed by Muslims before prayer. That this term in Mali is used as a euphemism for circumcision underscores the local belief that uncircumcised women, like uncircumcised men, are ritually unclean and unfit for prayer. Liselott Dellenborg reports that for Muslim Jola in Senegal, an uncircumcised woman's prayers are said not to "take" or to give her fewer "points" than a circumcised woman's prayers (2004, 82).[12]

Corinne Kratz reminds us that discourses about circumcision "are located more generally within histories of the body and understandings of the body as a site of signification" (1994, 341). Considering this, circumcision among the Mandinga must be understood in relation to beliefs about Islam, gender, and the life course. As women mature physically, they come into contact with the polluting substances of menstrual blood, the blood of childbirth, and bodily emissions of young children, all of which may limit their involvement in certain religious activities, such as prayer and fasting. For Mandinga women, female circumcision can thus be interpreted as a strategy for offsetting the impurity associated with physical maturation. By ritually altering their bodies as men do, women claim equal participation in Islam.

Further affirming the link between female circumcision and Islam, many Mandinga believe that the Qur'an prescribes the practice. While conducting

research in Guinea-Bissau and Portugal, I recorded several versions of the story
of the origin of female circumcision, a story that my informants claim is contained within the pages of Islam's most sacred text. Qur'anic scholars and healers
in both sites often assert, however, that the passage is an especially powerful and
secret one that can be seen and interpreted only by people "with a head" (who
possess supernatural powers), those blessed with *baraka* (God's grace), or those
who have studied the Qur'an for more than forty years.[13]

Although Mandinga and other African Muslims have construed female circumcision as a Muslim practice, there is no mention of it in the Qur'an and
only brief mention of it in the Hadith (texts describing the life and philosophy
of the Prophet Mohammed). The official view, then, is that female circumcision
did not originate in Islam but was later accepted by it (Kouba and Muasher
1985, 104). Many Muslims consider it an optional practice that is neither man-
dated nor punishable by Islam. According to this view, when female circumcision is performed it should be slight, since the clitoris contributes to the sexual
enjoyment of both husband and wife.[14]

The overarching importance attributed by Mandinga to the practice of
female circumcision, however, has to do not only with their identity as Muslims but also with their identity as Mandinga. This is especially true given the
powerful link that Mandinga make between ethnicity and Islam. In contrast
to other groups in West Africa such as the Limba of Sierra Leone (Ottenberg
1984) or the Mawri of Niger (Masquelier 1996), for whom conversion to Islam
is a rather recent phenomenon, for Mandinga in Guinea-Bissau and other parts
of the Senegambia Islam and "Mandinga-ness" have been long intertwined.
In the first and only ethnography to date of the Mandinga people of Guinea-
Bissau, written more than five decades ago, Antonio Carreira estimated that 80
percent of Mandinga defined themselves as Muslims. Furthermore, he asserted,
"Islam is rooted in the spirit of the Mandinga people" (1947, 193, my translation from Portuguese).

This interconnectedness of Islam and "Mandinga-ness" was evident upon
my first trip to the village of Bafata-Oio in 1996. I quickly learned that even the
most routine activities, such as breastfeeding an infant, greeting a relative, and
boiling rice for the evening meal, are infused with religious (Islamic) meaning.
Indeed, for all Mandinga I know in Guinea-Bissau, ethnicity (being Mandinga)
is inseparable from religious identity (being Muslim) (see Riesman 1998, 96, for
a similar argument for the Fulani people). From the point of view of Mandinga
women, refusing to undergo circumcision renders one's prayers worthless and
"spoils" ones identity as a Muslim. And if a woman is not a Muslim, she can
hardly call herself Mandinga. In fact, when I asked my informants if there were
non-Muslim Mandinga, they responded, "Yes, there are, but they are Soninke
[another ethnic group], not Mandinga."

After nearly ten years of working with Mandinga in Guinea-Bissau, I have
not yet met a Mandinga woman who opposes female circumcision. Indeed,

Mandinga women's views on the issue are surprisingly consistent, as everyone with whom I have spoken remains strongly in favor of retaining the practice. This can be sharply contrasted, however, with non-Muslims in the country, who feel strongly that the practice should end. They associate female circumcision with negative health consequences, such as infection and complications with childbirth. They also feel that the practice has negative social consequences, such as sexual promiscuity and prostitution. Mandinga men and women alike claim the opposite, that female circumcision "tames" women's sexuality, molding women into faithful and patient wives and mothers. As one Mandinga man and Qur'anic scholar from Bissau explained, "Female circumcision is a good thing because it calms women down and makes them more faithful to their husbands. Why do you think you never see a Muslim prostitute in Bissau?" In general, however, Mandinga men's views on female circumcision are more variable than women's views. Whereas women state confidently that the practice will never end, men often claim that it might. Ultimately, however, they stress that deciding the future of the practice should be left to the women.

DEBATING FEMALE CIRCUMCISION IN PORTUGAL

I have argued that the strong desire by Mandinga women to retain the practice of female circumcision is best explained by the tendency in Guinea-Bissau to conflate ethnicity and Islam. Being Mandinga means being Muslim, and being Muslim requires one to pray, ideally five times a day. Mandinga women in Guinea-Bissau assert that for their prayers to count, they must be "clean," meaning that they must be circumcised. Through the practice of female circumcision, Mandinga women in Guinea-Bissau reaffirm the fusion of ethnicity and Islam by permanently inscribing it onto their bodies.

In contrast, views on female circumcision in Portugal are more varied and contradictory. Support for or condemnation of the practice depends ultimately on the degree to which one believes that ethnicity (being Mandinga) and religious identity (being Muslim) are one and the same. Considering this, female circumcision has become a gendered debate. In contrast to men in Guinea-Bissau who consider female circumcision to be a "women's issue" whose fate must be decided by its practitioners, Mandinga men in Portugal often take a more aggressive stance toward the practice and are willing to use their power and influence in determining its future. Those men who have traveled to Saudi Arabia to make the pilgrimage to Mecca (*hijoo*) or to other Islamic nations to study Arabic contend that initiation and female circumcision—like many Mandinga life-course rituals (see Johnson 2002)—are African "customs," not Muslim ones. As such, they claim that the alleged link made by Mandinga in Guinea-Bissau between female circumcision and "cleanliness" (ritual purity) required for prayer is actually a misunderstanding resulting from the conflation of two identities that should remain separate: ethnicity (being Mandinga) and religious identity (being Muslim). While the former is acquired "naturally" through a father's name and a mother's breast milk, the latter is achieved through daily prayer, Qur'anic study, and the observation of Muslim dietary taboos (for example, avoiding pork and alcohol). Many of these men are thus beginning to oppose female circumcision for their daughters.

In contrast to men's views, which appear rather clear on the matter, women's views on female circumcision in Portugal remain divided and fraught with uncertainty. While many women continue to maintain the link between female circumcision and ritual purity necessary for prayer, others, especially those who have been influenced by men, are losing confidence in this link. Tunbulo Faati is the "mother" of the Badim Culubo, the Mandinga immigrant women's association mentioned earlier. Tunbulo told me that club members seldom discuss female circumcision because of its divisive potential. I suggest that this divisiveness—a recent phenomenon among Mandinga women—can be traced in part to negative portrayals of female circumcision in the media. Indeed, through my discussions with club members and other Mandinga in Portugal, regardless of gender, I learned that media images are currently playing a powerful role in how people conceptualize and speak about the practice of female circumcision. During my research in Lisbon, many of my informants made reference to a French documentary program aired on national Portuguese television shortly before my arrival in 1999. Whatever their views on female circumcision, my informants found this program deeply disturbing. Many expressed anger over seeing such a sacred element of their culture portrayed in a negative way on national television "for everyone to see."

What people found most disturbing about the program was its featuring of close-up views of women's genitals, bleeding from the practice of "female genital mutilation" recently performed on them. Mandinga maintain that out of respect, a man should not look directly at even his own wife's genitals. In light of this belief, many Mandinga women with whom I spoke questioned not only the morals of the photographers and producers of the documentary program but their mental state as well. They recounted countless stories of Portuguese colonial officers or, more recently, development workers, who ended up "spoiling their heads" (going insane) after attempting to film the practice of female circumcision in Guinea-Bissau. These women maintain that the sight of women's genitals—like that of the initiation masquerade figure and the circumcision knife—is "too strong" (that is, powerful) for human eyes or camera lenses to "capture." These women perceived the documentary program's close-up views of women's bleeding genitals, therefore, to be not only disrespectful and insulting but also dangerous and lacking in credibility.

Changing views about the practice of female circumcision also stem from the difficulties that African immigrants in Portugal confront in their daily lives, especially with racism and marginalization. Several people linked the airing of the documentary program to an increase in tension between African immigrants and Portuguese in Lisbon. One woman claimed that shortly after the airing of the program, a (Portuguese) cashier at a local grocery store refused to take money out of her hand. "She asked me to place the money on the counter because she was afraid to touch me," the woman explained. "She must have thought my hand would start bleeding just like the women's genitals in the program." Other women claimed that shortly after the airing of the program, they received more stares than usual when traveling on Lisbon's buses, ferries, and commuter trains. One woman told me that, on one occasion while on the Metro, she sat down next to a Portuguese man. He quickly changed seats, which led the woman to believe that he had probably seen the program.[15] Even non-Muslim Guineans and immigrants from other Lusophone countries who do not practice female circumcision were upset by the program and claimed to be suffering from its effects. For example, several people told me that after the documentary aired, Portuguese men stopped seeking relationships with African women because they assumed that they were all "mutilated."

During my stay in Lisbon, several local newspapers and magazines also featured articles on female circumcision in Africa. The May 1999 edition of the news magazine *Pública* featured an interview with Somali models Waris Dirie and Iman about their personal experiences of female circumcision; it was titled "A Savage Ritual" (R. Johnson 1999, my translation from Portuguese). Mandinga women's awareness of such media representations and their sensitivity toward them are powerful examples of how mediascapes, to use Arjun Appadurai's term (1996, 35), play upon the imagining of selves and societies. Appadurai argues that mediascapes eventually become transformed into metaphors by which people live (see Lakoff and Johnson 1980). For Mandinga in Lisbon, the metaphor of the "savage other" is a daily reality that has only intensified with the recent campaigns to end "female genital mutilation" in Africa and beyond.

In light of the preceding discussion, I now present three case studies from Portugal that concretely reveal the ambiguity and contradiction inherent in Mandinga views on the practice of female circumcision. The case studies demonstrate that female circumcision provides a lens for examining the debate surrounding ethnicity and Islam in Guinea-Bissau and Portugal. Is female circumcision a Mandinga practice or a Muslim one? Can an uncircumcised woman be a Muslim? Can an uncircumcised woman be Mandinga? The case studies also show that the future of female circumcision as practiced by Mandinga both "at home" and in the contemporary diaspora remains uncertain.[16]

ON LIES AND QUR'ANIC TRUTH(S)

Alaaji was born in Guinea-Bissau in the capital city of Bissau. He has been living in Portugal for ten years, where he works as a Muslim healer (*mooroo* in Mandinga; *astrólogo* in Portuguese) in his home in Queluz-Belas, a twenty-minute train ride from central Lisbon. In 1999 he made the pilgrimage to Mecca. According to Alaaji, one's views on female circumcision depend ultimately on his or her knowledge of Islam—particularly the sacred texts of the Qur'an, the holy book of Muslims. In his view, the debate surrounding female circumcision is a matter between those people who have studied Arabic officially, and thus understand the "deep" meaning of the Qur'an, and those whose training doesn't extend beyond the memorization of religious texts, as is common in village Qu'ranic schools. Since men in Guinea-Bissau generally study longer and more rigorously than do women, one's views on circumcision thus become a matter of gender. To cut or not to cut, as Alaaji sees it, is a debate between "enlightened" men and "unenlightened" women. While women believe that female circumcision is essential to their identity as Muslims, men "know" that the practice has nothing to do with Islam.

Despite the fact that Alaaji has studied in the Middle East, speaks and reads Arabic fluently, and has made the pilgrimage to Mecca, his views regarding the link between female circumcision and Islam are not as uniform and free of contradiction as they may appear. During my first recorded interview with Alaaji, for example, he stated clearly that there is no connection between female circumcision and Islam. "To say that a woman must be circumcised in order to pray is a lie," Alaaji explained. "The people who said that don't know anything. Once a boy is seven years old he should be circumcised so that he can pray. But if a woman is not circumcised, it does not ruin her Muslim-ness. Female circumcision has nothing to do with being Muslim."

In a follow-up interview, however, Alaaji recounted the story of the origin of the practice of female circumcision. In this story, the Prophet Ibrahim's young wife was circumcised by her older co-wife out of jealously and competition for Ibrahim's affection (for a variation of this story, see Johnson 2000). Although the older wife was confident that Ibrahim would refuse his young wife as a result of the act, God "accepted" the act, telling Ibrahim not to refuse her. Alaaji claims that the story is in the Qur'an but that its meaning is often misinterpreted. In his view, the story's presence in the Qur'an does not mean that Islam requires women to be circumcised in order to pray. Rather, the story defines female circumcision as an optional practice that is neither prescribed nor punishable by God. To clarify his view, Alaaji compared female circumcision to a decorative flower arrangement on his coffee table. Although not essential to daily life, the flower arrangement "makes the house more pleasant." Alaaji likened the aesthetic appeal of a flower arrangement to female circumcision's positive effects on female sexuality. He explained:

> An uncircumcised woman sleeps around more than a circumcised one. That is why the Prophet Mohammed said to take off just a little bit of that thing [the clitoris], to reduce it in order to remove uncleanliness. If a woman wants men too much, it ruins her Muslim-ness. Even when she is married, she will want to play with [have sex with] other men. It is *haraamoo* [forbidden] for a married woman to sleep with men other than her husband.

That is why God sent us circumcision. He never said that a woman must be circumcised in order to pray.

This reveals an intriguing contradiction. After initially stating that female circumcision has nothing to do with Islam, Alaaji later claimed that God himself sent the practice to the Mandinga people to "reduce" women's sexual appetites, making them better wives and, ultimately, better Muslims.

Furthermore, after discussing the positive effects of female circumcision on female sexuality, Alaaji later claimed that these positive effects are not necessarily attributable to the practice of female circumcision. In his view, a woman's "upbringing" (moral education) ultimately counts for more than whether she has had her genitals "reduced." Alaaji told me that he knows circumcised women who are less faithful to their husbands and who "want men more" than uncircumcised women. In his mind, people (Westerners) should shift their focus from ending female circumcision to ending the initiation rituals that have traditionally accompanied the practice. "Putting young girls in the bush for several months where they do not wash or pray and where they drum, dance with demons [traditional masquerade figures], and seek illicit affairs with leatherworkers and blacksmiths [the only male participants in girls' initiation rites] is un-Islamic and should be forbidden," Alaaji explained. In his view, it is the responsibility of parents, not an initiation ritual, to teach children to "know the eye." Women who continue to circumcise their daughters should do so without an accompanying initiation ritual.

Alaaji's views on the fate of female circumcision are open to change. If women themselves decide to end the practice, he stated that he would support their decision. At the same time, however, he is disturbed by the recent global efforts to end the practice, launched primarily by non-Muslims and Westerners. He claimed that such efforts provide the opportunity for *kristons* (non-Muslims) to "spoil" the name of Muslims by inventing "lies" about negative health consequences associated with female circumcision. He explained, "In our grandmothers' time, hundreds of girls were circumcised at the same time without the use of any 'white' (Western) medicines. Those same women all grew up and gave birth to us without ever going to the hospital." Alaaji cited further evidence for what he perceives as the erroneous association of female circumcision with health problems: "I treat Portuguese [female] clients for fertility and birthing problems almost every day, and these women have never been circumcised."

In Alaaji's view, singling out female circumcision as Africa's most urgent problem is unfair. He sited several more pressing problems, such as the lack of hospitals, the continual shortage of medicines, unsafe drinking water, and government corruption. He also claimed that *tokatchurs*—"animist" funerary ceremonies in Guinea-Bissau in which hundreds of cows may be killed and consumed in a single day—are more detrimental to society than is the practice of female circumcision. "But the government doesn't worry about these things,"

Alaaji explained. "They prefer to attack the Muslim traditions. Life in Guinea-Bissau is like one big soccer match; it's the Muslims against the non-Muslims, and each wants his team to win."

FEMALE CIRCUMCISION AND ILLUSIONS OF MEN

Aja was born near Bafata in Guinea-Bissau and came to Portugal with her parents when she was five years old. When I first met her, in 1999, she was nineteen years old and was completing high school in Outerela, about forty-five minutes by bus from central Lisbon. Aja and her father made the pilgrimage to Mecca together in 1999, and I attended an *Alaaji buuñaa*—a rite celebrating the return of the Mandinga pilgrims—held in Aja's honor upon her return. Over the years I have worked closely with Aja to learn about her experiences as a Mandinga immigrant woman and a Muslim in Portugal, and she has shared with me on a number of occasions her views on the practice of female circumcision.

Aja was circumcised in Guinea-Bissau when she was three years old. When I first asked her about the practice of female circumcision, she told me that she was opposed to it. "What we are born with, the way God made our bodies, no one has the right to change that," she asserted. Unlike many Mandinga women in Lisbon who continue to link female circumcision to ritual purity necessary for prayer and thus to Muslim identity, Aja claims that this association is false. "In order for a woman to be clean," she explained, "God said that she must perform ablution [ritual washing] and nothing more. There are many uncircumcised, Muslim women in the world and God grants their prayers. He answers them just the same." Like Alaaji, Aja attributes the alleged link between female circumcision and being Muslim to a lack of knowledge of Islam. "Many women from Guinea-Bissau believe that female circumcision is necessary for prayer because that is what their elders have told them," she explained. "They have never heard otherwise."

Although Aja does not believe that female circumcision is required for prayer, she agrees with Alaaji that the practice has positive effects on female sexuality. Circumcised women, according to Aja, are "calm." They stay at home as proper wives should, dedicating themselves to domestic chores, raising children, or small business affairs, such as selling clothing, jewelry, food, or other goods from back home. A circumcised woman doesn't worry about her husband's whereabouts, nor does she wait impatiently for his return.

Uncircumcised women, in contrast, have *iluson di omi,* a Kriolu term that Aja used to denote an extreme physical and emotional dependence on men, especially on one's husband. Aja finds this behavior especially common among Portuguese women, who are uncircumcised. She explained that when Portuguese men spend a lot of time away from the house, their wives immediately accuse them of having an affair. "Some Portuguese women even ask a friend to follow their husbands for a day and to report back on their whereabouts," Aja told me. "Others consult with African healers, obtaining medicines to help them discover their husbands' lovers." Aja blamed European women's unusual dependence on their husbands on an insatiable sex drive, which she sees as a consequence of their intact genitalia.[17] According to Aja, uncircumcised women are oversexed. They can rarely go a day without having sex and are forced to arrange lovers to satisfy their unyielding desire. She explains:

> Muslim women, women who are circumcised, they don't concern them-
> selves with men. They don't feel that same temptation—worrying until they
> are crazy about whether or not their husbands are having affairs, arranging
> lovers when their husbands go away, and eventually leaving them for other
> men. Muslim women don't have that illusion [obsession]. Uncircumcised
> women know [have sexual relations with] men when they are only fifteen
> years old, and many of them have children before they are married. Once
> they are twelve or fourteen years old, their body starts to itch. It itches be-
> cause it needs a man. It is not the same for circumcised women. Their bod-
> ies are normal. If they have a man, fine; if not, fine. They don't know men
> until they are around nineteen years old, and they don't have children until
> they are married.

For Aja, female circumcision corrects for an abnormal sexual desire, which in her view leads to an undesirable relationship between men and women, and especially between husbands and wives.[18] Unlike Alaaji, who feels that "normal" female sexuality can be achieved independently of female circumcision, however, Aja believes that it is the rite itself that accomplishes this. Many Mandinga immigrant women in Lisbon share her belief, often to the dismay of their male relatives.

In his work with the Kétu of Nigeria, Emmanuel Babatunde considers appropriate female sexuality to be the central issue explaining the practice of female circumcision, which occurs in the context of fertility rites. The Kétu make an important distinction between sex between lovers, which occurs out-side the context of marriage and is not intended for procreation, and sex be-tween husbands and wives, aimed at procreation, especially of sons who will continue the patriline (1998, 45). Babatunde shows that circumcision is but one of many Kétu life-course rituals that strive to minimize the dilemma be-tween male dominance and male dependence on women, thus emphasizing the lineage group over the husband-wife bond. As Babatunde states, the Kétu lin-eage system subordinates the roles and interests of individual family members to those of the wider kinship group and "puts a wedge" between husband and wife so that the bond between them does not become so consuming as to threaten the solidarity of the lineage (ibid., 73). Female circumcision is thought to play a primary role in this process: "[Female] circumcision is thought to lessen the pleasure of intercourse for the wife, since such pleasure is thought to reduce the lineage members' intense feelings of loyalty to the lineage by the creation of a strong man/wife bond. Circumcision is also taken as making clear that sexual intercourse is not an end in itself but a means of begetting children who will continue the lineage" (ibid., 73–4).

When I asked Aja if she planned to have her own daughters circumcised one day, she claimed that her decision would ultimately depend on where she decides to live. If she stays in Europe, she will not have them circumcised because female circumcision is "big trouble." "It is not the custom here," she asserted. If she returns to Guinea-Bissau to live, however, she will opt to have her daughters circumcised, since, as she put it, "it is our custom." In contrast to Alaaji, Aja feels that the link between female circumcision and initiation rituals is extremely important. In her view, the physical practice of circumcision loses all meaning once it is divorced from the "traditional" context of initiation rites. As such, if she eventually has her daughters (as well as her sons) circumcised, she would prefer that it take place in the context of these rites.

Commenting on the future of the practice, Aja speculated that the recent widespread publicity over female circumcision will soon decline and, eventually, the practice will come to an end. "Soon the elders who are in charge of things will be dead. Their sons and daughters will be concerned with other things, such as coming to Europe and making money. Initiation rituals and circumcision will no longer be the only things on their minds."

FATU'S DIFFICULT CHOICE

Fatu is a Mandinga woman in her mid-forties who came to Portugal in the late 1980s. When I first met Fatu, in 1999, she was living with her husband, Ali, and their youngest daughter, Aminata, in the neighborhood of Santa Cruz Damaia, located twenty minutes by train from central Lisbon. I joined Fatu and her cousin, Miriama, one afternoon for a meal of rice and peanut sauce. After eating, we lounged in Fatu's bedroom, chatting and watching Brazilian soap operas, a favorite pastime of Guinean immigrant women in Lisbon. The men gathered in the living room to make *ataaya,* Chinese green tea brewed to maximum strength and sweetened with sugar.

I asked Fatu if she was planning on attending the "coming-out" ceremony that was to be held in Setúbal the following weekend for two Mandinga boys who had recently been circumcised in the hospital. Our conversation drifted to girls' initiation rituals and female circumcision. Miriama told us that she was planning to send her daughter back home to Guinea-Bissau to have her circumcised in a traditional "bush" initiation ritual. "If she is not initiated [circumcised]," Miriama said, "no Muslim man will want to marry her, and I do not want my daughter to marry a *kriston* [a non-Muslim]." But Miriama worried about the risks—both physical and spiritual, most often seen as conjoined in the Mandinga case—associated with "traditional" initiation rituals. Would her daughter get enough food to eat during her stay there? Would she be strong enough to take the beatings by former initiates? Would the hand of the *ŋamaanoo* (traditional circumciser) be easy to "suffer," as it ideally should be?

Most of all, Miriama worried about the kind of circumcision that would be performed on her daughter should she be sent to Guinea-Bissau. She wanted her daughter to be circumcised in the "Mandinga way," in which the clitoris is "reduced" (that is, partial clitoridectomy) rather than in the "Fula way," in which a girl's genitals are "cleaned" (that is, excision, including cutting of the labia minora). Indeed, many Mandinga immigrant women in Portugal claim that the Fula people, because they practice a more severe form of female circumcision, are "ruining initiation for everyone." During my first stay in Guinea-Bissau in 1996 and 1997, a local physician informed me that methods of female circumcision among Fula and Mandinga do indeed vary. There is no official research supporting this claim, however, and Fula women in both Guinea-Bissau and Portugal deny that there is any difference in female circumcision as practiced by the two ethnic groups. Fula women commonly attribute Mandinga statements to the contrary to a history of ethnic rivalry between Fula and Mandinga. Nevertheless, Miriama's concern underscores the possibility that the practice of female circumcision in Guinea-Bissau may be less homogenous than once presumed (for example, by Urdang 1979, 185–186).

Fatu expressed concern for her own daughter, Aminata, who was five years old in 1999. Fatu explained that it was time to have Aminata circumcised but that her husband, a respected holy man who has been to Mecca, is against the practice and has forbidden her from doing so. Ali had assured her that women do not have to be circumcised in order to pray and that the practice has nothing to do with being Muslim. But Fatu doubted her husband's certainty about this issue. "Our elders say that the prayers of an uncircumcised woman are worthless," Fatu told me. "God doesn't hear them."

Fatu thus faced a difficult choice: should she have Amintata circumcised against her husband's will? Alternatively, should she respect Ali's wishes and run the risk of "spoiling" Aminata's identity as a Muslim? At the time, sending her daughter home was not a viable option for Fatu, as it was for her cousin, Miriama, because of financial constraints. If it were a possibility, Ali probably would not allow Aminata to make the trip alone, anyway. As a result, Fatu was considering having her daughter circumcised in Lisbon by one of three *ŋamaanoolu* (traditional circumcisers) presumed to be living and working there. Since news travels fast among members of the Guinean immigrant community, however, Fatu feared that if her daughter were circumcised in Lisbon, Ali would eventually find out. But at the time, it was a risk that she was prepared to take. "Circumcision is our custom," she explained. "My grandmother was circumcised, I am circumcised, why shouldn't my daughter be? How can we tell our elders—the people who gave birth to us—that we no longer want to follow their customs?" Although Fatu would not have to make a final decision for several years, this did not ease her anxiety surrounding her difficult choice. "If I wait until my daughter knows men [becomes sexually active] then it will be too dangerous to have her circumcised: if cut, her wound may never stop bleeding.[19]

CONCLUSION

I have argued that Mandinga in Guinea-Bissau imagine ethnicity and religious identity as fused, such that being Mandinga means being Muslim. In order for Mandinga women to be Muslims—and thus, full Mandinga persons—they must pray, and for their prayers to count, they must be "clean," a state they obtain by being circumcised. Through female circumcision, Mandinga women thus affirm the fusion of ethnicity and Islam by inscribing it onto their bodies. As a result of this fusion, views on female circumcision in Guinea-Bissau remain relatively uniform; women are overwhelmingly in favor of retaining the practice, and men feel that the fate of the practice should be left to women.

Migration to Europe and the experience of global Islam, however, have begun to unsettle the link between ethnicity and Islam traditionally made by Mandinga. More specifically, a heightened awareness of how Islam is practiced outside of Africa, coupled with global efforts to end female circumcision and media portrayals of the practice as a "savage ritual," have led many Mandinga in Portugal to separate being Mandinga from being Muslim. Those who study the Qur'an rigorously and aspire to be "modern" Muslims—more often men than women—argue that female circumcision is an "African" custom, not a Muslim one. In challenging the link between female circumcision and Muslim identity, many Mandinga men in Portugal are beginning to oppose the practice for their own daughters, often to their wives' dismay.

The case studies demonstrate, however, that it is not possible to equate views in Guinea-Bissau with "tradition" and views in Portugal with "change." Indeed, unsettling the relationship between ethnicity and Islam in Portugal cannot clearly be correlated with the end of—or even a decline in—the practice of female circumcision. Views on the practice in Portugal remain highly varied, complex, and often contradictory.

Although Alaaji describes female circumcision as an optional practice that has nothing to do with Islam, he feels that it has positive consequences in the realm of female sexuality: it "tames" sexual desire, making women more dedicated wives and mothers. For Alaaji, the problem is not female circumcision itself but the initiation rituals that have traditionally accompanied it. In the end, he feels that a woman's ability as a wife and mother has more to do with her upbringing than with a ritual.

Aja agrees with Alaaji that female circumcision, although not necessary for prayer, has positive effects on female sexuality. In contrast to Alaaji, however, she feels that the rituals of initiation and female circumcision are crucial for making women dedicated wives and mothers. Because they are uncircumcised, Portuguese women suffer an abnormally strong sexual desire, which in turn leads to an unhealthy relationship to their husbands. In the end, whether Aja will have her own daughters circumcised will have less to do with identity than with where she decides to live.

Although Fatu's views on the issue are most common among Mandinga women in Portugal, they are perhaps the most difficult to tease out. Despite her husband's assurance that female circumcision has nothing to with Islam, Fatu would rather follow the path of her ancestors by having her daughter circumcised than run the risk of "spoiling" her daughter's identity as a Muslim and as a Mandinga by not having her circumcised. But when, where, and how should she do it, and what if her husband were to find out?

The case studies reveal that the transnational debate surrounding female circumcision, ethnicity, and Islam is leading to tensions between men and women, between elders and youth, and between those who subscribe to "modern" Islam (as understood and practiced outside of Africa) and those who remain rooted in African "custom." In their attempt to mediate between the demands of tradition and the "will to be modern" (Gable 1995), Mandinga women in Portugal face difficult choices. The competing discourses surrounding these choices move back and forth between Africa and Europe and shape both how Mandinga imagine themselves as members of a distinct ethnic group and how they practice the world religion of Islam. Furthermore, they underscore the contested nature of ritual practice and the making of modern Mandinga identity.

NOTES

1. I have decided to use the term "female circumcision" in my work. Although this term is not by any means a perfect translation of the local Kriolu and Mandinga terms, it is a closer approximation than "female genital mutilation" or "female genital cutting." See Shell-Duncan and Hernlund (2000, 3–7) and Gruenbaum (2001, 3–4) for thorough discussions of the problems associated with terming the practice.
2. Initiation (and female circumcision) is but one of many life-course events through which Mandinga in both Guinea-Bissau and Portugal are currently debating ethnicity and Islam. Elsewhere (Johnson 2002) I consider birth and naming, the writing-on-the-hand ritual to initiate Qur'anic education of children, healing, pilgrimage, and funerals.
3. Research in Guinea-Bissau was generously funded by an International Predissertation Fellowship from the Social Science Research Council. I am thankful for institutional support offered by scholars at INEP (Instituto Nacional de Estudos e Pesquisa) in Bissau, especially from P. Karibe Mende. Research in Portugal was supported by fellowships from the U.S. Department of Education (Fulbright-Hays), the Social Science Research Council, and the Women's Studies Program at the University of Illinois at Urbana-Champaign. I would like to acknowledge my indebtedness to these organizations, as well as to Paulo Zagallo e Mello and Rita Bacelar at the Comissão Cultural Luso-Americana and Maria João Santos Silva at the U.S. Embassy in Lisbon for their logistical support in Lisbon. Generous summer research funds from Bucknell University allowed me to return to both field sites in 2003. An earlier draft of this chapter was presented at the ninety-eighth annual meeting of the American Anthropological Association in Chicago in 1999. Alma Gottlieb, Ned Searles, and Marc Schloss all read earlier drafts of this chapter, and I benefited from their insightful suggestions. Of course, I am most indebted to the people who have informed my research and continue to share their lives with me in both Guinea-Bissau and Portugal, especially the villagers of Bafata-Oio and the members of the *Badim Culubo* in Lisbon.
4. George Brooks (1993, 28–29) notes that, for centuries, acephalous "animist" groups speaking West Atlantic languages and practicing wet-rice agriculture have inhabited

coastal-riverine areas in Guinea-Bissau. In contrast, peoples inhabiting the interior savannah-woodland have been politically centralized and Islamicized. Carlos Lopes (1987, 10–11) asserts that the tendency to distinguish between indigenous coastal peoples and interior peoples in Guinea-Bissau is inherently political. Because interior peoples were organized under a state, Islamized, and exhibited political centralization and class divisions, the Portuguese regarded them as less "backward" than coastal peoples.

5. The Balanta are the largest ethnic group in Guinea-Bissau. My informants explained that this name comes from the Mandinga N'Balanta, meaning, "we refused [Islam]" (see also Forrest 1992, 10). According to Teixeira Da Mota (1954, 223), however, the name is the Balanta term for "people." Some Balanta (the Balanta-Mané) and Manjaco are Muslims today.

6. Despite their tendency to be viewed as "outsiders," the Mandinga have been powerful and influential agents in the history of Guinea-Bissau. At the height of its power in the fourteenth century, the Mali Empire expanded into the Senegambian region, founding more than twenty kingdoms along the Gambia and Casamance Rivers. At the fall of Mali in the seventeenth century, one of these kingdoms, Kaabu—which was located primarily in present-day Guinea-Bissau—replaced it in power and importance (Schaffer and Cooper 1987, 3–4; Quinn 1972, 10; see also Lopes 1999).

7. One could identify a fourth wave of immigration to Portugal, consisting of refugees who fled Guinea-Bissau during the "7 de Junho" war, an eleven-month armed conflict that began in June 1998 when a military junta led by Ansumane Mané attempted to oust João "Nino"Vieira, who had been Guinea-Bissau's president for nineteen years.

8. The Badim Culubo is a Mandinga women's organization that was founded in 1989. In 2003 it had more than seventy-five card-holding members (including four male "assistant" members) and more than two hundred "supporters." Badim is an orthographic variation of the Mandinga term baadiṇo, which refers to children who nursed from the same breast (full siblings or maternal half-siblings). The association's primary role—creating community by allowing members to "live together," as one informant put it—is thus expressed through the cultural idiom of maternal kinship. Among Mande peoples ofWest Africa, maternal kinship is a powerful symbol of "oneness"—of equality, loyalty, and affection—in contrast to paternal kinship, which implies difference and competition (see Bird and Kendall 1980, 14–15).

9. This is also true to some extent for boys. Although I know some Mandinga men who were circumcised "in the bush" in a traditional initiation ritual, most were circumcised in the hospital and "initiated" later in a ritual. Most of my male informants prefer hospital circumcisions to "bush" circumcisions for their own sons. See M. Johnson (2000, 230) for Mandinga women's views on the possibility of hospital circumcisions for girls.

10. Joshua Forrest (1992, 133) reports that major campaigns have been waged in Guinea-Bissau against female circumcision, a practice that the national leadership regards as "backward" (see also Urdang 1979, 183–188).

11. Richard Shweder argues that ethnicity or cultural group affiliation is the most important factor in determining whether a group practices (or doesn't practice) circumcision for both boys and girls (2000, 217). Ironically, the link between female circumcision and ethnic identity remains relatively unexplored. See Gruenbaum (2001, chapter 4) for a fascinating example from Sudan.

12. Discourses linking male and female circumcision and ritual purity are also prevalent among practitioners of indigenous African religions. Victor Turner (1962, 160–161) notes that among the Ndembu of Zambia boys are "made pure" through circumcision by the removal of their feminine attributes (that is, the foreskin). Among the Ndembu, "infantile filthiness" is contrasted with "clean maturity" (ibid., 173; see C. P. MacCormack 1979, 32, for a similar case among Mende girls in Sierra Leone). Janice Boddy argues that in Sudan, the heat and pain associated with infibulation are considered

"acts of feminine purification" (1989, 64). Mary Douglas's (1966) work on pollution is useful in understanding such discourses. Individuals are made "pure" when they are freed from the pollution and danger associated with categorical ambiguity.

13. Mandinga are not alone in linking female genital cutting and Islam. Anke van der Kwaak reports that many Somali women believe that the Qur'an prescribes female circumcision (1992, 780).

14. Eric Winkel writes that according to Islam, female circumcision is classified as *sunnah,* meaning "optional." In contrast, however, full clitoridectomy (removal of the clitoris) is "legally parallel to castration, and that is forbidden as an 'alteration of Allah's creation'" (1995, 4). See also Gruenbaum (2001, 60–66) for a thorough discussion of female circumcision and Islam.

15. See D'Alisera (2004, chapter 6) for a discussion of the "othering" potential of negative and stereotypical images of female circumcision in the media for Sierra Leonean Muslim women living in Washington, D.C.

16. Some of the names and places in these case studies have been changed to conceal the identity of my informants. This was not an easy decision to make, however, since most Mandinga I know are delighted about the possibility of appearing in published works about them and would be horrified by the idea of changing their names. My informants are beginning to understand the risk associated with anthropological research on sensitive subjects, however. In 2003 several of my informants told me that journalists had contacted them, asking them their views on "female genital mutilation." They assumed that the journalists learned about them through my work or that I had sent them.

17. Alma Gottlieb reminds us that sexual desire is culturally constructed. Indeed, whereas Americans generally believe that men have a stronger sex drive than do women, Muslims often believe the reverse. Gottlieb explains that the practices of female seclusion and female circumcision are thought in some cases to protect women from the possible negative consequences of their own strong desires (2002, 176–178).

18. Gosselin traces this to the Mande belief that the clitoris contains excessive concentrations of *nyama,* "the world's fundamental and awesome energy" (2000a, 54). For those who uphold this view, the clitoris, if not removed, is said to be dangerous to men (during intercourse) and infants (during birth).

19. Before my most recent trip to Portugal in 2003, Fatu's husband, Ali, had died unexpectedly. As customary among the Mandinga, Fatu was waiting to marry one of Ali's brothers, who was still in Guinea-Bissau. Aminata still had not been circumcised, and Fatu did not yet know her future husband's view on the issue.

CHAPTER 10

Infibulation and the Orgasm Puzzle

SEXUAL EXPERIENCES OF INFIBULATED
ERITREAN WOMEN IN RURAL ERITREA
AND MELBOURNE, AUSTRALIA

Mansura Dopico

ANTI–FEMALE GENITAL MUTILATION (FGM) advocacy litera-
ture and the global discourse on circumcision and sexual satisfaction portray
women who have undergone female genital cutting (FGC) as "mutilated,"
"frigid," or "unsatiable" (Shweder 2000, 210). Thus, there is an assumption that
almost all women who have undergone FGC have sexual problems or are unable to achieve pleasure from sex. Many opponents justify their views on the
basis of core assumptions and beliefs about the female anatomy and the role
of the clitoris in achieving sexual pleasure (Ahmadu, chapter 12 of this volume). Nevertheless, many women who have undergone FGC generally report achieving orgasm and sexual satisfaction, "an unpredictable response from
women who cannot, at least according to western medical discourse, enjoy the
act" (Kirby 1987, 44). Ahmadu (chapter 12 of this volume) writes, "if I had
not been sexually active prior to my own initiation . . . I would certainly be
confused by all the negative messages and misinformation." A similar sentiment
was echoed by one of my respondents who said, "I had no idea about circumcision and the clitoris, I just thought everybody was the same and that women
could only orgasm if they slept with men. . . . I also heard that the clitoris is the
only sensitive place on a woman and that puzzles me" (Lula, female, Australia,
quoted in Dopico 1997).

Western anti-FGM activists and other unaffected opponents who claim to
"know" the effects of circumcision on female sexuality (Ahmadu, chapter 12 of
this volume) may explain the fact that many women who have undergone FGC
and especially infibulation report achieving orgasm, for example, by claiming
that they are in utter denial about their experiences and that they are somehow
pretending to enjoy sex and orgasms when in fact they are suffering in silence (ibid.), or as reported by a Sudanese psychiatrist (cited in Lightfoot-Klein

1989a) have no idea what orgasms are and only think they are experiencing them, as it is a supposed physiological impossibility due to their impaired genitals. I wondered how women who have undergone infibulation felt about such assertions. In my research I ask how women who have undergone infibulation and are orgasmic and experience sexual pleasure reconcile their actual experiences with what they are supposed to experience according to these activists. Their views and experiences are often the last to be given attention when it comes to gaining information and data on the topic, especially if they are not in line with dominant ideology or do not reflect the ethnocentric views of anti-FGM writers (see also Ahmadu, chapter 12 of this volume); yet, I suspect, they might shed considerable light on this puzzle.

The sexual experiences of some women who have undergone infibulation have been documented, particularly by El Dareer (1982a, 1982b), Lightfoot-Klein (1989a), and Shandall (1967). All have recorded personal testimonies of Sudanese women who have undergone infibulation; some of the women reveal lack of sexual satisfaction and others report healthy and satisfying sexual experiences. I hope to provide an opportunity for Eritrean women and men to discuss their sexual experiences as people who have experienced infibulation directly or indirectly. In addition, focusing on Eritreans addresses the omission of cultural differences in research. No reported research in the area of sexual experiences and infibulation incorporates Eritrean perspectives. Additionally, research into the impact of infibulation on sexual gratification is more commonly rooted in an interpretation and analysis of Western concepts of sexuality or an analysis that assumes culture neutrality.

This chapter is based on the findings in a segment of my doctoral thesis that was developed as a tool for documenting the experiences of the participants in the study; it will serve to highlight the impact of infibulation on orgasm and sexual satisfaction. The specific aim was to elicit accounts of the personal sexual experiences of Eritrean women who have undergone infibulation. Specifically, I hope to develop a better understanding of the subject by constructing a synoptic account from the perspective of Eritrean women and men, a knowledge of specificity that can be applied to challenge current logic with respect to infibulation and orgasm/sexual satisfaction.

A purposive sample was sought to increase the range of data exposed, as well as to uncover the full array of multiple realities. The research population consists of married or divorced Eritrean women who have undergone infibulation and Eritrean males who are or have been married to women who have undergone infibulation. The study included ten female and five male respondents residing in Australia and the same number residing in Hal Hal, a rural part of Eritrea. This research was conducted in 2001, and was funded by the School of Social Work at Australia's James Cook University.

A background and medical history was used to collect demographic information. The core of this research, however, centers upon semistructured, open-ended,

TABLE 10.1

Gender, Age, Type of Marriage, Marital Status, and Education Levels of Australian Participants (pseudonyms have been used to maintain participants' anonymity)

Respondent	Gender	Age group	Type of marriage	Marital status	Educational level
Amna	Female	30–35	Love marriage	Married	B.A.
Hassina	Female	55–60	Arranged marriage	Married	Illiterate
Fatma	Female	40–45	Arranged marriage	Married	B.A.
Adela	Female	35–40	Love marriage	Married	B.A.
Lula	Female	40–45	Arranged marriage	Married	Postgraduate
Zenat	Female	35–40	Arranged marriage	Married	Postgraduate
Nura	Female	30–35	Arranged marriage	Divorced	Grade 12
Asha	Female	45–50	Love marriage	Married	Postgraduate
Nyla	Female	30–35	*Arranged love marriage	Married	Tertiary
Selam	Female	35–40	Love marriage	Married	Diploma
Mussa	Male	50–55	Arranged love M	Married	Postgraduate
Yusef	Male	30–35	Love marriage	Married	B.Sc.
Abdu	Male	30–35	Arranged love M	Married	Postgraduate
Hussien	Male	50–55	Arranged marriage	Married	B.A.
Sameer	Male	25–30	Arranged love M	Married	Postgraduate

*Arranged love marriage: Marriage was arranged and they fell in love afterward, before being married.

in-depth interviews. The interviews were focused in order to give participants an opportunity to explore a wide range of experiences relevant to the study. Respondents were encouraged to use the language they were most comfortable with because, as Spradley (1979) asserts, language is more than a means of communication about reality; it is a tool for constructing reality. Participants told their stories in Tigre or Tigrinia, the two major languages in Eritrea. Since I am adept in both languages, there was no need for an interpreter.

The interpretive and collaborative paradigms employed in this research are grounded in the actual experiences and language of the respondents. Participants defined marriage, orgasm, and sexual and marital satisfaction in their own

TABLE 10.2

Gender, Age, Type Of Marriage, Marital Status, and Education Levels of Rural Eritrean Participants (pseudonyms have been used to maintain participants' anonymity)

Respondents	Gender	Age group	Type of marriage	Marital status	Educational level
Nafisa	F	35–40	Arranged	Divorced	Nil
Aziza	F	30–35	Arranged	Divorced	Nil
Baraka	F	35–40	Arranged	Married	Nil
Massoda	F	30–35	Arranged	Married (second wife)	Nil
Um Mariam	F	45–50	Arranged	Widowed	Nil
Arhet	F	45–50	Arranged	Married	Nil
Zenab	F	45–50	Arranged	Married	Nil
Jamih	F	30–35	Arranged	Married	Nil
Fatma	F	30–35	Arranged	Married	Nil
Kadija	F	70–75	Arranged	Widowed	Nil
Idreiss	M	50–55	Arranged	Married	Nil
Benamir	M	40–45	Arranged	Married	Nil
Ibrahim	M	50–55	Arranged	Married	Nil
Hamid	M	35–40	Arranged	Married	Nil
Aziz	M	30–35	Arranged	Married	Nil

terms; thus the data consist solely of participants' phenomenological accounts of their sexual life and marital relationship.

Humans have the ability to enjoy sex that is unrelated to reproduction. Biopsychosocial aspects dictate whether this potential has an opportunity to be fulfilled, however. In addition to hormones and health conditions, interpersonal relationships, social constructs, and emotional status all influence the ability to reach sexual satisfaction. To investigate infibulation and its impact on sexual health and marital relationship, it is important to understand the views expressed in the dominant literature on women's sexuality and sexual and marital satisfaction.

GENERAL OVERVIEW OF DOMINANT LITERATURE

Our knowledge of female sexuality, the clitoris, and orgasm has been constructed within different "epistemological fields" or "epistemes," as Foucault (1973, xvii) calls them. For Foucault, all knowledge is "enmeshed in the clash of petty dominations," as well as in the larger battles that constitute our world. De Beauvoir (1953) demonstrates how literature transmits myths and creates standards that adversely affect women's realities. Writing more than forty years later, Tiefer (1995, 19) rejects the idea of a "universal, inborn sexual drive" by claiming that sexual scholarship is not and cannot be objective or detached from historical, cultural and political influences and proposed instead viewing sexuality as being shaped and scripted by sociocultural forces and learning. However, the treatment of sexuality and orgasm in the dominant literature, despite its emphasis on biopsychosocial factors, seems to deemphasize cultural differences by offering concepts that are clearly grounded in Western sexual values (Lavee 1991). Today, phallocentric values prevail in Western societies, influencing sexologists' perceptions. Thus, sexology as a science has been strongly influenced by social mores and the personal values of writers, researchers, and sex therapists (Ahmadu 2000; Tiefer 1995), which are often based on myth (Ellison 1984; Zilbergeld and Ellison 1980).

The Concept of Female Orgasm

The mere use of the term "female orgasm" may be considered a historical achievement. It denotes an acknowledgment that women have a physical response to sexual stimulus and implies that there is potential for women to have sexual satisfaction. Kinsey, Masters and Johnson, and others defined orgasm as a reflex that occurs when scale tension and blood flow to the pelvis reach a peak and are dispersed, the pubococcygeal (PC) muscle group spasms, and the heart rate accelerates rapidly and then slows down. It can vary greatly in its physical and psychological intensity (Keesling 1999). The neurology of orgasm involves elaborate collaboration between the genitals, the spine, and the brain, especially the limbic system, the brain's pleasure center. Some studies illustrate the mind-body collaboration during orgasm. After years of monitoring the physical aspects of orgasm, both Bohlen and Wagner (1983, cited in W. Gallagher 1986) concluded that its essence does not lie in the genitals, and they postulated that orgasm is a brain experience. Likewise, Cole (cited in W. Gallagher 1986) claims orgasm to be a psychophysiological phenomenon, primarily psychic with physiological correlates.

Although Masters and Johnson (1966) established what happens during sexual processes and what an orgasm looks like, the fact is that orgasms are so peculiar to the person experiencing them that they are often described by researchers as '"fingerprints" or "signatures."' In a similar vein, Krantz (1958) contends that female orgasm depends both on the woman's ability to surrender to sensation and on the idiosyncrasies of her physiology.

Importance of the Clitoris in Orgasm

The clitoris is commonly defined as having three parts—the glans, the hood, and the shaft; feminists arrived at a new view of the clitoris by using self-examination, personal observation, and meticulous analysis. Often definitions of the clitoris include not only these three parts but also all other parts of "the organ of female orgasm" (Federation of Feminist Women's Health Centre 1981). The clitoral system, it is argued, includes all those structures that function together to produce orgasm, including the vagina.

The clitoris has tremendous potential for arousal; what may affect sensitivity, however, is the supply of nerve endings and individual patterns of each clitoris, which explains the variation in women's preference for sexual stimulation. According to Krantz (1958) no two people, not even identical twins, have the same pattern and distribution of nerves. In some, the clitoris is more sensitive to touch than in others (L. Murray 1983, 58). Therefore, to say that it must be stimulated to orgasm is an oversimplification. There is some evidence that removal of the clitoris cannot inhibit either arousal or orgasm. For example, Weijmar-Schultz and colleagues (1989) found that patients who had undergone radical vulvectomy (due to tumors) could experience orgasm with elaborate foreplay, without their clitorises. The explanation might be found in the extensive nerve network linking the clitoris to the spinal column, leading researchers to conclude that there are two separate roots with nerve endings so plentiful that simply stimulating the area around the surgical site produces waves of sensations that result in orgasm (Murray 1983).

Weisberg (1984) states that the clitoris responds to sexual excitement by swelling and becoming erect, but the enlargement may be barely visible. He adds that the size of the clitoris has no impact on sexual performance or enjoyment. It has been noted that only rarely do women prefer direct stimulation of the clitoris (Masters and Johnson 1966), and that they are much more likely to stimulate the shaft of the clitoris or the mons in the area of the clitoris (Weisberg (1984), or the vagina (Ahmadu 2000), which produces waves of sensations that result in orgasm.

Types of Orgasm

Masters and Johnson (1966) concluded that all female orgasms involve the clitoris and are physiologically indistinguishable. Most authorities have interpreted these findings as defining a single, normative type of female orgasm. For example, Koedt (1970) and Westheimer (1994) conclude that the vaginal orgasm is a myth instigated by Freud. Koedt (1970) argues that the vagina is of no importance in female sexuality other than for menstruation, to receive a penis, to hold semen, and as a birth passage. The erotic nature of the vagina is denied, and any woman who claims to experience vaginal orgasm is a victim of deception or confusion (Koedt 1970).

Since the pioneer treatise of Masters and Johnson (1966), there have not been any major challenges to or corrections of their data. But in the 1980s, new theories emerged, and several writers departed from the "one model of orgasm" and posited the two-orgasm theory (for example, Bentler and Peeler 1979; C. Butler 1976; Singer and Singer 1972). The contradictory either/or orthodoxies were also refuted by Ladas and colleagues (1983), who argue that there is no one ideal way to experience orgasm and suggest that it is instead a continuum of experiences.

Most theorists, including Masters and Johnson (1966) and H. Kaplan (1974), describe only one reflexive pathway in sexual response. However, Perry and Whipple (1981) illustrate a second reflexive pathway, which includes the G–spot as its major source of stimulation, the pelvic nerve as its major pathway, and the musculature of the uterus, the bladder, the urethra, and the proximal portions of the PC muscle as its major spasmic/contraction manifestation. Hoch (1986) and Alzate and Hoch (1986), however, refute the evidence in support of the G–spot as a discrete anatomical structure on the anterior vaginal wall. Instead, Hoch claims that the entire anterior vaginal wall, rather than one specific spot, is erotically sensitive in most women (1986).

This does not diminish or dispute the importance of the clitoris, but it does highlight the equal importance of the vagina and demonstrates that there are at least two genital foci of erotic arousal in women, not only the clitoris. Likewise, normative data illustrate a great variety in the way in which women experience sexuality and what triggers orgasm. For example, Otto (cited in Lightfoot-Klein 1989a) argues that women are capable of experiencing seven distinct types of orgasm: clitoral, vaginal, breast, oral, G-spot, anal, and mental. Likewise, Marmor reports that some orgasms, for example, those obtained from nipple suction, nursing a baby, pressing (fully dressed) against another, a look, or a kiss, represent a discharge of the spinal center that has been initiated primarily by cerebral excitation (1954, 242). There is also documentation of women who are so excitable that they can reach a spasmic, pleasurable reaction merely using their own fantasy (Ogden 1994, 142), while at the other extreme some women apparently never experience orgasm despite various sources, lengths, and intensities of physical stimulation.

Over the past centuries, various experts have told women that they have no orgasms; then two kinds; then only one kind; then three or more kinds. In the early 1980s, however, orgasm was redefined as one basic response with different qualities and degrees of intensity and various primary areas of sensation (Federation of Feminist Women's Health Centre 1981). Equally, many sex therapists are now defining orgasm simply as a decrease in sexual tension, without listing specific criteria (W. Gallagher 1986).

Female Sexual Response and Orgasm

Available reports on the percentage of women who consistently experience orgasm tend to vary. C. Butler (1976), Fisher (1973), Hite (1976), Hunt (1974), and Wallin (1960) give the estimate range of 5 and 25 percent for women who never experience orgasm in coitus, although the lower figure is a more frequent estimate. Despite regular findings of certain percentages of women with anorgasmic patterns of response, some researchers still assume that lack of orgasm is an abnormal or an inadequate response. C. Butler (1976), Ford and Beach (1951), and H. Kaplan (1974) suggest that sexual response lacking in orgasmic features may, in fact, represent a normal variation in the wide range of female orgasmic sexual response.

THE ORGASM IMPERATIVE

For centuries, Western women were socialized to be sexually passive and to focus on male satisfaction during sexual intercourse (Hurlbert 1991). Under the influence of Masters and Johnson, however, sexual problems came to be regarded as disorders of intercourse that necessitate cure; this view was institutionalized in the American Psychiatric Association's Diagnostic and Statistical Manual of Mental Disorders (American Psychological Association 1987 and 1994). In an attempt to demystify sexuality, Masters and Johnson reduced it to the most atomistic of human activities; they focused explicitly on orgasm and, in turn, formulated women (and men) as "sexual machines" (Gardetto 1993, 244). Their frame of meaning articulated a new view of sexuality governed by the orgasm imperative (Bejin 1986).

The advent of the feminist movement in the 1960s helped women assert their claims as sexual beings, and thus the experience of orgasm came to be viewed by many women as both a right and a goal (Weinberg et al.). This has created a societal expectation that women should always experience orgasm during coitus, although scientific evidence indicates such a goal to be unrealistic (LoPiccolo and Stock 1986).

Sexual response is a biopsychosocial phenomenon (Leiblum 2000) and, rather than envisioning an orderly, linear progression of desire, arousal, and orgasm, it can be more accurately understood as consisting of both sexual and nonsexual elements that affect each phase (Basson 2000). It is argued that orgasm corresponds to expectation on both cultural and personal levels; thus it is likely that because Western women now expect and are expected to have orgasms, more of them do (Davidson and Moore 1994). Conversely, women who perceive orgasm during sexual intercourse to be an important component of sexual life feel like failures in not achieving this goal and that can evoke feelings of guilt (ibid.), which may eventually lead to loss of sexual desire (Hurlbert 1993).

Some elucidation of the variation in women's ability to experience orgasm may lie in the different levels of learned inhibition during social and psychological development, individual differences in stimulation thresholds, and other physiological processes (Jayne 1981). However, nonsexual interpersonal factors are extremely important in determining whether a woman will be sexually motivated (for example, if she is angry at or resentful toward a partner). In other words, the woman may be physiologically capable of becoming aroused but psychologically disinterested or unmotivated (Basson 2000).

Female participants in this survey stated that they engaged in the sexual act to be close and loving toward their partner, because it seemed like a good idea, to please their husband, to pave the way for a request, and as a duty. The results indicate that most participants were not distressed if they failed to reach orgasm. Orgasm was taken out of the equation; it was not a goal to be attained, as can be gathered from the following responses:

I don't have sex in order to have an orgasm. I just enjoy the sensation of the act and it almost always leads to orgasm. All the publicity about orgasm makes me sick. (Nyla, female, Australia)

Sometime back I read sex books and said to myself I should be experiencing this and that. On those days I viewed orgasm as a goal. I felt badly when I did not orgasm and started to doubt my womanhood. Yet in my head I knew that isn't true. I think I was striving for much less to than what I already had. I can say that leads to disappointment and may prevent the desired experience from occurring. Good sex is like sleep, if you try hard it does not happen. (Asha, female, Australia)

I am fed up right up to here with all the emphasis on orgasm nowadays. It is absolutely sickening; after thirty years of marriage and four lovely children, I certainly do not see anything so great about orgasm. Thank goodness that I am old (early fifties) and can go to bed and just sleep instead of having to wrestle with a lustful man if I do not want to. I feel sorry for all the young girls who are led to believe they are in for a great experience, a goal to be achieved. (Fatma, female, Australia)

The data analyses concerning feelings if orgasm was absent during coitus reveal that female participants did not attribute their lack of orgasm either internally (to themselves, their femininity, or their ability) or to circumcision (infibulation). Although some reported annoyance, anger, and frustration at being left behind, these emotions were mostly directed at interpersonal (partners) and situational factors. This could be attributed to the facts that Eritrean women are not expected to achieve orgasm or have pleasure from sex, and that labels such as female sexual dysfunction, which may increase anxiety and guilt for those women who lack orgasms during coitus, are not known or used by the wider community. "What is there to feel bad about? He can only do what he can, or he is satisfied and you have fulfilled your duty," was the response of most female participants in rural Eritrea.

Total acceptance of the partner, the knowledge that they were loved and cared for, and a belief in their ability to achieve orgasm under different conditions provided a tremendous source of strength for most female participants in Australia. Conversely, when those in good relationships, those with high self-esteem who feel good about their sexuality, did not have orgasms, they stated that they worked on overcoming the barriers.

To present a clearer understanding of female sexuality, sexual responses and the role of orgasm must be examined within the context of the woman's genetic inheritance, constitutional endowment, psychosexual development, and goals for fulfillment as an individual and women within the society and the culture in which she lives.

SEX ROLE EXPECTATIONS AND SEXUAL GUILT

Culture has a strong impact on sexual scripts, beliefs, and behaviors (Burgos and Diaz Perez 1986; Pavich 1986; Wilson 1986; Wyatt et al. 1976; Yap 1986) and also on what is considered normal. Thus, both values and sexual behavior are highly diverse, and no one society can be pointed out as representative. D'Emilio and Freedman (1988) found sexuality to be associated with a range of human activities and values, such as the procreation of children, attainment of physical pleasure, recreation or sport, personal intimacy, spiritual transcendence, or power over others. However, despite being embedded in early childhood interactions, personal sexual scripts continue to evolve in relationships with others (Engel et al. 1993).

Sexual guilt, which results from prohibitions and idealized goals, is a generalized expectancy for self-punishment when failing to attain one's internalized standards (Wyatt and Dunn 1991). Guilt inhibits or encourages different types of sexual behavior, and Hurlbert (1993) contends that it has a strong inhibiting influence on sexual development. Religious attitudes (Daniluk 1993), parents (Propper and Brown 1986), and peers (Sack et al. 1984) are found to be influential in increasing levels of sexual guilt. Religious rigidity is reported to be a contributing factor in impaired marital sexual functioning, including guilt, inhibition, and lower levels of sexual interest, activity, and responsiveness (Daniluk 1993).

All female respondents in this study have been tacitly trained from a very early age not to touch their genitals, as this is seen as sinful and immoral. The official message is, "Do not look, do not touch, and do not feel." The concept of intimacy and closeness shown by touching the genitalia has been absent. The vagina is an unmentionable part, and all female respondents referred to it as "privates," "down there," "you-know-where," or "it." As the following responses suggest, female respondents felt guilty for indulging in what are seen as forbidden sexual behaviors:

> We have tried some of the things you see in the sex movies. He used to go down on me. I enjoyed it. It was something new. After a while I did not want it any more, because all those old thoughts came back. I am not very religious but I do believe in what I hear and what the religious people say. Our religion clearly states that things like masturbation/stimulation, cunnilingus, touching, and so on should not be done, even with one's spouse. (Amna, female, Australia)

> I think this has something to do with the way I was brought up. I do not look at my body and I never take my clothes off and walk naked even in the bathroom. The body is not for exposure. Even during intercourse I cover my body. So during intercourse, instead of enjoying his hands on my body, I am busy stopping him subtly from venturing there. (Amna, female, Australia)

Although I tried and liked masturbation, I could not let myself enjoy it. My mind rejected it. I have a great deal of sexual hang-ups and confusion. I know much of what I have learned of sexuality has been slanted. I was trying very hard to dump that and to listen to my body, but I couldn't and can't. I think we are controlled by hypocrisy, and fear of change. We are in a state of transition; we cannot handle this new culture or our own culture correctly. (Amna, female, Australia)

Impact of Non-Eritrean (Western and Other) Views on Respondents

I believe Eritrea can be cited as a prototype of a sexually repressive culture; yet, like the rest of the world, Eritrean communities have not remained static. Traditional as well as modern communities have witnessed varying degrees of change in values, norms, attitudes, and behavior regarding sexual relations. As a result, some Eritreans exposed to Western views are experiencing contradictions between the capitalist and the traditional constructions of their bodies. The former seems to push them to be seductive, sexy and sexual, the later to be prudish, conservative, and asexual.

For example, Asha learned to masturbate to orgasm after her divorce. However, after remarrying she felt it was wrong to ask her husband to please her in this fashion, and, convinced that she would betray her cultural upbringing, she denied her sexuality for sometime. For every woman like Asha, there are many more who have been similarly influenced without being aware of it. In contrast to Asha, there is Lula, who said, "I do not like him to touch or kiss my genitals, and that is what I am supposed to like." Lula felt abnormal because she did not like clitoral stimulation, and Asha felt uncomfortable because she did. The fears of both women are perpetuated, if not generated, by the conflicting popular beliefs of their cultures.

As yet, sexuality has not moved from the realm of theology to that of science in the Eritrean community, and discourse on sexual behavior and sexuality is still the province of religious leaders and elderly women. The assumption is that the best mothers, wives, and managers of households know little or nothing of sexual indulgence. It is argued that it is indecent for a woman to understand the structure and functions of her own body. The exploration of areas of sexual behavior—for example, masturbation, kissing, and touching—is confined to the category of sin or vice. However, the questioning by some Australian respondents of the nature of such practices has contributed to the possibility that they may come to be regarded as normal.

There are some respondents, however, who have incorporated this new information to enhance their sexual lives. They see it as a means of independence and self-reliance to develop their sexuality and self-esteem. As Asha said, "If I don't orgasm I know it has nothing to do with me but with him."

I learned some new things about sex that I did not know before and decided to see if they work for me, and it created new heights for our relationship. I am always learning and trying new things. I feel no longer different. (Nyla, female, Australia)

In our culture we believe women have sex for the sake of the man, and men have sex because they need to. This is not so—it is not a one-way traffic—both have to enjoy it. The men also know and feel that we are only tolerating it for their sake. I read and learned a lot about sex and sexuality. Earlier on I used to get impatient and could not wait for him to finish, but now I taught myself to enjoy it, because I know I have a right to it. (Nura, female, Australia)

Sexual Satisfaction and Sexual Dissatisfaction

Western definitions of sexual satisfaction and dissatisfaction are considered problematic, as behaviors that are considered normal within one culture may be defined as deviant in another. The assertion that the experience of orgasm necessarily leads to a sense of sexual pleasure and gratification is problematic as well. Sexual satisfaction has been defined in terms of enjoyment and release or relief from sexual desire, yet Bohlen (1983), could not measure the pleasure associated with orgasm. Equally, it has been suggested that an experience of orgasm may not be necessary in order for a woman to experience "sexual release or relief" and that orgasm and satisfaction are not synonymous in women. Similarly, orgasm consistency and satisfaction are separate, but overlapping, dimensions of female sexual response (Bell and Bell 1972; Hite 1976). The fact remains that women persist in and prefer sexual activities that may not produce orgasm or may produce it inconsistently (Fisher 1973; Kinsey et al. 1953), rendering it problematic to explain sexual satisfaction in terms of a reward view of orgasm without considering dimensions beyond the purely physical, that is, the essential role that nonsexual considerations, such as the wish for intimacy and interpersonal harmony, play in motivating and maintaining much of a woman's sexual behavior.

A sense of enjoyment or satisfaction with one's sexual life is a highly personal sentiment. Asking women who believe they have no right to sexual satisfaction to make judgments about the quality of their sexual life requires them to articulate thoughts and feelings that are not usually the subject of their conscious reflection and in fact are opposite to their beliefs, as demonstrated by the following quotation: "I haven't really thought about it. In fact I do not think about it at all. I just plod on, going about my wifely duties from day to day. I don't ever think about my sexual life or satisfaction" (Aziza, female, Eritrea).

Quality of sexual life is a latent concept, and several female respondents reported that it is not a concept that people commonly use. As Fatma (female, Australia) pointed out, people do not regularly analyze their marital lives in sexual terms. On close examination, however, quality of sexual life was greatly related to participants' past sexual experiences, current expectations, and future aspirations, as the following responses indicate:

One does not know what a happy sex life is. No one thinks about it. You just assume that what you have is what it is supposed to be. You do not see people complaining, so you take it for granted that it is the norm. However, the condition of the relationship is very important. You need to be in a good state of mind to appreciate sex. Otherwise you just lift your skirt and pray that he ejaculates soon and jumps down. (Aziza, female, Eritrea)

The results of this study demonstrate the importance of considering several psychosocial dimensions when attempting to understand the meaning of a reported level of sexual satisfaction.

For female respondents, sexual satisfaction involved more than physical release or orgasm. It was claimed to come from being in tune with one's partner at that point in time. Orgasm or lack of orgasm was not found to have a great effect on sexual satisfaction, as could be ascertained from the following:

The penis is not a magic wand that creates great sex. Sexual satisfaction depends less on the way the man's penis touches the woman's privates and more on the way the man's spirit touches the woman's spirit. The key to sexual satisfaction is above the eyebrows, not below the pubis. (Asha, female, Australia)

Sexual satisfaction, as defined by the following respondents, is a psychological construct of subjective fulfillment. The responses demonstrate the individual's capacity to experience subjective contentment, happiness, and satisfaction despite not achieving orgasm, as well as dissatisfaction despite climaxing:

Orgasm cannot be taken as the sole criterion for determining the degree of satisfaction a female derives from sexual activity. Whether or not she herself reaches orgasm, many a female finds satisfaction in knowing that her husband has enjoyed the contact, and in realizing that she has contributed to his pleasure. (Asha, female, Australia)

When I was in a good and happy mood, it gave me great pleasure to make love to him even if it did not lead to orgasm. I was very satisfied to see him satisfied. It was as if I came only much more. You can say, being close, giving myself and receiving him unconditionally is sexual satisfaction for me. But when I was not in the mood and I came, I was not satisfied in my mind; I would not call this sexual satisfaction. (Amna, female, Australia)

Some female respondents reported resenting their partner or themselves when forced to have sex, even if it resulted in orgasm for them. Their refusal to enjoy sex under such conditions was intended to get even with their spouses. The following participants cut off their orgasms to spite their husbands:

We have so many conflicts and I take it to the bedroom. I just think all he wants is sex, so why should I give him pleasure by orgasming? I just do it with no feelings and try very hard not to come. So for me not coming is a reward and if I orgasm when I am not in the mood I see it as a defeat. (Asha, female, Australia)

If I have trouble with him and he wants sex, it is very difficult for me to enjoy it because I would be thinking that he only wants my body and that he will have it because I am his wife. At such times I purposely refuse to come. I resent him and at times hate him if I come. If I was in a happy mood, it gave me great pleasure to make love to him even if it did not lead to orgasm. (Zenat, female, Australia)

Most literature on marriage acknowledges that the sexual relationship has an impact on the quality of satisfaction experienced in the marriage (Fields 1983; Lederer and Jackson 1968). As Yusef, a male respondent from Australia, said, "If the sexual relationship is good, it accounts for 10 percent of the whole relationship, but if is unsatisfactory then it accounts for 90 percent and creates huge problems." A significant relationship has been evinced between trust and marital relationship and between trust and sexual satisfaction (Fields 1983; Kaplan 1974; Lederer and Jackson 1968).

IMPACT OF SEXUAL SATISFACTION ON MARITAL HAPPINESS OF PARTICIPANTS

Sexual and marital satisfaction judgments, to borrow Fox-Rushby and Parker's (1995) phrase, are culture-full, that is, they reflect the cultures within which they were made, as well as the values and beliefs of the environments responsible for their development. Female participants did not perceive sex, orgasm, or sexual satisfaction as the epitome of the potential for marital satisfaction. On the contrary, some female participants viewed sex as a source of guilt ("he is a good man and we have a wonderful life, so I make love to him out of guilt"), fear (he might take a second wife or mistress), punishment (the tortures of hell for breaking a religious obligation/contract), and oppression and inequality (since frequency and duration of the sexual activity is almost always decided by the male).

Respondents who reported being happily married indicated that having an orgasm was important/desirable, but that not having one was not that devastating and did not impact the quality of their marital life. On the contrary, marital satisfaction had an impact on sexual dissatisfaction. Female respondents saw sex as much more than orgasm; it was about dialogue, about listening, being kind and loving, and being thoughtful. The following response reinforces this view:

Sex was excellent between my first husband and I, but he was a jealous man, so I divorced him. See, fantastic sex did not lead to a happy marriage. Now I am married to a wonderful man, but he is useless in bed. My sex life is lousy, sometimes I fake to please him, but I have a happy marriage and I am satisfied. (Asha, female, Australia)

FIRST SEXUAL ENCOUNTERS AND SUBJECTIVE
RATINGS OF WEDDING MONTH PAIN

Infibulation reduces the vulvar opening, sometimes to a pinhole, making it necessary to cut or tear tissue before sexual penetration can take place. Thus, sex is thought to cause pain rather than pleasure. The results for wedding night experiences are consistent with findings from several other studies. All female respondents reported pain during the initial stages of their first sexual intercourse, which supports previous findings by El Dareer (1982a), El Saadawi (1980), and Hosken (1993). Although most respondents remembered and described their first sexual encounters as pure ordeal, there were marked differences in the degree of severity of reported pain. For some it was a "breeze," while for others it was "torture."

It hurts like hell and I cried my heart out. He did not take pity on me—why would he? Would a hyena leave meat? A man is like an animal, he just goes for it. So while I sob my heart out he struggles down there. It took him seven days of chipping to get there. His penis swelled and they treat him, but not me. The wound is only for a few days but after that it gets good. Even though sex afterwards is great, I would not go through the first few months for anything. (Kadija, female, Eritrea)

The pain was not the way people explain it to be, it was not that bad. Sure I had pain, but the process was very gradual. He used to leave me if I couldn't take it. Also we used creams, local anesthetic, Vaseline, and so on. (Nyla, female, Australia)

I can say my wedding night was the darkest day of my life. Even to this day I remember it and I feel bad. He was very rough and forceful and if I was ever to scream it would have been that night. I haemorrhaged all night but, stupid me, thought it was the semen and that it was normal. When I woke up in the morning I was soaked in blood and when I walked clots of blood dropped. I just collected the clots on the bed sheet and I sent it home to my mother. And for three months it was torture every time we had sex. (Fatma, female, Australia)

Mine was a breeze. One week after the wedding I checked myself in a hospital and had the operation under full anaesthetic and within a few days it was as good as gold. (Asha, female, Australia)

Most respondents endured the defibulating process stoically. They displayed laughter and humor while recalling the experiences; they likened the experience to "labor pain"—natural torture, but ultimately rewarding.

MALE EXPERIENCE

It is claimed that men who are married to or have sexual partners who have undergone infibulation might have unpleasant sexual experiences (Toubia

1995). The initial stages of sexual encounters, apart from the pain and distress they cause the woman, can also have negative affects on some men. For example, according to van der Kwaak (1992), the consequences of forceful and repeated intercourse to penetrate a tight infibulation may cause impotence in some men. Dirie and Lindmark (1991) reported one case of a penile ulcer that resulted from repeated forceful attempts at penetration.

The anxieties and apprehensions of male respondents were similar to those previously reported. They reported not only severe abrasions of the penis as a result of repeated attempts at penetration, but also fear of failure in accomplishing their duty as a groom (defibulation by penetration), which affects self-image. The wedding month was described as physically and mentally taxing, similar to findings reported by van der Kwaak, (1992) and Dirie and Lindmark (1991). It was also rewarding for those able to open their infibulated brides by repeated penetration, as it reaffirmed their manhood.

Although most male respondents interpreted their behavior as an acceptable act of the defibulating process, some reported being in turmoil for causing pain to another person but had to stop being sympathetic in order to get on with their duty as a new groom, and go through the process.

> It was very difficult because she really resists sleeping with you. It is quite frustrating. People are different and some men are kind and others are not when deflowering their bride. The poor girl suffers, but what can you do? That is the only way. You try to make her feel better by saying that "this is the normal thing, but we will be happy because we will multiply and have our children in our lap." (Benamir, male, Eritrea)

> I was prepared for it mentally and physically. We know what we have to do and pain for the girl is part of it, otherwise why did she get married? Also your mates are waiting for you every morning to find out if you have done it, so it is a matter of honor to do it as quick as you can. (Hamid, male, Eritrea)

OTHER RESEARCHERS' VIEWS ON FGC AND SEXUAL HEALTH

The dominant literature on female sexuality demonstrates the importance of considering a variety of factors, such as the biological, sociological, psychological, and interpersonal relationship issues related to the sexual satisfaction of women. Nevertheless, much of the literature used to support the negative impact of female circumcision on sexual health focuses on erogenous zones and tends to trivialize the importance of these factors.

Studies that systematically investigate the sexual responses of women in societies where FGC are practiced are rare (Vance 1991), and the limited information available challenges the assertion that the practice impedes sexual enjoyment (Obermeyer 1999). Lack of orgasm or sexual gratification is often cited as one of the long-term effects of the practice (Badri 1979; El Dareer 1982a). Other studies (for instance, Ahmadu 2000; Gruenbaum 1996) have shown that this is not uniform, however. Likewise, the available studies do not give a clear understanding of the altered sexual response in their respondents, and why some women with a particular FGC experience sexual pleasure while others do not.

Koso-Thomas (1987) examined the impact of FGC on arousal, sexual feelings, and possibility of reaching orgasm through genital stimulation in Sierra Leone. Results revealed lack of intense arousal by all respondents. Conversely, Ahmadu's (2000) respondents from the same country reported achieving orgasm by stimulating the vagina. Similarly, Badawi (1989) found that 25 percent of Egyptian women who have undergone infibulation could still attain orgasm through stimulation to the clitoral area. Toubia (1995) argues that some of the sensitive tissues of the body and the crura of the clitoris are embedded deeply and are not removed when excision takes place. Thus, even women who have undergone infibulation often have parts of the sensitive tissue of the clitoris and labia left intact, making the extent of sexual damage due to infibulation questionable and difficult to assess. This study supports that contention, as the following responses indicate:

> I have a lot of sensation down there, if touched; it is enough to send me to orgasm. I know it is stitched, but his finger can get there, trust me. I know that most men do stimulate their women this way, otherwise how will he arouse her? Mine is stitched right down, but I love to be stimulated there. No matter what, I always reach orgasm. We always find the spot; there is no worry in that department, I can assure you. (Adela, female, Australia)

> I can tell you, I have two different types of orgasms. One is when I use a vibrator down there, and the other when I sleep with my husband. But as far as the literature goes I am not supposed to feel anything in my clitoris. I swear you will hear me scream (orgasm) when I play with myself, which makes me think I must be weird. (Asha, female, Australia)

Many of Kere and Tapsoba's respondents (1994) reported pain and discomfort during intercourse, and although some experienced a degree of sexual arousal, most did not achieve orgasm. Equally, Shandall's (1967) study of Sudanese women observed that more than 80 percent of those who have undergone infibulation, compared to 10 percent of those with type I or no circumcision, did not identify or experience orgasm. A national survey, also in northern Sudan by El Dareer (1982a), yielded similar results, with 50 percent of respondents reporting no sexual pleasure, 23.3 percent being indifferent, and the remaining 26.7 percent finding sex pleasurable either always or sometimes. The percentage of women who found sex pleasurable sometimes in El Dareer's study is comparable to that reported for uncircumcised Western women in the United States, for example, by Fisher (1973), Hite (1976), and Uddenberg (1974).

Many argue that the relationship between FGC and lack of sexual satisfaction had been grossly exaggerated. Some studies that contradict some of the argument are, for example, Ahmadu's (2000 and chapter 12 of this volume), whose results negate the negative impact of the lack of clitoris on sexuality. Likewise, Khattab (1996) maintains that the majority of Egyptian women who have undergone FGC reported enjoying sex. Equally, Edgerton (1989) states that Kikuyu men and women claimed that women continue to be orgasmic after circumcision. Lightfoot-Klein's (1989a) Sudanese study found that 90 percent of respondents achieved orgasm or had done so at various periods of their married life. Similarly, a study of Egyptian women by Assaad (1980) revealed that 94 percent enjoyed sex, and Megafu (1983) found that 58.8 percent of circumcised Nigerian participants experienced orgasm in contrast to 68.7 percent of uncircumcised women. Another clinical study of women who have undergone all types of FGC in Egypt (Karim and Ammar 1966) reported that 41 percent achieved orgasm frequently, 30 percent experienced some pleasure and no orgasm, and 29 percent did not experience any sexual pleasure.

When respondents in my study were asked whether infibulation impedes sexual satisfaction, some women reported that the state of the mind, quality of marital relationship, and technical expertise of the partner have a greater impact on sexual satisfaction, while others believed culture, and not infibulation, to be the culprit.

> I orgasm almost all the time and I had no idea about circumcision and the clitoris before I came here [Australia]. Circumcision is not the problem; it is the lack of caring, sharing, and respect in the marriage, which creates conflict and that is the end of marital satisfaction and sexual satisfaction. (Lula, female, Australia)

> I do not think I am different to other women in what happens inside or outside my private parts. I have orgasms like the ones they describe in magazines so where is the harm? You need a good mind, not good sexual organ. (Amna, female, Australia)

> To me it does not matter whether one is infibulated or not. What is so different about being circumcised? The hole is there; the body is there, so, what has changed? Trust me, it is the person and your relationship with that person that matters. It is not only the missing clitoris, or the stitched labia that give women pleasure; there are so many other parts of the body that increase pleasure. If you lack a little bit down there, you increase on the lips, you touch the boobs, and that compensates. The only thing I can say is, it depends on the man if he is very experienced and knows how to please a woman and does not finish quick. (Asha, female, Australia)

Female participants did not appear to believe that every other (uncircumcised) woman in the world is constantly scaling the heights of sexual ecstasy while they are missing out as a result of infibulation. The following quote is apt:

I can experience orgasm even by pressing hard down there. I'm sure my clitoris is not affected from inside. All the talk about us being somewhat less sexual is rubbish and has been damaging to some extent. We are creatures of variety in sexual matters as in all other areas. (Adela, female, Australia)

A clear link between an unsatisfying sexual life and infibulation was absent, but female participants did state that circumcision might have an impact on sexual desire. They viewed this as beneficial, however, since it helped them keep their sexual desires and lustfulness under control and helped them project the desired feminine image.

Inherent in Eritrean culture is the presumption that women are passive receptors of male sexual activity and as such do not, and should not, have the desire or the capacity to respond as sexual beings. However, almost all female respondents in the study stated that they did get pleasure from sex but tried to underplay it; despite their efforts to conceal sexual pleasure, most reported that their spouses knew when they were satisfied.

FREQUENCY OF ORGASM

For cultural and practical reasons it was not possible, nor was it the purpose of this study, to objectively measure the effect of infibulation on women's ability to have orgasm in a controlled experimental setting. On questioning, however, almost all female participants claimed to regularly achieve or to have achieved orgasm sometimes in their sexual relationships. Women respondents from Australia and Eritrea made clear and definitive statements about orgasm and the conditions under which it was attained and not attained. Most rural Eritrean respondents claimed to have strong and frequent orgasm in the first few years of marriage. For this group, domesticity, motherhood, lack of privacy, and age were cited as reasons for the decrease in coital frequency, as well as orgasm.

Female participants in Australia reported experiencing orgasm during most of the sexual intercourse episodes in their current relationship if the environment was conducive. The factors found to be most critical in reaching orgasm were state of mind, interpersonal relationship, the environment in which sexual activity was taking place, purpose and motive for sexual interaction, perceived positive value of sexuality, and training in sensuality and relaxation. Female respondents who have a greater tendency to actively take charge of sexual encounters, those who use sexual aids such as vibrators, and those who enjoy erotica reported a higher frequency of coital orgasm. Sexual behaviors, including nature and duration of foreplay, were also recognized as significant contributors to orgasm:

The capacity for orgasm involves a number of learned responses and to develop this capacity, a woman needs to know about the physical aspects of her sexual response and must be handled appropriately. I learned to listen to my body and to convey that to my partner, so I orgasm almost all the time. (Adela, female, Australia)

Sex is like food; you have to enjoy eating it. It starts with the ingredients; the atmosphere has to be right. It is indulgence of the five senses and not only the vagina/clitoris. The nose has to smell, the eyes have to see, the mouth has to taste, the hands have to feel, and the ears have to hear nice things. When all these are working together you have perfection. It is not a last minute thing; you have to prepare for it, that is why I have set days for sex. (Selma, female, Australia)

Descriptions of Orgasm

Culture and religion may inhibit public discussion and sex education in Eritrea and among Eritreans abroad, but a more fundamental problem is language. There are no words for certain sexual things (interactions or outcomes); for example, in Tigre and Tigrenia, which are spoken in most parts of Eritrea, there is no word for "orgasm." Survey participants in Australia were found to have adopted an Arabic word, *ráha,* which means "relaxation." Nevertheless, there was little ambiguity in respondents' understanding of orgasm.

Although there is vagueness about orgasm evident in the "sort of like" ways it was described, most women were aware of when they were experiencing orgasm. When asked to describe an orgasm, most respondents resorted to similes, and words such as "tingly," "alive," "warm," "emotionally and physically relaxed," "floating," "fullness," and "ejaculation" were used as examples.

You feel like you are up there very high and then a moment of floating. I feel as if I am losing all my senses. I feel something chewing me inside which gives me intense pleasure. Then my whole body is relaxed. (Nyla, female, Australia)

It feels like an electric shock going through your body. It feels as if you have little ants inside and they are biting you in a sweet teasing way. (Baraka, female, Eritrea)

I tremble all over. I experience strong vaginal contractions and all that. When I finish I ejaculate; it is a total letting go. (Lula, female, Australia)

I never thought about it consciously, so it is difficult to describe what it feels like. Also in our time we used to try very hard not to let the man know that we were enjoying sex. Even if there was something happening we hid it. All I remember is how my body relaxes. (Aziza, female, Eritrea)

Views of Men Married to Women Who Have Undergone FGC

It is claimed that men who are married to or have sexual relations with women who have undergone female genital surgery might have unpleasant sexual experiences. For example, according to van der Kwaak (1992) the consequences of forceful intercourse to penetrate a tight infibulation may cause impotency in some men. Karim's (1994) Egyptian male respondents claimed that their excessive usage of alcohol and hashish was a result of dissatisfaction in their sexual interactions with their spouses. Similarly, Kéré and Tapsoba (1994) argue that men often seek extramarital affairs with uncircumcised women, as they are deemed to be complete and more satisfying. Of Shandall's (1967) polygamous Sudanese respondents, among whose wives only one had undergone infibulation while the others were uncircumcised or had undergone clitoridectomy, 88.7 percent claimed to prefer the uncircumcised wife or the one who had undergone clitoridectomy to the infibulated wife. While 20 percent stated that they could not keep up with the ordeal of defibulating their spouses after each childbirth, 12 percent reported enjoying sexual intercourse with a partner who had undergone infibulation. Conversely, almost all of El Dareer's (1982a) male respondents stated that both spouses had an enjoyable sexual life.

My study reveals the importance of commitment, communication, tenderness, and caring as paramount in the sexual satisfaction of female participants. As can be gathered from the responses of male respondents, the role of infibulation in sexual gratification was not recognized as the main factor impeding sexual satisfaction for them or their spouses:

> The loss of the clitoris will not be the main obstacle for her satisfaction; there are other more important factors. If you were to put the circumcised woman in a healthy atmosphere, she has the same chance as the uncircumcised woman. You see, even the perfect woman, the one that is not circumcised, might not get there. I cannot generalize and say that these two women have the same rate of response. The English woman is different to the French woman. It has to do with the way they are reared. For example, Amhara girls are supposed to have a great appetite for sex. It might be their diet or upbringing. So, you see, every woman is different. (Mussa, male, Australia)

> I call a woman who has not been circumcised "ever ready," because she is ready in a flash. Some of them cannot control themselves. Most of the times it is very exciting, it makes you feel good and big, but at times it makes you feel uneasy. I do not find that with the circumcised woman; she is as cool as they come. One has to handle her very differently in the initial stages, but once we are making love I do not find much difference. I do not think the circumcised woman is missing out if only she would let herself go. (Hussein, male, Australia)

> I have had many relationships with uncircumcised women, and I was worried that my sex life would be unsatisfying after marriage. My wife was infibulated, but to my surprise she was really good and was willing to experiment. She is the best; she knows how to please herself and is not shy to ask for what she wants. I do not know if other circumcised women are like her, but I would have to say circumcision has not affected her at all. (Bakri, male, Australia)

Although male subjects reported being satisfied with their sexual life and had positive attitudes toward sex and their partners, three Australian respondents who are married to women who did not comply with sex on demand reported a desire for more physical contact. Among the Australian sample the best predictors of sexual satisfaction were wives' open communication and wives' sexual desire (for frequency of intercourse).

Finally, when asked, "Do women who have undergone infibulation enjoy sex?" one respondent said:

> Of course she gets sexual enjoyment. What is the use of marriage if there is no satisfaction? I can tell when she gets satisfied. Partners can tell. Also, why would she lie under a man night after night if she gets nothing out of it? [One response might be because he is the main or sole wage earner and she would be hungry and homeless if she did not perform this role.] Duty or not, she would not oblige if she gets nothing out of sex. It is natural that a woman gets as much out of sex as a man does. Trust me, you can see it in her face. If a woman is without a man, her skin gets dull and she is miserable. The woman who has a man glows. Even if she smells him she gets satisfaction. (Ibrahim, male, Eritrea)

Conclusion

Knowledge of the physiology of sex facilitates the understanding of female sexual responses that involve the entire body, as well as emotions. Marmor (1954) postulates that where there is a freedom from psychological tension in the sexual act and a high degree of tender affection, love, and psychological excitement, cortical facilitation takes place and the result is an intense orgasmic response. Similarly, Ellis argues that "while the clitoris remains the most exquisitely sensitive of the sexual centres in woman, voluptuous sensitivity is much more widely diffused in woman, and the loss of the clitoris or of any of the structures involves no correspondingly serious disability for women" (1933, 132). Orgasm in women is a sensation localized in different regions. Some indicate the genital region or part of it as the center of this sensation; some indicate quite different parts of the body; and others again claim they feel it everywhere. Some women consider the cervix or the uterus to be the center of the sensation; others affirm an equally strong orgasm after the removal of both organs. Some women cite the clitoris as the zone of maximum pleasure; conversely, women who have undergone clitoris cauterization for medical reasons (tumors) are found not to have their orgasmic ability damaged. As early as 1948, Elkan and Pinner posited that the orgasmic sensation in the woman is not linked with any special part of her body as it is in the man. Thus, the existence of such differences should not be surprising. It is possible that the relationship between FGC and lack of sexual satisfaction has been grossly exaggerated, as Ahmadu (2000 and chapter 12 of this volume) contends, and that interpretations might be prejudiced by the insistence on the biological role of the clitoris in orgasm.

Despite the fact that they measured physical reactions only, Masters and Johnson (1966) use the term "orgasmic women" for women who have sexual satisfaction. Likewise, Barbach (1986) assumes that being orgasmic and being sexually satisfied are synonymous, and seems to understand orgasm as a moment of physical spasmic reaction. Measuring women's genital reactions to stimulation and defining them as orgasms is one thing; inferring that these are pleasurable is quite another. The term "orgasm" reflects a physical phenomenon whose absolute impact on sexual pleasure might be questionable, because there are some women in this study who report being sexually satisfied with or without orgasm. Respondents experienced sexual pleasures in many different ways, and a pattern that results in pleasure for one may cause pain and distress for another. Conversely, the same woman could vary in what she found pleasurable from one time to another. For example, relationship variables, individual dimensions, and general ecological factors were associated with orgasm and sexual satisfaction.

Familiarity with the literature on sexual responses, orgasm, and sexual satisfaction that demonstrate its biological, sociological, psychological, and religious/spiritual dimensions, and which continues to exert its influence on the interpretation of sexual satisfaction, leads me to be critical of the current FGM literature in its treatment of sexual satisfaction and its uncritical assertion of the devastating negative effects of FGC on health and sexuality. Furthermore, since it has been ascertained that the clitoris or part of the clitoris might still be intact in some cases of infibulation, it is problematic to accept anti-FGM views on sexual health.

In light of the findings of this study, it is difficult to accept the assumption that one single factor, infibulation, is responsible for inability to attain complete physiological sexual expression (orgasm), that the capacity for sexual enjoyment is dependent on an intact clitoris, and that orgasm is the key principal measure of healthy sexuality. By focusing exclusively on the clitoris and its function, this assumption fails to take into account the biopsychosocial aspects of sexuality and sexual satisfaction and the way in which individuals interpret sexuality and define sexual satisfaction. As Bell notes, "embedded in every act is an entire history of how we account for our own and others' behaviours, an ideational trail that would make sense of every moment we live" (1997, 45). I would argue that to insist on a uniform expression of sexual behaviors or beliefs is erroneous, because cultural values dictate the meaning of sexuality, the construction of a normal, healthy or adequate sexual relationship, and the perceptions and meaning of sexual satisfaction. However, culture is not static, and standards of morality and behavior are susceptible to change over time, whether as a result of evolution or of external force (Martin 1995). Thus, the meaning of sexual satisfaction is not constant, but dynamic. Each generation reinterprets it according to its culture and history. What once was considered satisfaction may no longer be valid.

Finally, this work calls into question the assertion that FGC hinders sexual satisfaction, because, regardless of an environment that is strongly adversarial and the many factors that impact negatively on women's capacity to enjoy sexual relationships, it shows high incidence and considerable frequency of orgasm among the women. Thus, as Ahmadu (chapter 12 of this volume) asks, how important is the clitoris to female sexuality? To keep referring to the frequently used anti-FGM arguments is to impede from the very start our progress toward a solution. It might therefore be easier and more beneficial to fit the arguments to the values of the communities practicing FGC, rather than attempting to teach them what a normal, good, or a healthy sexual life is.

CHAPTER 11

Experiencing Sex in Exile:
Can Genitals Change Their Gender?

ON CONCEPTIONS AND EXPERIENCES
RELATED TO FEMALE GENITAL CUTTING
(FGC) AMONG SOMALIS IN NORWAY

R. Elise B. Johansen

DURING A MEETING in Norway for immigrants from communities practicing female genital cutting (FGC), a Somali man proclaimed from the stage that his main grievance against the practice was that it leads to divorces, because it causes sexual frustration in both men and women. The women present were upset and furious: "How can he talk like that?" "Why do they remarry another circumcised virgin then, if it is so bad?" "How can women be satisfied in two minutes? Who will teach our two-minute-men how to treat women?" "FGC does not affect sexuality, it just takes longer." "I have no feeling in bed. I think it is because I was cut." "An uncut woman will run after men and have sex with anyone."

Some of these comments were stated loudly, others confided to the women close by. Some were expressed in fury, others as jokes, and yet others as intimate exchanges between friends. The comments point to the complexity and intensity of discussions about FGC and sexuality within the Somali community. The purpose of this chapter is to explore what statements such as these say about the way affected women and men perceive and discuss the relationship between FGC and personal sexual experience.

Sexuality was an important concern of my Somali informants when they were discussing FGC. Generally, the practice was believed to reduce women's sexuality in various ways, an effect that was regarded with ambivalence. On the one hand the informants saw FGC as a positive way to "domesticate" female sexuality. On the other hand, they saw this "domestication" as negative, believing it reduced women's sexual pleasure, which could in turn harm their marital relationships.

These concerns, and the often ambivalent worries, seemed to have intensified in the exile environment. In the informants' home countries, FGC was regarded as a natural and necessary ingredient in becoming a decent woman; it was tied up with basic cultural values relating to gender, sex, fertility, identity, morals, and beauty. In exile, they have been exposed to Western views of the practice as the destruction of genitals, sexuality, and even femininity itself. This has led to informants questioning some doxic cultural models of fundamental values regarding gender, genitals, and sexuality. Hence Somalis have had to ask whether circumcision carves women into complete, clean, and proper women—as it is understood in emic cultural models—or whether it deprives women of significant body parts, womanhood, and sexuality, as the Western view suggests. These questions were usually expressed as deeply personal concerns: How did *my* circumcision affect *my* sexual life? Would I have felt more had I not been circumcised? Would my marriage have been happier, or more difficult? Would my husband have loved me more, or less? Would he have married me? Has my circumcision made me complete, or destroyed me?

My informants, both men and women, focused mainly on three sexual "consequences" of FGC: the importance of virginity, the pain upon defibulation, and a reduction of sexual desire and pleasure. These concerns seemed to be at the root of a widespread ambivalence about FGC, as expressed by Hassan, a male informant: "FGC is bad because it removes the feelings from a woman. But at that time (as a young boy), we did not know about clitoris and lips and all that. We did not know that women had genitals as such or any sexual feelings. We just felt it [circumcision] was a simple solution to preserve their chastity." Although few juxtaposed this ambivalence as clearly as Hassan, the concerns were widespread, and hence form the basis and structure of this chapter.

CULTURE AND PERSONAL EXPERIENCE

In line with the emphasis placed on personal concerns and experiences by the informants, my approach to the relationship between FGC and sexuality focuses on how it is experienced personally. In contrast to many anthropological studies focusing on the "cultural construction of sexuality" in the form of commonly shared cultural models (but see also Ahmadu and Dopico, chapters 10 and 12 of this volume), this chapter will look mainly at how cultural models are lived and experienced on a personal level.

The context of these deliberations is life in exile, and hence cultural models of both home and host cultures, constitutes a part of the multiplex background within which people try to make sense of their personal experiences. Also significant here are the personal histories and relationships in which the person is involved over time. I will also consider biological aspects, both how they have been described in medical literature and as they are perceived among the informants. My aim is thus to try to bring into the analysis the multitude of biological, experiential, and cultural factors that affect personal experience and social discussion of FGC.

My focus on the particularistic has been inspired especially by Shore's writings on the relationship between personal experience and cultural models (Shore 1996 and 1998). I am also inspired by his emphasis on the multiplicity of cultural models that may both contradict and challenge each other and overlap and support each other.

In contrast to many anthropological presentations that seem to take it as self-evident that cultural models coincide with personal experience, Shore has highlighted a much more complex relationship between the two. First, it is important to remember that "[m]eaning—at least about any linguistic or cultural categories that matter to us—is always psychologically particular to the individual" (Chodrow 1995, 517). In relation to this I will focus mainly on the frequent discrepancies and gaps between personal experience and cultural models and the way in which individuals deal with these discrepancies. This may be particularly relevant in studies of sexuality, as sexual activity in most societies is performed in private and involves strong emotions that may lead to larger discrepancies between the "public" and the "private" than most other domains (Leavitt 1991; see also Tuzin 1991; Vance 1991). Thus, while "culture" may construct relatively shared understandings of body and sexuality in the public sphere, personal experiences may be at great variance with these. And these discrepancies may be significant to the individual in her effort to make sense of personal experiences and the cultural models. Furthermore, situations of change and exile may accentuate these gaps, as both personal experiences and cultural models become more multiple and questionable.

A second field of anthropological theorizing that has inspired this study is the increasing focus on culture as bodily experiences and "habitus" (Csordas 1994; Shore 1996; Solheim 1998). Culture is not only patterns of mental maps of meaning and symbolic significance; it is also embedded in bodily processes and experiences. This is particularly so in relation to sex and to FGC; hence it is vital to include personal bodily experiences in any analysis of sex and FGC. This means that the analysis should include both medical and emic understandings of the body.

Field and Method

The material in this chapter is part of a larger study among African immigrants in Norway affected by FGC.[1] The Somali were chosen as a main field of study because they are the most numerous immigrant group in Norway affected by FGC. This implies that most informants had experienced infibulation, as this practice is common among the Somali (Dirie and Lindmark 1992).

For the purpose of the present discussion, I will differentiate between two broad categories: excision and infibulation. Excision involves partial or total removal of the clitoris and/or labia minora (Types I and II in WHO's classification). In infibulation, excision is followed by scraping or cutting into the labia majora, after which the two sides are joined together to form a seal of skin covering most of the vulva. At the lower end a small orifice is left open to allow the flow of urine and menstruation (Type III in WHO's classification). However, recent clinical evidence suggests the presence of various amounts of clitoral tissue under the infibulated seal of many Somali women.

Fieldwork involved several methods and groups of informants. The data in this chapter are based mainly on repeated in-depth interviews with about forty-five Somali women and twenty-five Somali men, numerous informal conversations, spontaneous focus groups, and general participant observation in various social settings. The study has also been informed by a four-week study tour to Somali areas, and about four years of work as a leader of the national project against FGC in Norway.

A key element in debates on FGC is a tendency to polarization between those who focus mainly on "harmful effects" and those who mostly focus on emic meaning (Johansen 2006a). These polarizations seem somehow to mute the ambivalence I encountered in most informants, who generally saw FGC as both physically destructive and culturally meaningful, in sexual terms as simultaneously important for sexual morality and destructive to sexual pleasure. This ambivalence, many informants said, had already been present in their minds prior to migration, although at the time they rarely voiced their doubts about the practice. It was within the realm of doxa, an unquestioned culture.

The sensitivity and doxic character of the issues of sexuality and FGC may be a reason why social discourses on this subject often take indirect forms, such as rituals and humor. Both rituals and humor are modes of communication that are set aside from everyday modes of serious discourse while simultaneously being based on them, playing with them, and breaking them. In this way, humor and ritual often highlight and express basic cultural and personal concerns that may be muted or tabooed in the everyday serious modes of social discourse. Hence, although indirect or nonserious modes of communication, they may be a key to understanding central cultural and personal concerns.

ANALYTICAL APPROACHES IN STUDIES OF FGC AND SEXUALITY

FGC is a multiplex practice. It has a biological basis in that it consists of a physical operation on the genitals of each girl affected. It is performed to conform to cultural values held in the community and by those who have custody and power over the young girls. Each girl experiences genital cutting in a complex relationship between these and other significant aspects.

In anthropological studies of sexuality, the relative significance of biology and culture has changed historically, broadly speaking, from a focus on biological determinism to one of cultural constructionism (for a short summary see, for example, Löfstöm 1992 and Vance 1991; also Foucault 2000; Ortner and Whitehead 1981). In this way, sexuality has traveled the same route as gender, from being considered the "natural" expressions of "inborn female nature" to being seen as a cultural construction.

Parallel to these sexual studies, sexuality has been an integral part of many anthropological studies of initiation rituals. However, as sexuality here has tended to be a byproduct in rite-de-passage studies, it has rarely been theorized as a thing in itself, but rather as the symbolic expression of other central issues, such as gender, fertility, and kinship: "Sexuality has more to do with procreation than with pleasure and more specifically with the continuation of the patri-lineage" (Nelson 1987, 221). This emphasis on sexuality as a vehicle for and symbol of procreation and lineage brings FGC into the core of anthropological studies of kinship and ritual. However, some anthropologists may find it frustrating that "in essay after essay, the erotica dissolves in questions of rank, and images of male and female bodies, sexual substances, and reproductive acts are peeled back to reveal an abiding concern for military honors, the pig herd, and the estate" (Ortner and Whitehead 1981, 24), a concern still troubling anthropologists working on sexuality in the 1990s (Tuzin 1991; Leavitt 1991; Vance 1991).

A significant part of FGC studies is framed within studies of female initiation rituals; hence many of the aspects mentioned that relate to the bias in sexual studies are also frequent in anthropological studies dealing with FGC, including a tendency to deemphasize sexuality. In reference to van Gennep's claim that what part of the body is cut is irrelevant, that it could just as well have been the nose, Parker expresses her frustration at the anthropological tendency to disassociate sexuality and FGC by suggesting that "anthropologists are reluctant to admit that the genitals are not the nose" (Parker 1995).

One such central bias is the tendency to focus on the fertility side of the ritual's symbolic linkages between sex and fertility (Heald 1995). For example, Janice Boddy presents sex and fertility as opposites, with fertility taking the upper hand: "Pharaonic circumcision is a symbolic act which brings sharply into focus the fertility potential of women, by dramatically deemphasizing their sexuality" (Boddy 1989, 55). In contrast, Abdalla's study on infibulation in Somalia suggests that FGC highlights sexuality: "The principal effect of the operation is to create in young girls an intense awareness of her sexuality and anxiety concerning its meaning, its social significance" (Abdalla 1982, 51).

The magnitude of this tendency to highlight everything but sexuality has made me wonder whether anthropologists at times play the role of protagonist of non-Western cultures, trying to present them as more morally acceptable to Western notions (see also Narayan 1997). I believe that while children and fertility are vital to any culture, community, family, and even to most individual women and men, so also is sexuality. And this, I think, is not limited to Western culture, as suggested by Giddens and others. Quite the contrary: several recent studies support my research experiences in Africa and with Africans in Europe and show that sexuality is highly significant in itself in African cultures. It is often a cornerstone for moral concerns, in which personal, cultural, social, political, cosmological, and religious concerns all focus and intertwine (see, for example,

Ahmadu, chapter 12 of this volume; Ahlberg 1994; Caldwell and Caldwell 1987; Heald 1995; Hernlund 2003; for extensive later discourses see Arnfred 2004).

The scientific controversies concerning the relationship between FGC and sexuality pointed out here converge to a significant extent with the mundane discourses that flavor everyday conversations, political decisions, and media presentations in Norway.[2] As such, they constitute a part of the context in which women in exile are working out their sexuality.

That is, the perception most Norwegians have of African sexuality affect the way my informants are met by the host community and hence discourses among the Somalis. A key factor driving these controversies seems to be the polarization between the "sexual mutilation approach" and the "rite-de-passage approach." I will elaborate a little further on this, but to make my point clear I will simplify the arguments at the expense of showing due respect to the nuances and empirical variations in the various studies.

Those who take the "sexual mutilation approach" find the most important aspects of female genital mutilation (FGM), as they call it, to be the negative effects of the practice on women's health and human rights; they see the practice as the most extreme example of male and patriarchal control over female sexuality.[3] This view is mainly held by anti-FGM activists, as well as by feminist-oriented researchers. It generally attributes to FGC an almost total destruction of female sexual pleasure, grounded in a universal biological understanding of femininity and sexuality. A key factor here is the consideration of the clitoris as the main location of sexual pleasure; hence its removal is believed to remove the possibility of sexual enjoyment. With such a major emphasis on biological determination of sexuality, local cultural meanings are generally presented as irrelevant, misconceptions, myths, vehicles of patriarchal power, or ignorance and lack of knowledge. Cultural constructions of femininity are seen as "false consciousness" that stands in sharp contrast to "real femininity" built on universal biological structures (see also Ahmadu, Boddy, Dopico, and Rogers, chapters 12, 2, 10, and 6 of this volume).

The "rite-de-passage approach" considers descriptions and analyses of local meaning and functions of genital cutting to be a key scientific obligation. This approach is pursued by most social anthropologists and reflects how frequently the issue is dealt with mainly as an integral part of female initiation rituals (see, for example, H. L. Moore 1996). As the main focus of these studies generally has been the ritual as a whole, FGC is commonly understood as just one part of the ritual's overall function and symbolism (see Johansen 2006a). As such, until recently major emphasis tended to be placed on the nonsexual aspects of both FGC and initiation rituals.

All studies have also had to ponder the relative weight of biological and cultural structures in forming femininity, sex, gender, and sexuality. As suggested, the rite-de-passage approach mainly sees femininity and sexuality as culturally constructed (see, for example, Boddy 1989, 56), while generally deemphasizing or questioning the universal applicability of biological factors as described in sexology and medicine (see also Vance 1991, who strongly argues for a cultural constructionist perspective in studies of sexuality).

The discourse between the sexual mutilation approach and the rite-de-passage approach often appears as a polarization between an understanding of FGC as either physically destructive (the mutilation approach) or as culturally meaningful (the rite-de-passage approach) that tend to escalate (Johansen 2006b). When anthropologists in Norway have presented emic understandings of FGC, they have been portrayed in the mass media as a major danger to the human rights of young girls in Norway, as their studies of the cultural meaning of FGC are said to legitimize what is seen by others as an oppressive cultural structure (Skartveit 2002). This tendency toward polarization increases the challenge of addressing the sexual effects of FGC. It illustrates the urgency of taking into account the physical changes involved, the cultural underpinnings of the practice, other cultural models on sexuality and FGC, and the relationships in which sexual activity unfolds.

The long-term physical effects of FGC vary with the type of cutting, the age at which it is done, and the healing process. Removal of tissue, especially the clitoris, and scar formation may cause reduced responsiveness to physical stimulation in the clitoral area and thereby affect achievement of orgasm. The significance of the clitoris in sexual sensitivity and orgasm has been elaborately discussed by Ahmadu and Dopico in chapters 12 and 10 of this volume (see also Ahmadu 2000; Bakr 1982; Gruenbaum 2001). One aspect of this debate focuses on the function of the shaft of the clitoris, which remains within the body, even if the whole outer part of the clitoris is cut.[4] There is also limited knowledge of the sexual function of surrounding tissue, as well as of other erogenous zones and their ability to compensate for lost clitoral tissue.

Cutting may also lead to temporary or permanent oversensitivity and pain. The narrowing of the vaginal orifice in infibulation necessitates reopening (defibulation) to allow coitus. Most nonmedical methods of defibulation involve a lengthy and painful process that may affect sexual experience in both the short and the long term (see also Almroth et al. 2000; Dopico, chapter 10 of this volume; Johansen 2002; Talle 1993 and this volume).

Also affecting women's sexual experience are the cultural models of both FGC and sexuality. Emically, FGC is often considered to be a significant and constituent part of femininity and womanhood and a way to "domesticate" female sexuality. In very broad terms, cutting the clitoris is more often described as a means to reduce women's sexual desire in order to ensure virginity and fidelity, as seen in descriptions from Egypt (El Saadawi 1982; Thorbjørnsrud 1999), Ethiopia (Rye 2002), and Somalia (Ali 2003; Hicks 1982; Talle 1993). At other times, it is described as a way to "open the woman," making her sexually accessible, as among the Masaai (Talle 1994) and in Ethiopia (Rye 2002). As seen in Simon Rye's study, apparently contradictory views may thus coexist. Other

significant meanings are related to maturity, cleanliness (ritual and physical), en-
durance of pain, fertility, femininity, and religious and ethnic identity.

The closing of the vagina in infibulation is generally intimately linked with
ideals and ideas of virginity. The infibulation seal inhibits coitus unless a partial
reversal of the original operation is performed. Hence infibulation is believed
both to prevent premarital sex and to function as proof of morality, as an intact infibulation on the wedding night is taken as the only legitimate proof of
virginity. Other analyses relate infibulation to fertility (Boddy 1989), clan affiliation (Boddy 1989; Talle 1993), purity (religious and hygienic), and beauty
(Boddy 1989; Gruenbaum 1996; Talle 1993).

The key dilemma and ambivalence toward infibulation among the Somalis,
between the positive evaluation of FGC as a means to domesticate female sexuality and the negative evaluation of pain and reduced sexual pleasure, has probably
been highlighted and inspired by the encounter with the Norwegian society.

THE NORWEGIAN ENCOUNTER

Arriving in Norway, women and men from societies practicing FGC encounter Norwegian notions of gender, sexuality, and genitalia that differ significantly from those of their home societies. A central value in Norwegian culture
is the praise of everything "natural." The opposite of natural is not "cultural," but
rather "unnatural" or "fake" (Gullestad 1992) and, in terms of sexuality, "per-
verted" or "deviant." Sexuality is seen as inborn and natural and should be left to
develop "naturally." One expression of this is that, to the extent that Norwegians
question sex education in school, it is less out of fear of "moral degeneration"
than out of fear of systematizing and teaching something that ought to be left
to develop on its own terms. These considerations may increase the Norwegian
perception of FGC as immoral, not only because the practice is considered destructive and oppressive but also because it destroys "nature."

Present-day Norway may be characterized as having a comparatively liberal
view of women's sexuality, with a strong emphasis on women's sexual pleasure,
personal choice of both partners and activity, and little value attached to virginity at marriage. This liberal view of women's sexuality is closely related to a
strong ideology of gender equity.

These ideologies are not automatically attributed to African women living
in Norway, however. Norwegian views of the African "other" are ambiguous.
On the one hand, Africa is viewed as the home of the "noble savage," whose
culture and society have not been destroyed by modernization. In this context,
African sexuality is seen as free and uninhibited, unconstrained by a Christian,
particularly Lutheran, division of body and soul (Gotaas 1996; see also several
articles in Arnfred 2004). This parallels anthropological studies of sexual life of
the "noble savage" and discourses on "African sexuality." On the other hand,
African women, especially Muslims, are envisaged as totally formed by their
culture, a patriarchal society in which women are subordinated to men.[5] Veiling

and FGC, both of which are practiced by Somali women, are seen as the most extreme symbols of women's oppression.[6] Somali women are easily recognizable; they visibly stand out among other immigrant groups in Norway. They are generally the only veiled Africans and are thus usually recognized by their appearance. I also frequently encountered Norwegians passing moral judgments on Somali women based on what the Norwegians perceived to be correct Somali or Muslim culture, rather than on Norwegian ideologies of gender equity and equality. There appeared to be a widespread concern about "moral degeneration" of the Somali in relation to practices such as divorce, extramarital pregnancy, abortion, use of contraceptives for single women, and so on that were seen as less abhorrent when carried out by ethnic Norwegians.[7]

In Norway, FGC is both morally and legally condemned and periodically subject to extensive medical debates. Yet, at the time of my fieldwork and before, FGC was generally considered to be a "strange and barbaric" practice carried out in remote areas of Africa. Few considered it to be relevant in a Norwegian context.[8]

This public silence changed dramatically after a series of two documentary programs was shown on Norwegian television in the fall of 2000 (Figenshou 2000; Gylseth 2001; Talle, chapter 4 of this volume). Similar programs have since been made in Sweden (see Johnsdotter 2002 and chapter 5 of this volume).

The reactions among my Somali informants generally centered on the discomfort of raising such a sensitive issue in public and on increased fear of stigmatization. Jamila, a Somali woman, said, "Such public attention makes people think of us as handicapped, as evil beings who want our children to suffer." One woman said she felt Norwegians were "trying to see through my clothes." Others reported having been asked very private and intimate questions about the effect of FGC on their sexual life by rather distant acquaintances. Many preferred to reject the problem or refused to talk about it with Norwegians if they felt challenged.

We see, then, how moving into exile has brought the Somalis into contact with various and contrasting cultural models: Norwegian ideas of sexuality and gender relations as well as Norwegian ideas of African and Muslim women and society. The Somalis have also experienced tremendous changes within their own communities and families, and in gender relations, sexual experiences, and considerations of FGC. Living in exile also presents its own burdens. For some this includes fleeing from the war and leaving relatives and loved ones behind. In addition, many experience a tremendous decline in social status. Somalis in Norway also experience many social and economic problems, which are often dramatically presented in the media. The rather negative public stereotypes of the Somali constitute a part of the environment of their life in exile.

In contrast to the negative media picture, the women in my study expressed a positive image of, and pride in, their own culture. In particular, they praised the social ties and various cultural expressions, especially weddings and marriage rituals. Furthermore, women generally seemed to manage the transition to Norway better than did men, making use of opportunities for education, work, and economic independence. They also expressed a wish for greater gender equity and an increased emphasis on sexual pleasure for women. This change did not seem to lessen the cultural emphasis on virginity and sexual chastity, both of which were seen as significant aspects of women's identity as Somalis and Muslim (see also Aaretun 1998). But at the same time women frequently complained about tight social controls (see also Johnsdotter, chapter 5 of this volume).

Many mothers also expressed a concern that exposure to Norwegian society increased the risk of moral failure among young girls, and there was a general fear that girls and women might become "too Norwegian," and thus "bad" girls, and lose their "culture," Muslim identity, and morality. For example, young girls wearing Western clothes described how they were addressed in the street by religious men and reprimanded for dressing indecently, and adult women who behaved in "non-Somali" ways often described social sanctions and criticism. A fear of losing cultural identity and sexual morals was often expressed in the emphasis on premarital virginity and intra-ethnic marriage (see also Aaretun 1998). A few informants suggested that some parents, after originally wanting to dispense with the practice, had circumcised their daughters at a late age as a last resort to preserve her Somali identity and moral character.

Traditionally, women said, rumors of "improper" behavior among unmarried girls in Somalia could be refuted by the presentation of an intact infibulation. In Norway, this presentation was said to no longer be practiced; it seems genitals and virginity had become a more private matter, no longer open for public inspection. I suggest that the former role of infibulation in proving moral conduct is in the process of being replaced by other symbols, especially of codes of dressing (see Johansen 2006a, and Talle, chapter 4 of this volume).

Life in exile also opens up new possibilities for maneuvering within the moral codes. Aspects such as living at a distance from powerful relatives, possibilities for increased anonymity in Norwegian towns, and ambiguous marital status allow for a more flexible practice of certain moral codes. For example, the two parallel but distinct marital systems, the official Norwegian and the Muslim/traditional, seem to facilitate increased flexibility and freedom for women, since a woman can be simultaneously divorced or separated according to Norwegian law while remaining married according to Islamic or her Somali customary law. In this way, women can more easily negotiate increased independence from their husbands while simultaneously maintaining their respectability and fertility. A disadvantage from the women's point of view was that this also enabled some men to maintain multiple wives and made it more difficult for women to demand money or services from their men.

The differing expectations in the home and host cultures also contributed to widely different ways in which they presented themselves in various contexts. Some girls said they claimed another ethnic identity to avoid the stigma that arises when they are confronted about the issue of FGC by the host community. Some claimed to their non-Somali acquaintances to be uncircumcised, whereas within their own community they claimed they had been cut. For others, it was the other way around.

INFIBULATION: QUESTIONING A PAINFUL DOOR TO VIRGINITY
Virginity and Infibulation—Safeguarding Open Bodies

Virginity, considered to be extremely important by the vast majority of my Somali informants, was not considered an inborn quality but had to be culturally constructed through infibulation (see also Boddy 1989; Talle 1993). An intact infibulation was believed to both ensure and prove virginity, as the infibulated seal has to be physically broken to allow coitus. Some studies suggest the protection of virginity to be the major reason for FGC (Ali 2003). The morality of an uncut girl would be questioned; she would be feared to be "loose" and "oversexed." My informants conveyed similar ideas , suggesting that an "open," never-married girl would automatically be suspected of having engaged in premarital sex. The idea of a noninfibulated virgin seemed to present a puzzle to most Somalis. There appeared to be no way for them to differentiate between a woman who had never been infibulated and one who had been defibulated.

Following from this, sexual activity was generally understood as synonymous with coitus. It was only coitus, and especially pregnancy, that could be proven and thus endanger a girl's reputation. Many also deemed infibulation necessary to avoid sexual activity. Some young women, such as Nima, used this as a reason for refusing or delaying their own defibulation:

> I am infibulated still. I do not want to be defibulated. Why should I? Then people would think I was not a virgin. And I think virginity is important. I think my infibulation helps me to stay a virgin. I know it will be very painful to have sex, so it is easy for me to refrain. But of course the boys want it. I am a young modern girl. And my Norwegian boyfriends don't know that I am circumcised or what it means. So they don't understand that it [sex] is impossible for me.

Nima's resistance was thought provoking, as she was a very "progressive" girl, well educated, fashionably dressed, and socializing mainly with non-Somali friends. She had also made some efforts to fight FGC and had helped to rescue her younger sister from cutting. Nima's decision to remain infibulated demonstrates the emphasis that is put on infibulation as a physical reminder of moral standards (see also McGown 1999). Resistance against defibulating unmarried women was widespread, especially among teenage mothers. Similarly, some men, although opposed to infibulation on a general level, expressed doubts about the virginity and moral standards of an uncut potential wife. Most Somalis, especially men, seemed to see defibulation as an open invitation to promiscuity, as expressed by one woman: "We are now doing a social experiment with our young girls that are not cut. Time will show whether they become more promiscuous."[9] Physical hindrance thus seemed important or even necessary to prevent premarital sex, as sexual desire was described as easy to arouse and difficult to control mentally.

Virginity was intimately linked to morality in a significant way. The "danger" of an "open" woman seemed to be less a question of her missing her virginity than of premarital sex as evidence of moral failure. Women said that Somali men would often test the morality of a prospective bride by trying to persuade her to have sex. If she seemed willing, the man would consider her unreliable and break off the relationship. Many men made similar statements: "If she [any woman] agreed to go to bed with me, it means she could agree to go to bed with anyone. I could never trust such a woman," Abdi said. However, men were only concerned about virginity when marrying a girl who had never been married. When they were marrying a divorcee, virginity had no importance, as she had already proven her moral reliability. Thus, premarital virginity seemed more important as a guarantee of a moral standard than of sexual innocence in itself.

For infibulation to be seen as a proof and guarantee of virginity, it had to be performed prior to coitus. In Somalia, infibulation is mostly performed between the age of five and eight. There was a strong insistence on the part of my informants that the operation should be done prior to menarche, as the onset of menstruation was perceived to "open up" the woman's body and make her able to have sex (coitus).

Male informants heatedly refuted the possibility of postmenarche infibulation. The possibility of postmenarche infibulation and reinfibulation seemed to create in them a sense of intense discomfort and disbelief, as it cast doubt on the possibility of proving virginity through infibulation. Male concerns suggest that men perceive a closer link between infibulation and virginity than do women (see also Boddy 1989).

Parents emphasized the importance of infibulation in proving virginity as an assurance of their daughters' marriageability. This was the most commonly cited reason for the continuation of the practice and for resistance against postmenarche premarital defibulation. This concern also indicates an implicit demand for ethnic endogamy, as it is basically only Somali men who could be expected to demand infibulation. The possibility of cross-ethnic marriage was rarely discussed and when it was discussed was generally feared and disapproved of.[10] I would therefore suggest that, in exile, infibulation has gained a new significance as an ethnic marker and an incentive to ethnic endogamy.

But, although adult women seemed to fear the uncontrollability of a never-infibulated or defibulated vulva, they simultaneously claimed that there was no connection between infibulation and sexual conduct. "If a woman wants to have sex, the infibulation will not hinder her," many women said. This is supported by research, which gives no indication of significant differences in frequency of sexual activity (coitus) and FGC status (Morison et al. 1998; Okonofu et al.

2002). This may be related to the general attitude of growing resistance to in-fibulation. It seemed to gradually be losing its significance, as indicated by the story of Amber:

> I had a very small hole, the smallest among my peers, and I felt very proud of it. I thought I was the best of all the girls because of this. Then I came to Norway, and realized that most of my classmates were not circumcised. My small hole, which caused me so much pain every time I had to pee, was nothing to be proud of. Instead I felt ashamed and different. But I could not think of being opened. I feared, I think, that if I did so, [Somali] people would lose respect for me. They would think I was a loose girl, a girl with-out morals. I was twenty-seven when I finally decided to be opened. I was not planning to marry, and I did not have a boyfriend. But the small hole had no meaning for me anymore. It was just a frustration.

The increased demand for defibulation, also from unmarried girls such as Am-ber, suggests that defibulation's overall significance is diminishing among the exile population. Infibulation also seems to have become a more private mat-ter. Many associated values, such as premarital virginity, ethnic endogamy, and "proper Somali female identity" are still in demand, however, and these values may take different expressions.

Securing Enclosure: From Infibulation to Veiling

I suggest that, in some ways, modes of dress are increasingly replacing infib-ulation as a locus for moral conduct and identity. The clothing habits of Somali women, particularly veiling, have gone through significant changes in space and time (Akou 2004). Increased veiling has been a common trend in the period after the Somali civil war. Migration to Western countries seems to have further promoted this trend (ibid.; McGown 1999; Talle 2001 and chapter 4 of this vol-ume). Dress was a hot topic, often more so than FGC. The heat of the debate suggests that something important was at stake.

If we define veiling as dressing in ways that cover both skin and body shape, there seemed to be a systematic variance in its contextual use. The more the women were exposed to the Norwegian majority in public in mixed arenas, the more they veiled. Let me give two examples: An informant I had known for some time, who always used to be carefully covered in public, removed her scarf one day during my private visit to her house, with a twinkle of her eye, a joke, and comments that suggested that the disclosure was an act of increasing trust and intimacy in our relationship. In more African-dominated contexts, veiling was less extensive. For example, on another occasion, I was attending a confer-ence on FGC in Tanzania in which some of my Somali acquaintances from Norway also participated. As the conference proceeded through its five days, the women gradually reduced their veiling. By the last day, their head scarves had been reduced from framing their faces and covering their necks to small transparent scarves dangling from their ponytails. And on the last day, one of the women took a swim in a tiny bikini.

Women and children have also significantly increased the covering of their hair. Traditionally, the women said, women would start covering their hair after marriage, as could be seen in their photographs from home. The wedding ritual that is practiced in southern Somalia, *shaash saar*, literally means "covering head in scarves," which is the main content of the celebration. The practice of starting to veil upon marriage is interesting, as it means that bodily enclosure through veiling starts when their genital "veil" (infibulation) is broken. In exile, as well as in postwar Somalia, veiling often starts at an earlier age, often at age six or seven, and at least when girls approach puberty.

Furthermore, the proportion of women who cover their hair seems to be increasing, particularly in situations in which FGC is going to be discussed. The different dress styles in different arenas suggest that the most cited religious reason for veiling—that is, protection from male sexual lust—was less significant. Rather it was the presence of non-Somalis, rather than of Somali men, that influenced the code of dress.

We can see parallels to Boddy's analysis of the different levels or layers of veiling: from infibulation, to dress, to enclosure in the house, to a symbolic linkage between protection from sexual penetration by a "foreign" man to ethnic penetration by exposure and intrusion of external groups (Boddy 1989). Hence the dress styles of Somali women in exile seem to communicate different messages externally and internally.

Externally, the increased veiling in interethnic contexts may be seen partly as an expression of a sense of vulnerability and a need for protection and distance from the host community and partly as a way to present a respectable ethnic identity. We may here draw links to increased Islamization worldwide (McGown 1999).

Internally, however, increased veiling through dress may be seen as an alternative to veiling through infibulation. Moral conduct seems to be more often evaluated on the basis of decent dress and behavior and in the choice of friends and social circles. This may be one of the reasons why everyone agreed that Somali girls were kept under stricter surveillance in exile than had been usual in the home countries. In this way, some central values may be maintained: the significance of enclosure, protection from intrusion from outside, and protection of moral and ethnic identity, while the veil is changed from skin to cloth, from the woman's physical body to the applied attire.

Opening the Body

In order for a marriage to be consummated, the veil of infibulation has to be broken. This is an important event for both the girl and her family, because defibulation and marriage transform the girl from a closed virgin into an open, married, sexually active, and potentially fertile woman. Also, through her marriage, an important link is established with another lineage, which is thereby given the rights over her sexuality and fertility. The significance of the event for the girl, her family, and the community is evident from the fact that defibulation is the only aspect of infibulation that is given significant ritual attention.

Traditionally defibulation was supposed to be performed during the first week of marriage, after which the marriage should be consummated. The ritual that marks the event is held immediately after the wedding. Two alternate rituals are performed depending on local customs: the *xeero* ritual in the north and the shaash saar ritual, mentioned previously, in the south

"Xeero" is the term for the figurine that plays a major role in the ritual. Several xeeros are made by female relatives of the bride. Xeeros consist of a particular type of jar filled with a special dish of dried and fried camel meat in butter, covered by dough of dates, covered again, and formed into doll-like figurines. The figurine is made of two baskets that are placed together as a bottom and a lid; then the whole figure is covered again with a white cloth and ropes are tied outside before the figurine is dressed up in bridal attire, such as dress, head scarf, jewelry, shoes, and other ornaments. Much pride goes into both the preparation of the food and the intricacies of tying. The xeero ritual is a major celebration. Men from the groom's family are invited to untie the xeero and reveal its delicious contents, which are then eaten. The process of opening it is arranged as a competitive game, in which each man has his try, while being teased, hit, and blocked by the women. As the men fail to open the "doll," the women punish them by making them perform acts that make them look ridiculous.

As the untying of the xeero marks and coincides with the defibulation of the bride and the consummation of marriage, the ritual clearly symbolizes the opening of the bride for sexual accessibility; the inside food may symbolize her fertile potential, which from now on belongs to her husband's lineage. However, the ritual also symbolizes other aspects of defibulation and gender relations: it highlights female power, in the sense that it is women who tie up the bride that men have to struggle to untie, and during the ritual this is further marked by women hitting the men who are trying to achieve their goal. Hence it illustrates how men have to fight for access to a woman's (and her lineage's) sexuality and fertility. Through the beating, women also inflict pain on men that may parallel the pain both women and men generally experience during defibulation. Both male and female informants described the xeero ritual as hilarious, laughing as they talked about it.

In contrast, the actual defibulation was described quite differently. Defibulation requires that the infibulated scar has to be torn or cut open. This can be achieved either by the husband's penis (the ideal in southern Somalia) or by cutting (common in northern Somalia). To prevent reclosure of the wound and thus reinfibulation, coitus was said to be necessary during the healing period. This procedure, which often could take several days and even weeks, was described by both women and men as extremely painful, both physically and psychologically, and as a very negative start to married life (see also Dopico, chapter 10 of this volume; Johansen 2002; Talle 1993 and chapter 4 of this volume). Resulting wounds and infections were regarded as normal for women and not infrequent for men (see Almroth et al. 2001).

One may wonder why people use humor in a ritual that marks a significant but painful life event for women. Ritualized humor is frequently used in relationships and events that are simultaneously significant and problematic. This has been studied particularly in relation to African traditions of "joking relationships." Jokes and laughter create a distance between oneself and the statement made, both emotionally and morally. Moreover, the xeero ritual is the main socially accepted channel through which women can express their experiences of this personally and socially.

Most couples who got married in Norway had their defibulation done in hospitals. This reduced pain to a minimum as it was performed under an anesthetic, with stitching on the sides to prevent regrowth, pain-reducing medication, and the advice to abstain from intercourse until the wound had healed (usually from two to eight weeks).

After a successful defibulation, most couples depicted their sexual life as unproblematic. For a few, however, coitus was painful for years, and for others it was not possible at all. Jamila described her first four years of marriage as a series of painful intercourses. Although she married in exile, she and her husband resorted to defibulation through penile penetration both because it was their tradition and because of hospital waiting lists. During the first two months of their marriage, sexual intercourse was extremely painful because of open wounds and intense pressure as the husband tried to break through the vaginal seal. Jamila recalled how she often had to vomit and cry during intercourse, and she had constant wounds and pain in the vagina. After this initial period, the opening was sufficient for lovemaking in certain positions: "But we were young and in love and wanted to try different things, but then it was still very painful for me."

Although most Somali women lamented painful defibulations, they generally described them as a normal part of a woman's life, and there seemed to be little room to pity women who complained. Because defibulation and the accompanying pain mark an important change in women's lives, one could expect the pain of defibulation to be experienced as part of womanhood, of femininity itself; this seemed not to be the case, however. Although there is some cultural approval associated with enduring pain, particularly female hardship and pain—describing it as a woman's lot, and sometimes even glory (Adan 1996)—women did not seem to experience the pain of defibulation as relevant for their sensation of femininity—quite the contrary. One example is Jamila, who after her defibulation exclaimed,

> It was fantastic. Finally I felt like a woman. I had been a woman all the time, but I didn't feel it. Not until now. Sex was not painful any more. And my

husband was very happy. He said he loved me much more now. It was nice for him to see that I also enjoyed sex. Not to have any pain. It is a strange thing. I had to be an adult woman, and only after having two children was I to feel what it was like to be a real woman.

Jamila's story supports my suggestion that personal experience of womanhood does not necessarily correspond with cultural models. This might particularly be the case in exile, where both the infibulation itself and the pain associated with it are questioned, and women explore new roads to female gender identity that are affected by the Norwegian cultural models that see such painful experiences as degrading rather than glorifying.

Thus, infibulation and defibulation are closely related to central cultural values of virginity, women's possibility for marriage, and honor. The personal experience, however, was flavored simultaneously by cultural models inspiring pride, by pain, and by a sense of loss of meaning (see also Johansen 2002).

Reconsidering Sexual Pleasure: Perceptions of the Clitoris—Is It Changing Gender?

In discussing the effect of FGC on sexuality, one needs to take into account the various understandings of genitals, sex, and gender. The practice of genital cutting itself suggests that inborn genital differences are not considered sufficient to constitute proper women and men (Ahmadu 2000; Boddy 1989; Talle 1991and 1993). To make a girl a proper woman, her genitals have to be molded or carved to fit cultural standards. This means that a woman's body, her biology, not only her gender, is also perceived to be in need of cultural construction. Among the Somali, the natural genitals are seen as ambiguous, consisting of both male and female elements. The clitoris (*kinter*) is described as unclean, a male element, a "penis" out of place, so to speak. As a masculine element, however, the clitoris has been regarded as something out of place that has to be removed to purify the female sex, gender, and sexuality (Ahmadu 2000; Boddy 1982 and 1989; Talle 1991 and 1993). Grammatically, the word for it is also masculine.

Somali women informants drew various parallels between the clitoris and the penis. First, there is the size. An uncut clitoris was believed to grow, like a penis, at puberty. Such an organ is considered aesthetically repulsive and counter to the idea of proper female genitals. Several Somali women described how they were teased by other girls prior to their circumcision, with references to the size of their clitoris. Jamila, for example, recalled how her classmates dragged her behind the school wall, threatening to remove her skirt to demonstrate her shame to the whole school: "You still have it. Let us see your big clitoris. It must be this big," they teased her. When I asked women to estimate the size of an uncut clitoris, they usually indicated large rounded shapes, mostly around three to four centimeters in diameter, occasionally larger, and sometimes elongated like a penis. To make for clearer estimations I made extensive use of visual aids such as clay, pictures, and drawings in these discussions. When presented with various pictures and models of uncut clitorises, women always expressed surprise at their small sizes (see also Johnsdotter 2002). As Idil mumbled, "If it is that small, what's the point in cutting it?"

Secondly, the clitoris is associated with strong sexual drives and could thus lead its owners to promiscuity if not cut.[11] Some informants used expressions such as "battery," "engine," and "the seat of sexual drive" when describing it. Women often claimed that if the clitoris was left intact and the woman kissed or hugged a man, her sexual desire would be beyond control. There was a frequent equation between lack of circumcision and wanton behavior, sexual promiscuity, and uncontrollable sexual lust. One expression of this was a widespread belief that Norwegian women experience almost constant sexual craving. The view that a strong sexual urge leads to sexual promiscuity was common also among male informants. The male gender of the clitoris is associated with several male characteristics, such as growth, sexual urge, initiative, aggression, and promiscuity, all of which were seen as repulsive and ridiculous in women.

In exile, circumcised women are confronted with completely different ideas of the clitoris. Whereas the "male-like" qualities of the clitoris were frowned upon in Somali culture, they are seen as positive qualities in the West (see also K. Bell 2005), as the main seat of women's physical sexual pleasure and achievement of orgasm (Hite 1976; Langfeldt 1993).[12] This is related to the clitoris being the organ with the highest concentration of nerve endings. In fact it is the only human organ with no known function other than pleasure (see also Dopico, chapter 10 of this volume).

In Europe, the clitoris and associated female pleasure have become increasingly associated with femininity itself and with women's liberation (see also Rogers, chapter 6 of this volume). A recent example of this can be found in the world-famous *Vagina Monologues,* a play based on interviews with American women (Ensler 2000). One of the characters explains how, upon "discovering" her clitoris and the associated sexual pleasure, she came to see her clitoris not only as central to herself but also as constituting her core identity as a woman. The play further contrasts the European "discovery of the clitoris" with its removal in operations of genital cutting. To put it simply: whereas in Europe a "real" woman is a woman with an intact clitoris that gives her pleasure and orgasms, a "real" Somali woman should have no clitoris or "clitoral behaviors"—that is to say she should express no sign of desire for sexual activity or pleasure.

Since most types of FGC are described as partial or total removal of the clitoris, the operation is generally believed in the West to reduce or even destroy women's capability for sexual pleasure. This Western belief produces very uncomfortable situations for many circumcised women. Some informants report being questioned by Norwegian women about their sexual lives in derogatory and ways that reflected prejudice. Thus, in some ways, the missing clitorises have become the most visible part of Somali women's veiled bodies for the Norwegian majority.

Somali women may consider the clitoris as an out-of-place male element, as claimed in the cultural models from their home countries. Or they may consider it a core symbol of femininity, as professed in the society where they live in exile. Although the women's stories and perceptions varied significantly, they often described their circumcision as a loss—a loss of body parts, of sexual pleasure, of nature—and particularly as an experience of extreme pain (see Johansen 2002). Earlier I described how Amber gradually came to feel that her infibulation was a meaningless frustration, pushing her toward a decision to have a defibulation performed, as she describes here:

> I was defibulated a few months ago. After the operation I asked the doctor what it looked like. My circumcision had been very radical, he said. There was nothing left. No traces of clitoris or inner lips. I was so disappointed. I just cried and cried for hours. Only then did I realize that all this time, ever since I was circumcised, I had always had a dream that there would be something, at least a little bit left underneath. But there was nothing. I felt sad and worried.

Amber, after moving into exile, had come to see her genital cutting as a loss of significant body parts, rather than as cultural perfection or purification. This perception, she said, was caused by increasing knowledge of bodily functions that she had gained through health education. She had also, like many women, come to see "natural genitals" as more correct—morally, emotionally, and aesthetically.

Many Somali women in Norway have requested genital surgery to restore their genitals to their natural shape. Even Nima, who did not want to be defibulated, said that she would have wanted it if it had been possible to make her "look natural." The desire to be operated "back to normality" is mostly expressed as a matter of aesthetics. The women want to "look natural." This was the reason given by Suad who, desiring to "look natural" for her new, non-Somali husband, had a defibulation in her early forties. This increased demand for "naturalization" could be a response to the Norwegian focus on "nature." However, similar images are used as arguments against the practice in Africa, such as the argument that it is wrong to alter God's creation.

In the following section I will discuss perceptions of how my informants believed FGC was affecting sexual pleasure. Before doing so, however, I want to make it clear that I see sex as much more than biology, nerve endings, and clitorises; I believe that to focus too narrowly on biology would present a limited view of sexuality (see also Dopico, chapter 10 of this volume). Love, gentleness, caressing, and physical and emotional sensitivity and closeness may be as highly evaluated as clitoral sensations. As Fardosa explained, "I never liked sex, the coitus part, that is only a mess; but I like to feel close to a man, to hold and kiss each other." The tendency to forget these aspects of sexuality when discussing the sexual life of "the other" suggests another challenge to this research. Sexual pleasure is not only a question of open or closed bodies, virginity and pain; it is also embedded in the relationship in which the sexual activity is a part. This was often emphasized by my female informants, and will be discussed later in the chapter. First, however, I will investigate Somali perceptions on sexual pleasure and how these relate to FGC.

Perceptions of Sexual Pleasure

Literature on the sexual experiences of infibulated women varies from suggestions that more than 90 percent of infibulated women experience orgasm (Lightfoot-Klein 1989b) to claims that more than 90 percent have no pleasure in sex (El-Deefrawi et al. 2001; Hassan 2001). In a review of literature on FGC, Obermeyer concludes that the varying reports are sufficient to challenge the assumptions that capacity for sexual enjoyment is dependent on an intact clitoris and that orgasm is the principal measure of "healthy sexuality" (Obermeyer 1999).

Although the definition of what constitutes "healthy sexuality" or "sexual satisfaction" may vary significantly between persons and across cultures, a frequent measure is the extent to which women experience desire, pleasure, and orgasm. It is also fairly widely agreed within biomedical and sexology sciences that the clitoris plays a central role in this for most women. Hence it is probable that the sexual effect of genital cutting varies with physical factors, particularly the amount and type of tissue removed. Based on the known biological processes and functioning of the clitoris, its removal could significantly affect sexual sensitivity in the area, and probably the ability to experience orgasm. However, as many infibulated women are found to have significant parts of their clitorises intact under the infibulation scar, if the clitoris is a major factor in sexual satisfaction, infibulation may be less harmful than excision to sexual sensitivity.

Because of the development chronology of the nerve system, the age at which the operation is done may also be significant for sexual sensitivity. This also relates to sexuality as a learned behavior, in which good experiences become embodied, and pleasure can be more easily accessible over time. This may be why research has found women to enjoy higher sexual pleasure and reach orgasm more easily as they age, even though sexual desire may reduce (Conference on Female Sexuality 2000).

Significant new contributions to the scientific discourse on sexuality and FGC express doubts about the importance of the clitoris for sexual sensitivity and orgasm in genitally cut women (for example, Ahmadu 2000 and chapter 12 of this volume; K. Bell 2005; Dopico, chapter 10 of this volume). Others also suggest that some women feel they have a healthy and satisfactory sexual life without experiencing orgasm (Obermeyer 1999; Vance 1989). My measure of sexual satisfaction is based on perceptions and experiences as the informants presented them to me.

My female informants were divided almost half and half in the way they considered that their genital cutting had affected their sexual life. The slightly

larger group complained of reduced sexual feelings resulting from their circumcision. They expressed this as a feeling of loss that they regretted, a feeling
that they missed something, as Amina put it: "You know, circumcision affects
your sexual life. I feel less. I feel I miss something. When I talk to my Norwegian friends and they tell me how they feel, I see that there is something I am
missing." Many women expressed similar views. Edna, for example, when I first
met her during her labor with her first child, complained that the main complication of her circumcision was sexual deprivation. Her focus on sexual loss
in the process of her first delivery suggests that it was important to her. Zainab
also expressed a sense of loss, both of body parts and of the sexual feelings
associated with them: "The bad thing about infibulation is that they remove
something from your body, your sexual feeling. There is something missing.
Sometimes I joke with my sister-in-law that we should go back home and look
for 'our things,' the things they cut away from us. But, of course, there is no way
you can replace what has been removed." This sense of loss of a significant body
part was frequently expressed. As the clitoris was regarded as the most sexually responsive organ in the female body, most women regretted its removal
through circumcision.

There was, however, a growing knowledge that many infibulated women
actually may retain at least parts of the clitoris beneath the infibulated seal.
Women's wish for "total defibulation," to be opened "all the way up," was often
done to expose the clitoris, and hence, many hoped, to experience increased
sexual pleasure. Many were disappointed when they found that the clitoris had
been totally removed. Amina had experienced this, as she had felt an itching
bump at the site of the clitoris, recalling: "I was opened in the hospital . . . but
they did not open all the way up. The clitoris was hidden . . . so I went back to
be operated again, and I told them to open me all the way up. I was so disappointed when they found that there was no clitoris there. The bump I had felt
and that had been itching was just a clot of blood. I felt sad."

Most of the informants attributed their reduced sexual feelings to the absence of the clitoris. Others, however, were not so sure of this. Recall Jamila,
who experienced a new sexual enjoyment when, after defibulation, she could
indulge in sexual intercourse without pain. At first she did not consider that her
missing clitoris made a difference. But then she wondered, "Maybe I would have
felt more if I had it. But I can't know. I was always like this." Many shared this
expression of a vague sensation that there may be something missing but that it
is impossible to know since they had only experienced sex after circumcision.

Those who claimed sexual pleasure had not been reduced through circumcision often suggested that rather than being reduced, sexual pleasure was
"just different." Fatouma Ali, a Somali psychiatrist, claims that "Somali women
don't have less sexual feelings, but different," pointing to an increased sensitivity in other erogenous zones (Heller 2003). This view was shared by many of
my female informants. Although they considered the clitoris the most sexually

sensitive part in uncut women, they were also concerned with the fact that the whole body could be sexual: "If you are in love and young, just the touch of the fingertips can make you shake all over." Several described their breasts, abdomens, thighs, and buttocks as their most sensitive parts (see also Okonofu et al. 2002). Some informants also suggested that infibulated women may need a longer time to be aroused and satisfied.

Because little is known about the functioning of the remaining clitoral tissue in excised women and because some infibulated women may have various amounts of clitoris intact under the infibulated seal, it is difficult to know to what extent this feeling of loss of sexual sensitivity is directly related to the removal of tissue. Even less is known about the body's ability to compensate less feeling in one area (such as a cut clitoris) with increased sensitivity in another (such as nipples or abdomen), or to "repair" of clitoral nerves.

Another general challenge to understanding female sexuality is the widespread discrepancy between women's sexual function and cultural models. For example, there is a cross-culturally widespread ideal that women should orgasm through coitus alone, while research shows that few women do. Rather, most women need more varied physical stimulation. This gap between expectations and experience seems to constitute a central cause of much of women's (and men's) sexual frustrations in many places, including both Norway and Somalia. Hence cultural models on the "shoulds" and "should-nots" of sexual acts can affect women's access to, and knowledge of, other routes to sexual pleasure. For example, Shukri, who had experienced sexual excitement and pleasure during noncoital sexual contact, still feared she would not experience sexual pleasure during coitus.

The inculcation of sexual prudence since childhood can also affect a woman's ability both to show and to experience sexual pleasure. The Somali women I interviewed generally emphasized norms of sexual prudence. As words are our key to information about sexual satisfaction, we need to look into how such feelings are talked about and what words and cultural models are available to make sense of one's personal experiences. When asking women about Somali words for sexual pleasure (Norwegian *lyst,* which may also indicate desire), the women's first term was usually *dareen,* which is used to signify any feeling, and thus has to be specified. Other terms with a more direct connotation to sexual desire were *galmo, wasmo* ("coitus"), and most directly *kacsi* ("aroused"). These terms apparently were seen as synonymous, suggesting no clear distinctions between desire, pleasure, and activity.

Women always talked about desire, pleasure, and orgasm as slow and continuous processes and never mentioned any specific and time-limited or repeated sensations that could clearly mark orgasms. Nor did their terminology refer to orgasm as such. Only when I asked a linguistically interested man was I told of specific terms for orgasm itself: *shahwabax* and *biyabax.* Both words denote ejaculation in some way; *shahwabax* refers univocally to ejaculation of sperm and could thus only be used about male orgasm, whereas *biyabax* simply indicates ejaculation of fluid or water and could therefore also be used about women, he said. These terms for orgasm were never volunteered by women, but when presented to them seemed to be well known.

When women talked about their physical sexual reactions, they usually described vaginal humidity, "getting wet." Both women and men drew a parallel between female discharge of fluid (literally "water") and male ejaculation. Some women also expressed a view that both fluids were equally important for conception. However, women usually described the discharge of vaginal fluids as a slow and continuous flow, and as a sign of arousal and excitement, rather than a time-limited ejaculation like that associated with male orgasm. Thus it is possible that their concept of orgasm was closer to sexological concepts of sexual arousal and pleasure than orgasm as such. However, this may need further investigation.

These linguistic nuances suggest that there may be cross-cultural differences in how orgasm is understood, and hence in what can be expected in sexual life as well as what terms will be used. Research projects on orgasm do not always give sufficient information to clarify whether the informant and the researcher have the same understanding of the term and what sensation it refers to.[13] Hence it is difficult from words alone to estimate the extent to which women orgasm.

A frequent method of indirect speech about sexuality is the use of jokes and humor. Humor is a creative mode of communication that is simultaneously set aside from everyday modes of serious discourse while building on them. Humor offers a unique opportunity to play with social norms and discuss muted or taboo issues, including intimate personal experiences. But, importantly, without being held personally responsible, "it is just a joke" (Johansen 1992; Lear 1997). The frequent use of humor in sexual discourse may also be a way to reduce the tension and shyness involved in discussing such intimate matters.

My first encounter with social discourse on sexuality among Somali women was actually through a game played during a holiday camp arranged for Somali mothers and their children. Many mothers also brought along younger single women to assist them in the daily chores. After our children were tucked into bed, it was time for the adults to enjoy themselves, and Hawa introduced the game, Truth or Lie, which she considered to be of Norwegian origin. She twirled a bottle. It stopped, pointing at Asha, who was in her mid-thirties and pregnant with her fourth child. She was challenged: Would she answer any question by telling the truth or a lie? The social pressure to tell the truth was compelling, and Asha gave in. Hawa fired off the question "When did you have your last fuck?" Roars of laughter rang out from the women while Asha proudly announced that it was only two days ago, the evening prior to our departure. The question set the scene, and for several hours we played the game of intimate sexual interrogation. Idil, who had not seen her husband for a year, was challenged on sexual desires and actions in his absence and laughingly offered fruits and vegetables, and even the baby bottle used for twirling, as remedies. Laughing allusions to this incident colored our conversations for months thereafter. Through the game and the jokes, sensitive themes such as women's sexual desire and pleasure, mastur-bation, lesbian sex, premarital and extramarital sexual experiences, marital rela-tions, and being sexually desirable were raised and discussed.

In the game, women were supposed to present "the truth" about their sex lives, and I had the impression that many private experiences and concerns were revealed. I particularly sensed a difference in the self-presentation of the unmar-ried women. They presented a strong image of sexual prudence, in spite of tak-ing pride in having many suitors and boyfriends. The adult married women, on the other hand, whose stories brimmed over with rule-breaking behavior, also provoked and teased the young girls: "You didn't even kiss him? What sort of boyfriend was that? When I was your age...."

It is my impression that the games and jokes present something new in exile, a more positive evaluation and expectation of female sexual desire and pleasure. It also seems that exile has created a change in the acceptable ways of talking and joking about female sexuality. This relates both to the discrepancy between the jokes, games, and laughter, which present a positive and playful dis-course of sexuality in my Norwegian research, and sexual descriptions in terms of necessary evil, pain, and fertility, which are frequent in many other studies from societies practicing infibulation (Abdalla 1982; Boddy 1989; Gruenbaum 2001), as well as in my experiences in Somalia.

Sexual experience is basically private in character, however, and it can di-verge significantly from public expressions. Hence one cannot make a direct connection from such public discourses to private experiences. For example, Asha, who often joked of sexual matters and frequently showed me with pride gifts from her husband that she related to his sexual interest in her, also said that she generally tried to avoid sex as much as possible, as it was painful to her and gave her no pleasure.

MALE PERCEPTIONS OF FEMALE SEXUALITY

My female informants claimed that FGC is performed to satisfy men. Men are expected to demand that a prospective wife has been circumcised. However, this was never related to male sexual pleasure, as has been suggested elsewhere (Gruenbaum 1996 and 2001). With one exception, none of my female infor-mants believed that infibulation increased male sexual pleasure. On the contrary, they considered that the pain and delay associated with defibulation were also burdens for the men (see also Almroth et al. 2001; Dirie and Lindmark 1992; Rye 2002). Men's demands for a circumcised bride mainly concerned a desire for a *moral* wife.

The same view was found among the male informants. Men's main concern regarding FGC was about sexual complications, particularly the painstaking pro-cedure of defibulation, and their perception that FGC reduced women's "sexual responsiveness." Many men had experienced defibulations as painful to themselves, but first and foremost to their wives. As Abdi said, "How can I enjoy sex when it causes pain to my wife?" Abdi, a man in his late fifties, at first regarded the pain in defibulation as the only negative consequence of infibulation, having experienced it in his first marriage. He insisted that FGC had no further effect on women's sexuality and that infibulated women were warm and passionate, enjoying sexual intercourse as much as any other women. When asked if there was no difference in his encounters with his second (also former) wife, a Norwegian, his response changed, "Oh, you mean that. That's a completely different thing. Of course, if you think like that, then it is different. Very, very different." Abdi had recently married his second Somali wife, and he introduced me to her, as well as discussing our conversations with her. They seemed to be very much in love and showed great affection and care for each other. Once, after his wife had told me that she did not consider her sexual feelings to be affected by her circumcision, Abdi commented, in a voice of remorse, "You know, she doesn't know the difference. How can she know?"

A similar concern was expressed by Yonis, a man in his late twenties. He suggested that, as men often had more sexual experience, they would "compare" women with different genital states. Such experiences could, of course, not be discussed with their wives and therefore contributed, he said, to the silence on the topic in conversations between men and women: "You know there is a difference. But you can't say that to your wife, that 'other women I have been with have more feelings.' You cannot say such a thing in a marriage. So we don't talk about it. But we are both, me and my wife, against circumcision, especially me."

Male informants who thought that FGC reduced women's sexual pleasure usually associated it with the absent clitoris, as suggested by Zackaria: "A woman with an antenna [clitoris] is much more responsive and active in bed. . . . So most men prefer uncircumcised women for sex. But, for marriage they would go for one who is circumcised. It is safer that way."[14] His statement could need further contextual analysis in relation to the fact that the uncircumcised women he referred to here were the ones met during business trips to other parts of the country. It does, however, point to a distinction often made between sexual pleasure and the sexual morality as required in a wife as in the Madonna/whore complex.

In many ways, women's sexual desires and pleasures were presented not only as positive and exciting but also as dangerous and animalistic (see also R. Abusharaf 2000; Hernlund 2003; Johnson 2000 and chapter 9 of this volume; Thorbjørnsrud 1999). While men in Somalia sometimes used negative terminology about circumcised women, likening them to "mattresses," "cars without a battery," or "without an engine," uncircumcised women were just as often derogatively described as "running around and chasing men" or biting and screaming during intercourse, ruining their reputations and morals, and harming and scaring their husbands. Though these comparisons were often made in a jocular vein, they suggest some of the ambivalence and fear about women's sexuality.

The bases on which men evaluated their female partners' sexual pleasure may vary, but the most usual "measurement" seemed to be the extent to which the women moved during intercourse. There seemed to be a general belief, a cultural model, adhered to by both men and women that female sexual pleasure was directly related to physical movements in bed. That is, the more pleasure the more movement, and vice versa. One example of this was Shukri's fear that she would experience no sexual pleasure due to her circumcision; hence she would not move during intercourse, and her husband would be dissatisfied with her. In Somalia uncircumcised women (most probably from other ethnic groups) were often described as "dancing" in bed.

Many men and women, including Zackaria, also suggested that reduced responsiveness could be as much cultural as physical, reflecting the dictates of proper female conduct, trying to avoid showing sexual desire or excitement for fear of being regarded as "oversexed." The Western equivalent would be women's tendency to fake orgasm. Thus, whereby Somali moral culture would encourage hiding the sexual pleasure that women actually feel, European present-day sexual culture tends toward expressing more pleasure than is actually felt in order to satisfy cultural standards of femininity.

How the women actually felt, including to what extent their feelings or expressions of feelings were subdued because of cultural notions of prudence or physical changes, can obviously not be known from the men's statements. However, male perceptions of "good" or "desired" and "bad" or "feared" sexual behavior in their different categorizations of women throw some light on male concerns over female sexuality. And this concern suggests an increased emphasis on women's sexual pleasure and a concern that this may be hampered by FGC in exile.

Marriage in Exile—Changing Relations, Changing Sensations

One reason why the concerns over sexuality seem to change in exile may be found in the changing relationships of which sexuality is a part. Somali marriages seem to go through changes similar to those described in Giddens's analysis of the transformation of intimacy that has accompanied industrialization and modernization in the West (Giddens 1992). Giddens links this to greater equality between the sexes and the related assumption that sex should be a pleasurable act for both parties in order to function as a key to intimacy and as the glue of marriage. Similar changes were pointed out by many informants of both sexes. They were particularly attributed to changes in labor division within the family, from a clear gender-based division of labor in Somalia to increased interdependence and mixed gender contributions in Norway. These changes were said to affect marriages both positively and negatively, depending on how the couple coped with them.

These new demands on the couple often contributed to marital conflicts. Because many women felt the men's contribution to the family was minor, men's entire role was questioned. As Fardosa suggested, "I ask myself sometimes what the point of having a man is. It is just another person to cook and clean for. Somebody who bosses you around, but gives you nothing in return." There was a perception among Somalis that divorces have increased in exile.[15] Although divorces have historically been widespread and fairly socially accepted in the Somali society,[16] the causes of divorce, and particularly gender roles, seem to have changed significantly in exile (see also El-Solh 1993; Griffiths 1997). Whereas divorces in Somalia were generally understood to be initiated by men and feared by women, in Norway the situation was turned upside down. Now it is women who mostly initiate and benefit from divorces. Such drastic changes probably also affect the sexual and emotional relationship of the couple, in ways similar to those described by Giddens. This was suggested by Halima, from whom many Somali sought advice: "If the man contributes nothing, not money and not help to the wife in the house, then at least if he has sex with her, if he uses her body once in a while, she can forget about those other things."

For some women, women's sexual pleasure was not a theme in marriage. Fardosa, for example, considered sex just another burden in marriage and attributed her lack of pleasure to her infibulation. She did not, however, see this as unequivocally negative. She suggested instead that it strengthened women's position in marriage: "In some ways FGC is good for the woman, because you become more independent of the man. You don't miss him as much, and you don't degrade yourself by clinging to him and accepting anything" (see also Hernlund 2003; Johnson, chapter 9 of this volume).

Thus, it seemed that men experienced an increased sense of vulnerability to divorce, and this, combined with experiences of sexual encounters with noncircumcised women, may be a reason why men seemed more concerned about the influence of FGC on women's sexual pleasure. As a result of other changes in social relations, employment, and the need for female services such as cooking and cleaning, it seemed that men also experienced an increased need for women.

Concluding Remarks—Antennas and Barriers

Encountering a new society that presents cultural models that challenge those of their home culture, Somali women and men have been stimulated to reflect more upon and to voice their concerns. Their exile situation includes an encounter with contrasting models of gender, genitals, and sexuality, as well as an intense debate over whether FGC should continue. Women's concerns with sexual experiences in connection with FGC also include worries about the future prospects of their cut and uncut daughters.

It has been my intention to present a broad picture of the relationship between sexuality and FGC, allowing space for personal experiences in terms of both physical sensations and intimate relations. Sex is neither fully culturally nor fully physiologically determined; rather, it is experienced, explored, and lived in a complex interconnection with body, culture, and personal experiences and relations.

A major difference between home and exile is that "at home" women's sexual drives and pleasures are generally talked about as unwanted or irrelevant aspects of their lives or marriages. Similar attitudes have been reported by Aud Talle, especially from rural areas. In clear contrast is the different way women reacted when men publicly claimed that FGM reduces female sexual feelings. Whereas women in Somali areas seemed to accept such statements, they reacted with fury in Norway (see the opening paragraph of this chapter). This positive evaluation of women's sexual sensations in exile also seems to have created a sense of vulnerability and sorrow in women. The widespread sense of loss was a sensitive matter, as women did not always know whether they missed some sensations or what they could be like.

In addition, many Somali women felt great discomfort with the Norwegian emphasis on female sexual pleasure and the belief that circumcised women are deprived of such pleasure. Many experienced such allusions as humiliating. This may be one reason why women often presented different views on sexuality and FGM, depending upon whether they were alone in an interview or in a public social context.

It also seems that moving into exile transfers the relative weight of sexuality from social control (including checking the closed vagina in children and on the wedding night) to the increased importance of intimacy and sexual pleasure in marriage, coupled with a privatization of the vagina (no longer open to public inspection of an intact infibulation). There is also a change in marital relations, including a transfer of the fear of divorce from women to men. This seems to inspire an increase in male concern with female pleasure and intimacy, and an increase in women's expectations of sexual pleasure as a part of marriage.

Furthermore, migration seems to have given voice to some formerly doxic and tacit experiences and knowledges. Research in an exile community can help cast new light on cultural processes that were less accessible in the home context, because in exile they are voiced and debated to a higher extent. These debates may also give insight into some of the discrepancies between personal experiences and cultural models, making them more visible for research. The main concern for Somali men and women is, however, the opportunity this gave them to negotiate change, to move toward the abolition of a practice they felt to be difficult and painful.

There is a need for further analysis of FGM and infibulation in a broader framework of cross-cultural models of femininity. Forms of genital manipulation and cultural focus on women's genitals are in no way exclusive to societies practicing FGC. It seems to be a widespread idea that the female body is in need of physical alteration in order to meet local cultural standards. I think a key to increased understanding can be found in Solheim's analysis of the significance of a woman's body as a cultural core symbol for social borders in many societies (1998). She sees the female body as the ultimate symbol both of the "function" of women's own bodies as the means through which the world is understood (see also Csordas 1994; Shore 1996) and of how this is related to the symbolic construction of the body. Solheim goes beyond Douglas's analysis of the body as a model of society, suggesting that it is primarily the female body that serves this symbolic function. Because of the "openness" of a woman's body, in which her "inside overflows its shores—as milk, children, blood," how the woman's body in the sexual act is invaded from outside, and how women "surround men" and "take them in" (Solheim 1998, 74), the woman's body and its borders, particularly its sexual border, play a core symbolic function in society. Although Solheim's analysis focuses on Norwegian and modern Western culture, it draws parallels between all the Judeo/Christian/Muslim monotheistic cultures. Thus, to fully understand FGC we may have to deepen our understanding beyond the particularities of each culture. The failure to do so may be one reason why so many projects to stop FGC fail. They may alter the forms or conditions of the practice, but they do not challenge the very root of FGC: the worry over the openness of the female body, and hence the vulnerability of social structure, and hence society itself.

NOTES

The study was financed by the Norwegian research council (NFR), the Norwegian Ministry of Health and Social Welfare (SHD), and the National Center for Competency for Minority Health (NAKMI). My study affiliation was at the Section for Medical Anthropology at the University of Oslo. Thanks to my supervisor, Professor Johanne Sundby, and co-supervisor, Tordis Borchrevink. Thanks also to members of FOKO (Scandinavian Network for Research on FGC), including Heidi Skramstad, Lisen Dellenborg, Sara Johnsdotter, and Berit Thorbjørnsrud. Thanks also to Berit Austveg and Siri Vangen. The editors of this volume, Ylva Hernlund and Bettina Shell-Duncan, contributed with their careful reading, insightful comments, and intensive discussions. So also did Fuambai Ahmadu. But most of all I want to thank the women and men who opened their hearts and homes to share with me their experiences, concerns, and sense of humor.

This chapter is a shortened version of a paper with the same title appearing in my Ph.D. dissertation (Johansen 2006a).

1. This study focuses generally on women's experiences and reflections on their circumcision after immigration to Norway. For more results, see Johansen 2002; Johansen et al. 2004; Johansen in press; Vangen et al. 2002; Vangen et al. 2004.
2. To make my points clear, this presentation is a simplification of a much more nuanced debate, which is better presented elsewhere (see, for example, Gruenbaum 2001; Shell-Duncan and Hernlund 2000).
3. Several French activists have adopted the term "sexual mutilation" to emphasize the fact that most forms of FGC mainly or only cut organs significant for women's sexual pleasure. Hence they see sexual control of women as an emic key factor of FGC.
4. Descriptions of the clitoris are often unclear, confusing the clitoris, the clitoral hood (glance and prepuce), the prepuce, and the shaft (the internal parts). I generally employ

the term, as understood by my informants, to refer to the part that is visible externally (the clitoral hood).

5. For an interesting analysis of the dual view of African women as both "exotic" and oppressed, see Fadel et al. 2000. This theme is also frequently elaborated on by Queendom, a black women's theater group in Norway.

6. One example is the focus on women in all-covering black hijab in a TV program about FGC. The presentation is striking, as this dress is very rare in Norway and many infibulated girls wander the streets in jeans and tight T-shirts.

7. The Norwegian concern for what they perceived as moral degeneration of the Somali in exile was also expressed in terms of abuse of social assistance and concern for the single mothers. Statistical evidence, however, documents relatively little difference in the divorce rates in Norway and Somalia (Lewis 1962). See also note.

8. An act specifically prohibiting genital mutilation was passed in 1995. It also prohibits FGM carried out during trips abroad as well as reinfibulation after delivery.

9. Sixteen years of age is the age limit for operations without parents' consent. The most frequent reasons young girls and women gave for demanding defibulation was to ease the flow of menstruation and urine, to look "natural," and to engage in coitus.

10. Interethnic marriages is rare among Somalis in Norway.

11. There are some complicating elements, however. Whereas sexual drive is believed to reside in the clitoris, "sunna" circumcision, which often cuts more of the clitoris than infibulation, is not believed to affect sexual drives or pleasure in any significant way.

12. A cultural model of vaginal orgasm as somehow "better," morally or qualitatively, than clitoral orgasm, is known from many of the societies practicing FGC, as well as from Freud's writings (Abusharaf 2000; Karim and Ammar 1965).

13. Terms of reference to describe orgasm in general sexual studies are equally vague. Descriptions such as feelings of "dizziness," "pleasure," "sweetness," and "warmth" may describe both sexual pleasure in general as well as the orgasm itself.

14. Zackaria was from Ethiopia, but I include this statement because it expresses an evaluation similar to that made by many Somali men.

15. About 30 percent of Somali mothers are officially registered as single, that is divorced, widowed, or never married. The "real" number of single mothers may be smaller because of the various marital systems mentioned earlier in the chapter. That is, many mothers who were officially registered as single nonetheless defined themselves as married, as they were single according to Norwegian regulations but married according to Muslim tradition. Remarriage was frequent; hence many former divorcees were now married.

16. On divorces in "traditional Somalia," especially the northern regions, see Lewis (1962); on southern regions see Helander (1988). The sense of increased divorce and family instability was also frequently expressed in Somali areas (see also *Impact of the War on the Family*, a documentary film made by Somaliland Academy for Peace and Development (ADP); the film is about twenty-four minutes long and can be ordered through the organization's Web site, www.apd-somaliland.org.

CHAPTER 12

"Ain't I a Woman Too?"

CHALLENGING MYTHS OF SEXUAL
DYSFUNCTION IN CIRCUMCISED WOMEN

Fuambai Ahmadu

WHEN CIRCUMCISED WOMEN are asked whether they enjoy sex
or experience orgasms, some laugh at what seems a naïve question with an
obvious answer—of course they enjoy sex, why shouldn't they?[1] Others complain that sex is something they endure for the sake of marriage and contend
that they feel nothing except, often, pain. For some writers who are opposed to
female circumcision, this second response serves as further evidence that genital
cutting has an adverse effect on female sexuality. For most of these observers
there is an automatic, often unconscious, equation of female genital cutting with
sexual dysfunction. Many opponents justify their views on the basis of core assumptions and beliefs about the female anatomy and the role of the clitoris in
achieving sexual pleasure. However, a problem that is often overlooked is the
fact that many uncircumcised women also report never achieving orgasm. How
essential, then, is the clitoris to female sexuality?

In this chapter, I express concern about the negative psychosexual ramifications of anti–female genital mutilation (FGM) campaigns and stereotypes for
circumcised African women, particularly vulnerable teenagers and young adults,
many of whom are struggling with all sorts of conflicting messages regarding
their bodies and sexuality. These issues are especially poignant to circumcised
African girls and women living as immigrants in the Western[2] diaspora, where
attitudes toward these practices are most unforgiving. In the first section I briefly
recollect past observations of circumcised female relatives, friends, and acquaintances, their attitudes, views, and experiences concerning sexuality, and contrast
this with the experience of sexual "mutilation" reported by some circumcised
African immigrant women today. A major difference is evident in the way some
circumcised African girls and women in the diaspora are increasingly internal-
izing dominant Western stereotypes and prejudices about their bodies and are
now defining themselves in terms of these perceived shortcomings,[3] especially

in the arena of sexuality where female circumcision stands for a priori evidence of sexual dysfunction or repression.

Elsewhere in this chapter I make use of ethnographic data from semistructured interviews and focus group discussions with various categories of women in The Gambia, extrapolating anecdotes relating to individual attitudes and experiences of sexuality. This varied information enables us to consider ways in which excised women of different ages, ethnic groups, and social categories think and talk about their sexual experiences. Their open and intimate discussions reveal different experiences of sexual pleasure (or lack thereof) and perceptions about orgasm, as well as beliefs about social norms and expectations in relation to female sexuality. Data were taken from several focus groups of married women and sex workers from various ethnic groups and regions in The Gambia.[4] The information provided by circumcised women in The Gambia is considered against the state-of-the-art of Western scientific knowledge, in particular neurobiological processes involved in female orgasm. I hope to shed light on the question of the credibility of circumcised women who insist that they experience sexual pleasure and orgasm. In the final sections of this chapter I consider the problem of "objective knowledge" of subjective experiences, particularly where anti-FGM activists assume to know the effects of circumcision on female sexuality. Also, the increasingly popular idea of male perceptions of female circumcision and sexuality is addressed and challenged as often eliciting racist and sexist stereotyping of the "other."

POSITIONALITY
"Ain't I a Woman Too?"

In the mid-nineteenth century, Sojourner Truth, a female former slave who campaigned for the abolition of slavery as well as for the rights of women, stood up in a crowded women's suffrage convention and put forward this question in protest to her "invisibility" as a black female living in a racist society. bell hooks (1983) posed this same question in her book with this title, in an effort to highlight the "invisibility" of black women's experiences in white middle-class women's writings throughout the women's liberation movements of the last century. In this chapter I have borrowed the phrase to ask the same question of white (and black) educated middle-class "Western" women who gaze between the legs of circumcised African women, rendering them "invisible" as individuals with their own dynamic histories, cultures, and traditions.

What these more affluent "modern" women tend to "see" are their own history, struggles, and experiences of loss, subordination, disenfranchisement, and dysfunction (see Boddy, chapter 2 of this volume). Additionally, these same Western middle-class women spectators "implicitly have their bodies and their sexuality reconfirmed as normal and ideal" (ibid.). Rarely are affected African women themselves given the space to counter these prejudices. The only "authentic" voices that are allowed to be heard are those that confirm the dominant stereotypes and projections of more powerful women in the North on the experiences of African women in the South.[5] This is especially so when alternative voices threaten to contradict cherished "Western" assumptions about womanhood, or in this case, female sexuality, and to expose them for the cultural constructions they are rather than the universal experiences of women worldwide.

In this chapter, I write first and foremost as a first-generation Sierra Leonean/American who is circumcised. As an academic, I have devoted more than ten years to studying and writing about female initiation and circumcision from various perspectives. As a professional anthropologist I have worked on several research projects that have dealt in varying degrees with issues relating to the circumcision of girls and women in the field in West Africa, mainly within the Senegambia region. Thus, the issues I research and write about are not only of keen scholarly interest to me but are also informed by aspects of my personal knowledge and experiences. In particular, this volume on experiences of circumcised African women in the diaspora homes in on familiar problems we face in aspiring to integrate and assimilate, especially the experiences of culture clash and isolation as we strive to balance our different cultural identities with the realities of Western residence and citizenship. The issue of position is given particular force in a volume such as this in which scholars from different racial, cultural, professional, and disciplinary backgrounds engage in discussions on similar topics yet provide provocatively varied interpretations and emphases in their research.

Whether or not it is admitted, most scholars who are now focusing on individual experiences of circumcised women are influenced to some extent by what presumptions and experiences they have about sexuality, and this undoubtedly affects how they interpret, analyze, and emphasize women's various responses. As is well known in social science, researchers are inherently selective—those who have made up their minds about female circumcision one way or the other will tend to gravitate toward subjects that confirm their views, and they unwittingly question the credibility of those who say otherwise. Perhaps I may be forgiven if I have proven to be no exception. From my personal experience and from personal communications with circumcised women in London and in Washington, D.C., as well as through my extensive research in the field in West Africa, I do not see it as some sacrosanct "scientific" logic that tampering with the exposed part of the clitoris damages crucial sensory nerves to the extent that this necessarily reduces sexual feeling or desire. Nonetheless, I do appreciate and sympathize with the testimonies of circumcised women who may complain of sexual dysfunction. As with uncircumcised women facing sexual problems, I am inclined to conjecture that the sources are deeper and more complex than any neurological damage that excising the external clitoris purportedly causes.

Impact of Anti-FGM Campaigns in "Desexualizing" Circumcised Women

What do we invest in the clitoris that contemplating its loss augurs
such personal diminishment?

—(Boddy, this volume)

Some years ago, in an article for a popular women's magazine,[6] I noted that the
potential psychosocial damage of negative FGM campaigns on teenage girls and
women could be far worse than any impact of the physical act of cutting the
clitoris. Since this time, to my knowledge, there have been no systematic studies
that assess and document the impact of FGM campaigns on individual attitudes
and experiences of sexuality among circumcised female immigrants in Western
countries. There are some obvious methodological difficulties in conducting a
study that isolates the effects of campaigns on attitudes and behavior, but these
problems are not insurmountable. This volume is a step forward in that several
authors provide much-needed documentation through first-person accounts of
the individual experiences of circumcised women (see Dopico and Johansen,
chapters 10 and 11 of this volume).

In my own experience growing up in Washington, D.C., in the mid-1980s
into the early 1990s, my Sierra Leonean cousins, aunties, and girlfriends, including the JJCs,[7] seemed as obsessed with dating, boyfriends, and sex as many
"normal," "liberated" American women of the same age group.[8] The major difference is that we all had to sneak behind our parents' backs. Those who had
lost their virginity spoke as if they were enjoying sex, at least much of the time.
I remember sitting in a nightclub listening to one cousin reminiscing about
"Salone" and a "sugar daddy" she missed. She joked about how the older man
spent a lot of money on her but was lousy in bed. She told us how one day he
walked in on her as she was having multiple orgasms with one of her younger
and better-endowed boyfriends. At about the age of fifteen, I was usually the
youngest in these groups, so I would listen eagerly and attentively through stories of their sexual exploits and adventures, especially their vivid descriptions of
"orgasm," keenly wondering when I would experience it all for myself. I was
more drawn to my Sierra Leonean peers because, even with all the restrictions
and strict physical punishment they risked, they all seemed to be "at it" and they
discussed sex far more explicitly and vulgarly than my Western friends who, it
seemed, were given all the freedom to date openly or socialize on their own
with the opposite sex.

Ten, fifteen, twenty years on, however, researchers are reporting that some
circumcised women complain of lack of sexual pleasure and are associating this
with the side effects of their operations (for example, Johansen, chapter 11 of this
volume). Feelings of sexual dysfunction or "loss" are not limited to infibulated
women; even excised women are beginning to report problems with sexuality
or complain that they have no sexual "feeling." Ten years ago, given my personal

experiences as a circumcised woman, I would have attributed such reports to mere projection of researchers' own experiences and fears onto circumcised African women. But the fact is that some circumcised women, especially the younger generation of teenagers and women in their early to mid- twenties, *are* beginning to associate feelings of sexual dysfunction or inadequacy with experiences of circumcision. Even a few middle-aged excised women, who rarely speak of circumcision as particularly problematic, have shared with me their own spin on female circumcision and lack of sexual pleasure. Some of them express the view that circumcision has been a blessing to them, saving them from "shame" and "disgrace." Several women have claimed that although they no longer have any "feeling" for their husbands, they do not have any desire to "go out" and "find" sex elsewhere. In other words, because they no longer have any "feeling," they are capable of being blissfully celibate and can get on with the rest of their duties and responsibilities to their children and other family members.

Were my circumcised friends and cousins in D.C. in the 1980s and early 1990s in utter denial about their experiences? Were they somehow, within our small groups, in girly private conversations, pretending to enjoy sex and orgasms when in fact they were suffering in silence? Or, could it possibly be that they had no clue what orgasms were and only thought they were having them when actually they could never really physiologically know such heights of sexual delight? Or, were there cultural taboos against discussing sexual displeasure and the "pain" of circumcision, psychological prohibitions deep enough to terrorize them as far away as the capital city of the United States in the privacy of our bedrooms? If some of the oversensationalized messages promulgated by anti-FGM activists are to be believed, then clearly these Sierra Leonean girls, including myself, must be victims of "false consciousness" (see Boddy, chapter 2 of this volume) and "prisoners of ritual" (Lightfoot-Klein 1989a).

The fact is that circumcision, excision, or *Bondo* as the practice is referred to in Sierra Leone, just never came up in our adolescent chitchats about sex. Our discussions simply never went there, most likely because circumcision was not seen as relevant to enjoyment (or lack of enjoyment) of sex. In fact, at the time I had not undergone Bondo, although I knew my cousins and some of my friends had. I never knew that the clitoris was cut off during initiation and so could not presume anything about the effects of excision on my agemates. I could only "know" what I experienced vicariously as their enjoyment of romantic escapades and sexual encounters. I thought, at least at the time, that their attitudes toward sex were healthier and far more exciting than the seemingly rigid views of some of our older, more religiously conservative female relatives whose own sexual values are firmly grounded in the Abrahamic religious traditions. I often did hear older women allude to Bondo in specific contexts, for example when one woman would make a direct reference to another woman's private parts, usually during heated arguments which threatened to (and often did) degenerate into physical fights.

I have not exactly gone back to ask these same friends and cousins whether they were less than forthcoming about their experiences way back when. I took for granted that they were telling it like they experienced it, in the same way that I and some of my uncircumcised friends speak frankly about our own sexual encounters and romantic relationships. Should I now doubt the experiences of these circumcised Sierra Leoneans, now that I "know" all about the "harmfulness" of excision and the supposed diminishment of women's sexual enjoyment? The difficulty in doing so is that I did finally undergo Bondo at a much later stage than my cousins and therefore I am now also excised/circumcised. As I had no reason then, I certainly have no cause now to confuse feelings of sexual pleasure and arousal with experiences of pain and suffering.

Fortunately, my Sierra Leonean agemates and I came of age at the tail end of an epoch of general ignorance about these African traditional practices in the West—a pre-*Warrior Marks* era that was about to witness the worldwide "outing" of "FGM" in Africa. To many of us it seems that since the early 1990s, it has become the onus of righteous-thinking international feminist activists and other liberal-thinking persons, especially those working in the media, to expose the barbarism of FGM. These two decades heralded what has been dubbed the "white woman's burden" to liberate affected African women and a future generation of young girls from sexual oppression and human indignity. There has been no shortage of anti-FGM campaign materials, magazine articles, news specials, talk shows, hospital centers, social welfare offices and so on seeking to edify circumcised African women and girls regarding the harsh but necessary "truth" that we are sexually "mutilated." Once celebrated and feared in their traditional African communities as the custodians of "matriarchal" power (Ahmadu 2005), female circumcisers have been shamed, tried, imprisoned, and forced to accept and apologize for their supposed collusion in "patriarchal" crimes against their own gender.

In these post-*Warrior Marks* times, African women in the diaspora who hail from practicing communities are taking seriously notions of sexual dysfunction and are expressing types of sexual anxieties that were previously the exclusive preserve of supposedly frigid Western women left behind by the sexual revolution. Despite the fact that in most African cultures where female circumcision is practiced there is no concept of "frigidity" or "sexual dysfunction,"[9] some African women are beginning to blame the problems they face in their lives today, in their marriages or interpersonal relationships, on their circumcision operations, of which they may have very little or no memory.

For example, I once spoke to a friend who had led a very sexually active life in her late teens and twenties but complained that she went off sex with her husband because her clitoris had been "mutilated." As with many "modern" women in America, my friend's dwindling libido could well be associated with the hectic, demanding pace of *la vie quotidienne* or on the passion-killing drudgery that she, like most working-class immigrant women, endures on a daily basis:

the strains and stresses of trying to make ends meet, the endless cycle of working at menial jobs to pay bills while raising small children and trying to skim a little here and there to send back home to suffering (and relentlessly demanding) relatives. However, my "mutilated" girlfriend reasoned that her sudden loss of sexual desire must be the effect of hidden psychological and physical damages of a (long-forgotten) childhood genital surgery. After all, she said, this is what was discussed on an Oprah Winfrey show—*didn't I see that episode?*

Actually, I missed that particular TV program, but I was more interested in my friend's attempt at self-psychoanalysis. It seems to me that it is perhaps more than just the realities of daily living and getting older that are overlooked when some circumcised women "admit" to lack of sexual response. I suggest that the overall impact of negative messages about our bodies, beliefs, and cultural values contained in well-meaning anti-FGM campaigns (see Johansen, chapter 11 of this volume) are also beginning to color African women's views about female circumcision and sexuality. In other words, some reasons for my friend's (and possibly others') experiences of sexual inadequacy could be related to poor body image developed as a result of living in exile in communities with conflicting views and values about women's bodies. Hearing over and over again that infibulation is genital "mutilation" and is "unnatural" is understandably sufficient to send many young East African women in Scandinavia rushing for reversals of their operations, which are generously underwritten by the national health services (ibid.). While part of their motivation may be to reduce the trauma of first sexual intercourse or of child delivery later on, it is possible that many of these young girls and women just want to look, feel, and behave like "normal" women—that is, like the Norwegian, Swedish, or Danish ideals of being a "woman."

Wanting to transform the vagina to look and feel "normal" is not unique to East African immigrants. In some Western countries, most notoriously the United States, there has been a recent surge (and active promotion) of cases of otherwise healthy women undergoing surgery to achieve "designer vaginas."[10] Previously uncut Western women can undergo *painful* surgeries to get their clitorises tailored to their individual preferences, their various labiae trimmed down, their pelvic floor muscles nipped, tucked, and tightened to look more like their ideals in *Playboy* magazines and to feel like new "virgins." Instead of being condemned as FGM, these "modern" (versus "traditional") practices have a fashionable label that emphasizes the individual, aesthetic, commoditized values of the prototypical sexually liberated, modern Western woman. Ironically, in the name of sexual liberation, these wealthy or middle-class Western women spend thousands of dollars to become as "closed" as virgins, while ordinary Somali immigrants in Norway line up at hospitals to be "opened" at public expense, under the same banner. Unlike these "mutilated" African women, no one seems to question the credibility of Western women with surgical "designer vaginas" who report increased psychological and physical sexual satisfaction after drastic genital operations.

Thus, it is not surprising that some young African immigrant girls are ex-pressing concern about the appearance of their circumcised vaginas. Many are also complaining about differences in their body structures, about being too round or "fat" around the hips and thighs. In my late teens it was my Western friends (and myself) who seemed obsessed with body image, maintaining slim figures, the shape and size of breasts, buttocks, and so on. At that time I never once heard my Sierra Leonean friends complain about their body sizes or figures. According to some African male friends who are distraught about their ever-di-eting "sisters," there was a time when such obsession about body weight would have seemed un-African. Now, however, like many of their African American counterparts, more and more African immigrant girls seem to have bought into dominant white middle-class definitions of feminine beauty.

Many sex researchers note that the most powerful sexual organ is the brain. A woman's attitudes toward and expectations from sex, her culture and environ-ment, what she believes about herself, her body, her desires, her partner, and so on are all important nonphysiological determinants of sexual gratification. This gives emphasis to the challenges faced by circumcised African women living in the diaspora who have the added stigma of being different, of knowing that their bodies, what has been done to them, and their cultural beliefs and values regard-ing sex, are condemned by hostile host communities. I often wonder whether if I had not been sexually active prior to my own initiation I would not also doubt my sexual capacity and ability to experience pleasure and orgasm, espe-cially after being told over and over again by the Western media, "FGM experts," as well as the general society, that I am sexually "mutilated." I would certainly be confused by all these negative messages and misinformation. As many sex researchers have noted, particularly in relation to male sexual issues, fears about sexual dysfunction on their own can lead to or exacerbate actual experiences of dysfunction. Unfortunately, circumcised female adolescents and women have little access to straightforward, nonprejudicial, and nonpresumptuous informa-tion about the nature of their operations and all that makes up women's sexual anatomy, the clitoris and beyond, making it difficult to judge for themselves what links, if any, there are between circumcision and sexuality.

REDRESSING MYTHS ABOUT CIRCUMCISED WOMEN AND SEXUALITY

It is important to stress the main purpose of this section, which is to pro-vide further documented evidence of circumcised women's own voices on fe-male circumcision and sexuality. Many presumptions are automatically made about the sexuality of circumcised African women based on Western scientific or "Western folk" ideas about women's bodies and perhaps deeper prejudices about the types of societies from which these women hail. The evidence in this section further questions Western presumptions regarding female genital cutting and sexual dysfunction. It is important not only to note what women are saying but also how they talk about sexuality, the words and phrases they use to describe their behaviors and preferences. In The Gambia as well as other predominantly Muslim African countries where women tend to be perceived as sexually passive and repressed, many women are often unabashedly candid and matter-of-fact in discussions about sexuality.

Some of the data presented in this section are of a very explicit or graphic nature. I have edited out words and expressions that, in my own perception, may be considered too unpleasant for some readers. No attempt is made and none is possible at this point to generalize about the experiences of circumcised women in The Gambia, much less the diaspora, or to make systematic comparisons between their experiences and those of uncircumcised women. Further research is required to study more methodically the differences if any between circumcised and uncircumcised women in terms of their ideas and experiences of sexuality.[11]

Focus group discussions, and semistructured interviews with different categories of women in The Gambia reveal a wide range of sexual experiences and attitudes toward female sexuality. In this section I use excerpts from interviews with married women and sex workers of various ages and ethnic groups. In the focus groups I conducted, women's responses about their individual experiences fall into three general categories: women who report sexual enjoyment including orgasms; women who report never experiencing orgasms but nonetheless enjoy sex; women who report lack of orgasm, aversion to sex, and aversion to men in general.

SEXUAL ENJOYMENT AND EXPERIENCES OF ORGASM(S)

There was universal agreement in the separate focus groups of married women and sex workers that sex is meant to be enjoyed and that women are "naturally" designed to derive pleasure from sexual intercourse. However, women in both groups insisted that there are many cases or instances where they do not or cannot enjoy sex. Married women spoke in more general and allegorical terms about sexual fulfillment, whereas sex workers were much more enthusiastic in giving detailed and vivid descriptions of their individual experiences. Married women indicated that no specific word in the local language, Mandinka, is used to define a single concept of sexual enjoyment, but several laughed and used phrases such as "to fall down," "to go to that place over there," and "to tremble and then fall." Two elderly widowed women in the focus group declared that all married women are entitled to sexual pleasure and thus their husbands have a corresponding duty to satisfy them. They cited examples of husbands who were shamed in traditional courts for neglecting "to lie down" or "to sleep" with their wives. One of them, a *ngansimbaa*,[12] cited a case in which a husband with three wives claimed in his defense that he was just too worn out and that his wives were too demanding. She maintained that it was nevertheless against customary law and Sharia for this man to refuse to have sex with any one of them during their specified "turn" simply because of his exhaustion, lack of sexual interest, or any other reason.

Focus groups with young sex workers were much more revealing about different types and experiences of sexual pleasure and orgasm. The majority of respondents who claimed to experience orgasm said that "doing it for your-self," or masturbation, was the easiest and fastest means to reach climax. Sex workers particularly described stimulating themselves manually, or "rubbing up" on their partners, as usually inducing orgasm. Several of them said that they had no "feeling" with clients and could only enjoy sex through masturba-tion. When they were asked when and how they began masturbation, several of them said that they frequently watch "blue films" and learn how to do it from the actresses they see. Others reported that they have "always" mastur-bated in private.

> Me, I think I was just born with this itch. From the time I was small, I just like to rub myself. My other sisters sometimes used to catch me and tell my mother and she would beat me. But I still like to play with myself. I can get release very fast and easy. (Aji,[13] twenty-eight-year-old Mandinka, Farafenni)

> Since I was small I liked to do it. I had an uncle[14] who used to rub me there and I liked it. He would give me money and tell me to keep quiet. When my grandmother found out, the next month they took me for circumci-sion. But still I had a boyfriend in school and we used to play with ourselves behind the trees after study lesson. When I was fifteen one of my aunties caught me inside her room sleeping with my [wrapper] down and my legs open and my hand in my private. I think I was always a *chagga* [prostitute]. (Mariama, nineteen-year-old Jola, Manjai)

One sex-worker recounted how it took her several years to learn how to achieve orgasm through masturbation.

> As for my own experience, I did not taste anything like orgasm until many, many years. I had one white woman, she is [a lesbian] from U.K. She always comes here with another woman friend. She used to show me blue films, which makes me get good feeling, and then she climb on top of me and rub me up and start licking down there until I yell and scream and feel my body shaking. After that it took some time, but I learned how to pleasure myself; it can only take some minutes just to release tension. With some of my male customers I can have orgasm, it depends how I feel for them. Most of the time, I just want them to finish and pay me. (Princess, twenty-eight-year-old Yoruba,[15] Senegambia)

When asked about oral sex, most sex workers said they knew what it was and had tried and enjoyed it, although some expressed anxieties that the practice was un-African.

> Some of my white customers they do that [oral sex], and that makes me orgasm. I like that but you know we Africans, we say that is bad. Still I will

charge them more if they want to do that. (Fatoumatta, nineteen-year-old Fula, Basse)

Unlike Fatoumatta, of those who said they did enjoy it, only a few stated that they could experience orgasm through oral sex alone.

Most sex workers said that they enjoyed sexual intercourse, or at least they had at some points in their lives. Nearly all those who reported pleasure in sexual intercourse said that their level of enjoyment depended on what they felt for their partners as well as the latter's skill in satisfying them. For example, one sex worker narrated in detail how she was overjoyed having sex with her long-term lover.

> With Paul it is very good. He is a black British rasta [colloquialism for Rastafarian, or any man who wears dreadlocks] who comes here frequently on holidays and helps me with some of my problems.[16] He has a very big size you know, so we have to take it easy and we go very, very slow. This makes me so crazy. He takes his time to put it all the way inside and he knows how to move himself inside me and how to find that thing in there.... Hey, it's like I feel myself dying [laughs] ... and my whole body will faint when I ... squeeze in and down many times, fast, out of my control and I cry many tears like a baby and just lie down there.... One time, he got on top of me again and I could not believe I could even do anything anymore but I start to have this feeling again ... so me too I just squeeze myself around his thing and let him move again slowly until I beg him to stop because I knew I was going to die. He was going to kill me with that his sweet thing but he didn't stop and when I ejaculate[17] I scream so loud, people came to knock on my door to see what was happening to me. (Fatou, twenty-four-year-old Fula, Senegambia[18])

More than half of the sex workers interviewed had been married, usually as very young teenagers. Some of them, especially Fula women, said their marriages were arranged and that they were not at all happy with sexual relations with their husbands but they enjoyed themselves with boyfriends after their marriages fell apart. According to one young sex worker,

> My husband left me with twins. He was very poor and could not provide for us properly. So I had to go out to find something to feed us and my mother who was taking care of my children. My first boyfriend was a mature man who was already married. He did so many things for me. With him for the first time, I enjoy a man. He really took his time for me and love me. *Walai* [I swear], I have never tasted anyone like him since we broke off. (Sireh, twenty-two-year-old Fula, Basse)

Some sex workers said they had regular or occasional clients with whom they enjoyed sexual relations; most said that they rarely mixed business with pleasure, however.

From my own experience, it is better not to enjoy it with your customers. You can pretend to like it, you know, because men they like that. But you the woman, you are a chagga; which one of these men will marry you? And if you enjoy yourself there you will fall for the guy and just be disappointed. Better you just take care of your own needs by yourself at home. (Aji)

Pleasure what? That feeling has gone for a long time. Right now I am just dry between my legs. After six, seven, even ten customers for one day, and they pay you sometimes just fifteen dalasis [less than one U.S. dollar] and you are stressed because you cannot afford to even feed yourself, not to talk of send money home to your people—how can you enjoy pleasure there? Ah, no, *me,* business is business! Let it be sweet for the customer, maybe he will come back. But for me, I hate this work I am doing. It is only circumstances. (Kadija, thirty-five-year-old Fula, Farafenni[19])

Focus group discussions with younger married women were far more telling than those with older age categories.

I do enjoy having sex with my husband. He can make me feel very hot and the thing is sweet. But we don't talk about it. He knows from my eyes that he satisfies me. Sometimes I do want more, but I don't disturb him because he is tired. But then sometimes I accuse him of giving all the best to the other wife, so that when he is with me he has no energy. (Binta, twenty-nine-year-old Mandinka, Brikama)

Me and my husband were having sex before we got married. I always love to do it with him. Since we got married and now we have four children, it's not really the same. We both have slowed down. But I still desire him very much. I just have to touch his big thing and I feel aroused [laughs]. (Sainabou, thirty-five-year-old Fula, Brikama)

One sex-worker surprised a few remaining participants at the end of a focus group discussion when she made this remark:

Yes, it is even possible that you have this orgasm without anyone touching you. They say that boys when they are becoming a man they will have this thing, wet dream, and ejaculate whilst they are sleeping. Me too I used to experience this thing. I am sleeping and dreaming I am having sex and then suddenly I feel my body shaking and all these sensations around my vagina until I have this thing, orgasm, and I wake up feeling ashamed if in case anyone is looking.

Sexual Enjoyment without Experiencing Orgasm

Several authors have suggested that orgasm may not be as important to circumcised women's perceptions of sexual fulfillment, presumably, as compared to uncircumcised Western(ized) women. There are several ethnographic studies that

seem to indicate women's ambivalence toward sexual pleasure and preference
for the procreative value of sexuality and reinforcement of beliefs about purity,
modesty, and chastity (for example, Boddy, chapter 2 of this volume). Johansen
(chapter 11 of this volume) criticizes this academic devaluing of women's sexual
pleasure, yet she also goes on to cite examples of Somali women in Norway who
express satisfaction in purely relational aspects of marriage—warmth, security,
touching, cuddling, and so on. Johansen seems to have accepted at face value
that circumcision as well as cultural dictates have reduced women's capacity for
sexual enjoyment and inhibited their desires or expectations for sexual gratification. Johansen seems to express confusion, given her personal observations of
young Somali women at various functions, their seductive dancing and frank
discussions about male sexual organs and intercourse with their husbands.[20]
Dopico (chapter 10 of this volume), as well, gives examples of women who
privilege their husband's sexual satisfaction and see it as women's sociocultural
as well as personal duty to fulfill men's sexual needs.

But does this mean that, in general, circumcised women are not interested
in sexual pleasure or orgasm in the same way as Western(ized) women? Actually, it is not clear how these comments from circumcised informants differ in
significant ways from experiences of some, if not the majority, of uncircumcised
Western women.[21] As mentioned earlier in this chapter, some women did say
that sometimes they did not enjoy sex or that sexual enjoyment is not a prior-
ity in their lives and not a goal in lovemaking. However, none that I have come
across attribute this to any notion of sexual dysfunction generally or the effects
of circumcision in particular, even after some prodding by me or local female
interlocutors with whom I worked.

> As for me, this sex thing, I don't really like it. But I love my husband and I
> want to please him. I was a virgin when I transfer to him. I like it when he
> touches me and plays with me, but I don't really like it when he puts it in-
> side of me. Anyway he is very quick. Maybe he doesn't know how to do it.
> This is what my sister was advising me—that I should just close my eyes un-
> til he finishes. I have been to seek help even with *marabouts* and they always
> give me something for him to rub or to use. But I don't have the courage to
> confront him. He will be offended. I don't want to drive him away. (Isatou
> twenty-three-year-old Mandinka, Brikama)

> Sex enjoyment? With my old pa? There is nothing there. I used to enjoy the
> boyfriend I had before I got married but we never made love, just playing
> with one another. After I got married, after a few months I became preg-
> nant. After my first child, they said all of my [vagina] collapse. My husband
> said for this reason he had to take another wife. I don't mind. I used to beg
> him for sex, not for enjoyment there but to have other children so that my
> mates will not mock me. Now I have three children. This is all I think of,
> not sex. (Fatou, thirty-year-old Jola, Brikama)

Not all women know such a thing as pleasure. Many young girls run away to my compound saying they do not want to lie down with their husbands because they are afraid of sex, that it is painful. We [senior women] teach them that it takes time, then it will become sweet. We teach them how to approach their husbands to make them relax so they can both enjoy this thing much better. Many men do not know that when they just go on top of a woman like that, without making her ready, it can be painful for her. So we teach the girls when they are young to teach their husbands what they like. (a *ngamano*,[22] Brikama)

AVERSION TO SEX AND LACK OF ORGASM

Western sex journals and manuals are replete with anecdotes from Western women who for one reason or another have lost interest in sex and women who have significant anxieties and hang-ups that have inhibited them from enjoying sex—hence the concept of sexual dysfunction and "frigidity" in women. Like uncircumcised women, some circumcised women in The Gambia report that they do not enjoy or even desire sex at all for a variety of reasons that may include deeply imbedded negative early experiences.

Sex? I never enjoy it. I don't like it at all. When I was small my stepfather used to force himself on me when my mother was not around. Since then I do not like to go to any man. Even my husband was afraid of me. I told him to take another wife and to stop bothering me. Sometimes I go out [to meet other men] just for extra money for clothes and for my children's school fees as my husband has no job. He knows this but I don't care. He too he goes out with girlfriends, spending my money on them. Sex is just to get something from a man. That's all.

Nothing is there in this sex. I don't have any more feeling, you see. My husband, you see him, he drinks and he goes out with other women. Then when he comes home he will want to begin to beat me and the children. Then he wants to have sex. For me there is nothing there again. Just pain and headache.

DOES CULTURE MATTER?

My second point is that there is nothing natural about how the clitoris is construed. It is not self-evidently the female penis nor is it self-evidently opposed to the vagina. Nor have men always regarded clitoral orgasm as absent, threatening or unspeakable because of some primordial male fear of, or fascination with, female sexual pleasure. The history of the clitoris is part of the history of sexual differences generally and of the socialization of the body's pleasures. Like the history of masturbation, it is a story as much about sociability as about sex. (T. W. Laqueur 1989)

> Perceptions of, and attitudes towards, the clitoris, provide a powerful
> reflection of wider societal attitudes to female sexuality, whether this
> is seen as so dangerous that it must be eradicated, or simply needing
> to be brought into a greater complementarity with male sexual needs.
> (L. Berman and J. Berman 2005)

The purpose of this section is to question the tendency of some authors to equate cultural and religious norms concerning male and female sexuality with women's actual behaviors and experiences, as well as their motivations for continuing female circumcision. (see, for example, Mackie 2000). For example, underlying some of the anti-FGM literature and presumptions about sexual dysfunction is a conflation of dominant Muslim and African "traditional" ideals with women's actual behavior. In other words, because Islam or African "traditions" promulgate female (and male) chastity and modesty, an assumption is made that all circumcised women must be sexually passive and repressed as a result of these dominant religious and cultural models.

There is a plethora of interesting studies on cultural and historical constructions of sexuality. One paper, in particular, examines changing Western intellectual discourses on male and female sexuality and how these are linked with shifting views on male and female genital surgeries (K. Bell 2005). Bell lucidly unravels various scholarly and medical debates on the significance of the clitoris to female sexuality, as well as varying views on the nature of male and female sexuality that underlie the contradiction in current Western aversions to female genital surgeries versus general acceptance of male circumcision operations.

Another influential article, this one by Richard Shweder (2002), poses the very question "What about female genital mutilation? And why understanding culture matters in the first place." In this article Shweder effectively interrogates universalist premises of current anti-FGM campaigns, especially arguments that overemphasize "universal" notions of human rights and women's bodily "integrity" (see also Hernlund and Shell-Duncan, chapter 1 of this volume). Shweder's and Bell's studies, among others, show us how culture, or at least people's perceptions about their culture, does matter to some degree in shaping as well as in changing attitudes toward female (and male) sexuality and female (and male) genital cutting.

Some anthropologists, such as Henrietta Moore (1988 and 1994), have noted how people's "lived realities" can differ significantly from overt cultural norms and values; these anthropologists emphasize that this must be considered in discussions about the strategies, motivations, and subjective experiences of circumcised women (Moore, chapter 13 of this volume). Culture is itself constructed and shifting, and its link with actual behavior is always problematic. The mere fact that I conducted focus group discussions with active sex workers is an indication that, despite an open and public commitment to Islamic and African tradition in The Gambia, there are many people who do not behave according to dominant societal norms and values. Further, the data from these focus groups with female sex workers and non–sex workers alike indicate that many women are far from sexually passive and repressed and, in fact, have sexual experiences quite like many "normal," "modern," Western women, at least to my knowledge.

Culture is invoked by many insiders to justify tradition as well as by many outsiders to condemn or criticize the continuation of tradition; in both cases erroneous assumptions are made about female sexuality and the impact of female circumcision that do not always correlate with women's behaviors and expressed attitudes.

In The Gambia, several ethnic groups stress the importance of women's sexual virtue, premarital virginity, and monogamy in marriage (Ahmadu 2005). As in other countries where circumcision is practiced, women of all age groups and men for the most part profess that excision attenuates sexual desire in women (and men) so that they are better able to control sexual urges. This is said to ensure not only female premarital virginity but also, more important, fidelity in marriage (Mackie 2000). Among some Fula, mothers or grandmothers in certain cases request a procedure called "sealing" during a young girl's circumcision (Daffeh et al., 1999). This involves closing of the labia minorae, leaving a small hole for menstruation and urine, a practice that is similar to full infibulation. I often heard stories (from non-Fula) about how Fula girls are "virgins" at the time of marriage, yet become "promiscuous"[23] after "tasting" sex with their husbands.[24] I encountered men of other ethnic groups who said they "keep" Fula girlfriends or, more precisely, were having affairs with married Fula women. According to one such informant, Hassan, "these poor girls are married when they are so young to old men who cannot satisfy them. They go from left to right to find men who will give them pleasure."

Although I did not observe that Fula women were any more "promiscuous" than those from other ethnic groups, I did encounter a greater proportion of Fula girls working as sex workers in several regions of The Gambia. Interviews with these girls suggest that although chastity and sexual purity may be cultural ideals the reality was that many girls engage in sexual relations while still in primary school (usually around the age of twelve or thirteen), usually with schoolteachers or "sugar daddies" in the community. Among the Mandinka, as well, rising numbers of teenage pregnancies out of wedlock belie cultural pronouncements of female premarital chastity. Although I rarely encountered actual incidents or even rumors of Mandinka women having extramarital affairs, I cannot say for certain that this is uncommon.

In any case, none of the women in any of the ethnic groups I interviewed expressed the view that women are not entitled to sexual pleasure or that sexual enjoyment is the sole license of their husbands. In fact, the view expressed by many women (and men) and the one represented in ritual metaphors that associate the clitoris with the male penis is that of women's "naturally" heightened sexual proclivities. This is what is supposed to be minimized and purportedly brought under individual as well as social control through the effect of female excision (and male circumcision).[25]

Thus, it is a critical fallacy to view ideals of "virginity" and "chastity" as reasons for female circumcision, to associate this with a diminished likelihood for women having premarital or extramarital affairs, and, further, to link this with an erroneous assumption of women's lack of sexual response or "feeling."

My own symbolic analysis of female and male circumcision rituals and mythology in The Gambia reveals a convoluted body of metaphorical associations that concern sex and gender, particularly the role of androgyny in nature as well as the separation of sex and gender in the achievement of culture and gendered spheres of power (Ahmadu 2005). These symbolic constructions, I argue, do matter in terms of cultural justifications for and congruent experiential dimensions of female and male circumcision. And, as I have suggested, the underlying cultural principles and categorizations that make moral sense of female and male genital modification rituals do not include notions of women's sexual passivity or repression; these latter ideas most probably stem from Western psychoanalytic models that are often unconsciously superimposed on African "traditional" models.

Ironically, as I alluded to earlier, it is in the United States and Europe that I have encountered more women, uncircumcised and circumcised, talking openly about experiences of sexual dysfunction or of some physical/psychological inability to enjoy sex or experience orgasms. This is a particularly interesting observation for circumcised African women who say they have been "suffering in silence"; their experiences are shared by uncircumcised women. Some authors suggest that the peculiar nature of modern consumer cultures reinforces women's anxieties over their bodies and their sexuality (Schur 1988). According to Schur, women living in "Americanized" societies in which sex is viewed as a commodity are judged by their capacity to achieve orgasm(s), and this places undue pressure on individual women, which could result in increased sexual anxieties and feelings of dysfunction or inadequacy (see also Dopico, chapter 10 of this volume).

Currently, in Britain and the United States, and likely in other Western countries, pharmaceutical companies are offering and doctors are prescribing the female equivalent of male Viagra as a panacea for women's actual or perceived sexual inadequacies. Also, as mentioned earlier, although "cultural" female genital surgeries are for the most part illegal and publicly condemned in Western countries, very similar genital operations are permitted on Western(ized) women, and even hailed in some corners, for aesthetic reasons and sexual enhancement (see Hernlund and Shell-Duncan, chapter 1 of this volume, and Johnsdotter, chapter 5 of this volume).

Although culture is significant, it is not the sole or even main determinant of female sexuality or sexual response. Ideologies of female chastity and modesty do not condition women to repress their sexuality in Islamic or African "traditional" societies; moreover, Western cultural norms and expectations that emphasize women's unrestricted sexual pleasure and achievement of orgasm may encourage the opposite effect: women's sexual dysfunction resulting from excessive sexual performance anxieties. And, of course, the greatest irony of all is the increasing number of clinical female genital surgeries performed on women in the West for cultural reasons when the same are condemned for African women because "culture is no excuse for mutilation."

The "State of the Art" on Female Orgasm

Unlike some Western(ized) iconographic representations of the clitoris as the ultimate symbol of female sexual autonomy, biological science seems more uncertain about the role of this neurologically complex appendage to female sexual pleasure and orgasm (see also Dopico, chapter 10 of this volume). The main shortcoming of the current biological evidence is its almost exclusive reliance on the experiences of "normal," uncircumcised women, which is used to generalize or universalize the experiences of all women. Nonetheless, the experiences of circumcised women do not necessarily diverge from those of uncircumcised women, and thus, by extension, may not entirely contradict Western scientific or Western folk models of female sexuality. What emerges from this section is the argument that the *exterior clitoris* has far more symbolic than physiological value in terms of its role in inducing orgasm in women.

The Role of the Clitoris in Female Orgasm

Many sex researchers and other experts have provided varying descriptions and definitions of female orgasm based on women's responses about their subjective experiences. According to Masters and Johnson,

> Women often describe the sensations of an orgasm as beginning with a momentary sense of suspension, quickly followed by an intensely pleasurable feeling that usually begins at the clitoris and rapidly spreads throughout the pelvis. The physical sensations of the genitals are often described as warm, electric, or tingly, and these usually spread through the body. Finally, most women feel muscle contractions in their vagina or lower pelvis, often described as "pelvic throbbing." (1966)

Another sex researcher remarks,

> Female sexual arousal and orgasm is a complex process involving the entire woman, mind and body. The human mind receives in sexual stimuli from the body, processes it, and based on past learning and experience causes the body to respond to it. The brain may start the sexual arousal process in response to thought (sexual fantasy), visual stimuli (seeing a partner nude), audible stimulation (hearing a partner's voice), olfactory stimuli (the smell of a partner's body), and taste (the taste of a partner's body). The body may

start the arousal process as the result of a woman, or her partner, touching her genitals or breasts, the feel of air flowing across her exposed skin, or her clothes stimulating her breasts or genitals. The mind and body, while able to experience sexual arousal separately, cannot experience orgasm separately. Orgasm requires both the mind and body to work together. *Mental thought alone may result in orgasm, but you still feel the orgasm in your body* [emphasis added]. All the sexual stimulation and arousal may originate in one or the other, but orgasm takes place in both.[26]

Defining the clitoris itself is not always straightforward or apolitical (Dopico, chapter 10 of this volume). Nonetheless, most standard textbooks on human physiology or sexuality put forward a basic description of its location, size, appearance, and function. To summarize, the clitoris is located above the vaginal and urethral openings and is structurally connected to the labia minorae or inner lips of the vagina. In uncircumcised women, the visible "glans" of the clitoris, which is "hooded" by a "prepuce" formed by the meeting of the labia minorae, is only the outward and visible manifestation of much more extensive structures of "erectile" tissue, which form a padding over the pubic bone.[27] These concealed parts are anatomically and functionally linked to the vagina. The entire organ is heavily packed with nerve endings. Although the clitoral structure has roughly the same number of nerve endings as those of the penis, they are much more concentrated and closer together. When the clitoris is stimulated it becomes engorged and erect; when a high degree of arousal is reached it retracts, appearing to have reduced in size.

According to Dopico's synopsis (chapter 10 of this volume) of the literature on the "neurology of the clitoris," the three main parts of the clitoris are the glans, the hood, and the shaft. The shaft is responsible for "broadcasting powerful pleasure signals to the pelvic region" and the glans "has primary nerve connections with the pudendal nerve, which detects stimulation around the clitoris, labia, vaginal entrance, and anus, and sends signals to the brain." The pudendal nerve is also responsible for "transmitting signals from the brain to the pubococcygeal (PC) muscle, inducing the rhythmic contractions that are associated with the most common type of orgasm."

The average clitoral glans is about one-quarter of an inch (6 mm) in diameter, and the body of the clitoris is three-quarters of an inch (19 mm) in length. The portion of the clitoris that projects out from the pubic bone is one inch in length (25 mm) and one-quarter of an inch in diameter. There is, however, significant variation in size of the exterior clitoris. The clitoris in some women is very small and hard to locate within the folds of the labia and hood, and in others it is completely hidden under the hood and cannot be seen, but may be felt. In some women, the visible portion of the clitoris measures up to about two and one-half inches (6.3 cm) in length and nearly one inch (2.5 cm) in diameter. According to experts,

When [clitorises] are of this size, *they look just like a penis* [emphasis added]. The only difference is a groove along the bottom side of the clitoris, where the urethra would be located on a penis. While urine may not travel out the tip of these large clitorises, they do look and function like a penis. These women, as well as women in general, are capable of experiencing erections, the sensation of having a "hard-on," producing *ejaculate* in their paraurethral glands, *and even ejaculating.* Women with large clitorises are even able to engage in intercourse, by inserting their clitoris into their partner's vagina or anus.[28]

TYPES OF CIRCUMCISION

In Type I circumcision, or clitoridectomy, it is usually the hood or glans that is either incised or removed. In Type II, or excision, the hood, the glans, and the rest of the visible body of the clitoris are removed as are parts or all of the labia minorae. Type III is commonly referred to as infibulation and includes excision (although not always the case) and stitching together of the labia majorae, leaving a reduced entrance for the flow of menstrual blood and urine.

Type II is the most prevalent type in sub-Sahara Africa as a whole (see, for example, Shell-Duncan and Hernlund, 2000). Based on the size of the average clitoris, the proportion affected in radical excision or type II can be roughly estimated as 25 percent of the clitoris, which is not in any way near the entire clitoral structure, as many of us researchers often write, and perhaps mistakenly believe. Notwithstanding, questions remain: How much, if any, damage is done to remaining nerve endings that are said to filter through the glans and hood of the clitoris? What effect does any such impairment have on the functioning of the rest of the intricate organ that lies underneath the mons veneris—that is to say the shaft and the "two bundles of erectile tissues," as well as, importantly, the pudendal nerve that transmits pleasure signals to and carries them from the brain to induce orgasm?

These two questions—how much and what impact?—are made more complicated by the different types of operations and, more significantly, the individual neurobiological as well as psychosocial makeup of each girl or woman who undergoes a specific type of circumcision. Dopico (chapter 10 of this volume) notes that for all women,

> The clitoris has tremendous potential for arousal; what may affect sensitivity, however, is the supply of nerve endings and individual patterns of each clitoris, which explains the variation in women's preference for sexual stimulation. According to Krantz (cited in W. Gallagher 1986) no two people, not even identical twins, have the same pattern and distribution of nerves. In some, the clitoris is more sensitive to touch than in others (L. Murray 1983, 58). (Dopico, chapter 10 of this volume)

Dopico further highlights perhaps the most dramatic "finding," which promises vindication to many circumcised women who claim that they do in fact enjoy sex:

There is some evidence that removal of the clitoris cannot inhibit either arousal or orgasm. For example, Weijmar-Schultz and colleagues (1989) found that patients who had undergone radical vulvectomy (due to tumors) could experience orgasm with elaborate foreplay, without their clitorises. The explanation might be found in the extensive nerve network linking the clitoris to the spinal column, leading researchers to conclude that there are two separate roots with nerve endings so plentiful that simply stimulating the area around the surgical site produces waves of sensations that result in orgasm (L. Murray 1983). (Dopico, chapter 10 of this volume)

Simply stimulating the area around the surgical site produces waves of sensations that result in orgasm. I can recall the awkwardness and frustration of trying to convey this experience to skeptical Western colleagues, some of whom are also engaged in research on FGC, and at least one young male medical doctor and research student I worked with at the Medical Research Council (MRC) in The Gambia. Although most colleagues are sympathetic and open to my arguments about the cultural and symbolic significance of female initiation and excision, as well as to all my suggestions about Mande women's political and ritual power in The Gambia and Sierra Leone, they remain obviously doubtful that I know what I am talking about when it comes to orgasm. This is where many otherwise open-minded, unprejudiced, and tolerant scholars draw the line. As far as they are concerned, excision means amputation of sexuality, a partial if not absolute elimination of nerves and, thus, sensation. And, according to this "scientific" view, if nerves and sensation are removed or reduced, sexual pleasure and potential for orgasm, by logical extension, must also be reduced or eliminated altogether.

My usual response to friendly cynics is to point out that I have not experienced any change, either elimination or reduction, in sexual response following my own initiation. Thus, if there has been any nerve damage, it must be so minimal that it has not affected my perception or experience, and, if I cannot perceive any change, it does not make much difference to me, at least sexually, that I am circumcised. Some of them generously concede to me, being somewhat their educated, "Western(ized)" equal, that I must be *different* from *other* circumcised women, that somehow my pre-excision experience of sex means that I am more sexual or something, anything, as long as it does not contradict their cherished interpretations of scientific or folk theories of female sexuality.

In any case, the ethnographic evidence from my own research and the research of others indicates that I am not alone in my experiences. Many circumcised women report experiencing orgasm from *simply stimulating the area around the surgical site* and, incidentally, without the need for elaborate foreplay, if I may, just a good imagination and a few minutes of privacy. Thus, it is not just circumcised women who reach climax through indirect stimulation of the clitoris.

According to infamous sex researchers, most women (presumably uncircumcised) are unenthusiastic about direct stimulation of the clitoris (Masters and Johnson 1966) and prefer stimulation of the shaft of the clitoris or the mons in the area of the clitoris (Weisberg 1984, cited in Dopico, chapter 10 of this volume).

Dopico gives several individual examples of sexual responsiveness from her focus group discussions with infibulated married women in Australia. I have also encountered infibulated women in the diaspora who frankly admit to occasional or frequent masturbation that involves stimulation of the clitoral area. I interviewed a Somali university student some years ago in London who said that although she was opposed to female circumcision on moral grounds, she did not feel that her operation affected her ability to enjoy sex and experience orgasm. She said that she could stimulate herself to orgasm by using a vibrator against the top of her vagina. As she was infibulated and still a virgin, she did not want to undergo the pain of trying to insert the vibrator into her vagina. She expressed anxiety about having any premarital penetrative sex that would compromise her virginity, yet she said she had no real psychological issue with masturbation.

In short, the ethnographic data and anecdotes reveal that, like uncircumcised women, many women who have undergone different forms of genital surgeries do experience different types of orgasms through a variety of sexual techniques, with or without a partner, depending on individual psychosocial conditions. This is not to say that all excised women experience orgasm 100 percent of the time or that most experience any form of orgasm at all. Studies vary widely on the number or proportions of circumcised women who claim to experience orgasms. What the data in this chapter indicate is that, at the very least, the neurobiological capacity or potential for experiencing orgasm is not necessarily eradicated or noticeably reduced,[29] even in the severest forms of infibulation. It seems that whether this potential is maximized or even realized depends on important internal as well as external idiosyncrasies of each individual woman, circumcised or not.

Woman to Woman: A Question of "Objective" Knowledge

Women who have never experienced orgasm, and women who are not sure if they have, often ask, "What does an orgasm feel like?" This is a hard, if not impossible, question to answer. Imagine trying to explain to someone what it feels like to sneeze or yawn. Not easy to do. How our senses and brain interpret physical stimuli is subjective, that is dependent solely on the individual's perceptions. While we can measure the physical stimuli, we cannot measure how a person perceives it. Even if a woman is connected to monitoring equipment when she experiences 15 strong orgasmic contractions over a 10 second period of time, how do we know she experienced it more intensely than another woman who only has a 5 contraction orgasm lasting 4 seconds? The woman having the ten-second orgasm may be wondering why her orgasms are so weak! (Berman and Berman 2005)

The ethnographic and personal examples presented earlier in this chapter suggest tentative answers to questions about the extent and impact of various forms of cutting on circumcised women's neurobiological capacity to experience orgasm. Nonetheless, there still remains the problem of "objective knowledge" that relies on women's subjective experiences of sexuality. How is it possible for a researcher to "know" what her (or his) research subject is actually experiencing during sex—whether or not the latter is circumcised? On many occasions I have heard uncircumcised women dismiss the experiences of circumcised women who report having orgasms by questioning the latter's ability to adequately discern their sexual potential given that many, although not all, are circumcised as young girls, prior to having any previous sexual experience.

The assumption is that a circumcised woman could not possibly "know" what "real" orgasm feels like if she has never experienced sex with a "proper" clitoris in the first place. But then how would an uncircumcised researcher/observer/inquisitor "know" what her own experience of sex would be like without an outer clitoris, not to speak of the experiences of others? The bottom line is that it is impossible for any one woman, circumcised or not, to "know" what another woman, circumcised or not, is experiencing as sexual arousal or orgasm. I cannot say that I "know" for a fact what my circumcised female informants mean when they describe what appear to be experiences of orgasm, but then again I cannot say that I "know" with confidence what my uncircumcised friends mean by their own experiences.

Current techniques that "objectively" measure sexual response in "normal" women focus on factors such as the appearance of vaginal secretions, swelling of genitals including the external clitoris (although the greatest engorgement takes place in the shaft beneath the pubic bone), increase in heart rate, muscle spasms, and so on, all of which to some extent should be observable in circumcised women who report experiencing sexual pleasure and orgasm. Although it may raise serious ethical questions, such experimentations could shed more light on what differences may or may not exist between circumcised and uncircumcised women and between women with different types of genital operations.

For the moment, given ethical and other technical considerations, what most of us researchers have to work with are accounts of women's individual responses about their subjective experiences. Invariably, if unconsciously, many of us weigh the responses of research subjects on three levels: first, against subjective "knowledge" of our own bodily experiences; second, against subjective beliefs about what we interpret to be the experiences of others we know personally or have read or heard about; third, and importantly, against subjective interpretations of Western scientific or folk theories of female sexuality and orgasm.[30] The work of serious sex researchers have yet to include studies of circumcised women, yet such research could pose significant questions and perhaps offer important solutions to "problems" of sexual dysfunction among circumcised as well as uncircumcised female populations in general.

QUESTIONING "MALE PERCEPTIONS" OF CIRCUMCISED WOMEN

Men from practicing ethnic groups have received the brunt of criticism for "mutilation" of "their" women. According to many anti-FGM campaign strategists, targeting men and incorporating them into the eradication movement is critical. Because of deeply held assumptions about patriarchal origins and motives for various forms of female genital surgeries, some activists have promulgated misogynist notions of FGM and blamed men for demanding a practice that oppresses female sexuality. The not so implicit message is that uncircumcised women are more sexually responsive and, importantly, more liberated, and can express their sexuality unhindered by neurobiological and cultural limitations supposedly imposed on circumcised women by male-dominated societies.

The appeal of this argument to men in practicing cultures lies in its resonance with powerful cross-cultural stereotypes concerning the role of the clitoris in maximizing female sexual pleasure, stereotypes that are easily confirmed by dominant ideas about the "oversexed" clitoris in cultures where women are circumcised. Thus, male as well as female perceptions are caught up in these dominant discourses.

Several authors have considered views and attitudes of men from communities that practice female circumcision.[31] Some men discussed their own sexual preferences, others what they perceived as women's different levels of enjoyment and sexual response depending on whether they are circumcised, as well as their attitudes toward the types of women that circumcision or lack of circumcision produces. Men's responses vary from reaffirming existing presumptions and stereotypes about race or ethnicity and women's sexuality (for example, "other" women are more promiscuous than "our" women), about the role of the clitoris/excision in releasing/inhibiting women's sexuality (for example, uncircumcised women enjoy sex better than circumcised women), and how they value women accordingly (for example, "other"/uncircumcised women are good to play with versus "our"/circumcised women are better as wives).

In some of Johansen's examples (chapter 11 of this volume), some husbands and boyfriends describe their circumcised wives and girlfriends as "missing out" on sex, as being unresponsive and almost docile in bed. The comments made by Johansen's male informants must be seen in the context of a hostile anti-FGM atmosphere in Norway and strong cultural assumptions about the "naturalness" of sexuality and so on. Somali men's "traditional" beliefs and expectations about their wives' sexuality, which promulgate ideals of virginity and sexual ignorance prior to marriage, seem congruent with what they have read or "know" about the "realities" (according to Norwegian views) of FGM in eliminating women's sexuality. Johansen's male informants make references to experiences with supposedly more sexually knowledgeable uncircumcised women from nonpracticing African ethnic groups or women from Europe, North America, and other nonpracticing regions. What Johansen does not clearly bring out is the way in which some of these commentaries about "men's perceptions" reveal stark racist/sexist overtones in sexual comparisons they (are asked to) make between circumcised and uncircumcised women.

Among the Mandinka, there is an entire set of beliefs regarding the clitoris, sexual ambiguity, and promiscuity (Ahmadu 2005). Excision is said to remove masculinity from a girl, her male twin "head" (or penis), and the parallel male circumcision is supposed to remove a boy's female twin "soul" (or vulva/flesh). Uncircumcised persons are referred to as *solimaalu* and are said to be sexually licentious, because of their androgynous state. Since excision, like male circumcision, is required for marriage, excision is associated with being a wife. As a woman who has undergone excision, a Mandinka wife is said to be able to control her sexual urges and passions (see also Johnson, chapter 9 of this volume). Thus, there are many stereotypes that men and women hold on to about the supposed sexual restraint of circumcised wives compared with the promiscuity of uncircumcised mistresses or lovers. The Madonna/whore complex that Johansen refers to later on in her chapter of this volume is played out in the men's sexual narratives. Circumcised women are portrayed as restrained and unresponsive, yet (or therefore) they make respectable wives; uncircumcised women are seen as great to have as girlfriends or prostitutes but not to bring home as daughters-in-law for the men's mothers.

In The Gambia, beliefs about white or (uncircumcised) women's sexuality is no doubt influenced by the main sources of images available to them, pornographic video films and magazines, as well as hundreds of young, middle-aged, and elderly female tourists who flood the beaches and resorts of Senegambia, Fajara, Kotu, and Kololi each year in search of sexual liaisons with local young men known as bumsters. My research on sexual exploitation in The Gambia included two focus groups of Gambian men: current and former bumsters in one and professionals who had spent significant time studying or working in Scandinavia in the second. I have extrapolated those comments that express views about their experiences with white women versus African women and circumcised women versus uncircumcised women. Their views are tainted by strong racial and gender stereotypes, as well as by assumptions about the role of the "unruly" clitoris in determining women's sexual behavior.

Yah man . . . I used to have this *toubab*[32] lady, her buttocks was as round as this bath pan and used to jiggle like butter every time I did it to her. Man, these white ladies they can really appreciate this nice ting you know. But you see Gambian girls—these small girls—their mamas have cut their ting off so they don't feel anything. So, all they want is money, *hallis rek, kodo do-rong*.[33] They just spread open, you do what you want quickly and give them fifty or a hundred dalasis, or you send one bag of rice for the mama. So me, I don't care, man. Even the old toubab ladies, I prefer them. They have that sweet thing down there, it makes them behave like crazy, man. They don't have no problem, man. (Forty-year-old Wolof "rasta," former bumster, unemployed, Serrekunda)

These white women in Europe have no morals. You can get sex until your thing drop. They cannot leave black guys alone. They used to chase us in nightclubs in Oslo and then take us to their flats. After that they change their numbers so you don't call them again. Then they go out and look for different black guys. You feel used just to satisfy them sexually. I came home to marry a girl from my tribe [Wolof] that my mother chose for me. She used to be a good wife and knows how to please in the bedroom. But like any typical Wolof, she and her mother just wanted money and more money. Now she is abroad, who knows what she is doing. Maybe I need to try the circumcised girls, these Mandinkas or Fulas. But a Wolof man can never marry a Mandinka woman—they are below our class. But at least they may be steady. (Thirty-eight-year-old Wolof civil servant, spent seven years in Norway, lives in Serrekunda)

I used to date a Swedish girl. . . . One Christmas dinner, her sister followed me down to the wine cellar and grabbed my penis. She wanted me do it to her right there. She said she heard about me from her older sister and wanted to try. I told her in The Gambia we don't have this practice, it is not our culture, and then I left her there. This is why I came back home to marry a sober girl. My wife is a Fula. I am a Wolof. We dated for several years before we were married and I didn't know she was circumcised. She has orgasms just like any woman. But I trust her. I don't think [circumcision] makes any difference for her. But I will not allow her to circumcise my daughter, even though her family is always pressuring. You know it's just the Western culture you have to avoid for your children. But you shouldn't put them through this circumcision. (Fifty-two-year-old Wolof, businessman, spent twenty years in Sweden)

It's not just the white girls, even some of these Senegalese girls. Most of them come here as prostitutes and mislead Gambian girls. I dated one Senegalese, a Wolof. Her thing was so big and long, before I can even touch her she is having orgasms, just by rubbing it on my leg. Eh? No! What if I am not around? Any small breeze and she will disgrace herself in public. What man would she refuse? As for my personal view, it's better they cut this thing on girls so they can control themselves later on. (Twenty-seven-year-old Mandinka, security guard, Senegambia)

A couple of men stated that their experiences contradicted the common stereotypes about uncircumcised/circumcised women.

As for me, I once had a Senegalese girlfriend and she just lay there in bed. She too is a Wolof but all she knew how to do is to spread her legs. I have

been with an Aku girl who had only fifteen years and she is circumcised
but you wouldn't know because she is just too sexy. (Twenty-four-year-old
Mandinka, bumster, Senegambia)

Two of my wives, the half-caste [Lebanese/Jola] and the Fula, are circumcised, but the Wolof is not. I married Amie [Wolof] first. Even though I
am a Mandinka I knew I did not want a Mandinka wife. They are not as
sophisticated and educated and I didn't think they seem too experienced
in sex, even though I never even had a Mandinka girlfriend. You know the
Wolof are supposed to know how to really love a man and take care of a
man and please him sexually—you know we men joke about the fact they
have that thing down there. But truly I enjoy sex with my Fula wife, she is
much younger than the other two and she really likes sex and is willing to
try anything. I was surprised to find out my Lebanese wife was circumcised,
but she was brought up by her Jola relatives. She's beautiful, but she's much
more shy. So you see I don't believe this thing about circumcision. It really
depends on the women . . . I used to be married to a German a long time
ago and I also had a lot of other toubaab girlfriends, even a Japanese girl.
Some of them are very wild and you really enjoy it with them. Some of my
friends say it is because they are not circumcised, so they are crazy for sex,
especially from black men. But I don't know. Many times you see some of
our women, as well, dressing and behaving the same way they do and you
know they are circumcised, though they are going with different men. Just
look at those girls in Senegambia running after toubabs! It is the Western
culture and how they are exposed. (Ousmane, forty-three-year-old Mandinka businessman, Kanifing, spent ten years in Germany)

Interestingly, circumcised sex workers expressed far more doubts that in the
throes of passion many men can even tell the difference between a circumcised
or uncircumcised woman.

Some of my toubab customers, they don't care if you are a prostitute, what
they like is to [engage in oral sex]. Sometimes I think they will see I don't
have this thing but they don't even notice and I don't even care if they do,
because me too I am busy enjoying what they are doing. (Awa, twenty-six-
year-old Mandinka, Senegambia)

One toubab from England one time asked me if I was circumcised before
I even took off my clothes. He said he heard about it on a program in
London. I told him he is not supposed to ask a woman such a question.
He asked me whether I enjoy sex. I told him he is paying me for his own
enjoyment. In the end I lied to him and told him my tribe does not allow
female circumcision. He never knew the difference. After, he used to tell
me that he wanted to try sex with a circumcised girl. So, as fun, I brought
him my Wolof friend who is not circumcised. He still did not know the

difference. We did not like sex with him because he was not circumcised and he was old, but he was giving us a lot of money. (Astou, nineteen-year-old Fula, Senegambia)

However, another Fula girl mentioned how she was disgraced by her then-boyfriend because she was circumcised.

I once had a Wolof boyfriend and one time I caught him with another girl; she too is a Wolof. I confronted both of them in this nightclub where I saw them together and began insulting the two of them. I called the girl a dirty prostitute and a "solima [uncircumcised] with a big water hole." My boyfriend got up and slapped me and said what do I know, after all I don't have any sex between my legs, that if I can go and find it maybe he will stop going out with other girls. It was such a shame to me when he said that, since then I have never gone with a Wolof again! (Binta, twenty-two-year-old, Manjai)

These anecdotes expose the absurdity of taking men's comments about women's sexual experiences too seriously, especially when they are permitted the liberty of comparing the bodies and sexual performance of women of different races and ethnicities. The exercise itself evokes suspicion in that it seems to invite these racist and sexist commentaries.[34] Moreover, the race, sex, and ethnicity of the interviewer seem to influence how men respond to such questions. Often, in semistructured interviews, male (as well as female) informants from practicing ethnic groups presume I am an African American (which I am) and, therefore, uncircumcised. Some will speak condescendingly and apologetically or with open hostility against FGM. When later, depending on the discussions, I mention that I am also a Kono and circumcised, some brazenly dissociate themselves with earlier comments, insisting that female circumcision is an important part of cultural tradition and harmless to girls and women. Such turnabouts rarely occurred in interviews with men from nonpracticing ethnic groups. Many remain opposed to female circumcision and mesmerized that I accepted to undergo the traditional operation.

One Mandinka professor at Gambia College, with which I was affiliated during fieldwork, attempted an explanation. He said that he and several of his colleagues had no choice but to go with the Western intellectual status quo or be publicly ostracized. According to him, several well-known male professionals, including a renowned and popular local gynecologist, expressed concerns about excesses and misinformation propagated by FGM campaigns, only to be widely assailed and ridiculed by so-called women activists in the country. Another male lecturer explained to me that there are too many individuals chasing too little development funding coming into the country and a significant amount is geared toward campaigns to eliminate FGM. As male scholars, he said, it is already becoming more and more difficult to compete for funds targeted for "gender-this and gender-that," so none of them can afford to be on record for being politically incorrect about issues such as FGM.

In several other offices where I worked, Mandinka men would "whisper" one set of views in closed-door informal discussions and either remain quiet or make extra effort to appear anti-FGM in formal meetings. In one unusual case, during an official meeting I participated in, when the topic of FGM was raised, a woman representative of an eradication NGO based in Kenya dominated the discussions. The moment that a man happened to interject, making a point about the cultural importance of the practice to women in his ethnic group, the auditorium fell awkwardly tense and unnervingly silent. The more "knowledgeable" African female activist proceeded to set the man straight, reminding him that FGM is a violent crime against defenseless women which cannot not be justified by culture. Hence, it has become anathema in international development and many scholarly circles for anyone, male or female, circumcised *or* uncircumcised to speak up in any defense of female circumcision as a cultural practice.

CONCLUSION

The questions that findings of sexual enjoyment in circumcised women raise are unsettling precisely because they imply that what is presented as an indisputable physiological reality may itself be socially constructed. (Obermeyer, quoted in Boddy, chapter 2 of this volume)

That the external clitoris is key to women's sexual experience and liberation is as much a symbolic construction as the idea that its removal suppresses women's sexuality. As I hope this chapter has demonstrated, the significance of the exterior clitoris is not so much its neurobiological value in purportedly enabling female sexual enjoyment or orgasm—the latter can be achieved without it as far as the medical as well as anecdotal evidence suggests. Rather, as many writers have noted, what is invested in the clitoris in contemporary Western societies is an all-important symbolic value signifying that women are capable of, have a right to, and can enjoy sexual pleasure with or, importantly, without a man. Thus, some "traditionalist" circumcised African women criticize Western women's rediscovery of the clitoris as a way to deemphasize the sacredness of marriage and promote sexual licentiousness in the guise of women's autonomy.

This criticism perhaps makes more sense in light of dominant "traditional" beliefs about gender interdependence and complementarity in many African cultures, especially where female (and male) circumcision is practiced. In The Gambia, indigenous models of female sexuality do symbolically endow the clitoris with tremendous sexual power or energy equal to if not to rival that of men's. And, as I have shown in this chapter, these dominant views underscore attitudes concerning women's inherent capacity for sexual enjoyment. Local discourses about the external clitoris as a site of uncontrollable desire suggest why many women say it can be removed without affecting a woman's ability to enjoy sexual relations. Removing parts of the clitoral hood or the external glans is said to inhibit uncontrollable sexual behaviors (such as masturbation, nymphomania, and so on), which, I argue, are seen to violate sexual norms in marriage and thus deep-rooted interconnected beliefs about the nature of sex and gender. In any case, inhibiting sexual desire and antisocial sexual behavior, I offer, are not intended as the main goals of female genital surgeries in many practicing societies of which I am aware.

I have demonstrated in this chapter that in both Western and African "traditionalist" contexts, myths about the relevance of the clitoris to female sexuality are betrayed by women's different and varied experiences. In Western countries, many women with intact clitorises reportedly do not experience any type of orgasm in their lifetime, and complaints about sexual dysfunction or loss of sexual desire abound. In The Gambia, as in other African countries where female circumcision is widespread, "un-African" or "imported Western" sexual practices are clearly known and engaged in; women are not repressed and passive, even by "modern" Western standards.

Despite all the focus on women's sexual liberation and autonomy, most of my Western uncircumcised, heterosexual, female friends say that there is no substitute for the deep joy or intense pleasure experienced during lovemaking with a committed male partner in the context of a stable, monogamous relationship; my circumcised African female friends and relatives would most probably agree. The point to be made is that even with inherent differences between Western "scientific" and African "traditional" models of female sexuality there is great congruence in actual experiences of both uncircumcised and circumcised women.[35]

Many hardcore anti-FGM activists and radical feminists will not be assuaged by the findings and views expressed in this chapter. For many of them it is their taken-for-granted androcentric assumptions about female sexuality that fuel their outrage against female genital operations on African girls and women. However, the fact that the "female-circumcision-equals-female-sexual-dysfunction" thesis holds little resemblance to most circumcised women's lived realities does not necessarily mean a deathblow to eradication efforts in Western countries. Shweder's provocative articles highlight the arrogance, hypocrisy, and misdirection of international anti-FGM campaigns and makes prescriptions that would permit minor circumcisions of underage girls, just as circumcision operations are allowed for boys (2002 and forthcoming, see also Hernlund and Shell-Duncan, chapter 1 of this volume) while prohibiting or postponing extensive surgeries until an appropriate age of consent. For Boddy (chapter 2 of this volume), part of the problem lies in the fact that what one child may experience as a fulfilling "traditional" coming-of-age ceremony associated with her "home" country, another child born or raised in a "host" country may experience as traumatic violence and alienation. It is for this reason that Shweder's emphasis on an approved age of consent seems a compelling solution.

What is definitely needed are more culturally sensitive policies that reaffirm, not disparage, the values and body images of affected women, measures that show respect for their various cultural and "traditional" heritages. African girls and women who happen to be circumcised today are entitled to see themselves as okay the way they are, as "normal" and healthy and not as "mutilated" objects who are in some pathetic "search for missing clitorises."[36]

Many of us unequivocally reject as absurd the notion that our mothers and grandmothers are child abusers or mutilators and that all our menfolk are misogynists and sadistic oppressors of their wives and daughters. Some of us are even married to men who frown upon the continuation of these "old women's traditions." Most of us do not want our European- or American-born daughters to be targets of degrading anti-FGM stereotypes. And when these girls do mature and develop into young women, they should be given the option and right to choose with dignity whether or not to uphold their "traditional" customs; that is, whether or not to undergo a particular form of circumcision for cultural reasons, just as their Western counterparts are allowed to undergo any number of physically invasive operations for aesthetic or other supposedly *noncultural* reasons. Denying young Western(ized) African girls and women this freedom to choose is tantamount to refusing them fundamental, universal human rights—rights to their own bodies and to sexual autonomy, as well as to uphold their cultural identities, however they may define this.

Many African women in the diaspora who are circumcised do acknowledge circumcision for cultural reasons yet also support a woman's *inherent* capacity for sexual pleasure (including orgasms, for those who do experience them) and aspirations for sexual autonomy, although they may have different ways to define these. These values are not mutually exclusive. Many circumcised women eagerly and deferentially submit to their grandmothers' authority in a symbolic and ritual "tradition" that marks and celebrates their identities and inherent power *as African women*. They also experience sexual pleasure as a "natural," God-given gift.

I have no quarrel with Western women who hail possession of an external clitoris as affirmation of their sexual autonomy and equality with men. And for those uncircumcised and circumcised African women who are sold on this view, this too is fine. However, for African women of my grandmother's persuasion, it is eschewing the peripheral clitoris (or the disembodiment of the external phallus) that symbolizes a true separation from masculinity and thus defines, paradoxically, the quintessence of matriarchal power (Ahmadu 2005). It is unfortunate that some of our Western(ized) feminist sisters insist on denying us this critical aspect of becoming a woman in accordance with our unique and powerful cultural heritage. It is even more regrettable that in our consummate fear and virtual paralysis in challenging Western feminist interpretations of who we are and how we supposedly feel, as circumcised African women, we truly have assured our psychological mutilation.

NOTES

1. I use the terms "female circumcision," "female genital cutting," "female genital surgeries," or "operations" as generic descriptions for various types of traditional female genital operations. The term "FGM" is used to emphasize the language and position of international eradication movements. More specific terms such as "clitoridectomy," "excision," and "infibulation" are also used to describe specific types of operations.

2. I use the term "Western" in this chapter in the most general sense to refer to the liberal democracies of mainly North America and Western Europe; to the dominant moral, political, economic, and religious norms and values associated with these societies; and to emphasize the subtle ironies and contradictions inherent in prevailing assumptions about progress, modernity, enlightenment, and individual autonomy associated with these societies.

3. See, for example, Sia Amma's Web site, http://www.celebrateclitoris.com/.

4. The research on sex workers was conducted for a subregional survey focusing on the sexual exploitation of children in The Gambia and Senegal from February to August 2002. The Sexual Exploitation Study was coordinated by CODESRIA in Dakar, Senegal, and funded by UNICEF The Gambia and Senegal. Focus groups of married women were conducted during fieldwork for my Ph.D. dissertation at the Department of Anthropology, London School of Economics. This fieldwork was funded by the Wenner-Gren Foundation between January 1998 and June 1999.

5. See, for example, Abdalla (1982); El Dareer (1982b); Koso-Thomas (1987).

6. *Pride* (United Kingdom) magazine, 1995.

7. "JJC" stands for "Johnny Just Come," a common term of reference for Africans newly arrived to America.

8. Roughly between the ages of seventeen and twenty-five.

9. Similarly, there is often no term for female "orgasm." Sexual enjoyment for both sexes is taken for granted as a natural part of coitus or sex play.

10. See, for example, the article by Sara Klein at http://www.metrotimes.com/editorial/story.asp?=7405; see also Hernlund and Shell-Duncan, chapter 1 of this volume.

11. See Ahmadu 2005 for a more complex and thorough anthropological study of the cosmological and cultural sources of ideas and values concerning sexuality among The Mandinka in The Gambia.

12. Most senior female head of "traditional" women's affairs—that is, girls' circumcision and marriage ceremonies.

13. All names were changed to protect the identities of informants.

14. The speaker was referring to an agemate of her father.

15. Several sex workers in focus groups originate from neighboring countries. This respondent reported that she was originally from Benin, West Africa.

16. Meaning that he provides financial and practical assistance—accommodation, toiletries, clothing, and so on.

17. This term is more frequently used than the word "orgasm." Interestingly, many women (and men) also refer to vaginal secretions as "semen."

18. Of Senegalese origin. Although "Senegambia" is sometimes used to refer to the region of The Gambia and Senegal, here it refers to a periurban area near the capital where many tourist hotels are located.

19. Originally from Senegal.

20. See Ahmadu (2005) for a more in-depth critique of one author's interpretation of the social/symbolic meanings of infibulation as well as the psychosexual significance of defibulation vis-à-vis Somali women.

21. See Klein (2005) for a discussion of women who opt for "designer vaginas" (tighter and perkier to please or satisfy their partners).

22. A *ngamano is a* "traditional" female circumciser.

23. This could be related to beliefs that Fula women are some of the most beautiful and desirable women in West Africa.

24. It is important to stress that I only heard such comments from non-Fula, for example, Mandinka and Wolof, men as well as men from other African countries, including Nigerians and Sierra Leoneans residing in The Gambia. I heard the same disturbing narrations regarding Fula women's sexuality from Mandingo and Susu men in Guinea (Conakry). Most Fula women I asked about this said that it is probably true because of their "culture" and the fact that they marry so young.

25. One of the puzzles of excision and sexuality that I mentioned in a previous article on the Kono of Sierra Leone relates to local distinctions between sexual desire and sexual pleasure and the role of the clitoris in attenuating the former while having no impact on the latter (Ahmadu 2000). As with the Kono, my Gambian informants and participants in focus group discussions stated that circumcision enables a woman to comport herself properly in society (by not being enslaved to or controlled by sexual desires), yet they denied that removal of the clitoris reduces sexual pleasure and capacity for orgasm.

26. From the Web site of Drs. L. Berman and J. Berman (2005).

27. I have used quotation marks here to emphasize the masculine or androcentric terms that are used in the "scientific" literature to describe and define the clitoris. This tendency to "phallicize" the clitoris has also been noted by K. Bell (2005) and several others and, interestingly, correlates with my analysis of the rich and graphic symbolic imagery that is produced in Mandinka female and male circumcision rituals and Bambara/Mande creation mythology (Ahmadu 2005).

28. Berman and Berman (2005) Web site.

29. The question of "reduction" in sensation can only be reasonably answered by women themselves who have experienced orgasm prior to their operations and, presumably, have engaged in sexual relations afterward.

30. For instance, "folk" theories contained in books by Masters and Johnson as well as the Kinsey reports, popular books from the 1970s, such as *The Joy of Sex,* as well as women and men's consumer magazines, such as *Cosmopolitan* and *Playboy.*

31. See for example, (Dopico and Johansen, chapters 10 and 11) respectively of this volume.

32. Slang term used in Senegal and The Gambia to refer to white people or people believed to be from Europe or America. Terminology is also used to describe "naïve," wealthy, Westernized Africans.

33. Meaning "money only" in Wolof and Mandinka respectively.

34. The comments presented here are from sections of interviews concerned with sexual exploitation of underage girls. They were selected because of references men made to circumcision, race, and women's sexuality.

35. My emphasis in this chapter has been on the experiences and desires of heterosexual women. However, it must be noted that in The Gambia same-sex relations among women (as well as men) are acknowledged, albeit often dismissed as "un-African." Several circumcised African women admit to "playing" with other women and do not see their sexual preference for women as affecting their desire for, or duty to marry, a male partner. Marriage to the opposite sex is considered by most Africans to be a social and moral obligation—a *right* as well as *rite* of adulthood—which may or may not coincide with individual sexual practices and preferences despite overt cultural norms stressing heterosexuality and (women's) monogamy (see also Roscoe and Murray 2001).

36. Sia Amma Web site, http://www.celebrateclitoris.com.

CHAPTER 13

The Failure of Pluralism?

Henrietta L. Moore

WE MIGHT AGREE that culture matters, but how much should it matter, and to whom? Arguments about culture are always fraught, because they are perennially entangled in a debate about transcendence versus recognition. Should we live our lives according to principles that apply to the whole of humanity, or should we be guided by the historical specificity of lives lived? The circularity of these debates defies simple narratives or solutions.

In one familiar version, culture as tradition is figured as the antithesis of modernity. Colonial politics in the nineteenth and twentieth centuries claimed a civilizing mission based on portraying the non-Western world as in need of enlightenment and reform. Traditional culture was the mark of nonmodernity, and evidence for this was most often advanced in the form of female bodies and the treatment of women: the harem, female circumcision, sati, age at marriage, and marriage laws. Colonial officials everywhere felt able to denounce certain cultural practices as backward, shocking, uncivilized, and barbaric. As a number of writers have pointed out, there is more than a little continuity between those arguments and contemporary denouncements of female genital operations (Boddy 1998b; Erlich 1991; Walley 1997; Boddy and Rogers, chapters 2 and 6 respectively of this volume).

However, the West's ongoing effort to present itself as having transcended culture has long been recognized as the absent core of liberal politics. Claims to transcendence being little more than claims for the universality of a particular set of historical specificities. The West, it turns out, has culture just like everyone else. What falls out from this critique are a number of interrelated points. One is that culture is never simply culture, it is also always politics. In consequence, culture can never be self-evident, but is always open to radical interrogation and interpretation. In the contemporary moment, this means that culture is not the opposite of modernity, or indeed of globalization or capitalism, but constitutive of them. Whatever is defended in the name of culture now is not a statement about the past, but about the future present (see Piot, chapter 7 of this volume).

The relationship of culture to politics is historically an uncomfortable one, most especially when culture is understood as religion. Religion has been central to the formation of many modern national identities, but the ideal of the modern nation-state is one that has historically been closely bound up with secularization. The underlying premises—deriving by circuitous routes from the Enlightenment—being that the place of religion in modern life should be a private not a public one, that a modern society should be characterized by secularism, that the irrational and superstitious should be repudiated in favour of the scientific (see Chakrabarty 1995). However, religion has not withered in the face of modernity; indeed we have seen a dramatic reengagement with politicized religion in the closing decades of the twentieth century and one that promises to gather force in the twenty-first century. The relationship of religion to politics is thus occluded by the assumption that modern nation-states must, if they are to be democratic, also be secular, and this presents particular difficulties where religion and culture are conflated.

The modern nation-state regulates all aspects of individual life—including birth, marriage, and death—and it intervenes directly in the reform of society (Asad 1999, 191). As part of that process of reform, it insists that the law be adhered to. One consequence of these processes is that the state is intimately bound up not only with the constitution of social spaces and religious and cultural identities but also with their legal recognition and regulation. The state therefore has to deal directly with culture in situations of cultural diversity and moral plurality. As the fate of multiculturalism in the West so tellingly illustrates, the liberal state is caught by the irresolvable dilemma of upholding the primacy of liberal values while affirming cultural recognition. The most usual outcome is one where those who are deemed "to have culture" must accept the values and institutions of their country of residence in exchange for the "private" enjoyment of their culture and religion (cf. van der Veer 2002). Others, of course, are in the happy situation where the values and institutions of the country are already their culture or are formed around it (Rogers, chapter 6 of this volume).

The tension between universal value claims, cultural recognition, and moral plurality has been addressed by contemporary philosophy through the framework of a form of procedural liberalism (Seth 2001). The struggle is to find rules that could in principle regulate and adjudicate conflicts between competing conceptions of the good, rather than seeking to impose a form of metaphysical liberalism based on setting out constitutive universal values (cf. Rawls 1993). A major difficulty with procedural liberalism is that it is necessarily nonsubstantive, one might say virtually content free. It is premised on the assumption that the state will remain a neutral arbiter, or as near as possible, and will not make substantive moral or value claims. The result is a view of politics as a valueless space where all values can be considered and debated. However, this presupposes a view of society as being morally good when neutral. This is a highly problematic assumption for societies that see politics, law, and faith as indissoluble (Seth 2001, 71–73). It also provides no practical mechanism for dealing with differences—forms of moral and cultural diversity—that exceed the possibility of consensus within the space of a morally neutral politics. Issues concerning the intimate nature of selves and bodies—female genital operations, for example—frequently threaten to exceed consensual spaces and their possibilities.

Arguments within procedural liberalism also have a tendency to reduce values and conceptions of the good to questions of belief. This is partly related to the emphasis on the autonomous, individual subject who is the bearer of values and thus of rights within any possible consensual space. Within liberal nation-states, modern liberties rest on sets of rights and duties that are underpinned by assumptions about a given self that must be permitted to both make and defend itself (Asad 1999, 181 and 186). There is a tension here because a self that is conceived and defined as able to make and defend itself is a particular kind of self, and therefore not a value-free one. But selves are not just a matter of belief or of conscious choice; they are bound up with others, with experiences and aspirations, and with passions and desires. Insofar as there is a particular relationship between self and society, psyche and culture, it is not one that can be said to be freely and wholly chosen. Selves, our sense of ourselves, and therefore our identities are intimately connected to an intersubjective world formed out of our relations with others. This intersubjective world is both historically sedimented and subject to change, but participation in it cannot be simply glossed as a matter of belief. Thus, to reduce individual values and conceptions of the good to beliefs misses much that is important about identities and the relation between selves and others.

These reflections set the context for the theoretical issues raised by female genital operations, their changing nature and the views of those who practice, support, reform, study, and condemn them. It is evident that female genital operations question assumptions about liberalism and universal values directly, but more than that they challenge the validity of all forms of multiculturalism. The anxieties and fears of those who oppose them demonstrate the limits of a consensual and negotiated politics within the boundaries of the liberal nation-state. They are thus in a very real sense the paradigmatic moment both of cultural recognition and of its failures. There is a certain irony in this, because it comes at a time when the liberal project has been powerfully criticized on the grounds that its universal claims are not foundational, but contingent, and indeed exclusionary. Yet, as the contributors to this volume demonstrate, a review of the debates on female genital operations demonstrates that interrogations of the liberal project and its assumptions are not as radical as they may once have appeared.

Culture and Cosmopolitanism

It is a truism that we all live in a globalized and globalizing world. In certain accounts, the global is implicitly or explicitly contrasted with something called the local, which is itself glossed as the site of culture (see Moore 2004). Yet it is no longer possible, if it ever was, to think of cultures as bounded, fixed entities.

Cultures are hybrid, changing, mobile, and disjunct (see Appadurai 1996). The anthropological vantage point has always been a fictionalized one, but this is ever more evident as the experiences of other cultures, of travel, comparison, observation, intervention, and critique are extended to large numbers of people across the globe. Cultures are never simply local, although anthropologists in the past often presented them as though they were. The very idea of a rooted, native culture was the product of a traveling, comparative Western gaze (cf. Clifford 1988). Thus, the division of the world into the global and the local is an interested one, enmeshed in power relations, functioning as a distorted mirror image of an hierarchical distinction between culture and modernity (Rosaldo 1989; Chatterjee 1993). The binary is a disabling one, because it prevents us from understanding that the global and the local are mutually constitutive, that we do not in fact live in a world where we were once all local and then at a certain historical moment found ourselves interconnected. Those whom anthropology has presented as local have global experiences, understandings, and aspirations. Cosmopolitanism—in the sense of global experiences, perspectives, and aspirations—is to be found all over the world. People travel, they are forced, they settle, they work, and they move backwards and forwards across boundaries both national and cultural.

Contemporary anthropology frequently cites transnational cultures as evidence for the fact that cultures are not spatially bounded and fixed. But the very term "transnational" presupposes the existence of its opposite, an originary location, the national. Nations, however, do not map onto cultures. The fact of belonging and of having a culture cannot straightforwardly be glossed as the national or the local and then juxtaposed with the transnational and the global: "the citizens of one of those large 'imagined communities' of modernity we call nations are not likely to be centred on a common culture. . . . There is no single shared body of ideals and practices in India that sits at the heart of the lives of most Hindus and most Muslims, that engages all Sikhs and excites every Kashmiri, that animates every untouchable in Delhi and organizes the ambitions of every Brahmin in Bombay" (Appiah 1998, 100). There are no existing modern nations that are founded on a culture as a single set of shared practices and beliefs. Nations are heterogeneous, diverse, and full of contradiction and conflict; this has long been the case and is not just the result of transnational cultural flows and the movement of people, goods, and images around the world, although such movement has intensified the process. The national, like the local, cannot be treated as an originary, rooted location.

One of the difficulties here is the way in which social science discourses, and to a certain extent professional and popular discourses, frame their understandings of a globalized world, its institutions, and the lived experience of individuals. The binaries "local/global, national/transnational" are clearly insufficient in themselves to capture the mutually constituted, interpenetrated, and internally diverse nature of the processes at play, but they cannot simply be dismissed. Much contemporary work in anthropology has focused on the processes, mechanisms, and institutions that crosscut these binaries, but it has also had to recognize that the local and the national are continuously being constituted and reconstituted through these interconnections. For example, the Islamic diaspora in Europe is forcing nation-states to rethink the definition and horizons of the nation. Taking diverse viewpoints into account is not only a requirement for a liberal multicultural state, but a political necessity. While the Blair government in the United Kingdom has had to respond to charges of institutional racism, it has also had to deal with a massive withdrawal of support by Muslim voters following the decision to ally with the United States in the war against Iraq. Thus the national is constituted in terms of the transnational, the local in terms of the global.

However, this process is an uneven and contradictory one. In a parallel development, the head of the Commission for Racial Equality in the United Kingdom announced in April 2004 that multiculturalism should be abandoned. He explained his reasoning by saying that the term implied "separateness" and was no longer useful in contemporary Britain because "[w]hat we should be talking about is how we reach an integrated society, one in which people are equal under the law, where there are some common values." This point is a curious one, because multiculturalism is normally understood as the recognition of cultural diversity within the rule of the law, but as many critics of his argument were quick to point out the issue is not really recognition, but values. In other words, the real fear is of an excess of diversity leading to a loss of shared values. This was tellingly revealed by the admission that the ideal would be to replace multiculturalism with integration. "We need to assert there is a core of Britishness. For instance, I hate the way this country has lost Shakespeare. That sort of thing is bad for immigrants too. They want to come here not just because of jobs but because they like this country—its tolerance, its eccentricity, its Parliamentary democracy, its energy in the big cities. They don't want that to change" (Phillips 2004). What is evident is that British ethnic minorities and "immigrants" are effectively being exhorted to be more British, and in some way to put Britishness first. This seems rather more like assimilation than integration, a process usually recommended by the right rather than the liberal left.

What this points to is not only diversity but also intense debate in a context where the relationships between identities, viewpoints, beliefs, and ideological presuppositions are contradictory, unstable, and shifting. Culture is variously understood as nation, as ethnicity, and as religion, but adherents often switch between and collapse these understandings into each other (cf. Baumann 1999). Multiple allegiances mean that individuals and groups may hold firmly to complex and internally differentiated positions and want to defend, for example, both the tenets of the liberal state and an ethnic and/or religious identity. There is little value—as opponents and supporters of multiculturalism often fail to realize—in asking which comes first. These are lived relations bound up with history, sedimented values, experiences, and aspirations. Adherence to a form of life is not something that is necessarily rational, completely conscious, and/or thought out. Passion and desire are part of identification, and there are, for example, many devout Muslims who are also staunch defenders of the liberal democratic state and of the "British way of life," but when these aspects of identity and sets of values come into conflict, that conflict will be a lived embodied one, striking at the very core of self and group identity (Talle, chapter 4 of this volume). Culture—however it is understood—does imply difference, but this difference is no longer categorical or taxonomic, but rather increasingly interactive and interdependent.

There has been a good deal of discussion in anthropology about cross-cultural experience and understanding in the form of the debate on cosmopolitanism. Various authors have pointed out that cosmopolitanism is not merely a matter of traveling, of crossing boundaries and encountering other ways of life, but must entail some form of serious engagement with otherness and with a plurality of cultures (cf. Hannerz 1990). In writings on the new cosmopolitanism, there is a determined effort to avoid an oppositional binary between the "world citizen" and the "rooted native," between global and local perspectives, internationalism and patriotism (see Cheah and Robbins 1998). There is a clear recognition that just as there are divergent interpretations of what the local implies, so there are "divergent cosmopolitanisms," different views of global and globalizing worlds, and that most of these do not originate in the West (cf. Clifford 1988; Appadurai 1996). Yet there is little clarity about what these cosmopolitanisms entail. Minimally, they imply some kind of critique—often practical rather than theoretical—of ethnocentrism; they insist on a willingness to take others' values and beliefs into account. As a form of human understanding and/or empathy, there is little new in this, and a willingness to live with difference is hardly the product of contemporary transnationalism or globalization, since it is both the founding principle of most modern nation-states and the defining feature of cosmopolitanism since the Stoics. What analysts seem to be trying to convey is the emergence of a new range of tolerances, an openness to and a willingness to embrace emerging forms of modernity.

Processes of this kind or something like them are clearly at work. Take, for example, the rise of the gay movement as a world movement, or the adoption of new reproductive technologies across the globe. Such developments do not go uncontested, however, and opposition follows lines of fracture across and within communities, nations, classes, religions, genders, and generations. New forms of "secularism" in the broadest sense may be arising, but they are countered everywhere by increasingly essentialist and "ancestral" views of culture, by religious fundamentalism, ethnic exclusion, and ideological intransigence. As contemporaneous forms of modernity, secularisms and their opposites are indissolubly bound together, constantly producing and reproducing each other as the interior and exterior of the other.

One consequence of this is that the debate on female genital operations cannot simply be glossed as a controversy between "African women" and "Westerners," "traditionalists" and "feminists," Islam and the West (Gosselin, 2000a). These binaries do not capture the internally differentiated nature of groups, categories, and positions. What is evident is that the debate itself engages with a spectrum of views on conceptions of the good, the place of values in the lives of individuals and groups, and ideas about the nature of society. Claudie Gosselin's discussion of the situation in Mali (2000a) makes this point very well and draws out the fact that discussions about female genital operations are highly charged and are ways for Malians to debate and articulate the role of the state, the impact of Westernization, the nature of Islamic revivalism, and issues of gender, age, and class. Therefore, to reduce the debate about female genital operations to a battle between the titans of universalism and relativism is to silence many voices.

The views of individuals, and indeed groups, are trivialized when they are reduced to "cultural beliefs" or homogenized into single, fixed positions (cf. Talle, chapter 4 of this volume). Michelle Johnson demonstrates in her comparative study of Guinea-Bissau and Portugal (chapter 9 of this volume) that people's views are complex, differentiated, and often ambiguous, and that they are formulated in relation—sometimes in contradistinction—to the views of others. In her discussion of Mandinga women and men living in multiethnic communities in Portugal, she describes how individuals respond differentially to the transnational and national debates on female genital operations, producing tensions between women and men, old and young, "traditionalists" and "revivalists." Many individuals actively debate the difference between Mandinga personhood (being Mandinga) and religious identity (being Muslim), thus opening up the possibility of a distinction between "African traditions" and "modern Islam." One informant argued on the basis of his reading of the Qur'an that Islam does not require women to be "circumcised" in order to pray and thus there is no necessary connection between female genital operations and Islam. However, when discussing the value of "cutting" for the management of female sexuality, he implicitly invoked religious authority, arguing that "If a woman wants men too much, it ruins her Muslim-ness." Yet, on reflection, he concluded that a woman's "upbringing" will account more for her behavior than whether she has had her genitals "reduced." What this example illustrates is that individuals' values are composite and may be contradictory, and that they do not necessarily form a single set of coherent interconnected beliefs and practices. The actuality is that views, ideas, and opinions are open to change, that they are often ambiguous, and they reflect the struggle of individuals to resolve the tensions between and competing demands of religious education, international debates, economic circumstances, history, ethnic and religious discrimination, and cultural context.

In such circumstances, ambivalence may be a better metaphor for—and indeed a measure of—cosmopolitanism than general notions of the recognition and valuation of cultural difference. Sara Johnsdotter (chapter 5 of this volume) emphasizes that individuals—and indeed groups—may have both positive and negative feelings towards female genital operations. This ambivalence means that it is not possible simply to state that people are either for or against the practice. The specific experiences of Somali mothers living in Sweden mean that they reevaluate female genital operations in terms of the life chances of their daughters, of how these young women will be seen by their Swedish peers, and whether being uncircumcised will impair or enhance their marriage prospects. These strategic evaluations, however, run alongside more critical reflections about whether the practice is "natural" and/or "necessary," and whether it is a necessary component of Muslim religious identity and practice. Both Johns-dotter and Johnson argue that one of the major forces for change is the debate going on within the broader Muslim community and the contact with other Muslim groups and individuals who do not circumcise their daughters. This creates a space in which ideas about female genital operations can be reformulated in relation to Muslim identity. Thus, it is not the reforming zeal of Westerners or the legal structures of the liberal state that bring about change; in fact, such pressure as they seek to exercise can frequently result in resistance, anger, and back-lash. This is not to suggest that nonpracticing, non–Muslim women and men should not be campaigning on this issue or that states should not be legislating. What it does point to is that change is occurring, that culture and religious identity are not monolithic and fixed, and that cosmopolitanism cannot simply be glossed as recognizing cultural difference. Rather, cosmopolitanism needs to be understood as an openness and/or tolerance towards ambivalence within a wide range of competing discursive frames, none of which are entirely local or global, national or international, traditional or modern.

In the existing debate about cosmopolitanism, there is an implicit tendency in the writing of some authors to trivialize culture, and this is curious given that most of the protagonists are trying to do precisely the opposite. It arises directly from a propensity to reduce cultural differences to "values" or "beliefs." This has the unintentional effect of essentializing differences and divorcing them from practices. The nature of all forms of beliefs, values, and opinions, as has been argued, is that they are part of a lived relation to the world, and that this relation is not wholly a matter of individual choice either at the level of socioeconomic and political circumstances or at the level of unconscious motivation and desire. However, it is the divorcing of values and beliefs from the context of practice that "thins" culture almost to the point of incomprehensibility: "How could women do this to their own daughters?"; "How could people believe that religion demands this?" The result is that cultures appear incommensurable as the paradoxical consequence of trying to find ways to value them.

Both multiculturalism and certain forms of cosmopolitanism suffer from this because they have to consider cultures out of their lived context in order to value them equally with others. Lived practices, however, are not just a matter of carrying out actions that are the direct consequence of holding particular beliefs, as in "they do this because their culture is different from ours." A view, as Johnsdotter (this volume) points out, results either in calls for moral education or in a hierarchization of "modernity" versus "tradition." What a notion of lived practices draws attention to is the actual context in which individuals make decisions, take actions, and formulate beliefs and viewpoints. This involves not only understanding culture as history and as a series of identifications, experiences of embodiment, and self, but also considering these in relation to modes of livelihood, marriage strategies, political institutions, state legislation, and the like. This attention to context is what makes culture a "thick" notion, and makes it possible to consider those areas of rationality, reflection, and choice over which individuals have some control and other forms of determination over which they do not. As Johnsdotter and Obiora (chapters 5 and 3 respectively of this volume) point out, women who circumcise their daughters are involved in strategies and tradeoffs; in the context they find themselves in they are deciding how to act in the interests of what they define as the best and the good. This may sound like a truism, but it is of primary importance in the debate on female genital operations, as many authors in this volume point out, because of the way women are often portrayed as passive victims of culture, acting in the interests of ideology or religion or patriarchy, as though they had no view about such things. In addition, it also accounts for the diminished nature of much argument in the debate that reduces women to the general category "women," often making their bodies stand for them merographically (see Strathern 1991 and 1993), and completely occluding their age, class, ethnicity, religion, and broader socio-economic and political circumstances.

SEXUALITY AND AGENCY

Opponents of female genital operations frequently cite the loss of sexual pleasure as a consequence of the operation as one of the mainstays of their opposition. The issues of sexuality and sexual pleasure suffuse the international and national debates because they act as a location for the definition of what is normal. Discussions about the normality of bodies, pleasures, and sexualities are also ways of talking about the normality of culture, religion, and ethnicity, and vice versa (Rogers, chapter 6 of this volume). This provides for a very potent mix. Recent studies on female genital operations have emphasized that the effects of the operations on sexual response are varied (cf. Gruenbaum 2000; Lightfoot-Klein 1989b). This is in part because the operations are themselves varied, ranging from sunna through intermediate to pharaonic (infibulation) (cf. Gruenbaum 2000; Shell-Duncan and Hernlund 2000; WHO 1998). It is also because sexual pleasure and sexual satisfaction are not self-evident experiences, categories, or concepts. Much of the recent debate in the literature has focused on whether women who have had genital operations experience orgasm. There is evidence both from women's own accounts of their sexual pleasure and from women who were sexually experienced before circumcision that

many women do experience orgasm (cf. Ahmadu 2000 and chapter 12 of this
volume; Gruenbaum 2000; Lightfoot-Klein 1989b; Dopico; Johansen, chapter
11 of this volume).

Sexual pleasure is, however, an intimate experience that lends itself only
marginally to verbal articulation. Anthropologists, clinicians, and others asking
women about sexual pleasure and satisfaction have little more than their own
experiences to draw on. Reading and talking about other people's sexual experiences rarely provides a definitive understanding of whether one's personal
experience is strictly comparable to another's (Ahmadu and Dopico, chapters 11
and 10 respectively of this volume). So the "uncircumcised woman" talking to
the "circumcised woman" can have no certainty as to the nature and compara-
bility of their forms of sexual pleasure, just as the "circumcised woman" cannot
know definitively whether the "uncircumcised woman" experiences her forms
of sexual pleasure. The very idea of the "normal" sexual experience is one that
can only be approached critically through a genealogical understanding of how
forms of power create forms of knowledge; it has no meaning outside specific
discursive historical contexts. Thus, uncertainty will not be resolved simply by
appealing to science, by examining in minute detail the physiological responses
to stimulation in different parts or areas of women's bodies (Dopico, chapter 10
of this volume). This is very clearly demonstrated by the long debate in the West
about clitoral versus vaginal orgasm, and the attempt to discursively normalize women's sexual responses (ibid.). Physiological responses are not the same
thing as sexual satisfaction or pleasure, as many women have pointed out when
trying to account for their own experiences of sexual pleasure in terms of the
findings of sexologists and clinicians. Many Western women have reportedly
found the reduction of sexual pleasure and desire to physiological response in
one location of the body an uncomfortable and unsettling experience, rather
than an affirming one. We cannot therefore assume that clitoral orgasm is necessarily either the goal of sexual activity for women or the given and predictable
definition or epitome of sexual pleasure. In this context, it is far from surprising that circumcised women, and practitioners and supporters of female genital
operations are unwilling to have their experiences of sexual pleasure reduced to
clitoral orgasm or rather the lack of it (cf. Abusharaf 2000; Ahmadu 2000; Talle,
chapter 4 of this volume). Even more problematic is the assumption that sexual
pleasure and sexual satisfaction are synonymous. The evidence from research
in the West suggests that they are separate but overlapping aspects of women's
sexual responses (Dopico, chapter 10 of this volume). This means that we need
to take far more seriously than hitherto circumcised women's claims that sexual
satisfaction, and indeed pleasure, are linked for them to fertility, conception, and
socially reproductive sex.

Pleasure and satisfaction are difficult terms. Within any group of women,
circumcised or not, ethnically homogenous or not, of a single faith or not, there
will be a wide range of sexual experiences, understandings of pleasure and

satisfaction, ideas about the body, its sensations, bleeding, childbirth, and pain (Talle, chapter 4 of this volume). Culture as a notion is not of much assistance here unless we understand it as a lived context, a set of changing and sedimented relations between history, social structures, political economy, personal experiences, concepts of self, views of the body, and ideas about the bodies and selves of others. We need to comprehend and understand problems of scale. We cannot claim that English women have different ideas of sexual pleasure from Kenyan women. The categories are already too broad—both England and Kenya are ethnically and religiously diverse, and age and class are salient axes of difference with regard to sexuality and sexual pleasure—and differences within the group are likely to be as great as differences between them. The idea of cultural difference in this context, unless handled very carefully, is not an explanation for anything (ibid.).

The very notion of sexuality, as Foucault argued, is historically and discursively constructed within a field of power relations. Sexual practices, forms of embodiment and sexual pleasure are not preexistent or given ideas, experiences or entities, but forms of lived relations shot through with the workings of power. The anthropological debate on female genital operations has sought to capture some understanding of these sets of discursive practices by examining how genital operations "make sense" within specific lived contexts (cf. Boddy 1989; Gruenbaum 2000; Parker 1995; Talle 1993; C. J. Walley 1997). This process of contextualization is complex and involves working on multiple levels. Anthropological analyses frequently emphasize the importance of marriage, descent, and fertility in relation to genital operations, that is the specific connections that many cultures make between sexuality, marriage, reproduction, and the continuity of social groupings. Sexuality, and indeed sexual pleasure and sexual satisfaction, are connected for many women in these circumstances to fertility and reproduction within marriage, as noted earlier. The divorce of sexuality, sexual pleasure, and satisfaction from fertility, reproduction, and the continuity of lineages and other social groupings was a very slow and uneven process in Europe that took place over hundreds of years and remains unfinished, but the crucial factor in this process was easily available and effective contraception in the hands of women. Continuity of the lineage or social group and its continuing fertility are sources of esteem and power for many women in different contexts around the world (Boddy, Johansen, and Johnson, chapters 2, 11, and 9 respectively of this volume). Female genital operations mark the location of this power in the bodies of women, and they therefore represent powerfully condensed sets of significations. It is for this reason that genital operations are usually set within complex initiation and life transition rites and are connected to deeply sedimented religious symbols focused on fertility.

One view that is commonly found in cultures practicing female genital operations, albeit in a variety of specific guises, is that women's and men's bodies have anatomical similarities and that what is required for fertility and successful reproduction is to make them complimentary. Difference is literally inscribed on the bodies of women and men whose "natural" bodies are not sufficiently different for socially appropriate reproduction (Boddy and Johnson, chapters 2 and 9 respectively of this volume). Hence the often cited reason for genital operations that they are a means to contain women's sexuality within socially approved bounds, focusing it down on the social goals of marriage, fertility, and reproduction. In such contexts, women's bodies are moral entities, holographic versions of larger social bodies such as the village and the lineage, literally the living embodiment of the complementary forces that make life (Boddy, this volume).

Opponents of female genital operations, in recognizing these interconnections, have suggested that what is at issue here is male domination of women and patriarchal control. Elaborating on this, some have claimed that infibulation is done to enhance male sexual pleasure. Anthropologists, while not denying that female genital operations are conducted in societies where most material and symbolic resources are controlled by men, point out that men do not think that infibulation enhances their sexual pleasure, do not necessarily think that genital operations give them more personal control over women, and often see genital operations as a domain of women's "business," if not women's "power." Men frequently express considerable anxiety about defibulation (Johansen, chapter 11 of this volume) and are not automatic supporters of female genital operations. Their views, like those of women, are complex and sometimes contradictory, refracted through political and economic circumstances, education, ethnicity, religion, age, and class. They do not form a homogenous group within any single cultural context. Furthermore, the views of men, like those of women, are not straightforwardly derived from cultural precepts or values; individuals can hold views that are at odds with dominant cultural understandings and models, they may also hold contradictory and/or ambivalent views, as in the case of the Somali doctor discussed by Johansen (ibid.), who is opposed to infibulation but still sees attempts to ban circumcision as promoting sexual promiscuity and abortion.

It is clear that men's interests are different from women's in many contexts, but we cannot simply refer to men as a group without a carefully nuanced account of how personal and local understandings, models, and views intersect with broader discursive arenas. Here we are often dealing with what we might term the positive and negative ambivalence of cosmopolitanism. For example, Ahmadu (chapter 12 of this volume) relates the views of a number of men in The Gambia from practicing and nonpracticing groups concerning female sexual responsiveness. As she notes, many of the experiences and opinions expressed drew on sets of interlinked attitudes about race, ethnicity, and sexuality. In a complex multiethnic and multifaith context, which is also a major holiday destination for Western tourists, many of them seeking sexual relations with African men and women, discursive frames conflict, but they also resonate with and mimic each other. "Local" ideas about uncircumcised women not being able to control their sexuality and the "uncut" clitoris resembling the penis are seemingly frequently validated by the sexual experiences African men have with Western women, as well as with women from ethnic groups that do not practice female genital operations. Such women are seen and experienced as being sexually needy, overresponsive, and assertive. Thus, a curious resonance is established between Western discourses of liberated female sexuality and the relationship of the clitoris to sexual pleasure and agency and more "local" male discourses about the importance of removing the clitoris in order to bring sexuality under the woman's control as a means to ensure successful, socially reproductive sex.

Discourses in The Gambia on sexual responsiveness are also over-determined by international campaigns against female genital operations, national and international media coverage, pornographic films, and the stated views of tourists and other visitors. Many Gambian women and men are certainly cosmopolitan in their outlook in the sense that they are knowledgeable about other "cultures," have been exposed to competing discursive frames on sexuality and gender relations, may have lived overseas, and are engaged with the images and discourses produced by the media. Many Gambian men, in particular, know how to deploy different discursive frames in different contexts, and as Ahmadu makes clear we have to understand their expressed views about sexuality and circumcision in the context of the political economy of international aid (where money is available for eradication campaigns) and of tourism (where sex is an important source of income). The result, however, is both positive and negative forms of ambivalence about perceived differences rather than the recognition and valuation of cultural difference per se.

Considering the broader social-economic and political context of female genital operations makes it possible, as noted earlier, to analyze them as a set of practices. In this context, there is a clear need not just to focus on women and men as abstract sociological groups but also to analyze gender both as a sociological and symbolic category and as a lived relation (cf. H. L. Moore 1994). In this regard, we need as a minimum to locate gender in dynamic relation to forms of identification and experiences of embodiment and self, as well as marriage strategies, modes of livelihood, political institutions, state intervention, NGO discourses, and the like. Johansen (chapter 11 of this volume) shows how migration, low levels of male employment for Somalis in Norway, and consequent changes in the household division of labor have altered ideas about marriage, sexuality, and reproduction, with some informants reporting that sexuality and sexual satisfaction have become more of an issue within marriages. But changes in the nature of intimate relationships between women and men have to be seen not only in terms of certain features of political economy but also in the context of negative views of female genital operations in Norway, and concerns about possible state interventions in family life. Media exposés have made the members of immigrant cultures all too well aware not only of the way their "culture" is viewed by mainstream Norwegian society but also of how dominant discourses frame their cultural practices as "damaging," "inferior," "abusive," and so on (cf. Rogers and Talle, chapters 6 and 4 respectively of this volume). Thus, in considering female genital operations as a set of changing practices, we have to be able to analyze the interrelations between different scales, from self-understandings and gendered forms of identification, to the level of family life, marriage strategies, and interaction with the state and the wider society (Johnsdotter and Talle, chapters 5 and 4 respectively of this volume).

It is not just the analysis of the intersections of discourses and practices at different scales and of gender (both as a category and as a lived relation) that is at issue here, but the larger difficulty of the relationship between gender and agency. A number of authors in this volume criticize the way an unthinking focus on male domination or patriarchal control portrays women as passive victims of men. Such an assumption divorces women's actions and decisions from the context of daily practices and in so doing unintentionally trivializes them. How can we understand women's actions if they are reduced to simply doing what men tell them to do? More importantly, how can we account for the celebration and humor with which they greet girls who have successfully gone through circumcision, their tenacious adherence to "tradition" in some circumstances, and their ambivalence about whether to perform the operation on their daughters given what they know and their personal experiences of pain and suffering (Talle and Johnson, chapters 4 and 11 respectively of this volume)? What do women themselves mean when they say that they do things because "it is our culture," and what do anthropologists and others mean when they say "these women do it because it is their culture"?

There are a number of interrelated issues here. The first concerns the powerful discourse in the West that links women's agency to sexual freedom (Ahmadu, Boddy, and Rogers, chapters 12, 2, and 6 respectively of this volume). This makes female genital operations not only a modification of the body but also an attack on bodily integrity, on individual agency, and, ultimately, on the self. This accounts in large part for the moral outrage and horror genuinely felt by many opponents in the West. Women's bodies, however, are never free of larger significations, never just physical bodies. Rogers (this volume) gives a powerful account of how dominant discourses in Australia position circumcised women not as differently embodied but as "mutilated," and how the excision/removal of the clitoris, which in the dominant "white"/"Western" discourse represents agency and women's capacities as social/political subjects, acts to refigure circumcised women as bearers of "mutilated reason," as lacking the capacity to speak and to take political action on their own behalf. In the process, the bodies of uncircumcised "white" women are represented as normal, nonmutilated, and capable of agency. Talle (chapter 4 of this volume) discusses how the bodies of circumcised Somali women in London are bodies in pain, how the traces of pain from the original operation, defibulation, and childbirth are renewed and given different meanings by the pain of exile, displacement, the global and national debate on female genital operations, the interventions of the health service, and the gaze of outsiders on the street. Discourses shift sets of lived practices and these rework embodied understandings and forms of identification.

In the last thirty years much of feminist scholarship has been concerned with laying the groundwork for a theory of women's agency. The issue of female genital operations cuts right across this project because it is most often portrayed by opponents, many of whom are self-identified as feminists, as being an example of the subjugation of women to "tradition," "culture," "fundamentalism," "patriarchy," and "religious ideology." The role of the body in the making of self and its links to agency are complex, but as Rogers notes (see chapter 6 of this volume), the liberal, white opposition all too easily provides an account of the circumcised subject in the face of power as one whose agency is defective. What kind of alternative account can we give, therefore, of women's agency? There is a particular problem here because insofar as much feminist scholarship has criticized the unthought sexism and racism of liberalism and has provided specific critiques of universal theories of the subject, it still has to struggle with the fact that its own emancipatory project is in many ways a liberal one. This is because of an understanding of a self that assumes certain types of liberties, among the most important of which are the right to choose, to make oneself and thus to defend oneself and one's rights. This is one very powerful way of understanding the twentieth-century feminist slogan "The personal is the political." Within this model, male domination is at the very minimum an attack on self-determination.

Selves are not just a matter of choice or belief, however, but are bound up with other selves and with experiences, aspirations and desires. Feminist theory still finds it difficult to acknowledge and recognize the agency of female selves in contexts where agency is only conceived as possible within, and in fact entails the recognition of, complex sets of relations of autonomy, subordination, and dependence. This does not mean that feminist theory posits a subject who is free of subjectification. Much feminist theory is in fact a detailed account of the makings and remakings of gendered selves in the context of situated practices and forms of knowledge (cf. J. Butler 1990 and 1993; H. L. Moore 1994). However, as Saba Mahmood has argued, the notion of freedom is central to the imagined self of feminist agency. Feminist consciousness is about resisting dominant male cultural norms; the desire of the feminist self is to be free from relations of gender subordination (Mahmood 2001). The question of women's agency is made more problematic in the case of female genital operations because these operations are carried out by women and are often seen as demarcating a domain of women's power. For a feminist perspective, the question then arises as to why such women should be active in re-creating the grounds for their own subordination. The response is varied but often entails an argument that makes appeal to some notion of false consciousness (cf. Walley 1997), where women fail to recognize the conditions of their own subordination and, as a result, cannot be full agents. However, if we take the view that subjects as agents cannot preexist power relations, that they must necessarily be constituted within them, then we must recognize that it is the very relations of subordination that create the possibility both for subjectivity and for agency. Thus, the task is to strive analytically to recognize alternative forms of agency where they occur historically and within definitive relations of power, rather than to define some women as agents and others as lacking (Mahmood 2001).

Mahmood has argued in her analysis of Egyptian women involved in the mosque movement that one very important condition for agency is the idea that action does not arise out of natural dispositions but rather creates them. It is through repeated bodily acts that one trains desire and intellect to conform to cultural values and standards, and thereby evinces moral understanding (Mahmood 2001, 214). This is a form of self-making that is recognizable from the kind of argument made by Foucault in *Technologies of the Self,* a kind of aesthetic and moral self-fashioning that takes certain sorts of power and knowledge as transcendent (Foucault 1988). However, it is very far from the notion of self or agency espoused in much feminist writing. Its resonances with some of the connections established between identifications and female genital operations as forms of embodiment and self-fashioning in the context of specific relations of power are suggestive. Talle's discussion (chapter 4 of this volume) of how new forms of lived embodiment are arising for Somali women in London and how women, in some contexts, are refusing to circumcise their daughters, but simultaneously changing their comportment and dress to guard important cultural and religious values from the gaze of outsiders, to reposition those values for themselves in the context of the full glare of the globalized world, is a clear example of specific forms of self-fashioning and agency.

The anthropological challenge is to trace the connections, resonances, and recursive relationships between identifications, experiences of embodiment and self, and forms of agency. However, we need to do this not just for women who practice female genital operations, but also for those who oppose these practices. There is a need for a comparative anthropological project here. But we need to have a much more critical understanding of subjectivity and the discursive and lived relation to bodies, ethnicity, culture, and political economy of the opponents (Rogers, chapter 6 of this volume), because they are still too often treated as the "norm," as those who do not have "cultural traditions," as those whose forms of agency and reason are self-evident. The analysis of the relationship of clitoral sexuality to agency in the West is a starting point, as is the discussion of how many "Western" discourses continue to reposition themselves as the "normal" from which all difference is a variation. Such discourses should not, however, be simply glossed as a continuation of colonial discourses on "women" or "other cultures." To make this move disassociates these discourses from the social, economic, and political circumstances in which they are powerful today.

Recognizing continuity is crucial, but it is equally important that we should be aware of the differences. It is not enough simply to adhere to a position that says "racism is racism" or to say that "the 'other' is always constructed as the other of the West." We need to pay heed to the details of political economy and the changing power configurations in which forms of representation arise and discourses become powerful. We need to be alert to the specific circumstances and sets of practices in which groups who find themselves labeled as "mutilated," "migrant," "deviant," or "traditional," as well as those who label themselves "normal," "free," "tolerant," or "modern" are mutually implicated. We need a much more cogent analysis of power and its diverse effects than a general claim about "othering" gives us. It should be noted here that to make an argument that we need a detailed understanding of how and why particular discourses become powerful is not in any sense to endorse or justify them, but rather to take an essential step in establishing a critical genealogy.

What of those women who oppose female genital operations but are not white, Westerners, or feminists? How are we to understand the specific discursive fields and power relations within which they make choices as agents? Are we to assume that, unlike their sisters who continue to practice female genital operations, they have seen the light, given up their cultural traditions, and espoused liberal human rights!? In all the cultures and contexts of the world where female genital operations are practiced there are women and men who are opponents of these practices, but this does not mean that they are necessarily allying themselves with Western liberal traditions and ideas of human rights, or giving up on cultural and religious values (cf. Moghadam 1994). Their agency is not the result of having given up on false consciousness, but of setting forth new goals and aspirations in the context of changed ideas and circumstances. In many African countries, notably Kenya and The Gambia (cf. Hernlund 2000), women are involved in maintaining the rituals of female initiation and their associated teachings, but refraining from the actual physical operations. In other contexts, individuals are modifying the nature of the operations and setting them within emerging ritual forms. This process is not new, since female genital operations and their associated rituals have always changed over time (Walley 1997; Kratz, chapter 8 of this volume). If we locate the radical critique of oppositional discourses to female genital operations within an unexamined context of a general interrogation of Western racism, what frame are we forcing on oppositional non-Western voices? Even to set the enquiry in terms of the "West" versus the "rest" is to deploy fictive categories that we too often assume we know the meaning of, and thus we continue to divorce them from the actuality of contemporary power relations.

THE NATURE OF POLITICS

Female genital operations raise with particular force the question of the nature of politics in a globalized world. They focus our attention on the specific way in which the political is increasingly defined through a set of interlinked circuits that overdetermine the connections between culture, identity, and agency. While the debate on female genital operations might at first seem to be relatively narrow in its remit, it opens up a series of questions regarding the nature of contemporary cultural politics. In this regard the role of the state is key. Corinne Kratz and Charles Piot (chapters 8 and 7 respectively of this volume) both discuss asylum cases in the United States involving individuals seeking to avoid undergoing female genital operations. The national and international debates, especially the media coverage, provoked by these cases portrayed the individuals involved as pursuing personal freedom, as attempting to liberate themselves from oppressive cultural contexts. In the process, stereotypes of Africa and Africans were freely deployed, but particularly disturbing was the way African cultures were portrayed in the generality as patriarchal tribes with immutable cultural norms who oppress and mutilate their women.

The nature of the legal claims regarding asylum require that individuals be members of a social group that can be determined to be suffering persecution. This requirement had a variety of consequences in the specific cases involved, but it did have the impact of framing discursive constructions in terms of reified and abstract entities, notably that of culture. The legal cases thus relied to a significant extent on reifying and ossifying culture, something that resonated all too well with the stereotypes in media and public discourse. What these asylum cases affirm is how the production and circulation of knowledge in a globalized world depends on reified notions of difference. Despite the facts that extensive anthropological literature exists that could have been germane to the cases, and that other forms of expert testimony could have been available, the evidence produced was fragmentary, thin, and at considerable remove from direct experience of the cultures in question. Both Kratz and Piot take the view in this volume that the stereotypes and reified notions of culture deployed, in public debate, the media, and the court room, affected not only the standards of evidence but also the critical evaluation of that evidence.

What characterizes the globalized world is that everyone thinks they know about culture, and about the difference that cultural difference makes. Culture thus becomes a particular kind of reference point. In the case of the asylum seekers, they were widely depicted and discursively constructed as involved in a form of emancipatory agency akin to the liberatory forms of feminist agency discussed in this chapter. This certainly occluded any critical understandings of the individuals' motivations (Piot, chapter 7 of this volume) and focused attention on their struggle against cultural impositions at the expense of understanding the social and economic circumstances of their decisions to seek asylum in the United States. The heated debates surrounding these cases conclusively demonstrated that the recognition of cultural difference does not necessarily lead to new forms of hybrid cosmopolitanism, to a recognition of the value of cultural difference within an interconnected world, but tends rather to the reduction of difference to sets of autonomous reified units. Pluralism does not necessarily lead to recognition. This is, of course, the bind of multiculturalism, where the demand that all cultures should be equally recognized before the law results not in an understanding of the interconnections between cultures but instead emphasizes their differences as autonomous entities.

This is not to deny that cultural hybridization and interconnection are taking place as a result of globalization; clearly they are. However, whatever these forms of hybridization, cosmopolitan consciousness, and emerging secularisms are, they are everywhere accompanied by new forms of cultural fundamentalism, nationalism, and religious intolerance. Explaining this process poses a challenge, especially to feminism and to anthropology. Marilyn Strathern has suggested that anthropology and feminism have a tendency to undermine each other; where the one values difference and specificity, the other is premised on a universal basis for political action (Strathern 1987; see also Walley 1997; Piot, chapter 7 of this volume). Their relations are more intertwined then this binary analysis would suggest, however, because they are both based on forms of agency that retain a commitment to autonomy and ideas of self-fashioning. The notion of culture in anthropology—and indeed in the various discourses of contemporary cultural politics, both liberal and nonliberal—draws on the idea that humans make their own worlds, that they create understandings and moral realms for action. In this sense, the notion of culture presupposes a notion of agency based on self-fashioning or self-making within the context of group life, of community. Culture in many anthropological accounts is what makes us distinctively human, and it assumes that we can act in and on the world in a way that shapes it to our own purpose to a greater or lesser extent, and that makes us particular kinds of moral agents (cf. Cheah 1998). It is this notion of culture that so powerfully underlies identity politics and demonstrates why all forms of cultural fundamentalism, nationalism, and religious intolerance are based on strong premises regarding cultural autonomy, the right to be self-fashioning moral beings. There is more than a little irony in this, since such claims to cultural autonomy are the product of a critique of a universalist notion of culture; they are claims for an authentic tradition that is distinctive and is unoppressed by universalism, and yet they are based on a universalistic claim about autonomy and self-fashioning (Cheah 1998, 308).

The result is that all political claims for the recognition of distinctive life ways, beliefs, values, and so on are claims premised on the autonomy of cultures. In the context of globalization, and the social, economic, and political inequalities that both produce and are produced by it, such claims are given further force because it is so obvious that not all groups/societies/cultures in the world have equal access to the social, economic, and political forces that constitute the world system (Cheah 1998, 309). Thus, the more interconnected we all become, the more hybrid and more cosmopolitan, the more the calls for cultural autonomy will increase. Many activists in the developing world

implicitly recognize this interconnection when they argue that the eradication of female genital operations should take second place to the reduction of
poverty and international inequality. The point is equally well recognized by
those who use culturalist arguments—arguments based on authenticity and
autonomy—to counter international discourses on human rights and women's
rights: "[W]e have our own way of doing things that creates a distinctive moral
realm and requires recognition."

So the irony is that culture cannot be transcended by new forms of cosmopolitanism, secularism, or internationalism. Cultural pluralism is a failure in
its own terms because it is always based on preexisting ideas about authenticity
and autonomy which must needs undermine it. This is why we must agree with
Richard Shweder when he argues that female genital operations reveal the limits of pluralism and consensual politics, but disagree with him when he suggests
that this is only because they are such an extreme case of cultural difference
(Shweder 2000).

BIBLIOGRAPHY

Abankwah v. INS. 1999. 185 F.3d 18122 (2d Cir. 1999).

Abdalla, R. 1982. *Sisters in affliction: Circumcision and infibulation of women in Africa.* London: Zed Press.

Abdel Hadi, A. 1998. *We are decided: The struggle of an Egyptian village to eradicate female circumcision.* Cairo: Cairo Institute of Human Rights Studies.

———. 2006. "A community of women empowered: The story of Dier El Barsha." In *Female circumcision: Multicultural perspectives,* ed. R. Abusharaf. Philadelphia: University of Pennsylvania Press.

Abu Lughod, L. 1986. *Veiled sentiments: Honor and poetry in a Bedouin society.* Berkeley: University of California Press.

Abusharaf, R. 1999. "Beyond 'The External Messiah Syndrome': What are Sudanese people doing to end ritualized genital surgeries?" Paper presented at the Annual Meeting of the American Anthropological Association, session on Female Genital Cutting: Local Dynamics of Global Debates.

———. 2006. *Female circumcision: Multicultural perspectives.* Philadelphia: University of Pennsylvania Press.

Abusharaf, R. M. 1995. "Rethinking feminist discourses on female genital mutilation: The case of Sudan." *Canadian Woman Studies* 15:52–54.

———. 1996. "Revisiting feminist discourses on female infibulation: Responses from Sudanese indigenous feminists." Paper presented at the annual meeting of the American Anthropological Association, San Fransisco.

———. 1998. "Unmasking tradition: A Sudanese anthropologist confronts female 'circumcision' and its terrible tenacity." *The Sciences* 38:22–27.

———. 2000. "Revisiting feminist discourses on infibulation: Responses from Sudanese feminists." In *Female "circumcision" in Africa: Culture, controversy, and change,* ed. B. Shell-Duncan and Y. Hernlund. Boulder, CO: Lynne Rienner.

Accad, E. 1989. *L'Excisée.* Washington, DC: Three Continents Press.

Adams, M., M. Idris, N. Marshall, and T. Posthma. 1996. "Eritrean women's group education campaign against female circumcision (1993–1994)." Unpublished report.

Adan, A. H. 1996. "Women and words. The role of women in Somali oral literature." *Comparative Studies of South Asia, Africa, and the Middle East* 2:81–92. Durham, NC: Duke University Press [journal].

African Women's Working Group [on Female Circumcision] (AWWG). 1996a. "Accompanying statement to the distribution of the report on community legal information project on female circumcision."

———. 1996b. "Report on community legal information project on female circumcision."

———. 1997. "Important notice." Disseminated July–August, 1997

Ahlberg, B. M., I. Krantz, G. Lindmark, and M. Wasame. 2004. "'It is only a tradition': Making sense of eradication interventions and the persistence of female 'circumcision' within a Swedish context." *Critical Social Policy* 24:50–78.

———. 2005. "A reply to Johnsdotter and Essén." *Critical Social Policy* 25:591–596.

Ahlberg, B. M. 1994. "Is there a distinct African sexuality? A critical response to Caldwell." *Africa* 64:220–242.

Ahmadu, F. 1995. "Rites and wrongs: Perspectives of African women on female circumcision." *Pride*, April/May, 43–46.

———. 2000. "Rites and wrongs: An insider/outsider reflects on power and excision." In *Female "circumcision" in Africa: Culture, controversy, and change*, ed. B. Shell-Duncan and Y. Hernlund. Boulder, CO: Lynne Rienner.

———. 2005. "Cutting the anthill: The symbolic foundations of female and male circumcision rituals among the Mandinka of Brikama, The Gambia." Ph.D. diss., Department of Anthropology, London School of Economics.

Akou, H. M. 2004. "Nationalism without a nation: Understanding the dress of Somali women in Minnesota." In *Fashioning Africa: Power and the politics of dress*, ed. J. Allman. Bloomington: Indiana University Press.

Ali, A. M. 2003. "A study of the factors perpetuating infibulation among Somali Muslims in Mandera District, Kenya." Master's thesis, Kenyatta University.

All Africa Press Service. 1997. "Religous leader reaffirms opposition to female

Circumcision." All Africa Press Service. Cairo, August 4.

Allotey, P., L. Manderson, and S. Grover. 2001. "The politics of female genital surgery in displaced communities." *Critical Public Health* 11:189–201.

Almroth, L., V. Almaroth-Berggren, O. Mahmood Hassanein, N. El Hadi, S. S. Eldin Al-Said, S. S. Alamin Hsan, U. B. Lithell, and S. Bergstrom. 2000. "A community based study on the change of practice of female genital mutilation in a Sudanese village." *International Journal of Gynaecology and Obstetrics* 53:1455–1460.

———. 2001. "Male complications of female genital mutilation." *Social Science and Medicine* 53:1455–1460.

Almroth, L., H. Holmgren, V. Berggren, and S. Bergström. 2005. "Frågan om stympning av flickor fordrar uppmärksamhet och forskning" [The question of mutilation of girls requires attention and research]. *Läkartidningen* 102:2426–2427.

Alzate, H., and Z. Hoch. 1986. "The 'G spot' and 'female ejaculation': A current appraisal." *Journal of Sex and Marital Therapy* 12:211–220.

Amadiume, I. 1987. *African matriarchal foundations: The case of Igbo societies*. London: Karnak House.

American College of Obstetricians and Gynecologist s (ACOG) Committee Opinion. 1995. "Female genital mutilation." *International Journal of Gynaecology and Obstetrics* 49:209.

American Psychological Association. 1987. *Diagnostic and statistical manual of mental disorders*. 3rd ed. Washington, DC.

———. 1994. *Diagnostic and statistical manual of mental disorders*. 4th ed. Washington, DC.

Ammar, H. 1954. *Growing up in an Egyptian village: Silwa, Province of Assam*. London: Routledge and Kegan Paul.

Amnesty International. 1994. *Report*.

———. 1997a. *Australia. Deaths in custody: How many more?* International Secretariat.

———. 1997b. *Female genital mutilation: A human rights information pack*. AI Index: ACT 77/05/97.

Anokye, F. 1999. "Genital mutilation made in America." *The Ghanaian Chronicle*, May 24–25, p. 10.

Anonymous. 1982. "Female circumcision: Because it's always been done." *The Economist*, September 18, 42.

————. 1992. "Mutilation by any name." *The Economist*, April 25, 46.

————. 1999a. "Female genital cutting: Is it a crime or culture?" *The Economist*, February 13, 45.

————. 1999b. "U.S. professor exposes deceit on Ghana." *The Ghanaian Chronicle*, October 4, www.ghana.web.com/GhanaHomePage/NewsArchive/artikel.php3?ID=8748.

————. 2005. "Adelaide Abankwah" [entry under the category "Imposters"]. Wikpedia en.wikipedia.org/siki/Adelaide_Abankwah (accessed July 15, 2005).

Appadurai, A. 1990. "Disjuncture and difference in the global cultural economy." *Theory, Culture and Society* 7:295–310.

————. 1996. *Modernity at large: Cultural dimensions of globalization*. Minneapolis: University of Minnesota Press.

Appiah, K. A. 1992. *In my father's house: Africa in the philosophy of culture*. New York: Oxford University Press.

————. 1998. "Cosmopolitan patriots." In *Cosmopolitics: Thinking and feeling beyond the nation*, ed. P. Cheah and B. Robbins. Minneapolis: University of Minnesota Press.

Ardayfio-Schandorf, E., and K. Kwafo-Akoto. 1990. *Women in Ghana: An annotated bibliography*. Accra: Woeli Publication Services.

Ardener, S. 1986. "The representation of women in academic models." In *Visibility and power: Essays on women in society and development*, ed. L. Dube, E. Leacock, and S. Ardener. New York: Oxford University Press.

Aretun, A. 1998. *Bland sjalar och fotbollar—en studie av somaliska ungdomar, etnisk identitet och tilhörighet*. Institute of Social Anthropology, University of Göteborg.

Armstrong, S. 1991. "Female circumcision: Fighting a cruel tradition." *New Scientist* 129:42–47.

Arnfred, S. 2004. *Re-thinking sexualities in Africa*. Uppsala: Nordic Africa Institute.

Asad, T. 1999. "Religion, nation-state, secularism." In *Nation and religion: Perspectives on Europe and Asia*, ed. P. Van der Veer and H. Lehman. Princeton, NJ: Princeton University Press.

Assaad, M. B. 1980. "Female circumcision in Egypt: Social implications, current research, and prospects for change." *Studies in Family Planning* 11:3–16.

Atoki, M. 1995. "Should female circumcision continue to be banned?" *Feminist Legal Studies* 3:223–235.

Aziz, F. A. 1980. "Gynecologic and obstetric complications of female circumcision." *International Journal of Gynaecology and Obstetrics* 17:560–563.

Baasher, T. 1979. "Psychological aspects of female circumcision." In *Traditional practices affecting the health of women and children*, 71–105. Alexandria, Egypt: WHO/EMRO technical publication no. 1.

Babatunde, E. 1998. *Women's rites versus women's rights: A study of circumcision among the Ketu Yoruba of South Western Nigeria*. Trenton, NJ: Africa World Press.

Badawi, M. 1989. "Epidemiology of female sexual castration in Cairo, Egypt." *Truth Seeker*, July/August, 31–34.

Badri, A. E. S. 1984. "Female circumcision in the Sudan." *Ahfad Journal* 1:11–21.

Badri, G. 1979. "The views of gynaecologists, midwives and college students on female circumcision." In *proceedings of the symposium on the changing status of Sudanese Women*. Omdurman, Sudan: Ahfad University College for Women.

Bakr, S. A. 1982. "Circumcision and infibulation in the Sudan." *In Traditional practices affecting the health of women and children*, ed. T. Baasher, R.H.O. Bannermann, H. Rushwan, and I. Sharaf. Technical publication vol. 2, no. 2. Alexandria, Egypt: World Health Organization, Regional Office for the Eastern Mediterranean.

Balk, D. 1996. *Toward a demographic understanding of ritual female genital practices in the Sudan*. Program on Population, East-West Center.

————. 2000. "To marry and bear children? The demographic consequences of infibulation in Sudan." In *Female "circumcision" in Africa: Culture, controversy, and change*, ed. B. Shell-Duncan and Y. Hernlund, 55–72. Boulder, CO: Lynne Rienner.

Barbach, G. L. 1986. *For each other*. New York: Signet.

Bardach, A. L. 1993. "Tearing off the veil." *Vanity Fair*, August, 122–127, 154–158.

Barnes, V., and J. Boddy. 1994. *Aman: The story of a Somali girl*. Toronto: Knopf.

Basson, R. 2000. "The female sexual response: A different model." *Journal of Sex and Marital Therapy* 26:51–65.

Baumann, G. 1999. *The multicultural riddle: Rethinking national, ethnic, and religious identities*. New York: Routledge.

Beauvoir, S. de. 1953. *The second sex*. New York: Vintage Books.

Beidelman, T. O. 1997. *The cool knife: Imagery of gender, sexuality, and moral education in Kaguru initiation ritual*. Washington DC: Smithsonian Institution Press.

Bejin, A. 1986. "The decline of the psychoanalyst and the rise of the sexologist." In *Western sexuality*, ed. P. Aries and A. Bejin. Oxford: Basil Blackwell.

Bell, A. 1997. *The heart and mind in human sexual behavior*. Northvale, NJ: Jason Aronson.

Bell, K. 2005. "Genital cutting and Western discourses on sexuality." *Medical Anthropology Quarterly* 19 (2): 125–148.

Bell, R., and P. Bell. 1972. "Sexual satisfaction of married women." *Medical Aspects of Human Sexuality* 6:136–144.

Bentler, P., and W. Peeler. 1979. "Models of female orgasm." *Archives of Sexual Behavior* 8:405–423.

Berman, J., and L. Berman. 2005. http://www.hisandherhealth.com/jenniferbio.html.

Bird, C. S., and M. B. Kendall. 1980. "The Mande hero: Text and context." In *Explorations in African systems of thought*, ed. I. Karp and C. S. Bird. Washington, DC: Smithsonian Institution Press.

Bloul, R. A. 1996. "Victims or offenders? 'Other' women in French sexual politics." *European Journal of Women's Studies* 3:251–268.

Boddy, J. 1982. "Womb as oasis: The symbolic content of pharaonic circumcision in rural nothern Sudan." *American Ethnologist* 9:682–698.

————. 1989. *Wombs and alien spirits: Women, men, and the Zar cult in Northern Sudan*. Madison: University of Wisconsin Press.

————. 1991. "Body politics: Continuing the anti-circumcision crusade." *Medical Anthropology Quarterly* 5:15–17.

————. 1994. "Afterword: Some background to Aman." In *Aman: The Story of a Somali Girl*, ed. L. Barnes and J. Boddy. Toronto: Knopf.

————. 1995. "Managing tradition: "Superstition" and the making of national identity among Sudanese women refugees." In *The pursuit of certainty: Religious and cultural formulations*, ed. W. James. London: Routledge.

————. 1998a. "Remembering Amal: On birth and the British in Northern Sudan." In *Pragmatic Women and Body Politics*, ed. M. Lock and P. Kaufert. Cambridge: Cambridge University Press.

————. 1998b. "Violence embodied? Female circumcision, gender politics, and cultural aesthetics." In *Rethinking violence against women*, ed. R. E. Dobash and R. P. Dobash. Thousand Oaks, CA: Sage.

————. 2007. *Civilizing women: British crusades in colonial Sudan*. Princeton, NJ: Princeton University Press.

Bohlen, J. G. 1983. "State of the science in sexual physiological research." In *Challenges in sexual science*, ed. C. M. Davis. Philadelphia: Society for the Scientific Study of Sex.

Bonaparte, M. 1953. *Female sexuality*. New York: International Universities Press.

Bordo, S. 1989. "The body and the reproduction of femininity: A feminist appropriation of Foucault." In *Gender/body/knowledge: Feminist reconstructions of being and knowing*, ed. A. M. Jaggar and S. R. Bordo. New Brunswick, NJ: Rutgers University Press.

———. 1993. *Unbearable weight: Feminism, Western culture, and the body*. Berkeley: University of California Press.

Boulware-Miller. 1985. "Female circumcision: Challenges to the practice as a human rights violation." *Harvard Women's Law Journal* 8:155–177.

Bourdieu, P. 1977. *Outline of a theory of practice*, trans. R. Nice. Cambridge: Cambridge University Press.

———. 1986. "The forms of capital." In *Handbook of theory and research for the sociology of education*, ed. J. Richardson. New York: Greenwood Press.

———. 1990. *The logic of practice*. Stanford, CA: Stanford University Press.

———. 1991. *Language and symbolic power*. Ed. J. B. Thompson. Trans. G. Raymond and M. Adamson. Cambridge: Polity Press in association with Basil Blackwell.

Bourne, J., and T. Edmans. 2000. "Feminine sorrows: African women's health clinic in Waltham Forest, for women experiencing difficulties resulting from female genital mutilation." Community Health Project and Refugee Advice Centre, Redbridge and Waltham Forest Health Authority, London.

Boyle, E. H. 2002. *Female genital cutting: Cultural conflict in the global community*. Baltimore, MD: Johns Hopkins University Press.

Branigin, W., and D. Farah. 2000a. "Asylum seeker is imposter, INS says." *Washington Post*, December 20, A1.

———. 2000b. "Genital-mutilation woman exposed as a fraud."/ www.ghanaweb.com/ GhanaHomePage/NewsArchive/printnews.php?ID=12743 (accessed August 5, 2005).

Breitung, B. 1996. "Interpretation and eradication: National and international responses to female circumcision." *Emory International Law Review* 10 (2). www.law.emory.edu/ EILR/volumes/win96/breitung.html.

Broche-Due, V. 1993. "Making meaning out of matter: Perceptions of sex, gender and bodies among the Turkana." In *Carved flesh/cast selves: Gendered symbols and social practices*, ed. V. Broche-Due, I. Rudie, and T. Bleie. Oxford: Berg.

Brooks, G. E. 1993. "Historical perspectives on the Guinea-Bissau region, fifteenth to nineteenth centuries." In *Mansas, escavos, grumetes e gentio: Cacheu na encruzihada de civilizações* [Rulers, slaves, seamen, and African societies: Cacheu on the crossroads of civilization], ed. C. Lopes. Bissau, Guinea-Bissau: Institito Nacional de Estudos e Pesquisa.

Bruner, E. 1999. "Return to Sumatra: 1957, 1997." *American Ethnologist* 26:461–477.

Burgos, N., and Y. Diaz Perez. 1986. "An exploration of human sexuality in the Puerto Rican culture." *Journal of Social Work Human Sex* 4:135–150.

Burstyn, L. 1996. "Asylum in America: does fear of female genital mutilation qualify?" *Washington Post*, March 17, C5.

Butler, C. 1976. "New data about female sexual response." *Journal of Sex and Marital Therapy* 2:40–46.

Butler, J. 1990. *Gender troubles: Feminism and the subversion of identity*. London: Routledge.

———. 1993. *Bodies that matter*. London: Routledge.

Caldwell, J., and P. Caldwell. 1987. "The cultural context of high fertility in sub-Saharan Africa." *Population and Development Review* 13:409–434.

Carr, D. 1997. *Female genital cutting: Findings from the Demographic and Health Surveys Program*. Calverton, MD: Macro International.

Carreira, A. 1947. *Mandingas da Guiné Portuguesa* [Mandingas of Portuguese Guinea]. Lisbon: Sociedade Industrial de Tipografia Limitada.

Central Intelligence Agency. 2005. "Gunea-Bissau." *The world factbook*. Washington, DC: Central Intelligence Agency.

Chakrabarty, D. 1995. "Radical histories and question of Enlightenment rationism: Some critiques of subaltern studies." *Economic and Political Weekly*, April 8, 751–759.

Chalmers, B., and B. K. Hashi. 2000. "Somali women's birth experiences in Canada after earlier genital mutilation." *Birth* 27:227–234.

Chatterjee, P. 1993. *The nation and its fragments: Colonial and postcolonial histories.* Princeton, NJ: Princeton University Press.

Cheah, P. 1998. "Given culture." In *Cosmopolitics: Thinking and feeling beyond a nation*, ed. P. Cheah and B. Robbins. Minneapolis: University of Minnesota Press

Cheah, P., and B. Robbins. 1998. *Cosmopolitics: Thinking and feeling beyond the nation.* Minneapolis: University of Minnesota Press.

Chodorow, N. J. 1995. "Gender as a personal and cultural construction." *Signs: Journal of Women in Culture and Society* 23:516–543.

Clifford, J. 1988. *The predicament of culture: Twentieth-century ethnography, literature, and art.* Cambridge, MA: Harvard University Press.

Cohen, J., and C. H. Bledsoe. 2002. "Immigrants, agency, and allegiance: Some notes from anthropology and from law." In *Engaging cultural differences: The multicultural challenge in liberal democracies*, ed. R. Shweder, M. Minow, and H. R. Markus. New York: Russell Sage Foundation.

Cohen, J., M. Howard, and M. Nussbaum. eds. 1999. *Is multiculturalism bad for women?* Princeton, NJ: Princeton University Press.

Coleman, C. 1997. "The fight against female genital mutilation." *Self*, January, 126–129, 142–143.

Coleman, D. L. 1998. "The Seattle compromise: Multicultural sensitivity and Americanization." *Duke Law Journal* 47:717–783.

Collinet, P., D. Stien, D. Vinatier, and J. L. Leroy. 2002. "Management of female genital mutilation in Djibouti: The Peltier Hospital experience." *Acta Obstetrica et Gynecologica Scandinavica* 81:1074–1077.

Collins, P. H. 2000. *Black feminist thought.* 2nd ed. New York: Routledge.

Comaroff, J. 1985. *Body of power, spirit of resistance: The culture and history of a South African people.* Chicago: University of Chicago Press.

Comaroff, J., and J. Comaroff. 1993. "Introduction." In *Modernity and its malcontents: Ritual and power in postcolonial Africa*, ed. J. Comaroff and J. Comaroff. Chicago: University of Chicago Press.

Commonwealth of Australia. 1997. *Bringing them home: A guide to the findings and recommendations of the national inquiry into the separation of Aboriginal and Torres Straight Islander children from their families.* National Inquiry into the Separation of Aboriginal and Torres Strait Islander Children from their Families. Sydney, Australia: Human Rights and Equal Opportunity Commission.

Conference on Female Sexuality. 2000. Research presented at Conference on female sexuality, sora Maria, Oslo, May 12–13.

Cook, R. 1979. "Damage to physical health from pharaonic circumcision (infibulation) in females." In *Traditional practices affecting the health of women and children.* Alexandria, Egypt: World Health Organization WHO/EMRO technical publication no. 2.

Coomaraswamy, R. 2004. "Fighting violence against women as and international right." Paper presented at the University of Washington Speaker Series: Human Rights from the Bottom Up, Seattle, March 8.

Costello, M. 2004. "Two in U.S. accused of genital mutilation." http://www.womense-news.org/article.cfm/dyn/aid/1718.

Cowan, J. K., M.-B. Dembour, and R. Wilson, eds. 2001a. *Culture and rights: Anthropological perspectives.* Cambridge: Cambridge University Press.

———. 2001b. "Introduction." In *Culture and rights: Anthropological perspectives*, ed. J. K. Cowan, M. B. Dembour, and R. A. Wilson. Cambridge: Cambridge University Press.

Crawley, M. 2005. "Africa spurns female circumcision." *Christian Science Monitor*, April 4.

Csordas, T. S. 1994. "The body as representation and being-in-the-world." In *Embodiment and experience. The existential ground of culture and self*, ed. T. S. Csordas. Cambridge: Cambridge University Press.

Daffeh, J., S. Dumbuya, and A. Sosseh-Gaye. 1999. *Listening to the voice of the people: A situation analysis of female genital mutilation in The Gambia*. Banjul, The Gambia: WHO [World Health Organization], UNFPA [United Nations Fund for Population Activities], UNICEF [United Nations Children's Fund].

Dakubu, M. E. 1988. *The languages of Ghana*. London: Kegan Paul International for the International African Institute.

D'Alisera, J. 2004. *An imagined geography: Sierra Leonan Muslims in America*. Philadelphia: University of Pennsylvania Press.

da Mota, T. A. 1954. *Guiné Portuguesa*. Lisbon: Agéncia Geral do Ultramar.

D'Andrade, R. 1995. "Moral models in anthropology." *Current Anthropology* 36:399–408.

Daniluk, J. 1993. "The meaning and experience of female sexuality: A phenomenological analysis." *Psychology of Women Quarterly* 17:53–69.

Daniszewski, J. 1997. "Female circumcision ban nullified." *Los Angeles Times*, June 25.

Danticat, E. 2005. "A crime to dream." *The Nation*, May 2, 13–16.

Davidson, J., and N. Moore. 1994. "Guilt and lack of orgasm during sexual intercourse: Myth versus reality among college women." *Journal of Sex Education and Therapy* 20:153–174.

Delaney, C. 1990. The Hajj: Sacred and secular. *American Ethnologist* 17 (3): 513–530.

Dellenborg, L. 2004. "A reflection on the cultural meanings of female circumcision: Experiences from fieldwork in Casamance, Southern Senegal." In *Re-thinking sexualities in Africa*, ed. S. Arnfred. Uppsala: Nordic Africa Institute.

Dembour, M. B. 2001. "Following the movement of a pendulum: Between universalism and relativism." In *Culture and rights: Anthropological perspectives*, ed. J. K. Cowan, M. B. Dembour, and R. A. Wilson. Cambridge: Cambridge University Press.

D'Emilio, J., and E. Freedman. 1988. *Intimate matters: The history of sexuality in America*. New York: Harper and Row.

Derrick, L. 2001. "Genital landscaping, labia remodeling and vestal vagina: Female genital mutilation or female genital surgery?" *Jenda: A Journal of Culture and African Women Studies* 1. http://www.jendajournal.com/vol1.1/dvagina.html.

Derrida, J. 1981. *Positions*. Chicago: University of Chicago Press.

———. 1990. "The force of law: The mystical foundation of authority." *Cardozo Law Review* 11:921–1045.

de Sainte-Maurice, A. 1997. *Identidades reconstruidas: Cabo-verdianos em Portugal*. Oeiras: Celta Editora.

Dick, D. 2001. "Second to none? Australia and indigenous human rights." *Alternative Law Journal* 26:22–26.

Diop, N. J., and I. Askew. 2006. "Strategies for encouraging the abandonment of female genital cutting." In *Female circumcision: Multicultural perspectives*, ed. R. Abusharaf. Philadelphia: University of Pennsylvania Press.

Diop, N. J., M. M. Faye, A. Moreau, J. Cabral, H. Benga, F. Cisse, B. Mane, I. Baumgarten, and M. Melching. 2003. "The Tostan program: Evaluation of a community based education program in Senegal." Unpublished report.

Dirie, M., and G. Lindmark. 1991. "Female circumcision in Somalia and women's motives." *Acta Obstetrica et Gynecologica Scandinavica* 70:581–585.

Dopico, M. 1997. "Hear me talk." Honors dissertation, Department of Social Work, James Cook University, Australia.

Dorkenoo, E. 1994. *Cutting the rose—female genital mutilation: The practice and its prevention*. London: Minority Rights Group.

Dorkenoo, E., and S. Elworthy. 1992. *Female genital mutilation: Proposals for change.* London: Zed.

Douglas, M. 1966. *Purity and danger: An analysis of the concepts of pollution and taboo.* London: Routledge and Kegan Paul.

———. 1973. *Natural symbols.* New York: Vintage Press.

DuBois, M. 1991. "The governance of the Third World: A Foucaldian perspective on power relations in development." *Alternatives* 16:1–30.

Dugger, C. 1996a. "African ritual pain: Genital cutting." *New York Times*, October 5, A1.

———. 1996b. "New law bans genital cutting in United States." *New York Times*, October 12, A1.

———. 1996c. "A refugee's body is intact but her family is torn." *New York Times*, September 11, A1, 8–9.

———. 1996d. "U.S. frees African fleeing ritual mutilation." *New York Times*, April 25, A1, B7.

———. 1996e. "U.S. grants asylum to woman fleeing genital mutilation rite." *New York Times*, June 14, A1, B2.

———. 1996f. "Woman's plea for asylum puts tribal ritual on trial." *New York Times*, April 15, A1, B4.

Ebert, R. 2004. "Moolaade." *Chicago Sun Times*, December 3. http://rogerebert.suntimes.com/reviews.

Edgerton, R. 1989. *Mau Man: An African crucible.* New York: The Free Press.

Egan, T. 1994. "An ancient ritual and a mother's asylum plea." *New York Times*, March 4, B12.

Ehrenreich, B., and D. English. 1979. *For her own good: 150 years of the experts' advice to women.* Garden City, NY: Anchor Books.

El-Bashir, H. 2006. "The Sudan National Committee on the eradication of harmful traditional practices and the campaign against female mutilation." In *Female circumcision: Multicultural perspectives*, ed. R. Abusharaf. Philadelphia: University of Pennsylvania Press.

El Dareer, A. 1982a. "A study on prevalence and epidemiology of female circumcision to date." Paper delivered at seminar on traditional practices affecting the health of women and children in Africa, Alexandria, Egypt.

———. 1982b. *Woman, why do you weep? Circumcision and its consequences.* London: Zed Press.

El-Deefrawi, M. H., G. Lofty, K. F. Dandash, R. A. H., and M. Eyada. 2001. "Female genital mutilation and its psychosexual impact." *Journal of Sexual and Marital Therapy* 27:465–473.

El Hassan, A. M. 1990. "The influence of education on female circumcision." *Ahfad Journal* 7:70–73.

Elkan, E., and M. D. Pinner. 1948. "Evolution of female orgastic ability: A biological survey." *International Journal of Sexology* 2:1–13.

Ellis, H. 1933. *Psychology of sex: A manual for students.* New York: Long and Richard Smith.

Ellison, C. 1984. "Harmful beliefs affecting the practice of sex therapy with women." *Psychotherapy* 21:327–334.

El Saadawi, N. 1980. *The hidden face of Eve.* London: Zed Press.

———. 1982. *The hidden face of Eve.* Boston: Beacon Press.

El-Sohl, C. F. 1993. "Be true to your culture: Gender tensions among Somali Muslims in Britain." *Immigrants and Minorities* 12:21–46.

Engel, J., M. Saracino, and M. Bergen. 1993. "Sexuality education." In *Handbook of family life education: The practice of family life education*, ed. M. E. Arcus, J. D. Schvaneveldt, and J. J. Moss. Vol. 2. Thousand Oaks, CA: Sage.

Ensler, E. 2000. *The vagina monologues.* London: Virago.

Erlich, M. 1991. "Circoncision, excision et racisme" [Circumcision, excision and reacism]. *Nouvelle Revue D'Ethnopsychiatrie* 18:125–140.

Essén, B. 2001. "Perinatal mortality among immigrants from Africa's Horn: The importance of experience, rationality, and tradition for risk assessment in preganacy and childbirth." Ph.D. diss., Department of Obstetrics and Gynecology, Malmo University Hospital, Lund University.

Essén, B., B. Bodker, N.O. Sjoberg, J. Langhoff-Roos, G. Greisen, P.O. Ostergren, and S. Gudmundsson. 2002. "Are some perinatal deaths in immigrant groups linked to sub-optimal perinatal care services?" *British Journal of Obstetrics and Gynaecology* 109:677–682.

Essén, B., and S. Johnsdotter. 2004. "Female genital mutilation in the West: Traditional circumcision versus genital cosmetic surgery." *Acta Obstetrica et Gynecologica Scandinavica* 83:611–613.

Essén, B., S. Johnsdotter, B. Hovelius, S. Gudmundsson, N.O. Sjoberg, J. Friedman, and P. O. Ostergren. 2000. "Qualitative study of pregnancy and childbirth experiences in Somalian women resident in Sweden." *British Journal of Obstetrics and Gynaecology* 107:1507–1512.

Essén, B., N.-O. Sjöberg, S. Gudmundsson, P.-O. Östergren, and P. G. Lindqvist. 2005. "No association between female genital circumcision and prolonged labour: a case control study of immigrant women giving birth in Sweden." *European Journal of Obstetrics and Gynecologal Reproduction Biology* 121:182–185.

Essén, B., and C. Wilken-Jensen. 2003. "How to deal with female circumcision as a health issue in the Nordic countries." *Acta Obstetrica et Gynecologica Scandinavica* 86:683–686.

Fábos, A. H. 2001. "Embodying transition: FGC, displacement, and gender-making for Sudanese in Cairo." *Feminist Review* 69:90–110.

Fadel, U., P. Hervik, and G. Vestgaard. 2000. "De besvaerlige somaliere" [The troublesome Somalis]. In *Den generende forskjellighed. Danske svar paa den stigende multikuluralism* [Embarrassing difference: Danish responses to growing multiculturalism], ed. P. Hervik. Copenhagen: Hans Reitzels Forlag.

Falcon, M. 2000. "Female genital surgery goes public." *USA Today*, March 3. In *Jenda: A Journal of Culture and African Women Studies* (2001) 1. http://www.jendajournal.com/vol1.1/dvagina.html.

Falk Moore, S. 1994. "The ethnography of the present and the analysis of process." In *Assessing cultural anthropology*, ed. R. Borofsky. New York: McGraw-Hill.

Family Law Council. 1994a. *Female genital mutilation: A discussion paper*. Canberra, Australia.

———. 1994b. *Female genital mutilation: A report to the attorney-general*. Canberra, Australia.

Fausto-Sterling, A. 1997. "How to build a man." In *The gender/sexuality reader*, ed. R. Lancaster and M. di Leonardo. New York: Routledge.

Federation of Feminist Women's Health Centre. 1981. *A new view of a women's body*. New York: Simon and Schuster.

Ferguson, J. 1990. *The anti-politics machine: "Development," depoliticization, and bureaucratic power in Lesotho*. Minneapolis: University of Minnesota Press.

Fernandez-Romano, C. 1999. "The banning of female circumcision: Cultural imperialism or a triumph for women's rights?" *Temple International and Comparative Law Journal* 1:137–161. http://www.heinonline.org.HOL/page?handle=hein.journals/tclj13 (accessed May 9, 2006).

Fields, N. 1983. "Satisfaction in long-term marriages." *Social Work* 28:37–41.

Figenshou, T. U. 2000. *Er dette innvandrernes tilstand? Rikets tilstand og kvinnelig omskjæring*. Bachelor's thesis, University of Oslo, Faculty of Journalism.

Fisher, S. 1973. *The female orgasm: Psychology, physiology, fantasy*. New York: Basic Books.

Fokkena, L. 1994. "Female genital mutilation: The circumcising of women stirs up worldwide debate." Originally published in *Acculturation* in 1994. www.avalon.net/~laurafo.fgm.htm.

Ford, C. S., and F. Beach. 1951. *Patterns of sexual behavior*. New York: Harper.

Forrest, J. B. 1992. *Guinea-Bissau: Power, conflict and renewal in a West African nation.* Boulder, CO: Westview Press.

Foucault, M. 1973. *The order of things: An archeology of the human sciences.* New York: Vintage Books.

———. 1979. *Discipline and punish.* New York: Vintage.

———. 1980. *Power/knowledge: Selected interviews and other writings, 1972–1977.* New York: Pantheon Books.

———. 1988. *Technologies of the self.* London: Tavistock.

———. 1990. *The history of sexuality: An introduction.* First published in English in 1978. Vol. 1. New York: Vintage.

———. 2002. *Seksualitetens historie.* Oslo: EXIL.

Fox-Rushby, J., and M. Parker. 1995. "Culture and the assessment of health-related quality of life." *European Review of Applied Psychology* 45:257–263.

Fraser, D. 1995. "The first cut is (not) the deepest: Deconstructing "female genital mutilation" and the criminalization of the other." *Dalhousie Law Journal* 18:310–375.

Fraser, N. 1989. *Unruly practices: Power, discourse and gender in contemporary social theory.* Minneapolis: University of Minnesota Press.

Friedman, J. 1995. "Global system, globalization and the parameters of modernity." In *Global Modernities*, ed. S. L. Mike Featherstone and Roland Robertson, 69–90. London: Sage.

Gable, E. 1995. "The decolonization of consciousness: Local skeptics and the 'will to be modern' in a West African village." *American Ethnologist* 22 (2): 242–257.

Gallagher, C., and T. Laqueur, eds. 1987. *The making of the modern body.* Berkeley: University of California Press.

Gallagher, W. 1986. "The etiology of orgasm." *Discover* 7:51–59.

Gallard, C. 1995. "Female genital mutilation in France." *British Medical Journal* 310:1592–1593.

Gallo, P. G., and M. Abdisamed. 1985. "Female circumcision in Somalia: Anthropological traits." *Anthropologische Anzeiger* 43:311–326.

Gardetto, D. C. 1993. "Engendered sensations: Social construction of the clitoris and female orgasm, 1650–1975." Ph.D. diss., University of California, Davis, 1992. Abstract in *Dissertation Abstracts International*, A: The Humanities and Social Sciences 53, 9 (March): 3372 A.

Geertz, C. 1973. *The interpretation of cultures.* New York: Basic Books.

———. 1983. "From the native's point of view: On the nature of anthropological understanding." In *Local knowledge: Further essays in interpretive anthropology*, ed. C. Geertz. New York: Basic Books.

Geographical. 1991. "Female circumcision exposed in Britain." *Geographical* [magazine of the Royal Geographic Society] 63:16–18.

Geschiere, P. 1997. *The modernity of witchcraft: Politics and the occult in postcolonial Africa.* Charlottesville: University of Virginia Press.

Ghadially, R. 1991. "All for 'Izzat': The practice of female circumcision among Bohra Muslims." *Manushi* 66.

Ghanian [sic] found guilty in mutilation hoax. 2003. ghanaweb.com/GhanaHomePage/News/Archive/printnews.php?ID=31605 (accessed August 8, 2005).

Giddens, A. 1992. *The transformation of intimacy: Sexuality, love and eroticism in modern societies.* Oxford: Polity Press.

———. 1994. "Living in a post-traditional society." In *Reflexive modernization: Politics, tradition and aesthetics in modern social order*, ed. U. Beck, A. Giddens, and S. Lash. Stanford, CA: Stanford University Press.

Gilliam, A. 1991. "Women's equality an national liberation." In *Third World women and the politics of feminism*, ed. C. T. Mohanty, A. Russo, and L. Torres, 215–236. Bloomington: University of Indiana Press.

Giorgis, B. W. 1981. *Female circumcision in Africa.* Addis Ababa: United Nations Economic Commission for Africa, African Training and Research Centre for Women.

Glaberson, W. 2002. "Woman who sought U.S. asylum is arrested." *New York Times*, September 10, B3.

Gluckman, M. 1958. *Analysis of a social situation in modern Zululand.* Rhodes-Livingston Paper no. 28. Manchester, UK: Manchester University Press. (Originally published 1940)

Godelier, M. 1986. *The .mental and the material: Thought economy and society.* London: Verso.

Goodman, E. 1996. "Mutilated by her culture." *Boston Globe*, April 7, 69.

Gordon, D. 1991. "Female circumcision and genital operations in Egypt and the Sudan: A dilemma for medical anthropology." *Medical Anthropology Quarterly* 5:3–14.

Gorov, L. 1999. "The latest fad from La-La Land: A 'designer vagina.'" *Jenda: A Journal of Culture and African Women Studies* 1. http://www.jendajournal.com/v011/dvagina.html.

Gosselin, C. 1996. "The politics of doing feminist ethnography on excision." Unpublished paper, University of Toronto.

———. 1999. "'Light like fire': Excision and women's sexuality in urban Mali." Paper presented at the Annual Meeting of the American Anthropological Association, session on Female Genital Cutting: Local Dynamics of a Global Debate, Chicago.

———. 2000a. "Feminism, anthropology and the politics of excision in Mali: Global and local debates in a postcolonial world." *Anthropologica* 42:43–60.

———. 2000b. "Handing over the knife: Numu women and the campaign against excision in Mali." In *Female "circumcision" in Africa: Culture, controversy, and change*, ed. B. Shell-Duncan and Y. Hernlund. Boulder, CO: Lynne Rienner.

Gotaas, N. 1996. *Farger i natten: Sosial kategorisering og stereotypisering i møtet mellom afrikanere og nordmenn på utesteder i Oslo* [Colors in the night: Social categorization and stereotyping in the encounter between Africans and Norwegians inpublic places in Oslo]. NIBR report 1966:19. Oslo: Norwegian Institute for Urban and Regional Research.

Gottlieb, A. 2002. "Interpreting gender and sexuality: Approaches from cultural anthropology." In *Exotic no more: Anthropology on the front lines*, ed. J. MacClancy. Chicago: University of Chicago Press.

Grande, E. 2004. "Hegemonic human rights and African resistance: Female circumcision in broader comparative perspective." *Global Jurist Frontiers* 4:article 3. http://www.bepress.com/gj/frontiers/v0114/iss2/art3.

Greer, G. 1999. "Why genital cutting goes on." *Newsweek* (Atlantic edition), July 5, 64.

Grewal, I., and C. Kaplan. 1996. "*Warrior Marks*: Bolab Womanism's neocological discourse in multicultural context." *Camera Obscura: A Journal of Feminism, Culture and Media Studies* 39:5–33.

Griaule, M. 1965. *Conversations with Ogotenmêli: An introduction to Dogon religious ideas.* London: Oxford University Press for the International African Institute.

Griffiths, D. 1997. "Somali refugees in Tower Hamlets: Clanship and new identities." *New Community* 23:5–24.

Grisaru, N., S. Lezer, and R. H. Belmaker. 1997. "Ritual female genital surgery among Ethiopian Jews." *Archives of Sexual Behavior* 26:211–215.

Grise, M. 2001. "'Scarred for life?' Representations of Africa and female genital cutting on American television and news magazines." In *Images of Africa: Stereotypes and Realities*, ed. D. Mengara. Trenton, NJ: Africa World Press.

Grosz, E. 1987. "Notes toward a corporeal feminism." *Australian Feminist Studies* 5:1–16.

———. 1990. "Inscriptions and body maps: Representations and the corporeal." In *Feminine/Masculine and Representation*, ed. T. Threadgold and A. C. Francis. St. Leonards, New South Wales: Allen and Unwin.

———. 1994. *Volatile bodies: Toward a corporeal feminism*. St. Leonards, New South Wales: Allen and Unwin.

Gruenbaum, E. 1982. "The movement against clitoridectomy and infibulation in Sudan: Public health policy and the women's movement." *Medical Anthropology Newsletter* 13:4–12.

———. 1988. "Reproductive ritual and social reproduction: Female circumcision and the subordination of women in Sudan." In *Economy and class in Sudan*, ed. N. O'Neill and J. O'Brien. Avebury, UK: Aldershot.

———. 1991. "The Islamic movement, development, and health education: Recent changes in the health of rural women in central Sudan." *Social Science and Medicine* 33:637–645.

———. 1996. "The cultural debate over female circumcision: The Sudanese are arguing this one out for themselves." *Medical Anthropology Quarterly* 10:455–475.

———. 2000. "Is female 'circumcision' a maladaptive cultural pattern?" In *Female "circumcision" in Africa: Culture, controversy, and change*, ed. B. Shell-Duncan and Y. Hernlund. Boulder, CO: Lynne Rienner.

———. 2001. *The female circumcision controversy: An anthropological perspective*. Philadelphia: University of Pennsylvania Press.

Gullestad, M. 1992. *The art of social relations. Essays on culture, social action and everyday life in modern Norway*. Oslo: Scandinavian University Press.

Gunning, I. R. 1991. "Modernizing customary international law: The challenge of human rights." *Virginia Journal of International Law* 31:211–247.

———. 1992. "Arrogant perception, world-traveling and multicultural feminism: The case of female genital surgeries." *Columbia Human Rights Law Review* 23:188–248.

———. 2002. "Female genital surgeries: Eradication measures at the Western local level—a cautionary tale." In *Genital cutting and transnational sisterhood: Disputing U.S. polemics*, ed. S. James and C. Robertson. Urbana: University of Illinois Press.

Gupta, A., and J. Ferguson. 1992. "Beyond 'culture': Space, identity, and the politics of difference." *Cultural Anthropology* 7 (1): 6–23.

Gylseth, S. 2001. *Metoder og presentasjonsformer i Kadrasaken* [Methods and forms of representation in the Kadra case]. Oslo: Høyskolen i Oslo.

Hage, G. 1998. *White nation: Fantasies of white supremacy in multicultural society*. New South Wales: Pluto Press.

Hale, S. 1994. "A question of subjects: The 'female circumcision' controversy and the politics of knowledge." *Ufahamu* 22:26–35.

Hall, M., and B. A. Ismail. 1981. *Sisters under the sun: The story of Sudanese women*. London: Longman.

Halldén, A. 1979. *Kvinnlig omskärelse [female circumcision]*. SIDA [Swedish International Development Agency] LF/ALLF 171 79 049.

Hamilton, L. 1999. "A theory of true interests." *Government and Opposition* 34:516–46.

Hannerz, U. 1990. "Cosmopolitans and locals in world culture." *Theory, Culture and Society* 7:237–251.

Hansen, J. O. 2005. "Ancient rite or a wrong? Genital cutting of girls becomes an issue in Georgia, nationwide." *Atlanta Journal-Constitution*, March 2.

Hartsock, N. 1998. *The feminist standpoint revisited*. Boulder, CO: Westview Press.

Hashi, K. O., and J. Silver. 1994. "No words can express: Two voices on female genital mutilation." *Canadian Woman Studies* 14:62–64.

Hassan, A. A. R. 2001. "Summary on the impacts of the research on female genital mutilation (FGM) psychosocial-sexual consequences and attitude change in Khartoum North and East Nile." Sudan National Committee on Traditional Practices.

Hastrup, K. 1995. *A passage to anthropology. Between experience and theory.* London: Routledge.

Hastrup, K., and P. Hervik, eds. 1994. *Social experience and anthropological knowledge.* London: Routledge.

Hayes, R. O. 1975. "Female genital mutilation, fertility control, women's roles, and the patrilineage in modern Sudan: A functional analysis." *American Ethnologist* 2:617–633.

Hays, T. 2002. "Mutilation horror, or hoax?" *CBS News.* January 14. http://www.cbsnews.com/stories/2003/01/14/national/main536361.shtml?CMP=ILC-SearchStories.

Heald, S. 1995. "The power of sex: Some reflections on the Caldwells' African sexuality thesis." *Africa* 65:489–505.

———. 1999. *Manhood and morality: Sex, violence and ritual in Gisu society.* New York: Routledge.

Hedin, C. 1994. *Islam i vardagen och världen [Islam in everyday life and in the world].* Stockholm: Arena.

Helander, B. 1988. "The slaughtered camel. Coping with fictitious descent among the Hubeer of southern Somalia." Ph.D. diss., Department of Social Anthropology, University of Uppsala.

Heller, E. 2003. *Broken silence.* Copenhagen: A film by Heller Production.

Hernlund, Y. 1999. "Ritual negotiations and cultural compromise: an alternative initiation in The Gambia." Paper presented at the Annual Meeting of the American Anthropological Association, session on Female Genital Cutting: Local Dynamics of a Global Debate, Chicago.

———. 2000. "Cutting without ritual and ritual without cutting: Female 'circumcision' and the re-ritualization of initiation in the Gambia." In *Female "circumcision" in Africa: Culture, controversy, and change,* ed. B. Shell-Duncan and Y. Hernlund. Boulder, CO: Lynne Rienner.

———. 2003. "Winnowing culture: Negotiating female 'circumcision' in The Gambia." Ph.D. diss., Department of Anthropology, University of Washington.

Hicks, E. K. 1982. *Infibulation: Female mutilation in Islamic northeastern Africa.* New Brunswick, NJ: Transaction Publishers.

Hill, M. T. 2003. "Development as empowerment." *Feminist Economics* 9:117–135.

Hinge, H. 1995. "Mild omskaering er okay" [Mild circumcision is okay]. *Exil* 4:28–31.

Hite, S. 1976. *The Hite Report: A nationwide study of female sexuality.* New York: Dell.

Hobsbawm, E., and T. Ranger, eds. 1983. *The invention of tradition.* Cambridge: Cambridge University Press.

Hoch, Z. 1986 "Vaginal erotic sensitivity by sexological examination." *Acta Obstetrica et Gynecologica Scandinavica* 65:767–773.

Holy, L. 1991. *Religion and custom in a Muslim society: The Berti of Sudan.* Cambridge: Cambridge University Press.

Honig, B. 1999. "My culture made me do it." In *Is multiculturalism bad for women?* ed. J. Cohen, M. Howard, and M. Nussbaum. Princeton, NJ: Princeton University Press.

hooks, b. 1981. *Ain't I a woman? Black women and feminism.* Boston: South End Press.

Horowitz, C., and C. Jackson. 1997. "Female 'circumcision': African women confront American medicine." *Journal of General Internal Medicine* 12:491–499.

Horton, R. 1967. "African traditional thought and Western science." *Africa* 37:50–71.

Hosken, F. 1978. "The epidemiology of female genital mutilation." *Tropical Doctor* 8:150–156.

———. 1982. *The Hosken Report: Genital and sexual mutilation of females.* 3rd ed. Lexington, MA: Women's International Network News.

———. 1993. *The Hosken Report: Genital and sexual mutilation of females.* 5th ed. Lexington, MA: Women's International Network News.

————. n.d. "Genital and sexual mutilation of females." Women's International Network News summary distributed at United Nations Decade for Women Conference, Nairobi, 1985.

Hosken, F. P. 1994. Editorial, "Male violence against women—A growing global cancer." *Women's International Network News* 20:1–2.

————. 1995. *The universal childbirth picture book*. Lexington, MA: Women's International Network News.

Hu, W. 1999. "Woman fearing mutilation savors freedom." *New York Times*, August 20, A21.

Huelsman, B. R. 1976. "An anthropological view of the clitoral and other female genital mutilations." In *The Clitoris*, ed. T. P. Lowry and T. S. Lowry. St. Louis, MO: Warren Green.

Human Rights Dialogue. 2003. "Introduction." In *Human Rights Dialogue 2.10*, http://www.cceia.org/viewMedia.php/prmID/1044.

Hunt, M. 1974. *Sexual behavior in the 1970s*. New York: Dell.

Hurlbert, D. F. 1991. "The role of assertiveness in female sexuality: A comparative study between sexually assertive and sexually non-assertive women." *Journal of Sex and Marital Therapy* 17:183–190.

————. 1993. "A comparative study using orgasm consistency training in the treatment of women reporting hypoactive sexual desire." *Journal of Sex and Marital Therapy* 19:41–55.

Idris, M. (on behalf of the AWWG). 1996. Letter to Shirley Pinnell (DHS).

Ignatieff, M. 1999. "Whose universal values? Crisis in human rights." Amsterdam: Praemium Erasmianum Foundation.

Immigration and Refugee Board. 1996. *Guideline 4: Women refugee claimants fearing gender-related persecution, chairperson's guidelines*. Ottawa, Canada, November 13.

In Re: Abankwah v. INS (2d Cir. 1999), A74–881–776 (BIA 1998).

In Re: Kasinga, A73-A76–695 (BIA 1996).

————. Reply Brief for Respondent.

————. Transcript of hearing, www.courttv.com/library/rights/mutilation/html.

Ismail, N.H.A. 1999. *Urinary leakage and other complications of female genital mutilation(FGM) among Somali girls in Sweden*. Degree project report series. Uppsala, Sweden: Uppsala University.

Ivan, P. 1997. "Female circumcision: Reasons, rights and relativism." Ph. D. diss., Department of Philosophy, University of Ottawa.

Jackson, M. 1977. *The Kuranko: Dimensions of social reality in a West African society*. London: C. Hurst.

————. 1998. *Minima ethnographica: Intersubjectivity and the anthropological project*. Chicago: University of Chicago Press.

Jacobs, A. 1999. "U.S. frees African woman who fled genital cutting." *New York Times*, July 20, B3.

James, S., and C. Robertson. eds. 2002. *Genital cutting and transnational sisterhood: Disputing U.S. polemics*. Urbana: University of Illinois Press.

Jayne, C. 1981. "A two dimensional model of female sexual response." *Journal of Sex and Marital Therapy* 7:3–30.

Jen-Loy. n.d. "Pushing the perfect pussy." *Jenda: A Journal of Culture and African Women Studies*, 1:http://www.jendajournal.com/v011.1/dvagina.html.

Johansen, R. E. B. 1992. *Humor og seksualitet blant norsk ungdom* [Humor and sexuality among Norwegian youth]. NAVF's Program for Ungdomsforskning. UNGforsk, report n0.2/92. Oslo.

————. 2002. "Pain as a counterpoint to culture: Toward an analysis of pain associated with infibulation among Somali immigrants in Norway." *Medical Anthropology Quarterly* 16:312–340.

————. 2006a. "Experiences and perceptions of pain, sexuality and childbirth: A study of female genital cutting among Somalis in Norwegian exile, and their health providers." Ph.D. diss., medical anthropology, Institute of General Practice and Social Medicine, University of Oslo.

————. 2006b. "Care for infibulated women giving birth in Norway: An anthropological analysis of health workers management of a medically and culturally unfamiliar issue." *Medical Anthropology Quarterly* 20 (4): 516–544.

Johansen, R. E. B., Barre A. Vangen, S; Sundby S. 2004. "Bare et lite snitt—Ulike perspektiver ved behandling av kvinner som er omskåret/infibulert" [Just a small cut: Different perspectives on treating women who have been circumcised/infibulated]. *Tidsskr Nor Lægeforen* [Journal of the Norwegian Medical Association] 124:2506–2508 .

Johnsdotter, S. 2002. "Created by God: How Somalis in Swedish exile reassess the practice of female circumcision." Ph.D. diss., Department of Social Anthropology, Lund University.

————. 2004. "FGM in Sweden: Swedish legislation regarding 'female genital mutilation' and implementation of the law." European Commission Daphne Project research report, Lund University.

Johnsdotter, S., A. Carlborm, A. Elmi, and A. O. Geesdiir. 2000. *Som gud skapade oss: Forhallningssätt till kvinnlig omskärelse bland somalier i Malmo [As we were created by God: Attitudes to female circumcision among Somalis in Malmo].* Malmo: Program Sexuell hälsa.

Johnsdotter, S., and B. Essén. 2005. "It *is* only a tradition: Making sense of Swedish Somalis' narratives of female circumcision and avoiding submission to hegemonic political discourse." *Critical Social Policy* 25:578–596.

Johnson, D., and G. Zdenowski. 2000. "Mandatory justice: Compulsory imprisonment in the Northern Territory." *Australian Centre for Independent Journalism* 145.

Johnson, M. 2000. "Becoming a Muslim, becoming a person: Female 'circumcision,' religious identity, and personhood in Guinea-Bissau." In *Female "circumcision" in Africa: Culture, controversy, and change*, ed. B. Shell-Duncan and Y. Hernlund. Boulder, CO: Lynne Reinner.

————. 2002. "Being Mandinga, being Muslim: transnational debates on personhood and religious identity in Guinea-Bissau and Portugal." Ph.D. diss., Department of Anthropology, University of Illinois.

————. 2006. "'The proof is on my palm': Debating ethnicity, Islam, and ritual in a new African diaspora." *Journal of Religion in Africa* 36 (1): 50–77.

Johnson, R. 1999. "Um ritual selvagem: Uma conversa entreas modelos Somalis Waris Dirie e Iman" [Victim of a savage ritual: A conversation with Somali models Waris dirie and Iman]. *Pública* 155 (May 9): 27–34.

Joseph, R. 2002. "War, state-making, and democracy in Africa." In *Beyond state crisis: Africa and post-Soviet Eurasia in comparative perspective*, ed. M. Beissinger and C. Young. Washington, DC: Woodrow Wilson Center Press.

Kaphle, S. R. 2000. *Report of qualitative research on the communication channels in use in Somalia.* Report for UNICEF Somalia office, July–December 2000.

Kaplan, C. 1999. "Resisting biomedicine: Intersex activism and transnational FGM discourse." Paper presented at the Annual Meeting of the American Anthropological Association, session on Female Genital Cutting: Local Dynamics of a Global Debate, Chicago.

Kaplan, D., S. Lewis, and J. Hammer. 1993. "Is it torture or tradition?" *Newsweek*, December 20, 124.

Kaplan, H. 1974. *The new sex therapy.* New York: Brunner and Mazel.

Kapur, R. 2002. "The tragedy of victimization rhetoric: Resurrecting the 'native' subject in international/post-colonial feminist legal politics." *Harvard Human Rights Journal* 15:1–37.

Karim, M. 1994. *Circumcisions and mutilations: Male and female.* Cairo: National Population Council.

Karim, M., and R. Ammar. 1965. *Female circumcision and sexual desire.* Cairo: Ains Shams University Press.

———. 1966. "Female circumcision and sexual desire." *Shams Medical Journal* 17:2–39.

Kassamali, N. J. 1998. "When modernity confronts traditional practices: Female genital cutting in Northeast Africa." In *Women in Muslim societies: Diversity within unity*, ed. H. L. Bodman and N. Tohidi. Boulder, CO: Lynne Rienner.

Kassindja, F., and L. M. Bashir. 1998. *Do they hear you when you cry.* New York: Delacorte Press.

Keesling, B. 1999. "Beyond orgasmatron." *Psychology Today* 32:58.

Kellner, N. 1993. "Under the knife: Female genital mutilations as child abuse." *Journal of Juvenile Law* 14:118–132.

Kennedy, J. G. 1978. "Circumcision and excision ceremonies." In *Nubian ceremonial life*, ed. J. Kennedy. Berkeley: University of California Press.

Kéré, L. A., and I. Tapsoba. 1994. "Charity will not liberate women." In *Private decisions, public debate*. London: Panos Press.

Khattab, H. 1996. *Women's perceptions of sexuality in rural Giza.* Monographs in reproductive health. Cairo: The Population Council.

Kinsey, A., W. Pomeroy, and C. Martin. 1953. *Sexual behavior in the human female.* Philadelphia: Saunders.

Kirby, V. 1987. "On the cutting edge: Feminism and clitoridectomy." *Australian Feminist Studies* 5:35–55.

Kissane, K. 1993. "We must set limits for the sake of little girls." *The Age*, December 3.

Kjöller, H. 2002. "Oskyldigt misstänkt måste också höras" [A suspect, although innocent, must also be interrogated]. *Dagens Nyheter*, October 11.

———. 2005. "Intimkirugi inför räta" [Intimate surgery on trial]. *Dagens Nyheter*, February 22. http://www.dn.se/DNet/road/Classic/article/0/jsp/print.jsp?&a=381960.

Klein, S. 2005. "Does this make my labia look fat? Medicine and marketing collide below the belt." *Metrotimes*, March 9, 2005. http://www.metrotimes.com/editorial/story.asp?id=7405.

Knudsen, C. O. 1994. *The falling dawadawa tree: Female circumcision in developing Ghana.* Hojbjerg, Denmark: Intervention Press.

Koedt, A. 1970. "The myth of the vaginal orgasm." In *Notes from the Second Year*, ed. S. Firestone and A. Kodet. New York: Women's Liberation.

Koso-Thomas, O. 1987. *The circumcision of women: A strategy for eradication.* London: Zed Press.

Kouba, L. J., and J. Muasher. 1985. "Female circumcision in Africa: An overview." *African Studies Review* 28 (1): 95–110.

Krantz, K. 1958. "Innervation of the human vulva and vagina: A microscopic study." *Obstetrics and Gynaecology* 34:382–396.

Kratz, C. 1991. "Amusement and absolution: Transforming narratives during confession of social debts." *American Anthropologist* 93:826–851.

———. 1993. "We've always done it like this . . . except for a few details: 'Tradition' and 'innovation' in Okiek ceremonies." *Comparative Studies in Society and History* 35:30–65.

———. 1994. *Affecting performance: Meaning, movement, and experience in Okiek women's initiation.* Washington D.C: Smithsonian Institution Press.

———. 1999a. "Contexts, controversies and dilemmas: Teaching circumcision." In *Great ideas for teaching about Africa*, ed. M. Bastian. Boulder, CO: Lynne Rienner.

———. 1999b. "Female circumcision in Africa." in *Encarta Africana*, ed. K. A. Appiah and H. L. Gates Jr. Redmond, WA: Microsoft.

———. 2001. "Conversations and lives." In *African words, African voices*, ed. D. W. Cohen, S. Miescher, and L. White. Bloomington: Indiana University Press.

———. 2002. *"The ones that are wanted": Communication and the politics of representation in a photographic exhibit*. Berkeley: University of California Press.

———. 2003. "Circumcision, pluralism and dilemmas of cultural relativism." In *Applying anthropology: An introductory reader*, ed. A. Podolefsky and P. Brown. New York: McGraw-Hill.

Kuper, A. 1999. *Culture: The anthropologists' account*. Cambridge, MA: Harvard University Press.

Kymlicka, W. 1999. "Liberal complacencies." In *Is multiculturalism bad for women?* ed. J. Cohen, M. Howard, and M. Nussbaum. Princeton, NJ: Princeton University Press.

Ladas, A., J. Perry, and B. Whipple. 1983. *The G Spot and other recent discoveries about human sexuality*. New York: Holt Rinehart and Winston.

Lakoff, G., and M. Johnson. 1980. *Metaphors we live by*. Chicago: University of Chicago Press.

Langfeldt, T. 1993. *Sexologi*. Oslo: Gyldendal.

Langton, M. 2001. "Domination and dishonour: A treaty between our nations." *Postcolonial Studies* 4:13–26.

Laqueur, T. 1990. *Making sex: Body and gender from the Greeks to Freud*. Cambridge, MA: Harvard University Press.

Laqueur, T. W. 1989. "Amor Veneris, vel Dulcedo Appeletur." in *Fragments for a history of the human body, part three*, ed. R. Naddaff and N. Tazi. New York: Zone Books.

Lavee, Y. 1991. "Western and non-Western human sexuality: Implications for clinical practice." *Journal of Sex and Marital Therapy* 17:203–213.

Lavie, S., and T. Swedenburg. 1996. "Introduction: Displacement, diaspora, and geographies of identity." In *Displacement, diaspora, and geographies of identity*, ed. S. Lavie and T. Swedenburg. Durham, NC: Duke University Press.

Lear, D. 1997. *Sex and sexuality. Risk and relationships in the age of AIDS*. Thousand Oaks, CA: Sage.

Leavitt, S. C. 1991. "Sexual ideology and experience in Papua New Guinea Society." *Social Science and Medicine* 33:897–907.

Leiblum, S. R. 2000. "Redefining female sexual response." *Contemporary Ob/Gen* 5 (11): 120–129.

Lederer, J., and D. Jackson. 1968. *The mirages of marriage*. New York: Norton.

Leonard, L. 1999. "'We did it for pleasure only': Hearing alternative tales of female circumcision." Paper presented at the annual meeting of the American Anthropological Association, session on Female Genital Cutting: Local Dynamics of Global Debates, Chicago.

Levin, B., ed. 1996. *Sex i sverige. Om sexuallivet i Sverige 1996* [Sex in Sweden. About sexual life in Sweden]. Stockholm: Folkhälsoinstitutet (Public Health Institute).

Lewis, I. M. 1961. *A pastoral democracy: A study of pastoralism and politics among the northern Somali of the Horn of Africa*. London: Oxford University Press for the International African Institute.

———. 1962. *Marriage and the family in northern Somaliland*. Kampala, Uganda: East African Institute for Social Research East African Studies, no. 15.

Leye, E., and J. Deblonde. 2004. *Legislation in Europe regarding female genital mutilation and the implementation of the law in Belgium, France, Spain, Sweden and the UK*. Ghent: International Centre for Rreproductive Health, Ghent University.

Lightfoot-Klein, H. 1983. "Pharaonic circumcision of females in the Sudan." *Medicine and Law* 2:353–360.

———. 1989a. *Prisoners of ritual: An odyssey into female genital circumcision in Africa*. New York: Harrington Park Press.

————. 1989b. "The sexual experience and marital adjustment of genitally circumcised and infibulated females in the Sudan." *Journal of Sex Research* 26:375–392.

Lightfoot-Klein, H., and E. Shaw. 1990. "Special needs of ritually circumcised women patients." *Journal of Obstetric, Gynecologic and Neonatal Nursing* 20:102–107.

Lindsay, S. 1996. "Hand drumming: An essay in practical knowledge." In *Things as they are: New directions in phenomenological anthropology*, ed. M. Jackson, 196–212. Bloomington: Indiana University Press.

Lionnet, F. 1992. "Identity, sexuality, and criminality: 'Universal rights' and the debate around the practice of female excision in France." *Contemporary French Civilization* 16:294–307.

Löfstöm, J. 1992. "Sexuality at stake: The essentialist and constructionist approaches to sexuality in anthropology." *Suomen antropologi* 17 (3): 13–26

Lopes, C. 1987. *Guinea-Bissau: From liberation struggle to independent statehood*. Boulder, CO: Westview Press.

LoPiccolo, J., and W. Stock. 1986. "Treatment of sexual dysfunction." *Journal of Consulting and Clinical Psychology* 54:158–167.

MacCormack, C. 1980. "Proto-social to adult: A Sherbro transformation." In *Nature, culture and gender*, ed. C. MacCormack and M. Strathern. Cambridge: Cambridge University Press.

MacCormack, C. P. 1979. "Sande: The public face of secret society." In *The new religions of Africa*, ed. B. Jules-Rosette. Norwood, NJ: Ablex.

MacGaffey, J., and R. Bazenguissa-Ganga. 2000. *Congo-Paris: Transnational traders on the margins of the law*. Bloomington: Indiana University Press.

Machado, F. L. 1994. "Luso-Africanos em Portugal: Nas margens de etnicidade" [Luso-Africans in Portugal: On the margins of ethnicity]. *Sociologia: Problemas e Practicas* [Sociology: Problems and Practice] 16:111–134.

————. 1998. "Da Guiné-Bissau a Portugal: Luso-Guineenses e imigrantes" [From Guinea-Bissau to Portugal: Luso-Guineans and immigrants]. *Sociologia: Problemas e Prácticas* [Sociology: Problems and Practice] 26:9–56.

Mackie, G. 1996. "Ending footbinding and infibulation: A convention account." *American Sociological Review* 61:999–1017.

————. 2000. "Female genital cutting: The beginning of the end." In *Female "circumcision" in Africa: Culture, controversy, and change*, ed. B. Shell-Duncan and Y. Hernlund. Boulder, CO: Lynne Rienner.

————. 2003. "Female genital cutting: A harmless practice?" *Medical Anthropology Quarterly* 17:135–158.

Macklin, A. 1994. "*Canada Attorney General v. Ward*: A review essay." *International Journal of Refugee Law* 6:362–681.

————. 2006. "The double-edge sword: Using the criminal law against female genital mutilation in Canada." In *Female circumcision: Multicultural perspectives*, ed. R. Abusharaf. Philadelphia: University of Pennsylvania Press.

Mahmood, S. 2001. "Feminist theory, embodiment, and the docile agent: Some reflections on the Egyptian Islamic revival." *Cultural Anthropology* 16:202–236.

Malkin, M. 2002. "Hillary and the great clitoridectomy hoax." *Capitalism*, capmag.com/article.asp?ID=1878 (accessed August 6, 2005).

Mandara, M. 2000. "Female genital cutting in Nigeria: Views of Nigerian doctors on the medicalization debate." In *Female "circumcision" in Africa: Culture, controversy, and change*, ed. by B. Shell-Duncan and B. Hernlund. Boulder, CO: Lynne Rienner.

Mann, J. 1996. "When judges fail." *Washington Post*, January 19, E3.

Marmor, J. 1954. "Some considerations concerning orgasm in the female." *Journal of the American Psychosomatic Society* 16:240–245.

Marr, D., and M. Wilkinson. 2003. *Dark victory*. St. Leonards, New South Wales: Allen and Unwin.

Martin, D. A. 2005. "Adelaide Abankwah, Fauziya Kasinga, and the dilemmas of plitical asylum." In *Immigration stories*, ed. D. A. Martin and P. H. Schuck, 245–277. New York: Foundation Press.

Martin, E. 1987. *The woman in the body: A Cultural analysis of reproduction*. Boston: Beacon Press.

———. 1991. "The egg and the sperm: How science has constructed a romance based on stereotypical male-female roles." *Signs: Journal of Women in Culture and Society* 16:485–501.

Martin, T. 1995. "Case vignette: Child abuse or acceptable cultural norms: 'Response.'" *Ethics and Behavior* 5:290–292.

Mascia-Lees, F., and P. Sharpe. 1992a. "Introduction: Soft-tissue modification and the horror within." In *Tattoo, torture, mutilation, and adornment: The denaturalization of the body in culture and text*, ed. F. Mascia-Lees and P. Sharpe. Albany: State University of New York Press.

———. 1992b. "The marked and the un(re)marked: Tattoo and gender in theory and narrative." In *Tattoo, torture, mutilation, and adornment: The denaturalization of the body in culture and text*, ed. F. Mascia-Lees and P. Sharpe. Albany: State University of New York Press.

Masland, T., L. Gubb, and C. Cooper. 1999. "The ritual of pain." *Newsweek* (international edition), July 5, 61.

Mason, C. 2001. "Exorcising excision: Medico-legal issues arising from male and female genital surgery in Australia." *Journal of Law and Medicine* (Australia) 9:58–67.

Masquelier, A. 1996. "Identity, alterity and ambiguity in a Nigerian community: Competing definitions of "true" Islam." In *Postcolonial identities in Africa*, ed. R. Werbner and T. Ranger. London: Zed.

Masters, W., and V. Johnson. 1966. *Human sexual response*. Boston: Little Brown.

Matory, J. L. 1994. *Sex and the empire that is no more: Gender and the politics of metaphor in Oyo Yoruba religion*. Minneapolis: University of Minnesota Press.

Matter of Abankwah. Transcript, file A 74 881 776.

McCarthy, S. 1999. "No activism, no asylum." *Ms.*, October/November, 21–22.

McGown, R. B. 1999. *Muslims in the diaspora: The Somali communities of London and Toronto*. Toronto: University of Toronto Press.

———. 2003. "Writing across difference: Standing on authentic ground." *Journal of Muslim Minority Affairs* 23:163–171.

Megafu, U. 1983. "Female ritual circumcision in Africa: An investigation of the presumed benefits among Ibos of Nigeria." *East African Medical Journal* 40:793–800.

Melching, M. 2001. "Abandoning female genital cutting in Africa." In *Eye to eye: Women practising development across cultures*, ed. S. Perry and C. Schenck. London: Zed Books.

Merry, S. E. 2001. "Changing rights, changing culture." In *Culture and rights: Anthropological perspectives*, ed. J. K. Cowan, M. B. Dembour, and R. A. Wilson. Cambridge: Cambridge University Press.

Metcalf, B. D., ed. 1996. *Making Muslim space in North America and Europe*. Berkeley: University of California Press.

Meyers, D. T. 2000. "Feminism and women's autonomy: The challenge of female genital mutilation." *Metaphilosophy* 31:469–491.

Mikva, A. 2000. "The wooing of our judges." *New York Times*, August 26, opposite editorial page.

Miller, A. M. 2000. "Sexual but not reproductive: Exploring the junction and disjunction of sexual and reproductive rights." *Health and Human Rights* 4:69–109.

———. 2004. "Sexuality, violence against women, and human rights: Woman make demands and ladies get protection." *Health and Human Rights* 7:17–47.

Miller, A. M., and C. M. Vance. 2004. "Sexuality, human rights, and health." *Health and Human Rights* 7:5–15.

Miller, G. P. 2002. "Circumcision: Cultural legal analysis." *Virginia Journal of Social Policy and the Law* 9:497–585.

Minority Rights Group. 1980. *Female circumcision, excision and infibulation: The facts and proposals for change*, report no. 47. London: Minority Rights Group

Minow, M. 2002. "About women, about culture: About them, about us." In *Engaging cultural differences: the multicultural challenge in liberal democracies*, ed. R. Shweder, M. Minow, and H. R. Markus. New York: Russell Sage Foundation.

Mire, S. 1994. *Fire eyes*. New York: Filmakers Library.

Moghadam, V. 1994. *Identity politics and women: Cultural reassertions and feminisms in international perspective*. Boulder, CO: Westview Press.

Mohamed, M. (on behalf of AWWG). 1996. "The implications of the legislation of FGM for the affected communities."

Mohamud, O. A. 1991. "Female circumcision and child mortality in urban Somalia." *Genus* 67:203–223.

Mohanty, C. 1991. "Under Western eyes: Feminist scholarship and colonial discourses." In *Third World women and the politics of feminism*, ed. C. Mohanty, A. Russo, and L. Torres. Bloomington: Indiana University Press.

———. 1994. "Under Western eyes: Feminist scholarship and colonial discourse." In *Colonial discourse and postcolonial theory: A reader*, ed. P. Williams and L. Chrisman. New York: Columbia University Press.

Money, J., and P. Tucker. 1975. *Sexual signatures*. Boston: Little Brown.

Moore, H. L. 1988. *Feminism and anthropology*. Minneapolis: University of Minnesota Press.

———. 1994. "Fantasies of power and fantasies of identity: Gender, race, and violence." In *A passion for difference: Essays in anthropology and gender*, ed. H. L. Moore. Cambridge: Polity Press.

———. 1996. *Space, text, and gender: An anthropological study of Marakwet of Kenya*. New York: Guilford Press.

———. 1999. "Anthropological theory at the turn of the century." In *Anthropological theory of today*, ed. H. Moore. Oxford: Polity Press.

———. 2004. "Global anxieties: Concept-metaphors and pre-theoretical commitments in anthropology." *Anthropological Theory* 41 (1): 71–88.

Moore, S. F. 1978. "Law and social change: The semi-autonomous social field as appropriate object of study." In *Law as process*, ed. S. F. Moore. London: Routledge and Kegan Paul.

Morgan, R., and G. Steinem. 1979. "The international crime of genital mutilation." *Ms.*, March, 65–100.

Morison, L., A. Dirir, S. Elmi, J. Warsame, and S. Dirir. 2004. "How experiences and attitudes relating to female circumcision vary according to age on arrival in Britain: A study among young Somalis in London." *Ethnicity and Health* 9:75–100.

Morison, L., S. Dirir, J. Warsame, A. Dirir, and S. Elmi. 1998. *Experiences, attitudes and views of young, single Somalis living in London of female circumcision*. Report from a collaborative project between the London Black Women's Health Action Project and the London School of Hygiene and Tropical Medicine.

Morison, L., and L. Scherf. 2003. "Correspondence on the association between female genital cutting and correlates of sexual and gynaecological morbidity in Endo State, Nigeria." *BJOG: An International Journal of Obstetrics and Gynaecology* 110:1137–1140.

Morison, L. C., C. Scherf, G. Ekpo, K. Paine, B. West, R. Coleman, and G. Walraven. 2001. "The long-term reproductive health consequences of female genital cutting in rural Gambia: A community-based survey." *Tropical Medicine and International Health* 6:643–653.

Moszinsky, P. 2003. "Sudan to tighten law on female genital mutilation." *British Medical Journal* 327:580.

Mugo, M. 1997. "Elitist anti-circumcision discourse as mutilating and anti-feminist." *Case Western Law Review* 47:461–480.

Murphy, D. E. 2000. "I.N.S. says African women used fraud to gain asylum." *New York Times*, December 21, C21.

Murray, J. 1974. "The Kikuyu female circumcision controversy, with special reference to the Church Missionary Society's 'sphere of influence.'" Ph.D. diss., University of California, Los Angeles.

———1976. "The Church Missionary Society and the 'female circumcision' issue in Kenya, 1929–1932." *Journal of Religion in Africa* 8:92–104.

Murray, L. 1983. "The clitoris nobody knows." *Forum* 12:57–63.

Musalo, K., J. Moore, and R. Boswell, eds. 2001. *Refugee law and policy: A comparative and international approach*. Durham, NC: Carolina Academic Press.

Myers, R. A., F. I. Omorodion, A. E. Isenalumhe, and G. I. Akenzua. 1985. "Circumcision: Its nature and practice." *Social Science and Medicine* 21:581–588.

Narayan, U. 1997. *Dislocating cultures: Identities, traditions, and Third World feminism*. New York: Routledge.

National Immigration Law Center. 2005. "9th Circuit finds that female genital mutilation constitutes ongoing persecution." *Immigrants' Rights Update* 19:2.

National Public Radio. 2000. "INS fraud." Reported by Margot Adler. *All things considered*, December 21. http://www.npr.org/templates/story/story.php?storyId=1115851.

Navarro, M. 2004. "The most private of makeovers." *New York Times*, November 28.

Nelson, N. 1987. "Selling her kiosk: Kikuyu notions of sexuality and sex for sale in Mathare Valley, Kenya." In *The cultural construction of sexuality*, ed. P. Caplan. London: Tavistock Press.

Nilsson, L. 2005. "Missnöjd med dina blydläppar? Boka könsstympning idag!" [Dissatisfied with your labia? Make an appointment today for genital mutilation!] *ETC* 2.

NIRVA. 1991. Race discrimination Commissioner, Human Rights and Equal Opportunity Commission. *Racist violence: Report of the national inquiry into racist violence in Australia*, 387–398. Canberra: Australian Government Publishing Service.

Nour, Nawal M. 2005. "Female genital cutting is both a health and human rights issue." In *Our bodies, ourselves: A new edition for a new era*. The Boston Women's Health Book Collective. New York: Simon and Schuster.

Ntiri, D. W. 1991. "Experimenting with family life centers in Africa's development: A case study of rural women in Somalia, East Africa." *International Journal of Sociology of the Family* 21:73–88.

———. 1993. "Circumcision and health among rural women of southern Somalia as part of a family life survey." *Health Care for Women International* 14:215–226.

Nukunya, G. K. 1992. *Tradition and change in Ghana*. Accra: Ghana Universities Press.

Nussbaum, M. 1996. "Double moral standards?" *Boston Review* 21:5.

———. 1999. *Sex and social justice*. New York: Oxford University Press.

Obermeyer, C. M. 1999. "Female genital surgeries: The Known, the unknown, and the unknowable." *Medical Anthropology Quarterly* 13:79–105.

———. 2003. "The health consequences of female circumcision: Science, advocacy, and standards of evidence." *Medical Anthropology Quarterly* 17:394–412.

Obiora, L. A. 1996. "The little foxes that spoil the vine: Revising the feminist critique of female circumcision." *Canadian Journal of Women and Law* 9:46–73.

———. 1997. "Bridges and barricades: Rethinking polemics and intransigence in the campaign against female circumcision." *Case Western Law Review* 47:275–378.

————. 1998. "Toward an auspicious reconciliation of international law and comparative law." *American Journal of Comparative Law* 46:649–652.

————. 2001. "Female excision: Cultural concerns and feminist legal theory." In *International encyclopedia of social and behavioral sciences*, ed. N. J. Smelser and P. B. Baltes. Amsterdam and New York: Elsevier.

————. 2004. "Suppri, Suppri, Suppri Oyibo: Interrogating some deficits of gender mainstreaming." *Signs: Journal of Women in Culture and Society* 29:649–652.

Office of Women's Affairs (OWA). 1996a. "Community Legal Information Project: Summary."

————. 1996b. Letter to AWWG.

Ogden, G. 1994. *Women who love sex*. New York: Pocket Books.

Okeyo, A. P. 1981. "Reflections on development myths." *Africa Report* March–April:7–10.

Okin, S. 1999a. "Is multiculturalism bad for women?" In *Is multiculturalism bad for women?* ed. J. Cohen, M. Howard, and M. Nussbaum. Princeton, NJ: Princeton University Press.

————. 1999b. "Reply." In *Is multiculturalism bad for women?* ed. M. Howard and M. Nussbaum. Princeton, NJ: Princeton University Press.

Okonofu, F. E., U. Larsen, F. Oronsaye, R. C. Snow, and T. E. Slanger. 2002. "The association between female genital cutting and correlates of sexual and gynaecological morbidity in Endo State, Nigeria." *British Journal of Obstetrics and Gynaecology* 109:1089–1096.

Olliver, D. 2000. "Female genital surgery goes public." *Jenda: A Journal of Culture and African Women Studies* 1. http://www.jendajournal.com/v011.1/dvagina.html.

Olsson, I. 2000. "Bred kamp mot kvinnlig konsstympning: Uppemot 8 000 flickor beräknas vara i riskzonen" [Struggle on a broad front against female genital mutilation: Nearly 8,000 girls in Sweden are estimated to be at risk]. *Läkartidningen* [The Physician's Journal] 97:4694–4695.

Olwig, K. F., and K. Hastrup. 1997. "Introduction." In *Siting culture: The shifting anthropological object*, ed. K. F. Olwig and K. Hastrup. London: Routledge.

Omar, A., A. Elmi, S. Johnsdotter, and A. Carlborm. 2001. "Siduu Eebbe noo abuuray: Soomaalida Malmo aragtida ay ka gabaan gudniinka dumarka" [As we were created by God: Attitudes to female circumcision among Somalis in Malmo]. Internal report, Department of Sociology, Lund University.

Ortner, S. B. 1974. "Is female to male as nature is to culture?" In *Woman, culture and society*, ed. M. Rosaldo and L. Lamphere. Palo Alto, CA: Stanford University Press.

————. 1996. *Making gender: The politics and erotics of culture*. Boston: Beacon Press.

————. 1999. "Thick resistance: Death and the cultural construction of agency in Himalaya mountaineering." In *The fate of "culture": Geertz and beyond*, ed. S. B. Ortner, 136–159. Berkeley: University of California Press.

Ortner, S. B., and H. Whitehead, eds. 1981. *Sexual meanings: The cultural construction of gender and sexuality*. Cambridge, MA: Cambridge University Press.

Ottenberg, S. 1984. "Two new religions, one analytical frame." *Cahiers d'Études Africaines* 96:437–454.

————. 1989. *Boyhood rituals in an African society: An interpretation*. Seattle: University of Washington Press.

Oyĕwùmi R., ed. 2003. *African women and feminism: Reflecting on the politics of sisterhood*. Trenton, NJ: Africa World Press.

Parekh, B. 1999. "A varied moral world." In *Is multiculturalism bad for women?* ed. C. J., M. Howard, and M. Nussbaum. Princeton, NJ: Princeton University Press.

Parker, M. 1995. "Rethinking female circumcision." *Africa* 65:506–523.

Pavich, E. G. 1986. "A Chicana perspective on Mexican culture and sexuality." *Journal of Social Work Human Sex* 4:47–65.

Pederson, S. 1991. "National bodies, unspeakable acts: The sexual politics of colonial policy-making." *Journal of Modern History* 63:647–680.

Pegler, T. 1993." Court told of assault on sisters." *The Age* (Melbourne, Australia), December 2.

Perry, D. 2004. "Muslim child disciples, global civil society, and children's rights in Senegal: The discourses of strategic structuralism." *Anthropology Quarterly* 77:47–86.

Perry, J. D., and B. Whipple. 1981. "Pelvic muscle strength of female ejaculators: Evidence in support of a new theory of orgasm." *Journal of Sex Research* 17:22–39.

Peterson, V. S. 2002. "Rewriting (global) political economy." *International Feminist Journal of Politics* 4:1–30.

Peyrot, M. 1991. "Tribal practices pose dilemma for Western society." Originally in *Le Monde*, March 8–11. Translation in *Guardian Weekly*, March 24, 1991. Reprinted in *Passages*, issue 3, 1992.

Phillips, T. 2004. "I want an integrated Britain." *London Times*, April 3, Home News, 1.

Piot, C. 1999a. *Remotely global: Village modernity in West Africa.* Chicago: University of Chicago Press.

———. 1999b. "Representing Africa in the Kasinga asylum case." Paper presented at the Annual Meeting of the American Anthropological Association, session on Female Genital Cutting: Local Dynamics of a Global Debate, Chicago,.

Plaut, V. C. 2002. "Cultural models of diversity in America: The psychology of difference and inclusion." In *Engaging cultural differences: The Multicultural challenge in liberal democracies*, ed. R. Shweder, M. Minow, and H. R. Markus. New York: Russell Sage Foundation.

Pollitt, K. 1999. "Whose culture?" In *Is multiculturalism bad for women?* ed. J. Cohen, M. Howard, and M. Nussbaum. Princeton, NJ: Princeton University Press.

Population Reference Bureau. 2001. *Abandoning female genital cutting: Prevalence, attitudes, and efforts to end the practice.* Washington, DC: Population Reference Bureau.

Posnansky, M. 1998. "Affidavit of Professor Merrick Posnansky." *Review of Law and Women's Studies* 7:418–428.

Post, R. 1999. "Between norms and choices." In *Is multiculturalism bad for women?* ed J. Cohen, M. Howard, and M. Nussbaum. Princeton, NJ: Princeton University Press.

Powell, R., E. Leye, A. Jayatody, F. N. Mwangi Powell, and L. Morison. 2004. "Female genital mutilation, asylum seekers and refugees: The need for an integrated Eurpoean Union Agenda." *Health Policy* 70:151–162.

Prop. 1998/99:70. *Könsstympning: Borttagande av kravet på dubbel straffbarhet* [Genital mutilation: Removal of the requirement of double criminality]. Governmental bill Prop. 1998/99:70. Stockholm: Socialdepartmentet [Ministry of Health and Social Affairs].

Propper, S., and R. Brown. 1986. "Moral reasoning, parental sex attitudes, and sex guilt in female college students." *Archives of Sexual Behavior* 15:331–340.

Pugh, D. 1983. "Bringing an end to mutilation." *New Statesman*, November 11, 8–9.

Quinn, C. A. 1972. *Mandingo kingdoms of the Senegambia: Traditionalism, Islam, and European expansion.* Evanston. IL: Northwestern University Press.

Rahman, A., and N. Toubia. 2000. *Female genital mutilation: A guide to laws and policies worldwide.* New York: Zed Books.

Rasmussen, S. J. 2003. "When the field space comes to the home space: New constructions of ethnographic knowledge in a new African diaspora." *Anthropological Quarterly* 76:7–32.

Rawls, J. 1993. *Political liberalism.* New York: Columbia University Press.

Rehman, S. 2000. "Glimrende journalistikk eller glitrende offerporno?" [Glittering journalism or gleaming victim porno?] *Fundamental.net* [Web magazine], http://www.fundamental.net/2000/11/14/1602.html (accessed May 1, 2002).

Renteln, A. D. 1988. "Relativism and the search for human rights." *American Anthropologist* 90:56–68.

————. 2002. "In defense of culture in the courtroom." In *Engaging cultural differences: The multicultural challenge in liberal democracies*, ed. R. Shweder, M. Minow, and H. R. Markus. New York: Russell Sage Foundation.

Riesman, P. 1998. *Freedom in Fulani social life: An introspective ethnography*. Chicago: University of Chicago Press.

Rikets-tilstand [The state of the country]. 2000. NRK (Nork Rikskringkasting [Norwegian Broadcasting Corporation]), October 2000.

Rosaldo, R. 1989. *Culture and truth: The remaking of social analysis*. Boston: Beacon Press.

Roscoe, W., and S. O. Murray. 2001. *Boy-wives and female husbands: Studies in African homosexualities*. Palgrave Macmillan.

Rosenthal, A. M. 1993. "Female genital torture." *New York Times*, November 12, A33.

————. 1996. "On my mind: Fighting female mutilation." *New York Times*, April 12, A31.

Rousseau, C., M. S. Taher, M. J. Gange, and G. Bibeau. 1998. "Between myth and madness: The premigration dream of leaving among young Somali refugees." *Culture, Medicine and Psychiatry* 22:385–411.

Rye, S. 2002. "Circumcision in urban Ethiopia: Practices, discourses and contexts." Ph. D. diss., Institute of Social Anthropology, University of Oslo.

Sachs, S. 1999. "Fears of rape and violence: Women newly seeking asylum." *New York Times*, August 1, Week in Review.

Sack, A., J. Keller, and D. Hinkle. 1984. "Premarital sexual intercourse: A test of the effects of peer group, religiosity, and sexual guilt." *Journal of Sex Research* 20:168–185.

Sacks, K. 1976. "State bias and women's status." *American Anthropologist* 78:565–569.

Sager, L. 2002. "Culture of property." In *Engaging cultural differences: The multicultural challenge in liberal democracies*, ed. R. Shweder, M. Minow, and H. R. Markus. New York: Russell Sage Foundation.

Sahlins, M. 1999. "Two or three things I know about culture." *Journal of the Royal Anthropological Institute* 5 (3): 399–421.

Said, E. 1978. *Orientalism*. London: Penguin Books.

Sanderson, L. M. 1981. *Against the mutilation of women: The struggle against unnecessary suffering*. London: Ithaca Press.

Sargent, C. 1989. *Maternity, medicine, and power: Reproductive decisions in urban Benin*. Berkeley: University of California Press.

————. 1991. "Confronting patriarchy: The potential for advocacy in medical anthropology." *Medical Anthropology Quarterly* 5:24–25.

Schaffer, M., and C. Cooper. 1987. *Mandinko: The ethnography of a West African holy land*. Rev. ed. Prospect Heights, IL: Waveland Press. (Originally published 1980.)

Scheper-Hughes, N. 1991. "Virgin territory: The male discovery of the clitoris." *Medical Anthropology Quarterly* 5:25–28.

————. 1992. *Death without weeping: Everyday violence in Brazil*. Berkeley: University of California Press.

Schierup, C.-U. 1993. *På kulturens slagmark. Mindretal og storretal taler om Danmark* [On the battleground of culture: Minorities and majorities talk about Denmark]. Esbjerg: Sydjysk Universitetsforlag.

Schroeder, P. 1994. "Female genital mutilation: A form of child abuse." *New England Journal of Medicine* 331:739–740.

Schur, E. M. 1988. *The Americanization of sex*. Philadelphia: Temple University Press.

Scroggins, D. 2005. "The Dutch-Muslim culture war: Ayaan Hirsi Ali has enraged Muslims with her attacks on their sexual mores." *The Nation*, June 27.

Sen, A. 1999. *Development as freedom*. New York: Random House, Anchor Books.

Seth, S. 2001. "Liberalism and the politics of (multi)culture: Or, plurality is not difference." *Postcolonial Studies* 4:65–77.

Shandall, A. 1967. "Circumcision and infibulation of females." *Sudan Medical Journal* 5:178–212.

Shaw, C. M. 1995. *Colonial inscriptions: Gender, race and class in colonial Kenya.* Minneapolis: University of Minnesota Press.

Shaw, E. 1985. "Female circumcision." *American Journal of Nursing* 85:684–687.

Shell-Duncan, B. 2001. "The medicalization of female 'circumcision': Harm reduction or promotion of a dangerous practice?" *Social Science and Medicine* 52:1013–1028.

———. 2002. "Conceptual and methodological issues in studying sociocultural determinants of female genital cutting." Paper presented at the Conference for the Advancement of Research on Female Genital Cutting, Bellagio, Italy, May.

Shell-Duncan, B., and Y. Hernlund. 2000. "Female 'circumcision' in Africa: Dimensions of the practice and debates." In *Female "circumcision" in Africa: Culture, controversy, and change,* ed. B. Shell-Duncan and Y. Hernlund. Boulder, CO: Lynne Rienner.

Sheridan, M. B. 2002. "Ghanaian woman convicted of fabricating tale." *Washington Post,* January 17, B3.

Shore, B. 1996. *Culture in mind.* New York: Oxford University Press.

———. 1998. "How culture means. Personal meaning and cultural models." Lecture given at the University of Oslo, June 17, 1998.

Shweder, R. 1991. *Thinking through cultures: Explorations in cultural psychology.* Cambridge, MA: Harvard University Press.

———. 2000. "What about 'female genital mutilation'? And why understanding culture matters in the first place." *Daedalus* 129 (4): 209–232.

———. 2002. "What about female genital mutilation? And why understanding culture matters in the first place." In *Engaging cultural differences,,* ed. R. Shweder, M. Minow, and H. R. Markus. New York: Russell Sage Foundation.

———. Forthcoming. "When cultures collide: Which rights? Whose tradition of values? A critique of the global anti-FGM campaign." In *Global justice and the bulwarks of localism: Human rights in context,* ed. C. Eisgruber and A. Sajo. Leiden and Boston: Martinus Nijhoff.

Shweder, R., M. Minow, and H. R. Markus, eds. 2002. *Engaging cultural differences: The multicultural challenge in liberal democracies.* New York: Russell Sage Foundation.

Sikes, G. 1998. "Why Are women who escape genital mutilation being jailed in America? *Marie Claire* campaign." *Marie Claire,* May, 52–56.

Silverman, E. 2004. "Anthropology and circumcision." *Annual Review of Anthropology* 33:419–445.

Simons, M. 1993. "Mutilation of girls' genitals: Ethnic gulf in French court." *New York Times,* November 23, A13.

Singer, J., and I. singer. 1972. "Types of female orgasm." *Journal of Sex Research* 8:255–267.

Skartveit, H. 2002. "Omskaerign og piercing" [Circumcision and piercing]. *VG* [Verdens Gang], August 8.

Skramstad, H. 1990. *The fluid meanings of female circumcision in a multiethnic context in Gambia: Distribution of knowledge and linkages to sexuality.* Working paper, Christian Michelson Institute, Bergen, Norway.

Slack, A. T. 1984. "Female circumcision: A critical appraisal." *Human Rights Quarterly* 10:437–486.

Snively, J. 1994. "Female bodies, male politics: Women and the female circumcision controversy in Kenyan colonial discourse." Master's thesis, Department of Anthropology, McGill University.

Solheim, J. 1998. *Den åpne kroppen. Om kjønnssymbolikk i moderne kultur* [The open body: About gender symbolism in modern culture]. Oslo: Pax Forlag.

Spencer, W., ed. 1994. *Global studies: The Middle East.* Guilford, CT: Dushkin.

Spivak, G. C. 1985. "Three women's texts and a critique of imperialism." *Critical Inquiry* 12:242–261.

———. 1988. "Can the subaltern speak?" In *Marxism and the interpretation of culture*, ed. C. Nelson and L. Grossberg. Urbana: University of Illinois Press.

Spradley, J. 1979. *The ethnographic interview*. New York: Holt, Rinehart and Winston.

Stephens, S. 1995. *Children and the politics of culture*. Princeton, NJ: Princeton University Press.

Stoeltje, B. 1997. "Asante queen mothers: A study in female authority." In *Queens, queen mothers, priestesses, and power: Case studies in African gender*, ed. F. Kaplan. New York: Annals of the New York Academy of Sciences.

Stoller, P. 2002. *Money has no smell: The Africanization of New York City*. Chicago: University of Chicago Press.

Strathern, M. 1987. "An awkward relationship: The case of feminism and anthropology." *Signs: Journal of Women in Culture and Society* 12:276–292.

———. 1988. *The gender of the gift: Problems with women and problems with society in Melanesia*. Berkeley: University of California Press.

———. 1991. *Partial connections*. Savage, MD: Rowman and Littlefield.

———. 1993. "Making incomplete." In *Carved flesh/cast selves: Gendered symbols and social practices*, ed. V. Broche-Due, I. Rudie, and T. Bleie. Oxford: Berg.

Suárez-Orozco, M. 2002. "Everything you ever wanted to know about assimilation but were afraid to ask." In *Engaging cultural differences: The multicultural challenge in liberal democracies*, ed. R. Shweder, M. Minow, and H. R. Markus. New York: Russell Sage Foundation.

Sudan Government. 1982. *Principal Report*. Vol. 1 of *The Sudan Fertility Survey, 1979*. Khartoum: Department of Statistics.

Summerfield, H. 1993. "Patterns of adaptation: Somali and Bangladeshi women in Britain." In *Migrant women: Crossing boundaries and changing identities*. Vol. 7 of *Cross cultural perspectives on women*, ed. G. Buijs. Oxford: Berg.

Summerfield, R. 2004. "A private perfection." *Calgary Herald*, April 15.

Talle, A. 1974. "Barabaig: Economic Dilemmas in the Combination of Livestock Keeping and Agriculture." Thesis, Department of Ethnography, University of Oslo.

———. 1991. "Kvinnlig könsstympning: ett sätt att skapa kvinnor och män" [Female genital mutilation: A way to create women and men]. In *Från kön till genus: Kvinnligt och manligt i ett kulturellt perspektiv* [From sex to gender: Female and male in a cultural perspective], ed. D. Kulick. Stockholm: Carlssons.

———. 1993. "Transforming women into 'pure' agnates: Aspects of female infibulation in Somalia." In *Carved flesh, cast selves: Gender symbols and social practices*, ed. V. Broch-Due, I. Rudie, and T. Bleie. Oxford: Berg.

———. 1994. "The making of female fertility: Anthropological perspectives on a bodily issue." *Acta Obstetrica et Gynecologica Scandinavica* 73 (3): 280–283.

———. 2001. "'But it *is* mutilation': Antropologi og vansklige temaer" [Anthropology and complicated issues]. *Norsk Antropologisk Tidskrift* 12:25–33.

Tamir, Y. 1996. "Hands off clitoridectomy." *Boston Review* 21:3–4.

———. 1999. "Siding with the underdogs." In *Is multiculturalism bad for women?* ed. J. Cohen, M. Howard, and M. Nussbaum. Princeton, NJ: Princeton University Press.

Theorin, M. B. 2001. "Könsstympningen måste stoppas" [The genital mutilation must be stopped]. *Sydsvenskan*, June 8, 2.

Thiam, A. 1983. "Women's fight for the abolition of sexual mutilation." *International Social Science Journal* 35:747–756.

Thomas, L. 1997. "Imperial concerns and 'women's affairs': State efforts to regulate clitoridectomy and eradicate abortion in Meru, Kenya, c. 1920–1950." *Journal of African History* 39:121–145.

————. 2000. "'Ngaitana (I will circumcise myself)': Lessons from colonial campaigns to ban excision in Meru, Kenya." In *Female "circumcision" in Africa: Culture, controversy, and change*, ed. B. Shell-Duncan and Y. Hernlund. Boulder, CO: Lynne Rienner.

————. 2003. *Politics of the womb: Women, reproduction, and the state in Kenya.* Berkeley: University of California Press.

Thomas, L. M. 1996. "'Ngaitana (I will circumcise myself)': The gender and generational politics of the 1956 ban on clitoridectomy in Meru, Kenya." *Gender and History* 8:338–363.

Thompson, G. 1999a. "Lawmakers want an asylum rule for sex-based persecution." *New York Times*, April 26, B8.

————. 1999b. "No asylum for a woman threatened with genital cutting." *New York Times*, April 25, A25.

Thorbjørnsrud, B. 1999. *Controlling the body to liberate the soul: Towards an analysis of the Coptic Orthodox concept of the body.* Oslo: Unipub forlag/Academika.

Tiefer, L. 1995. *Sex is not a natural act and other essays.* Boulder, CO: Westview Press.

Tostan. 2005. Tostan: Women's Health and Human Rights. *www.tostan.org*.

Toubia, N. 1985. "The social and political implications of female circumcision: The case of Sudan." In *Women and the family in the Middle East: New voices of change*, ed. E. W. Fernea. Austin: University of Texas Press.

————. 1988. "Women and health in Sudan." In *Women of the Arab world: The coming challenge.* London: Zed Press.

————. 1994. "Female circumcision as a public health issue." *New England Journal of Medicine* 331:712–716.

————. 1995. *Female genital mutilation: A call for global action.* 2nd ed. New York: Rainbo/ Women Ink.

Toubia, N., and S. Izette. 1998. *Female genital mutilation: An overview.* Geneva: World Health Organization (online edition).

Toubia, N. F., and E. H. Sharief. 2003. "Female genital mutilation: Have we made progress yet?" *International Journal of Gynaecology and Obstetrics* 82:251–261.

Troup, M. 1993. "Rupturing the veil: Feminism, deconstruction and the law." *Australia Feminist Law Journal* 1 (August): 63–88.

Turner, V. 1962. "Three symbols of passage in Ndembu circumcision ritual: An interpretation." in *Essays on the ritual of social relations*, ed. M. Gluckman. Manchester, UK: Manchester University Press.

Turone, F. 2004. "Controversy surrounds proposed Italian alternative to female genital mutilation." *British Medical Journal* 328. http://bmj.bmjjournals.com/cgi/content/full/328/7434/247-b.

Tuzin, D. 1991. "Sex, culture and the anthropologist." *Social Science and Medicine* 33:867–874.

Uddenberg, N. 1974. "Psychological aspects of sexual inadequacy in women." *Journal of Psychosomatic Research* 18:33–47.

United Nations. 1986. *Report of the working group on traditional practices affecting the health of women and children.* United Nations Sub Commission for the Prevention of Discrimination and the Protection of Minorities Special Working Group on Traditional Practices Item 19.

United States Department of Justice. 1996. *http://www.usdoj.gov.eoir/efoia/kasinga7.pdf.*

United States Department of State. 1996. *Togo Country Report on Human Rights Practices 1996*, http://www.state.gov/www/global.human_rights/1996_hrp_report/togo.html.

————. 2004. *Human Rights Reports*, www.state.gov/g/drl/hr/c1470.htm (accessed September 2005).

Urdang, S. 1979. *Fighting two colonialisms: Women in Guinea-Bissau.* New York: Monthly Review Press.

Valderrama, J. 2002. "Female genital mutilation: Why are we so radical?" *The Lancet*, February 9:359 (on-line version).

Vallgren, C. 2001. "Unga flickor könsstympas—utomlands [Young girls are genitally mutilated—abroad]." *Aftonbladet*, September 5, p. 11.

van der Kwaak, A. 1992. "Female circumcision and gender identity: A questionable alliance?" *Social Science and Medicine* 35 (67): 777–787.

van der Veer, P. 2002. "Transnational religion: Hindu and Muslim movements." *Global Networks* 2:95–109.

van Dijk, R. 1997. "From camp to encompassment: Discourses of transsubjectivity in the Ghanaian Pentecostal diaspora." *Journal of Religion in Africa* 27 (2): 135–159.

Vance, C. 1989. "Social construction theory: Problems in the history of sexuality." In *Homosexuality, which homosexuality? International Conference on Gay and Lesbian Studies*, ed. D. Altman et al. London: GMP.

———. 1991. "Anthropology rediscovers sexuality: A theoretical comment." *Social Science and Medicine* 33:875–884.

Vangen, S., R. E. B. Johansen, Stoltenbery, Sundby, and Stray-Pedersen. 2004. "Qualitative study of perinatal care experiences among Somali women and local health care professionals in Norway." *European Journal of Obstetrics and Gynecology and Reproductive Biology* 112:29–35.

Vangen, S., C. Stoltenberg, R. E. B. Johansen, J. Sundby, and B. Stray-Pederson. 2002. "Perinatal complications among ethnic Somalis in Norway." *Acta Obstetrica et Gynecologica Scandinavica* 81:317–322.

Verzin, J. A. 1975." Sequelae of female circumcision." *Tropical Doctor* 5:163–169.

Wachira, C. 1995. "Kenya Custom: Dilemma of Female Circumcision." January 24, *Newsgroup:Soc.culture.african* [news group posting].

Waldman, A. 1999. "Woman who feared genital cutting adapts to new freedom." *New York Times*, July 21.

Walker, A. 1992. *Possessing the secret of joy*. New York: Harcourt Brace Jovanovich.

Walker, A., and P. Parmar. 1993. Warrior Marks: *Female genital mutilation and the sexual blinding of women*. New York: Harcourt Brace.

Walley, C. 2002. "Searching for 'voices': Feminism, anthropology, and the global debate over female genital operations." In *Genital cutting and transnational sisterhood: Disputing U.S. polemics*, ed. S. James and C. Robertson. Urbana: University of Illinois Press.

Walley, C. J. 1997. "Searching for 'voices': Feminism, anthropology, and the global debate over female genital operations." *Cultural Anthropology* 12:405–438.

Wallin, P. 1960. "A study of orgasm as a condition of women's enjoyment of intercourse." *Journal of Sexual Psychology* 51:191–198.

"We Are Not Savages." 2003. Chief Nana Kwa Bonko V. www.ghanaweb.com/GhanaHomePage/News/Archive/printnews.php?ID=31766 (accessed August 8, 2005).

Weijmar-Schultz, W., H. van de Wiel, J. Klatter, B. Sturm, and J. Nauta. 1989. "Vaginal sensitivity to electric stimuli: Theoretical and practical implications." *Archives of Sexual Behavior* 18:87–95.

Weisberg, M. 1984. "Physiology of female sexual function." *Clincial Obstetrics and Gynecology* 27:697–705.

Weisberg, M., R. Swensson, and S. Hammersmith. 1983. "Sexual autonomy and the status of women: Models of female sexuality in U.S. sex manuals from 1950 to 1980." *Social Problems* 30:312–324.

Welch, C. E., Jr. 1995. *Protecting human rights in Africa: Strategies and roles of nongovernmental organizations*. Philadelphia: University of Pennsylvania Press.

Werbner, P. 1990. *The migration process: Capital, gifts, and offerings among British Pakistanis*. Oxford: Berg.

Westheimer, R. 1994. *Dr. Ruth's encyclopaedia of sex*. Jerusalem: Jerusalem Publishing House.

Whimp, K. 1997. *Final report into the Royal Commission into aboriginal deaths in custody: A summary*. Australian Legal Information Institute.

WHO [World Health Organization]. 1979. "Traditional practices affecting the health of women and children." WHO/EMRO technical publication no. 2. Khartoum, February 10–15.

———. 1982. *Female circumcision: Statement of WHO position and activities*. World Health Organization.

———. 1986. A traditional practice that threatens health—Female circumcision. *WHO Chronicle* 40:31–36.

———. 1996. *Female genital mutilation: Report of a WHO technical working group*. World Health Organization.

———. 1998. *Female genital mutilation: An overview*.

———. 1999. *Female genital mutilation: Programmes to date: What works and what doesn't. A review*. Geneva: World Health Organization WHO/CHS/WMH/99.5. www.who.int/reproductive-health/publications/fgm.

———. 2006. "Female genital mutilation and obstetric outcome: WHO collaborative prospective study for African countries." WHO Study Group on Female Genital Mutilation and Obstetric Outcome [E. Banks, O. Meiriki, T. Farley, O. Akande, and H. Bathija]. *The Lancet* 367 (June 3, 2006): 1835–1841. www.thelancet.com

Widmark, C., C. Tishelman, and B. M. Ahlberg. 2000. "A study of Swedish midwives' encounters with infibulated African women in Sweden." *Midwifery* 18:113–125.

Widstrand, C. G. 1964. "Female infibulation." *Occasional Papers of Studia Ethnographica Upsaliensia* 20:95–124.

Wikan, U. 1995. *Mot en ny norsk underklasse: Innvandrere, kultur og integrasjon* [Toward a new Norwegian lower class: Immigrants, culture and integration]. Oslo: Gyldendal Norsk Forlag.

———. 1999. Culture: A new concept of race. *Social Anthropology* 7:57–64.

———. 2002. "Citizenship on trail: Nadia's case." In *Engaging cultural differences: The multicultural challenge in liberal democracies*, ed. R. Shweder, M. Minow, and H. R. Markus. New York: Russell Sage Foundation.

Wiklund, H., A. S. Aden, U. Hogberg, M. Wikman, and L. Dahlgren. 2000. "Somalis giving birth in Sweden: A challenge to culture and gender specific values and behaviours." *Midwifery* 16:105–115.

Wilson, P. M. 1986. "Black culture and sexuality." *Journal of Social Work Human Sex* 4:29–46.

Winkel, E. 1995. "A Muslim perspective on female circumcision." *Women and Health* 23:1–7.

Winter, B. 1994. "Women, the law and cultural relativism in France: The case of excision." *Signs: Journal of Women in Culture and Society* 19:939–974.

Wollstonecraft, M. 1971. *A vindication of the rights of women*. New York: Source Book Press. (Originally published 1792.)

World Bank. 1998. "Senegalese woman remake their culture." Indigenous knowledge (IK) notes, no. 3. December 1998. http://www.worldbank.org/afr/ik/iknotes.htm.

———. 2000. "Putting an end to female genital cutting in Guinea." Development Marketplace, World Bank. http://web.worldbank.org/WBSITE/EXTERNAL/OPPORTUNITIES/GRANTS/DEVMARKETPLACE/,,contentMDK:20193125~menuPK:867620~pagePK:180686~piPK:180184~theSitePK:205098,00.html.

———. 2002. *Empowerment and poverty reduction: A sourcebook*. Washington, DC: World Bank.

Worseley, A. 1938. "Infibulation and female circumcision: A study of a little-known custom." *Journal of Obstetrics and Gynecology* 45:686–691.

Wyatt, G., and K. Dunn. 1991. "Examining predictors of sex guilt in multiethnic samples of women." *Archives of Sex Research* 20:471–485.

Wyatt, G., R. Strayer, and W. Lobitz. 1976. "Issues in the treatment of sexuality dysfunction couples of Afro-American descent." *Psychotherapy, Theory, Research, Practice* 13:44–50.

Wymark, E. 2003. *Från främling till bror* [From stranger to brother]. *Menorah* 4.

Yalçun-Heckmann, L. 1993. "Are fireworks Islamic? Towards an understanding of Turkish migrants and Islam in Germany." In *Syncretism/anti-syncretism: The politics of religious synthesis*, ed. C. Stewart and R. Shaw. London: Routledge.

Yankah, K. 1995. *Speaking for the chief: Okeyeame and the politics of Akan royal oratory*. Bloomington: Indiana University Press.

Yap, J. G. 1986. "Philippine ethnoculture and human sexuality." *Journal of Social Work Human Sex* 4:121–134.

Yoder, P. S. 2004. *Female genital cutting in the demographic and health surveys: A critical comparative analysis*. Washington DC: Macro International.

Yount, K. 2004. "Symbolic gender politics, religious group identity, and the decline in female genital cutting in Minya, Egypt." *Social Forces* 82:1063–1090.

Yount, K., and D. Balk. n.d. "Health and social effects of female genital cutting: The evidence to date." Unpublished paper.

Zilbergeld, B., and C. Ellison. 1980. "Desire discrepancies and arousal problems in sex therapy." In *Principles and practices of sex therapy*, ed. S. R. Leiblum and L. A. Pervin. New York: Guilford Press.

About the Contributors

FUAMBAI AHMADU, a Sierra Leonean/American, completed her doctorate at the department of anthropology, London School of Economics, on the symbolic meanings of female and male circumcision rituals among the Mandinka in The Gambia. Dr. Ahmadu has worked as a research consultant and principal investigator in The Gambia for various UN organizations and research institutes, including UNICEF, the Medical Research Council, and CODESRIA (Dakar). Her current research interests include women's sexual and reproductive health, conceptualizing gender in African societies, and women's roles in African economic development.

JANICE BODDY got her Ph.D. from the University of British Columbia and is professor of anthropology at the University of Toronto. She began fieldwork in Sudan in 1976–77 and returned in 1983–84 and briefly in 1994. She is the author of *Wombs and Alien Spirits: Women, Men and the Zar Cult in Northern Sudan* (1989), articles on the body, spirit possession, feminism, and popular anthropology, and coauthor of *Aman: the Story of a Somali Girl* (1994). Her latest book is *Civilizing Women: British Crusades in Colonial Sudan* (Princeton University Press, 2007).

MANSURA DOPICO, B.S.W. (1st Class Honours), is a doctoral candidate in social work/social policy at James Cook University, Cairns campus, and manager of The Early Intervention Service, department of child safety, Cairns, Australia.

YLVA HERNLUND, is a research associate in anthropology at the Center for Studies in Demography and Ecology at the University of Washington in Seattle, Washington, where she also received her Ph.D. She has been doing research in The Gambia since 1988, focusing on reactions to and debates around campaigns against FGM, and on alternative ritual. She is currently working with Bettina Shell-Duncan and a team of local fieldworkers on a three-year research study in The Gambia and Senegal that examines decision making around female circumcision; and is affiliated with Gambia College and Université Chiekh Anta Diop in Dakar.

R. ELISE B. Johansen received her Ph.D. at the department of medical anthropology, University of Oslo, on a study of female genital cutting among Somali immigrants and their health care providers in Norway (2006). She is currently at the World Health Organization to manage research projects on female genital mutiliation. For four years she was in charge of the Norwegian government project against FGC in Norway (the OK Project, 2001–2005). Her previous research has centered around sexuality and reproductive health, including a study on humor and sexuality among Norwegian youth and life-stage rituals relating to sexuality and birth among Maconde immigrants in Tanzania. Her master's thesis focused on music and dance in multiethnic nation building in the Ivory Coast (1989).

SARA JOHNSDOTTER, a social anthropologist, is a research fellow at the department of health and society, Malmö University, Sweden. Her doctoral thesis, "Created by God: How Somalis in Swedish Exile Reassess the Practice of Female Circumcision," was completed in 2002 at Lund University. She is currently working on a research project focusing on female genital cutting in relation to sexual ideologies and discursive changes of experiences and concepts of sexuality due to migration to the West among circumcised women. Since 1996, she has conducted research in cooperation with Dr. Birgitta Essén, specialist in gynecology. Among other issues, they have analyzed and raised a debate about the relation between Western anti-FGM legislation and the permissive attitude toward the growing occurrence of "designer vaginas" among Western women.

MICHELLE JOHNSON, Ph.D., is a cultural anthropologist specializing in religion and ritual in West Africa and in the "new" African diaspora. She conducts her research with Mandinga in Guinea-Bissau and with immigrants from Guinea-Bissau living in Portugal. She is currently an assistant professor of anthropology at Bucknell University.

CORINNE KRATZ, Ph.D, is professor of anthropology and African studies and co-director of the Center for the Study of Public Scholarship at Emory University in Atlanta. She writes and teaches about culture and communication, ritual, performance, photography, museums and exhibitions, and other forms of cultural display and representation. She has been doing research in Kenya since 1974, has curated exhibitions, and is the author of *The Ones that Are Wanted: Communication and the Politics of Representation in a Photographic Exhibition* and *Affecting Performance: Meaning, Movement, and Experience in Okiek Women's Initiation,* as well as a series of articles on international controversies concerning genital cutting.

HENRIETTA L. Moore is professor of social anthropology at the London School of Economics. She has written and lectured on social theory, epistemology, feminist theory, anthropology, gender, space, development and social enterprise.

She has a continuing long-term research engagement with Africa, focused on gender, livelihood strategies, social transformation and symbolic systems. Recent research and publications on Africa have included work on fertility, symbolism, witchcraft and technology. Her publications include *Feminism and Anthropology* (Polity 1986); *A Passion for Difference* (Polity 1994) and *Anthropological Theory Today* (Polity 1999). She is a Fellow of the Royal Society of Arts and Academician of the Learned Societies for the Social Sciences."

LESLYE OBIORA joined the University of Arizona College of Law in 1998. She obtained her professional degree from the University of Nigeria and her graduate degrees from Yale and Stanford law schools. She has written extensively on human rights, gender equity, development, and jurisprudence and teaches courses that inform her research interests. Recently, she was a residential fellow at the Institute for Advanced Studies at Princeton, the Rockefeller Study Center in Bellagio, Italy, and at the Djerassi Resident Artist Program and was recruited by the World Bank to manage a gender and law program. The founder of the Institute for Research on African Women, Children and Culture and the pioneer of Strategic Philanthropy Initiative for Nigeria (SPIN), Professor Obiora maintains an active speaking schedule.

CHARLES PIOT is Creed C. Black Associate Professor in the Department of Cultural Anthropology and the Program in African & African American Studies at Duke University. He does research on the political economy and history of rural West Africa. His book *Remotely Global: Village Modernity in West Africa* (1999) attempts to re-theorize a classic out-of-the-way place as within the modern and the global. He is currently engaged in research on the way human rights discourse, democratization, development, and charismatic Christianity are articulating with and transforming West African political cultures.

JULIET ROGERS, B.A. Soc.Sci (Hons), M.A. C.A.Th., is completing her Ph.D. in the faculty of law and management at La Trobe University, Melbourne, Australia. She currently consults to community organizations in organizational dynamics, mediation, and staff development.

BETTINA SHELL-DUNCAN currently is an associate professor of anthropology and international health at the University of Washington. She began fieldwork in Africa in Kenya in 1989 and currently maintains an ongoing research program on multiple aspects of maternal and child health. Her work on female genital cutting was initiated in 1995, focusing on issues including behavior change in the process of settlement and development, and medicalization. She became a consultant for the World Health Organization in 2001 and is currently the principle investigator of a WHO- and NSF-sponsored project on behavior change. This three-year project, done in collaboration with Ylva Hernlund, focuses on the dynamics of decision making regarding female genital cutting in Senegal and The Gambia. Shell-Duncan and Hernlund are also the coeditors of an earlier (2000) volume, *Female "Circumcision" in Africa: Culture, Controversy and Change.*

AUD TALLE is a professor it the department of social anthropology at the University of Oslo, Norway. Based upon long-term fieldwork in East Africa, she has written extensively on issues related to pastoralism, gender, and social change. She also has an interest in medical anthropology. Currently, she is involved in fieldwork among Somalis in the diaspora.

INDEX